Knowledge and Technology Adoption, Diffusion, and Transfer:

International Perspectives

Ali Hussein Saleh Zolait
University of Bahrain, Kingdom of Bahrain

Managing Director:	Lindsay Johnston
Senior Editorial Director:	Heather A. Probst
Book Production Manager:	Sean Woznicki
Development Manager:	Joel Gamon
Acquisitions Editor:	Erika Gallagher
Typesetter:	Lisandro Gonzalez
Cover Design:	Nick Newcomer

Published in the United States of America by
Information Science Reference (an imprint of IGI Global)
701 E. Chocolate Avenue
Hershey PA 17033
Tel: 717-533-8845
Fax: 717-533-8661
E-mail: cust@igi-global.com
Web site: http://www.igi-global.com

Library of Congress Cataloging-in-Publication Data

Knowledge and technology adoption, diffusion, and transfer: international perspectives / Ali Hussein Saleh Zolait, editor.
    p. cm.
  Includes bibliographical references and index.
  Summary: "This book is filled with original scientific and quality research articles on management information systems, technology diffusion, and business systems application aspects of e-commerce, e-government, and mobile application"-- Provided by publisher.
  ISBN 978-1-4666-1752-0 (hardcover) -- ISBN 978-1-4666-1753-7 (ebook) -- ISBN 978-1-4666-1754-4 (print & perpetual access) 1. Knowledge management. 2. Management information systems. 3. Information technology--Management. 4. Technology transfer. 5. Diffusion of innovations. I. Zolait, Ali Hussein Saleh, 1972-
  HD30.2.K63614 2012
  658.4'038011--dc23
                                    2012002476

British Cataloguing in Publication Data
A Cataloguing in Publication record for this book is available from the British Library.

The views expressed in this book are those of the authors, but not necessarily of the publisher.

Table of Contents

Preface xv

Chapter 1

Harnessing Information and Communication Technologies for Diffusing Connected Government
Applications in Developing Countries: Concept, Problems and Recommendations 1

    E. Ruhode, Cape Peninsula University of Technology, South Africa
    V. Owei, Cape Peninsula University of Technology, South Africa

Chapter 2

An Efficient and Simple Algorithm for Matrix Inversion 21

    Ahmad Farooq, King Khalid University, Saudi Arabia
    Khan Hamid, National University of Computer and Emerging Sciences (NUCES), Pakistan

Chapter 3

Thirst for Business Value of Information Technology 29

    Govindan Marthandan, Multimedia University, Malaysia
    Tang Chun Meng, Multimedia University, Malaysia

Chapter 4

Adoption of Short Messaging Service (SMS) in Malaysia 44

    Ainin Sulaiman, University of Malaya, Malaysia
    Ali Hussein Saleh Zolait, University of Malaya, Malaysia

Chapter 5

A Study of the Systemic Relationship Between Worker Motivation and Productivity 56

    J. J. Haefner, Walden University, USA
    Christos Makrigeorgis, Walden University, USA

Chapter 6

E-Government Initiative in the Sultanate of Oman: The Case of Ubar 73

    Khamis Al-Gharbi, Sultan Qaboos University, Oman
    Ahmed Al-Kindi, Sultan Qaboos University, Oman

Chapter 7
Mobile Commerce Use among UK Mobile Users: An Experimental Approach Based
on a Proposed Mobile Network Utilization Framework 78
  Asem Moqbel, Cardiff University, UK
  Mirella Yani-De-Soriano, Cardiff University, UK
  Shumaila Yousafzai, Cardiff University, UK

Chapter 8
An Efficient and Generic Algorithm for Matrix Inversion 112
  Ahmad Farooq, King Khalid University, Saudi Arabia
  Khan Hamid, National University of Computer and Emerging Sciences (NUCES), Pakistan
  Inayat Ali Shah, National University of Computer and Emerging Sciences (NUCES), Pakistan

Chapter 9
Saving DBMS Resources While Running Batch Cycles in Data Warehouses 118
  Nayem Rahman, Enterprise Data Warehouse Engineering-ETL, Intel Corporation

Chapter 10
Internet Adoption from Omani Organizations' Perspective: Motivations and Reservations 133
  Khamis Al-Gharbi, Sultan Qaboos University, Sultanate of Oman
  Ahlam Abdullah AlBulushi, Sultanate of Oman

Chapter 11
Electronic Training Methods: Relative Effectiveness and Frequency of Use
in the Malaysian Context 140
  Veeriah Sinniah, University of Malaya, Malaysia
  Sharan Kaur, University of Malaya, Malaysia

Chapter 12
Problems of Initiating International Knowledge Transfer: Is the Finnish Living
Lab Method Transferable to Estonia? 154
  Katri-Liis Lepik, Estonian Business School, Estonia
  Merle Krigul, Estonian Business School, Estonia
  Erik Terk, Tallinn University, Estonia

Chapter 13
Mobile Commerce Use among UK Mobile Users Based on a Proposed Mobile
Network Utilization Framework: An Experimental Approach – Part 2 166
  Asem Moqbel, Cardiff University, UK
  Mirella Yani-Di-Soriano, Cardiff University, UK
  Shumaila Yousafzai, Cardiff University, UK

Chapter 14
A Study on the Internet Security and its Implication for E-Commerce in Yemen 200
  Ali Hussein Saleh Zolait, University of Malaya, Malaysia
  Abdul Razak Ibrahim, University of Malaya, Malaysia
  Ahmad Farooq, King Khalid University, Saudi Arabia

Chapter 15
Supply Chain Management Practices and Firm Performance: An Empirical Study
of the Electronics Industry in Malaysia 214
    Abdul Razak Ibrahim, University Malaya, Malaysia
    Ali Hussein Zolait, University Malaya, Malaysia
    Veera Pandiyan Sundram, University Malaya, Malaysia

Chapter 16
Traditional Job-Related Factors and Career Salience in IT-Based Workplace 222
    Aminu Ahmad, Abubakar Tafawa Balewa University, Nigeria
    Hartini Ahmad, Universiti Utara Malaysia, Malaysia

Chapter 17
The Impact of Technology Anxiety on the Use of Mobile Financial Applications 231
    Cheon-Pyo Lee, Fairmont State University, USA

Chapter 18
The Influence of Internet Security on E-Business Competence in Jordan: An Empirical Analysis........244
    Amin Ahmad Shaqrah, Alzaytoonah University of Jordan, Jordan

Chapter 19
Human Talent Forecasting using Data Mining Classification Techniques 261
    Hamidah Jantan, Universiti Teknologi MARA (UiTM), Malaysia, & Universiti Kebangsaan
        Malaysia (UKM), Malaysia
    Abdul Razak Hamdan, Universiti Kebangsaan Malaysia (UKM), Malaysia
    Zulaiha Ali Othman, Universiti Kebangsaan Malaysia (UKM), Malaysia

Chapter 20
Computing Gamma Calculus on Computer Cluster 275
    Hong Lin, University of Houston-Downtown, USA
    Jeremy Kemp, University of Houston-Downtown, USA
    Padraic Gilbert, University of Houston-Downtown, USA

Chapter 21
Determinants of the Use of Knowledge Sources in the Adoption of Open Source
Server Software 287
    Kris Ven, University of Antwerp, Belgium
    Jan Verelst, University of Antwerp, Belgium

Compilation of References 305

About the Contributors 336

Index..339

Detailed Table of Contents

Preface...xv

Chapter 1

Harnessing Information and Communication Technologies for Diffusing Connected Government
Applications in Developing Countries: Concept, Problems and Recommendations.............................1
    E. Ruhode, Cape Peninsula University of Technology, South Africa
    V. Owei, Cape Peninsula University of Technology, South Africa

Improving information management practices is a key focus for many organisations across both the public and private sectors. An information society begins with a connected government and ICTs are the bedrock and founding pillars of such societies. To assist public administrators think beyond traditional e-government, this study describes a concept of connected government, whose philosophy rests on the integration story that happens behind the scenes of the visible web interface as well as the collaboration among government agencies. Diffusion of Innovations theory is the conceptual framework underpinning this study. The connected government phenomenon is also put into perspective by the systems theory that is explained in this study. This article describes a case study of an organisation in a developing country environment where even the basic e-government services are barely extant. This study was done to determine the connectedness within and across government agencies, with the idea of stimulating some thinking within and among public administrators, around the possibility that a connected government can indeed be established in a developing country setting. The study exposes shortcomings to e-government diffusion not only of the organisation under investigation, but also of other similar enterprises in developing countries within the same context. The paper concludes by proposing a set of recommendations toward diffusing connected government applications as an antidote to identified problems.

Chapter 2

An Efficient and Simple Algorithm for Matrix Inversion 21
    Ahmad Farooq, King Khalid University, Saudi Arabia
    Khan Hamid, National University of Computer and Emerging Sciences (NUCES), Pakistan

In this paper, a new algorithm is proposed for finding inverse and determinant of a given matrix in one instance. The algorithm is straightforward in understanding and manual calculations. Computer implementation of the algorithm is extremely simple and is quite efficient in time and memory utilization. The algorithm is supported by an example. The number of multiplication/division performed by the algorithm is exactly n^3; however, its efficiency lies in the simplicity of coding and minimal utilization of memory. Simple applicability and reduced execution time of the method is validated form the numerical experiments performed on test problems. The algorithm is applicable in the cases of pseudo inverses for non-square matrices and solution of system of linear equations with minor modification.

Chapter 3
Thirst for Business Value of Information Technology 29
Govindan Marthandan, Multimedia University, Malaysia
Tang Chun Meng, Multimedia University, Malaysia

For years information technology (IT) has helped companies improve organizational efficiency and effectiveness. Today's IT plays a more strategic role in building capabilities for sustaining and creating competitive advantages. The increasing importance of IT has led many organizations to integrate it into their daily operations. To justify the ever-increasing spending on IT, organizations have been searching for evaluation methods to prove the business value of IT. However, this is a challenging undertaking, as there are contradictory answers to questions on whether it is worthwhile to pay substantial sums for IT. To gain insight into the reasons behind the contradictory answers, this paper first reviews conflicting research results of past studies on IT business value. It then explains the term IT productivity paradox. Last, it provides five reasons why IT business value is not fully reflected in the way business managers expect it to be.

Chapter 4
Adoption of Short Messaging Service (SMS) in Malaysia... 44
Ainin Sulaiman, University of Malaya, Malaysia
Ali Hussein Saleh Zolait, University of Malaya, Malaysia

Short Messaging Service (SMS) being an almost instantaneous communication medium that connects people is now a phenomenon that has grown and spread around the globe at an amazing speed. Given the current trend of SMS usage and its potential growth, this paper provides an insight into SMS adoption. The study attempts to delineate the demographics and usage profile of SMS users in Malaysia, as well as explaining the factors influencing SMS adoption in Malaysia by using a modified version of the Technology Acceptance Model (TAM), which was originally introduced by Davis (1989). The study presents the demographic and usage profile in terms of gender, age, occupation, monthly personal income, extent of SMS usage and so forth of 489 SMS users from four institutions of education in the Klang Valley and Selangor. The present research uses and validates the scales for variables developed by earlier studies, namely perceived usefulness, perceived ease of use, perceived enjoyment, and perceived fees, which are hypothesized to be fundamental determinants of behavioural intention. The scale items for the said variables were tested for reliability, correlation and regression. The application of correlation analysis reveals a significant relationship among the independent variables, namely, perceived usefulness, perceived enjoyment, and perceived ease of use with the dependent variable that is behavioural intention. With regards to the level of importance derived from regression analysis, usefulness ranks the highest, followed by ease of use and enjoyment in explaining SMS adoption in Malaysia. Perceived fees do not seem to have a significant relationship with behavioural intention. Some implications, limitations and recommendations for future research are also discussed.

Chapter 5
A Study of the Systemic Relationship Between Worker Motivation and Productivity 56
J. J. Haefner, Walden University, USA
Christos Makrigeorgis, Walden University, USA

Three well known theories on worker motivation have proliferated in the literature and practice over the past 50 years, namely Theories X, Y, Z, Expectancy Theory, Equity Theory, Justice Theory, and Goal-Setting Theory, to name a few. We propose a Fourth Theory that is based on the fundamental principles of open systems theory that function in holistic fashion into the phenomenon of systemic motivation. When fully engaged, systemic motivation can influence workers to become more productive than in a system that does not engage. It is the central construct that has been missing in motivation theory. This paper briefly explains systemic motivation and demonstrates its potential in a case study where a motivation effect resulted in an additional $1 million in product throughput.

Chapter 6

E-Government Initiative in the Sultanate of Oman: The Case of Ubar 73

Khamis Al-Gharbi, Sultan Qaboos University, Oman
Ahmed Al-Kindi, Sultan Qaboos University, Oman

There are many interesting initiatives regarding the use of internet technologies in e-government that are taking place in developing countries. A number of studies have been conducted in recent years regarding the adoption and use of internet technologies in e-government. However, most of these studies focused on the developed countries. There are many interesting initiatives regarding the use of internet technologies in e-government that are taking place in the developing countries and yet have received very little research attention. The Sultanate of Oman is currently working on a project called e-Oman to provide e-government, e-commerce, e-learning and other e-services. The hope is to enhance the quality of services offered by the government to its citizens. The purpose of this paper is to highlight e-government Initiatives in Oman.

Chapter 7

Mobile Commerce Use among UK Mobile Users: An Experimental Approach Based
on a Proposed Mobile Network Utilization Framework 78

Asem Moqbel, Cardiff University
Mirella Yani-De-Soriano, Cardiff University
Shumaila Yousafzai, Cardiff University

In this paper, the authors examine UK mobile users' perceptions of m-commerce utilization. For this purpose, the authors devise a Mobile Network Utilization Model empirically tested in experimental settings. The empirical findings reveal strong support for the capability of the proposed utilization model in measuring the concept of Mobile Task-Technology Fit (MTTF) and explaining the utilization of m-commerce services among UK mobile users. In particular, their research finds that MTTF and m-commerce utilization are dependent on the interactions between the key components of a wider mobile network, namely mobile users, mobile devices, mobile tasks, mobile operators, as well as mobile vendors. The authors identify 15 factors as a result of such interaction and the importance of these factors in explaining MTTF and the utilization of m-commerce services.

Chapter 8

An Efficient and Generic Algorithm for Matrix Inversion 112

Ahmad Farooq, King Khalid University, Saudi Arabia
Khan Hamid, National University of Computer and Emerging Sciences (NUCES), Pakistan
Inayat Ali Shah, National University of Computer and Emerging Sciences (NUCES), Pakistan

This work presents an improvement on the simple algorithms of matrix inversion (Farooq & Hamid, 2010). This generalized algorithm supports selection of pivot randomly in the matrix thus supporting partial and full pivoting. The freedom in pivot selection can be used in minimizing the numerical error and prioritizing the variable to find the solution first. The algorithm is more suitable for finding inverse and determinant of dense matrices. The algorithm requires a mechanism for selection of pivot (e.g., selection of absolute maximum value) in the available sub-matrix and the mechanism to get the inverse from the final resultant matrix by rearranging the rows and columns. A method for assigning the sign of the determinant is also given. The algorithm is explained through solved examples. The number of arithmetic calculations performed by the algorithm is of O (n³) however. The efficiency and simplicity of coding remains the same as of the original algorithm.

Chapter 9
Saving DBMS Resources While Running Batch Cycles in Data Warehouses 118
Nayem Rahman, Enterprise Data Warehouse Engineering-ETL, Intel Corporation

In a large data warehouse, thousands of jobs run during each cycle in dozens of subject areas. Many of the data warehouse tables are quite large and they need to be refreshed at the right time, several times a day, to support strategic business decisions. To enable cycles to run more frequently and keep the data warehouse environment stable the database system's resource utilization must be optimal. This paper discusses refreshing data warehouses using a metadata model to make sure jobs under batch cycles run on an as-needed basis. The metadata model limits execution of the stored procedures in different analytical subject areas to source data changes in the source staging subject area tables, and then implements refreshes of analytical tables for which new data has arrived from the operational databases. The load is skipped if source data has not changed. Skipping unnecessary loads via this metadata driven approach enables significant database resources savings. The resource savings statistics based on an actual production data warehouse demonstrate an excellent reduction of computing resources consumption achieved by the proposed techniques.

Chapter 10
Internet Adoption from Omani Organizations' Perspective: Motivations and Reservations.............. 133
Khamis Al-Gharbi, Sultan Qaboos University, Sultanate of Oman
Ahlam Abdullah AlBulushi, Sultanate of Oman

In this paper, to the authors determine the motivations and reservations for Internet/E-business adoption within the organizations in Oman. For this purpose, questionnaires were used to collect the data from the organizations that have adopted Internet and the organizations that have not adopted Internet applications. The results and analysis of the data show that the main reasons for adopting Internet applications in Oman are to simplify process, improve communication with staff, keep up with competitors, and reduce the use of paper. The lack of skill and security problems is the main reservation for not adopting the Internet.

Chapter 11
Electronic Training Methods: Relative Effectiveness and Frequency of Use
in the Malaysian Context 140
Veeriah Sinniah, University of Malaya, Malaysia
Sharan Kaur, University of Malaya, Malaysia

This study comparatively examines the relative effectiveness and frequency of use of modern and conventional training methods, as much rhetoric has surrounded the use of techniques like distance learning and computer-based training methods. The responses from 200 employees suggest that no significant difference exists with respect to frequency of use, but a significant difference exists in terms of effectiveness. The result shows that on-the-job training (OJT) methods are widely used and are perceived as the most effective method, whereas distance learning is not widely used because it is perceived as less effective. This study also reveals that a significant difference exists between modern training methods and conventional training methods in terms of attaining training objectives. OJT is given the highest rating for attaining training objectives.

Chapter 12

Problems of Initiating International Knowledge Transfer: Is the Finnish Living
Lab Method Transferable to Estonia? 154

    Katri-Liis Lepik, Estonian Business School, Estonia
    Merle Krigul, Estonian Business School, Estonia
    Erik Terk, Tallinn University, Estonia

Regional competitiveness is a policy priority of the European Union. This article explores cross-border knowledge transfer for regional integration and development. The focus of this research is the role of cross-border co-operation in development of innovative forms of co-operation, initiating and supporting knowledge transfer. The article presents a theoretical-methodological analysis of new complex tasks and theoretical paradigms emerging in the context of increasing integration and convergence of cross-border co-operation: method's innovation approach, knowledge and knowledge transfer. A cross-border co-operation organisation's potential model for enhancement of complex regional co-operation has also been described based on Helsinki-Tallinn Euregio's case. The article then focuses on investigating the international transferability of the Living Lab's method. The article concludes by presenting the opportunities and principles of activities of a cross-border co-operation organisation to support the knowledge transfer process.

Chapter 13

Mobile Commerce Use among UK Mobile Users Based on a Proposed Mobile
Network Utilization Framework: An Experimental Approach – Part 2 166

    Asem Moqbel, Cardiff University, UK
    Mirella Yani-Di-Soriano, Cardiff University, UK
    Shumaila Yousafzai, Cardiff University, UK

This paper examines UK mobile users' perceptions of m-commerce utilization. For this purpose, the study has devised a Mobile Network Utilization Model that was empirically tested in experimental settings. The empirical findings revealed strong support for the capability of the proposed utilization model in measuring the concept of Mobile Task-Technology Fit (MTTF) and explaining the utilization of m-commerce services among UK mobile users. In particular, the research found that MTTF and m-commerce utilization are dependent on the interactions between the key components of a wider mobile network, that is mobile devices, mobile tasks, mobile operators, as well as mobile vendors. Fifteen factors were identified as a result of such interaction and the importance of these factors in explaining MTTF and the actual utilization of m-commerce services was empirically asserted.

Chapter 14

A Study on the Internet Security and its Implication for E-Commerce in Yemen 200

    Ali Hussein Saleh Zolait, University of Malaya, Malaysia
    Abdul Razak Ibrahim, University of Malaya, Malaysia
    Ahmad Farooq, King Khalid University, Saudi Arabia

This study examines the use of the Internet for business purposes in Yemen, where main sectors of banking and private trade organizations are observed. Through interviews, a thorough study is performed concerning the Internet facilities available in Yemen, the literacy and use of Information Communication Technology (ICT) in organizations, the level of e-commerce adopted, the main hurdles in the adoption of e-commerce, and measures required to increase the adoption of e-commerce. The study finds that both organizations realize the importance of e-commerce for their business. The main causes in the delay of e-commerce adoption by some are the discrepancies in the infrastructure, high costing of the Internet facilities, bureaucratic hurdles in obtaining the facilities, and the non-availability of a secure environment. Beyond concerns about Internet security, their awareness of security hazards and protection measures is minimal. In light of the data collected, the study has come up with certain recommendations for the interested authorities to improve e-commerce in Yemen.

Chapter 15
Supply Chain Management Practices and Firm Performance: An Empirical Study
of the Electronics Industry in Malaysia 214
    Abdul Razak Ibrahim, University Malaya, Malaysia
    Ali Hussein Zolait, University Malaya, Malaysia
    Veera Pandiyan Sundram, University Malaya, Malaysia

Supply chain management (SCM) is the integration and strategic alliance involving all the value-creating elements in the supply, manufacturing, and distribution processes from raw material extraction, the transformation process, and end user consumption. This paper explores the SCM activities carried out by electronic manufacturing organizations in Malaysia and determines the correlation between SCM practices and firm performance. A self-administrated questionnaire based survey technique was employed to ascertain the status of SCM adoption and the practices in SCM that are significant for Malaysian electronics manufacturers. The findings suggest that the adoption of SCM activities is reasonably moderate.

Chapter 16
Traditional Job-Related Factors and Career Salience in IT-Based Workplace 222
    Aminu Ahmad, Abubakar Tafawa Balewa University, Nigeria
    Hartini Ahmad, Universiti Utara Malaysia, Malaysia

Despite growing academic and practical concerns about IT-transformed workplaces, little research empirically investigates these concerns. This paper adopts a unique approach to address these concerns by evaluating the appropriateness of traditional drivers of career salience in high IT working environments. Building on established measures of role stress, participation in decision making, job involvement and career salience, questionnaires were distributed to staff working in high IT organizations in Nigeria. Multiple regressions were run from a valid response of 223, resulting in the three traditional drivers accounting for 25% of the variance in career salience. Similarly, standardized β coefficients indicate on job involvement (0.46) makes unique significant contribution to career salience. This finding is in line with sociotechnical theory—that changes in technical sub-system affect the social sub-system and vice versa. The finding also provides indirect exploratory support for the decreasing importance of non-IT factors in the evolving digital workplace. Other implications, limitations and direction for future research are highlighted.

Chapter 17
The Impact of Technology Anxiety on the Use of Mobile Financial Applications 231
    Cheon-Pyo Lee, Fairmont State University, USA

Mobile Commerce activities will not expand without the proper support of mobile financial applications (MFA), including mobile banking, mobile brokerage service, mobile money transfer, and mobile micro-payments. MFA is expected to have a great impact on the future of mobile commerce industries and makes purchasing activities more flexible and convenient, also creating new markets. However, despite the advent of these MFA technologies and the availability of various mobile services, the adoption of mobile financial applications across the globe is still relatively low. In this regard, this study investigates the role of technology anxiety (TA) in the adoption of MFA and resolves the discrepancy between the apparent interest in and low adoption of MFA. The results of a broad survey of 595 mobile payment users in Korea indicate TA negatively moderates the influence of intention on actual usage in addition to the direct negative influence on intention to use MFA. Also, the author found that TA significantly differs depending on the frequency of use and gender. However, contrary to a common notion that older people are more anxious in context to new technologies, TA has been found to be higher among young people.

Chapter 18

The Influence of Internet Security on E-Business Competence in Jordan: An Empirical Analysis........244
    Amin Ahmad Shaqrah, Alzaytoonah University of Jordan, Jordan

The purpose of this study is to investigate the relationship between internet security and e-business competence in Jordan. The proposed conceptual model examined the antecedents and consequences of e-business competence of its empirical validity, the sample of 152 banking and exchange firms, and tests the posited structural equation model. Results consistently support the validity of the proposed conceptual model, finding that both organizations realize the importance of e- business for their business and are willing to proceed further with e- business. In this regard, businesses are highly concerned about internet security, their awareness of security hazards, and minimal internet performance, concluding that public awareness of the ICT is very low. In light of the data collected, the study has proposed certain recommendations for the interested authorities to improve e- business in Jordan.

Chapter 19

Human Talent Forecasting using Data Mining Classification Techniques 261
    Hamidah Jantan, Universiti Teknologi MARA (UiTM), Malaysia, & Universiti Kebangsaan Malaysia (UKM), Malaysia
    Abdul Razak Hamdan, Universiti Kebangsaan Malaysia (UKM), Malaysia
    Zulaiha Ali Othman, Universiti Kebangsaan Malaysia (UKM), Malaysia

Talent management is a very crucial task and demands close attention from human resource (HR) professionals. Recently, among the challenges for HR professionals is how to manage organization's talents, particularly to ensure the right job for the right person at the right time. Some employee's talent patterns can be identified through existing knowledge in HR databases, which data mining can be applied to handle this issue. The hidden and useful knowledge that exists in databases can be discovered through classification task and has been widely used in many fields. However, this approach has not successfully attracted people in HR especially in talent management. In this regard, the authors attempt to present an overview of talent management problems that can be solved by using this approach. This paper uses that approach for one of the talent management tasks, i.e., predicting potential talent using previous existing knowledge. Future employee's performances can be predicted based on past experience knowledge discovered from existing databases by using classification techniques. Finally, this study proposes a framework for talent forecasting using the potential Data Mining classification techniques.

Chapter 20

Computing Gamma Calculus on Computer Cluster 275
    Hong Lin, University of Houston-Downtown, USA
    Jeremy Kemp, University of Houston-Downtown, USA
    Padraic Gilbert, University of Houston-Downtown, USA

Gamma Calculus is an inherently parallel, high-level programming model, which allows simple programming molecules to interact, creating a complex system with minimum of coding. Gamma calculus modeled programs were written on top of IBM's TSpaces middleware, which is Java-based and uses a "Tuple Space" based model for communication, similar to that in Gamma. A parser was written in C++ to translate the Gamma syntax. This was implemented on UHD's grid cluster (grid.uhd.edu), and in an effort to increase performance and scalability, existing Gamma programs are being transferred to Nvidia's CUDA architecture. General Purpose GPU computing is well suited to run Gamma programs, as GPU's excel at running the same operation on a large data set, potentially offering a large speedup.

Chapter 21
Determinants of the Use of Knowledge Sources in the Adoption of Open Source
Server Software 287
    Kris Ven, University of Antwerp, Belgium
    Jan Verelst, University of Antwerp, Belgium

Previous research suggests that the adoption of open source server software (OSSS) may be subject to knowledge barriers. In order to overcome these barriers, organizations should engage in a process of organizational learning. This learning process is facilitated by exposure to external knowledge sources. Unfortunately, this leaves open the question of which factors determine which knowledge sources are used by organizations. In this study, the authors have performed an exploratory study on the determinants of the use of knowledge sources in the adoption of OSSS. The conceptual model developed in this study was based on the absorptive capacity theory. Data was gathered from 95 organizations to empirically investigate this model. Results provide a quite consistent view on how external knowledge sources are used by organizations in the adoption of OSSS. Moreover, results provide more insight into the context in which the adoption of OSSS takes place.

Compilation of References 305

About the Contributors 336

Index 339

Preface

Nowadays, it is impossible to live without the use of information technology innovations which became a necessity in many people's lives. Innovations are fast spreading and invaded many aspects of people's life. Accordingly, gaining in-depth understanding on the adoption process of technology, its diffusion mechanism, and transfer of technology in the marketplace is vital for the success of individuals and organizations to have easy and better quality of life. "Knowledge and Technology Adoption, Diffusion, and Transfer: International Perspectives" is a collection packed with variety of original scientific and quality research articles on innovations and new practice of Information Technology (IT). Scholarly works in this collection address several issues pertaining to management information systems, technology diffusion, and business systems application aspects of e-commerce, e-government, and mobile applications. As a forum of multi-disciplinary and interdisciplinary dialogue, collection addresses research on all aspects of innovation diffusion in the field of business computing technologies and their past, present, and future use. The collection is very important as an international educational forum because it covers topics that serve as a vital source of information on technology diffusion for researchers and practitioners alike. The main obstacle and challenge faced in the development of this collection is how to produce an international and unified point of view that combine IT knowledge, technology adoption, diffusion, and IT transfer that is affluent in gaining reader's attention.

In order to overcome this challenge, editor built a solution based on an initiative idea which is to combine and cluster materials of the collection in several themes. Moreover, in this collection the editor brings together many international scholars who share their experience, giving explanation and in depth insight to several issues of information technology, including opportunities, challenges, and technology determinants of diffusion. Several studies in this collection stand on issues from Europe to Asia, from America to Africa. Also, a quite number of researchers come from different contexts such as Malaysia, Oman, South Africa, Estonia, Nigeria, Yemen, Jordan, Belgium, United Kingdom, and the United States who discussed and put the IT fundamentals of this collection. They discussed issues related to the deployment of numbers of technologies which are very important for each country. Therefore this book is a collection of studies which can be attributed as global in its contents, authors, and technology's topics. The contributors are very delighted to put in the hand of readers a variety of research in information technology and practical papers representing a variety of subjects in field of technology diffusion. This collection organized around different themes that discuss very in need information technology researches in different emerging IT topics. The focus of collection main theme is to show how to develop and maintain a prosperous Information Technology Knowledge (ITK), using IT-based solutions in global and multi-cultural environments. This collection will be a good contribution to overcome the lack of understanding of technologies by both individual and practisers, and will motivate to seek out a way to create a new knowledge system based on a deep understanding of fundamental principles of technology diffusion. Six themes represent this book as follows.

Theme one, reserved to present mobile application adoption and authors will discuss materials pertaining to the impact of technology anxiety on the use of mobile financial applications. Also, this theme discusses a proposed mobile network and mobile commerce use among UK mobile users. The adoption of Short Messaging Service (SMS) in Malaysia is one of mobile application discussed in the theme.

Moqbel et al. examine UK mobile users' perceptions of m-commerce utilization. A mobile network utilization model empirically tested in experimental settings and the result reveals strong support for the capability of the proposed utilization model in measuring the concept of Mobile Task-Technology Fit (MTTF) and explaining the utilization of m-commerce services among UK mobile users. According to Moqbel et al. (*Mobile Commerce Use among UK Mobile Users: An Experimental Approach Based on a Proposed Mobile Network Utilization Framework, p.78*), utilization of m-commerce is dependent on the interactions between the key components of a wider mobile network, namely mobile users, mobile devices, mobile tasks, mobile operators, as well as mobile vendors. The authors identified 15 factors as a result of such interaction, and they discussed the importance of these factors in explaining MTTF, as well as the utilization of m-commerce services. Furthermore, in the second contribution, Moqbel et al. (*Mobile Commerce Use among UK Mobile Users Based on a Proposed Mobile Network Utilization Framework: An Experimental Approach – Part 2, p.166*) devised a Mobile Network Utilization Model that was empirically tested in experimental settings, to examine UK mobile users' perceptions of m-commerce utilization. The study revealed strong support for the capability of the proposed utilization model in measuring the concept of Mobile Task-Technology Fit (MTTF) and explaining the utilization of m-commerce services among UK mobile users.

Then, Cheon-Pyo Lee (*The Impact of Technology Anxiety on the Use of Mobile Financial Applications, p.231*) from Fairmont State University - USA, investigates the role of Technology Anxiety (TA) in the adoption of Mobile Financial Applications (MFA) and resolves the discrepancy between the apparent interest in and low adoption of MFA. Cheon-Pyo Lee found that TA significantly differs depending on the frequency of use and gender. However, contrary to a common notion that older people are more anxious in context to new technologies, TA has been found to be higher among young people. Also, the research indicates that TA negatively moderates the influence of intention on actual usage in addition to the direct negative influence on intention to use MFA. While, Short Messaging Service (SMS) being an almost instantaneous communication medium that connects people is now a phenomenon that has grown and spread around the globe at an amazing speed.

Given the current trend of SMS usage and its potential growth, Sulaiman and Zolait (*Adoption of Short Messaging Service (SMS) in Malaysia, p.44*), from University of Malaya researched the SMS adoption in Malaysia and provided an insight into SMS adoption. The study delineated the demographics and usage profile of SMS users in Malaysia, as well as explained the factors influencing SMS adoption in Malaysia by using a modified version of the Technology Acceptance Model (TAM). The study presented the demographic and usage profile in terms of gender, age, occupation, and monthly income of person. They discussed the extent of SMS usage and usefulness of SMS, which is the highest ranking, followed by ease of use and enjoyment in explaining SMS adoption in Malaysia. Perceived fees do not seem to have a significant relationship with behavioural intention.

Theme Two, E-Government initiatives, discusses e-government initiatives and presents case study from the Sultanate of Oman. In full, this theme's studies discussed many issues such as concepts, problems, and recommendations for diffusing government applications in developing countries. For instance, in the conceptual framework built on the Diffusion of Innovations Theory, Ruhode and Owei (*Harnessing Information and Communication Technologies for Diffusing Connected Government Applications in Developing Countries: Concept, Problems and Recommendations, p.1*), from Cape Peninsula University of Technology, South Africa, described a concept of connected government, whose philosophy rests on the integration story that happens behind the scenes of the visible web interface as well as the collaboration among government agencies. The study proposed set of recommendations toward diffusing connected government applications as an antidote to identified problems.

Al-Gharbi and Al-Kindi (*E-Government Initiative in the Sultanate of Oman: The Case of Ubar, p.73*) from Sultan Qaboos University, Oman, researched an interesting initiative of e-government that is taking place in one of the developing countries and the adoption and use of Internet technologies in e-government. The authors presented Sultanate of Oman, which is currently working on e-Oman project meant to be portal that provides e-government, e-commerce, e-learning, and other e-services. The researchers believe that the e-Oman will enhance the quality of services offered by the Omani government to its citizens. While in the second chapter of the second theme, Al-Gharbi and Al-Bulushi used quantitative research and analysis, and attempted to determine the motivations and reservations for Internet/E-business adoption within the organizations in Oman. The researchers found that the main reasons driving the adoption of Internet applications in Oman are to simplify process, improve communication with staff, keep up with competitors, and reduce the use of paper. According to Al-Gharbi and Al-Bulushi (*Internet Adoption from Omani Organizations' Perspective: Motivations and Reservations, p.133*), the lack of skill and security problems is the main reservation for not adopting the Internet by organizations in Oman for conducting E-business.

Sinniah and Kaur (*Electronic Training Methods: Relative Effectiveness and Frequency of Use in the Malaysian Context, p. 140*), from University of Malaya, Malaysia, examined the use of modern and conventional training methods like distance learning and computer-based training methods. The study shows that on-the-job training (OJT) methods are widely used in Malaysia and are the most effective method, whereas distance learning is not widely used because it is considered less effective. This study also reveals that OJT is given the highest rating for attaining training objectives.

Theme Three is Security, and Shaqrah from Alzaytoonah University of Jordan – Jordan (*The Influence of Internet Security on E-Business Competence in Jordan: An Empirical Analysis, p. 244*), investigates the Internet security and e-business competence in Jordan as the first chapter of this theme. The author found that Jordanian organizations realize the importance of e-business to the growth of their business. Furthermore, businesses are highly concerning Internet security, awareness of security hazards, and minimal Internet performance, concluding that public awareness of the ICT is very low. Zolait et al. (*A Study on the Internet Security and its Implication for E-Commerce in Yemen, p.200*) examine the use of the Internet for business purposes with much focus on two main business organizations which they are banking and private trade organizations. They researched the Internet facilities, the literacy and use of Information Communication Technology (ICT) in organizations, the level of e-commerce adopted, the main hurdles in the adoption of e-commerce, and measures required to increase the adoption of e-commerce. The researched the causes behind the delay in e-commerce adoption.

Theme Four is knowledge & DBMS, and in the first chapter of this section, Ven and Verelst from the University of Antwerp - Belgium (*Determinants of the Use of Knowledge Sources in the Adoption of Open Source Server Software, p.287*) employed the absorptive capacity theory to research knowledge barriers and the adoption of open source server software (OSSS) by organizations. The study discussed the importance of exposure to external knowledge sources in facilitating the process of organizational learning. Rahman (*Saving DBMS Resources While Running Batch Cycles in Data Warehouses, p.118*) discusses refreshing data warehouses using a metadata model to make sure jobs under batch cycles run on an as-needed basis. The metadata model limits execution of the stored procedures in different analytical subject areas to source data changes in the source staging subject area tables, and then implements refreshes of analytical tables for which new data has arrived from the operational databases. The resource savings statistics based on an actual production data warehouse demonstrate an excellent reduction of computing resources consumption achieved by the proposed techniques.

Lepik et al. (*Problems of Initiating International Knowledge Transfer: Is the Finnish Living Lab Method Transferable to Estonia?, p.154*) explore cross-border knowledge transfer for regional integration and development. They examined issues pertaining to the role of cross-border co-operation in development of innovative forms of co-operation, initiating and supporting knowledge transfer. The study presents cross-border co-operation organisation's potential model for enhancement of complex regional co-operation. Lepik et al. described opportunities and principles of activities of a cross-border co-operation organisation to support the knowledge transfer process. Jantan et al. (*Human Talent Forecasting using Data Mining Classification Techniquesm p.261*) researched talent management and human resource (HR) professionals. They discussed issues pertaining to employee's talent patterns, talent identification and the use of existing knowledge in HR databases and data mining to manage organization's talents. According to Jantan et al., the hidden and useful knowledge that exists in databases can be discovered through classification task and has been widely used in many fields. Furthermore, Jantan et al. presented an overview of talent management problems using classification techniques, using previous existing knowledge for predicting potential talent. Additionally, Jantan et al. discussed the use of past experience knowledge in understanding employee's performances in the future using an existing databases and classification techniques. Finally, study suggested a framework for talent forecasting using the potential data mining and classification techniques.

In the first chapter in Theme Five, Information Technology, Ibrahim et al. (*Supply Chain Management Practices and Firm Performance: An Empirical Study of the Electronics Industry in Malaysia, p.214*), from University Malaya - Malaysia, explore the Supply Chain Management (SCM) activities carried out by electronic manufacturing organizations in Malaysia. They examine issues pertaining to SCM practices and firm performance. Aminu and Hartini from University Utara Malaysia, Malaysia, researched high IT organizations in Nigeria and the measures of role stress, participation in decision making, job involvement and career salience, to evaluate the appropriateness of traditional drivers of career salience in high IT working environments. The study found that changes in technical sub-system affect the social sub-system and vice versa. In addition, it provides indirect exploratory support for the decreasing importance of non-IT factors in the evolving digital workplace.

Marthandan and Meng from Multimedia University – Malaysia (*Thirst for Business Value of Information Technology, p.29*), had discussed the business value of information technology. Therefore, the authors reviewed conflicting research results of past studies on IT business value and then explained the term IT productivity paradox. Accordingly, they concluded with five reasons why IT business value is not fully reflected in the way business managers expect. Haefner and Makrigeorgis from Walden University – USA (*A Study of the Systemic Relationship Between Worker Motivation and Productivity, p.56*), researched theories on worker motivation that have being proliferated in the literature and practiced over the past 50 years, namely Theories X, Y, Z, Expectancy Theory, Equity Theory, Justice Theory, and Goal-Setting Theory. They argue that when fully engaged, systemic motivation can influence workers to become more productive than in a system that does not engage. They consider it as essential construct that has been missing in motivation theory. The study explains systemic motivation and demonstrates its potential in a case study where a motivation effect resulted in an additional $1 million in product throughput.

Theme Six: Computing and Algorithm, starts with a chapter by Lin et al. (*Computing Gamma Calculus on Computer Cluster, p.275*), who researched high-level programming model, Gamma Calculus, which allows simple programming molecules to interact, creating a complex system with minimum of coding. Gamma calculus modeled programs were written on top of IBM's TSpaces middleware, which is Java-based and uses a "Tuple Space" based model for communication, similar to that in Gamma. A parser was written in C++ to translate the Gamma syntax. This was implemented on UHD's grid cluster (grid.uhd.edu), and in an effort to increase performance and scalability, existing Gamma programs are being transferred to Nvidia's CUDA architecture. General Purpose GPU computing is well suited to run Gamma programs, as GPU's excel at running the same operation on a large data set, potentially offering a large speedup.

Farooq et al. (*An Efficient and Generic Algorithm for Matrix Inversion, p.112*) present research that show an improvement on the simple algorithms of matrix inversion. They discussed an algorithm that is more suitable for finding inverse and determinant of dense matrices. The algorithm requires a mechanism for selection of pivot (e.g., selection of absolute maximum value) in the available sub-matrix and the mechanism to get the inverse from the final resultant matrix by rearranging the rows and columns. They provided a method for assigning the sign of the determinant and the algorithm is explained through solved examples. On the other hand, Farooq and Hamid continued research on the same topic resulted on introducing a new algorithm for finding inverse and determinant of a given matrix in one instance. The algorithm is straightforward in understanding and manual calculations. Computer implementation of the algorithm is extremely simple and is quite efficient in time and memory utilization. The algorithm is supported by an example. The algorithm is applicable in the cases of pseudo inverses for non-square matrices and solution of system of linear equations with minor modification.

Ali Hussein Zolait
University of Bahrain, Kingdom of Bahrain

Chapter 1
Harnessing Information and Communication Technologies for Diffusing Connected Government Applications in Developing Countries:
Concept, Problems and Recommendations

E. Ruhode
Cape Peninsula University of Technology, South Africa

V. Owei
Cape Peninsula University of Technology, South Africa

ABSTRACT

Improving information management practices is a key focus for many organisations across both the public and private sectors. An information society begins with a connected government and ICTs are the bedrock and founding pillars of such societies. To assist public administrators think beyond traditional e-government, this study describes a concept of connected government, whose philosophy rests on the integration story that happens behind the scenes of the visible web interface as well as the collaboration among government agencies. Diffusion of Innovations theory is the conceptual framework underpinning this study. The connected government phenomenon is also put into perspective by the systems theory that is explained in this study. This article describes a case study of an organisation in a developing country environment where even the basic e-government services are barely extant. This study was done to determine the connectedness within and across government agencies, with the idea of stimulating some thinking within and among public administrators, around the possibility that a connected government can indeed be established in a developing country setting. The study exposes shortcomings to e-government diffusion not only of the organisation under investigation, but also of other similar enterprises in developing countries within the same context. The paper concludes by proposing a set of recommendations toward diffusing connected government applications as an antidote to identified problems.

DOI: 10.4018/978-1-4666-1752-0.ch001

INTRODUCTION

Improving information management practices is a key focus for many organisations, across both public and private sectors (Robertson, 2005). The PC Magazine defines information management as a discipline that analyzes information as an organizational resource. The discipline covers the definitions, uses, value and distribution of all data and information within an organization whether processed by computer or not. The following is a more contemporary definition of information management given by Duffey and Assad (1989, p. 6):

(Information management) is the planning, organising, developing and controlling of the information and data in an organisation (at both corporate and individual levels) and of the people, hardware, software, and systems that produce the information and data.

Duffey and Assad's definition implies that information management is a broader concept that includes information sharing within and across organisations. Impact Consulting (2007) report that one of the most organisation-focused benefits of electronic information management is information sharing. Many government systems specialists argue that government and public institutions are not simple but complex and mammoth bureaucratic establishments with a set of information silos that erect barriers to the access of information and make the provision of services cumbersome and frustrating (Kumar et al., 2007). However, with the emergence and proliferation of Information and Communication Technologies (ICTs), Gichoya (2005), argues that it is possible to improve efficiency and effectiveness of internal administration within governments and to relocate government services from government offices to locations closer to the citizens. This relates well to an earlier insistence by Tapscott (1995), that ICTs support the "age of network intelligence",

reinventing businesses, governments and individuals. Throughout the world, use of ICTs for government reinvention is increasing, though developing countries are still in the early stages of full-scale ICT deployment.

While ICTs have been harnessed in many governments throughout the world, the European Commission (2003) reported the emergency of 'islands' of government that are frequently unable to interoperate due to fragmentation resulting from uncoordinated efforts at all levels of public administration. Information sharing across government agencies provides new opportunities to enhance governance, which can include improved efficiency, new services, increased citizen participation, and an enhanced global information infrastructure. Referring to knowledge sharing and information, the Canadian International Development Agency's Knowledge-Sharing Plan (2007) explains that it is an effort at "knowledge pooling" amongst diverse participants across all sectors of the economy in order to consolidate existing knowledge and generation of fresh intellectual capital with a view to improving programming in governance and development (CIDA, 2007).

The main objective of this article is to examine the diffusion of connected government applications in government organisations in developing countries. The study draws from the systems theory of management where the entire government is perceived as one system with several constituent parts like departments and agencies, people, software, hardware and procedures. A case study approach is adopted where the role of ICTs in promoting inter-organisational information sharing culture is examined. The study is limited to a single organisation, whose inter-organisational relationships will be thoroughly investigated. This article is mainly motivated by our experience with disjoint government agencies in developing countries where getting a full cycle of services is not easy. The main purpose of this article then is to address the concept of connected government as a way of promoting information sharing within government agencies. This paper therefore makes a significant contribution to the body of knowledge in e-government as the concept of connected government is virtually unknown in a developing country setting, especially in Africa.

The structure of the paper is as follows: The next section describes the theoretical framework underpinning this study and brings to the fore the connected government concept and the systems theory. Diffusion of Innovation theory, connected government concept and the systems theory are all explained in this section. Section 3 explains the case study approach to research and its relevance to this particular study. The case under investigation is also described in section 3 as well as the research problem and the research method. Section 4 gives a detailed discussion of the findings followed by an explanation of the analysis of the findings section 5. During analysis of the findings, problems and issues are identified and recommended solutions to these problems and issues are presented in section 6. Section 7 is a discussion of the findings followed by conclusion in section 8.

THEORETICAL FRAMEWORK

Diffusion of innovations theory was selected in this article to explain diffusion of connected government applications in developing countries. The systems theory is also explained to bring the connected government phenomena into perspective. These theories are described in the following subsections:

DIFFUSION OF INNOVATIONS THEORY

Diffusion of Innovations Theory (DOI) is defined by Rogers (1962) as the process by which an innovation is communicated through certain channels over time among the members of a social system. An innovation is an idea, behaviour, or object that is perceived as new by its audience (Robinson, 2009). According to Rogers (1995), the core assumption of diffusion research centres on the conditions which increase or decrease the likelihood that a new idea, product, or practice will be adopted by members of a given culture. In the context of this study, connected government is an innovation which is widely perceived to modernise government operations. DOI is therefore applied in this study to examine the diffusion of connected government applications in a developing country context.

Rogers (1995) holds that the diffusion of innovation theory consists of four elements which are:

i.   Innovation: an idea, practices, or objects that is perceived as knew by an individual or other unit of adoption
ii.   Communication channels: the means by which messages get from one individual to another
iii. Time: the three time factors are:
      a. Innovation-decision process
      b. Relative time with which an innovation is adopted by an individual or group
      c. Innovation's rate of adoption
iv.   Social system: a set of interrelated units that are engaged in joint problem solving to accomplish a common goal. The members or units of a social system may be individuals, informal groups, organizations, and/or subsystems. The social system constitutes a boundary within which an innovation diffuses.

The amount of time it takes for people to adopt the innovation led to the categorisation of adopters into five groups. Members of each category typically possess certain distinguishing characteristics as follows:

i.   Innovators: venturesome, educated, have the ability to cope with a high degree of uncertainty about an innovation and they control substantial financial resources

ii. Early adopters: social leaders, successful, respected and highly educated

iii. Early majority: seldom hold positions of opinion leadership, are deliberate before adopting a new idea, have many informal social contacts and seldom hold positions of opinion leadership

iv. Late majority: cautious and sceptical, traditional and have lower socio-economic status

v. Laggards: usually suspicious of innovations and possess no opinion leadership. Neighbours and friends are the main sources of information, and the fear of debt is atypical characteristic of this group.

The rate of adoption of innovations is impacted by five factors: relative advantage, compatibility, trialability, observability, and complexity (Rogers, 1995). The first four factors are generally positively correlated with rate of adoption while the last factor, complexity, is generally negatively correlated with rate of adoption (Rogers, 1995). The actual rate of adoption is governed by both the rate at which an innovation takes off and the rate of later growth. According to Rogers (1995), low cost innovations may have a rapid take-off while innovations whose value increases with widespread adoption (network effects) may have faster late stage growth. Innovation adoption rates can, however, be impacted by other phenomena. For instance, the adaptation of technology to individual needs can change the nature of the innovation over time. In addition, a new innovation can impact the adoption rate of an existing innovation and path dependence may lock potentially inferior technologies in place.

The connected government phenomenon is a new innovation within the developing country context. This study recognises DOI as a theory applicable to the diffusion of this innovation. The next sub-section defines and contextualises the connected government concept.

CONNECTED GOVERNMENT CONCEPT AND THE SYSTEMS THEORY

Australia's Management Advisory Committee (2004) report that "the distinguishing characteristic of whole of government (connected government) work is that there is an emphasis on objectives shared across organisational boundaries, as opposed to working solely within an organisation. It encompasses the design and delivery of a wide variety of policies, programs and services that cross organisational boundaries". The connected government concept realizes the need to position the entire government as one integrated enterprise, underpinned by interoperability among its constituent departments and agencies. Simply put, connected government enables government to work as an integrated body that shows only one face to the public (United Nations, 2006). Extending government as one enterprise to public information consumers can be illustrated by the systems theory in information management. The systems theorists focus on viewing the enterprise as a whole and as an interrelationship of its parts (Lussier, 2000). They define a system as a goal-directed collection of interrelated, interdependent and interacting parts existing in an environment with boundaries. In other words, systems theory is a framework that can be used to analyse a group of objects working together to achieve one goal. A major characteristic of the systems theory is that it emphasises the importance of all of the parts of the enterprise working together and acknowledges the interconnections of the enterprise with its envirnment. According to Cook and Hunsaker (2001), one of the significant aspects of the systems approach is that it allows the level of analysis to run up and down the organisation hierarchy and from the outside environment to individual behaviour. The development of a connected government results in the creation of one system or entity with several interconnected parts. Such a government, according to Singh (2008) will have a single sign-on portal, unified health records, connected schools and other institutions and a value chain approach.

The concept of connected government can be understood in the context of e-government. As generally accepted, e-government is the use of information technology to support government operations, engage citizens, and provide government services. While this definition captures the essence of e-government, Dawes (2002) unpacks e-government to expose the following four dimensions:

E-services: The electronic delivery of government information, programs, and services often (but not exclusively) over the Internet

E-democracy: The use of electronic communications to increase citizen participation in the public decision-making process

E-commerce: The electronic exchange of money for goods and services such as citizens paying taxes and utility bills

E-management: The use of information technology to improve the internal management of government.

Similar to Dawes' four dimensions of e-government is Heeks' three application domains of e-government that are shown in Figure 1.

Heeks (2001) summaries e-government domains as follows:

- *e-Society:* To enable relationships and interactions beyond boundaries, among public agencies, private sector and civil community in general
- *e-Citizens and e-Services:* To realize connections and interrelationships among governments and citizens and to deliver automated services
- *e-Administration:* For automation and computerization of administrative tasks and for realization of strategic connections among internal processes, departments and functions

The connected government philosophy's thrust rests upon the last dimension of Dawes's definition, that is, e-management and Heeks' domain of e-administration. While the target of e-government encompasses four main groups: citizens, businesses, governments (other government and public agencies) and employees (Ndou, 2004), the emphasis of connected government is on the integration story that happens behind the scenes of the visible web interface (UN, 2008). Connected government lies at the confluence of Dawes' and Heeks' views, therefore it embraces

Figure 1. E-government domains (Adapted from Heeks, 2001)

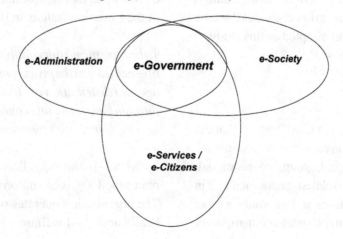

both. According to the UN e-Government Survey Report (2008, p. 3), the concept of connected government is "derived from the e-government-as-a-whole concept which focuses on the provision of services at the front-end, supported by integration, consolidation and innovation in back-end processes and systems to achieve maximum cost savings and improved service delivery". In this context, value is created for citizens, business and other consumers of government information and services. By having related agencies across different levels of governments and also different agencies with different functionality communicate with each other, these consumers, according to Layne and Lee (2001), will then view the government as an integrated information base.

A connected government infrastructure enables seamless sharing of information across departments and agencies. The focus of connected government is not to replace any system that is already in place, but to make them communicate with each other in as seamless and transparent manner as possible, in order for processes to be streamlined, thereby increasing value to information consumers. In light of this; the National Blood Services of Zimbabwe (NBSZ) was selected for this article as a case study. The NBSZ has a direct obligation to pass on information to the parent ministry, which is the ministry of health and child welfare. A successful connected government implementation at NBSZ or any other government establishment depends on effective information management. The next section discusses the case study approach that was adopted in this study.

CASE STUDY

As a research strategy, Yin (2003) assets that the case study is used in many situations to contribute to knowledge of individual, group, organisational, social, political, and related phenomena. Yin (2003, pp. 13-14) defines a case study as "an empirical enquiry that investigates a contemporary phenomenon within its real-life context, especially when the boundaries between object of study and context are not really evident". Dul and Hak (2007) add savour to Yin's definition by expressing that scores obtained in case studies are analysed in a qualitative manner. A remarkable strength of case study research is that it yields in-depth information of the phenomena under investigation. Stake (1995) and Yin (2003) identified at least six sources of evidence in case studies, namely: documents, archival records, interviews, direct observation, participant-observation and physical artifacts. This allows for a rich description of the phenomena under study as it occurs in the natural environment.

According to Feagin et al. (1991), a case study is an ideal methodology when a holistic, in-depth investigation is needed. A case study selected in this study is a problem-oriented one, which analyses a real life situation where existing problems need to be solved. As discussed earlier, a single case study is considered sufficient in this study to expose the connected government requirements of organisations. The following subsection describes NBSZ as the unit of analysis.

CASE DESCRIPTION

The NBSZ is one of the several government-owned organisations in Zimbabwe. The purpose of NBSZ as an organisation can be summed up in their mission statement that says,

To be recognized internationally as the institution of excellence in the procurement, processing, storage and distribution of blood and blood products through innovative and contemporary technology in compliance with international standards

NBSZ is the only licensed operator in human blood services and products in Zimbabwe. The organisation operates within the ministry of health and child welfare. One of the company's core values says, "The voluntary non-remunerated blood donor drives the organisation and the needs of the donor will be central to the operations of the NBSZ". Blood donors are either institutions or individuals. The Service operates according to international standards as set out by the World Health Organisation (WHO). According to NBSZ Quality Policy, ISO 9001:2000 forms the organisation's foundation of the Quality Management System encompassing Health, Safety and Environmental concerns. Within the context of this study, NBSZ exchanges data and information with other organisations as the WHO, the parent ministry, hospitals, medical school, National Social Security Authority (NSSA) and others. NBSZ has five centres throughout the country located in Harare, Bulawayo, Gweru, Masvingo, and Mutare.

RESEARCH FRAMEWORK

The telephonic interview with the systems administrator was conducted on November 20, 2008. The organisation had more than 80 users and 70 Personal Computers (PCs) on the wide area network (WAN) covering five cities—Harare, Masvingo, Bulawayo, Gweru, and Mutare. NBSZ runs an IBM database application called Progress that stores blood records. Data that is recorded is blood donor (companies, schools, and individuals), stocks of blood, testing results, notification letters and other relevant information. The Progress system is also integrated with Pastel Software that processes the organisation's financials. Both the WAN and Local Area Network (LAN) are widely used as employees share network resources like printers and fax machines. Documents are also shared through file sharing facility across the WAN. Emails are extensively used especially in communicating with blood donors externally and with other employees internally.

RESEARCH PROBLEM

As a result of our experience with the Zimbabwe government's products and services, the following issues are noted:

i.   There is absence of information sharing strategies within the departments and ministries in the Government of Zimbabwe

ii.   There is much evidence of computerisation and embracing of ICTs across the public sector, but there is lack of collaboration in the implementation of ICT-based tools

iii. Most citizens of Zimbabwe, particularly the young to middle-aged, are well enlightened about technological developments in other countries but are not enjoying the same benefits from their government. They can only make use of online resources of other countries when necessary, but the same resources from their government are not available online

The above issues bring to the fore the statement of research problem for this study, which is the following:

Government Ministries and Departments in Zimbabwe do not have a whole-of-government approach to information sharing in order to create an information pool from where information can be harvested and shared for the benefit of the citizens, the business community, international community and other stakeholders, as well as for fostering good governance.

The main question that this study seeks to answer is: what role can ICTs play in the establishment of a connected government in a developing country context? The next subsection explains the research method that was used.

RESEARCH METHOD

In order to gain an in-depth operational realism of the systems in the government agencies in Zimbabwe, we conducted telephonic interview with the Systems Administrator who was acting as the Information Technology manager of the National Blood Services Zimbabwe (NBSZ). The choice of information technology administrator was made on the premise that he had knowledge of both organisational and technical architecture framework for information management within the organisation. It is in this view that the systems administrator was selected to provide required information. The systems administrator is a middle administration position in the organization, which meant that apart from technical information, the interviewee had sufficient knowledge about management issues. The informant supplied valuable information with regard to information sharing and ICT infrastructures in the organisation and inter-organisation networking methods. Appendix A shows qquestions that we sought to gather primary data on. Literature search on the organisation was mainly done on the NBSZ website (http://www.bloodbank.co.zw/), which is well maintained and sufficiently informative. The site has information ranging from general to detailed. General information is that regarding core purpose, mission, health and safety policies and quality policies; while detailed information pertains to blood donation process, graphical views of donated blood amounts, statistical reports on blood usage and available counselling services. The website has helped a great deal in reaching the blood donor community.

FINDINGS

Findings from the investigation were grouped into two categories, which are e-administration and inter-organisational collaboration. The rationale behind the two categories is that connected government applications become effective when they improve internal information management as well as facilitating communication with other organisations.

E-ADMINISTRATION (E-MANAGEMENT)

As discussed earlier, e-Administration (or e-Management according to Dawes, 2002), is the thrust of the connected government concept. The Progress system at NBSZ takes care of back-end processing and reports on blood stocks, usage, donors, etc are extracted for internal use from the system. The main handicap though is that the system is inflexible and can only produce pre-defined reports. It does not provide for end user computing where managers can define their own ad hoc and summary reports. However, information processing problems mainly relate to human organisational issues rather than technical. Absence of a leaner organisation structure in NBSZ rendered movement of information within and across boundaries very difficult. Traditional rigid structures have been maintained in Zimbabwe over many years. Information systems that do not promote innovation and sharing within departments are basically a result of the traditional structure and management styles that have characterised much government practice to date (Haricharan, 2005). Organisations with high bureaucratic structures prevent collaboration and community interaction. Modernisaion of public entities has positive implications such as convenient and timely access to public information, rapid access to information, quick service through interaction, enhanced participation of employees and other stakeholders, cost-reduction through online access to required information and improved overall efficiency and effectiveness.

INTER-ORGANISATIONAL COLLABORATION

NBSZ has a need to share information with other departments and organisations particularly those within the same ministry of heath and child welfare. For statistics purposes, the parent ministry requires information from NBSZ like amount of blood in stock. Of equal significance to the ministry is information on contaminated blood in categories of TB, Hepatitis and HIV/AIDS. This information is extracted from the Progress system at NBSZ and passed manually to the ministry. There is however no direct information exchange with other organisations like the National Aids Council (NAC) whose core business is on HIV/AIDS statistics.

The systems administrator at NBSZ did not indicate any formal networking with NGOs that work directly with HIV/AIDS. Some of the NGOs running HIV/AIDS mitigation programmes in Zimbabwe are the Zimbabwe Aids Network (ZAN), ZNNP+ and SAfAIDS. While these NGOs are engaged in the creation, processing, management and dissemination of HIV/AIDS information (Matizirofa & Smith, 2006), there is no direct networking and sharing of information with the NBSZ. On the same vein, the Progress system does not produce reports for external use as required by academic and research institutions such as the University of Zimbabwe's faculty of Medicine or the Medical Research Council of Zimbabwe. Therefore, information exchange between NBSZ and academic and research institutions is barely consistent.

ANALYSIS OF FINDINGS

Rogers (2003) asserts that instead of focusing on persuading individuals to change, DOI sees change as being primarily about the evolution or "reinvention" of products and behaviours so they become better fits for the needs of individuals and groups (Robinson, 2009). According to Rogers (2003), the success of an innovation depends on how well it evolves to meet the needs of more and more demanding people. It follows therefore that reinvention is a key principle in diffusion of innovations. The following subsections present analysis of the findings according to DOI's four elements which are innovation, communication channels, time and social system.

INNOVATION

In this study, the networked or connected government is referred to as the innovation. The innovation is diffusing slowly within the government social systems but no formal diffusion method has been devised. At NBSZ and other government institutions in Zimbabwe, e-administration and ultimately collaboration of systems, which are the findings of this study, are hindered by a number of challenges. Some of these challenges which also apply to most developing countries in Africa are prohibitive cost of computers and networking equipment, poor technological infrastructure (inadequate access technologies and poor national and international bandwidth), inadequate electricity, human capital flight, poor ICT literacy and closed systems in some organisations like the NBSZ. The underlying factor on these challenges is believed to be the political and economic despair Zimbabwe is reeling under. The WAN at NBSZ study connects offices that are in towns and cities while the majority of smaller stations are electronically isolated. NBSZ's blood donor community and individuals, schools and other institutions spread throughout the country cannot access information and other resources which are regularly posted on the NBSZ web site. Organisations cannot establish communication links in rural and marginalized areas because of lack of electricity. Zimbabwe is currently in a state of economic and political isolation, so it is therefore very difficult to finance any electrification projects due to severe foreign currency shortage. The Rural Electrification Programme whose master plan was approved by cabinet in 1997 and funded by the African Development Bank (Mapako & Prasad, 2004) was a noble venture until financial resources ran dry. Zimbabwe is currently a net importer of electricity which is the determinant in rolling out ICTs to the whole country. Internally, Zimbabwe can generate 750 megawatts (MW) from Lake Kariba, 920MW from Hwange Power Station and 300MW from other smaller stations at Munyati, Bulawayo and Harare. The domestic power consumption requirement is estimated at more than 2700MW, so the remainder is imported from the Democratic Republic of the Congo (DRC), Zambia, Mozambique and South Africa.

COMMUNICATION CHANNELS

Communication is a process in which participants create and share information with one another to reach a mutual understanding (Rogers, 1995). There is general agreement among management and staff at NBSZ that the closed system in the organisation must be replaced. Although there is no formal way of communicating connected government as a new technological idea at NBSZ, the need for an enterprise system was identified and discussed in formal meetings. Prohibitive costs of computer equipment and software have often been sited as a major drawback in acquiring an open system that can be integrated with other systems.

TIME

The relative time with which connected government is adopted or its rate of adoption at NBSZ or any other government institution in Zimbabwe are affected by many factors. Firstly, the innovation itself is not fully developed as explained in the first element of innovation. Secondly, the holistic nature of the whole-of-government approach re-

quires e-literacy at all levels of management and user communities in government institutions. The low rate of computer literacy and pre-requisite skills to use new technological tools and applications is a notable challenge in Zimbabwe. Thirdly, the human resource capacity in many organisations in Zimbabwe and particularly government institutions is very fluid. A detailed examination of substantial brain drain in Zimbabwe can reveal that the direct impact of significant outflows of human capital have had a negative effect on projects implementation at organisational and national levels.

SOCIAL SYSTEM

The social system is not only constituted by the NBSZ user community, but also by other organisations that share information with it. While the social system constitutes a boundary within which an innovation diffuses, it is important to point out that the social systems in Zimbabwean organisations have been affected by high staff turnover caused by human capital flight. Despite the fact that NBSZ has a stand-alone information technology unit, staff turnover during the time of this investigation was extremely high. Baldwin and Curley (2007) argue that the diffusion of innovative ideas need not be random or accidental but can be deliberately directed, managed, and accelerated within organisations. However, severe political and economic pressure exerted on Zimbabwean companies and individuals has led to mass exodus of qualified people. Zimbabwe has lost more than four million people to neighbouring countries and overseas in less than a decade. USAID (2007) reported that Zimbabwe's scientific and technological capacity is comparable to regional benchmarks, but integration of new technologies through foreign investment is partly being blocked by flight of skilled workers. The problem of human capital in Zimbabwe brings our attention to another dimension that affects the organisational social system, that of low rate of computer literacy and pre-requisite skills to use new technological tools and applications. This is a particular problem in the developing countries, where the chronic lack of qualified staff and inadequate human resources training has been a problem for years (UNPA & ASPA, 2001). Government employees and their managers have less knowledge and appreciation of ICTs as compared to their counterparts in the private sector where e-commerce has established itself.

RECOMMENDATIONS

During the analysis of the findings, it has emerged that many challenges are faced when efforts are made towards diffusing connected government applications in public enterprises in Zimbabwe. The three concepts discussed earlier—the systems theory, Dawes' four dimensions of e-government and Heeks' three application domains of e-government—can be used to propose solutions to challenges identified during analysis of findings. At the confluence of the three concepts is a government with coherent internal workings while providing seamless products and services to consumers. The concepts' thrust is interoperability of government entities which can only be facilitated by improving technological infrastructure in Zimbabwe's government organisations. The information and network architecture at one government agency should allow for flexibility and interoperability with other departments. Standard data definitions must be established and enforced across networks to facilitate cross-transfer of information. A standardization plan should be formulated for system-wide network, data exchange, system standards, etc. As the need for a connected government emerges, then communication and integration-oriented technologies become more imperative. Replacing closed systems with open Enterprise Resource Planning (ERPs) software, Customer Relationship Managenement (CRMs)

systems and integrated databases will facilitate collaboration of the whole public sector, resulting in improvement of user-focused services as well as internal and external delivery effectiveness. These large modelling systems will facilitate the processing and sharing of diverse management information such as human resources information, marketing, procurement, financial reporting, etc. The command-based progress software at NBSZ does not permit any communication with other software such as Pastel which is used for the financial processing within the same organisation. This is a similar case with other public organisations in Zimbabwe where islands of information are processed and stored in legacy systems that do not connect to other software. A study on ERPs by Seddon (2005), suggests that ERP systems provide benefits such as improved information visibility, personnel and inventory reduction, productivity improvement and new improved processes. The main source of different and unrelated software is that most systems are imported into the country. There are also no guiding principles at government level regarding acquisition and deployment of these systems.

Figure 2 shows a recommended matrix structure of organisations with which the NBSZ can exchange information on HIV/AIDS. Collaborative systems can facilitate seamless information exchange as shown in Figure 2. In the diagram, HIV/AIDS information which originates at NBSZ is shared with the ministry of health, academic and research bodies, NGOs, the NAC, and WHO. All the other institutions can also share information as shown in the diagram.

Cost of computers, ICT equipment and software is a major concern to cash-strapped organisations in Zimbabwe. Firstly, the government can encourage importation of computers and computer parts by removing import taxes on such equipment. Such a move can help suppress prices to the levels where organisations can afford to think towards digital revolution. Government can also initiate computer assembly projects as

Figure 2. NBSZ HIV/AIDS inter-agency information flow

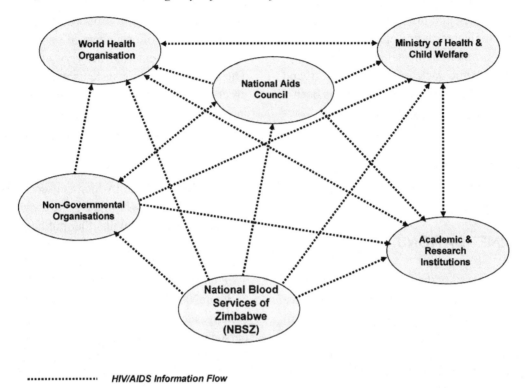

··················· **HIV/AIDS Information Flow**

in the case of the Madaraka computer project in Kenya. Though the Madaraka project's success is still questionable (Wanjiku, 2008), it is important to understand that the underlying idea when implemented properly, can yield phenomenal results. Secondly the Government of Zimbabwe, like Kenya and Ghana, can also organise to receive used but recyclable computers from developed countries as Japan, the US and European countries for free. The government can also fund and initiate open source software development initiatives in Zimbabwe in order to save a lot of money currently used on Windows software licensing. The Zimbabwe government can be spurred by the example of other developing countries, such as India, that seem to be "riding the ICT wave" successfully. India and indeed many other countries, has established technology park concept, commonly known as technoparks to promote research and development (R&D) especially in software development. Many developing countries such

as Turkey, China, Malaysia, Singapore, Taiwan, Thailand, have sought to emulate these successes and reap the benefits of ICT-led growth for their own economies. Applications that are locally developed in these technoparks are then deployed to various private and public organisations, fostering interoperability within and across these entities. The Turkish government passed a technology development zones law in 2001 whose thrust was to promote the establishment of technoparks under the guidance and lead of universities. According to this law, companies are encouraged to invest more into R&D and software development through tax incentives and according to this law, any kind of software development activity is considered an R&D activity. Phenomenal expansion of ICT applications (e.g., e-commerce, e-learning and telemedicine etc.) especially in rural and remote areas in Turkey has been witnessed since then.

The problem of poor technological infrastructure can be solved by improving the national and international bandwidth. Broadband technologies such as fibre optics though expensive, are the best way to building a reliable technological infrastructure. Following the establishment of technological infrastructures, the creation of portals, websites and gateways would be the only way to implementing a connected government. These are web-based tools for better information sharing, coordination and planning among donors and governments. A connected government's full potential, at least in the consumers' view, can be achieved by lateral integration of government electronic services across different enterprises' functional walls. The roadway to reaching this level is the establishment of a government portal, which by definition, is a website that constitutes the central access or entry point to all available government information and electronic services. The portal should make available an array of on-line services including government information publicity, government and citizen interaction, government service for individuals, government service for business, culture services, etc. Basic services that many e-government portals throughout the world are offering, but not yet available in Zimbabwe are: voter registration, ordering birth, death, and marriage certificates, filing state taxes, hunting and fishing licenses, accessing to medical information, etc. It is however important to mention that mail servers, web servers, routers, switches, base stations etc all need electricity to operate. So it is necessary that we have adequate electricity to power the servers that will serve the web pages. It is therefore obvious that the Government of Zimbabwe should resuscitate the present power generation plants at Hwange, Kariba and Munyati. Other forms of energy generation like solar, wind, biogas and even nuclear energy should also be explored.

The problem of low ICT literacy rate can be overcome if the government would make a deliberate policy to implement e-literacy programs. The impact of human capital flight would also not have as catastrophic as it is today had the Zimbabwean population been e-literate. The Gyandoot project of India is a very good case where community-based e-literacy programs have been successfully implemented. In this project, roving entrepreneurs teamed up with government to bring Internet-based government services to remote villages.

DISCUSSION

Zimbabwe's capacity to deliver on the sustainable development front, including e-government initiatives, has been acutely weighed down by unprecedented political and economic turmoil the country is reeling under. The government's controversial land reform programme has reportedly been the cause of significant damage to the commercial farming sector rendering the country a net importer of food after having traditionally been the source of jobs, exports, and foreign exchange (Isaacs, 2007). This led to the isolation of Zimbabwe from the international community. Zimbabwean economy has since year 2000 been beset with crises, characterised by an unsustainable fiscal deficit, an overvalued exchange rate, rampant inflation, above 80 per cent unemployment, decline in manufacturing and agricultural production due to farm invasions, company closures, human capital flight, and many other problems.

Political tension in Zimbabwe then led to strict regulation laws in such areas as telecommunications and media. The postal and telecommunications regulatory authority of Zimbabwe (POTRAZ) created monopolies in the telecommunications sector which eventually failed to meet their service obligations. The three data and voice careers which are Telone, Powertel and Transmedia enjoy unmatched monopoly but their services have significantly dropped. The net effect of government decisions on telecommunications is poor technological infrastructure throughout the country. National and international bandwidth for internet services is very low making it difficult for the government to offer even basic e-government services.

Structural transformations of government enterprises are the entry point into serious discussion of the change agenda especially concerning connected government. Artkinson (2003) argues that "Bureaucracy—with its rigid rules and focus on regulating the process rather than the outcomes—is more often an impediment to effective and innovative service provision". Horizontal systems of management, where people interact and share ideas, information and resources are the most suitable for enterprises in an information economy. Hence, horizontal or flat organization structures offer what vertical bureaucratic structures never can deliver, that is the direct, horizontal connection with people. In developing countries there are significant demographic differences in both the access to, and use of the Internet, for personal, professional, or political purposes, either at home, at work, or in the community (Riley, 2004). This difference makes it impossible to effectively implement and deploy connected government applications as the majority of consumers of government services do not have access to the e-services. Explaining the challenges of digital divide, the United Nations World Public Sector Report (2003), says, "The potential of e-government as a development tool hinges upon three prerequisites—a minimum threshold level of technological infrastructure, human capital and e-connectivity—for all. E-government readiness strategies and programmes will be able to be effective and "include all" people only if, at the very minimum, all have functional literacy and education, which includes knowledge of computer and Internet use; all are connected to a computer; and all have access to the Internet. The primary challenge of e-government for development therefore, is how to accomplish this". According to Riley (2004), the concept of the digital divide is based on the hypothesis that there are both "information-haves" and "information-have-nots"

in the Internet Age. This is very true in Zimbabwe as the NBSZ only reaches people in urban areas more often than rural folks because of the wide digital divide. Low rates of access to ICTs in rural areas of developing countries are a concern to proponents of connected government concept. The IT Administrator made it clear that e-mail is the mode of communication they normally use to reach blood donors. In addition, the NBSZ web site is full of informative material about blood transfusion which however can only be accessed by technology-literate part of the community. While the NBSZ has made significant efforts to physically reach many remote parts of Zimbabwe, it however remains a point of concern that these electronically inactive people are not fully aware of the significance of the blood transfusion development programme.

NBSZ or any other organisation that is committed to working in partnership with other agencies involved in providing services to the public requires an inter-organisation policy on information sharing. An Information Sharing policy or protocol sets out a framework for information sharing across the respective organisations. The policy commits the partner organisations to draw up information sharing agreements to meet specific business needs in an agreed format. Such policy would make it easy for organisations such as NAC, ZAN or Research institutions to electronically extract HIV/AIDS data from the NBSZ database. This policy is concerned with the planning, introduction and use of IT resources for the benefit of all public enterprises. The new paradigm of value creation in the information-based economy requires information system strategies that create the platform to integrate and optimize the value chains in the extended institutions. We concur with Dawes' (2007) regarding her proposed contents of such an information system strategy. Dawes says it should "emphasize the principles, standards, and infrastructure that make it possible for all agencies to work in consistent ways. This might include legal and policy infrastructure, telecommunications infrastructure, standards for data and technologies, rules and mechanisms for information use and sharing, and a host of other elements". According to Gilbert (2003), an information sharing policy is a scaleable security measure because it can exist at any level of an organization; from global corporate mandate down to workgroup issue-specific policy

CONCLUSION

Conclusion to the study is presented in three subsections as follows: summary, limitations, and related further study.

SUMMARY

An information society begins with a connected government and ICTs are the bedrock and founding pillars of such information societies. In this paper, we introduced the connected government concept which is a new philosophy in e-government implementation. The focus of this concept is that governments should manage their back-end processes which are the backbone of information integration and collaboration. Whereas the traditional e-government focused on e-services, connected government emphasizes the value of those services. A theoretical framework to this study was presented through the relevance of the diffusion of innovations theory to the adoption of connected government applications. The connected government phenomenon is also put into perspective by the systems theory which is explained in this study. We then presented an investigation, a case study of NBSZ, a government-owned organisation in Zimbabwe determine the connectedness within and across government agencies, with the idea of stimulating some thinking within and among public administrators, around the possibility that a connected government can indeed be established in a developing country setting. Naturally, service

delivery inhibitors were exposed as e-government initiatives have not yet been fully accepted and diffused in the developing world. We documented these shortcomings and suggested their possible causes as we believed that the identification of such problems is a small step on the road towards an integrated and networked government.

A set of proposed solution to problems was presented in the paper. The establishment of digital infrastructures as network connections, subsequent implementation of modeling technologies and government portal were among the recommended solutions. Others were the elimination of bureaucratic structures and the formulation of a sound information sharing policy to guide sharing of information within and across organisations.

The study presented in this article is deemed by the authors to be applicable not only to the Zimbabwe environment, but to all other developing countries in similar setting especially in Africa.

LIMITATIONS

As with all case study research, there are limitations to the interpretation of the results in attempting to generalise these analyses to a broader community of organisations. In this study, although government institutions in Zimbabwe face similar challenges, the choice of one organisation to investigate the diffusion of connected government applications may have introduced a bias. Inhibiting factors affecting connected government implementation at NBSZ may not necessarily be the same across all government agencies in Zimbabwe. Another limitation of this study may be a scarcity of hard quantitative information with regard to the actual contribution a connected government can have in the context of the Zimbabwean economy.

RELATED FURTHER STUDIES

This study considered a single case study in the investigation of the diffusion of connected government applications in Zimbabwe. We have exposed the inhibitors to the deployment of connected government applications within public institutions in Zimbabwe. We have also presented our recommended solutions to overcome the hindrances. Further research is however needed on how the Zimbabwe government can employ ICTs to extend electronic service delivery to citizens particularly under the current economic environment. On the same note, further research is required that can spell out the actual quantifiable benefits of investing in connected government applications in the developing economies such as Zimbabwe

REFERENCES

Akther, M. S., Onishi, T., & Kidokoro, T. (2007). E-Government in a developing: Citizen-centric approach for success. *International Journal of Electronic Governance*, *1*(1). doi:10.1504/IJEG.2007.014342

Anderson, G. L., Herr, K., Nihlen, A. S., & Noffke, S. E. (2007). *Studying your own school: An educator's guide to practitioner action research*. Thousand Oaks, CA: Corwin Press.

Artkinson, D. R. (2003). *Network government for the digital age*. Washington, DC: Progressive Police Institute.

Baldwin, E., & Curley, M. (2007). *Managing it innovation for business value: Practical strategies for it and business managers*. Intel Press.

Canadian International Development Agency. (2007). *Knowledge-Sharing Plan*. Retrieved February 2009 from http://www.acdi-cida.gc.ca/CIDAWEB/acdicida.nsf/En/EMA-218122154-PR4

Chan, O. J. (2005). Enterprise information systems strategy and planning. *The Journal of American Academy of Business, 2*.

Cook, C. W., & Hunsaker, P. L. (2001). *Management and organisational behaviour*. New York: McGraw-Hill.

Davision, M. R., Wagner, C., & Ma, C. K. L. (2005). From government to e-government: A transition model. *Information Technology & People*, *18*(3), 280–299. doi:10.1108/09593840510615888

Dawes, S. S. (2002). *The future of e-government*. Retrieved March 20, 2009, from http://www.vinnova.se/upload/EPiStorePDF/vri-06-11.pdf

Dul, J., & Hak, T. (2007). *Case study methodology in business research*. Oxford, UK: Butterworth-Heinemann.

Ebrahim, Z., & Irani, Z. (2005). E-government adoption: architecture and barriers. *Business Process Management Journal*, *11*(5), 589–611. doi:10.1108/14637150510619902

European Commission. (2003). *Linking-up Europe: The importance of interoperability for e-Government services*. Retrieved July 20, 2009, from http://europa.eu.int/ISPO/ida/

Gichoya, D. (2005). Factors affecting the successful implementation of ICT projects in government. *Electronic Journal of E-Government*, *3*(4), 175–184.

Gilbert, C. (2003). *Guidelines for an information sharing policy*. Bethesda, MD: SANS Institute.

Haricharan, S. (2005). *Knowledge management in the South African public sector*. Retrieved July 5, 2009, from http://www.ksp.org.za/holonl03.htm

Heeks, R. (2002). *eGovernment in Africa: Promise and practice* (iGovernment Working Paper Series Paper No. 13). Manchester, UK: University of Manchester.

Heeks, R. (2003). *e-Government Special – Does it Exist in Africa and what can it do?* Retrieved September 8, 2009, from http://www.balancingact-africa.com/news/back/balancing-act93.html#headline

Ifinedo, P. (2005). Measuring Africa's e-readiness in the global networked economy: A nine-country data analysis. *International Journal of Education and Development Using ICT, 1*(1).

Impact Consulting. (2007). *A CLICK AWAY: The benefits of managing programme information electronically.* Retrieved November 8, 2009, from http://www.sangonet.org.za/conference2007

Infodev. (2002). *The E-Government handbook for developing countries.* Retrieved September 30, 2009, from http://www.egovbarriers.org

Isaacs, S. (2007). *Survey of ICT and education in Africa: Aimbabwe country report.* Retrieved November 8, 2009, from http://www.infodev.org/en/Document.437.pdf

Kaaya, J. (2004). Implementing e-government services in east africa: assessing status through content analysis of government websites. *Electronic Journal of E-Government, 1*(2).

Kock, N. (2008). *Levels of adoption in organizational implementation of e-collaboration technologies.* Hershey, PA: IGI Publishing.

Kumar, V., Mukerji, B., Butt, I., & Persaud, A. (2007). Factors for Successful e-Government Adoption: a Conceptual Framework. *Electronic Journal of E-Government, 5*(1), 63–76.

Layne, K., & Lee, J. (2001). Developing fully functional E-government: A four stage model. *Government Information Quarterly, 18*(2), 122–136. doi:10.1016/S0740-624X(01)00066-1

Lussier, R. N. (2000). *Management fundamentals: Concepts, applications, skill development.* Springfield, MA: Springfield College.

Marche, S., & McNiven, J. D. (2003). E-Government and E-Governance: The Future isn't what it used to be. *Canadian Journal of Administrative Sciences, 20*(1), 74–86.

Ndou, V. (2004). E-Government for Developing Countries: Opportunities and Challenges. *Electronic Journal on Information Systems in Developing Countries, 18*(1), 1–24.

Parajuli, J. (2007). A content analysis of selected government web sites: A case study of Nepal. *Electronic Journal of E-Government, 5*(1).

Riley, T. B. (2004). *E-government, the digital divide and information sharing: Examining the issue.* Commonwealth Centre for E-Governance.

Robinson, L. (2009). *Understanding diffusion of innovations.* Retrieved February 20, 2009, from http://www.enablingchange.com.au

Rogers, E. M. (1962). *Diffusion of Innovations.* New York: Free Press.

Rogers, E. M. (1995). *Diffusion of Innovations* (4th ed.). New York: Free Press.

Ruhode, E., Owei, V., & Maumbe, B. (2008, May). *Arguing for the Enhancement of Public Service Efficiency and Effectiveness Through e-Government: The Case of Zimbabwe.* Paper presented at the IST-Africa Conference, Windhoek, Namibia.

Seddon, P. B. (2005). *Are ERP systems a source of competitive advantage?* New York: John Wiley & Sons.

Singh, N. (2008, July). *Moving from silos to virtual government.* Paper presented at the GoveTech 2008 Conference, Durban, South Africa.

Stake, R. E. (1995). *The Art of Case Study Research*. Thousand Oaks, CA: Sage Publications.

Tapscott, D. (1995). Leadership needed in age of networked intelligence. *Boston Business Journal, 11*(24).

Tellis, W. (1997). Introduction to Case Study. *Qualitative Report, 3*(2).

UN. (2008). *E-Government Survey Report*. Retrieved June 10, 2009, unpan1.un.org/intradoc/groups/public/documents/UN/UNPAN028607.pdf

Uzoka, F. E., Shemi, A. P., & Seleka, G. G. (2007). Behavioural influences on e-commerce adoption in a developing country context. *Electronic Journal of Information Systems in Developing Countries, 31*(4), 1–15.

Wanjiku, R. (2008, September). Still waiting for Madaraka PC. *ComputerWorld Kenya*.

Yin, R. K. (2003). Case study research design and methods. *Applied Social Research Methods Series, 5*.

APPENDIX A

Interview Questions (Table 1)

QUESTION	ANSWER
1. How many users are in your organisation	
2. How many PCs (including laptops) does your organisation have?	
3. Which tasks do you use your computers for? (Tick all that apply)	Desktop Applications
	Line of business application
	Billing/accounting
	E-mail
	Web research
	Other (Specify)
4. Do you do the following? (Tick all that apply):	Share a printer, fax machine, or other office equipment?
	Share documents, client information and an appointment calendar?
	Use the Internet for work purposes
	Access company e-mail from anywhere
	Retrieve business information when travelling?
	Work with employees in different business locations
5. What kind of computer network does your organisation currently have?	Peer-to-peer
	Server-based
6. Do you have a website?	
7. If your answer above is Yes, do you post downloadable information on your website – for use by your customers, suppliers or other organisations?	
8. If your answer above is Yes, what type of downloadable information do you post?	
7. Do you have any need to share information with other ministries/departments?	
8. If your answer above is Yes, which ministries and or departments do you exchange information with?	
9. Do you have in information sharing policy or Strategy document?	
10. In general (do not include details), what kind of information do you exchange?	
11. How do you currently exchange information?	
12. How does your business connect to the Internet?	Dial-up (e.g 56k modem)
	High Speed (e.g Cable, DSL)
	No internet connection yet
13. What Operating Systems do you run on your PCs?	
14. What Network Operating Systems do you run?	

QUESTION	ANSWER
15. What tools do you use for Data Management & Analysis	Business Intelligence
	Database/Data Warehouse
	Knowledge Management
	Other (Specify)
16. What tools do you use for Enterprise Back Office?	
17. How do you rate ICT literacy and ICT skills in your organisation?	Poor
	Good
	Satisfactory
	Excellent
18. Do you have a stand-alone IT department?	
19. If your answer above is yes, indicate how many of the following you have in the IT department	Technicians/Operators
	Programmers/Database/Network Administrators
	Senior Managers in IT

This work was previously published in International Journal of Technology Diffusion, Volume 1, Issue 1, edited by Ali Hussein Saleh Zolait, pp. 1-19, copyright 2010 by IGI Publishing (an imprint of IGI Global).

Chapter 2
An Efficient and Simple Algorithm for Matrix Inversion

Ahmad Farooq
King Khalid University, Saudi Arabia

Khan Hamid
National University of Computer and Emerging Sciences (NUCES), Pakistan

ABSTRACT

In this paper, a new algorithm is proposed for finding inverse and determinant of a given matrix in one instance. The algorithm is straightforward in understanding and manual calculations. Computer implementation of the algorithm is extremely simple and is quite efficient in time and memory utilization. The algorithm is supported by an example. The number of multiplication/division performed by the algorithm is exactly n^3; however, its efficiency lies in the simplicity of coding and minimal utilization of memory. Simple applicability and reduced execution time of the method is validated form the numerical experiments performed on test problems. The algorithm is applicable in the cases of pseudo inverses for nonsquare matrices and solution of system of linear equations with minor modification.

INTRODUCTION

The problem of finding inverse is one of the important problems in applied sciences and engineering. There are several methods available for finding inverses and for solving system of linear equations like iterative methods, Gauss elimination procedure and decomposition methods (Burden, 2001; Fill, 1997; Najafi, 2006; Rao, 1971). Recently many researchers worked on the area of matrix inversion (Chang, 2006; Mikkawy, 2006;

DOI: 10.4018/978-1-4666-1752-0.ch002

Vajargah, 2007). If inverse of coefficient matrix A in a given linear system is known then the solution can be found by $X = A^{-1}b$. In fact, the inversion of matrix is more generic requirement than the solution of linear system of equations in numerical linear algebra. Many algorithms exist to obtain numerical inversion for the given nonsingular matrix. A survey of these algorithms shows that efficiency, accuracy and simplicity of these algorithms can still be improved. However, most of these algorithms focus on particular types of matrices such as positive definite, diagonally dominant, banded and symmetric matrices etc.

In this work a new algorithm is developed for finding inverse of a given matrix. This approach is simpler and efficient than the exiting techniques and is applicable in general irrespective of the structure of the matrix. The manual calculations are straightforward and computer implementation is extremely easy. The memory utilization is minimal, i.e., it stores only the original matrix and replaces it gradually by the inverse. The most important and unique features of the algorithm is the ability of finding inversion and determinant in one go.

The rest of the paper is organized as follows. In section 2 we are presenting the simple algorithm. To emphasize the simplicity of computer implementation the code is also given in this section. Section 3 demonstrates the use of the algorithm through a numerical example. Section 4 is devoted to comparing computational complexity of the algorithm. In section 5 the performance results of the technique applied to the inversion of various matrices is given. Finally some conclusions are given in section 6.

(A). SIMPLE ALGORITHM FOR MATRIX INVERSION

The algorithm assumes to take a square matrix $A = [a_{i,j}]$ of dimension n. The inverse is calculated in n iterations. In each iteration p, all the existing elements $a_{i,j}$ of A change to new values $a'_{i,j}$. After the last iteration i.e. when $p = n$, $a'_{i,j}$ will be the elements of the inverse. The determinant of the matrix (denoted by d) is also calculated iteratively through successive multiplication of the pivot selected in each iteration. In this algorithm the pivots are selected diagonally starting from $a_{1,1}$ to $a_{n,n}$. If any pivot is found to be zero i.e., $a_{p,p} = 0$ then inverse cannot be calculated. If an inverse is calculated then d will contain the determinant of A.

A simple improvement to the algorithm is to go to the next diagonal element (in case of zero pivot) and revisit the zero diagonal element later. Probably by that time it would become non zero. Note that in step 7 of the following algorithm $a'_{i,p}$ on the LHS means that the latest value of the pivot row is to be used in the calculations.

- Let $p = 0$, $d = 1$;
  Step 2: $p \Leftarrow p + 1$
  - If $a_{p,p} = 0$ then cannot calculate inverse, go to step 10.
  - $d' \Leftarrow d \times a_{p,p}$
  - Calculate the new elements of the pivot row by:

$$a'_{p,j} \Leftarrow \frac{a_{p,j}}{a_{p,p}}, \quad where \quad j = 1, \cdots, n, \quad j \neq p$$

Calculate the new elements of the pivot column by:

$$a'_{i,p} \Leftarrow -\frac{a_{i,p}}{a_{p,p}}, \quad where \quad i = 1, \cdots, n, \quad i \neq p$$

Calculate the rest of the new elements by:

$$a'_{i,j} \Leftarrow a_{i,j} + a_{p,j} \times a'_{i,p}, \quad where \quad i = 1, \cdots, n, j = 1, \cdots, n \ \& \ i, j \neq p$$

Calculate the new value of the current pivot location:

$$a'_{p,p} \Leftarrow \frac{1}{a_{p,p}}$$

- If $p < n$ go to step 2 (n the dimension of the matrix A).
- Stop. If inverse exists- A contains the inverse and d is the determinant.

LEMMA

Let A be a non singular matrix of size 2 and M_1 is obtained from A through acting suitable matrix transformations. Whereas, $M_2 = A^{-1}$ is obtained from M_1 through acting and inserting suitable matrix transformation, then

1. F_1 the matrix obtained through the 1st iteration of the algorithm coincides with M_1.

2. $F_2 (=A^{-1})$ the matrix obtained through the 2nd iteration of the algorithm, coincides with M_2.

Proof: $A = \begin{bmatrix} a_{11} & a_{12} \\ a_{21} & a_{22} \end{bmatrix}$

Let $T_1\left(-\dfrac{1}{a_{11}}\right) = \begin{bmatrix} \dfrac{-1}{a_{11}} & 0 \\ 0 & 1 \end{bmatrix}$, let

$S_1(a_{22}) = \begin{bmatrix} 1 & a_{12} \\ 0 & 1 \end{bmatrix}$, let $X_1(x,y) = \begin{bmatrix} x & y \\ 0 & 1 \end{bmatrix}$

$T_1 A T_1 = \begin{bmatrix} \dfrac{1}{a_{11}} & \dfrac{-a_{12}}{a_{11}} \\ \dfrac{-a_{21}}{a_{11}} & a_{22} \end{bmatrix} = A_{1lr}$

$A_{1lr} S_1 = \begin{bmatrix} \dfrac{1}{a_{11}} & 0 \\ \dfrac{-a_{21}}{a_{11}} & \dfrac{|A|}{a_{11}} \end{bmatrix} = A_1'$

$X_1 A_1' = \begin{bmatrix} x & y \\ 0 & 1 \end{bmatrix} \begin{bmatrix} \dfrac{1}{a_{11}} & 0 \\ \dfrac{-a_{21}}{a_{11}} & \dfrac{|A|}{a_{11}} \end{bmatrix} = \begin{bmatrix} \dfrac{x}{a_{11}} - \dfrac{a_{21}}{a_{11}}y & \dfrac{|A|}{a_{11}}y \\ \dfrac{-a_{21}}{a_{11}} & \dfrac{|A|}{a_{11}} \end{bmatrix} = F_1 \qquad \cdots A$

$Let \begin{bmatrix} \dfrac{x}{a_{11}} - \dfrac{a_{21}}{a_{11}}y & \dfrac{|A|}{a_{11}}y \\ \dfrac{-a_{21}}{a_{11}} & \dfrac{|A|}{a_{11}} \end{bmatrix} = \begin{bmatrix} \dfrac{1}{a_{11}} & \dfrac{a_{12}}{a_{11}} \\ \dfrac{-a_{21}}{a_{11}} & \dfrac{|A|}{a_{11}} \end{bmatrix}$

This gives

$$x - a_{21}y = 1 \qquad \cdots 1$$
$$|A|y = a_{12} \qquad \cdots 2$$

by solving 1 and 2 we get

$$y = \frac{a_{12}}{|A|}, x = \frac{a_{22}\, a_{11}}{|A|}$$

by putting the value of x and y in equation X_1 and multiplying with A_1' we get F_1 so

$$X_1(T_1 A T_1)S_1 = A_1 = \begin{bmatrix} \dfrac{1}{a_{11}} & \dfrac{a_{12}}{a_{11}} \\ \dfrac{-a_{21}}{a_{11}} & \dfrac{|A|}{a_{11}} \end{bmatrix} = F_1$$

let $A_1 = \begin{bmatrix} \dfrac{1}{a_{11}} & \dfrac{a_{12}}{a_{11}} \\ \dfrac{-a_{21}}{a_{11}} & \dfrac{|A|}{a_{11}} \end{bmatrix} = \begin{bmatrix} b_{11} & b_{12} \\ b_{21} & b_{22} \end{bmatrix}$ let

$T_2\left(\dfrac{-1}{b_{22}}\right) = \begin{bmatrix} 1 & 0 \\ 0 & \dfrac{-1}{b_{22}} \end{bmatrix}$ let $S_2 = \begin{bmatrix} 1 & 0 \\ b_{21} & 1 \end{bmatrix}$, let

$X_2(x_0, y_0) = \begin{bmatrix} 1 & 0 \\ x_0 & y_0 \end{bmatrix}$

$$T_2 A_1 T_2 = \begin{bmatrix} b_{11} & \dfrac{-b_{12}}{b_{22}} \\ \dfrac{-b_{21}}{b_{22}} & \dfrac{1}{b_{22}} \end{bmatrix} = A_{2lr}$$

$$(A_{2lr}) S_2 = \begin{bmatrix} b_{11} & \dfrac{-b_{12}}{b_{22}} \\ \dfrac{-b_{21}}{b_{22}} & \dfrac{1}{b_{22}} \end{bmatrix} \begin{bmatrix} 1 & 0 \\ b_{21} & 1 \end{bmatrix}$$

$$= \begin{bmatrix} \dfrac{|A_1|}{b_{22}} & \dfrac{-b_{12}}{b_{22}} \\ 0 & \dfrac{1}{b_{22}} \end{bmatrix} = A_2'$$

$$X_2 A_2' = \begin{bmatrix} 1 & 0 \\ x_0 & y_0 \end{bmatrix} \begin{bmatrix} \dfrac{|A_1|}{b_{22}} & \dfrac{-b_{12}}{b_{22}} \\ 0 & \dfrac{1}{b_{22}} \end{bmatrix}$$

$$= \begin{bmatrix} \dfrac{|A_1|}{b_{22}} & \dfrac{-b_{12}}{b_{22}} \\ \dfrac{b_{21}}{b_{22}} & \dfrac{1}{b_{22}} \end{bmatrix} = F_2$$

$$= \begin{bmatrix} 0 & 1 \\ 1 & 0 \end{bmatrix} \begin{bmatrix} 1 & 0 \\ x_0 & y_0 \end{bmatrix} \begin{bmatrix} 0 & 1 \\ 1 & 0 \end{bmatrix} \begin{bmatrix} 0 & 1 \\ 1 & 0 \end{bmatrix} \begin{bmatrix} \dfrac{|A_1|}{b_{22}} & \dfrac{-b_{12}}{b_{22}} \\ 0 & \dfrac{1}{b_{22}} \end{bmatrix}$$

$$\begin{bmatrix} 0 & 1 \\ 1 & 0 \end{bmatrix}$$

$$= \begin{bmatrix} 0 & 1 \\ 1 & 0 \end{bmatrix} \begin{bmatrix} \dfrac{|A_1|}{b_{22}} & \dfrac{-b_{12}}{b_{22}} \\ \dfrac{b_{21}}{b_{22}} & \dfrac{1}{b_{22}} \end{bmatrix} \begin{bmatrix} 0 & 1 \\ 1 & 0 \end{bmatrix}$$

$$= \begin{bmatrix} y_0 & x_0 \\ 0 & 1 \end{bmatrix} \begin{bmatrix} \dfrac{1}{b_{22}} & 0 \\ \dfrac{-b_{12}}{b_{22}} & \dfrac{|A_1|}{b_{22}} \end{bmatrix} = \begin{bmatrix} \dfrac{1}{b_{22}} & \dfrac{b_{21}}{b_{22}} \\ \dfrac{-b_{12}}{b_{22}} & \dfrac{|A_1|}{b_{22}} \end{bmatrix}$$

let $x_0 = y$ & $y_0 = x$

$$= \begin{bmatrix} x & y \\ 0 & 1 \end{bmatrix} \begin{bmatrix} \dfrac{1}{b_{22}} & 0 \\ \dfrac{-b_{12}}{b_{22}} & \dfrac{|A_1|}{b_{22}} \end{bmatrix} = \begin{bmatrix} \dfrac{1}{b_{22}} & \dfrac{b_{21}}{b_{22}} \\ \dfrac{-b_{12}}{b_{22}} & \dfrac{|A_1|}{b_{22}} \end{bmatrix}$$

$$y = \dfrac{b_{21}}{|A_1|} = x_0, \ x = \dfrac{b_{11} b_{22}}{|A_1|} = y_0$$

$$= \begin{bmatrix} \dfrac{b_{11} b_{22}}{|A_1|} & \dfrac{b_{21}}{|A_1|} \\ 0 & 1 \end{bmatrix} \begin{bmatrix} \dfrac{1}{b_{22}} & 0 \\ \dfrac{-b_{12}}{b_{22}} & \dfrac{|A_1|}{b_{22}} \end{bmatrix} = \begin{bmatrix} \dfrac{1}{b_{22}} & \dfrac{b_{21}}{b_{22}} \\ \dfrac{-b_{12}}{b_{22}} & \dfrac{|A_1|}{b_{22}} \end{bmatrix}$$

$$\begin{bmatrix} 0 & 1 \\ 1 & 0 \end{bmatrix} \begin{bmatrix} \dfrac{1}{b_{22}} & \dfrac{b_{21}}{b_{22}} \\ \dfrac{-b_{12}}{b_{22}} & \dfrac{|A_1|}{b_{22}} \end{bmatrix} \begin{bmatrix} 0 & 1 \\ 1 & 0 \end{bmatrix}$$

$$= \begin{bmatrix} \dfrac{|A_1|}{b_{22}} & \dfrac{-b_{12}}{b_{22}} \\ \dfrac{b_{21}}{b_{22}} & \dfrac{1}{b_{22}} \end{bmatrix} = F_2$$

(B). CODE (IN C LANGUAGE)

In the following lines, the above algorithm is shown implemented in C language. The objective of giving the code here is mainly to demonstrate the simplicity of the algorithm. The code could be further optimized for performance in terms of time and memory in various ways. *MatB* in the code represent the original matrix provided to the function which will iteratively convert to the inverse. The dimension of the matrix is represented by *size*. Whereas *MAX* is assumed to be a *#def* constant this should be assigned a value equal to the maximum possible dimension of the matrix. If desired *MAX* could be replaced by appropriate numeric value, the function will return a float value. A nonzero return-value represents the determinant of the matrix and a zero return value indicates that the inverse could not be calculated and *MatB* does not contain the inverse (Refer to Algorithm 1).

NUMERICAL EXAMPLE

Let assume that we want to calculate the inverse of matrix *A*.

$$A = \begin{bmatrix} 2 & 1 & 3 \\ 1 & 3 & -3 \\ -2 & 4 & 4 \end{bmatrix}$$

The dimension of the matrix is 3. Therefore, inverse will be calculated in 3 iterations. In iteration 1 we select $a_{1,1}$ as pivot (step 3). Therefore row 1 and column 1 are the pivot row and column.

$$\begin{bmatrix} 2 & 1/2 & 3/2 \\ 1 & 3 & -3 \\ -2 & 4 & 4 \end{bmatrix}$$

$$\begin{bmatrix} 2 & 1/2 & 3/2 \\ -1/2 & 3 & -3 \\ 1 & 4 & 4 \end{bmatrix}$$

Algorithm 1.

```
float inverseMat(float MatB[MAX][MAX], int size)
{
    float pivot, det=1.0;
    int i, j, p;
    for(p=1; p <= size; p++)
    {
    pivot = MatB[p][p];
       det= det * pivot;
       if (fabs(pivot) < 1e-5)   return 0;
for (i = 1; i<= size; i++)
            MatB[i][p] = -  MatB[i][p] / pivot;
       for (i = 1; i<= size; i++)
            if (i != p)
            for (j= 1; j <= size; j++)
                 if (j != p)
                 MatB[i][j] = MatB[i][j] + MatB[p][j] * MatB[i][p];
    for (j= 1; j <= size; j++)
            MatB[p][j] =  MatB[p][j]/ pivot;
       MatB[p][p] = 1/ pivot;
    }
    return det;
}
```

$$\begin{bmatrix} 2 & 1/2 & 3/2 \\ -1/2 & 5/2 & -9/2 \\ 1 & 5 & 7 \end{bmatrix}$$

$$\begin{bmatrix} 1/2 & 1/2 & 3/2 \\ -1/2 & 5/2 & -9/2 \\ 1 & 5 & 7 \end{bmatrix}$$

ITERATION 1

The new pivot row values (except the pivot) are calculated using step 5.

The new pivot column values (except the pivot) are calculated using step 6.

The values of the elements excluding pivot row and pivot column are calculated using step 7.

The new value of the pivot is calculated using step 8. The current value of the determinant is 2 i.e., the pivot of first iteration (as per step 4).

$$\begin{bmatrix} 1/2 & 1/2 & 3/2 \\ -1/2 & 5/2 & -9/2 \\ 1 & 5 & 7 \end{bmatrix}$$

$$\begin{bmatrix} 1/2 & 1/2 & 3/2 \\ -1/5 & 5/2 & -9/5 \\ 1 & 5 & 7 \end{bmatrix}$$

$$\begin{bmatrix} 1/2 & -1/5 & 3/2 \\ -1/5 & 5/2 & -9/5 \\ 1 & -2 & 7 \end{bmatrix}$$

ITERATION 2

In iteration 2 we select $a_{2,2}$ as pivot (step 3). Therefore, row 2 is the pivot row and column 2 is the pivot column.

The new pivot row values (except the pivot) are calculated using step 5

The new pivot column values (except the pivot) are calculated using step 6.

$$\begin{bmatrix} 3/5 & -1/5 & 12/5 \\ -1/5 & 5/2 & -9/5 \\ 2 & -2 & 16 \end{bmatrix}$$

$$\begin{bmatrix} 3/5 & -1/5 & 12/5 \\ -1/5 & 2/5 & -9/5 \\ 2 & -2 & 16 \end{bmatrix}$$

The values of the elements excluding pivot row and pivot column are calculated using step 7.

The new value of the pivot is calculated using step 8. The partial value of the determinant so far is $2 \times \dfrac{5}{2} = 5$ (as per step 4).

$$\begin{bmatrix} 3/5 & -1/5 & 12/5 \\ -1/5 & 2/5 & -9/5 \\ 2 & -2 & 16 \end{bmatrix}$$

$$\begin{bmatrix} 3/5 & -1/5 & 12/5 \\ -1/5 & 2/5 & -9/5 \\ 1/8 & -1/8 & 16 \end{bmatrix}$$

$$\begin{bmatrix} 3/5 & -1/5 & -3/20 \\ -1/5 & 2/5 & 9/80 \\ 1/8 & -1/8 & 16 \end{bmatrix}$$

$$\begin{bmatrix} 3/10 & -1/10 & -3/20 \\ -1/40 & 7/40 & 9/80 \\ 1/8 & -1/8 & 16 \end{bmatrix}$$

$$\begin{bmatrix} 3/10 & 1/10 & -3/20 \\ 1/40 & 7/40 & 9/80 \\ 1/8 & -1/8 & 1/16 \end{bmatrix}$$

ITERATION 3

In iteration 3 we select $a_{3,3}$ as pivot (step 3). Therefore, row 3 is the pivot row and column 3 is the pivot column.

The new pivot row values (except the pivot) are calculated using step 5

The new pivot column values (except the pivot) are calculated using step 6.

The values of the elements excluding pivot row and pivot column are calculated using step 7.

The new value of the pivot is calculated using step 8. The current value of the determinant is $5 \times 16 = 80$ (as per step 4).

$$A^{-1} = \begin{bmatrix} 3/10 & 1/10 & -3/20 \\ 1/40 & 7/40 & 9/80 \\ 1/8 & -1/8 & 1/16 \end{bmatrix}$$

At the end of third iteration we obtain the inverse of the matrix. The determinant of the matrix is $|A| = 2 \times \dfrac{5}{2} \times 16 = 80$ (as per step 4).

ANALYSIS OF CALCULATIONS PERFORMED

Observing the simple algorithm given in 2(a) the number of maximum arithmetic operations required for inversion of an n by n matrix can be calculated quite easily.

Number of multiplications/division:

$n-1$ divisions for pivot row,
$n-1$ divisions for pivot column,
$(n-1)^2$ multiplications for rest of the elements and
1 division of pivot.

All these multiplications/divisions to be performed n times.

Therefore, total multiplications/divisions are
$n(2(n-1) + (n-1)^2 + 1) = n^3$.

Number of addition/subtraction:

0 for pivot row,
0 for pivot column,
0 for pivot and
$(n-1)^2$ additions for rest of the elements.

All these addition/subtraction to be performed n times.

Therefore, total summations are
$n(n-1)^2 = n(n^2 - 2n + 1) = n^3 - 2n^2 + n$.

Determinant requires $n-1$ multiplications.

COMPARATIVE RESULTS OF COMPUTER SIMULATION

The algorithm was tested for comparison of operational timing estimates with Gauss Jordan method (see Table 1). The simulations were performed on portable laptop with following specifications:

- Operating System: Microsoft Windows XP Professional (5.1, Build 2600)
- Processor: Intel(R) Pentium(R) M Processor 1.73 GHz
- Memory: 512 MB DDR RAM

CONCLUSION

This work has presented an algorithm for matrix inversion. The algorithm is straightforward for manual calculations and extremely simple for computer programming. It can calculate the inverse and the determinant in one instance and requires only *n-1* extra multiplication for the calculation of determinant. There are indications that the algorithm can be used with improvements in variety of situation e.g., solution of simultaneous equations, calculations of determinants only, calculating error bounds on the elements of the inverse etc.

The algorithm requires exactly n^3 multiplications/divisions to calculate the inverse; however,

Table 1.

Size of Matrix	Gauss Jordan	New Technique
30*30	0.016	0
50*50	0.032	0
100*100	0.26	0.015
150*150	0.54	0.047
200*200	1.13	0.125
250*250	2.05	0.234

its efficiency lies in the minimal utilization of memory and very simple computer coding, requiring only basic arithmetic operation.

ACKNOWLEDGMENT

The authors are indebted to the review, comments and Lemma suggested by Prof. Toru Nakahara of Saga University, Japan.

REFERENCES

Burden, R. L., & Fairs, J. D. (2001). *Numerical Analysis* (7th ed.). Pacific Grove, CA: Brooks/Cole.

Chang, F. C. (2006). Inverse of a perturbed matrix. *Applied Mathematics Letters, 19*, 169–173. doi:10.1016/j.aml.2005.04.004

Fill, J., & Fishkind, D. E. (1997). Moore-Penrose generalized inverse for sums of matrix. *Annual Mathematical Statistics, 18*.

Mikkawy, M. E., & Karawia, A. (2006). Inversion of general tridiagonal matrices. *Applied Mathematics Letters, 19*, 712–720. doi:10.1016/j.aml.2005.11.012

Najafi, H. S., & Solary, M. S. (2006). Computational algorithms for computing the inverse of a square matrix, quasi-inverse of a non-square matrix and block matrices. *Applied Mathematics and Computation, 183*, 539–550. doi:10.1016/j.amc.2006.05.118

Rao, C., & Mitra, S. K. (1971). Generalized inverse of matrices and its applications. New York: Wiley.

Vajargah, B. F. (2007). New advantage to obtain accurate matrix inversion. *Applied Mathematics and Computation*. doi:.doi:10.1016/j.amc.2006.12.060

This work was previously published in International Journal of Technology Diffusion, Volume 1, Issue 1, edited by Ali Hussein Saleh Zolait, pp. 20-27, copyright 2010 by IGI Publishing (an imprint of IGI Global).

Chapter 3
Thirst for Business Value of Information Technology

Govindan Marthandan
Multimedia University, Malaysia

Tang Chun Meng
Multimedia University, Malaysia

ABSTRACT

For years information technology (IT) has helped companies improve organizational efficiency and effectiveness. Today's IT plays a more strategic role in building capabilities for sustaining and creating competitive advantages. The increasing importance of IT has led many organizations to integrate it into their daily operations. To justify the ever-increasing spending on IT, organizations have been searching for evaluation methods to prove the business value of IT. However, this is a challenging undertaking, as there are contradictory answers to questions on whether it is worthwhile to pay substantial sums for IT. To gain insight into the reasons behind the contradictory answers, this paper first reviews conflicting research results of past studies on IT business value. It then explains the term IT productivity paradox. Last, it provides five reasons why IT business value is not fully reflected in the way business managers expect it to be.

INTRODUCTION

A study of the economic impact of IT in 82 countries and regions (IDC, 2007) reported that worldwide IT spending had reached US$1.24 trillion in 2007 and is expected to grow 6.1% a year between 2007 and 2011. In Asia Pacific, IT spending had reached US$242 billion in 2007 and is expected to grow 6.1% per year between

2007 and 2011. For different business objectives, organizations will continue to invest in IT. Ward (1990) proposes an applications portfolio approach to differentiate four types of IT investments, each type supports different business objectives and complements different business strategies. Ross and Beath (2002), along the dimensions of strategic objectives and technology scope, categorize IT investments into four types: transformation, renewal, process improvement and experiments, describing how technology is used

DOI: 10.4018/978-1-4666-1752-0.ch003

to fulfill short-term profitability and long-term growth objectives. Fitzgerald (1998) describes two types of IT projects, i.e. efficiency projects and effectiveness projects. An efficiency project intends to reduce operational costs by automation, while an effectiveness project endeavors to improve business processes, which eventually leads to organizational effectiveness. Joshi and Pant (2008) classify IT projects into four types: purely discretionary, mainly discretionary, mainly mandatory, and purely mandatory, explaining that organizations have full flexibility in making IT investments at times, but there are situations when they have no choice but to make mandatory IT investments, e.g. Y2K or government regulation compliance.

To seek funding approval of IT projects, business managers write business cases. To write a good business case, Ward et al. (2008) emphasize the need to first identify business drivers and IT investment objectives, followed by identification of benefits and measures. The value of each benefit can then be explicitly stated. They reckon that when investment objectives are achieved, expected benefits will naturally be realized. Bannister and Remenyi (2000) describe two types of value: value in exchange and value in use. In accounting practices, an item has an exchange value. However, the business value of IT is exhibited in its use. Renkema and Berghout (1997) suggest that people form a judgment about the value of information systems (IS) by evaluating the financial and non-financial consequences, positive or negative, as a result of IS. There are growing concerns about business value of IT (Demirhan, 2005) and strategic exploitation of IT (Freedman, 2003). Alinean, in a 2005 survey, identified one of the priorities of global 100 companies as IT value management. The pressure to remain competitive is forcing many organizations to consider a result-oriented approach (Epstein & Buhovac, 2006). Where the central question is: Will there be a return on investment (ROI)?

On the premise that organizations have been spending a lot of money on IT and facing difficulties in evaluating investment returns, business value of IT has been a hot debatable topic and still remains a question among IT researchers, IT specialists and business managers (Kohli & Grover, 2008). In a controversial article, "IT Doesn't Matter", Carr (2003) argues that IT is becoming a commodity and that it will not be delivering any discriminate competitive advantage anymore. He suggests that it is thus important to calculate returns on investment to make sure any spending on IT is essential. Disagree with Carr's proposition that IT doesn't matter, Urwiler and Frolick (2008) argue the reason why business managers have considerable difficulty conceptualizing IT value is because there is no framework available for that purpose. Learning from Maslow's Hierarchy of Need model, they propose an IT value hierarchy to describe five different levels of IT value. From lowest to highest, the levels are infrastructure and connectivity needs, stability and security needs, integrated information needs, competitive differentiation, and paradigm shifting. The higher levels of IT value are supported by Bannister and Remenyi (2005) who claim that IT helps create strategic value in different aspects, and in some cases, is a necessity to sustain and grow a business.

Although it is critical to be able to demonstrate value generated from IT investments, there is no single method comprehensive enough for evaluation purposes (Kanungo et al., 1999). There have been past studies attempted to measure performance and relevant business value of IT, however, the formula to weight both sides of a balance is no straightforward. Past studies are yet to draw a definite conclusion about the correlation between IT investment and firm performance (Tangpong, 2008). At times, conflicting findings were reported (Thatcher & Pingry, 2007). Some have positive findings to report. For example, having analyzed 57 customer-related IT investment announcements of 17 firms, Dardan et al. (2006/2007) reported that investment in customer-related IT improved customer satisfaction and yielded positive abnormal shareholder return. Another study by Merono-Cerdan (2008), involving 151 managers of SMEs in Spain, reported that groupware positively affected organizational performance. Liu and Tsai (2007) surveyed 500 managers working in Taiwanese hi-tech companies. Results showed that after the introduction of knowledge management system, there was an average 5.1% to 10% improvement in operating performance. Rivard et al. (2006) analyzed 96 survey responses from CEOs of Canadian SMEs to report that IT contributed positively and significantly to market performance and profitability respectively. Byrd et al. (2006), having surveyed CIOs of 94 US firms and analyzed data gathered from Compustat, reported that IT helped reduce total operational costs. Shu and Strassmann (2005) analyzed data of 12 banks between 1989 and 1997 to report that IT was the only input variable, among other input variables, to return positive marginal gain. They were also quick to point out as the banking industry was a heavy user in using IT for information-related routine activities, banks might see better value in replacing labor with IT.

However, Kim et al. (2008) reported conflicting findings after analyzing cost efficiency and organizational growth of 100 top IT spending firms in China electronic industry. Cost efficiency was measured by ROA, ROE, and profit margin, while organizational growth by sales growth and EPS growth. The only positive and significant correlation was found between IT and profit margin, all other performance measures showed insignificant correlations. Beccalli (2007) analyzed 3,456 observations between 1995 and 2000 of 737 European banks in five EU countries, attempting to find correlations between IT and ROA, ROE, cost efficiency, and profit efficiency. Mixed results were reported. There was a negative and significant correlation between IT and ROA as well as profit efficiency. The correlation between IT and ROE was positive and significant, but that between IT and cost efficiency was

negative and not significant. Hendricks, et al. (2007) analyzed ERP, SCM, CRM Investment announcements between 1995 and 1999. Results showed that for ERP, there was some evidence of improvement in profitability but not in stock return. For SCM, both positive abnormal returns and profitability observed. For CRM, there was no evidence of positive abnormal returns and profitability. Lin (2007) examined financial data of 155 publicly traded U.S. banking firms to report that IT contributed positively and significantly to firm performance as measured by MVA, EVA, Tobin's Q, market-to-book value. However the correlation was insignificant for ROE. Nicolaou and Bhattacharya (2006) examined dataset of 83 ERP adopting firms to report mixed results. ERP adoption had positive effect on ROA, ROI, OIA, ROS and OIS, negative effect on SGAS and # of employees divided by sales, and insignificant effect on CGSS. A study published by Mckinsey Global Institute (2001) on U.S. productivity growth in the 1995-2000 period, investigating relationship between IT investment and productivity of various industry sectors, reported that only six out of 59 industries illustrated positive correlation and the remaining 53 industries showed no significant correlation. These contradictory results have helped fuelled a does-IT-worth-it debate or an IT productivity paradox.

To clear the confusion surrounding IT business value and challenge Carr's assertion that IT doesn't matter, this paper examines the reasons why it is difficult for organizations to see the business value of IT fully. The next section explains the term IT productivity paradox, followed by a section on the reasons why it is difficult to see IT's business value reflected the way business managers expect it to be. The five reasons are: ambiguous identity of IT business value, blurred reflection of IT business value, misunderstood value realization process, poor business-IT alignment, and complications from mediating factors.

IT PRODUCTIVITY PARADOX

The term IT productivity paradox is commonly used to describe the situation where it is difficult to explain whether there is a positive correlation between IT investment and productivity (Brynjolfsson, 1993). In IT productivity studies, production theory is used to examine the correlation between IT and productivity. Productivity studies examine how efficient IT is in transforming inputs into outputs. Inputs refer to hardware investment, IT capital, or IT expenditures, whereas outputs consist of different surrogate measures of growth, e.g. profitability, revenue, and market value. There can be many forms of productivity, but frequently labor productivity is the main focus (Oz, 2005).

There have been considerable studies trying to explain the paradox—some showed positive results, some negative and some mixed. For example, Kudyba and Diwan (2002), in an IT productivity study, applied the Cobb-Douglas production function to analyze firm-level data between 1995 and 1997. Non-IT Capital, IT capital, non-IT labour, and IT labour were used as inputs; sales revenue and value-added were the outputs. The result was encouraging: productivity had improved during the 3-year period as a result of advances in computing and telecommunications. Timmer and Ark (2005) analyzed investment series of ICT goods of 14 EU countries to examine aggregate labor productivity growth (i.e. GDP per hour worked). They reported that between 1995 and 2001, higher ICT capital input caused the US labor productivity growth to be more than half of that of EU. Huang (2005) analyzed dataset of 175 observations of 34 banks for total factor productivity. IT capital was found to be a substitute for non-computer labor and non-IT capital. Computer employees and IT capital contributed to higher productivity than non-computer employees and non-IT capital. Stiroh (2002) analyzed 1987-2000 output data and 1987-1999 capital data of 57 US industries. Results showed that there was a robust link between IT and productivity gains. IT intensive industries experi-

enced a productivity acceleration that was about 2% point greater than other industries. Suggesting that production efficiency was an important and useful performance measure of IT value, Lin and Shao (2000) examined the relationship between IT investment and production efficiency. Using secondary data of large US corporations between 1988 and 1992 gathered from the Computerworld and Standard & Poor's Compustat II database, they reported that IT had a positive effect on production efficiency. Brynjolfsson and Hitt (1996) analyzed IS spending of 367 large firms between 1987 and 1991 to study contribution of IS to productivity at firm level. Applying a production function, inputs considered in the study were computer capital, non-computer capital, IS labor, and other labor. Their analysis showed positive results - IS spending contributed positively to firm output. With a gross marginal product of 81%, computer capital followed closely that of other capital investments. IS labor spending also contributed as much output as non-IS labor spending. In conclusion, they claimed that productivity paradox was no longer an issue in 1991.

Some of the studies reported mixed results or IT contributed to very little or no productivity growth. A study to examine the impact of IT on productivity of Japanese commercial banks reported that there were productivity gains from the use of IT, however, it was difficult to ascertain its correlation with profitability and asset growth (Swierczek & Shrestha, 2003). Osei-Bryson and Ko (2004) analyzed 1,130 observations between 1975 and 1994 of 63 hospitals. Results showed that investment in IT capital had a positive impact on productivity only if the amount invested was above a threshold. If below the threshold, IT capital had a negative impact on productivity. Rei (2004) analyzed Portuguese Annual Data for Labor Productivity to examine labor productivity growth. No evidence was found between ICT investment and labor productivity growth. Using firm-level IT spending data of 370 large firms, Hitt and Brynjolfsson (1996) examined how IT contributed to productivity, consumer value, and business profitability. To measure IT spending, the variable IT stock, consisted of two components: computer capital and IS labor, was used. Computer capital referred specifically to the total spending on central processors and all PCs. IS labor referred to the labor section of total IS budget. The results showed that IT had helped increase productivity and create consumer value but did not help improve business profitability. Lee and Menon (2000) examined financial data of hospitals between 1976 and 1994, collected by the Washington State Department of Health, to study the relationship between different levels of IT investment and process efficiency as well as productivity. Capital was segregated into IT capital and non-IT capital, while IT salaries formed IT labor. To measure process efficiency, three types of efficiencies were examined: overall efficiency, technical efficiency, and allocative efficiency. They reported positive correlation between IT capital and productivity, but negative correlation between IT labor and productivity. Hospitals experienced high technical efficiency used more IT capital than those experienced low technical efficiency. Interestingly, they found non-IT capital contributed positively much more than IT capital to productivity. They reasoned that as the sample consisted of only hospitals, thus naturally, medical capital would contribute to higher productivity than IT capital.

REASONS WHY IT BUSINESS VALUE IS NOT FULLY REFLECTED

Kohli and Grover (2008) conclude what we know about IT value: IT does create value, IT create value under certain conditions, IT-based value manifest itself in many ways, IT-based value is not the same as IT-based competitive advantage, IT-based value could be latent, mediating factors between IT and value, and causality for IT value is elusive. Although there is a general understanding

that IT provides organizations with benefits, in making a decision to invest in IT, the real challenge lies at identifying them, measuring them, and describing the proper conditions for them to happen (Tillquist & Rodgers, 2005). Brynjolfsson and Yang (1996) question that although recent studies have managed to establish a positive correlation between IT and productivity, but there are still two issues remained to be solved. First, do we have enough evidence to dismiss IT productivity paradox altogether? And second, what about the evaluation criteria? They offer four explanations why it is difficult to reflect the true business value of IT: measurement error of inputs and outputs in traditional measurement approaches, the effect of time lag in benefit realization, redistribution of IT benefits across functional areas and business processes makes tracing difficult, and mismanagement of IT.

Recognizing the complexity in evaluating business value of IT, this section attempts to provide five reasons on why it is difficult for organizations to see fully the business value of IT investments. The five reasons are ambiguous identity of IT business value, blurred reflection of IT business value, misunderstood value realization process, poor business-IT alignment, and complications from mediating factors.

AMBIGUOUS IDENTITY OF IT BUSINESS VALUE

Arguing that the term IS business value has not been properly defined in past studies, Cronk and Fitzgerald (1999) define the term as "the sustainable value added to the business by IS, either collectively or by individual systems, considered from an organizational perspective, relative to the resource expenditure required." They claim that without first define the term, its interpretation can come in diverse forms. Melville et al. (2004) define IT business value as the impact of IT on organizational performance, including both efficiency and competitive impacts, observed at functional and organizational levels. For a broader view, Cronk and Fitzgerald (1999) propose to examine IS business value from the organizational rather than individual perspective. The same view is supported by Tangpong (2008) and Kohli and Grover (2008). Weill and Olson (1989) explain that different definitions of IT and disparate organizational performance measures have made comparison of results across studies difficult with added complexity.

BLURRED REFLECTION OF IT BUSINESS VALUE

Opinions differ on why there are conflicting results in past studies. Some propose that contradictory findings reported in IT performance studies can be attributed to a confusion of three different terms: efficiency, quality and productivity. Efficiency refers to efficiency in using resources to produce a product or service where as productivity refers to the input-output ratio. Quality refers to product or service quality. An investment in IT might help improve productivity but not necessary quality. Quality improvement could in fact sometimes lead to higher production costs and poorer productivity (Thatcher & Oliver, 2001).

Some researchers oppose the use of productivity as a measure of IT value, claiming that it refers to a narrow labour productivity scope and ignore special characteristics of IT capital, e.g. a learning cycle for benefits realization (MacDonald et al., 2000; Yorukoglu, 1998). Instead, an assessment should be about business performance but not productivity (Sircar et al., 2000). Focusing on productivity alone would result in inconsistent findings in distinguishing the true value of IT investments. The benefits of IT, both qualitative and quantitative, should be measured before and after implementation (McBride & Fidler, 2003). Considering the intangible benefits conventional

approaches are not able to capture, there is a higher level of measurement problem (Brynjolfsson & Yang, 1996).

Brynjolfsson and Hitt (1998) attribute the difficulty in evaluating business value of IT to how organizations perceive IT value, which can differ from company to company. Grover et al. (1998) studied 313 contemporary US organizations to examine IS investments and the factors influencing these investments. They found out that competitive business environment had forced companies to adopt IS from a more strategic perspective and, as a result, companies could be looking at a totally different set of value than before. Farbey et al. (1992) stresses that strategic dimension of IS adds further difficulties to evaluation of IS investment returns.

To examine how IT investment is linked to productivity and organizational transformation, Brynjolfsson and Hitt (2000) reviewed firm-level past studies, suggesting that at firm level it was clearer to see how different companies use IT and the relevant operational context. They reported that on one hand a portion of IT value comes from the complementary changes, such as business processes, which in turn potentially made the organization more efficient. On the other hand, IT investment helps increase productivity, reduce costs and improve quality that could lead to intangible benefits, e.g. convenience, timeliness, quality, and variety. Their analysis showed that IT could be associated with increases in intangible benefits, for example variety, customer convenience and service, which could be difficult to define and measure. They proposed that we should understand more about intangible costs and benefits, and then learn how to evaluate them.

Business value of IT does not necessarily come from a particular area in the organization but could be many times more from the integration of functional areas or strategic business units. In evaluating IT business value, the context will help to identify evaluation criteria of different dimensions that are deemed appropriate for an effective evaluation (Cronk & Fitzgerald, 1999). In studying IT business value, measurement of inputs and outputs need to be improved in terms of accuracy. This could be an uphill task as some of the outputs are intangible. As diverse IT payoffs are observed across industries and firms, there is a need to conduct further research for better understanding of IT business value (Dedrick et al., 2003).

To understand why there are conflicting results among IT payoffs studies and to shed light on the topic, Kohli and Devaraj (2003) did a meta-analysis of 66 firm-level empirical studies between 1990 and 2000. They divided IT payoff studies into two groups – one showed positive effect and the other negative effect. To conduct a meta-analysis, they classified the dependent variables into three groups: productivity, profitability, or both. They reported that productivity-based measures appeared to be positively associated with IT investment, suggesting that productivity-based measures might capture payoff better. On the other hand, profitability-based measures could be confounded by other factors, e.g. sample size, data source, and industry type, that might influence firm-level profitability. Other influencing factors included choice of dependent variables, type of statistical analysis, and research design. In conclusion, they suggested that future IT payoff studies should explain clearly the sample size, independent and dependent variables, and statistical significance of correlation coefficients.

The results of IT value studies could also differ accordingly to the research questions addressed and dataset used (Hitt & Brynjolfsson, 1996). The use of aggregate output statistics does not accurately reflect the true value of IT as intangible benefits were not normally accounted for in aggregate statistics. With aggregate data, it is almost impossible to differentiate IT value across individual companies, to describe how firms use IT, and to identify the mediating effects of firm or industrial characteristics on IT productivity

(Hitt & Brynjolfsson, 1996). Dedrick et al. (2003) reviewed more than 50 return-on-IT-investment articles between 1985 and 2002 to study IT productivity paradox. The articles were reviewed at three levels of analysis: country, industry and firm. At firm level, there was no evident link between IT investment and profitability. Unable to quantify or capture some intangible or hidden benefits could be an explanation for the lack of evidence. However, at industry level IT investments had contributed to higher labor productivity. The correlation was more apparent in IT intensive industries. At country level, IT investment had contributed to improved economic growth.

MISUNDERSTOOD VALUE REALIZATION PROCESS

Tiernan and Peppard (2004) explain that one reason why business managers do not see IT value is because they do not understand value creation process of IT, from planning to realization stages. In the process of using IT to achieve business objectives, we see value being created. Business managers need to understand about IT value management—what to expect and how to evaluate. Only when the benefits realized exceed the costs, then value is created. Most business managers have the misconception that once an IT has been implemented, benefits would come along the way naturally—a reason why business managers have spent time on technology implementation, but not on benefits management. The value of IT comes from the use of it, but not from its implementation.

IS investments do not necessarily bring better financial performance in a short time period. Over time, when organizations have learned and become familiar with the new IS, better performance prevails (Kivijarvi & Saarinen, 1995). Alshawi et al. (2003) point out the difficulties we face in evaluating IT investments and assessing it real value could be due to our rather limited understanding of IT benefits. To understand IT benefits, we must first differentiate between outcomes and benefits. An outcome is the first-stage result of a new IT implementation which would then lead to a second-stage result, i.e. the benefit. An outcome is not necessarily a benefit and a benefit is what the outcome eventually leads to. For example, an outcome of having a new printer is the ability to print faster; an outcome which helps produce a benefit, i.e. a happier user.

A new technology goes through different life cycle stages. When the technology is at the introductory stage, companies that have adopted the technology might experience significant gains in productivity with the new production capability. However, the technology will then become a threshold investment across companies in the industry as the technology becomes mature and more companies are adopting the technology. Over time the productivity gains enjoyed by the early adopters will slowly disappear when most companies would observe similar output level. In some cases, output prices might have dropped over a longer time period of 10-15 years (Oz, 2005). It is also suggested that above an investment threshold level, companies could see their IT investments contribute positively to productivity, but not below the threshold level (Osei-Bryson & Ko, 2004).

POOR BUSINESS-IT ALIGNMENT

As pointed out by Dos Santos and Sussman (2000), the inability to fully exploit IT for business objectives and mitigate change resistances in implementing IT are reasons why organizations fail to see value. To reap full benefits, the alignment between IS and business strategies is an important consideration. Poor management of IS can also lead to little or no performance gains (Kivijarvi & Saarinen, 1995). A business gains the most from a new IT implementation only when the system delivers benefits that are

fulfilling business objectives. To see better business value of IT, we would need to pay attention to business-IT alignment. Traditional appraisal methods have placed too much emphasis on the quantitative aspect. However we are seeing more qualitative-based benefits which are heavily linked to organizational strategies (Alshawi et al., 2003).

In study of top 530 organizations in Australia investigating strategic use of IT in organizations, Sohal and Ng (1998) found out that in general organizations understand the strategic aspect of IT, however they did not fully exploit IT to reap benefits fully from their IT investments and did not align IT strategically with business objectives. The conclusion was that organizations might have experienced operational but not strategic improvements. In many cases, the focus of an IT investment was on cost reduction but not strategic benefits. In another study of Australia's top 500 businesses to compare between manufacturing and service industries of their performance measurement practices, Sohal et al. (2001) concluded that both industries received moderate benefits from their IT investments, mainly on productivity improvements and costs reduction. Research findings also showed that service industry used IT better than the manufacturing industry in value creation. They observed the reason why manufacturing industry was behind service industry was because of a misalignment between IT capabilities and organizational needs. They pointed out companies could reap better benefits from their IT investments if they align business needs and IT capabilities closely.

COMPLICATIONS FROM MEDIATING FACTORS

The association between IT investment and firm performance is not a direct calculation as it is also complicated with other mediating factors. Value of IS in organization can be mediated by organizational factors for different results (Cronk

& Fitzgerald, 1999). In order to see transformation of IT investment into firm performance, several factors, e.g. top management commitment to IT, previous firm experience with IT, user satisfaction with systems, and turbulence of the firm political environment, need to be considered. IT does not contribute equally to all companies. Instead, organizational factors are playing mediating roles between strategic IT and firm performance (Weill, 1992). To study the relationship between IS and organizational performance, Ragowsky et al. (2000) collected data from 310 and 197 Israel and U.S. manufacturing firms respectively. For each firm, data were obtained about the benefits of two specific IS applications, that is, customer order management and purchasing management, as perceived by senior managers. Operating characteristics of the firms such as number of suppliers, purchase order lead time, and customer lead time were also examined. They reported that operating characteristics of individual companies played a role in realizing different benefits from specific IS applications.

It might be appropriate to present the relationship as a two-stage model where IT directly influences the mediating factors, which in turn influence organizational performance (Chen & Zhu, 2004). Hassan and Saeed (1999) propose a process oriented approach, which considers management processes, organizational capabilities, and IT-business linkages, to study the relationship between IT and organizational performance as well as future IT-business direction. They reason that the impacts of IT come from its ability to help develop organizational competences, e.g. cost efficiency, new product development, quality improvement, and customer-focused. Improvements seen in functional areas with IT-transformed business processes, together with complementary organizational changes, will eventually lead to enhanced performance at organizational level (Melville, et al. 2004). At firm level, the mediating effects of complementary investments, e.g. business process redesign, job training, and

decision-making structure, on the correlation between IT and organizational performance are worth examining (Dedrick et al., 2003). In addition, organizational factors such as size, type and financial strategies would also influence how and what organizations benefit from their IS investments (Kivijarvi & Saarinen, 1995).

Arguing that a direct relationship between IT investment and productivity as examined in past studies was too simple, Francalanci and Galal (1998) did a study to examine the mediating effect of worker composition on the relationship between IT investment and productivity of life insurance companies. Worker composition was defined as ratio of the number of clerical, managerial, and professional position and total number of employees. Productivity was measured as premium income per employee and the ratio of total operating expense to premium income. IT expense was measured as the ratio of firm-level IT expenses to total premium income. Using a dataset between 1986 and 1995 of 52 U.S. life insurance companies, they reported that higher IT investment would bring greater productivity when accompanied with changes in worker composition. Improved productivity was evident for an IT investment when the number of clerical and professional workers was reduced. However productivity deteriorated when the number of managerial workers was reduced. They concluded that higher IT expenses might have either a positive or negative effect on productivity, depending on changes in worker composition.

With a dataset, consisted of capital stock of computers and public financial information, of 527 large U.S. firms between 1987 and 1994, Brynjolfsson and Hitt (2003) analyzed the effect of computerization on productivity and output growth. In 1-year period, the contribution of computerization to productivity and output growth was reported to be consistent with that of computer investments. However, over a five to 7-year period, the contribution had increased five times. They explained that the big increase was largely due to the complementary changes associated with computerization. Computerization, together with complementary changes, would offer organizations long term, intangible benefits. In productivity studies, capital expenditure on complementary changes was not reflected in the productivity calculation and this had caused misrepresentation of IT productivity.

To illustrate that IT does not generate benefits, but the organizational transformation and changes enabled by IT are the ones that bring benefits, Dhillon (2000) studied two system implementations to understand how benefits were being managed. Case one was about an IT system supporting organizational processes in a British hospital. Case two was about a customer service system in a computer manufacturing organization. Based on the case studies, they recommend that before making an IT investment, proposed benefits should first be identified. By doing so, companies understand better the purpose of investing in an IT solution, knowing clearly what they intend to get out from the system. The second consideration is about where the benefits actually occurred, i.e. benefits location. They suggested that it is important to plan for the benefits intended and make the necessary arrangements for change management. In other words, benefits will come only if companies have considered carefully the intended benefits, tightly coupled with the investment objectives and necessary business changes.

CONCLUSION

Apparently, before making an IT investment, a good evaluation method is much needed for better IT investment decision making (Joshi & Pant, 2008) and to study how IT can help create business value as well as the types of intended value (Curtis et al., 2003). As highlighted by Kohli and Grover (2008), "unless we can identify how and where IT is contributing to value creation, we cannot measures it; unless we can measure it, we

cannot demonstrate value, thus failing to dispel prophecies of diminishing IT value." The ability to prescribe what benefits we are expecting in an IT investment helps make better investment decision (Love et al., 2004). Only when we are able to compare between realized and expected benefits, then we can evaluate whether an IT investment has brought positive, neutral or negative returns (Fearon & Philip, 1999). Understanding the five reasons behind the difficulty for full reflection of IT business value could help business managers to dismiss the "IT doesn't matter" myth.

REFERENCES

Alshawi, S., Irani, Z., & Baldwin, L. (2003). Benchmarking Information Technology Investment and Benefits Extraction. *Benchmarking, 10*(4), 414–423. doi:10.1108/14635770310485015

Bannister, F., & Remenyi, D. (2000). Acts of Faith: Instinct, Value and IT Investment Decisions. *Journal of Information Technology, 15*(3), 231–241. doi:10.1080/02683960050153183

Bannister, F., & Remenyi, D. (2005). Why IT Continues to Matter: Reflections on the Strategic Value of IT. *Electronic Journal Information Systems Evaluation, 8*(3), 159–168.

Beccalli, E. (2007). Does IT Investment Improve Bank Performance? Evidence from Europe. *Journal of Banking & Finance, 31*(7), 2205–2230. doi:10.1016/j.jbankfin.2006.10.022

Brynjolfsson, E. (1993). The Productivity Paradox of Information Technology. *Communications of the ACM, 36*(12), 67–77. doi:10.1145/163298.163309

Brynjolfsson, E., & Hitt, L. M. (1996). Paradox Lost? Firm-level Evidence on the Returns to Information Systems Spending. *Management Science, 42*(4), 541–558. doi:10.1287/mnsc.42.4.541

Brynjolfsson, E., & Hitt, L. M. (1998). Beyond the Productivity Paradox. *Communications of the ACM, 41*(8), 49–55. doi:10.1145/280324.280332

Brynjolfsson, E., & Hitt, L. M. (2000). Beyond Computation: Information Technology, Organizational Transformation and Business Performance. *The Journal of Economic Perspectives, 14*(4), 23–48.

Brynjolfsson, E., & Hitt, L. M. (2003). Computing Productivity: Firm-Level Evidence. *The Review of Economics and Statistics, 85*(4), 793–808. doi:10.1162/003465303772815736

Brynjolfsson, E., & Yang, S. (1996). Information Technology and Productivity: A Review of the Literature. *Advances in Computers, 43*, 179–214. doi:10.1016/S0065-2458(08)60644-0

Byrd, T. A., Lewis, B. R., & Bryan, R. W. (2006). The Leveraging Influence of Strategic Alignment on IT Investment: An Empirical Examination. *Information & Management, 43*(3), 308–321. doi:10.1016/j.im.2005.07.002

Carr, N. G. (2003). IT Doesn't Matter. *Harvard Business Review, 81*(5), 41–49.

Chen, Y., & Zhu, J. (2004). Measuring Information Technology's Indirect Impact on Firm Performance. *Information Technology and Management, 5*(1-2), 9–22. doi:10.1023/B:ITEM.0000008075.43543.97

Cronk, M. C., & Fitzgerald, E. P. (1999). Understanding IS Business Value: Derivation of Dimensions. *Logistics Information Management, 12*(1/2), 40–49. doi:10.1108/09576059910256240

Curtis, G. A., Melnicoff, R. M., & Mesoy, T. (2003). Value Discovery: A Better Way to Prioritize IT Investments. *Accenture Outlook Journal.*

Dardan, S., Stylianou, A., & Kumar, R. (2006/2007). The Impact of Customer-Related IT Investments on Customer Satisfaction and Shareholder Returns. *Journal of Computer Information Systems, 47*(2), 100–111.

Dedrick, J., Gurbaxani, V., & Kraemer, K. L. (2003). Information Technology and Economic Performance: A Critical Review of the Empirical Evidence. *ACM Computing Surveys, 35*(1), 1–28. doi:10.1145/641865.641866

Demirhan, D. (2005). Factors Affecting Investment in IT: A Critical Review. *Journal of Information Technology Theory and Application, 6*(4), 1–13.

Dhillon, G. (2000). Interpreting Key Issues in IS/IT Benefits Management. In *Proceedings of the 33rd Annual Hawaii International Conference on System Sciences,* Maui, Hawaii (Vol. 7, pp. 7036).

Dos Santos, B., & Sussman, L. (2000). Improving the Return on IT Investment: The Productivity Paradox. *International Journal of Information Management, 20*(6), 429–440. doi:10.1016/S0268-4012(00)00037-2

Epstein, M. J., & Buhovac, A. R. (2006). What's in IT for You (and Your Company)? *Journal of Accountancy, 201*(4), 69–75.

Farbey, B., Land, F., & Targett, D. (1992). Evaluating Investments in IT. *Journal of Information Technology, 7*(2), 109–122. doi:10.1057/jit.1992.16

Fearon, C., & Philip, G. (1999). An Empirical Study of the Use of EDI in Supermarket Chains Using a New Conceptual Framework. *Journal of Information Technology, 14*(1), 3–21. doi:10.1080/026839699344719

Fitzgerald, G. (1998). Evaluating Information Systems Projects: A Multidimensional Approach. *Journal of Information Technology, 13*(1), 15–27. doi:10.1080/026839698344936

Francalanci, C., & Galal, H. (1998). Information technology and worker composition: Determinants of productivity in the life insurance industry. *Management Information Systems Quarterly, 22*(2), 227–241. doi:10.2307/249396

Freedman, R. (2003). Helping Clients Value IT investments. *Consulting to Management, 14*(3), 33–39.

Grover, V., Teng, J. T. C., & Fiedler, K. D. (1998). IS Investment Priorities in Contemporary Organizations. *Communications of the ACM, 41*(2), 40–48. doi:10.1145/269012.269019

Hassan, S. Z., & Saeed, K. A. (1999). A Framework for Determining IT Effectiveness: An Empirical Approach. In *Proceedings of the 32nd Annual Hawaii International Conference on System Sciences* (Vol. 7, pp. 7034).

Hendricks, K. B., Singhal, V. R., & Stratman, J. K. (2007). The Impact of Enterprise Systems on Corporate Performance: A study of ERP, SCM, and CRM System Implementations. *Journal of Operations Management, 25*(1), 65–82. doi:10.1016/j.jom.2006.02.002

Hitt, L. M., & Brynjolfsson, E. (1996). Productivity, Business Profitability, and Consumer Surplus: Three Different Measures of Information Technology Value. *Management Information Systems Quarterly, 20*(2), 121–142. doi:10.2307/249475

Huang, T. H. (2005). A Study on the Productivities of IT Capital and Computer Labor: Firm-level Evidence from Taiwan's Banking Industry. *Journal of Productivity Analysis, 24*(3), 241–257. doi:10.1007/s11123-005-4933-4

IDC. (2007). *The Economic Impact of IT, Software, and the Microsoft Ecosystem on the Global Economy*. Microsoft.

Joshi, K., & Pant, S. (2008). Development of a Framework to Assess and Guide IT Investments: An analysis based on a Discretionary-Mandatory Classification. *International Journal of Information Management, 28*(3), 181–193. doi:10.1016/j.ijinfomgt.2007.09.002

Kanungo, S., Duda, S., & Srinivas, Y. (1999). A Structured Model for Evaluating Information Systems Effectiveness. *Systems Research and Behavioral Science, 16*(6), 495–518. doi:10.1002/(SICI)1099-1743(199911/12)16:6<495::AID-SRES238>3.0.CO;2-R

Kim, J. K., Xiang, J. Y., & Lee, S. (2008). The Impact of IT Investment on Firm Performance in China: An Empirical Investigation of the Chinese Electronics Industry. *Technological Forecasting and Social Change, 76*(5), 678–687. doi:10.1016/j.techfore.2008.03.008

Kivijarvi, H., & Saarinen, T. (1995). Investment in Information Systems and the Financial Performance of the Firm. *Information & Management, 28*(2), 143–163. doi:10.1016/0378-7206(95)94022-5

Kohli, R., & Devaraj, S. (2003). Measuring Information Technology Payoff: A Meta-Analysis of Structural Variables in Firm-level Empirical Research. *Information Systems Research, 14*(2), 127–145. doi:10.1287/isre.14.2.127.16019

Kohli, R., & Grover, V. (2008). Business Value of IT: An Essay on Expanding Research Directions to keep up with the Times. *Journal of the Association for Information Systems, 9*(1), 23–39.

Kudyba, S., & Diwan, R. (2002). Research Report: Increasing Returns to Information Technology. *Information Systems Research, 13*(1), 104–111. doi:10.1287/isre.13.1.104.98

Lee, B., & Menon, N. M. (2000). Information Technology Value through Different Normative Lenses. *Journal of Management Information Systems, 16*(4), 99–119.

Lin, B. W. (2007). Information Technology Capability and Value Creation: Evidence from the US Banking Industry. *Technology in Society, 29*(1), 93–106. doi:10.1016/j.techsoc.2006.10.003

Lin, W. T., & Shao, B. B. M. (2000). Relative Sizes of Information Technology Investments and Productive Efficiency: Their Linkage and Empirical Evidence. *Journal of the Association for Information Systems,* 1-35.

Liu, P. L., & Tsai, C. H. (2007). Effect of Knowledge Management Systems on Operating Performance: An Empirical Study of Hi-Tech Companies using the Balanced Scorecard Approach. *International Journal of Management, 24*(4), 734–743.

Love, P. E. D., Irani, Z., & Edwards, D. J. (2004). Industry-Centric Benchmarking of Information Technology Benefits, Costs and Risks for Small-To-Medium Sized Enterprises in Construction. *Automation in Construction, 13*(4), 507–524. doi:10.1016/j.autcon.2004.02.002

MacDonald, S., Anderson, P., & Kimbel, D. (2000). Measurement or Management?: Revisiting the Productivity Paradox of Information Technology. *Quarterly Journal of Economic Research, 69*(4), 601–617.

McBride, N., & Fidler, C. (2003). An Interpretive Approach to Justification of Investment in Executive Information Systems. *Electronic Journal of Information Systems Evaluation, 6*(1).

McKinsey Global Institute. (2001). *US Productivity Growth, 1995-2000.* Retrieved from http://www.mckinsey.com/mgi/publications/us/index.asp

Melville, N., Kraemer, K., & Gurbaxani, V. (2004). Review: Information Technology and Organizational Performance: An Integrative Model of IT Business Value. *Management Information Systems Quarterly, 28*(2), 283–322.

Merono-Cerdan, A. L. (2008). Groupware Uses and Influence on Performance in SMEs. *Journal of Computer Information Systems, 48*(4), 87–96.

Nicolaou, A. I., & Bhattacharya, S. (2006). Organizational Performance Effects of ERP Systems Usage: The Impact of Post-Implementation Changes. *International Journal of Accounting Information Systems, 7*(1), 18–35. doi:10.1016/j.accinf.2005.12.002

Osei-Bryson, K. M., & Ko, M. (2004). Exploring the Relationship between Information Technology Investments and Firm Performance Using Regression Splines Analysis. *Information & Management, 42*(1), 1–13.

Oz, E. (2005). Information Technology Productivity: In Search of a Definite Observation. *Information & Management, 42*(6), 789–798. doi:10.1016/j.im.2004.08.003

Ragowsky, A., Stern, M., & Adams, D. A. (2000). Relating Benefits from Using IS to an Organization's Operating Characteristics: Interpreting Results from Two Countries. *Journal of Management Information Systems, 16*(4), 175–194.

Rei, C. M. (2004). Causal Evidence on the "Productivity Paradox" and Implications for Managers. *International Journal of Productivity and Performance Management, 53*(1/2), 129–142. doi:10.1108/17410400410515034

Renkema, T. J. W., & Berghout, E. W. (1997). Methodologies for Informaiton Systems Investment Evaluation at the Proposal Stage: A Comparative Review. *Information and Software Technology, 39*(1), 1–13. doi:10.1016/0950-5849(96)85006-3

Rivarda, S., Raymond, L., & Verreault, D. (2006). Resource-based View and Competitive Strategy: An Integrated Model of the Contribution of Information Technology to Firm Performance. *The Journal of Strategic Information Systems, 15*(1), 29–50. doi:10.1016/j.jsis.2005.06.003

Ross, J. W., & Beath, C. M. (2002). Beyond the Business Case: New Approaches to IT investment. *MIT Sloan Management Review, 43*(2), 51–59.

Shu, W., & Strassmann, P. A. (2005). Does Information Technology Provide Banks with Profit? *Information & Management, 42*(5), 781–787. doi:10.1016/j.im.2003.06.007

Sircar, S., Turnbow, J. L., & Bordoloi, B. (2000). A Framework for Assessing the Relationship between Information Technolgy Investments and Firm Performance. *Journal of Management Information Systems, 16*(4), 69–97.

Sohal, A. S., Moss, S., & Ng, L. (2001). Comparing IT Success in Manufacturing and Service Industries. *International Journal of Operations & Production Management, 21*(1/2), 30–45. doi:10.1108/01443570110358440

Sohal, A. S., & Ng, L. (1998). The Role and Impact of Information Technology in Australian Business. *Journal of Information Technology, 13*(3), 201–217. doi:10.1080/026839698344846

Stiroh, K. J. (2002). Information Technology and the U.S. Productivity Revival: What Do the Industry Data Say? *The American Economic Review, 92*(5), 1559–1576. doi:10.1257/000282802762024638

Swierczek, F. W., & Shrestha, P. K. (2003). Information Technology and Productivity: A Comparison of Japanese and Asia-Pacific Banks. *The Journal of High Technology Management Research, 14*(2), 269–288. doi:10.1016/S1047-8310(03)00025-7

Tangpong, C. (2008). IT-Performance Paradox Revisited: Resource-Based and Prisoner's Dilemma Perspectives. *Journal of Applied Management and Entrepreneurship, 13*(1), 35–49.

Thatcher, M. E., & Oliver, J. R. (2001). The Impact of Technology Investments on a Firm's Production Efficiency, Product Quality, and Productivity. *Journal of Management Information Systems, 18*(2), 17–45.

Thatcher, M. E., & Pingry, D. E. (2007). Modeling the IT Value Paradox. *Communications of the ACM, 50*(8), 41–45. doi:10.1145/1278201.1278204

Tiernan, C., & Peppard, J. (2004). Information Technology: Of Value or a Vulture? *European Management Journal, 22*(6), 609–623. doi:10.1016/j.emj.2004.09.025

Tillquist, J., & Rodgers, W. (2005). Using Asset Specificity and Asset Scope to Measure the Value of IT. *Communications of the ACM, 48*(1), 75–80. doi:10.1145/1039539.1039542

Timmer, M. P., & Arky, B. (2005). Does Information and Communication Technology Drive EU-US Productivity Growth Differentials? *Oxford Economic Papers, 57*(4), 693–716. doi:10.1093/oep/gpi032

Urwiler, R., & Frolick, M. N. (2008). The IT Value Hierarchy: Using Maslow's Hierarchy of Needs as a Metaphor for Gauging the Maturity Level of Information Technology Use within Competitive Organizations. *IS Management, 25*(1), 83–88.

Ward, J. (1990). A Portfolio Approach to Evaluating Information Systems Investments and Setting Priorities. *Journal of Information Technology, 5*(4), 222–231. doi:10.1057/jit.1990.46

Ward, J., Daniel, E., & Peppard, J. (2008). Building Better Business Cases for IT Investments. *MIS Quarterly Executive, 7*(1), 1–15.

Weill, P. (1992). The Relationship between Investment in Information Technology and Firm Performance: A Study of the Valve Manufacturing Sector. *Information Systems Research, 3*(4), 307–333. doi:10.1287/isre.3.4.307

Weill, P., & Olson, M. H. (1989). Managing Investment in Information Technology: Mini Case Example and Implications. *Management Information Systems Quarterly*, *13*(1), 3–17. doi:10.2307/248694

Yorukoglu, M. (1998). The Information Technology Productivity Paradox. *Review of Economic Dynamics*, *1*(2), 551–592. doi:10.1006/redy.1998.0016

This work was previously published in International Journal of Technology Diffusion, Volume 1, Issue 1, edited by Ali Hussein Saleh Zolait, pp. 28-40, copyright 2010 by IGI Publishing (an imprint of IGI Global).

Chapter 4
Adoption of Short Messaging Service (SMS) in Malaysia

Ainin Sulaiman
University of Malaya, Malaysia

Ali Hussein Saleh Zolait
University of Malaya, Malaysia

ABSTRACT

Short Messaging Service (SMS) being an almost instantaneous communication medium that connects people is now a phenomenon that has grown and spread around the globe at an amazing speed. Given the current trend of SMS usage and its potential growth, this paper provides an insight into SMS adoption. The study attempts to delineate the demographics and usage profile of SMS users in Malaysia, as well as explaining the factors influencing SMS adoption in Malaysia by using a modified version of the Technology Acceptance Model (TAM), which was originally introduced by Davis (1989). The study presents the demographic and usage profile in terms of gender, age, occupation, monthly personal income, extent of SMS usage and so forth of 489 SMS users from four institutions of education in the Klang Valley and Selangor. The present research uses and validates the scales for variables developed by earlier studies, namely perceived usefulness, perceived ease of use, perceived enjoyment, and perceived fees, which are hypothesized to be fundamental determinants of behavioural intention. The scale items for the said variables were tested for reliability, correlation and regression. The application of correlation analysis reveals a significant relationship among the independent variables, namely, perceived usefulness, perceived enjoyment, and perceived ease of use with the dependent variable that is behavioural intention. With regards to the level of importance derived from regression analysis, usefulness ranks the highest, followed by ease of use and enjoyment in explaining SMS adoption in Malaysia. Perceived fees do not seem to have a significant relationship with behavioural intention. Some implications, limitations and recommendations for future research are also discussed.

DOI: 10.4018/978-1-4666-1752-0.ch004

1. INTRODUCTION

SMS is a very important instant communication tool that can be used to serve several purposes. SMS can be used by businesses for advertising and promotion by which they can obtain instant feedback about their products. Also, governments can use it to communicate interested issues with the people as well as for conducting elections (SMS voting). Furthermore, the high number of opportunities to use creative and innovative marketing activities, as highlighted by Haghirian, et al., (2008) in mobile commerce (m-commerce), implies that marketers need to gain insights into relevant issues of consumer behaviour in the SMS context. Also, SMS banking is another application of mobile technology, which was investigated by Amin (2007) who conducted an analysis of mobile credit card usage intention in the Malaysian context.

M-commerce, a natural extension to electronic-commerce, includes any business activity conducted over a wireless telecommunication network, which includes B2C and B2B commercial transactions as well as the transfer of information and services via wireless mobile devices, especially in intra-business (Turban, 2006). Similar to other e-commerce applications, m-commerce can be done via the Internet, via private communication lines or over other computing networks. Currently, wireless devices used in mobile commerce include two-way pagers/short messaging service (SMS), wireless application protocol (WAP)-equipped cellular phones, personal digital assistants (PDA), Internet-enabled laptop computers with wireless access capacity and so forth.

Comparing the three platforms of m-commerce, namely, WAP, GPRS and SMS, SMS is the most popular platform and it was discovered that the use of the short messaging service (SMS) has exceeded all initial expectations (Bauer et al., 2005). This has indirectly resulted in mobile phones being used as an important market instrument compared to other mobile devices. SMS popularity is mainly due to its cost as it is the cheapest information delivery mode. Studies by the Malaysian Communications and Multimedia Commission (MCMC) found that, in Quarter 1, 2006, Malaysia ranked second with 56.6 persons owning a mobile phone per 100 inhabitants in comparison to other ASEAN countries (Communication and Multimedia, 2006). The growth of SMS-related services over the past several years reflects the enormous potential of the Malaysian wireless data communication market. This study is, therefore, timely to elucidate the rationale behind the adoption of SMS as a form of communication.

The Short Messaging Service (SMS) is generally understood as text read on small mobile phone screens, typically capable of presenting 15 to 20 characters per line. The messages are written with a numeric keypad on the phone, normally requiring more than one key press per character, with messages restricted to 160 characters in length (Svendsen et al., 2006). It has been classified as a form of communication service within mobile commerce, grouped together with voice call, MMS, video and e-mail (Harris et al, 2005) that allows people and organizations to send and receive short text messages from a mobile phone in near real time. SMS, is an almost instantaneous communication medium that connects people and is now a phenomenon that has grown and spread around the globe at an amazing speed compared to other types of mobile commerce services. SMS is extensively used, not only for communication purposes, but also as a major marketing effort due to its low cost. As a highly interactive medium, SMS enables the recipient of the message to reply to it immediately, which establishes a direct dialogue between the advertiser and the potential customer. This enables companies to offer personalized, timely and relevant information, which in turn strengthens both the customer relationship and the emotional relationship between a brand and its customers (Nysveen et al., 2005). SMS owes its popularity to its low cost mode of information delivery and its instantaneous communication medium, which operates on a "store and forward concept". With the increased number of mobile subscribers in the world, SMS has gained its popularity and become an integral part of people's lives (Pastore, 2002 quoted in Lai, 2004), and has significant implications for communication and information transmission. This study will attempt to answer the following research question. What are the factors that influence the adoption of the short messaging service? Based on the aforesaid research question, the following objective is developed; to determine factors influencing the adoption of the short messaging service.

2. ADOPTION OF SMS

Previous studies have examined ways in which everyday life activities influence mobile phone use and to a certain extent SMS usage (Harris et al., 2005; Gilligan & Heinzmann, 2004; Davis, 1989). The current study attempts to examine the factors that influence behavioural intention to use SMS as an instantaneous communication tool by mobile users in Malaysia. This is because the Malaysian experience of mobile applications like SMS might provide a model for other countries. According to SKMM (2007), it is a norm for most Malaysians to carry a mobile with them everywhere they go (SKMM, 2007). As of March 31, 2007, there were 20,808,797 mobile subscriptions on the 6 digital networks operating in Malaysia. Furthermore, SKMM (2007), wrote "Malaysians are avid texters. This has proven true over the years that short messaging services (SMS) or multimedia messaging services (MMS) have been introduced. A steady increase of hand phone users who send an average of 5 or more SMS or MMS a day was noted over the period 2004 to 2007. In fact a solid 50.4% of hand phone users sent more than 5 SMS or MMS per day".

Drawing on this body of research, a number of factors affecting SMS usage have been extracted.

First, the cost of mobile calls and SMS messages is likely to affect the adoption of SMS. Harris et al. (2005) discovered a relatively low level of SMS usage in Hong Kong as the cost of calls, beyond the free allowance, is about 7.5 times cheaper than in the UK.

Second, the adoption phase of mobile phones, according to Gilligan and Heinzmann (2004), could also be one of the factors affecting SMS usage. In the early phases of mobile phone take-up, mobile phones were used more for voice communication than for SMS. As users became more familiar with using the phone, they also became more familiar with other functions/services available on the phone, such as SMS. Therefore, SMS usage could be influenced by the period of ownership of the mobile phone.

Third, apart from using SMS as a communication tool for sending and receiving messages, as the vast majority of SMS users do (Gilligan & Heinzmann, 2004), there is an increasing number of SMS commercial services such as Voting (e.g. Malaysian reality shows such as *Akademi Fantasia*, *Malaysian Idol* and so forth), news alerts, sports results and ringtones/logos. The use of SMS in conjunction with television in the last couple of years has undoubtedly promoted the use of SMS in many countries, including Malaysia (Gilligan & Heinzmann, 2004). Hussin (2005) reported that the third season of *Akademi Fantasia*, created such a craze among the Malaysian public, especially youth, that it raked in RM1.7 million through audience SMS responses for the final round. Thus, this type of television programme, which employs SMS services, coupled with the collaboration of mobile operators through a single short code to access the SMS voting, irrespective of network operator, encourages SMS usage.

Fourth, SMS usage can also be influenced by cultural factors such as modes of commuting, sensitivity to privacy and cultural events. Modes of commuting to work and the related free time available to key in messages can influence SMS usage, for instance, public transport commuters

Figure 1. Technology acceptance model. Source: (Davis, 1989)

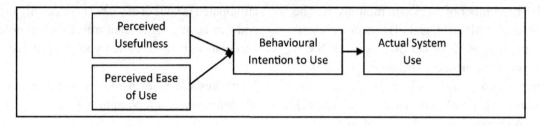

have more time available to send an SMS than people driving to work. Hence, groups or countries that have more of a commuter culture may have more opportunity to send messages when travelling. Another potential cultural factor may be that in some countries or areas, where people are less sensitive to privacy and willing to make voice calls in public, people may prefer to use their mobile more for voice communication than SMS.

TAM was originally developed by Davis (1989) to explain the individual's adoption of traditional technology (e.g. spreadsheet, email and software development tools) in an organizational setting (Davis, 1989) and has since become the most prominent model employed to explain the adoption and usage of technology by individuals. As mentioned earlier, TAM focuses on two theoretical constructs; *Perceived Usefulness* (PU) and *Perceived Ease of Use* (PEOU). PU is the degree to which a person believes that using a particular system will enhance their performance (Davis, 1989). A system high in perceived usefulness is one in which a user believes in the existence of a positive performance relationship. In contrast, PEOU refers to "the degree to which a person believes that using a particular system would be free of effort" (Davis, 1989). These constructs are of significant importance (Davis, 1989) since people's tendency to use or not use an application depend on the extent to which they believe it will help them perform their job better. The central idea underlying TAM is that a person's behavioural intention (BI) to use a 'system' is determined

primarily by its two constructs i.e. PU and PEUO. The model can be further illustrated by Figure 1.

Davis (1989) found that ease of use is an antecedent to usefulness rather than a parallel and is a direct determinant of usage. The causality of which can be shown as follows: ease of use → usefulness → usage chain. This means that the easier a system is to interact with, the less effort needed to operate it, and the more effort one can allocate to other activities, thus, contributing to overall job performance. This model has been tested for reliability and validity by Adam et al. (1992) who replicated this model and confirmed its reliability as well as the validity of the constructs used for both usefulness and ease of use scales. The applicability of TAM has been demonstrated in several countries including the United Kingdom (Al-Gahtani, 2001), Hong Kong (Chan & Lu, 2004) and was used to explain several perspectives ranging from the adoption of wireless Internet (Yu, Liu & Yao, 2003), online shopping (Gefen, 2003; Gefen, Karahanna, & Straub, 2003), web-based learning (Gong, Xu, & Yu, 2004), ERP implementation (Amoako-Gympah & Salam, 2004), Internet banking (Wang, Wang, Lin, & Tang, 2003; Chan & Lu, 2004) as well as instant messaging services (Wang, Hsu, & Fang, 2004).

2.1 Extent of Usage

The extent of usage, as defined by Lai (2004), is "the number of SMS sent monthly, the frequency of SMS sent and customer's self-categorization of his or her own usage of SMS". Hence, the questions asked in determining the extent of usage are, i) The number of SMS sent monthly, ii) The frequency of SMS sent, and iii) Customer's self-categorization of his or her own usage of SMS. The positive influence of behavioural intention on the extent of usage has been proven by Para-suraman et al. (1988) and Brady et al. (2002). It is hypothesized that behavioural intention is positively correlated with the extent of usage. Hence the first hypothesis is:

Hypothesis 1: *The frequency or extent of SMS usage is positively related to the behavioural intention to use SMS.*

2.2 Usefulness

Usefulness is defined as the total value a user perceives from using a new technology (Kim et al., 2005) i.e. the user believes that the device has some desirable functions that it can perform. Individuals evaluate the consequences of their behaviour in terms of perceived usefulness and base their choice of behaviour on the desirability of the usefulness. The usefulness construct has been used extensively in information systems and tech-nology research, and has strong empirical support as an important predictor of technology adoption (Matheison, 1991). It is then hypothesized that:

Hypothesis 2: *Usefulness is positively related to the behavioural intention to use SMS*

2.3 Enjoyment

Individuals, who experience immediate pleasure or joy from using the technology and perceive any activity using the technology to be personally enjoyable in its own right, aside from the instru-mental value of the technology, are more likely to adopt the technology and use it more extensively than others (Davis, 1989). Enjoyment refers to the extent to which the activity of using a product is perceived to be enjoyable in its own right, apart

from any performance consequences that may be anticipated (Davis et al., 1992). Since enjoyment and fun have a significant effect on technology acceptance, it is therefore hypothesized that:

Hypothesis 3: *Enjoyment is positively related to the behavioural intention to use SMS.*

2.4 Ease of Use

Even if potential users believe that SMS is useful, they may, at the same time, believe that SMS is too hard to use and that the performance benefits of usage are outweighed by the effort of using it. In addition to usefulness and enjoyment, SMS is theorized to be influenced by perceived ease of use. This variable has been adopted from Davis (1989), which refers to the degree to which an individual believes that using a particular system would be free of physical and mental effort. This follows from the definition of "ease", which is the freedom from difficulty or great effort. Davis (1989) claimed that an application that is perceived to be easier to use than another is more likely to be accepted by users. Therefore, the hypothesis is as follows:

Hypothesis 4: *Ease of use is positively related to the behavioural intention to use SMS.*

2.5 Perceived Fee

Technology users in an organizational setting use technology for work purposes and the cost of mandatory adoption and usage is borne by the organization. However, SMS adopters are individuals who play the dual roles of technology user and service consumer. Most of them adopt and use SMS for personal purposes, and the cost of voluntary adoption and usage is borne by the individual. Potential adopters of SMS are mobile service consumers who will consider prices and evaluate SMS usage based on its benefits and costs. Since the fee or charge structure for SMS is either *pay-as-you-use* (prepaid) or subscription-based pricing (post-paid), cost is an important factor to the consumer. According to the Adaptation Level Theory, instead of having perfect information about prices, customers possess internal reference prices and make a comparison with these prices (Grewal et al., 1998). In the case of SMS, one would probably compare with the prices of mobile phone calls and stationary Internet usage. The result of this comparison forms one's perception of the fee. It is therefore proposed that perceived fee directly influences the behavioural intention. Thus, the following hypothesis is:

Hypothesis 5: *Perceived fee is positively related to behavioural intention to use SMS.*

Behavioural intention, which is a component of the theory of reasoned action developed by Fishbein and Ajzen (1980), refers to a function of both attitudes towards behaviour and subjective norms towards the behaviour that has been found to predict actual behaviour. For instance, one's attitude about SMS combined with the subjective norms about SMS, each with their own weight, will lead to one's intention to use SMS (or not), which will then lead a person to actual SMS usage. Parasuraman et al. (1988) suggested that favourable behavioural intention is associated with the service provider's ability to get its customers to remain loyal to them and to recommend the service to other customers. As such, behavioural intention in the context of this study is regarded as, and, as defined by Lai (2004), "the use of more SMS in the future and recommending other people to use it".

3. RESEARCH METHODOLOGY

A convenience sampling was employed for the study. The sample was confined to students, who are hand phone, users from four institutions of education in the Klang Valley and Selangor. The

above geographical areas were chosen because the subscriber base comprising the Klang Valley and Selangor accounts for 34.5 percent of the total mobile phone users in Malaysia (Hand phone User Survey, 2004). Furthermore, 81.9 percent of the mobile subscribers are from the urban sector. Students were chosen as respondents because young adults have been found to be faster adopters of mobile commerce in general (Lee et al., 2002; SKMM, 2007). This study used a questionnaire survey as the primary form of obtaining responses from mobile users in the Klang Valley and Selangor about their perception of SMS adoption. This survey approach was chosen because it provides a quick, inexpensive, efficient and accurate means of assessing information about the population. Other research designs were not adopted for various reasons. First, the manipulation of variables is not required as such experimental methods are not appropriate. Second, not many studies have been conducted related to this research area, and, thus, the secondary data approach alone is not sufficient. Third, the observation approach was not viable as many things could not be observed. Attitudes, opinions, motivations and other intangible states of mind of people cannot be recorded by observation.

The questionnaire was designed to measure the mobile users' behaviour intention towards the usage of SMS in Malaysia. A 5-point Likert scale ranging from 1 (Strongly Disagree) to 7 (Strongly Agree) was used. Respondent's were required to indicate their level of agreement with each statement. The statements measured constructs that were deemed relevant in measuring SMS adoption. Among the constructs measured were 'behavioural intention', 'perceived usefulness', 'perceived ease of use', 'perceived enjoyment' and 'perceived fees'. The input for the SMS behaviour statements was derived from Brady et al. (2002), Lai (2004), and Kim et al. (2005). Again, a few adjustments were made to the original questions to suit the research context, for example, Kim et al. (2005) used the same constructs to measure the adoption of mobile Internet and not SMS.

In order to provide an adequate level of confidence in the study, 1,000 questionnaires were distributed and the survey was conducted over a six-week period using the self-administered drop-off method during the months of January and February 2007. This method was chosen for the data collection as it was less expensive in terms of manpower as well as time needed. A key person in each of the education institutions was engaged to act as the contact person and the distributing agent. A total of 510 responses were obtained from the fieldwork. Out of the total responses received, 21 were invalid or were incomplete and as such were rejected. In total 489 questionnaires were used for the final analysis.

4. RESEARCH FINDINGS

To test the hypotheses proposed earlier, correlation analysis and multiple regression analysis were conducted. The correlation analysis and multiple regression analysis are shown in Tables 1 and 2, respectively.

From the table above, there are statistical significant relationships among all the variables except for the relationship between behavioural intention (Factor I) and extent of usage (FU); ease of use (Factor III) and extent of usage (EU); and perceived fees (Factor V) and extent of usage (EU). The strongest relationships, in order of sequence, were between behavioural intention (Factor I) and usefulness (Factor II) ($r = 0.578$); usefulness (Factor II) and ease of use (Factor III)

Table 1. Correlation analysis between the variables

Variables	Factor I Behavioural Intention	Factor II Usefulness	Factor III Ease of Use	Factor IV Enjoyment	Factor V Perceived Fees
Factor II Usefulness	0.578(**)				
Factor III Ease of Use	0.473(**)	0.515(**)			
Factor IV Enjoyment	0.463(**)	0.559(**)	0.470(**)		
Factor V Perceived Fees	0.135(**)	0.236(**)	0.356(**)	0.130(**)	
EU Extent of SMS usage	-0.067	-0.126(**)	-0.015	-0.184(**)	0.031

** Correlation is significant at the 0.01 level.

Table 2. All variable regression

Model	Predictors (Independent Variables)	Standardized Coefficients Beta	Sig.
1	Usefulness	0.390	0.000
	Ease of Use	0.223	0.000
	Enjoyment	0.169	0.000
	Perceived Fees	-0.061	0.114
	Extent of SMS usage	0.000	0.990

Dependent Variable: Behavioural Intention (Factor I)
Adjusted $R^2 = 0.386$

($r = 0.515$); and usefulness (Factor II) and enjoyment (Factor IV) ($r = 0.559$). The relationships with medium strength were between behavioural intention (Factor I) and ease of use (Factor III) ($r = 0.473$); behavioural intention (Factor I) and enjoyment (Factor IV) ($r = 0.463$); ease of use (Factor III) and enjoyment (Factor IV) ($r = 0.470$); and ease of use (Factor III) and perceived fees (Factor V) ($r = 0.356$). Lastly, the relationships with the lowest strength were between behavioural intention (Factor I) and perceived fees (Factor V) ($r = 0.135$); usefulness (Factor II) and perceived fees (Factor V) ($r = 0.236$); enjoyment (Factor IV) and perceived fees (Factor V) ($r = 0.130$); usefulness (Factor II) and extent of usage (EU) ($r = -0.126$); and enjoyment (Factor IV) and extent of usage (EU) ($r = -0.184$). All the statistically significant relationships were positively related (for example an increase in one variable is associated with an increase in another variable) except for the relationships between usefulness (Factor II) and extent of usage (EU) and between enjoyment (Factor IV) and extent of usage (EU), which were negatively related (an increase in one variable is associated with a decrease in other variable).

According to Table 1, Factor II, Factor III and Factor IV had a significance level of 0.000, which was less than the selected significance level of 0.05. This indicated that there were significant relationships between the dependent variable Factor I and the predictors Factor II, Factor III and Factor IV. The Adjusted R^2 figure inferred that 38.6% of the variance in the dependent variable could be explained by the predictors, while the remaining 61.4% was explained by other factors.

The standardized coefficients value for Usefulness ($\beta = 0.390$) was the highest among the predictors, which indicated that usefulness was the most important variable in predicting behavioural intention. This was followed by ease of use ($\beta = 0.223$) and enjoyment ($\beta = 0.169$). Surprisingly, 'perceived fees' was not statistically significant in explaining the variance in behavioural inten-

tion, despite the correlation analysis results that showed a positive relationship between the two variables. Similar to the correlation result, frequency or extent of usage did not show any statistical significance when it was regressed with behavioural intention.

The results have successfully tested and supported the hypotheses except for H1 and H5. The first hypothesis, H1: 'The adoption of SMS usage is related to the behavioural intention to use SMS' was not supported since its correlation and regression significance levels were more than the selected significance level of 0.05. There was a lack of support for H5: 'Perceived fee is related to the behavioural intention to use SMS' as the correlation analysis showed a weak positive relationship between the two variables ($r = 0.135$). Further analysis to test H5 using multiple regression indicated an insignificant relationship between perceived fees and behavioural intention (significance value was 0.114, which is more than $p = 0.05$). The other three hypotheses namely H2: Usefulness is related to the behavioural intention to use SMS; H3: Enjoyment with regards to the use of SMS is related to the behavioural intention to use SMS; and H4: ease of use of SMS is related to the behavioural intention to use SMS; were all supported as the relationships between the variables were statistically significant (significance level lesser than $p = 0.05$). The Pearson Correlation Coefficients (r) and Standardized Coefficients Beta (β) for the three hypotheses were as follows, H2: $r = 0.578, \beta = 0.39$; H3: $r = 0.463, \beta = 0.169$; and H4: $r = 0.473, \beta = 0.223$.

5. DISCUSSION AND CONCLUSION

The results assert that SMS adoption is determined by the perception of usefulness, ease of use, enjoyment, and perceived fee. The more the users believe that SMS has some desirable function that it can perform the more they will use SMS in the future and the more they will recommend others to use SMS (behavioural intention). Usefulness appeared to be the strongest determinant for behavioural intention of SMS with r equal to 0.578 ($\beta = 0.390$), which strongly supported H2. This result further supported the reason of usefulness construct, which is used extensively in information systems and technology research, and has strong empirical support as an important predictor of technology adoption (e.g. Matheison, 1991).

The second strongest determinant of SMS adoption is ease of use with r equal to 0.473 ($\beta = 0.223$). Ease of use is determined by users' perceptions as to whether using SMS is free from physical, mental and learning effort. The greater the perception of ease of use by the users about SMS, the greater the behavioural intention is, thus, H4 was supported and reinforced earlier studies (Kim et al., 2005). Other than factors like low cost, easy manipulation and navigation, ubiquity and instantaneous response, SMS ease of use has been greatly enhanced by the cooperation between mobile phone service providers, after 1998, that permits SMS centres to send messages to each other as illustrated by Doyle (2000).

Support for H3 validated the hypothesis that enjoyment with regards to the use of SMS is related to behavioural intention of SMS ($r = 0.463$, $\beta = 0.169$). This is consistent with the findings by Davis et al. 1992, whereby, individuals, who experience immediate pleasure or joy from using any technology (including SMS) are more likely to adopt the technology and use it more extensively than others. Enjoyment is, as expected, a motivator and an effective determinant of behavioural intention.

Surprisingly, perceived fees emerged as the independent variable with the weakest relationship with behavioural intention, with r equal to 0.135, which was below 0.290 (low relationship as defined by Cohen, 1998). The weak relationship perhaps explained its statistically insignificant predictor for SMS adoption when it was regressed with behavioural intention. This finding suggested that monetary cost did not serve as a barrier to adoption.

Further, it differed with Kim et al. (2005), in which perceived fees was the top concern for M-Internet adoption, as users are deterred more by the costs than they are attracted by the benefits (usefulness and enjoyment). Perhaps, SMS in Malaysia is in the early stages of adoption whereby usefulness is still the top concern. This is unlike Singapore where the consumers have already deemed the service useful and consequently other factors like usage fee become significant.

The absence of a significant effect of the adoption of usage on behavioural intention was rather surprising and warrants further investigation in light of the importance of this variable in prior studies (e.g. Davis et al., 1989). This might be due to the reclassification of usage categories to avoid violating the assumptions of the chi-square analysis or it may simply be difficult for users to accurately report the number of times they send messages. Ideally, future research will take measures of actual usage, for instance, obtaining access to the user's mobile phone bills; however, such an approach is often impractical because it is burdensome and encroaches on the privacy of the respondents. Notwithstanding the above, there was a weak relationship between adoption of usage and usefulness and enjoyment. One possible explanation is that users develop their attitudes about SMS usefulness through prolonged usage.

The findings also held many practical implications. This research has served to broaden our understanding of the factors influencing SMS adoption from the perspective of users or customers. The benefits such as usefulness and enjoyment are the most important drivers of SMS adoption and should not be neglected in the development of new functions and enhancement of service features. Rather than creating services based on the perception of usefulness and demand by experts, service providers should conduct regular market research to discover consumer needs and wants and transform the findings into services useful to consumers. Findings from this study offer empirical support that pricing strategy/manipulating perceived fees is clearly not the only means of increasing behavioural intent, ease of use and enjoyment are equally essential. This may be an important consideration when developing pricing policies and marketing strategies for more innovative and value-added SMS.

With multi-media mobile messaging services emerging and given the similarity between new mobile messaging services and current short messaging services, understanding the current SMS users' behaviour towards the current SMS service is important for telecommunication service providers as customers would probably use the SMS quality to judge and form expectations of the new mobile messaging services. As such, service providers may use the quality of SMS services as a benchmark to meet the customer's expectation in delivering new mobile messaging services.

Nevertheless, there are limitations in this study that may restrict the generalizability of the findings, which could be addressed in future studies. First, the samples were students. The study was confined to students who are mobile users residing in Kuala Lumpur and Selangor. Mobile phone users from other parts of the country were excluded from the research due to time and cost constraints. Consequently, the study is subject to the limitations and possible biases that exist when only one geographic area is selected that may not be representative of the total mobile users. Moreover, most of the respondents in this study are highly educated; as such they may not be representative of Malaysian society as a whole. Future research on less educated users will offer further insights into the adoption of SMS.

Despite these limitations, this research paper serves as an important pilot study into the potential of SMS usage in Malaysia. It is hoped that businesses keen on entering the wireless marketplace will find this preliminary research useful in establishing business models and understanding the nature of the industry in Malaysia. Further research can be conducted over a more heterogeneous sample of Malaysians with a bet- ter formulated and in depth survey so as to yield more representative results.

REFERENCES

Adams, D. A., Nelson, R. R., & Todd, P. A. (1992). Perceived usefulness, ease of use and usage of information technology: A replication. *Management Information Systems Quarterly*, *16*(2), 227–247. doi:10.2307/249577

Al-Gahtani, S. S. (2001). The Applicability of TAM Outside North America: An Empirical test in the United Kingdom. *Information Resources Management Journal*, *14*(3), 37–46.

Amin, H. (2007). An analysis of mobile credit card usage intentions. *Information Management & Computer Security*, *15*(4), 260–269. doi:10.1108/09685220710817789

Amoako-Gyampah, K., & Salam, A. (2004). An extension of the technology acceptance model in an ERP implementation environment. *Information & Management*, *41*(6), 731–745. doi:10.1016/j.im.2003.08.010

Bauer, H. H., Reichardt, T., Barnes, S. J., & Neumann, M. M. (2005). Driving consumer acceptance of mobile marketing: A theoretical framework and empirical study. *Journal of Electronic Commerce Research*, *6*(3), 181–192.

Brady, M. K., Cronin, J. J., & Brand, R. R. (2002). Performance only measurement of service quality: A replication and intention. *Journal of Business Research*, *55*, 17–31. doi:10.1016/S0148-2963(00)00171-5

Chan, S., & Lu, M. (2004). Understanding Internet banking adoption and use behaviour: A Hong Kong perspective. *Journal of Global Information Management*, *12*(3), 21–43.

Davis, F. D. (1989). Perceived usefulness, perceived ease of use, and user acceptance of information technology. *Management Information Systems Quarterly, 13*(3), 319–340. doi:10.2307/249008

Davis, F. D., Bagozzi, R. P., & Warshaw, P. R. (1992). Extrinsic and intrinsic motivation to use computers in the workplace. *Journal of Applied Social Psychology, 22*(1), 1111–1132. doi:10.1111/j.1559-1816.1992.tb00945.x

Doyle, S. (2000). Software review: Using short messaging services as a marketing tool. *Journal of Database Marketing, 8*(3), 273–277. doi:10.1057/palgrave.jdm.3240043

Fishbein, M., & Ajzen, I. (1980). *Understanding Attitudes and Predicting Social Behavior*. Upper Saddle River, NJ: Prentice-Hall.

Gefen, D. (2003). TAM or just plain habit: a look at experienced online shoppers. *Journal of End User Computing, 15*(3), 1–13.

Gefen, D., Karahanna, E., & Straub, D. W. (2003). Trust and TAM in online shopping: An integrated model. *Management Information Systems Quarterly, 27*(1), 51–90.

Gilligan, R., & Heinzmann, P. (2004). *Exploring how cultural factors could potentially influence ICT use: An Analysis of European SMS and MMS use* (Cultural Difference Workgroup COST 269 Rep. No. 4). Ljubljana, Slovenia: COST.

Grewal, D., Monroe, K. B., & Krishnan, R. (1998). The effects of price comparison acquisition value, transaction value and behavioral intentions. *Journal of Marketing, 62*(2), 46–59. doi:10.2307/1252160

Harris, P., Rettie, R., & Cheung, C. C. (2005). Adoption and usage of m-commerce: A cross-cultural comparison of Hong Kong and the United Kingdom. *Journal of Electronic Commerce Research, 6*(3), 210–224.

Hussin, B. (2005, August 9). A sure thing. *The Sun (Baltimore, Md.)*, 9.

Kim, H. W., Chan, H. C., & Gupta, S. (2005). Value based adoption of mobile Internet: An empirical investigation. *Decision Support System*.

Lai, T. T. (2004). Service quality and perceive value's impact on satisfaction, intention and usage of short message service. *Information Systems Frontiers, 6*(4), 353–368. doi:10.1023/B:ISFI.0000046377.32617.3d

Lee, Y., Lee, I., Kim, J., & Kim, H. (2002). A cross-cultural study on the value structure of mobile Internet usage: comparison between Korea and Japan. *Journal of Electronic Commerce Research, 3*(4), 227–239.

Lu, J., Yu, C., Liu, C., & Yao, J. (2004). Technology Acceptance Model for wireless Internet. *Internet Research: Electronic networking application and Policy, 13*(3), 206-222.

Mathieson, K. (1991). Predicting user intentions: Comparing the technology acceptance with the theory of planned behavior. *Information Systems Research, 2*(3), 173–191. doi:10.1287/isre.2.3.173

Nysveen, H., Pedersen, P., Thorbjornsen, H., & Berthon, P. (2005). Mobilizing the brand- The effects of mobile services on brand relationship and main channel use. *Journal of Service Research, 7*(3), 257–276. doi:10.1177/1094670504271151

Parasuraman, A., Zeithaml, V. A., & Berry, L. L. (1988). SERVQUAL: A multiple item scale for measuring consumer perception of service quality. *Journal of Retailing, 64*(1), 12–40.

SKMM. (2007). *Hand Phone Users Survey 2007*. Selangor, Malaysia: Author.

Svendsen, G. B., & Johnsen, J. A. K. (2006, January 4-7). *Use of SMS in office environment*. Paper presented at the 39th Annual Hawaii International Conference on System Science, Kauai, Hawaii.

Turban, E., King, D., Lee, J. K., & Viehland, D. (2006). *Electronic Commerce - A Managerial Perspective* (4th ed.). Upper Saddle River, NJ: Pearson-Prentice Hall.

Wang, C., Hsu, Y., & Fang, W. (2004). Acceptance of technology with network externalities: An empirical study of Internet instant messaging services. *Journal of Information Technology Theory and Application*, 6(4), 15–28.

Wang, Y., Wang, Y., Lin, H., & Tang, T. (2003). Determinants of user acceptance of Internet banking: An empirical study. *International Journal of Service Industry Management*, 14(5), 501–519. doi:10.1108/09564230310500192

Wong, C. C., & Hiew, P. L. (2005). *The Current State and the Evolutionary Pathway of Telcos in Malaysia*. Paper presented at the 2005 Hawaii International Conference on Business.

This work was previously published in International Journal of Technology Diffusion, Volume 1, Issue 1, edited by Ali Hussein Saleh Zolait, pp. 41-51, copyright 2010 by IGI Publishing (an imprint of IGI Global).

Chapter 5
A Study of the Systemic Relationship Between Worker Motivation and Productivity

J. J. Haefner
Walden University, USA

Christos Makrigeorgis
Walden University, USA

ABSTRACT

Three well known theories on worker motivation have proliferated in the literature and practice over the past 50 years, namely Theories X, Y, Z, Expectancy Theory, Equity Theory, Justice Theory, and Goal-Setting Theory, to name a few. We propose a Fourth Theory that is based on the fundamental principles of open systems theory that function in holistic fashion into the phenomenon of systemic motivation. When fully engaged, systemic motivation can influence workers to become more productive than in a system that does not engage. It is the central construct that has been missing in motivation theory. This paper briefly explains systemic motivation and demonstrates its potential in a case study where a motivation effect resulted in an additional $1 million in product throughput.

BACKGROUND ON MOTIVATION THEORY

Motivational theories that adhere to the extreme principles of full management control and employee empowerment (Maslow, 1998) have proven insufficient explanations for employee motivation. Drucker (2007) noted that motivation is a fundamental responsibility of management and added

that Theory X control was minimally effective, and observed that managers who apply Theory X management techniques in fact de-motivated workers. In general, however, he considered the debate over Theory X and Theory Y a "sham battle" (p. 222), and studied Japanese management systems in an effort to describe possible alternate approaches for motivating employees. Maslow (1998) had already discovered new trends in motivation and presented the first paper on Theory Z. William Ouchi (1981) also went beyond McGregor's

DOI: 10.4018/978-1-4666-1752-0.ch005

theories X & Y, and wrote *Theory* Z, to explain Japanese motivation systems. He suggested that productivity is a function of human interpersonal familiarity and confidence. These conditions influence creativity and involve workers in such a way that they improve productivity.

Ouchi observed a distinct difference between the typical Japanese company and the typical American company, the most distinct being the bond between worker and company as a consequence of practices such as lifetime employment. This bond generates a security at the very core of motivation. This is very consistent with Maslow's hierarchy of needs (Maslow, 1968, 1998) which places, for example, safety (that includes job security) only above the basic physiological human needs. Recently, Jeffrey Liker (2004) described the basis for Toyota's success, and attributed it to the philosophy of understanding human motivation. Ouchi (1981) observed a similar theme in companies that he researched. Liker, however, simply says that Toyota uses all types of motivation, and Ouchi links motivation to culture. Neither has provided a tenable systemic model though they have provided an abundance of a posteriori evidence of motivation outcome differences.

Given that Japanese managers have created an effective motivation system (Deming, 1986; Ouchi, 1981; Johnson, 1982; Sakaiya, 1991), relying on simplistic Theory X and Theory Y explanations for worker motivation seems grossly inadequate. Ouchi (1981), Johnson (1982), and Deming (1986) all observed a phenomenon too rich to be the result of mere supervisory discretion. Von Bertalanffy (1968) would concur by explaining that a weakness in scientific inquiry and research has been compartmentalization, or a tendency to have a narrow focus that excludes relevant influences and possible interactions that might provide a clearer understanding of what is being studied. Furthermore, Steel and König (2006) specifically noted the absence of integration theories in studies of human motivation. Ambrose and Kulik (1999) surveyed Motives and

Needs Theory, Expectancy Theory, Equity and Justice Theory, Goal-Setting Theory, Cognitive Evaluation Theory, and others, and concluded that there has been no central construct to bind the theories. Therefore, we are compelled to sift through current motivation research and propose a Fourth Theory of Motivation.

MOTIVATION SUBSYSTEMS

Current research suggests that motivation is systemic (Ouchi, 1981; Liker, 2004; Haefner, 2008; Drucker, 2006; Maslow, 1998; Mizuno, 1984; Deming, 1986; Meyer & Vandenberghe, 2004; Langfred & Moye, 2004; Quigley, Tesluk, Locke, & Bartol, 2007), but what are the elements of a motivation system? From these authors, and others, the elements that contribute to motivation have been constructed into the systemic model shown in Table 1. It shows four motivational subgroups, and the elements within those subgroups. The subgroups are leadership, environment, individual psychology, and deterrence orientation.

SYSTEMIC MOTIVATION

The leadership in any organization directly controls two of the four motivation subsystems, and has a profound responsibility in systemic motivation. Moreover, one of the subsystems, deterrence orientation, sets the foundation principles and philosophies by which people are going to be treated. All other motivation subsystems are a function of deterrence orientation, as it is the force that engages or deters the other motivational subsystems. Deterrence orientation determines the degree of motivational saturation, or the mass of positive motivation in play. If we were to describe the motivation system in graphic form, it would appear as Figure 1. Deterrence orientation, leadership, and a brief overview of the motivational subsystems and elements follow.

Table 1. An assessment table of motivational and a deterrent category.

Leadership	Environment	Individual	Deterrence Orientation
Enabling Formulation	Org. Values & Dynamics	Self-efficacy	Valued Work
Task Significance	Interest Alignment	Prosocial Motivation	Enlightened HR Policy
Natural Work Units	Trust	Commitment	Fact-based Management
Intellectual Stimulation	Autonomy	Self-monitoring	Quality Systems
Regulatory Foci	Shared Norms	Agreeableness	Consistency in Task Significance & Performance
Participative Decision-Making	Normative Intrinsic	Positive Mood & Attitude	High Perceived Utility
Job Design	Group Rewards	Intrinsic Motivation	High Task Interdependence
Extrinsic Motivation		Self-determination	Task Simplicity
Goal Setting		Goal Regulation	Low Formalization

Note: The opposite of non-deterrent behavior will be deterrent behavior.

Figure 1. Motivation subsystem within an organization.

MOTIVATION SYSTEM INTERRELATIONSHIP

All of the elements in the motivation subgroups are interrelated. They work with one another in dynamic fashion, and function in accordance with Laszlo's (1996) supraorganic and von Berta-lanffy's (1968) open systems theory. The interplay between deterrence orientation and leadership drives the dynamic interrelationship between individual psychology and environment. Leadership, individual psychology, and environment then function as a holarchic interaction and maintain themselves (see Figure 2) through dynamic adaptive capability, responsiveness to other systems and subsystems, and are self-creative (Laszlo, 1996). Moreover, the motivation system is a subsystem of the larger system called the organization as seen in Figure 3.

Figure 2. Motivation interrelationship.

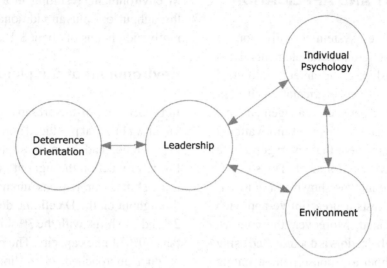

Figure 3. The motivation subsystem encased by degree of deterrence.

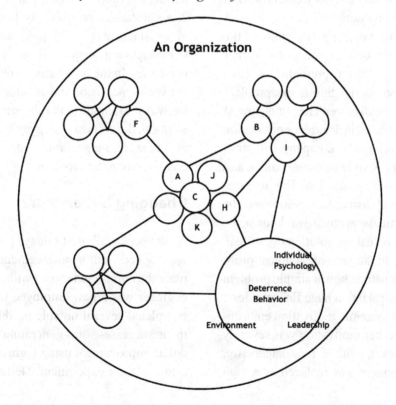

Figure 3 demonstrates other subsystems within an organization system. Some common organizational subsystems are accounting, human resources, engineering, and production. Each of these act according to the same systems principles as the motivation system. They affect one another, interact with one another, can diminish or enhance the contributions of other subsystems, and can undermine the output of the system in moments of system disequilibrium.

A CASE STUDY AND APPLICATION

This study examines systemic motivation as described by the subgroups and elements listed in Table 1, leadership, environment, individual psychology, and deterrence orientation. It contrasts the difference between management that inhibits motivation and creates a low motivational (low M); and management that leverages a high motivation (high M) environment. The study is consistent with the models shown in Figures 1, 2, and 3, and suggests a prescriptive approach that can be replicated. Moreover, the contrast between those two behaviors is documented using production throughput, a response, demonstrating the potential for a model of systemic motivation. This study forms a foundation for further research on motivation and productivity.

In this section we present a case study of the affects of two motivational systems on worker productivity. This opportunity presented itself as a result of a serious production throughput problem at a major battery manufacturer. The initial, low M environment was encased in deterrence orientation management behavior. The company had strict rules with a Theory X style of management, and the workers had union protection. The management style was so abrasive, that even when the solution to this particular problem was known, the worker would not reveal the solution out of fear. These conditions, in the face of technical problems, clearly demonstrate how a simple problem can spin out of control into a huge financial loss; all due to a low M systemic motivation environment. In effect, worker motivation was severely suppressed. However, with a new supervisor, the low M environment was replaced by a high M environment, resulting in a recovery of the throughput loss, plus an additional, unprecedented motivation bonus of about $ 1 million.

Environment of Suspicion

In 1995, a state-of-the-art Japanese battery manufacturing line that produced hundreds of batteries per minute, had been sub-optimized and was losing production throughput on the second and third shifts. For reasons unknown, production throughput on the D cell line deteriorated on the 2nd and 3rd shifts, with the 3rd shift producing less than 50% of line capacity. The net loss in salable product approached $9 million per year.[1] The units produced per shift, in average batteries-per-person (bpp) [2] throughput is shown in Table 2, a substantial productivity loss. The mystery of satisfactory 1st shift production contributed to management suspicions about 2nd and 3rd shift personnel. In the union environment, the tension between supervision and maintenance, in particular, was substantial. In the absence of a production solution, the working integrity between workers, maintenance, and supervision deteriorated, further compounding the problem.

Changing Supervisors

As the peak (fall pre-holiday) production period approached, senior management decided to replace the normal supervisor with an engineer. The engineer was a new employee who had already completed several notable production improvement successes, one generating over a million dollar improvement using regression analysis on a formulation experiment. He had an advanced

Table 2. Average Production Throughput per Person per Shift

	Shift 1	Shift 2	Shift 3
Units per Shift	153000	107100	76500
Avg. Units/Employee	25500	17850	10929

Figure 4. Week 1 motivational elements.

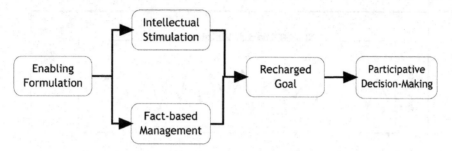

degree from the University of Wisconsin's College of Engineering, with specialization in systems and quality engineering. The University of Wisconsin's program was well-grounded in industrial statistics, fact-based decision-making, Deming philosophy, and a problem solving model that is more flexible than 6 Sigma's DMAIC.[3]

Fixing Production

The engineer/supervisor (ES) immediately began a collaborative, fact-based approach to study the production problem. On the first night, he let the production workers know that there must be a solution. Otherwise, there would not be shift to shift production throughput differences. He then requested the assistance of the maintenance worker who was reluctant, even a bit edgy, because of prior bad experiences and doubt[4]. The ES disregarded the attitude and used the maintenance worker's expertise to conduct a process sensitivity study to bracket production parameters. By the end of the first shift, the bounds of the production parameters were known. The next night, the maintenance worker was not so reluctant to help. For the remainder of the week, he and the ES gradually identified the production parameters the created acceptable product. By the end of the week, 3rd shift production improved to the level of the 2nd shift. Motivational elements that were applied during the first week were fact-based management, intellectual stimulation (having technical skills helpful for solving the problem), enabling formulation,

goal setting, and participative decision-making (see Figure 4). A relationship of trust was also beginning to develop.

The ES was leveraging modularity and the constitutive potential of the system. He engaged the key maintenance person to help restore production. A new pattern was being established, the high-flux principle, by collaboration between maintenance and supervision. This changed the nature of line workers tasks because they did not have to clean up after line failures. This blend of maintenance skill, the engineer's problem solving and technical ability, and workers engaging in an improving system, created synergy. The constitutive power of systems came into play and changed the nature of worker and management relationships. The basis was being laid for further development of systemic motivation.

By the end of week two, the 3rd shift average number of units per worker had increased to near full production. The problem appeared to have been solved. However, there was still the mystery of why the 1st shift had no problems. The answer to this had to do with the control procedure at the cathode forming station.[5] To control cathode production, operators were given three statistical process $\bar{X}$ & R control charts that monitored cathode height, weight, and width. Figure 5 shows the weight chart. To control the process for weight, for example, the operator would make an adjustment if weight went above or below the nominal target value. The 1st shift's charts looked similar to the chart in Figure 5. However, the 3rd shift'

Figure 5. Weight statistical process control chart

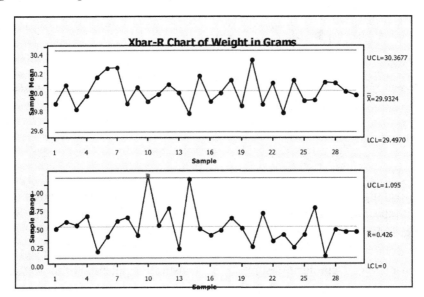

corrected process had a very different control chart. Figure 6 shows the shifts one and three side by side. The control chart shows a shift.

When the 1st shift and 3rd shift data was put on the same control chart, cathode weight was clearly higher on the 3rd shift. Yet, both shifts were now running full production (see Figure 6). Figure 7 shows the same data with statistical control limits calculated for the individual shifts. The control limits are different suggesting that there

Figure 6. Post solution weight comparison 1st shift to 3rd shift

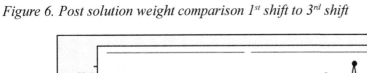

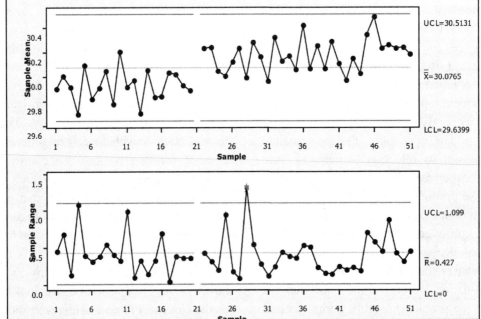

Figure 7. 1ˢᵗ shift control chart vs. 3ʳᵈ shift control chart.

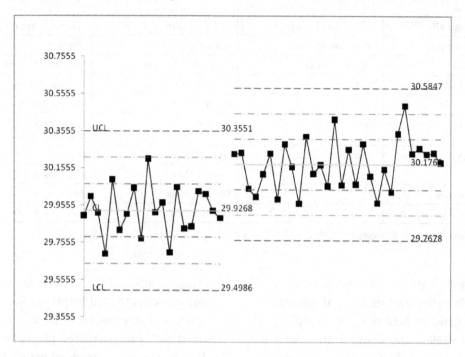

are two different processes. A simple trial proved that the 1ˢᵗ shift settings did not work. The ES visited the 1ˢᵗ shift operator to inquire why their chart was different.

The 1ˢᵗ shift operator who controlled the cathode process told the ES that she knew what process parameters worked. She also knew that the target means on the control charts did not work. In order to make the control charts look good, she made a temporary adjustment to the process, collected parts, readjusted the process parameters back, recorded the data from the altered process and went on with her job. She didn't let management know because of fear. It was obvious to her that the control chart process parameters were wrong. When the manager who set up the process was informed that the control charts were wrong, he became enraged and publically embarrassed himself. His behavior affirmed the operator's perception.

The cause for cathode breakage was that the 3ʳᵈ shift operators were trying to adjust the process to a bogus control chart. The process ran with nominal weight much higher than the original control parameter. The 1ˢᵗ shift operator knew this, and adjusted the weight lower to make the control chart look acceptable. She then set the process back there where it made good cathodes. The second and third shifts didn't know what she was doing and when they conducted their first control checks, they found the weight too high. They adjusted the weight down. When they did this, cathodes weakened and began breaking. As the operators made more adjustments, the process was less and less reliable. This is demonstrated by the sequence of up and down data points in the middle of the shift three portion of the chart. The points alternate nine times, a statistical improbability (see Figure 6). This is typical of processes that are tweaked back and forth due to over adjustment.

The affect of deterrent management orientation at this company was a low M environment. Only six of a possible thirty five motivational elements were engaged. Poor leadership deterred the other motivational elements; in effect, demonstrating

Table 3. An assessment table of motivational and a deterrent category

Leadership	Environment	Individual	Negative
Enabling Formulation	Org. Values & Dynamics	Self-efficacy	Valued Work
Task Significance	Interest Alignment	Prosocial Motivation	Enlightened HR Policy
Natural Work Units	Trust	Commitment	Fact-based Management
Intellectual Stimulation	Autonomy	Self-monitoring	Quality Systems
Regulatory Foci	Shared Norms	Agreeableness	Consistency in Task Significance & Performance
Participative Decision-Making	Normative Intrinsic	Positive Mood & Attitude	High Perceived Utility
Job Design	Group Rewards	Intrinsic Motivation	High Task Interdependence
Extrinsic Motivation		Self-determination	Task Simplicity
Goal Setting		Goal Regulation	Low Formalization

Note: The highlighted items are engaged motivational elements.

von Bertalanffy's progressive mechanization, or movement from holistic to individual summative, albeit dysfunctional, behavior. For example, goal setting was useless and de-motivating with an unattainable goal. Ineffective natural work units with high task interdependence backfired in the face of production throughput problems. Organization values, dynamics, and task simplicity had no meaning in these conditions. (see Table 3)

The ES conducted meetings with all of the shift operators and maintenance to understand the proper operating parameters. New control chart targets were established resulting in an effective quality control system. Shift-to-shift working relations improved. Secrecy and anxiety were removed. Process tweaking and unnecessary adjusting of process parameters stopped. System equilibrium and task consistency were established, and perceived utility increased. These, in turn improved the individual psychology element of commitment (see Figure 8).

Aligning Interests

After full production was achieved, there remained two impediments to full production. One was related to working the night shift, and the other was related to the time of year, harvest season,

and how it affected the workers associated with farming. Both affected employees' ability to get to work and stay awake while at work. The ES relaxed work rules so that employees could drink coffee or soda on the production line. Candy and gum were also allowed, though company rules prohibited those. Workers were also encouraged to take slightly longer breaks to nap for a few minutes. These rule changes did not seem to affect productivity.

The most challenging obstacle to production had to do with harvest season. The factory was

Figure 8. Week two motivational elements

located in a rural, dairy farming region. During harvest, farm men and women had to accelerate their work contributions. It was not unusual for the men to harvest throughout the day and into the evening. While they were in the fields, the women picked up chores normally done by the men, milking the cows, and caring for the animals, and other farm chores. Depending, on weather variability, it was not unusual for farms to operate in near crisis. That affected several of the women working the night shift. Some nights, they were barely able to stay awake, and were subject to disciplinary procedures for dozing off. The woman responsible for starting D-Cell production was one such person. She was sometimes late to work due to oversleeping. This prevented production from starting on time and lowered the throughput rate. Under normal circumstances, she would have been fired. That would have caused hardship on her family income that was needed to support the farm. When she was at work, she was an excellent worker. There were no issues with her during the non-harvest season. The ES discussed the issues with her and made an agreement that she would not be disciplined if she called whenever she was going to be late.

The entire production team was extended the same privilege with the understanding that the team would modify job responsibilities to cover positions whenever someone was going to be late or absent. Workers job skills were identified so that any position could be covered in the event of any worker's tardiness or absenteeism. The result was that full production was usually maintained. Motivation elements that emerged from this strategy are shown in Figure 9. These fall within environmental motivational factors category of which one of the most important is interest alignment where worker interests and needs merge with company interests and needs. It is a win/win situation if interests are properly identified and alignment is achieved. These modified practices exhibited the systems principles of modularity and flux.

Figure 9. Addressing worker interests.

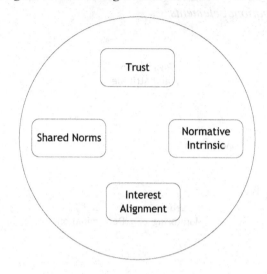

The Tipping Point

Gladwell (2002) theorized that latent behaviors reside in people. When the right conditions exist, the behaviors can be released. A tipping point occurs, and a latent behavior becomes epidemic, having widespread, and unique effects. The conditions leading to tipping are a carrier, a message or behavior that gains acceptance, and environmental context. All three conditions emerged in the D-Cell production line. The ES provided the message, the production problems were resolved, and the motivational system was dramatically altered. Changes in the motivation system created a new normative environment that resulted in something unanticipated and unique, individual psychology motivational elements began to emerge (see Figure 10).

Within two months, the first production record was set. The individual production workers self-organized. They exhibited the principle of requisite variety, or self-creation, autopoiesis. The principle of requisite variety means that control of any system has limitations. Control cannot be exercised if the lines for control exceed the magnitude of what is being communicated. When a system is broken, the lines of communication

Figure 10. Emerging individual psychology motivational elements.

become overloaded. This seems to have been the case, because the solution to the actual problem was known by at least one operator. Once, system equilibrium was achieved, the workers became self-motivated. As a team they made the decision to break production records. There were no meetings or motivation sessions, they just worked efficiently and took advantage of opportunity. They learned ways to make things more efficient specifically because they were given autonomy and the company's interest aligned with their interest. This created a learning opportunity, and

maybe even a game, to see how work activity could be rearranged and still meet production demands. Toward the end of the ES's tenure, the D-Cell workers were so intent on setting another production record that they continued to work into their cleanup period and did not stop until the next shift was in place and ready to work.

Table 4 shows an improvement in motivation within the organization. Most of the motivational elements were engaged, high M, high motivational saturation. This was the result of the ES instituting the leadership component concurrent with creating a non-deterrent orientation environment. This modified the environment, affected and improved the line workers' individual psychology so that they became self-motivated and absorbed in the experience of flow (Csikszentmihalyi, 1993). The work itself became engaging and a systemic motivational energy resulted in self-efficacy. Maslow (1999) describes what the workers experienced as self-validation or peak experience.

The original objective for changing supervisors was to return 3rd shift production to a normal level. However, the manner in which that goal was accomplished had an unanticipated effect, a motivation effect (see Figure 11). The result was nearly one million dollars of additional, unanticipated production throughput.

Table 4. Motivational elements in production.

Leadership	Environment	Individual	Negative
Enabling Formulation	Social Interaction	Self-efficacy	Valued Work
Task Significance	Interest Alignment	Prosocial Motivation	Enlightened HR Policy
Natural Work Units	Trust	Commitment	Fact-based Management
Intellectual Stimulation	Autonomy	Self-monitoring	Quality Systems
Regulatory Foci	Shared Norms	Agreeableness	Consistency in Task Significance & Performance
Participative Decision-Making	Normative Intrinsic	Positive Mood & Attitude	High Perceived Utility
Job Design	Group Rewards	Intrinsic Motivation	High Task Interdependence
Extrinsic Motivation		Self-determination	Task Simplicity
Goal Setting		Goal Regulation	Low Formalization

Figure 11. Motivation effect

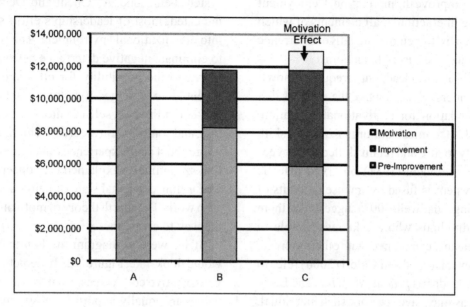

CONCLUSION: THE FOURTH THEORY OF MOTIVATION – A CENTRAL CONSTRUCT

The changes that occurred on the 3rd shift are an example of system dynamics described by von Bertalanffy (1968), Laszlo (1996), and Skyttner (2001). In von Bertalanffy's language, what occurred was a constitutive system reorganizing itself. Motivation was a catalyst subsystem that moved through a predictable sequence of activity. The motivation subsystem stopped entropy (the 2nd Law of Thermodynamics) and reestablished equilibrium. Leadership was a principal component. By providing technical support that helped remove impediments to production, and modifying the work environment, a new motivational system emerged. It freed workers to be responsive to other motivational affects, and created a growth interaction resulting in greater productivity, exactly what motivation theory would suggest.

The Fourth Theory

The Fourth Theory of motivation is an extension of theories X, Y, and Z. Through the work of Maslow, Csikszentmihalyi, and Pinker, and open systems theorists such as von Bertalanffy, Laszlo, and Skyttner, a new understanding of motivation is beginning to emerge. It recognizes that worker motivation is based in the interaction of normal human psychology, leadership, and the work environment; and that these can reach fruition only in an environment of free of deterrence. It is not culturally dependent, though some cultures and organizations have stumbled upon many of the key elements in the motivational model, and are using them effectively to improve worker performance. Those organizations and cultures have competitive advantage.

The Fourth Theory is also a model. The elements of the model are universal, repeatable, and predictable. Motivational saturation is the degree to which positive elements are effective within an organization. High motivation saturation optimizes a positive worker environment, high M. The theory suggests that organizations can deploy strategies to improve the motivation. Deployment involves the interaction of all elements of which the first step is to remove negative deterrence orientation in supervisory behaviors.

Leadership has to lead, but it requires knowledgeable leaders who can make the changes that lay the foundation for motivational saturation. This includes technical and organizational skill, or the ability to hire and retain skilled employees at every level. Ouchi (1981) observed that the Japanese system is fused by intense amounts of cross-training. Gladwell (2002) suggests that there are key individuals who are knowledgeable in specific areas and can connect with others to create tipping points. Durand and Calori (2006) refer to this type of leader as *practically wise*. The ES in the case study may have been one such individual. He demonstrated that leadership can establish the foundation for the organizational environment.

Environment, traditionally, has been referred to as culture. Inability to change culture has become the scapegoat for many organizational change failures. This need not be. What may have been missing is the understanding how subsystem interactions affect change, the motivation sub-

system being one. As Ouchi and Deming have indicated, most of leadership's effort should go into organizational environment. The first task is to eliminate negative deterrence behaviors. That increases the possibility for other motivational potential to emerge. Eventually, self-efficacy, self-determination, self-monitoring, goal regulation, and commitment are free to emerge. Maslow wrote about peak experiences and self-validation. Csikszentmihalyi explained the concept of flow, a near transcendental state of being in total sync with work. The fourth theory of motivation shows the way to create these.

If we were to diagram the Fourth Theory, it would look like Figure 12. It depicts a system with positive core values. Centered around those values are equally important subsystems, leadership, environment, and individual psychology. Their linkage is fragile, denoting the nature of dynamic systems. Positive core values are needed to maintain cohesiveness between the individual subsystems. Otherwise they are autonomous and free to disassociate from the system according to the dynamic of the open systems principle of progressive mechanization. Leadership is a balancing

Figure 12. The Fourth Theory of motivation

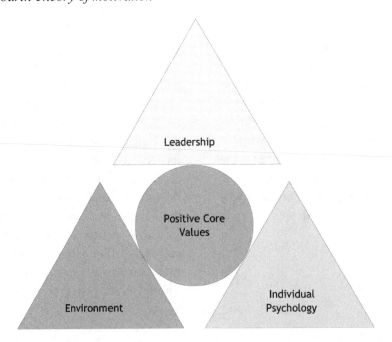

action based on positive core values. If core values are properly leveraged, they can decisively orient the three subsystems and create equilibrium in their interactions. With proper leadership, motivational saturation can be maintained. This is the best possible situation for any company facing competitive threats. A motivated workforce in a crisis will do much more for a company than a de-motivated workforce.

REFERENCES

Aguayo, R. (1990). *Dr. Deming the American who taught the Japanese about quality.* New York: Lyle Stuart.

Akao, Y. (1990). *Quality function deployment: Integrating customer requirements in product design.* Cambridge, MA: Productivity Press.

Akao, Y. (1991). *Hoshin kanri: Policy deployment for successful TQM.* Cambridge, MA: Productivity Press.

Ambrose, M. L., & Kulik, C. T. (1999). Old friends, new faces: Motivation research in the 1990s. *Journal of Management, 25,* 231–292. doi:. doi:10.1177/014920639902500302

Arauz, R., & Suzuki, H. (2004). ISO 9000 performance in Japanese industries. *Total Quality Management, 15*(1), 3–33.

Barrick, M. R., Parks, L., & Mount, M. K. (2005). Self-monitoring as a moderator of the relationships between personality traits and performance. *Personnel Psychology, 58*(2), 745–767. doi:10.1111/j.1744-6570.2005.00716.x

Becker, K. H., & Seidl, D. (2007). Different kinds of openings of Luhmann's Systems Theory: A reply to la Cour et al. *Organization, 14*(6), 939–944. doi:10.1177/1350508407082268

Bettencourt, L. A., & Ulwick, A. W. (2005). The customer centered innovation map. *Harvard Business Review, 86*(5), 109–114.

Bynner, W. (1944). *The way of life: According to Lao Tzu.* New York: Capricorn Books.

Cook, R. E., & Scott, W. R. (2000). *The quality movement & organizational theory.* Thousand Oaks, CA: Sage.

Crawford, R. (1991). *In the era of human capital.* New York: HarperBusiness.

Credit Union League and CUNA and Affiliates. (1994). *Total Quality Management.* Dubuque, IA: Kendall/Hunt Publishing.

Csikszentmihalyi, M. (1993). *The evolving self.* New York: Harper Perennial.

Deming, W. E. (1986). *Out of the Crisis.* Cambridge, MA: MIT CAE.

Diamond, J. (1999). *Guns, germs, and steel: The fates of human societies.* New York: W. W. Norton.

Diamond, J. (2005). *Collapse: How societies choose to fail or succeed.* New York: Penguin Books.

Drucker, P. F. (2007). *People and performance.* Boston: Harvard Business School Press.

Durand, R., & Calori, R. (2006). Sameness, otherness? Enriching organizational change theories with philosophical considerations on the same and the other. *Academy of Management Review, 31*(1), 93–114.

Durant, W., & Durant, A. (1968). *The lessons of history.* New York: Simon and Schuster.

Ehrlick, C. (2006). The EFQM-model and work motivation. *Total Quality Management, 17*(2), 131–140.

Forde, C., Slater, G., & Spencer, D. A. (2006). Faring the worst? Threat, participation and workplace productivity. *Economic and Industrial Democracy, 27*(3), 369–398. doi:10.1177/0143831X06065961

Gitlow, H. S., & Gitlow, S. J. (1987). *The Deming guide to quality and competitive position.* Englewood Cliffs, NJ: Prentice-Hall.

Gladwell, M. (2002). *The tipping point: How little things can make a big difference.* New York: Little Brown and Company.

Gottschalg, O., & Zollo, M. (2007). Interest alignment and competitive advantage. *Academy of Management Review, 32*(2), 419–437.

Grant, A. (2008). Does intrinsic motivation fuel the prosocial fire? Motivational synergy in predicting persistence, performance, and productivity. *The Journal of Applied Psychology, 93*(1), 48–58. doi:10.1037/0021-9010.93.1.48

Grant, A. (2008). The significance of task significance: Job performance effects, relational mechanisms, and boundary conditions. *The Journal of Applied Psychology, 93*(1), 108–124. doi:10.1037/0021-9010.93.1.108

Grayson, C. J., & O'Dell, C. (1988). *American business: A two-minute warning.* New York: Free Press.

Hackman, J. R., & Wageman, R. (2000). Total quality management: Empirical, conceptual, and practical issues. In R. E. Cole & W. R. Scott (Eds.), *The Quality Movement & Organization Theory* (pp. 23-48). Thousand Oaks, CA: Sage.

Haefner, J. J. (2008, July). *Beyond theory Z: Motivation in the knowledge-value era.* Poster session presented at the Walden University Ph. D. Summer Session Academic Residency Research Symposium.

Haefner, J. J., & Bartel, T. J. (1993). A structured approach. *The TQM Magazine, 3*(5), 19–26.

Halberstam, D. (1986). *The reckoning.* New York: William Morrow and Company.

Hawkins, P. (2007). *Blessed unrest.* New York: Viking.

Herrnstein, R. J., & Murray, C. (1994). *The bell curve.* New York: Free Press Paperbacks.

Hunt, M. (2007). *The story of psychology.* New York: Anchor Books.

Ishikawa, K. (1982). *Guide to Quality Control.* Tokyo: Asian Productivity Organization.

Jung, C. G. (1958). *The undiscovered self.* New York: Signet.

Juran, J. M., & Gryna, F. M. (1951). *Juran's quality control handbook.* New York: McGraw-Hill.

Kark, R., & Kijk, D. V. (2007). Motivation to lead, motivation to follow: the role of self-regulatory focus in leadership processes. *Academy of Management Review, 22*(2), 500–528.

Keller, M. (1989). *Rude awakening: The rise, fall, and struggle for recovery of General Motors.* New York: William Morrow and Company.

King, B. (1989). *Hoshin planning: The developmental approach.* Methuen, MA: Goal/QPC.

Kocabiyikoglu, A., & Popescu, I. (2007). Managerial motivation dynamics and incentives. *Management Science, 53*(5), 834–848. doi:10.1287/mnsc.1060.0640

Kodama, F. (1991). *Analyzing Japanese high technologies.* London: Pinter Publishers.

Kuhn, L. (2007). Why use complexity theories in social inquiry? *World Futures, 63,* 156–175. doi:10.1080/02604020601172525

Kumar, S., Ressler, T., & Ahrens, M. (2005). Systems thinking, a consilience of values and logic. *Human Systems Management, 24*(4), 259–274.

la Cour, A., Vallentin, S., Hojlund, H., Thyssen, O., & Rennison, B. (2007). Opening systems theory: A note on the recent special issue of Organization. *Organization, 14*(6), 929–938. doi:10.1177/1350508407082267

Land, G. T. L. (1973). *Grow or die: The unifying principle of transformation.* New York: Dell Publishing.

Langfred, K., & Moye, N. A. (2004). Effects of task autonomy on performance: An extended model considering motivation, informational, and structural mechanisms. *The Journal of Applied Psychology, 89*(6), 934–945. doi:10.1037/0021-9010.89.6.934

Laszlo, E. (1996). *The systems view of the world.* Cresskill, NJ: Hampton Press.

Leleur, S. (2007). Systemic planning: Dealing with complexity by a wider approach to planning. *E:CO, 9*(1/2), 2-10.

Lemonides, J. S. (2007). Toward an Adlerian approach to organizational intervention. *Journal of Individual Psychology, 63*(4), 399–413.

Liker, J. K. (2004). *The Toyota way: 14 management principles from the world's greatest manufacturer.* New York: McGraw-Hill.

Lord, R. L., & Farrington, P. A. (2006). Age-related differences in the motivation of knowledge workers. *Engineering Management Journal, 18*(3), 2026.

Lounsbury, M., & Ventresca, M. (2004). The new structuralism in organization theory. *Organization, 10*(3), 457–480. doi:10.1177/13505084030103007

Luhmann, N. (2006). System as difference. *Organization, 13*(1), 37–57. doi:10.1177/1350508406059638

Maslow, A. H. (1968). *Toward a psychology of being.* New York: John Wiley & Sons.

Maslow, A. H. (1998). *Maslow on Management.* New York: John Wiley & Sons.

Matsumoto, K. (1993). *The rise of the Japanese corporate system.* New York: Kegan Paul International.

Menezes, L. M., & Wood, S. (2006). The reality of flexible work systems in Britain. *International Journal of Human Resource Management, 17*(1), 106–138.

Meyer, J. P., Becker, T. E., & Vandenberghe, C. (2004). Employee commitment and motivation: A conceptual analysis and integrative model. *The Journal of Applied Psychology, 89*(6), 991–1007. doi:10.1037/0021-9010.89.6.991

Michaelson, C. (2005). Dialogue. *Academy of Management Review, 30*(2), 235–238.

Midgley, G. (2003). Five sketches of postmodernism: Implications for systems thinking and operational research. *Journal of Organisational Transformation & Social Change, 1*(1), 47–62. doi:10.1386/jots.1.1.47/0

Misencik, K. (2004). *Introduction to Freud.* Retrieved March 3, 2008, from http://classweb.gmu.edu/nclc130/s04/s04KMFreud.ppt

Mizuno, S. (1984). *Company-wide total quality control.* Tokyo: Asian Productivity Association.

Morcol, G. (2005). A new systems thinking: Implications of the sciences of complexity for public policy and administration. *Public Administration Quarterly, 29*(3/4), 297–320.

Nakamura, S. (1991). *The new standardization: Keystone of continuous improvement in manufacturing.* Portland, OR: Productivity Press.

Ouchi, W. G. (1981). *Theory Z: How American business can meet the Japanese challenge.* New York: Avon.

Pinker, S. (2002). *The blank slate.* New York: Penguin Books.

Pyzdek, T. (2001). *The six sigma handbook.* New York: McGraw-Hill.

Quigley, N. R., Tesluk, P. E., Locke, E. A., & Bartol, K. M. (2007). A multilevel investigation of the motivational mechanisms underlying knowledge sharing and performance. *Organization Science, 18*(1), 71–88. doi:10.1287/orsc.1060.0223

Richardson, K. A. (2004). Systems theory and complexity: Part 1. *E:CO, 6*(3), 75-79.

Richardson, K. A. (2004). Systems theory and complexity: Part 2. *E:CO, 6*(4), 77-82.

Richardson, K. A. (2005). Systems theory and complexity: Part 3. *E:CO, 7*(2), 104-114.

Richardson, K. A. (2007). Systems theory and complexity: Part 4. *E:CO, 9*(1/2), 166.

Sakaiya, T. (1991). *The knowledge-value revolution.* New York: Kodonsha International.

Sayer, A. (1992). *Method in social science: A realist approach.* New York: Routledge.

Senge, P. M. (1990). *The fifth discipline: The art and practice of the learning organization.* New York: Doubleday.

Skyttner, L. (2001). *General systems theory: Ideas and application.* River Edge, NJ: World Scientific Publishing.

Solow, D., & Szmerekovsky, J. G. (2007). The role of leadership: What management science can give back to the study of complex systems. *E:CO, 8*(4), 52-60.

Steele, M. D. (2003). Margins count: Systems thinking and cost. *AACE International Transactions,* 1-5.

Trochim, W. M. K., & Cabrera, D. (2005). The complexity of concept mapping for policy analysis. *E:CO, 7*(1), 11-22.

Tsai, W., Chen, C., & Liu, H. (2005). An integrative modeling linking employee positive moods and task performance. *Academy of Management Best Conference Paper, OB,* H1-H6.

Uchimaru, K., Okamoto, S., & Kurahara, B. (1993). *TQM for technical groups.* Portland, OR: Productivity Press.

von Bertalanffy, L. (1968). *General system theory.* New York: George Braziller.

Walton, M. (1990). *Deming management at work.* New York: Perigree Books.

Wang, T. W. (2004). From general system theory to total quality Management. *The Journal of American Academy of Business, 4*(1/2), 394–400.

Weber, M. (2002). The protestant ethic and the "spirit" of capitalism: And other writing. New York: Penguin Books.

ENDNOTES

[1] Line speeds varied based on battery size. The data in the paper is based on a slower line speed. The actual throughput losses were higher.

[2] The data is taken from the average productivity rate per shift. The production rate was amazingly consistent day to day. It appeared as if the process decayed for each hour after the day shift.

[3] DMAIC is define, measure, analyze, improve, control.

[4] At the end of the production season, the line workers threw a party for the ES. The maintenance worker explained that on the first night of the ES's presence, he hated him. However, he conceded that the ES "knew what he was doing" and conveyed deep respect.

[5] The cathode is a tube that is inserted inside the steel battery can. If it does not have the proper strength and density, it will crumble on insertion. This was the failure mode.

This work was previously published in International Journal of Technology Diffusion, Volume 1, Issue 1, edited by Ali Hussein Saleh Zolait, pp. 52-69, copyright 2010 by IGI Publishing (an imprint of IGI Global).

Chapter 6
E–Government Initiative in the Sultanate of Oman:
The Case of Ubar

Khamis Al-Gharbi
Sultan Qaboos University, Oman

Ahmed Al-Kindi
Sultan Qaboos University, Oman

ABSTRACT

There are many interesting initiatives regarding the use of internet technologies in e-government that are taking place in developing countries. A number of studies have been conducted in recent years regarding the adoption and use of internet technologies in e-government. However, most of these studies focused on the developed countries. There are many interesting initiatives regarding the use of internet technologies in e-government that are taking place in the developing countries and yet have received very little research attention. The Sultanate of Oman is currently working on a project called e-Oman to provide e-government, e-commerce, e-learning and other e-services. The hope is to enhance the quality of services offered by the government to its citizens. The purpose of this paper is to highlight e-government Initiatives in Oman.

INTRODUCTION

Recent studies have suggested many benefits from using Internet technologies in e-government. These benefits include improved quality customer service, increase number of customers, improve business processes, better relationship with customers, efficiency, time savings, and cost effective-

ness (Dearstyne, 2001). Furthermore, Khalid and Affisco (2002) cited the need for more efficiency in public sectors as the most driving force behind e-government initiatives. However, a number of studies have reported many challenges that might face e-government initiatives in developing countries. One of the main challenges is poor infrastructure in telecommunication, e-business, financial, and legal system. In addition, the lack of organizational culture, awareness, education,

DOI: 10.4018/978-1-4666-1752-0.ch006

language, social and psychological factors might add more barriers to the e-government initiatives (El-Nawawy & Ismail, 1999; Schmid et al, 2001; Sharma et al., 2002). Carter and Belanger (2004) argue that the success of e-government initiatives is not only depending on the government support but also on citizen willingness to accept and use the services. The purpose of this paper is to highlight e-government Initiatives in Oman.

E-GOVERNMENT DEFINITION AND IMPLEMENTATION

E-government is defined by (Luling, 2001, p. 43) as "online government services, that is, any interaction one might have with any government body or agency, using the Internet or the World Wide Web". Basically e-government represents the use of modern information technology (MIT) and telecommunication technology (TT) to exchange information and process across computer networks, especially the Internet Silcock (2001). The purpose of e-government in Oman is to:

- Improve the relationship with the citizen
- Provide round the clock services
- Cut departmental hierarchies
- Reduce queuing in many ministries' offices
- Provide a single point contact to speed up services

Studies describe e-government initiatives that serve a range of constituencies including: 1) Government-to-Citizen (G2C) applications such as the provision of online information and services, 2) Government-to-Business (G2B) applications such as electronic procurement, 3) Government-to-Employee (G2E) applications such as human resource internets, and 4) Government-to-Government (G2G) applications that provide integration between government agencies (e.g., between ministries). The Omani government vision is as follows: "The leveraging

of information technology and communications in providing collaborative services to public and private sectors and citizens through electronic means has been the driving force to move forward the Sultanate to the knowledge-based economy and achieve sustainable development" (Digital Society Strategy, 2002, p. 2).

The government has followed the following strategy in order to implement the above vision.

The strategy included the implementation of

- *E-Government Architecture, Applications and Service Delivery Model*
- *Security, Audit and Continuity Planning*
- *E-Legislation (Trust and Confidence)*
- *National Telecommunications and E-Payments Infrastructure*
- *E-Government Initiatives*
- *Flagship Projects (Quick Wins)*
- *Environment*
- *Resourcing*
- *Marketing and Awareness* (Oman IT Executive Committee (2002-2003)

Balutis (2001) identified the following phases for e-government implementation:

- Phase 1: Dissemination of information.
- Phase 2: Provision of forms.
- Phase 3: Ability to perform transactions.
- Phase 4: Government transformation (e.g., resulting in processes that cross organizational boundaries in order to provide citizens with information and "seamless service").

The Omani experience in implementing e-government initiatives based their methodology on the above phases but with local emphasis where the following phases were used:

- Phase 1: Availability of information (one way direction: to the user).

- Phase 2: Providing interaction mechanisms (i.e. email) for all users.
- Phase 3: Electronic Transaction through the Ubar portal as discussed below.
- Phase 4: Final transformation where Ubar becomes the gateway for all government services provided electronically to the users.

Figure 1 shows the architecture of the initiative as designed by the Omani Ministry of Economy. The figure illustrates The central nature of the Nervous System provides access to government services through various ways. For example, the portal module provides needed services to citizens, visitors and other customers electronically, while traditional methods of serving the people would continue in parallel.

METHODOLOGY

Since the scope of this paper is limited, the methodology used to gather data is based on interviews and document (literature) analysis. The

interviews were conducted here in Oman, with key participants who are responsible for some of the initiatives (i.e. Ubar). Also, literatures and studies regarding the initiatives were used to present the findings in this paper.

RESEARCH APPROACH

Case study research is an accepted research strategy in the Information Systems (IS) discipline. Many researchers have used the case study approach as their research strategy (see, Gable, 1994; Yin, 1994). The case study approach refers to an in-depth study or investigation of a contemporary phenomenon using multiple sources of evidence within its real-life context (Yin, 1994). According to Leidner and Jarvenpaa (1993), "Case study research is appropriate in situations where the research question involves a 'how', 'why', or exploratory 'what' question, the investigator has no control over actual behavioral events, and the focus is on contemporary as opposed to historical phenomenon".

Figure 1. Oman e-government initiative architecture (Al Ismaily, 2004)

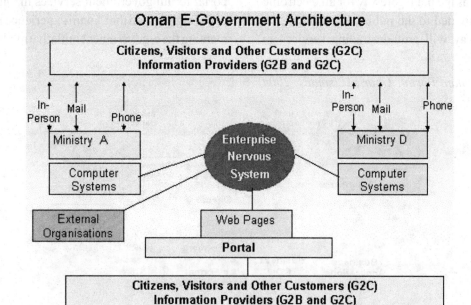

ICT SECTOR IN OMAN

According to the United Nation 2008 E-Government Readiness Report, Oman has jumped up to 28 points in this ranking position from 112th position in 2005 to 84th position in 2008. Oman ranks 60th position in the E-participation Index (out of 192 countries) with an index value of 0.2045 (www.ameinfo.com). The number of Internet subscribers and mobile subscribers are rising dramatically over the past few years (Naqvi and AL-Shihi, 2009). According to the ministry of national economy-Oman (2008) statistical bulletin, the number of Internet subscribers is over 2.6 millions in 2007.

This rise is a reflection of "the pace of progress through initiatives' to build of ICT infrastructure, over electronic services and build capacity within the country to harness the power of technology" remarked by CEO of ITA (www.ameinfo.com).

CASE STUDY (UBAR)

The government of the Sultanate of Oman embarked on an e-government initiative with a project named after the ancient Omani city of Ubar. The Ubar portal (Figure 2) is to be used by government institutions as the main gateway for all electronic services provided to the public. In addition, the Ubar gateway will provide trading services to the private sector, both locally and globally. The government vision is to make these services available electronically anytime and anywhere. In order for the service to be friendly, it must be rich, personalized, unified, and highly customizable experience to its users. The medium to reach Ubar in an efficient and user friendly manner is either by the web or by the mobile device where any portal visitor may request a service through a click of a button. Information and processes may then be made available to the client through a number of automated, sequenced, and synchronized service delivery steps in a seamless and transparent manner (http://www.ita.gov.om/english/government.html). In addition to its various features, Ubar would provide a secure environment where users' identities are protected by an authentication secure mechanism (i.e. digital signatures).

CONCLUSION

This paper presents the Omani experience in designing and implementing the e-government initiative. The paper covers the early stages of this implementation and introduces a case study (Ubar) which is considered the future gateway portal for all government services in Oman. The paper highlighted the Omani experience in implementing the e-government initiative methodology

Figure 2. Omani Portal: Ubar (Al Ismaily, 2004)

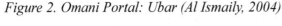

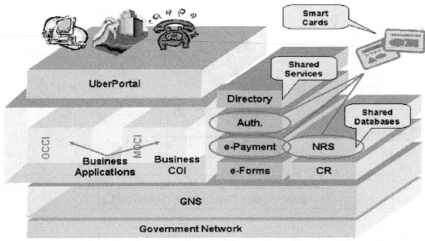

which consisted of the following four phases; 1) Availability of information (one way direction: to the user), 2) Providing interaction mechanisms (i.e. email) for all users, 3) Electronic Transaction through the Ubar portal as discussed below, and 4) Final transformation where Ubar becomes the gateway for all government services provided electronically to the users. This research illustrates the government vision in trying to enhance the quality of services offered to its citizens.

REFERENCES

Al Ismaily, S. (2004). *The Goals and A Progress Report.* DIGITAL OMAN.

Balutis, A. P. (2001). E-government 2001, Part I: Understanding the challenge and evolving strategies. *Public Management, 30*(1), 33–37.

Carter, L., & Belanger, F. (2004). *Citizen adoption of electronic government initiatives.* Paper presented at the 37th Hawaii International Conference on System Sciences.

Collins, J., & Millen, R. (1995). Information systems outsourcing by large American industrial firms: Choices and impacts. *Information Resources Management Journal, 8*(1), 5–13.

Dearstyne, D. (2001). E-business, e-government & information proficiency. *Information Management Journal, 35*(4), 16–24.

Digital Society. (2002). *Executive summary.* Muscat, Oman: Government of Oman.

El-Nawawy, M. A., & Ismail, M. M. (1999). Overcoming Deterrents and Impediments to e-commerce in Light of Globalization: The Case of Egypt. In proceedings of INET99, June 22-25, San Jose, California.

Gable, G. (1994). Integrating Case Study and Survey Research Methods: an Example in Information Systems. *European Journal of Information Systems, 3*(2), 112–126. doi:10.1057/ejis.1994.12

http://www.ameinfo.com/147106.html#story

Khalid, S., & Affisco, J. (2002, June 23-25). *Reporting on E-Government Initiatives in Canada and the United States.* Paper presented at the Third Annual Global Information Technology Management (GITM) World Conference, New York.

Leidner, D., & Jarvenpaa, S. (1993). The information Age Confronts Education: Case studies on Electronic Classrooms. *Information Systems Research, 4*(1), 24–54. doi:10.1287/isre.4.1.24

Luling, D. (2001). Taking it online: Anyway, anyplace. Tennessee anytime. *Journal of Government Financial Management, 50*(2), 42–49.

Oman IT Executive Committee. (2002-2003). *Report, Sultanate of Oman.* Muscat, Oman: Government of Oman.

Silcock, R. (2001). What is e-government? *Parliamentary Affairs, 54,* 88–101. doi:10.1093/pa/54.1.88

Yin, R. (1994). *Case Study Research Design and Methods* (2nd ed.). Newbury Park, CA: Sage.

This work was previously published in International Journal of Technology Diffusion, Volume 1, Issue 1, edited by Ali Hussein Saleh Zolait, pp. 70-74, copyright 2010 by IGI Publishing (an imprint of IGI Global).

78

Chapter 7
Mobile Commerce Use among UK Mobile Users:
An Experimental Approach Based on a Proposed Mobile Network Utilization Framework

Asem Moqbel
Cardiff University, UK

Mirella Yani-De-Soriano
Cardiff University, UK

Shumaila Yousafzai
Cardiff University, UK

ABSTRACT

In this paper, the authors examine UK mobile users' perceptions of m-commerce utilization. For this purpose, the authors devise a Mobile Network Utilization Model empirically tested in experimental settings. The empirical findings reveal strong support for the capability of the proposed utilization model in measuring the concept of Mobile Task-Technology Fit (MTTF) and explaining the utilization of m-commerce services among UK mobile users. In particular, their research finds that MTTF and m-commerce utilization are dependent on the interactions between the key components of a wider mobile network, namely mobile users, mobile devices, mobile tasks, mobile operators, as well as mobile vendors. The authors identify 15 factors as a result of such interaction and the importance of these factors in explaining MTTF and the utilization of m-commerce services.

INTRODUCTION

With slight variations mainly over the technological nature of the medium, m-commerce has been defined by a number of scholars as the trading of goods and services over mobile Internet devices.

In their article, Wu and Hisa (2004) defined mobile commerce as a monetary-value transaction that is carried out over a wireless telecommunication network. Makki et al. (2002) asserted this view and attributed the growing demand on wireless Internet services to the increasing growth of wireless net-

DOI: 10.4018/978-1-4666-1752-0.ch007

Copyright © 2012, IGI Global. Copying or distributing in print or electronic forms without written permission of IGI Global is prohibited.

works. Other scholars, however, have emphasized the broad dissemination of the mobile hardware when defining m-commerce. They argued for m-commerce as being the commercialization of services delivered over handheld devices such as mobile phones and Personal Digital Assistants (PDAs) (Sadeh, 2002; Mennecke & Strader, 2002; Dholakia & Dholakia, 2004; Shin et al., 2006). Still other scholars have favored a combination of the two views when defining m-commerce. Barnes (2002), for example, argued that "[m] odern wireless communications represent the convergence of two key technology trends of the 1990s: portability and networking." In this view, the nature of m-commerce is multi-dimensional since its emergence is not only attributed to advancements in the Internet technologies but also to a corresponding set of inventions in the telecommunication technologies.

Clearly, the advent of m-commerce is a natural phenomenon of the wireless convergence. Many have regarded such a form of electronic trade as "a natural extension" of electronic commerce (Coursaris et al., 2003) or "a subset of e-commerce" (Dholakia & Dholakia, 2004; Ngai & Gunasekaran, 2007; Siau & Shen, 2003). Others have seen it as a totally different form of trade stressing the wireless nature of the medium and drawing on the distinction between wired and wireless Internet (Bhasin, 2005). The debate on the nature of m-commerce is still current since more technological advancements seem to add to its uniqueness as a newly emerging business model.

In the greatest part of the literature, there remains, however, a strong emphasis on the increasing importance of m-commerce as a thriving force with great future potential in the realm of electronic commerce. Bertrand et al. (2001) expect a possible surge in the mobile-based electronic commerce due to the growing number of value-added mobile services and the increasing world-wide adoption of mobile Internet. Successful adoption of m-commerce with particular reference to Nordic Countries (e.g Kristoffersen & Ljungberg, 1999) and Japan's NTT DoCoMo (e.g. Bertrand et al., 2001; Anwar, 2002; Barnes, 2002; Funk, 2006) have been cited by many as examples to substantiate such a possible surge in m-commerce services in the years to come. Certain advanced regions and countries such as Western Europe and the USA, however, have been slow to embrace the m-commerce phenomenon. Scholars such as Makki et al. (2003) and Anckar and D'Incau (2002) have attributed such a slow response to the technical infrastructure, low speed wireless access links, as well as high costs associated with m-commerce implementation. This is also complicated by the absence of integration between mobile players' sophisticated infrastructure and applications development on the one hand and their wireless data service provision on the other (Seager, 2003).

The current paper, however, undertakes a consumer perspective as it utilizes a lab-based experiment to examine consumers' perceptions of m-commerce and explore the scope of its services adoption in the UK market. The experimental research aims to identify areas of interest in the mobile task-technology fit (MTTF) and ultimately measure users' utilization of m-commerce services. Building on some information system models, a conceptual framework was developed for the purpose of this research integrating relevant constructs perceived as central to answering the research questions and ultimately m-commerce adoption.

Theoretical Grounds

Frameworks and conceptual models of mobile information systems (Mobile IS) are very scant. The reasons are abound among which the novelty of the phenomenon, the non-commercial adoption of the innovation as a business model, as well as the interdependent nature of the medium exhibiting several players of contractual nature ranging from system manufacturers to service providers, mobile vendors, regulators, as well as mobile end users.

Though the traditional information systems (IS) have witnessed the emergence of several models and frameworks attempting to explain its acceptance as well as usage (e.g. Davis, 1989), mobile information systems suffer from a shortage in such theoretical frameworks. Some of the existing mobile IS frameworks have entirely adopted traditional IS models in their endeavors to elucidate the adoption of mobile technologies (e.g. Junglas et al., 2008). Other models have either modified or extended such traditional IS frameworks to best fit the mobile information medium (e.g. Lee et al., 2007). Both streams, however, have reflected an understanding that mobile information systems are unique in their nature though the attempted elucidations of such uniqueness have predominately been based on traditional IS frameworks. They have also been pre-occupied with tackling the utilization of mobile information systems within organizational settings – an area in which such a medium is not fully utilized. Therefore, there has been an urging need for developing mobile IS frameworks to explain the adoption of mobile technologies and services among mobile end users being the societal sector mostly targeted with m-commerce services.

In their nature, mobile systems are mainly end user-centered, a phenomenon explained by the exponential diffusion of mobile devices among end users all over the globe. The existing m-commerce applications are mainly targeted to accommodate end users' needs and hence priority should be given to the development of mobile end user frameworks. To address such a shortcoming, a mobile system framework was developed to explain the nature of m-commerce services adoption among mobile end users.

THE RATIONALE FOR A MOBILE TECHNOLOGY FRAMEWORK

Mobile technology boosts a challenge for the information technology models designed for work settings. Such models were aimed at explaining the relationships between organizations' tasks and their informational systems in order to measure job-related constructs such as individual performance and system utilization. The ubiquitous nature of the mobile medium, however, has the potential to redefine such relationships between the constructs and might disclose layers of embedded interrelationships that remained unattended to within the research corpus of information systems. In addition, the mobile use context varies by the mobility of the medium and hence frames mobile users in various use situations requiring different cognitive responses to utilize the technology and perform the mobile task at that given time and place.

Being part of the mobile context, m-commerce is different from other technology innovations that are mainly characterized by restrictions to place, time, and use situation. M-commerce operates in a mobile environment where the impact and interaction of mobile technology, mobile services, as well as mobile context outline the behavior of users and define their use framework. Hence, the requirements for utilizing m-commerce are contingent to the span of control imposed by the immediate context of use. For these reasons, theories such as the TAM (Davis, 1986) championing perfect use conditions are not entirely applicable. Urbaczewski et al. (2002) confirm this view when they assert that any attempt to validate or invalidate theories such as the TAM in the mobile context would be premature if no effort is made to gain an understanding of the complex phenomenon of adoption of mobile technology as a complex socio-technical process. The underlying assumption of the TAM constructs of perceived usefulness (PU) and perceived ease of use (PEOU) is that their positive perception is the sole determinant of technology utilization. Hence, there is an apparent negligence of the impact of the multi-dimensionality of the use context. The TAM clearly implies the supremacy of its two major constructs as motivators freeing the user from the other opposing forces of the use context. In this sense, the TAM context is mainly organizational (Goodhue and Thompson 1995; Dishaw and Strong, 1999) where job performance is the ultimate translation of technology acceptance – a phenomenon that is not entirely applicable to mobile technology and hence m-commerce where adopters are mainly end users.

The issue of job performance as a measure of technology acceptance has been widely criticized due to the relative absence of volitional use conditions in organizational settings (Stafford et al., 2004, cited in Lu et al., 2005). Voluntariness in usage was also an issue that has been criticized in the Theory of Reasoned Action (TRA) resulting in a modification of the theory's original model by adding the construct of perceived behavioral control as a determinant of behavioral intentions and use (Ajzen & Fishbein, 1973). This modification has come to be known as the Theory of Planned Behavior (TPB) (Ajzen, 1985, 1991). More recently, Venkatesh and Davis (2000) revised the original TAM proposing a TAM2 framework that included the construct of subjective norms as a determinant of PU.

Lu et al. (2005) further argue that the TAM related models focused on building a generic model for explaining general technology acceptance. A generic model may not accurately explain the process of adopting a specific system and tend to neglect one important variable – the impact of personal innovativeness on adoption (Ibid). A model such as the Task-Technology Fit (TTF) (Goodhue and Thompson, 1995), on the other hand, includes user abilities as a core component, but the empirical research carried out by the authors did not explore the moderating nature of personal innovativeness as a mediating force between the two major parts of the model, namely, the task and technology. Our proposed framework accounts for the interaction effect resulting from the user moderating mobile tasks and mobile technology. We claim that a fit between the mobile task and technology is relative to an individual's personal innovativeness as

well as the perception of and variation in the use context. Though studies such as Lee et al. (2004) have accounted for individual differences when measuring the TTF in use situations, they still share the commonality of applying the model to organizational settings in which the absence of volitional use is likely to distort the impact of TTF on both performance and use. Moreover, modeling the context of use to organizational settings could vary in extent and significance to that of end users'. These studies have also overlooked the impact of the use context on users' perception of the TTF and the inverse impact of such a use context on users' perceived abilities.

Though the TTF resembles the TAM in that they both presume perfect use conditions mainly in organizational settings, our proposed model for m-commerce adoption is not entirely preoccupied with the technicalities of the system (i.e., the Technical Fit) but also extends to include a wider 'Network Fit' where the user is part of a bigger and interrelated network of technology developers, service providers, and service users. The two sub fit models (technical and network) are also integral parts of a larger socio-technical context. Moreover, beside the technical consideration of the medium and users' familiarity with the technology, the framework factors in the impact of the larger mobile use context as a determinant of technology utilization.

As an information system framework, however, the TTF enjoys an advantage over the TAM model. While the former explicitly accounts for the information system task as a major determinant of the fit with the technological medium, the latter overlooks its criticality though its importance might implicitly be perceived as embedded under its construct of PU (Dishaw and Strong, 1999). After all, the two models were developed for stationary information systems and technologies.

Studies that have tested the TTF model on mobile information systems are very sparse. They are also pre-occupied with organizational tasks and the utilization of mobile technology in work settings. Gebauer and Shaw (2004), for example, applied the TTF to a newly implemented mobile e-procurement system introduced to aid the existing electronic procurement application of a Fortune 100 company. Gebauer et al. (2006) asserted that the existing studies on mobile information systems have addressed the basic concept of TTF but the concept has not been integrated systematically. In their research paper, the authors suggested the study of managerial tasks as the basis for analyzing mobile systems. Though the authors provided a systematic allocation of tasks based on their inherent nature of routineness and non-routineness, the study remained limited to managerial tasks whereby their performance was seen as part of the job rather than a voluntary choice (Dishaw & Strong, 1999).

Moreover, the study by Lee et al. (2007) explored the impact of individual differences among insurance agents on the performance of insurance tasks using the PDA technology. Although the study reported a major impact of individual differences on the performance of insurance tasks among the 238 surveyed insurance agents, it remained prone to the criticism that task performance in organizational settings is not entirely volitional. Besides, the study's organizational context distorted a precise measurement of the validity of the TTF and its applicability to mobile information systems though cognitive fit and computer self-efficacy were employed as explanatory measures of technology utilization and task performance. Perhaps the more recent study by Junglas et al. (2008) has gone a step further in recreating a more authentic mobile context whereby tasks were divided on the basis of their sensitiveness and insensitiveness to location and technology was epitomized according to locatability and mobility. The major drawback of the study, however, was the deliberate elimination of the impact of individual differences as the study recruited its participants entirely from an information system class. By doing this, the study intended to test for the fit between mobile technology and mobile

task without seeing individual abilities as having a major influence on moderating the fit between the task and technology. Furthermore, though the authors strived to provide ideal mobile context conditions to test for the fit between the proposed tasks and technologies, they overlooked the impact of the use context in determining the extent of fit between the tasks and technology used.

CONCEPTUAL MOBILE TECHNOLOGY FRAMEWORK AND HYPOTHESIZED RELATIONSHIPS

To address this urging need, we proposed a research framework for the utilization of mobile technology for m-commerce purposes incorporating constructs from information system models such as the TTF and our own. The conceptual framework employs the TTF model as a core component of a bigger network fit which is in turn incorporated into a larger socio-technical context. The logic for such a comprehensive framework is explained by the multi-dimensional nature of the mobile use context involving the existence and collaboration of many players forming an interrelated use network and assuming different though interlinked roles. The interaction between the constructs of individual fits within the framework have also been seen as crucial where, for example, individual differences are considered as having a moderation capability that affects the interaction between mobile task and mobile technology. The result is an extent of fit relative to the level of an individual's personal innovativeness. Similarly, the level of fit between the task and technology is impacted by the larger fit of the network in which the relative influence of mobile operators and vendors emerge as inevitable. Figure 1 presents a diagrammatic representation of our proposed framework along with the hypothesized interrelationships.

To this end, the following can be hypothesized.

Figure 1. Mobile network utilization framework

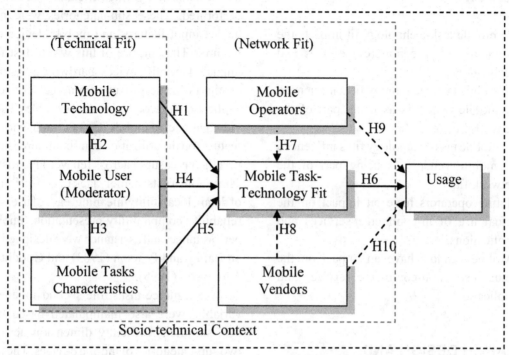

Note: Assumed indirect relationships are indicated with dotted lines.

Technical Fit

Mobile Technology

H1: The characteristics of mobile devices contribute to the fit with mobile tasks and hence the actual use of m-commerce services and applications.

H1a: The input features of mobile devices affect MTTF and hence the actual use of m-commerce services and applications.

H1b: The output features of mobile devices affect MTTF and hence the actual use of m-commerce services and applications.

Mobile Users

H2: Mobile users' skills and abilities impact their perceptions of the difficulty of mobile tasks.

H3: Mobile users' skills and abilities impact their perceptions of mobile devices' compatibility with mobile tasks.

H4: Following from H2 and H3, mobile users' skills and abilities affect their perceptions of the mobile task-technology fit (MTTF).

Tasks Characteristics

H5: The characteristics of mobile tasks contribute to the fit with mobile devices and hence the actual use of m-commerce services and applications.

H5a: Simple mobile tasks are likely to reflect greater fit with mobile devices and hence affect the actual use of mobile m-commerce services and applications.

H5b: Complex mobile tasks are likely to reflect lesser fit with mobile devices and hence the actual use of m-commerce services and applications than simple mobile tasks.

Network Fit

H6: The mobile task-technology fit impacts the actual use of m-commerce services and applications.

H7: The mobile task-technology fit is influenced by mobile operators as being part of the network fit.

H8: The mobile task-technology fit is influenced by mobile vendors as being part of the network fit.

H9: Mobile operators have an impact on the actual use of m-commerce services and applications.

H10: Mobile vendors have an impact on the actual use of m-commerce services and applications.

RESEARCH DESIGN AND METHODOLOGY

To answer the research questions and the conceptual framework hypotheses, a laboratory experiment was devised whereby the concept of fit, highlighted in the different levels of the research framework, was measured through manipulating specific characteristics of the tested m-commerce tasks and mobile devices. These manipulations in the characteristics of m-commerce tasks and mobile technology were aimed at measuring the impact of 'Technical Fit' on the utilization of m-commerce services and applications. Other elements of the framework such as MTTF, mobile operators, and mobile vendors were also introduced as part of the experimental questionnaire in which subjects were asked to assess the impact of the wider 'Network Fit' on the utilization of m-commerce services.

Technology and Task Manipulations

Technology, as one of our independent variables, was manipulated through dividing mobile devices' characteristics into two sub-categories based on the mechanisms by which m-commerce tasks were performed. These sub-categories were mobile device input features and mobile device output features. The purpose of this was to test for the impact of mobile devices' hardware and software on the utilization of m-commerce services and applications (i.e. our dependent variable). The individual impact of mobile devices' input and output features on the utilization of m-commerce services was then measured across ten MTTF constructs. These constructs, namely lack of confusion, level of detail, locatability/meaning, ease of use, system reliability, compatibility, presentation, timeliness, performance, and assistance were designed based on Bailey and Pearson (1983) and Goodhue and Thompson (1995).

M-commerce tasks, the second independent variable, were also manipulated based on the task simplicity/difficulty dimension across the two sub-categories of mobile devices. The results were four tasks in total. Two tasks: simple and difficult, were then performed focusing on the mobile device's input features while holding its output features constant. The other two tasks: simple and difficult, were also performed but this time with the focus being on the mobile device's output features while holding the input features constant. The testing of task simplicity and difficulty was also carried out across the same ten constructs in an attempt to predict m-commerce tasks fit with mobile devices and ultimately the impact of this fit on m-commerce utilization.

The mobile task-technology manipulations resulted in four experimental groups to whom four m-commerce tasks were randomly assigned. Group 1 carried out 'Simple Task 1' (sending a text message with pre-defined parameters to a designated mobile phone number). In designing this simple task, an emphasis was placed on the ultimate utilization of mobile devices' input features so as to test them across the ten constructs set forth for this purpose. We attempted to control and minimize the impact of mobile devices' output features through focusing much of the subjects' attention on an input-oriented task where a considerable use of capitalizations, punctuations, characters, symbols, and numbers was emphasized. The purpose was to provide accurate measurements of 'the simple task versus mobile device's input features' dimension.

Experimental group 2 performed 'Simple Task 2' (navigating into the 'message inbox' of the mobile device and browsing through a pre-sent SMS. The design of this simple task was to test for the impact of mobile devices' output features (display and screen size) on the utilization of m-commerce services. The task aimed at controlling to a minimal level the use of mobile devices' input features as the task only involved reading a text message. Moreover, the emphasis on stimulating the subjects' minds to look for a flight booking confirmation number in the text message and to write it down on a sheet of paper was to encourage maximum utilization of the device output features (screen and display).

Experimental group 3 was asked to perform 'Difficult Task 3' (logging into a designated email account, re-typing and sending a pre-defined email to a designated email account). The testing of the mobile-device-mobile-task fit in task 3 was carried out along 'the difficult task versus mobile device input features' paradigm. The subjects were asked to re-type and send a carefully designed email script the aim of which was to test the usability of the mobile device input features. As it was the case with Simple Task 1, the email script consisted of characters, numbers, symbols, punctuations, as well as capitalizations. 'Difficult Task 3' was

designed with the same conditions of 'Simple Task 1' except for the level of task difficulty as opposed to task simplicity. The control and manipulation mechanisms are otherwise identical. Furthermore, the emphasis on performing 'Difficult Task 3' on the interface of an email service provider website was to increase the level of task difficulty and hence its performance on the interface. The standardization of the email interface to a single email service provider was also essential to eliminate the impact of differences in website layouts and designs on the performance of the task.

Experimental group 4 carried out 'Difficult Task 4' (logging into a standardized mobile website; checking for weather forecasts according to pre-defined search parameters; and writing down weather details to verify task completion). The paradigm of testing the task was formulated around the dimension of 'difficult task versus mobile device output features.' For this experimental group, the task was designed so that maximum testing conditions of the usability of mobile devices' output features were to be attained. The weather checking process involved navigating through multiple Web pages within the standardized Website where browsing and scrolling through the mobile screen were inevitable. Moreover, the standardization of the mobile Website interface was to ensure accurate measurement of the task performance among the group subjects. Table 1 presents a tabular representation of the mobile experiment task-technology taxonomy.

Table 1. Experimental task-technology taxonomy

TTF		Mobile Technology Characteristics	
		Device Input Features	**Device Output Features**
Mobile Task characteristics	**Simple**	Experimental Group 1 (Simple task 1)	Experimental Group 2 (Simple Task 2)
	Difficult	Experimental Group 3 (Difficult task 3)	Experimental Group 4 (Difficult task 4)

Source: This research

Table 2. Characteristics of mobile operators and mobile vendors

Mobile Operator	Characteristics
	Network Coverage
	Connection Speed
	Range of services
	Pricing of services
	Level of integration with mobile devices, vendors, and users.
	Customers loyalty to mobile operator
	Characteristics
Mobile Vendor	Functionality of the mobile website
	Range of services
	Pricing of services
	Level of integration with mobile device, operators, and users.
	Customers loyalty to mobile vendor

Subjects

Subjects of the experiment were mainly students from various disciplines at a large UK university. Though experiments involving students as the experimental subjects are often criticized of being unrepresentative of the general public due to lower external validity issues and hence their generalizable results are seen as less credible (Saunders et al., 2007), laboratory experiments can still provide accurate results considering the novelty of certain technology applications such as those of m-commerce which are not quite well known to the general public. Besides, lab-based experiments ensure greater control over the experiment variables and hence increase their internal validity which is crucial for testing novel innovations with which the general public is less familiar. Furthermore, subjects were paid for their participation in the experiment to encourage genuine participation. As being part of the research framework, subjects' impact on the concept of fit between mobile tasks and mobile technology was evaluated through measuring subjects' computer self-efficacy and analyzing their demographic data.

Mobile Operators and Vendors

Being part of the 'Network Fit,' both mobile operators and mobile vendors were hypothesized as having effect on users' perception of MTTF and ultimately on m-commerce task performance. Six mobile operator and five mobile vendor constructs were developed based on the literature review and our own so as to test for the claimed impact or the lack of it thereof. Table 2 shows the tested dimensions of mobile operators and mobile vendors.

Questionnaire Development

The questionnaire was carefully developed and designed as an integrated part of the experimental tool devised to answer the research questions and hypotheses. For the purpose of this research, questionnaires were used to collect data from the experiment. The strength of questionnaires lies in the fact that they enable the standardization of responses and hence more accurate analysis of the collected data (Saunders et al., 2007).

DATA ANALYSIS AND FINDINGS

Participants' Demographics

In total, forty participants took part in the experiment deployed for collecting data for the purpose of this study. The data collection process revealed an almost even split between male and female participants. Nineteen of the participants were males while the remaining twenty one were females accounting for 47.5 and 52.5 percent respectively. Participants spread across three main age groups (18-25, 26-35, 36-45) out of four age groups used in the experiment-related questionnaire with 24 participants clustered around the 18-25 age group alone (60 percent). Of the remaining participants, 32.5 percent (i.e., 13 participants) belonged to the 26-35 age group while the other 7.5 percent of participants (i.e., 3 participants) belonged to the 36-45 age group. A possible explanation of the absence of participants in the 'Over 46' age group could be entailed to the weak representation of this age group among student population from which participants were mainly sampled. Table 3 summarizes the sample characteristics.

Reliability Analysis

The constructs of the research framework were tested using Cronbach's alpha for internal consistency and reliability. The analysis was carried out across the four experimental treatments to test for the 'Technical Fit' and 'Network Fit' of the research model. Table 4 presents the alpha values of the research framework constructs across the four experimental groups.

Though some scholars argue for an alpha value of 0.60 as marginally acceptable, the majority tend to emphasize a value of 0.70 or higher (Garson, 2008). As reflected in the table above, the Cronbach's alpha values for the research framework constructs showed higher internal

Table 3. Sample characteristics

Characteristic	Number of Sample	Percent
Gender		
Male	19	47.5
Female	21	52.5
Age		
18-25	24	60
26-35	13	32.5
36-45	3	7.5
Over 46	-	-
Education Level		
High School	-	-
Diploma	-	-
University Undergraduate	22	55
University Postgraduate	18	45
Income		
Unemployed	20	50
Under £10,000	8	20
£10,000 - £15,000	6	15
Over £15,000	6	15
Mobile Phone Ownership		
Yes	40	100
No	-	-
Number of Mobile Phones Owned		
One	28	70
Two	9	22.5
More than Two	3	7.5
Duration of Mobile Phone Ownership		
Under One Year	12	30
One to Two Years	4	10
Two to Three Years	4	10
Over Three Years	20	50

consistency levels except for mobile vendors' variables where the alpha value is 0.634 and hence might not be as reliable though marginally acceptable.

Table 4. Research framework reliability analysis

Research Framework Characteristic	Number of Constructs	Cronbach's Alpha Value
Mobile Device Input Features	10	0.805
Mobile Device Output Features	10	0.913
Simple Mobile Tasks	10	0.943
Complex Mobile Tasks	10	0.935
Mobile Operators	6	0.772
Mobile Vendors	5	0.634
User's Computer self-efficacy	10	0.903

Factor Analysis

To individually correlate an extensive number of constructs such as the ones deployed to test the several parts of the research framework can complicate the identification of patterns in the correlated relationships. To address this issue, the statistical reduction technique of factor analysis was employed to simplify and accurately identify the relationships between the research framework variables.

The Research Framework 'Technical Fit'

The 'Technical Fit' of the research framework comprised of three major parts as its core components: mobile device characteristics, mobile tasks characteristics, and mobile users.

Mobile Device Characteristics

The characteristics of mobile devices were examined using ten constructs across the dichotomous classification of Mobile Device Input Features and Mobile Device Output Features. Three factors were extracted for mobile device input features with eigenvalues over the desired value of 1. They were 'Usability of Mobile Device Input Features,' 'Efficiency of Mobile Device Input Features,' and 'Performance of Mobile Device Input Features.'

Their cumulative explanation potential of the variance between the tested original variables totaled to 68.726 percent. Similarly, two eligible factors were extracted for mobile device output features. They were 'Usability of Mobile Device Output Features' and 'Straightforwardness of Mobile Device Output Features.' Tables 5 and 6 show the factor analyses results for the ten constructs of mobile device input and output features.

MOBILE TASKS' CHARACTERISTICS

Mobile tasks characteristics were also dichotomously classified based on their level of difficulty into Simple Mobile Tasks and Complex Mobile Tasks. As it was the case with mobile device features, the same ten constructs were used to measure the fit of the two types of mobile tasks with mobile devices.

The presence of high correlation values between the ten constructs used to test for the concept of fit of simple mobile tasks with mobile devices heralded the existence of inter-variable relationships. The results from factor analysis exhibited in Tables 7 and 8 show that the high correlations (see appendix 1 and 2) across the variables are significant enough to enable the explanation of most of the variance between variables by a single extracted factor in the case of Simple Mobile Tasks

Table 5. Factor analysis for mobile device input features

Original Variables	Mobile Device Input Features					
	Extracted Factors			Eigenvalue	% of Variance	Cumulative %
	F1- Usability of Mobile Device Input Features			3.839	38.390	38.390
		F2- Efficiency of Mobile Device Input Features		1.892	18.917	57.307
			F3- Performance of Mobile Device Input Features	1.142	11.418	68.726
	Variables' Loadings on Extracted Factors					
Lack of confusion	.097	-.821	-.219			
Level of Detail	.103	-.789	-.137			
Locatability	.681	-.402	-.078			
Ease of Use	.896	.240	-.042			
Reliability	-.007	.094	.929			
Compatibility	.563	-.091	.522			
Presentation	.523	-.164	.415			
Timeliness	-.298	-.754	.248			
Performance	.139	-.816	.123			
Assistance Level	.596	-.103	.034			

* Significant loading value over 0.44

(67.143%) and two factors in Complex Mobile Tasks (77.040%).

Evident from Table 7, all variables loaded positively on the simple mobile tasks' extracted factor. Hence, the name 'Mobile Tasks Straightforwardness' was attributed to the extracted factor as all original variables tackled mobile tasks simplicity from different perspectives. The two extracted factors of complex mobile tasks, on the other hand, reflected varying significance (see Table 8). Nine out of the original ten variables have positive significant loading values on factor 1. The remaining variable almost entirely loaded on factor 2. There are no relational cross-loading, which means that the two factors were fully distinct though they differed in their variance explanation strength of the overall ten variables. As the nine variables that loaded positively on factor 1 signify the difficulty level of mobile tasks, the name 'Mobile Tasks Complexity' can be attributed to extracted factor 1. Moreover, since factor 2 is solely concerned with the level of assistance required to accomplish the complex mobile task, the factor can rightfully be termed 'Assistance level for Complex Mobile Tasks.'

Mobile Users' Technological Characteristics

The research framework hypothesized that mobile users have a moderation impact on the perception of fit between m-commerce services and mobile

Table 6. Factor analysis for mobile device output features

Original Variables	Mobile Device Output Features				
	Extracted Factors		Eigenvalue	% of Variance	Cumulative %
	F1- Usability of Mobile Device Output Features		5.777	57.771	57.771
		F2- Straightforwardness of Device Output Features	1.284	12.839	70.610
	Variables' Loadings on Extracted Factors				
Lack of confusion	.797	.000			
Level of Detail	.875	.035			
Locatability	.597	.515			
Ease of Use	.604	.451			
Reliability	.751	-.288			
Compatibility	.731	.261			
Presentation	.898	-.176			
Timeliness	.774	-.006			
Performance	.721	.267			
Assistance Level	-.045	.943			

* Significant loading value over 0.44

Table 7. Factor analysis for simple mobile tasks

Original Variables	Simple Mobile Tasks			
	Extracted Factors	Eigenvalue	% of Variance	Cumulative %
	F1- Mobile Tasks Straightforwardness	6.714	67.143	67.143
	Variables' Loadings on Extracted Factor			
Lack of confusion	.787			
Level of Detail	.807			
Locatability	.770			
Ease of Use	.897			
Reliability	.899			
Compatibility	.892			
Presentation	.856			
Timeliness	.794			
Performance	.781			
Assistance Level	.687			

* Significant loading value over 0.44

Table 8. Factor analysis for Complex Mobile Tasks

Original Variables	Complex Mobile Tasks				
	Extracted Factors		Eigenvalue	% of Variance	Cumulative %
	F1- Mobile Tasks Complexity		6.509	65.088	65.088
		F2- Assistance level for Complex Mobile Tasks	1.195	11.952	77.040
	Variables' Loadings on Extracted Factors				
Lack of confusion	.978	-.239			
Level of Detail	.876	-.094			
Locatability	.671	.348			
Ease of Use	.950	-.289			
Reliability	.883	-.091			
Compatibility	.800	.291			
Presentation	.704	.310			
Timeliness	.713	.170			
Performance	.795	.234			
Assistance Level	.047	.916			

* Significant loading value over 0.44

devices. Two separate methods were designed to test for the significance of such a moderation effect. These were the duration of participants' technological exposure to the mobile context and their computer self-efficacy.

Descriptive Analysis of Participants' Technological Characteristics

This section will discuss some descriptive measures to check for the possible significance of the 'Duration of Mobile Device Ownership' variable on moderating mobile users' perception of MTTF. In general, the mean scores of the perception of fit between mobile devices and m-commerce tasks tended to be higher among participants who recorded an ownership of a mobile device(s) for over three years. However, for the purpose of this study, we ignored the impact of the two middle categories of 'The Duration of Mobile Device Ownership' variable (i.e., 'One to Two Years' and 'Two to Three Years') for two reasons. The first

reason is that each category only recorded four participants resulting in too a small percentage (10% each). The second reason is that the time span between the two middle categories was presumed as less significant compared to the other two categories forming the extremes of the ordinal scale (Under One Year and Over Three Years). Besides, the 'Under One Year' and 'Over Three Years' recorded 12 and 20 participants respectively (i.e., 30% and 50%). Table 9 shows a projection of the mean and standard deviation scores of the ten constructs of mobile devices' input and output features for the ('Under One Year' and 'Over Three Years') categories.

As evident from Table 9, the higher mean and less standard deviation scores of the 'Over Three Years' category asserted that participants who owned a mobile device(s) for over three years reflected a tendency to perceive a higher fit rate between mobile devices and m-commerce tasks across the ten constructs as compared to participants who owned a mobile device(s) for less than

Table 9. Descriptive statistics for duration of mobile device ownership

Dependent Variable		No. of participants	Mean	Std. Deviation	Std. Error
Device Inputs Lack of Confusion	1 Under One Year	12	3.42	1.165	.336
	4 Over Three Years	20	3.55	.826	.185
Device Inputs Level of Detail	1 Under One Year	12	3.00	1.206	.348
	4 Over Three Years	20	3.35	.813	.182
Device Inputs Locatability	1 Under One Year	12	3.50	1.243	.359
	4 Over Three Years	20	3.75	.550	.123
Device Inputs Ease of Use	1 Under One Year	12	4.00	.853	.246
	4 Over Three Years	20	3.90	.788	.176
Device Inputs System Reliability	1 Under One Year	12	2.75	.754	.218
	4 Over Three Years	20	3.40	.883	.197
Device Inputs Compatibility	1 Under One Year	12	3.00	.853	.246
	4 Over Three Years	20	3.60	.883	.197
Device Inputs Presentation	1 Under One Year	12	3.50	.798	.230
	4 Over Three Years	20	3.80	.834	.186
Device Inputs Timeliness	1 Under One Year	12	3.00	1.206	.348
	4 Over Three Years	20	2.90	1.071	.240
Device Inputs Performance	1 Under One Year	12	3.00	1.348	.389
	4 Over Three Years	20	3.50	.889	.199
Device Inputs Assistance	1 Under One Year	12	4.58	.669	.193
	4 Over Three Years	20	4.00	.725	.162
Device Outputs Lack of Confusion	1 Under One Year	12	3.25	1.138	.329
	4 Over Three Years	20	3.80	.894	.200
Device Outputs Level of Detail	1 Under One Year	12	3.00	.953	.275
	4 Over Three Years	20	3.50	1.192	.267
Device Outputs Locatability	1 Under One Year	12	3.33	1.073	.310
	4 Over Three Years	20	3.20	1.005	.225
Device Outputs Ease of Use	1 Under One Year	12	3.58	.793	.229
	4 Over Three Years	20	3.50	1.000	.224
Device Outputs System Reliability	1 Under One Year	12	3.17	.835	.241
	4 Over Three Years	20	2.95	1.099	.246
Device Outputs Compatibility	1 Under One Year	12	3.17	.937	.271
	4 Over Three Years	20	3.25	.910	.204
Device Outputs Presentation	1 Under One Year	12	3.08	.996	.288
	4 Over Three Years	20	3.15	1.226	.274
Device Outputs Timeliness	1 Under One Year	12	2.75	1.288	.372
	4 Over Three Years	20	2.70	1.261	.282
Device Outputs Performance	1 Under One Year	12	3.33	.888	.256
	4 Over Three Years	20	3.15	1.089	.244
Device Outputs Assistance	1 Under One Year	12	4.33	.778	.225
	4 Over Three Years	20	3.80	.894	.200

one year. Similar higher mean and less standard deviations scores were also recorded among the over-three-year mobile device owners than the under-one-year owners as far as mobile tasks are concerned (see Table 10). This means that the perception of m-commerce tasks fit with mobile devices was higher among participants who owned mobile phones for a longer period.

It can therefore be concluded from above that descriptive analysis substantiated the hypothesized impact of users' mobile technology skills on their perception of fit between mobile devices and m-commerce tasks. This is consistent with the moderation effect hypothesis of the research framework. Such a validation will be further ascertained by testing the perception of fit between mobile devices characteristics and m-commerce services against the possible impact of users' computer self-efficacy measures.

Mobile Users' Computer Self-Efficacy

Participants' computer self-efficacy (Compeau & Higgins, 1995) was tested using ten questions that asked participants to hypothetically assume ten different use situations. As the use of mobile device was constant throughout the ten use situations, the correlation values showed strong associations between the ten different use situations (see Table 11). This significance implied the possible impact of users' computer self-efficacy on the actual utilization of m-commerce services.

Factor analysis confirmed such strong associations and two factors were extracted as significant (see Table 12).

As can be seen from Table 12, factor 1 reflected greater significance with 5.666 eigenvalue and a variance explanation capability of 56.659 percent. Factor 2, on the other hand, achieved a marginal significance value of 1.081 on the Eigen Test and a variance percentage of only 10.809 percent. Altogether, the two factors projected a total variance explanation potential of 67.468 per cent among the ten variables.

Moreover, the loading use situations have split evenly between the two factors with use situations 1, 2, 3, 7, and 8 loading significantly to factor 1 and use situations 3, 5, 6, 9, and 10 loading significantly to factor 2 (see Table 13).

While all use situations loading to factor 1 shared the assumption that different mobile device self-help features were available during task performance, use situations loading to factor 2 were all assuming access to assistance from others – whether it be skillful people or customer service departments – to enable the performance of mobile tasks. Therefore, the two extracted factors can be termed 'Mobile Device Self-Help Features' and 'Mobile Device Help-Desk Features' respectively.

Furthermore, though the split was even in use situations, the variance explanation of factor 1 was almost six times stronger. The logic behind this is that participants' responses tended to be positively skewed towards the use situations with self-help features being available, thus reflecting higher confidence levels in their ability to handle mobile devices (factor 1). This also means that responses were negatively skewed towards the advice-based help features (factor 2) reflecting participants' reluctance to request for help in performing m-commerce services (Table 14).

REGRESSION ANALYSIS FOR THE NETWORK FIT AND M-COMMERCE UTILIZATION

In the research framework, the three components of the 'Network Fit,' namely MTTF, mobile operators, and mobile vendors were also hypothesized as having an impact on the utilization of m-commerce. As actual utilization of m-commerce cannot be recreated in experimental settings, perceived utilization circumstances were used to measure such an impact of the 'Network Fit' components. In this way, measured utilization can best resemble real use circumstances. Four

Table 10. Descriptive statistics for duration of mobile device ownership across mobile tasks' two dimensions of simplicity and difficulty

Dependent Variable		No. of participants	Mean	Std. Deviation	Std. Error
Simple Task Lack of Confusion	1 Under One Year	12	3.92	.900	.260
	4 Over Three Years	20	4.10	.788	.176
Simple Task Level of Detail	1 Under One Year	12	3.83	.835	.241
	4 Over Three Years	20	4.05	.945	.211
Simple Task Locatability	1 Under One Year	12	3.58	.900	.260
	4 Over Three Years	20	3.55	.999	.223
Simple Task Ease of Use	1 Under One Year	12	3.75	1.055	.305
	4 Over Three Years	20	3.95	.826	.185
Simple Task System Reliability	1 Under One Year	12	3.67	1.073	.310
	4 Over Three Years	20	3.80	.951	.213
Simple Task Compatibility	1 Under One Year	12	3.58	1.084	.313
	4 Over Three Years	20	4.05	.826	.185
Simple Task Presentation	1 Under One Year	12	3.25	.965	.279
	4 Over Three Years	20	3.85	.933	.209
Simple Task Timeliness	1 Under One Year	12	3.58	1.379	.398
	4 Over Three Years	20	3.60	1.273	.285
Simple Task Performance	1 Under One Year	12	3.67	1.073	.310
	4 Over Three Years	20	3.90	.788	.176
Simple Task Assistance	1 Under One Year	12	4.50	.798	.230
	4 Over Three Years	20	4.15	.875	.196
Difficult Task Lack of Confusion	1 Under One Year	12	2.00	.953	.275
	4 Over Three Years	20	2.35	.933	.209
Difficult Task Level of Detail	1 Under One Year	12	2.33	.888	.256
	4 Over Three Years	20	2.60	1.095	.245
Difficult Task Locatability	1 Under One Year	12	2.50	.905	.261
	4 Over Three Years	20	2.30	.923	.206
Difficult Task Ease of Use	1 Under One Year	12	2.17	1.193	.345
	4 Over Three Years	20	2.20	1.005	.225
Difficult Task System Reliability	1 Under One Year	12	2.08	.996	.288
	4 Over Three Years	20	2.45	1.099	.246
Difficult Task Compatibility	1 Under One Year	12	2.58	1.311	.379
	4 Over Three Years	20	2.45	1.050	.235
Difficult Task Presentation	1 Under One Year	12	2.50	1.087	.314
	4 Over Three Years	20	2.75	1.118	.250
Difficult Task Timeliness	1 Under One Year	12	2.42	.996	.288
	4 Over Three Years	20	2.10	1.021	.228
Difficult Task Performance	1 Under One Year	12	2.75	1.138	.329
	4 Over Three Years	20	2.70	1.129	.252
Difficult Task Assistance	1 Under One Year	12	3.33	1.073	.310
	4 Over Three Years	20	2.85	1.040	.233

Table 11. Pearson's product-moment correlation coefficient for mobile users' computer self-efficacy variables

		User's Computer Self-Efficacy 1	User's Computer Self-Efficacy 2	User's Computer Self-Efficacy 3	User's Computer Self-Efficacy 4	User's Computer Self-Efficacy 5	User's Computer Self-Efficacy 6	User's Computer Self-Efficacy 7	User's Computer Self-Efficacy 8	User's Computer Self-Efficacy 9	User's Computer Self-Efficacy 10
User's Computer Self-Efficacy 1	Pearson Correlation	1	.505(**)	.640(**)	.506(**)	.179	.491(**)	.718(**)	.696(**)	.493(**)	.453(**)
User's Computer Self-Efficacy 2	Pearson Correlation	.505(**)	1	.560(**)	.540(**)	.189	.563(**)	.382(*)	.453(**)	.485(**)	.220
User's Computer Self-Efficacy 3	Pearson Correlation	.640(**)	.560(**)	1	.636(**)	.458(**)	.572(**)	.596(**)	.659(**)	.568(**)	.280
User's Computer Self-Efficacy 4	Pearson Correlation	.506(**)	.540(**)	.636(**)	1	.473(**)	.680(**)	.604(**)	.473(**)	.737(**)	.409(**)
User's Computer Self-Efficacy 5	Pearson Correlation	.179	.189	.458(**)	.473(**)	1	.479(**)	.360(*)	.246	.414(**)	.257
User's Computer Self-Efficacy 6	Pearson Correlation	.491(**)	.563(**)	.572(**)	.680(**)	.479(**)	1	.629(**)	.469(**)	.837(**)	.583(**)
User's Computer Self-Efficacy 7	Pearson Correlation	.718(**)	.382(*)	.596(**)	.604(**)	.360(*)	.629(**)	1	.702(**)	.702(**)	.564(**)
User's Computer Self-Efficacy 8	Pearson Correlation	.696(**)	.453(**)	.659(**)	.473(**)	.246	.469(**)	.702(**)	1	.454(**)	.377(*)
User's Computer Self-Efficacy 9	Pearson Correlation	.493(**)	.485(**)	.568(**)	.737(**)	.414(**)	.837(**)	.702(**)	.454(**)	1	.507(**)
User's Computer Self-Efficacy 10	Pearson Correlation	.453(**)	.220	.280	.409(**)	.257	.583(**)	.564(**)	.377(*)	.507(**)	1

** Correlation is significant at the 0.01 level (2-tailed).

* Correlation is significant at the 0.05 level (2-tailed).

Source: This research

Table 12. Factor analysis for mobile users' skills measures

Component	Initial Eigenvalues			Extraction Sums of Squared Loadings			Rotation Sums of Squared Loadings(a)
	Total	% of Variance	Cumulative %	Total	% of Variance	Cumulative %	Total
1	5.666	56.659	56.659	5.666	56.659	56.659	4.833
2	1.081	10.809	67.468	1.081	10.809	67.468	4.182
3	.917	9.167	76.634				
4	.740	7.399	84.033				
5	.443	4.428	88.462				
6	.322	3.216	91.678				
7	.278	2.778	94.455				
8	.266	2.663	97.118				
9	.176	1.757	98.876				
10	.112	1.124	100.000				

Table 13. Pattern Matrix for mobile users' skills measures

	Component	
	1	2
User's Computer Self-Efficacy 1	.953	-.114
User's Computer Self-Efficacy 2	.606	.129
User's Computer Self-Efficacy 3	.661	.248
User's Computer Self-Efficacy 4	.333	.626
User's Computer Self-Efficacy 5	-.226	.877
User's Computer Self-Efficacy 6	.273	.730
User's Computer Self-Efficacy 7	.686	.275
User's Computer Self-Efficacy 8	.920	-.106
User's Computer Self-Efficacy 9	.295	.697
User's Computer Self-Efficacy 10	.271	.448

constructs were used during the data collection process to test for the perceived utilization of m-commerce among participants. These constructs were the frequency of simple m-commerce services use over mobile devices, the frequency of complex m-commerce services use over mobile devices, the impact of mobile operators' quality of services on m-commerce utilization, as well as the impact of mobile vendors' quality of services on m-commerce utilization. The first two constructs were both designed to test for the MTTF impact on m-commerce use, while the third and fourth constructs aimed at measuring the effect of mobile operators and mobile vendors on the utilization of mobile services among participants respectively.

MTTF Impact on M-Commerce Utilization

The impact of MTTF on the use of m-commerce services was measured against two perceived utilization constructs, namely the frequency of usage of simple m-commerce services and the frequency of usage of complex m-commerce services over mobile devices. To test for such an impact, multiple regression and analysis of variance (ANOVA) were performed for each construct.

Evident from Table 15, there were strong positive relationships (R, 0.617) between simple m-commerce services utilization (the dependent variable) and the extracted factors of MTTF (the independent variables). In addition, the coefficient of determination (R^2, 0.380) implied that 38 percent of the variance in simple m-commerce services utilization was explained by the perception of fit

Table 14. Factor analysis for Mobile Users' Computer Self-Efficacy

Original Variables	Mobile Users' Computer Self-Efficacy					
	Extracted Factors			Eigenvalue	% of Variance	Cumulative %
	F1- Mobile Device Self-Help Features			5.666	56.659	56.659
		F2- Mobile Device Help-Desk Features		1.081	10.809	67.468
	Variables' Loadings on Extracted Factors					
User's Computer Self-Efficacy 1	.953	-.114				
User's Computer Self-Efficacy 2	.606	.129				
User's Computer Self-Efficacy 3	.661	.248				
User's Computer Self-Efficacy 4	.333	.626				
User's Computer Self-Efficacy 5	-.226	.877				
User's Computer Self-Efficacy 6	.273	.730				
User's Computer Self-Efficacy 7	.686	.275				
User's Computer Self-Efficacy 8	.920	-.106				
User's Computer Self-Efficacy 9	.295	.697				
User's Computer Self-Efficacy 10	.271	.448				

* Significant loading value over 0.44

between m-commerce tasks and mobile devices. Moreover, the ANOVA reported an F-value of 2.379 at a significant level of p<0.05 purporting that there is less than five in a hundred chances that the significant difference between m-commerce utilization and mobile users' perception of MTTF occurred by chance.

As several extracted factors of MTTF were used, it is possible that not all of these factors contributed to the prediction of m-commerce services utilization. To test for this, the beta values of the standardized coefficients (see Table 16) were referred to as they usually state the contributions of independent variables in the explanation of variance in the dependent variable. Tradition-

ally, it is agreed that Beta values at a significant level less than P<0.05 report unique contributions of independent variables while Beta values with significance levels over P>0.05 do not make unique predictions of the dependent variable. Rather, they suggest overlapping with other independent variables (Miller, 2002).

In this context, only two MTTF extracted factors, namely Usability of Mobile Device Input Features and Mobile Tasks Complexity reported Beta values of 0.441 and 1.157 at significance levels of p<0.05 and p<0.001 respectively. The other independent variables greatly overlapped in their prediction of m-commerce utilization.

Table 15. Regression and ANOVA results of MTTF impact on m-commerce utilization (simple m-commerce services)

	R	R²	F	Sig.
Regression	.617(a)	.380	2.379	.040(a)

Source: This research

Similarly, a regression analysis and ANOVA of the effect of MTTF extracted factors on the utilization of 'complex m-commerce services' were also conducted to test for the assumed relationship (see Table 17). As manifested in the following table, a coefficient R of 0.628 suggested a strong association between mobile users' perception of MTTF and the utilization of complex m-commerce services. In addition, almost 40 percent of the variation in the utilization of complex m-commerce tasks was explained by mobile users' perception of fit between mobile devices and m-commerce tasks. Moreover, a significant F-Value of 2.521 at a significant level of $p<0.05$ was also evident in the ANOVA analysis.

This also confirms that there are less than five in a hundred chances that the significant difference between mobile users' utilization of complex m-commerce services and their perception of fit between mobile tasks and mobile devices was due to chance. However, as it was the case with simple m-commerce utilization, it is possible that the several independent variables might not all be responsible for the unique difference. An investigation of the standardized Beta values in the Coefficients table (see Table 18) revealed that only the independent variable of 'Device Input Features' Performance' was responsible for the significant difference (B 2.048, $p<0.05$). The Beta values of the majority of independent variables,

Table 16. Coefficients of MTTF impact on m-commerce utilization (simple m-commerce services)

	Unstandardized Coefficients		Standardized Coefficients	t	Sig.
	B	Std. Error	Beta	B	Std. Error
Device Input Features Usability	.221	.099	.441	2.233	.033
Device Input Features Efficiency	.160	.114	.319	1.396	.173
Device Input Features Performance	-.145	.082	-.289	-1.770	.087
Device Output System Usability	-.322	.174	-.643	-1.851	.074
Device Output Features Straightforwardness	.066	.105	.132	.627	.535
Mobile Tasks Straightforwardness	-.085	.098	-.171	-.868	.392
Mobile Tasks Complexity	.579	.162	1.157	3.574	.001
Mobile Tasks Assistance Level	-.124	.098	-.247	-1.266	.215

Table 17. Regression and ANOVA results of MTTF impact on m-commerce utilization (complex m-commerce tasks)

	R	R²	F	Sig.
Regression	.628(a)	.394	2.521	.031(a)

on the other hand, suggested significant overlapping in their impact on the utilization of complex m-commerce services.

It is, therefore, clear from above that the perception of fit between mobile tasks and mobile devices has an impact on mobile users' utilization of m-commerce services which is also consistent with the research framework hypotheses.

MOBILE OPERATORS' IMPACT ON M-COMMERCE UTILIZATION

The research framework also hypothesized the impact of mobile operators as part of the 'Network Fit' on the actual use of m-commerce services. The two extracted factors (Mobile Operators' Quality of Services and Mobile Operators' Network Efficiency) out of the original six constructs were used as independent variables in the test for the assumed effect on the use of m-commerce services (the dependent variable).

As it is noticeable from Table 19, the coefficient (R, 0.422) revealed a tendency of a strong positive relationship between m-commerce utilization and participants' perception of mobile operators. The coefficient of determination R^2 also reported that participants' perception of mobile operators explained almost 18 percent of the variance in m-commerce services use. Furthermore, the F-value of 4.014 at the acceptable significance level of $p<0.05$ also asserted the existence of such an association well beyond the possibility of attributing it to mere chance.

To test for the source of the unique significance, however, the standardized Beta values for the two independent variables of mobile operators were computed (see Table 20). Mobile Operators' Network Efficiency (network coverage and connection speed) provided a larger positive Beta value of 0.409 at a significant level of $p<0.05$ thus implying stronger unique contribution to the explanation of the variance in m-commerce utilization than that of Mobile Operators' Quality of

Table 18. Coefficients of MTTF impact on m-commerce utilization (complex m-commerce services)

	Unstandardized Coefficients		Standardized Coefficients	t	Sig.
	B	Std. Error	Beta	B	Std. Error
Device Input Features Usability	.060	.139	.084	.431	.669
Device Input Features Efficiency	-.065	.161	-.091	-.403	.690
Device Input Features Performance	.235	.115	.331	2.048	.049
Device Output System Usability	-.365	.244	-.513	-1.494	.145
Device Output Features Straightforwardness	-.029	.148	-.041	-.196	.846
Mobile Tasks Straightforwardness	.013	.138	.018	.092	.927
Mobile Tasks Complexity	-.116	.228	-.162	-.508	.615
Difficult Mobile Tasks Assistance Level	.191	.138	.269	1.391	.174

Table 19. Regression and ANOVA results of mobile operators' impact on m-commerce utilization

	R	R^2	F	Sig.
Regression	.422(a)	.178	4.014	.026(a)

Source: This research

Services variable. Therefore, it can be concluded that there existed a considerable positive impact of mobile users' perception of mobile operators (particularly in terms of network efficiency and connection speed) on the actual use of m-commerce services.

MOBILE VENDORS' IMPACT ON M-COMMERCE UTILIZATION

The research framework also hypothesized an impact of mobile vendors on the actual utilization of m-commerce services among mobile users. Out of the original five mobile vendors' constructs used to test for the impact on MTTF, only one factor (Functionality of Mobile Vendors' User Interfaces) was extracted using factor analysis. This variable was used as the independent variable in the regression analysis computed to measure

the impact of mobile vendors on the utilization of m-commerce services (the dependent variable).

The coefficient R of 0.438 revealed a rather strong positive relationship between m-commerce utilization and participants' perception of mobile vendors. As also can be noticed from the coefficient of determination (R^2, 0.192), almost 20 percent of the variance in m-commerce utilization can entirely be explained by the functionality of user interfaces of mobile vendors. Moreover, the F-value of (9.044, $p < 0.005$) in Table 21 confirmed such a unique significance.

The results from the table above assert that there are less than five in a thousand chances that the significant relationship between mobile users' perception of mobile vendors and the utilization of m-commerce can be attributed to chance. As also can be noticed from the Beta value (0.438) in Table 22, the functionality of mobile vendors' user interfaces reflected a strong contribution to

Table 20. Coefficients of mobile operators' impact on m-commerce utilization

	Unstandardized Coefficients		Standardized Coefficients	t	Sig.
	B	Std. Error	Beta	B	Std. Error
Mobile Operators' Quality Of Service	.036	.104	.052	.343	.734
Mobile Operators Network Efficiency	.281	.104	.409	2.689	.011

Source: This research

Table 21. Regression and ANOVA results of mobile vendors' impact on m-commerce utilization

	R	R²	F	Sig.
Regression	.438(a)	.192	9.044	.005(a)

Source: This research

Table 22. Coefficients of mobile vendors' impact on m-commerce utilization

	Unstandardized Coefficients		Standardized Coefficients	t	Sig.
	B	Std. Error	Beta	B	Std. Error
Mobile Vendors' Interface Functionality	.281	.093	.438	3.007	.005

the prediction of m-commerce utilization among participants:

It can also be concluded that the functionality of mobile vendors' user interfaces has a positive impact on the utilization of m-commerce services among mobile users which is also consistent with the research hypothesis.

CONCLUSION AND RECOMMENDATIONS

In general, the research proposed and empirically validated a Mobile Network Utilization Framework. More specifically, the research found that mobile users' utilization of m-commerce services and applications is relative to their perceptions of the concept of fit between mobile devices, mobile services, mobile operators, as well as mobile vendors. It also found through empirical evidence that both the 'Technical Fit' and 'Network Fit' of the Mobile Network Utilization Framework are crucial elements of the mobile use context.

'Technical Fit' Findings

The research found supporting evidence for the interaction effect of the three main components of the 'Technical Fit' of the research framework, namely mobile users, mobile devices, and mobile tasks.

Mobile Users

The research revealed that mobile users' perceptions of the concept of MTTF varied across the dimensions of users' exposure to mobile technology and their computer self-efficacy. As hypothesized, users' different skills and abilities have a moderation effect on their perceptions of fit between mobile devices and mobile services. It became clear from the analysis that mobile users with longer periods of exposure to mobile technology tended to perceive higher rates of

fit between mobile devices and m-commerce services. Moreover, people with high computer self-efficacy showed tendency to adopt complex m-commerce tasks more than people with low computer self-efficacy.

In addition, the research disclosed two factors of mobile users' computer self-efficacy that are crucial to the concept of MTTF and the utilization of m-commerce services. These factors were 'Mobile Device Self-help Features' and 'Mobile Device Help-Desk Features.' The majority of participants in the experiment revealed a higher tendency of adopting m-commerce services provided various self-help features such as built-in help features and mobile device manuals are available. Moreover, participants reflected more confidence in using mobile devices with the least amount of help from customer service departments or experienced users in the field. This is in line with the hypothesized positive impact of mobile users' exposure to mobile technology on MTTF. The perception of fit between mobile devices and m-commerce tasks tended to be higher among participants who recorded an ownership of a mobile device(s) for longer time periods.

Mobile Devices

The research found empirical evidence of the importance of the dichotomous classification of mobile devices characteristics into 'Input' and 'Output' Features. For the former, the study identified three important factors that are vital to measuring the impact of mobile devices' input features on the perception of fit with mobile tasks and ultimately m-commerce utilization. These factors were 'Usability of Mobile Device Input Features,' 'Efficiency of Mobile Device Input Features,' and 'Performance of Mobile Device Input Features.' This means that the importance of mobile devices' input features to the utilization of m-commerce services lay in their usability to mobile users; efficiency in accomplishing mobile services under different use circumstances; as well as capability of processing mobile tasks and services. Similarly, the research also identified two factors spanning the criticality of mobile devices' output features to mobile users' perceptions of MTTF as well as the use of m-commerce services. These two factors were 'Usability of Mobile Device Output System' and 'Straightforwardness of Mobile Device Output Features.' According to the empirical findings, these two factors were essential to the presentation and ultimately performance of m-commerce services on the mobile device output mechanisms.

Mobile Tasks

The empirical research asserted the suitability of classifying mobile services according to their level of simplicity and complexity. It also found that the level of simplicity or complexity of mobile services is vital to mobile users' perception of fit between mobile technology and mobile tasks. It showed that the more complex the mobile service, the lower the fit rate between mobile devices and mobile services and vice versa. On these bases, the empirical test disclosed the factor of 'Mobile tasks Straightforwardness' as very essential to perceiving higher fit rate between mobile devices and mobile services. This also held true for m-commerce services utilization. On the other hand, the perception of MTTF was seen to be lower among complex mobile services. Both the perception of fit between mobile devices and mobile tasks as well as the utilization of m-commerce services were found to be relative to two crucial factors that the research identified. These factors were 'Mobile Tasks Complexity' and 'Assistance level for Complex Mobile Tasks'

In general, mobile users reflected higher level of confidence in performing simple mobile services without the need for technical assistance. The findings also showed that mobile users exhibited reluctance to ask for help from others when performing mobile services particularly with the ones that were perceived as complex.

'NETWORK FIT' FINDINGS

The research experiment showed empirical evidence of the impact of the three components of the 'Network Fit,' namely, mobile operators, mobile vendors, and MTTF on the utilization of m-commerce services.

Mobile Operators

Data analysis reflected strong support for the impact of mobile operators on both mobile users' perception of MTTF and the utilization of m-commerce services. More specifically, the impact was evident in two major areas, that is, Mobile Network Efficiency and Mobile Operators' Quality of Services. Mobile users showed greater association between m-commerce utilization and mobile operators' network efficiency particularly their network coverage and connection speed. The quality of services such as the range of services and pricing were also seen as major elements in the actual performance of mobile services.

Mobile Vendors

Mobile vendors were also perceived as significant in the fit between mobile devices and mobile services as well as in the utilization of m-commerce services. Such a perceived influence was greatly present in mobile users' perception of mobile data presentation on mobile devices. The empirical test found that 'User Interfaces Functionality' was the most significant element of mobile vendors' impact on mobile users' utilization of m-commerce services. Moderate support was also found for the range of services and pricing.

Mobile Task-Technology Fit (MTTF)

The research empirical approach also revealed direct impact of mobile users' perception of MTTF on the actual utilization of m-commerce services. In addition, strong empirical evidence of the overall effect of mobile users, mobile devices, mobile tasks, mobile operators, and mobile vendors on the formation of users' perception of MTTF was also witnessed. The empirical test further revealed that the concept of MTTF is dependent on the interaction between the key components of a wider mobile network, namely mobile users, mobile devices, mobile tasks, mobile operators, as well as mobile vendors (Table 23).

Academic Contributions

This research has proposed and empirically validated a Mobile Network Utilization Model for measuring the actual utilization of m-commerce services among UK mobile end users. Unlike previous studies of mobile technologies adoption, the current study has emphasized through empirical evidence the importance of 'Network Fit' in explaining m-commerce utilization and its criticality to the overall mobile use context. Moreover, the study has identified fifteen factors that are vital elements of the Mobile Network Utilization Model. These factors are as follows:

1. Usability of Mobile Device Input Features
2. Efficiency of Mobile Device Input Features
3. Performance of Mobile Device Input Features
4. Usability of Mobile Device Output Features
5. Straightforwardness of Mobile Device Output Features
6. Straightforwardness of Mobile Tasks
7. Complexity of Mobile Tasks
8. Assistance level for Complex Mobile Tasks
9. Mobile Device Self-help Features
10. Mobile Device Help-Desk Features
11. Mobile Operators' Network Efficiency
12. Mobile Operators' Quality of Services
13. Functionality of Mobile Vendors' User Interfaces
14. Mobile Vendors' Quality of Services
15. Mobile Users' Duration of Exposure to Mobile Technologies.

Empirically speaking, the above factors reflected validated significance in explaining the utilization of m-commerce services. In fact, these factors defined the interaction process between the key players of the mobile network, namely mobile users, mobile devices, mobile tasks, mobile operators, as well as mobile vendors.

Managerial Implications

The study has validated a practical utilization model that can assist mobile key players in understanding mobile end users' perceptions of mobile devices and m-commerce services. The model can therefore be used to inform the development of mobile devices; the design of mobile applications; as well as the improvement of mobile services. It also provided insight into the crucial role of integration between key players in the mobile use context, namely mobile users through exposure to mobile technology; mobile manufactures through mobile devices' input and output features capabilities; mobile providers through network efficiency and quality of services; as well as mobile vendors through the functionality and quality of user interfaces. The study has also identified fifteen crucial factors (see previous section) that can better aid mobile marketers in understanding both mobile services adopters and potential users. They can also be utilized in the design of m-commerce services and applications to better suit mobile end users.

Research Limitations

The tradeoff between internal and external validity is always present in experimental research (Zikmund, 2000). While this study recognized the importance of generalizable results, the internal validity was very essential to accurately measure m-commerce utilization. Moreover, the use of students as experimental subjects has often been criticized of being less representative of the general public. Yet, students were sampled

Table 23. Components and extracted factors of the mobile network utilization framework

Framework Components	Main Component	Sub Components	Extracted Factors
Technical Fit	**Mobile Devices**	**Mobile Device Input Features**	Usability of Mobile Device Input Features
			Efficiency of Mobile Device Input Features
			Performance of Mobile Device Input Features
		Mobile Device Output Features	Usability of Mobile Device Output Features
			straightforwardness of Device Output Features
	Mobile Tasks	**Simple Mobile Tasks**	Straightforwardness of Simple Mobile Tasks
		Complex Mobile Tasks	Complexity of Mobile Tasks
			Assistance Level for Complex Mobile Tasks
	Mobile Users' Skills	**Mobile Users' Computer Self-Efficacy**	Mobile Device Self-help Features
			Mobile Device Help-desk Features
Network Fit	**Mobile Operators**	**Network Efficiency**	Mobile Operators' Network Efficiency
		Services	Mobile Operators' Quality of Services
	Mobile Vendors	**User Interfaces**	Functionality of Mobile User Interfaces
		Services	Mobile Vendors' Quality of Services
	Mobile TTF	**Mobile Devices**	5 factors (3 Input Features factors + 2 Output Features factors)
		Mobile Tasks	3 factors (1 Simple Mobile Tasks factor + 2 Complex Mobile Tasks factors)
		Mobile Users' Skills	3 factors (2 Mobile Users' Computer Self-Efficacy factors + 1 Duration of Exposure to Mobile Technology factor)
Utilization	**Technical Fit**	Mobile Devices	5 factors (3 Input Features factors + 2 Output Features factors)
		Mobile Tasks	3 factors (1 Simple Mobile Tasks factor + 2 Complex Mobile Tasks factors)
		Mobile Users	3 factors (2 Mobile Users' Computer Self-Efficacy factors + 1 Duration of Exposure to Mobile Technology factor)
	Network Fit	Mobile Operators	2 factors (1 Mobile Network Efficiency + 1 Mobile Operators Quality of Services)
		Mobile Vendors	2 factors (1 Mobile User Interfaces' Functionality + 1 Mobile Vendors Quality of Services)
		Mobile TTF	11 factors (5 Mobile Devices factors: 3 are Input Features factors + 2 Output Features factors) + (3 Mobile Tasks factors: 1 Simple Mobile Tasks factor + 2 Complex Mobile Tasks factors) + (3 Mobile Users' factors: 2 Mobile Users' Computer Self-Efficacy factors + 1 Duration of Exposure to Mobile Technology factor)

randomly from across the university rather than a single class or department. Besides, participants were paid an agreed sum for their participation and use of own mobile devices. Unlike organizational settings where the use of information systems can be part of the actual job, choosing students as the subjects of the experiment ensured a voluntary atmosphere of participation. Overall, using students as experimental subjects was also helpful to ensure proper experimental settings to control for extraneous influences.

Directions for Future Research

The empirically tested Mobile Utilization Network Model provides opportunities for measuring the utilization of m-commerce services in different use contexts across different geographical, cultural, and socio-technical settings. It also provides scope for testing the impact of the model on mobile users' preferences of specific mobile devices and services. Moreover, the cultural aspect of mobile use can be explored as part of the socio-technical continuum.

The research has also identified a set of factors that are essential to the actual utilization of m-commerce services. Both the individual and collective impact of these factors can be investigated in areas such as the design of mobile user interfaces, the development of mobile applications, as well as improvements to mobile devices' current limitations. Further research can also be done on the 'Network Fit' where the impact of mobile operators and mobile vendors can be further studied. Since this study explored the actual utilization, the model can also be used to survey behavioral intentions of m-commerce adoption among potential mobile users.

REFERENCES

Ajzen, I. (1985). From intentions to actions: a theory of planned behavior. In Kuhi, J., & Beckmann, J. (Eds.), *Action-control: from cognition to behavior* (pp. 11–39). Heidelberg, Germany: Springer.

Ajzen, I. (1991). The theory of planned behavior. *Organizational Behavior and Human Decision Processes*, *50*(2), 179–211. doi:10.1016/0749-5978(91)90020-T

Ajzen, I., & Fishbein, M. (1973). Attitudinal and normative variables as predictors of specific behavior. *Journal of Personality and Social Psychology*, *27*, 41–57. doi:10.1037/h0034440

Anckar, B., & D'Incau, D. (2002). Value creation in mobile commerce: Findings from a consumer survey. *Journal of Information Technology Theory and Application*, *4*(1), 43–64.

Anwar, S. T. (2002). DoCoMo and m-commerce: a case study in market expansion and global strategy. *Thunderbird International Business Review*, *44*(1), 139–164. doi:10.1002/tie.1043

Bailey, J. E., & Pearson, S. W. (1983). Development of a tool for measuring and analyzing computer user satisfaction. *Management Science*, *29*(5), 530–545. doi:10.1287/mnsc.29.5.530

Barnes, S. J. (2002). The mobile commerce value chain: analysis and future developments. *International Journal of Information Management*, *22*, 91–108. doi:10.1016/S0268-4012(01)00047-0

Bertrand, V., Caplan, A., Fernandez-Moran, E., & Letelier, C. (2001). M-commerce: who will reap the profits? *Kellogg Tech Venture 2001 Anthology*.

Bhasin, M. L. (2005). E-Commerce and M-Commerce Revolution: Perspectives, Problems and Prospects. *The Chartered Accountant*, 824-840.

Compeau, D. R., & Higgins, C. A. (1995). Computer self-efficacy: development of a measure and initial test. *Management Information Systems Quarterly*, *19*(2), 189–211. doi:10.2307/249688

Coursaris, C., Hassanein, K., & Head, M. (2003). M-commerce in Canada: an interaction framework for wireless privacy. *Canadian Journal of Administrative Sciences*, *20*(1), 54–73.

Davis, F. (1986). *A technology acceptance model for empirically testing new end-user information systems: theory and results*. Unpublished doctoral dissertation, Sloan School of Management, Massachusetts Institute of Technology.

Davis, F. (1989). Perceived usefulness, perceived ease of use, and end user acceptance of information technology. *Management Information Systems Quarterly, 13*(3), 318–339. doi:10.2307/249008

Dholakia, R. R., & Dholakia, N. (2004). Mobility and markets: emerging outlines of m-commerce. *Journal of Business Research, 57,* 1391–1396. doi:10.1016/S0148-2963(02)00427-7

Dishaw, M. T., & Strong, D. M. (1999). Extending the technology acceptance model with task–technology fit constructs. *Information & Management, 36*(1), 9–21. doi:10.1016/S0378-7206(98)00101-3

Fishbein, M., & Azjen, I. (1975). *Belief, attitude, intention, and behavior.* Reading, MA: Addison-Wesley.

Funk, J. L. (2006). The future of mobile phone-based Intranet applications: a view from Japan. *Technovation, 26,* 1337–1346. doi:10.1016/j.technovation.2005.08.009

Garson, D. (2008). *Scales and standard measures.* Retrieved July 18, 2008, from http://www2.chass.ncsu.edu/garson/pa765/standard.htm

Gebauer, J., & Shaw, M. J. (2004). Success factors and impacts of mobile business applications: results from a mobile e-procurement study. *International Journal of Electronic Commerce, 8*(3), 19–41.

Gebauer, J., Shaw, M. J., & Gribbins, M. L. (2006). *Task-Technology Fit for mobile information systems.* Retrieved July 15, 2008, from http://www.business.uiuc.edu/ Working_Papers/papers/06-0107.pdf

Goodhue, D. L., & Thompson, R. L. (1995). Task-Technology Fit and individual performance. *Management Information Systems Quarterly, 19*(2), 213–236. doi:10.2307/249689

Junglas, I., Abraham, C., & Watson, R. T. (2008). Task-technology fit for mobile locatable information systems. *Decision Support Systems.* doi:10.1016/j.dss.2008.02.007

Kristoffersen, S., & Ljungberg, F. (1999). "Making place" to make IT work: empirical explorations of HCI for mobile CSCW. In *Proceedings of the International ACM SIGGROUP Conference on Supporting Group Work,* Phoenix, AZ (pp. 276-285).

Lee, C. C., Cheng, H. K., & Cheng, H. H. (2007). An empirical study of mobile commerce in insurance industry: task–technology fit and individual differences. *Decision Support Systems, 43,* 95–110. doi:10.1016/j.dss.2005.05.008

Lee, Y. E., & Benbasat, I. (2004). A framework for the study of customer interface design for mobile commerce. *International Journal of Electronic Commerce, 8*(3), 79–102.

Lu, J., Yao, J. E., & Yu, C. S. (2005). Personal innovativeness, social influences and adoption of wireless Internet services via mobile technology. *The Journal of Strategic Information Systems, 14*(3), 245–268. doi:10.1016/j.jsis.2005.07.003

Makki, S. A. M., Pissinou, N., & Daroux, P. (2002). Mobile and wireless Internet access. *Computer Communications, 26,* 734–746. doi:10.1016/S0140-3664(02)00208-6

Miller, R. L., Acton, C., Fullerton, D. A., & Maltby, J. (2002). *SPSS for social scientists.* Hampshire, UK: Palgrave Macmillan.

Ngai, E. W. T., & Gunasekaran, A. (2007). A review for mobile commerce research and applications. *Decision Support Systems, 43,* 3–15. doi:10.1016/j.dss.2005.05.003

Sadeh, N. (2002). *M-Commerce: technologies, services, and business models.* New York: John Wiley & Sons.

Saunders, M., Lewis, P., & Thornhill, A. (2007). *Research methods for business students* (4th ed.). London: Prentice Hall.

Seager, A. (2003). M-commerce: an integrated approach. *Telecommunications International*, 36-38.

Shin, Y., Jeon, H., & Choi, M. (2006). Analysis of the consumer preferences toward m-commerce applications based on an empirical study. IEEE Computer Society. *International Journal on Hybrid Information Technology*, *1*, 654–659.

Siau, K., & Shen, Z. (2003). Building customer trust in mobile commerce. *Communications of the ACM*, *46*(4), 91–94. doi:10.1145/641205.641211

Urbaczewski, A., Wells, J., Sarker, S., & Koivisto, M. (2002). Exploring cultural differences as a means for understanding the global mobile Internet: a theoretical basis and program of research. In *Proceedings of the 35th Annual Hawaii International Conference on System Sciences (HICSS-35.02)*. Washington, DC: IEEE Computer Society.

Venkatesh, V., & Davis, F. R. (2000). A theoretical extension of the technology acceptance model: four longitudinal field studies. *Management Science*, *46*(2), 188–204. doi:10.1287/mnsc.46.2.186.11926

Wu, J.-H., & Hisa, T. (2004). Analysis of e-commerce innovation and impact: a hypercube model. *Electronic Commerce Research and Applications*, *3*, 389–404. doi:10.1016/j.elerap.2004.05.002

Zikmund, W. G. (2000). *Business research methods*. Fort Worth, TX: Dryden Press.

APPENDIX 1

Pearson's Product-Moment Correlation Coefficient for simple mobile tasks variables

		Simple Task Lack of Confusion	Simple Task Level of Detail	Simple Task Locatability	Simple Task Ease of Use	Simple Task System Reliability	Simple Task Compatibility	Simple Task Presentation	Simple Task Timeliness	Simple Task Perf/ Intrst/ Dedicat	Simple Task Assistance
Simple Task Lack of Confusion	Pearson Correlation	1	.771(**)	.574(**)	.625(**)	.650(**)	.623(**)	.579(**)	.550(**)	.583(**)	.503(**)
	Sig. (2-tailed)		.000	.000	.000	.000	.000	.000	.000	.000	.001
	N	40	40	40	40	40	40	40	40	40	40
Simple Task Level of Detail	Pearson Correlation	.771(**)	1	.543(**)	.643(**)	.664(**)	.646(**)	.641(**)	.506(**)	.714(**)	.481(**)
	Sig. (2-tailed)	.000		.000	.000	.000	.000	.000	.001	.000	.002
	N	40	40	40	40	40	40	40	40	40	40
Simple Task Locatability	Pearson Correlation	.574(**)	.543(**)	1	.721(**)	.685(**)	.729(**)	.591(**)	.601(**)	.338(*)	.508(**)
	Sig. (2-tailed)	.000	.000		.000	.000	.000	.000	.000	.033	.001
	N	40	40	40	40	40	40	40	40	40	40
Simple Task Ease of Use	Pearson Correlation	.625(**)	.643(**)	.721(**)	1	.723(**)	.849(**)	.830(**)	.706(**)	.647(**)	.546(**)
	Sig. (2-tailed)	.000	.000	.000		.000	.000	.000	.000	.000	.000
	N	40	40	40	40	40	40	40	40	40	40
Simple Task System Reliability	Pearson Correlation	.650(**)	.664(**)	.685(**)	.723(**)	1	.801(**)	.700(**)	.701(**)	.717(**)	.702(**)
	Sig. (2-tailed)	.000	.000	.000	.000		.000	.000	.000	.000	.000
	N	40	40	40	40	40	40	40	40	40	40

continued on following page

		Simple Task Lack of Confusion	Simple Task Level of Detail	Simple Task Locatability	Simple Task Ease of Use	Simple Task System Reliability	Simple Task Compatibility	Simple Task Presentation	Simple Task Timeliness	Simple Task Perf/ Intrst/ Dedicat	Simple Task Assistance
Simple Task Compatibility	Pearson Correlation	.623(**)	.646(**)	.729(**)	.849(**)	.801(**)	1	.737(**)	.643(**)	.634(**)	.589(**)
	Sig. (2-tailed)	.000	.000	.000	.000	.000		.000	.000	.000	.000
	N	40	40	40	40	40	40	40	40	40	40
Simple Task Presentation	Pearson Correlation	.579(**)	.641(**)	.591(**)	.830(**)	.700(**)	.737(**)	1	.711(**)	.684(**)	.491(**)
	Sig. (2-tailed)	.000	.000	.000	.000	.000	.000		.000	.000	.001
	N	40	40	40	40	40	40	40	40	40	40
Simple Task Time-liness	Pearson Correlation	.550(**)	.506(**)	.601(**)	.706(**)	.701(**)	.643(**)	.711(**)	1	.625(**)	.439(**)
	Sig. (2-tailed)	.000	.001	.000	.000	.000	.000	.000		.000	.005
	N	40	40	40	40	40	40	40	40	40	40
Simple Task Perf/Intrst/Dedi-cat	Pearson Correlation	.583(**)	.714(**)	.338(*)	.647(**)	.717(**)	.634(**)	.684(**)	.625(**)	1	.428(**)
	Sig. (2-tailed)	.000	.000	.033	.000	.000	.000	.000	.000		.006
	N	40	40	40	40	40	40	40	40	40	40
Simple Task As-sistance	Pearson Correlation	.503(**)	.481(**)	.508(**)	.546(**)	.702(**)	.589(**)	.491(**)	.439(**)	.428(**)	1
	Sig. (2-tailed)	.001	.002	.001	.000	.000	.000	.001	.005	.006	
	N	40	40	40	40	40	40	40	40	40	40

** Correlation is significant at the 0.01 level (2-tailed).
* Correlation is significant at the 0.05 level (2-tailed).

APPENDIX 2

Pearson's Product-Moment Correlation Coefficient for difficult mobile tasks variables

		Difficult Task Lack of Confusion	Difficult Task Level of Detail	Difficult Task Locatability	Difficult Task Ease of Use	Difficult Task System Reliability	Difficult Task Compatibility	Difficult Task Presentation	Difficult Task Timeliness	Difficult Task Performance/ Interest/ Dedication	Difficult Task Assistance
Difficult Task Lack of Confusion	Pearson Correlation	1	.829(**)	.574(**)	.832(**)	.764(**)	.750(**)	.673(**)	.548(**)	.752(**)	.093
	Sig. (2-tailed)		.000	.000	.000	.000	.000	.000	.000	.000	.569
	N	40	40	40	40	40	40	40	40	40	40
Difficult Task Level of Detail	Pearson Correlation	.829(**)	1	.647(**)	.696(**)	.675(**)	.702(**)	.653(**)	.481(**)	.652(**)	.200
	Sig. (2-tailed)	.000		.000	.000	.000	.000	.000	.002	.000	.217
	N	40	40	40	40	40	40	40	40	40	40
Difficult Task Locatability	Pearson Correlation	.574(**)	.647(**)	1	.553(**)	.585(**)	.796(**)	.639(**)	.535(**)	.667(**)	.421(**)
	Sig. (2-tailed)	.000	.000		.000	.000	.000	.000	.000	.000	.007
	N	40	40	40	40	40	40	40	40	40	40
Difficult Task Ease of Use	Pearson Correlation	.832(**)	.696(**)	.553(**)	1	.797(**)	.734(**)	.483(**)	.671(**)	.620(**)	.078
	Sig. (2-tailed)	.000	.000	.000		.000	.000	.002	.000	.000	.632
	N	40	40	40	40	40	40	40	40	40	40
Difficult Task System Reliability	Pearson Correlation	.764(**)	.675(**)	.585(**)	.797(**)	1	.697(**)	.595(**)	.644(**)	.635(**)	.243
	Sig. (2-tailed)	.000	.000	.000	.000		.000	.000	.000	.000	.130
	N	40	40	40	40	40	40	40	40	40	40

continued on following page

		Difficult Task Lack of Confusion	Difficult Task Level of Detail	Difficult Task Locatability	Difficult Task Ease of Use	Difficult Task System Reliability	Difficult Task Compatibility	Difficult Task Presentation	Difficult Task Timeliness	Difficult Task Performance/ Interest/ Dedication	Difficult Task Assistance
Difficult Task Compatibility	Pearson Correlation	.750(**)	.702(**)	.796(**)	.734(**)	.697(**)	1	.677(**)	.673(**)	.729(**)	.510(**)
	Sig. (2-tailed)	.000	.000	.000	.000	.000		.000	.000	.000	.001
	N	40	40	40	40	40	40	40	40	40	40
Difficult Task Presentation	Pearson Correlation	.673(**)	.653(**)	.639(**)	.483(**)	.595(**)	.677(**)	1	.582(**)	.841(**)	.391(*)
	Sig. (2-tailed)	.000	.000	.000	.002	.000	.000		.000	.000	.013
	N	40	40	40	40	40	40	40	40	40	40
Difficult Task Timeliness	Pearson Correlation	.548(**)	.481(**)	.535(**)	.671(**)	.644(**)	.673(**)	.582(**)	1	.723(**)	.320(*)
	Sig. (2-tailed)	.000	.002	.000	.000	.000	.000	.000		.000	.044
	N	40	40	40	40	40	40	40	40	40	40
Difficult Task Performance/ Interest/ Dedication	Pearson Correlation	.752(**)	.652(**)	.667(**)	.620(**)	.635(**)	.729(**)	.841(**)	.723(**)	1	.367(*)
	Sig. (2-tailed)	.000	.000	.000	.000	.000	.000	.000	.000		.020
	N	40	40	40	40	40	40	40	40	40	40
Difficult Task Assistance	Pearson Correlation	.093	.200	.421(**)	.078	.243	.510(**)	.391(*)	.320(*)	.367(*)	1
	Sig. (2-tailed)	.569	.217	.007	.632	.130	.001	.013	.044	.020	
	N	40	40	40	40	40	40	40	40	40	40

** Correlation is significant at the 0.01 level (2-tailed).
* Correlation is significant at the 0.05 level (2-tailed).

Chapter 8
An Efficient and Generic Algorithm for Matrix Inversion

Ahmad Farooq
King Khalid University, Saudi Arabia

Khan Hamid
National University of Computer and Emerging Sciences (NUCES), Pakistan

Inayat Ali Shah
National University of Computer and Emerging Sciences (NUCES), Pakistan

ABSTRACT

This work presents an improvement on the simple algorithms of matrix inversion (Farooq & Hamid, 2010). This generalized algorithm supports selection of pivot randomly in the matrix thus supporting partial and full pivoting. The freedom in pivot selection can be used in minimizing the numerical error and prioritizing the variable to find the solution first. The algorithm is more suitable for finding inverse and determinant of dense matrices. The algorithm requires a mechanism for selection of pivot (e.g., selection of absolute maximum value) in the available sub-matrix and the mechanism to get the inverse from the final resultant matrix by rearranging the rows and columns. A method for assigning the sign of the determinant is also given. The algorithm is explained through solved examples. The number of arithmetic calculations performed by the algorithm is of $O(n^3)$ however. The efficiency and simplicity of coding remains the same as of the original algorithm.

INTRODUCTION

Farooq and Hamid (2010) presented an algorithm for matrix inversion which is simpler and efficient than the exiting techniques (Saad, 2000; Chang, 2006; Mikkawy, 2006; Vajargah, 2007) and is applicable in general irrespective of the structure of the matrix. They demonstrated that manual calculations of the algorithm are straightforward and computer implementation is extremely easy. The algorithm also utilizes minimal memory. However, the algorithm is limited in the pivot selection by allowing the pivot selection diagonally only. This work presents an extension of the same algorithm by making it generic in pivot selection.

DOI: 10.4018/978-1-4666-1752-0.ch008

An important feature of the algorithm is the ability to allow the user to select pivot off-diagonally during inversion. The pivots can be selected from anywhere within the legal candidates of the matrix elements using the group theory of permutations and projections. The legality of the pivot is determined by the fact that during the inverse process a row or a column can be selected only once for a pivot. The selection of the pivot can be left to the choice of the user for example to go for a maximum absolute value of an element to improve numerical accuracy.

The rest of the paper is organized as follows. In section 2 we are presenting the generic algorithm. Also a 3 x 3 matrix is inversed (and determinant calculated) by the algorithm using two different sequences of pivot selection. Future work is indicated in section 3 and the paper is concluded in section 4. Finally some references are given in the end.

The Generic Algorithm of Matrix Inversion

In many situations of matrix inversions and solution of equations it may be required to go off diagonal for some or all of the pivot elements because of the following reasons:

a. The diagonal element is zero and cannot be selected as pivot. However, if we can look for elements other than the diagonal, then in non-singular matrices we will always find a non-zero element for pivot.

b. To improve the accuracy of the result we may look for particular type of values for pivots. Let say selecting the element having maximum absolute value.

c. We are interested in particular row or column to be selected first for pivot, for example, in solution of equation the value of a variable is required to be evaluated first.

However, if pivots are selected off-diagonal the resultant matrix (after the application of the inversion algorithm) will contain the elements of the inverse but intermingled. To get the inverse, the rows and the columns of the resultant matrix have to be rearranged. Similarly the off-diagonal selection of pivots will affect the sign of the determinant and correct sign have to be determined.

In the generic algorithm the selection of pivots for the inversion of matrices and the calculation of their determinants are controlled by permutation group theory. If we take a matrix of order n then for the inverse we have to select exactly n pivots. Let $X = \{1, 2, 3..., n\}$ is the set of pivot selections. Then S_n is the set of all bijections (possible permutations of pivot selection) on the set X. S_n forms a group under the binary operation of composition of functions i.e., for any bijections ρ, $\sigma \in S_n$, $\rho \circ \sigma \in S_n$ where "$\circ$" is the composition. Moreover for $\gamma \in S_n$, γ^{-1} will denote its inverse. The number of elements in the given S_n are equal to $n!$. In this context cycles and transpositions have their usual meanings.

During the inverse calculation, pivot selection is made according to some criterion. This could be to improve accuracy, efficiency or achieve priority in the calculation of some variable. Whatever sequence, γ of pivot selection is made it will be on the set S_n i.e., $\gamma \in S_n$. Therefore, the inverse of the matrix A is then obtained when we alter the rows of the resultant matrix according to γ and columns of the resultant matrix according to γ^{-1}.

Note that for any $\gamma \in S_n$ the number of non-identity permutations are either even or odd, accordingly the number of transpositions are even or odd. The signature of $\gamma \in S_n$ is defined as follows;

$$Sgn(\gamma) = \begin{cases} 1, & \textit{if the number of transpositions are even} \\ -1, & \textit{if the number of transpositions are odd} \end{cases}$$

The determinant of A is given by,

$$|A| = Sgn(\gamma) \prod_{\gamma \in S_n} a_{i,\gamma(i)} \text{, where all}$$

$a_{i,\gamma(i)}$, $i = 1, 2, 3, \cdots, n$ are the pivot elements and $\gamma \in S_n$.

Note that during this process if a pivot element is found to be zero then certainly, matrix is not invertible.

The Algorithm

- Let $p = 0$, $d = 1$, $s = \{\}$.
  Step 2: $p' \Leftarrow p + 1$.
  - Select a nonzero pivot according to some criterion; (let say maximum of row p). Let the row of the pivot be r and column of the pivot be c. Note that the algorithm allows a particular row or column to be selected only once for pivot selection during the whole process of inversion.
  - If there cannot be selected a nonzero pivot then
  $d = 0$ and go to step 14 (inverse does not exist).
    - Append (r, c) to the permutation list s.
    - $d' \Leftarrow d \times a_{r,c}$
    - Calculate the new elements of the pivot row by:

$$a'_{r,j} \Leftarrow \frac{a_{r,j}}{a_{r,c}} \text{, where } j = 1, \cdots, n, \quad j \neq c$$

Calculate the new elements of the pivot column by:

$$a'_{i,c} \Leftarrow -\frac{a_{i,c}}{a_{r,c}} \text{, where } i = 1, \cdots, n, \quad i \neq r$$

Calculate the rest of the new elements by:

$$a'_{i,j} \Leftarrow a_{i,j} + a_{r,j} \times a'_{i,c} \text{, where } i = 1, \cdots, n, \\ j = 1, \cdots, n \quad \& \quad i \neq r, j \neq c$$

Calculate the new value of the old pivot location by:

$$a'_{c,r} \Leftarrow \frac{1}{a_{c,r}}$$

- If $p < n$ go to step 2 (n the dimension of the matrix A).
- Rearrange the rows of A according to the transpositions s and rearrange the column of A according to the inverse transpositions of s.
- If the number of transpositions in s is odd then:

$$d' \Leftarrow -d$$

- Stop. If $d \neq 0$ then A contains the inverse and d' is the determinant otherwise A is singular.

Numerical Example 1

$$A = \begin{bmatrix} 1 & 1 & 3 \\ 1 & 3 & -3 \\ -2 & -4 & -4 \end{bmatrix}$$

Let take matrix A and choose the pivot elements for inversion according to $\gamma = \rho = (13) \in S_3$.

$$\begin{bmatrix} 1 & 1 & 3 \\ 1 & 3 & -3 \\ -2 & -4 & -4 \end{bmatrix}$$

According to the given permutation $\gamma = \rho = (13)$, we choose $a_{1,3} = 3$ as pivot.

$$\begin{bmatrix} 1/3 & 1/3 & 1/3 \\ 2 & 4 & 1 \\ -2/3 & -8/3 & 4/3 \end{bmatrix}$$

The resultant matrix is obtained after performing the calculations of first iteration.

$$\begin{bmatrix} 1/3 & 1/3 & 1/3 \\ 2 & 4 & 1 \\ -2/3 & -8/3 & 4/3 \end{bmatrix}$$

According to the given permutation $\gamma = \rho = (13)$, we choose $a_{3,1} = -2/3$ as pivot.

$$\begin{bmatrix} 1/2 & -1 & 1 \\ 3 & -4 & 5 \\ -3/2 & 4 & -2 \end{bmatrix}$$

The resultant matrix is obtained after performing the calculations of second iteration.

$$\begin{bmatrix} 1/2 & -1 & 1 \\ 3 & -4 & 5 \\ -3/2 & 4 & -2 \end{bmatrix}$$

According to the given permutation $\gamma = \rho = (13)$, we choose $a_{2,2} = -4$ as pivot.

$$\begin{bmatrix} -1/4 & -1/4 & -1/4 \\ -3/4 & -1/4 & -5/4 \\ 3/2 & 1 & 3 \end{bmatrix}$$

The resultant matrix obtained after performing the calculations of third and last iteration.

$$A^{-1} = \begin{bmatrix} 3 & 1 & 3/2 \\ -5/4 & -1/4 & -3/4 \\ -1/4 & -1/4 & -1/4 \end{bmatrix}$$

Since in this case $\rho^{-1} = \rho = (13)$, by using step 12 i.e. interchanging row 1 and row 3 and then interchanging column 1 and column 3 of the resultant matrix, the inverse of the matrix A is obtained.

It is obvious that for $\gamma = \rho = (13)$, there is only one transposition (odd) and $Sgn(\rho)$ is negative, therefore, as per step 13 the determinant of A is given by:

$$|A| = Sgn(\rho) \prod_{\rho \in S_3} a_{i\rho(i)} = -\left(a_{2,2} a_{1,3} a_{3,1}\right) =$$

$$-\left(3 \times -\frac{2}{3} \times -4\right) = -8$$

Numerical Example 2

$$A = \begin{bmatrix} 1 & 1 & 3 \\ 1 & 3 & -3 \\ -2 & -4 & -4 \end{bmatrix}$$

Let take matrix A once again and choose the pivot elements for inversion according to $\gamma = \alpha = (123) = (12)(13) \in S_3$.

$$\begin{bmatrix} 1 & 1 & 3 \\ 1 & 3 & -3 \\ -2 & -4 & -4 \end{bmatrix}$$

According to the given permutation $\gamma = \alpha = (123)$, we choose $a_{1,2} = 1$ as pivot.

$$\begin{bmatrix} 1 & 1 & 3 \\ -2 & -3 & -12 \\ 2 & 4 & 8 \end{bmatrix}$$

The resultant matrix obtained after performing the calculations of first iteration.

$$\begin{bmatrix} 1 & 1 & 3 \\ -2 & -3 & -12 \\ 2 & 4 & 8 \end{bmatrix}$$

According to the given permutation $\gamma = \alpha = (123)$, we choose $a_{2,3} = -12$ as pivot.

$$\begin{bmatrix} 1/2 & 1/4 & 1/4 \\ 1/6 & 1/4 & -1/12 \\ 2/3 & 2 & 2/3 \end{bmatrix}$$

The resultant matrix obtained after performing the calculations of second iteration.

$$\begin{bmatrix} 1/2 & 1/4 & 1/4 \\ 1/6 & 1/4 & -1/12 \\ 2/3 & 2 & 2/3 \end{bmatrix}$$

According to the given permutation $\gamma = \alpha = (123)$, we choose $a_{3,1} = 2/3$ as pivot.

$$\begin{bmatrix} -3/4 & -5/4 & -1/4 \\ -1/4 & -1/4 & -1/4 \\ 3/2 & 3 & 1 \end{bmatrix}$$

The resultant matrix obtained after performing the calculations of third iteration.

We apply step 12 to get the rows and columns of the inverse correctly arranged. Since in this case $\alpha^{-1} = \beta$, we will interchange the rows of the resultant matrix according to α and the columns of the resultant matrix according to β. As

$\alpha = (123) = (12)(13)$, therefore, we interchange row 1 & 2 and then row 1 & 3. For the columns $\beta = (132) = (13)(12)$, therefore, we interchange column 1 & 3 and then column 1 & 2. Accordingly the inverse of A obtained from the above resultant matrix is given below:

$$A^{-1} = \begin{bmatrix} 3 & 1 & 3/2 \\ -5/4 & -1/4 & -3/4 \\ -1/4 & -1/4 & -1/4 \end{bmatrix}$$

As $\gamma = \alpha = (123) = (12)(13)$ showing that there are only two transpositions (even) and $Sgn(\alpha)$ is positive, therefore, the determinant is given by:

$$|A| = Sgn(\alpha) \prod_{\alpha \in S_3} a_{i\alpha(i)} = +\left(a_{1,2} a_{2,3} a_{3,1}\right)$$

$$= \left(1 \times -12 \times \frac{2}{3}\right) = -8$$

FUTURE WORK

Work is in progress to improve further the algorithm for calculation of determinants exclusively and calculation of pseudo inverses. The algorithm can find solution of system of linear equations and inverse simultaneously. Initial investigation shows that in case of solution of linear equations the number of calculations required can be reduced substantially. The algorithm is making many calculations independent of each other in every iteration; this demonstrates that it can be quite easily modified for parallel processing. There are indications that the algorithm can be used to identify bounds on the numerical error which is necessary while testing the stability of numerical schemes.

CONCLUSION

This work has presented an improvement on the simple algorithm for matrix inversion of Farooq and Hamid (2010). It provides freedom to select pivots from among the elements of the matrix thus allowing partial or full pivoting. The selection criteria for pivots can be used to select elements of the matrix to improve numerical accuracy or to select the variables to calculate the value first.

REFERENCES

Chang, F. C. (2006). Inverse of a perturbed matrix. *Applied Mathematics Letters, 19,* 169–173. doi:10.1016/j.aml.2005.04.004

Dongarra, J. J., & Eijkhout, V. (2000). Numerical linear algebra algorithms and software. *Journal of Computational and Applied Mathematics, 123,* 489–514. doi:10.1016/S0377-0427(00)00400-3

Farooq, A., & Hamid, K. (2010). An efficient and simple algorithm for matrix inversion. *International Journal of Technology Diffusion, 1*(1), 20–27.

Mikkawy, M. E., & Karawia, A. (2006). Inversion of general tridiagonal matrices. *Applied Mathematics Letters, 19,* 712–720. doi:10.1016/j.aml.2005.11.012

Saad, Y., & Vorst, H. A. (2000). Iterative solution of linear systems in the 20th century. *Journal of Computational and Applied Mathematics, 123,* 1–33. doi:10.1016/S0377-0427(00)00412-X

Vajargah, B. F. (2007). New advantage to obtain accurate matrix inversion. *Applied Mathematics and Computation.* doi:10.1016/j.amc.2006.12.060

This work was previously published in International Journal of Technology Diffusion, Volume 1, Issue 2, edited by Ali Hussein Saleh Zolait, pp. 36-41, copyright 2010 by IGI Publishing (an imprint of IGI Global).

Chapter 9
Saving DBMS Resources While Running Batch Cycles in Data Warehouses

Nayem Rahman
Enterprise Data Warehouse Engineering-ETL, Intel Corporation

ABSTRACT

In a large data warehouse, thousands of jobs run during each cycle in dozens of subject areas. Many of the data warehouse tables are quite large and they need to be refreshed at the right time, several times a day, to support strategic business decisions. To enable cycles to run more frequently and keep the data warehouse environment stable the database system's resource utilization must be optimal. This paper discusses refreshing data warehouses using a metadata model to make sure jobs under batch cycles run on an as-needed basis. The metadata model limits execution of the stored procedures in different analytical subject areas to source data changes in the source staging subject area tables, and then implements refreshes of analytical tables for which new data has arrived from the operational databases. The load is skipped if source data has not changed. Skipping unnecessary loads via this metadata driven approach enables significant database resources savings. The resource savings statistics based on an actual production data warehouse demonstrate an excellent reduction of computing resources consumption achieved by the proposed techniques.

INTRODUCTION

Data warehousing is a product of recent technological advances which fulfills the business needs of organizations (Wixom & Watson, 2001). It has appeared as a key platform to provide integrated management of decision support data in

organizations (Shin, 2003). The data warehouse is used to hold historical and cross-functional data. Organizations use data warehouses as their integrated enterprise repository of data coming from disparate operational sources. As the business environment has become more global and competitive the data warehouse has proved to be a very critical technology for an organization to better manage and leverage its information,

DOI: 10.4018/978-1-4666-1752-0.ch009

which in turn helps an organization to become more competitive, better understand its customers, and more rapidly meet market demands (Furlow, 2001; Wixom & Watson, 2001). Organizations use data warehouses for a variety of tasks such as planning, target marketing, decision making, data analysis, and customer services. They are changing the way business is conducted (Shin, 2003). Data warehousing continues to be very popular as many organizations are realizing its benefits (Furlow, 2001).

Until recently the data warehouses were usually refreshed after hours when business users went home. The business environment has become global, complex, and volatile and as a result nightly refresh is no longer practical. Business activities continue twenty four by seven as nighttime in one part of the globe is the day time of the other parts of the globe. The data warehouse users continue to look for up to date information more frequently. As a result we have to refresh data warehouses more frequently, every few hours. The good news is that through hardware advances such as massive parallel processing, and parallel database technology, it is now possible to load, maintain, and access databases of terabyte size (Wixom & Watson, 2001) in reasonable times. Thus data warehousing and other advances in information technology are now solving some of the very difficult technical problems and make it possible to organize, store, and retrieve huge volumes of information for a given decision (Cooper et al., 2000). In order to achieve this multiple facets needs to be considered. In addition to that data warehouse design, extract-transform-load (ETL) development, and load strategy need to be efficient. We need strategies as to how to save database management system (DBMS) resources during load processes in order to make the DBMS available to analytical tools and query processing while the load is running. All of these innovations are affecting how organizations conduct business, especially in sales and marketing, allowing companies to analyze

the behavior of individual customers rather than demographic groups or product classes (Wixom & Watson, 2001).

In data warehouses the main users are the analytical community, namely, business people running reporting and analytical web tools. Data warehouse systems resources are designed for use by these tools, enabling business people to make all sorts of decisions based on data warehouse information. It is critical that enough computing resources be available for use by the analytical community to retrieve and process information into intuitive presentations (i.e., reads). In operational databases, the primary candidates to use computing resources are operational needs and requirements (i.e., writes). Any reporting and analytical tools get secondary considerations. However, in the case of data warehouses the analytical tools are primary candidates and get high priority in using computing resources. This means that the data warehouse batch processing should use the minimum resources possible. Data warehousing has evolved to hold huge volumes of historical as well as cross-functional data. Today, the knowledge workers such as business users, analysts and managers are more dependent on data warehouses for business information. These users' information needs must be fulfilled on a priority basis by providing query results within a reasonable time in order for businesses to remain competitive.

Although an enterprise data warehouse has the potential to deliver competitive advantage, success is not necessarily guaranteed. The success of a data warehouse depends on data quality, data freshness, and accessibility to data by the analytical community with reasonable response times. In fact, a survey revealed that more than 60 percent of companies owning a data warehouse rated the system as having only limited success in meeting user expectations (Stedman, 1998). The survey by Watson and Wixom (2001) showed that the ability of many existing data warehouses to provide users with easy and timely access to quality data is limited. After an enterprise data warehouse is implemented successfully more applications engage the data warehouse and the number of users increase. The author of this paper observed that in a production enterprise data warehouse after the first few projects or applications got implemented successfully the more and more applications started to embrace data warehouse technology gradually over the years. Successful implementation for first few projects in data warehouse gave confidence to other projects and applications to take advantage of modern data warehouse technology. The data warehouse systems are in general robust in nature and based on advanced technology such as failover, clustering and parallel processing.

One important aspect of data warehousing is the acquisition of data in the warehouse as soon as the data changes at the source. Data warehouse customers want to see the changes near real time. Business organizations need tables to be refreshed frequently to have the most up to date data. Data freshness needs are moving from a weekly to daily to every few hours in order to meet customer expectations. This means that batch cycles need to be run more frequently, at a regular interval. Running batch cycles more frequently means more computing resource consumption for loading purposes. However, increasing the frequency of data warehouse refreshes reduces the number of source tables which will have newer data each cycle. So, there is an opportunity to reduce resource consumption by loading only those tables for which source data has changed. The author of this paper observed that in a large production data warehouse about 40% of the tables in the source staging area of data warehouse do not get changed at certain batch windows. The more frequent the cycle runs the less the percent of tables get changed. Running stored procedures without checking source data change causes unnecessary loads at the expense of DBMS resource consumption (Rahman, 2005).

The data warehouse load processes should use minimal DBMS resources. This is very

important because analytical tools should have enough resources available to run the reports and get results returned within a reasonable time. The query response time should be short. In this paper we propose making the load processes very efficient so that they consume significantly less resources. Making the load process metadata driven can help batch cycles run faster. In an enterprise data warehouse (EDW) where thousands of jobs run daily it is obvious that the jobs should run via batch process. In applications for which the real-time refresh of the data warehouse under source change is not critical, the source updates are usually maintained in batch fashion to reduce the maintenance overhead (Liu et al., 2002). The experimental results (Liu et al., 2002) showed that the batch technique outperforms the sequential one. Now how do we make batch cycles take less time?

There are two steps to get data to the analytical subject areas in a data warehouse. First, data is acquired from the operational data store and then landed into the staging (Cooper et al., 2000; Ejaz and Kenneth, 2004) subject area tables in the data warehouse via different database utilities and ETL tools. The analytical subject areas are refreshed by pulling data from the staging subject areas using transformations and stored procedures. In the load process we need to make sure that the database system resources such as CPU time and IO utilization are minimal. This can be done by bypassing unnecessary loads such as skipping stored procedure execution when source data has not changed. Given the improvement of database technologies the DBMS could be given an expanded role to play as a data transformation engine as well as data store (Rami & Nabila, 2002).

The purpose of this paper is to show how data warehouse analytical subject area refreshes can be made efficient by focusing on a metadata model driven and DBMS software based functionality. The paper proposes methods that provide the opportunity to complete batch cycles faster. Here we propose certain methodologies for analytical subject area refresh: (1) Make load process completely metadata driven; (2) Bypass ETL Transformation or stored procedure execution when source data has not changed.

This paper is organized as follows: Section 2 briefly discusses the goal of our proposed data warehouse update approach and related work done in this area. Section 3 discusses our proposed techniques. Section 4 provides resources savings statistics based on batch cycles runs in a production data warehouse. Section 5 summarizes and concludes the paper.

LITERATURE RESEARCH

The data warehousing is a prominent technology in information technology (IT). Data warehousing and data management have been identified as one of the six physical capability clusters of IT-infrastructure services required for strategic agility (Weill et al., 2002). Significant research work has been done on different aspects of data warehousing over the last one decade. Most previous work on data warehousing focused on design issues (Hanson & Willshire, 1997; Chao, 2004; Dey et al, 2006; Ram and Do, 2000; Storey and Goldstein, 1993; Evermann, 2008; García-García & Ordonez, 2010; Georgieva, 2008), ETL tools (Karakasidis et al., 2005; Schwarz et al., 2001; Simitsis et al., 2005), data maintenance (Labio et al., 2000) strategies relating to view materialization (Agrawal et al., 1997; Chirkova et al., 2006; Hwang and Kang, 2005; Lee and Kim, 2005; Lee et al., 2001; Mohania and Kambayashi, 2000; Zhuge et al., 1995; Zhuge et al., 1997), and implementation issues (Widom, 1995).

Research work has also been done on data warehouse load efficiency, SQL performance (Payton & Handfield, 2004; Lam and Lee, 2006; Martin and Powley, 2007), and maintaining a stable and healthy data warehousing environment. Many efforts have been undertaken in order to make the data environment efficient from a performance

and resource consumption standpoint. Yan, J. et al. (2006) propose dimensionality reduction to save memory and CPU resources and also propose dimensionality reduction algorithms. Armstrong (2007) studies minimizing of data movement in order to increase user accessibility, minimize data latency and improve performance of the entire data warehouse. Chirkova et al., (2006) address the problem that given a database and set of queries, how to find a set of views that can compute the answers to the queries, such that the amount of space, in bytes, required to store the view-set is minimal on the given database. The authors point out that the problem is important for applications such as distributed databases, data warehousing, and data integration. Hill & Ross (2009) present a method for transforming some outer joins to inner joins and describe a generalized semi-join reduction technique in order to improve performance and response time.

The work in (Carey et al., 1989) addresses the problem of priority scheduling in a database management system by investigating the architectural consequences of adding priority to a DBMS. This helps shifting resources to more critical queries than load jobs. Dung et al. (2007) experiment the performance evaluation of an integrated web data warehouse application. Beszedes et al. (2003) suggested the technique of program-code compression because the reduced-sized code can have a positive impact on network traffic and embedded system costs such as memory requirements and power consumption. Taufer et al. (2002) identify communication software inefficiency within the DBMS relating to crucial performance issues of OLAP workloads on clusters.

Elnaffar (2002) proposes autonomous and self-tuning DBMSs that are capable to manage their own performance by automatically recognizing the workload (Holze & Ritter, 2007) type and then reconfiguring their resources according to workload. The author presents an approach to automatically identifying a DBMS workload as either OLTP or DSS. Ghazal et al. (2009) presented an algorithm that dynamically chooses between saving and re-using compiled plans versus always re-compiling queries. Powley et al. (2008) examine query throttling techniques as method to control workload. In this approach, a workload class may be slowed down during execution in order to release system resources that can be used by higher priority workloads (Powley, et al., 2008). Ganguly et al., (1992) show that a cost model can predict response time with some features of query execution parallelism. The decreasing cost of computing allows for reducing the response time of decision support queries by virtue of parallel execution to exploit inexpensive resources (Ganguly et al., 1992).

Soror et al. (2008) addresses the problem of optimizing the performance of database management systems by manipulating the configurations of the virtual machines in which they run. Krompass et al. (2007) propose a workload management system for managing the execution of individual queries based on customer service level objectives. Business Intelligence query workloads which run on very large data warehouses contain queries with execution times ranging from seconds to hours (Krompass et al., 2009). The authors present a systematic study of workload management policies to enable a system to: (1) recognize long-running queries and categorize them in terms of their impact on performance and (2) determine and take (automatically!) the most effective control actions to remedy the situation. Dayal et al. (2009) and Sharaf and Chrysanthis (2009) explore how to manage database workloads containing mixture of OLTP-like queries that run for fraction of a second as well as business intelligence queries that run for a longer time.

Data warehouse workload and resource usage requirements cannot be handled just by workload management. Effective measures need to be taken in terms of efficient query and load procedures. Related work in the literature mainly focuses on developing techniques for a dedicated workload management system. In this paper, we present

techniques to cause load processes to consume fewer resources. We focus on bypassing load when there is no data change in upstream tables. We address the problem of DBMS resource consumption by load processes caused by the increase of the frequency of batch cycle runs necessary to provide up to date data. This is an important issue that has received little attention so far, but that arises very often in practice. True, the data warehouse systems have priority scheduling techniques to allow maximum resource to analytical tools and queries, and also schedule non critical applications or jobs lower in priority in resource utilization. The database research community has proposed approaches that use economic models to allocate multiple resources, such as main memory buffer space and CPU shares, to workloads that run concurrently on a DBMS (Zhang et al., 2008). But, that is really shifting resources from one area to another area. To cause batch cycles to use fewer resources it is critical to make batch cycles efficient. ETL developers can play an important role in making load processes innovative and efficient. In this instance, we may consider several things such as metadata driven batch cycles run, and optimization of transformation logic inside the stored procedures. Before running any job in the batch process it is important to check if data has changed in source tables affected.

Data warehouse resource savings is an important issue for efficient data warehouse management. In data warehouses, workloads are query intensive with mostly ad hoc, complex queries can access millions of records and perform numerous scans, joins and aggregates. Query throughput and response times are more important than transaction throughput (Chaudhuri & Dayal, 1997). In order to reserve more resources for queries we propose an efficient load process that would allow the data warehouse system to save computing resources in batch processes thus releasing them for analytical queries. So, skipping loads when necessary would help save resources.

A data warehouse system is required to handle diverse complex queries, ad hoc queries as well as processing of millions of rows. This means the system needs to provide differentiated levels of service to ensure that critical work takes priority. In order to meet these needs, it is necessary that load jobs consume less resource than analytical queries which are being executed in the system at the same time. In this paper we examine the essence of running each individual job in a batch process. In our approach, a metadata table is used to hold information about the source tables of each analytical table. When a batch job kicks off, at the very beginning a utility procedure runs against the metadata table to identify changes in source data. This metadata information will determine whether the batch jobs should execute the load stored procedure. By skipping a stored procedure execution valuable computing resources can be released to be used instead by higher priority workloads.

DATA WAREHOUSE REFRESH METHODOLOGIES

Data warehousing is a collection of decision support technologies, aimed at enabling the knowledge worker (executive, manager, and analyst) to make better and faster decisions (Chaudhuri & Dayal, 1997). This paper discusses how to make batch jobs for the analytical subject area refresh with minimal resources utilization. We propose highly-efficient methods for data warehousing, focusing on a metadata model using database management systems (DBMS) based functionality.

In data warehouses data come from heterogeneous sources including legacy systems, online transaction processing (OLTP), enterprise resource planning (ERP) applications, MPS system and more. The source data is loaded into a warehouse staging area (Cooper et al., 2000) as raw data to be processed and transformed. It is later loaded into actual analytical subject area tables. The source data arrives in the staging subject area tables as an incremental data feed via ETL tools or other database-specific utilities. The data is loaded in the staging tables as batch files. Data are sent from the source system with a cutoff timestamp based upon changed date and time in the source system. This as-of cutoff timestamp is also known as observation timestamp. An observation timestamp contains the date and time when the consistent set of triggered data was loaded into the staging table. The triggered timestamp is always less than or equal to observation timestamp. Staging area tables normally have a one to one relationship with the operational database tables. As a result these staging table loads are simple to comprehend. These table loads normally do not involve any transformation.

Metadata-Based Batch Processing

Once data arrives in the staging area of the data warehouse the batch processes start to refresh analytical subject areas which are used by analytical tools. The logical and physical data model is designed to facilitate and improve performance of analytical queries. The analytical tables can be loaded with data from multiple source tables in the staging area. These analytical tables are sometime called cooked tables in that reporting queries do not have to repetitively perform inefficient joins, complex transformations, and aggregations. This can result in analytical table loads which are complex and computing resources intensive. Efficiently loading data into an analytical table which pulls data from multiple staging tables requires checking metadata to see if data has changed is any of the source tables.

We allow the DBMS to play an expanded role as a data transformation engine as well as a data store as proposed by Rami and Nabila (2002). DBMS-based stored procedures are used to load the analytical subject areas, via batch processes, with data from the staging subject areas. The source data does not change in all tables during each cycle refresh. In a large production data warehouse, it was observed that data change occurred in 40% of the tables during a 4-hour refresh window (Rahman, 2007). As the frequency of batch cycles run increases, the percentage of tables with changed data will likely decrease. That means the batch cycles for downstream analytical subject areas need to run fewer stored procedures to load tables in a batch. An ETL metadata model can provide useful information about whether analytical tables have new data in the source tables. We propose to reduce data latency by providing methods capable of frequent batch runs via a metadata driven approach and incremental refreshes. Data latency is the interval between the time an event occurs and the time it is perceived by the user (Golfarelli et al., 2004).

With required information from the metadata model, the batch cycles kick off the jobs to do a full or incremental load or skip the load when it is determined that the source data has not changed. Thus, many jobs in an analytical subject area can skip loads and the data warehouse resource usage will be minimized. So, the cycle runs will be faster and the data warehouse computing resource (CPU and IO) utilization will be optimized.

The Metadata Functionality

Data warehouse metadata are "data about data" that relates to the refresh of the warehouse. Metadata is critical for implementing a data warehouse (Kim et al., 2000). Metadata is particularly important because data warehouse activities such as data integration from multiple autonomous and heterogeneous data sources, data transformation, and OLAP, are enabled by metadata (Fan & Poulovassilis, 2003). Metadata might describe each fact contained within the warehouse as to when it was last updated, or the source of the fact (Katic et al., 1998). Due to the increasing complexity of data warehousing, metadata management has received increasing research focus (Fan & Poulovassilis, 2003).

In our approach, the analytical subject areas are refreshed with support from a metadata model. We used a few metadata tables such as 'subj_area_tbl_fl_hist' (Figure 2) for source staging area table load information, 'src_load_log' (Figure 1) which captures last load timestamp for downstream analytical subject area table load, and 'load_chk_log' (Figure 2) which holds the list of analytical tables along with other load parameters for each subject area. The 'subj_area_tbl_fl' holds all load metrics for staging area tables such as subject area name, table name, as-of source date, as-of source time, insert row count, update row count, and delete row count. The 'load check log' table holds all required metrics for analytical subject area tables such as 'subj_area_nm', 'trgt_tbl_nm', 'load_strt_ts', 'load_enable_ind', and 'load_type_cd'. The 'src_load_log' table holds information such as 'trgt_subj_area_nm', 'trgt_tbl_nm', 'trgt_tbl_line_nbr', 'src_subj_area_nm', 'src_tbl_nm', and 'src_load_observation_upd_ts'.

Figure 1 shows that for a target table (second column) one or more source tables are used. This table is populated by an ETL developer who is

Figure 1. Source observation timestamp for target table refresh on '2009-12-29 20:00:00'

	TargetSubjArea	TargetTable	LineNumber	SourceSubjArea	SourceTable	LastObservationTs
1	Capital_DRV	dim_asset_cost_acct	101	Finance_CRS	fin_gl_acct_co	2009-12-17 02:00:00
2	Capital_DRV	dim_asset_cost_acct	102	Finance_CRS	acct_grp_depr_area_dtl	2008-09-18 02:00:00
3	Capital_DRV	dim_asset_depr_acct	101	Finance_CRS	fin_gl_acct_co	2009-12-17 02:00:00
4	Capital_DRV	dim_asset_depr_acct	102	Finance_CRS	fix_asset_val_adj_acct	2007-11-13 14:00:00
5	Capital_DRV	dim_asset_depr_area_chrt	101	Asset_CRS	asset_depr_area_chrt	2007-11-12 19:00:00
6	Capital_DRV	dim_asset_depr_gl_acct	101	Finance_CRS	acct_grp_depr_area_dtl	2008-09-18 02:00:00
7	Capital_DRV	dim_asset_depr_term	301	Asset_DRV	asset_depr_term	2009-12-29 19:42:11
8	Capital_DRV	dim_asset_gl_acct_dtrmn	101	Finance_CRS	fix_asset_val_adj_acct	2007-11-13 14:00:00
9	Capital_DRV	dim_asset_gl_acct_dtrmn	102	Finance_CRS	acct_grp_depr_area_dtl	2008-09-18 02:00:00
10	Capital_DRV	dim_asset_gl_acct_dtrmn	103	Asset_CRS	asset_depr_area_chrt	2007-11-12 19:00:00

Figure 2. Utility stored procedure to detect source data change

```
REPLACE PROCEDURE Dwmgr_Xfrm_MET.pr_utl_chk_tbl_changed(
IN subj_area VARCHAR(30),
IN trgt_tbl VARCHAR(30),
INOUT src_cur_ts  TIMESTAMP(0),
INOUT src_lst_ts  TIMESTAMP(0))
-----------------------------------------------------------------------
BEGIN
DECLARE min_tbl_line, max_tbl_line BYTEINT ;

L1: LOOP

-- Checking metadata for source data change
LOCKING Dwmgr.v_dwm_subj_area_tbl_fl_hist  FOR ACCESS
LOCKING Dwmgr_Xfrm_MET.v_src_load_log FOR ACCESS

SELECT CAST(MAX(CAST(a.asof_src_dt AS CHAR(10))||' '||CAST(a.asof_src_tm AS CHAR(8))) AS TIMESTAMP(0))
INTO :src_cur_ts
FROM  Dwmgr.v_dwm_subj_area_tbl_fl_hist a, Dwmgr_Xfrm_MET.v_src_load_log b
WHERE a.subj_area_nm = b.src_subj_area_nm
AND a.tbl_nm = b.src_tbl_nm
AND a.row_cnt > 0
AND b.trgt_subj_area_nm = :subj_area
AND b.trgt_tbl_nm = :trgt_tbl
AND b.trgt_tbl_line_nbr = :min_tbl_line ;

IF  src_cur_ts > src_lst_ts THEN
  UPDATE Dwmgr_Xfrm_MET.v_src_load_log b
  SET src_cur_upd_ts = :src_cur_ts
  WHERE b.trgt_subj_area_nm = :subj_area
  AND b.trgt_tbl_nm = :trgt_tbl
  AND b.trgt_tbl_line_nbr = :min_tbl_line ;
END IF;

SET min_tbl_line = min_tbl_line + 1;

IF  (min_tbl_line > max_tbl_line) THEN
  LEAVE L1;
END IF;

END LOOP L1;

LOCKING Dwmgr_Xfrm_MET.v_src_load_log FOR ACCESS
SELECT MAX(src_cur_upd_ts), MAX(src_last_upd_ts)
INTO :src_cur_ts, :src_lst_ts
FROM Dwmgr_Xfrm_MET.v_src_load_log
WHERE trgt_subj_area_nm = :subj_area
AND trgt_tbl_nm = :trgt_tbl;
-----------------------------------------------------------------------
END;
```

assigned to work on the stored procedures for each target table. The one-time population of this table consists of all required source tables, from one to many source subject areas. Metadata is inserted into this table for each target table (column 2). For each source table the latest data change is shown in the last column (last observation timestamp). A line sequence number (column 3) assigned to identify the source tables under each target table. The line numbers for each target table are used by a utility stored procedure to pull last source table change timestamp for each source table and update the last column in Figure 1. The latest observation timestamp is updated in the last column in Figure 1, when the target table batch

job kicks off. In order to activate a target table load at least one of the source tables must have new or changed data. The target table, 'dim_asset_depr_term' uses only one source table (Figure 1, Row 7) with latest source data change as-of '2009-12-29 19-42-11'. So, as part of '2009-12-29 20:00:00' target subject area refresh the target table will be refreshed. On the other hand, under the same target subject area refresh the other target tables listed in Figure 1 will not be refreshed as none of them have source data changed during the last four hours. The target subject area refresh occurs every four hours.

Checking Source Data Change

This work proposes using database-specific software such as stored procedures and macros to refresh data warehouse analytical area tables. There are separate stored procedures or macros written to perform full or incremental refreshes. Both full and incremental refreshes are made metadata driven. Instead of a metadata-driven approach the downstream analytical subject area table refreshes could be made DBMS trigger-driven, that is, refreshing tables when a data change is detected in source staging tables. However, triggers are not quite suitable since they can slow down the system, and cause performance impact (Gardner, 1998). Metadata-driven batch refreshes are more efficient than trigger driven loads, especially when the data warehouse is quite large with thousands of tables needing to be updated during certain time intervals (Rahman, 2007). Figure 2 shows a few metadata tables that are used to get information regarding source data change timestamp and a list of source tables used by individual downstream target tables.

In order to make the analytical subject area refreshes metadata-driven, we execute a few DBMS-based utility stored procedures to get the last source table load timestamps and other relevant load parameters from the metadata table(s) to execute full and incremental refresh stored procedures. A wrapper procedure first calls a utility procedure to get last source table load timestamp from the metadata table. It also checks the target table last load observation timestamp. By comparing both timestamps it determines whether source data has changed. If the source-load timestamp is equal to the last loaded timestamp of the target table that means the source data has not changed and the table load can be skipped. Therefore, the full or incremental refresh stored procedure execution is bypassed.

In Figure 2, the code block gets the last load timestamp of each of the source tables (primary, secondary, dimension, lookup, etc.) under one

or several different source subject areas that are referenced in the stored procedures to load the target table (example: Figure 1). Based on that information the source table load timestamps are pulled. The code block within the loop in Figure 2 gets executed repeatedly by line-number in Figure 1 to pull the latest source data change timestamp for each of the source tables to load each target table.

The utility stored procedure also pulls the last load timestamp for the target table (SQL at the bottom of Figure 2). Based on source and the target table observation timestamp if any of the source table load timestamps is found greater than the corresponding target table last load timestamps that means new data has arrived in some source tables and a full or incremental load stored procedure gets activated depending on load type code to load the target table.

If the source last load timestamp is equal to the target table last load timestamp that means source data has not changed. The target table load is skipped and the stored procedure execution is bypassed. If the source load current timestamp is greater than target table last load timestamp, it makes an attempt to load the target table via full or incremental load stored procedure depending on load indicator information in the metadata table. The default load is incremental load if no indicator value is provided.

COMPUTING RESOURCE USAGE AND SAVINGS

In a data warehouse where thousands of queries run by batch processes, analytical and ad-hoc queries and applications run at a given time, the computing resources are the most precious resources. These computing resources need to be optimized to keep the data warehousing environment stable and running. The analytical community cannot tolerate long running queries or delayed results. Response time of queries is one of the most impor-

Figure 3. Computing resource consumption by full, delta, & skipping stored procedure runs

Subject Area	Target Table	CPU usage by FULL sps	CPU usage by Full sps	CPU usage by Delta sps	IO usage by Delta sps	CPU save by Delta sps	IO save by Delta sps	CPU usage to skip sps	IO usage to skip sps	CPU save by skpping sps	IO save by skpping sps
Capital_DRV	dim_asset	260.78	544930	0.00	0	0.00	0	19.18	58471	241.60	486459
Capital_DRV	dim_asset_depr_term	567.66	1361556	102.28	282056	465.38	1079500	3.93	4066	563.73	1357490
Capital_DRV	dim_mtrl	336.01	932084	62.00	311765	274.01	620319	8.34	51575	327.67	880509
Capital_DRV	dim_wrkr	56.33	298637	0.00	0	0.00	0	7.66	22100	48.67	276537
Capital_DRV	fact_asset_depr_post	2078.52	2354844	961.00	2354456	1117.52	388	3.8	4162	2074.72	2350682
Capital_DRV	fact_asset_prprt_val	1046.90	1418033	120.62	273667	926.28	1144366	9.66	34315	1037.24	1383718
Capital_DRV	fact_ctrl_doc_captl_spnd	1712.73	2117581	135.07	592896	1577.66	1524685	5.5	4142	1707.23	2113439
Capital_DRV	fact_intco_asset_xfer_trns	1830.98	1594034	97.21	116597	1733.77	1477437	4.08	4075	1826.90	1589959
Capital_DRV	fact_purch_ord_gds_rcpt	2651.61	2305142	92.74	406366	2558.87	1898776	5.57	4191	2646.04	2300951
Total		10541.52	12926841	1570.92	4337803	8653.49	7745471	67.72	187097	10473.80	12739744

tant indicators of data warehouse stability and its success. The knowledge workers lose confidence in the system if the enterprise data warehouse cannot return information within a reasonable time, especially when it comes to tactical decision making. Transaction latency expressed as a deadline is the most commonly used form of SLA, reflecting the user's expectation for the transaction to finish within a certain amount of specified time (Sharaf & Chrysanthis, 2009).

In order to ensure the data warehouse is stable, scalable, and queries run efficiently many organizations institute a governing body to oversee the operation and running of the data warehouses. They closely monitor the deployment of objects such as views, stored procedures and macros to make sure they perform efficiently in the data warehouse. In most cases all code that lands on data warehouses goes through a code review process to make sure they are optimized. As a cross-check the DBA (database administrators) team constantly monitors queries and load procedures to make sure the data warehouse is stable and running efficiently.

In terms of data warehouse computing resource usage such as CPU and IO the analytical reporting queries should get priority over data warehouse load procedures. In this work we make an effort to minimize the resource utilization of batch processes. More specifically, this work concentrates on resource savings in analytical subject area refreshes with data from staging subject areas. In batch processing resource consumption relates to full load or incremental (aka, delta) load or skip-load. As normal, the full refreshes take more resources than incremental refreshes. The skip-load bypasses executing both full and incremental load stored procedure execution. The skip-load happens when source data has not changed for a target table load. In order to check if source data has changed a few utility procedures need to run which involves minimal resource consumption. Figure 3 provides comparative resource consumptions and relative resource savings for individual target table load.

Figure 3 shows the variation of computing resource consumption by individual load stored procedures. In row-one (for table, dim_asset), the target table load happens via full refresh due to data quality and integrity reasons. However, when source data does not change the batch process skips running the full stored procedure. For full load the stored procedure uses 260.78 CPU seconds (IO usage is 544,930) and to skip the load it uses only 19.18 CPU seconds (IO usage is 58471). A few utility procedures need to run to check if source data changed and that causes some resources consumption of 19.18 CPU seconds. In row-five (for table fact_asset_depr_post), the stored procedure for full load takes 2,078.52 CPU seconds (IO usage, 2,354,844), stored procedure for incremental (aka, delta) load takes 961.00 CPU seconds (IO usage, 2,354,456) and when it skips the load it takes only 3.8 CPU seconds (IO usage, 4,162).

Figure 4. Comparative average resource consumption and savings per cycle

Based on three subject areas (Asset, Project, Capital)	Total CPU second	Total I/O in KB
Full Refresh – Ran 150 Procedures	58.3 K	111,261
2nd Refresh - With 44 Procedures bypassed	41.7 K	64,731
3rd Refresh - With 40 Procedures bypassed	44.1 K	71,292
4th Refresh - With 39 Procedures bypassed	45.3 K	70,761
5th Refresh - With 40 Procedures bypassed	44.8 K	71,430
6th Refresh - With 37 Procedures bypassed	46.3 K	78,459
Average Savings by skipping Procedures	20.8 K	39,926
Percentage of Savings by skipping Procedures	23.77%	35.89%

Thus, in Figure 3, we see that skipping loads saves almost 90% of resource consumptions. For nine tables in Figure 3, the total CPU consumption for full load is 10,541.52 CPU seconds (total IO, 12926841). For delta load, the total CPU consumption is 1,570.92 (total IO, 4337803). And skip load uses only 67.72 CPU seconds (total IO, 187,097). The last two columns show the CPU and IO savings achieved when skipping the loads. In Figure 3, for nine tables the total computing resource savings achieved are 10,473.80 CPU seconds and 12,739,744 for IO. The Figure 3 shows only a partial list of tables under one subject area for one cycle refresh. In a large data warehouse, there are hundreds of subject areas that run multiple times a day. So, the total computing resources saving achieved through model-driven refresh methodology can be quite significant.

An experiment was conducted in a real-world production environment. All batch jobs under three subject areas (Asset, Project, and Capital) ran six times in a row with four-hour time intervals. A total of 150 jobs ran in three subject areas each time to load 150 target tables. The first cycle refresh was done with full refreshes. For subsequent cycle refreshes metadata was re-set and activated so a particular job would run full procedure if there was no delta procedure for it and also source data has changed; a delta procedure would run if one existed and source data has changed; no full or delta stored procedure would run and load would be skipped if the source data had not changed for that target table.

Figure 4 shows that total CPU and IO consumption was 58.3 K seconds and 111,261 respectively. For the next five cycle refreshes the bypassing of stored procedures were 44, 40, 39, 40, and 37. The corresponding CPU and IO usage were also shown in column 3 and 4. The average percentage of CPU and IO savings by skipping stored procedures execution per cycle based on five subsequent cycles (after first cycle run) under three subject areas (consisting of 22, 30, and 98 jobs) was 23.77% (CPU) and 35.89% (IO). In other words, on average a little less than one-fourth CPU and one third of IO savings were achieved based on statistics collected.

CONCLUSION

The objective of this paper was to suggest ways to achieve computing resource savings in refreshing the data warehouse. We have concentrated on the problem of making the batch cycles run faster, cycle time shorter, and DBMS resource utilization optimal. We have come up with techniques of analytical subject area refreshes by utilizing a metadata model. With incremental data feeds in the staging tables in the warehouse, the analytical subject areas are refreshed faster with batch processes that run as frequently as needed and with minimal resources utilization. The experimental results revealed that with the help of our refresh techniques, the batch processing had excellent performance and significant reduction of CPU and IO utilization. Our proposed techniques are suitable for any database engine. Finally, our approach helps reduce data latency by virtue of faster cycles runs and thereby increasing frequency of batch runs.

ACKNOWLEDGMENT

The author thanks his colleagues Dale M. Rutz and Jim Sims who provided thoughtful review comments on earlier version of this paper and anonymous referees for their useful comments which have led to this improved version of the paper.

REFERENCES

Agrawal, D., Abbadi, A., Singh, A., & Yurek, T. (1997). Efficient View Maintenance at Data Warehouse. *SIGMOD Record*, *26*(2), 417–427. doi:10.1145/253262.253355

Armstrong, R. (2007), When and Why to Put What Data Where. Teradata Corporation White Paper, 1-5.

Beszedes, A. (2003). Survey of Code-Size Reduction Methods. *ACM Computing Surveys*, *35*(3), 223–267. doi:10.1145/937503.937504

Carey, M. J., Jauhari, R., & Livny, M. (1989), Priority in DBMS Resource Scheduling, In Proceedings of the 15th international conference on Very Large Data Bases, Amsterdam, The Netherlands (pp. 397 – 410).

Chao, C. (2004). Incremental Maintenance of Object Oriented Data Warehouse. *Information Sciences*, *1*(4), 91–110. doi:10.1016/j.ins.2003.07.014

Chaudhuri, S., & Dayal, U. (1997). An Overview of Data Warehousing and OLAP Technology. *SIGMOD Record*, *26*(1). doi:10.1145/248603.248616

Chirkova, R., Li, C., & Li, J. (2006). Answering Queries using Materialized Views with Minimum Size. *The VLDB Journal*, *15*(3), 191–210. doi:10.1007/s00778-005-0162-8

Cooper, (2000). Data Warehousing Supports Corporate Strategy at First American Corporation. *Management Information Systems Quarterly*, *24*(4), 547–567. doi:10.2307/3250947

Dayal, U., Kuno, H., Wiener, J.L., Wilkinson, K., Ganapathi, A. & Krompass, S. (2009), Managing Operational Business Intelligence Workloads. ACM SIGOPS Operating Systems Review archive, 43 (1), 92-98.

Dey, D., Zhang, Z., & De, P. (2006). Optimal Synchronization Policies for Data Warehouse. *Information Journal on Computing*, *18*(2), 229–242.

Dung, X. T., Rahayu, W., & Taniar, D. (2007). A high performance integrated web data warehousing. *Cluster Computing*, *10*, 95–109. doi:10.1007/s10586-007-0008-9

Ejaz, A., & Kenneth, R. (2004), Utilizing Staging Tables in Data Integration to Load Data into Materialized Views. In Proceedings of the First International Symposium on Computational and Information Science (CIS'04), Shanghai, China, (pp. 685-691).

Elnaffar, S. S. (2002), A methodology for auto-recognizing DBMS workloads. In Proceedings of the 2002 conference of the Centre for Advanced Studies on Collaborative research, Toronto, Ontario, Canada.

Evermann, J. (2008). An Exploratory Study of Database Integration Processes. *IEEE Transactions on Knowledge and Data Engineering*, *20*(1). doi:10.1109/TKDE.2007.190675

Fan, H., & Poulovassilis, A. (2003), Using AutoMed Metadata in Data Warehousing Environments. In Proceedings of the 6th ACM international workshop on Data warehousing and OLAP, New Orleans, Louisiana, USA, 86 - 93.

Furlow, G. (2001), The Case for Building a Data Warehouse. IT Professional, 3(4,), 31-34.

Ganguly, S., Hasan, W., & Krishnamurthy, R. (1992), Query Optimization for Parallel Execution. In Proceedings of the 1992 ACM SIGMOD international conference on Management of data, San Diego, California, United States, 9 - 18.

García-García, J., & Ordonez, C. (2010). Extended aggregations for databases with referential integrity issues. *Data & Knowledge Engineering, 69,* 73–95. doi:10.1016/j.datak.2009.08.008

Gardner, S. R. (1998). Building the Data Warehouse. *Communications of the ACM, 41*(9). doi:10.1145/285070.285080

Georgieva, T. (2008). Discovering Branching and Fractional Dependencies in Databases. *Data & Knowledge Engineering, 66,* 311–325. doi:10.1016/j.datak.2008.04.002

Ghazal, A., Seid, D., Bhashyam, R., Crolotte, A., Koppuravuri, M., & Vinod, G. (2009), Dynamic Plan Generation for Parameterized Queries. In Proceedings of SIGMOD'09, Providence, RI, USA.

Golfarelli, M., Rizzi, S., & Cella, I. (2004). *Beyond data warehousing: what's next in business intelligence?* DOLAP.

Hanson, J. H., & Willshire, M. J. (1997), Modeling a faster data warehouse. International Database Engineering and Applications Symposium (IDEAS 1997).

Hill, G., & Ross, A. (2009). Reducing outer joins. *The VLDB Journal, 18,* 599–610. doi:10.1007/s00778-008-0110-5

Holze, M., & Ritter, N. (2007), Towards Workload Shift Detection and Prediction for Autonomic Databases. In Proceedings of PIKM'07, Lisbon, Portugal.

Hwang, D. H., & Kang, H. (2005). XML View Materialization with Deferred Incremental Refresh: the Case of a Restricted Class of Views. *Journal of Information Science and Engineering, 21,* 1083–1119.

Karakasidis, A., Vassiliadis, P., & Pitoura, E. (2005), ETL Queues for Active Data Warehousing. In Proceedings of the 2nd International Workshop on Information Quality in Information Systems, IQIS 2005, Baltimore, MD, USA.

Katic, N., Quirchmayr, G., Schiefer, J., Stolba, M., & Tjoa, A. M. (1998). *A Prototype Model for Data Warehouse Security Based on Metadata.* IEEE Xplore.

Kim, T., Kim, J., & Lcc, H. (2000). *A Metadata-Oriented Methodology for Building Data warehouse: A Medical Center Case.* Seoul, Korea: Informs & Korms.

Krompass, S., Kuno, H., Dayal, U., & Kemper, A. (2007), Dynamic Workload Management for Very Large Data Warehouses – Juggling Feathers and Bowling Balls. In Proceedings of the 33rd international conference on Very large data bases, Vienna, Austria, 1105-1115.

Krompass, S., Kuno, H., Wiener, J. L., Wilkinson, K., Dayal, U., & Kemper, A. (2009), Managing Long-Running Queries. In Proceedings of the 12th International Conference on Extending Database Technology: Advances in Database Technology, Saint Petersburg, Russia, 132-143.

Labio, W., Yang, J., Cui, Y., Garcia-Molina, H., & Widom, J. (2000), Performance issues in Incremental Warehouse Maintenance. In Proceedings of the VLDB, Cairo, Egypt.

Lam, K., & Lee, V. C. S. (2006). On Consistent Reading of Entire Databases. *IEEE Transactions on Knowledge and Data Engineering, 18*(4).

Lee, K. Y., & Kim, M. H. (2005), Optimizing the Incremental Maintenance of Multiple Join Views. In Proceedings of the 8th ACM International Workshop on Data Warehousing and OLAP (DOLAP'05), Bremen, Germany.

Lee, K. Y., Son, J. H., & Kim, M. H. (2001), Efficient Incremental View Maintenance in Data Warehouses. In Proceedings of the Tenth International Conference on Information and Knowledge Management (CIKM'01), Atlanta, Georgia, USA.

Liu, B., Chen, S., & Rundensteiner, E. A. (2002), Batch Data Warehouse Maintenance in Dynamic Environments. In CIKM'02, 68-75.

Martin, P., & Powley, W. (2007), An Approach to Managing the Execution of Large SQL Queries. In Proceedings of the 2007 conference of the center for advanced studies on Collaborative research, Richmond Hill, Ontario, Canada, 268 - 271.

Mohania, M., & Kambayashi, Y. (2000). Making Aggregate Views Self-Maintainable. *Journal of Data and Knowledge Engineering, 32*(1), 87–109. doi:10.1016/S0169-023X(99)00016-6

Payton, F. & Handfield, R. (2004, Spring), Strategies for Data Warehousing. MIT Sloan Management Review.

Powley, W., Martin, P., & Bird, P. (2008), DBMS Workload Control using Throttling: Experimental Insights. In Proceedings of the 2008 conference of the center for advanced studies on collaborative research, Ontario, Canada.

Rahman, N. (2005), Intelligent Metadata Model in a Teradata Warehousing Environment. The 2005 Teradata PARTNERS User Group Conference and Expo, Orlando, FL, USA.

Rahman, N. (2007). Refreshing Data Warehouses with Near Real-Time Updates. *Journal of Computer Information Systems, 47*(3), 71–80.

Ram, P., & Do, L. (2000), Extracting Delta for Incremental Data Warehouse Maintenance. In Proceedings of the 16th International Conference on Data Engineering, San Diego, CA.

Rami, R., & Nabila, B. A. (2002), Query-based Data Warehousing Tool. ACM Fifth International Workshop on Data Warehousing and OLAP (DOLAP 2002) McLean, VA, USA.

Schwarz, H., Wagner, R., & Mitschang, B. (2001), Improving the Processing of Decision Support Queries: The Case for a DSS Optimizer. In proceedings of the International Database Engineering & Applications Symposium. (IDEAS '01).

Sharaf, M. A., & Chrysanthis, P. K. (2009), Optimizing I/O-Intensive Transactions in Highly Interactive Applications. In Proceedings of the 35th SIGMOD international conference on Management of data, Providence, Rhode Island, USA, 785-798.

Shin, B. (2003). An Exploratory Investigation of System Success Factors in Data Warehousing. *Journal of the Association for Information Systems, 4*, 141–170.

Simitsis, A., Vassiliadis, P., & Sellis, T. (2005), Optimizing ETL Processes in Data Warehouses. In Proceedings of the 21st International Conference on Data Engineering (ICDE'05).

Soror, A. A., Minhas, U. F., & Aboulnaga, A. (2008), Automatic Virtual Machine Configuration for Database Workloads. In Proceedings of the 2008 ACM SIGMOD international conference on Management of data, Vancouver, Canada, 953-966.

Stedman, C. (1998). Warehousing Projects Hard to Finish. *Computerworld, 32*(12), 29.

Storey, V. C., & Goldstein, R. C. (1993). Knowledge-Based Approaches to Database Design. *Management Information Systems Quarterly, 17*(1), 25–46. doi:10.2307/249508

Taufer, M., Stricker, T., & Weber, R. (2002), Scalability and Resource Usage of an OLAP Benchmark on Clusters of PCs. In Proceedings of SPAA'02, Winnipeg, Manitoba, Canada.

Weill W., Subramani, M. & Broadbent, M. (2002, Fall), Building IT Infrastructure for Strategic Agility. MIT Sloan Management Review.

Widom, J. (1995), Research Problems in Data Warehousing. In proceedings of the 4th Int'l Conference on Information and Knowledge Management (CIKM).

Wixom, B. H., & Watson, H. J. (2001). An Empirical Investigation of the Factors Affecting Data Warehousing Success. *Management Information Systems Quarterly, 25*(1), 17–41. doi:10.2307/3250957

Yan, J. (2006). Effective and Efficient Dimensionality Reduction for Large-Scale and Streaming Data In Preprocessing. *IEEE Transactions on Knowledge and Data Engineering, 18*(3).

Zhang, M., Martin, P., & Powley, W. (2008), Using Economic Models to Allocate Resources in Database Management Systems. In Proceedings of the 2008 conference of the center for advanced studies on collaborative research, Ontario, Canada.

Zhuge, Y., García-Molina, H., Hammer, J., & Widom, J. (1995), View Maintenance in a Warehousing Environment. In Proceedings of the 1995 ACM SIGMOD International Conference on Management of Data (SIGMOD'95), San Jose, CA USA.

Zhuge, Y., Wiener, J. L., & Garcia-Molina, H. (1997), Multiple View Consistency for Data Warehousing. In Proceedings of the Thirteenth International Conference on Data Engineering, Birmingham U.K.

This work was previously published in International Journal of Technology Diffusion, Volume 1, Issue 2, edited by Ali Hussein Saleh Zolait, pp. 42-55, copyright 2010 by IGI Publishing (an imprint of IGI Global).

Chapter 10
Internet Adoption from Omani Organizations' Perspective:
Motivations and Reservations

Khamis Al-Gharbi
Sultan Qaboos University, Sultanate of Oman

Ahlam Abdullah AlBulushi
Sultanate of Oman

ABSTRACT

In this paper, to the authors determine the motivations and reservations for Internet/E-business adoption within the organizations in Oman. For this purpose, questionnaires were used to collect the data from the organizations that have adopted Internet and the organizations that have not adopted Internet applications. The results and analysis of the data show that the main reasons for adopting Internet applications in Oman are to simplify process, improve communication with staff, keep up with competitors, and reduce the use of paper. The lack of skill and security problems is the main reservation for not adopting the Internet.

INTRODUCTION

"The Internet is an extremely important new technology, and it is no surprise that it has received so much attention from entrepreneurs, executives, investors and business observers" (Porter, 2001, p. 1). While the Internet and the World Wide Web (www) as mainstream communication tools have been widely used throughout the world by various organizations (Kula & Tatoglu, 2003, p. 324), some others are as Sadowski noted, "barely

interested in adopting Internet" (Kula & Tatoglu, 2003, p. 325). Those organizations have got different reasons and aspects in order to adopt Internet application or not.

The purpose of this study is to explore the adoption and non adoption of the Internet and e-business applications in Oman through a sample of organizations that have adopted Internet and others that have not. Drawing on the reasons that drives an organization to adopt/not adopt Internet, the benefits and opportunities that they gain through it and what are the challenges that may prevents an organization to adopt Internet application.

DOI: 10.4018/978-1-4666-1752-0.ch010

LITERATURE REVIEW

Internet /E-Business

Using the Internet or the "Global Network" (Kula & Tatoglu, 2003, p. 324), is one of the opportunities arising from the increase of the electronic communications through the different applications of information technology Since the growth of the usage of the Internet through the globe passed 1 billon for the first time in 2006 (Chaffey, 2007, p. 4), many of the of the business have adopted their process using Internet through Electronic business and Electronic commerce.

E-business is about conducting business electronically over the Internet which could include different activities such as communication, marketing, and collaboration (Navarroa et al., 2007) and E-business as Plessis & Boon emphasized is about creating an electronic Internet-based platform to allow customers, suppliers, and employees to collaborate with one other through the sharing of data, information and knowledge (Navarroa et al., 2007).

In addition, as Johnston noted, the knowledge regarding implementing E-business or adopting Internet in general are very important to an organization since the **e**-business is the result of a virtual interaction between an organization and its partners (Navarroa et al., 2007). Although **e**-business provides organizational members with a better understanding of the market they are playing in; as Tolman noted, very little is achieved if they do not link these understandings with the thoughts that an individual has about a particular situation or problem of interest (Navarroa et al., 2007).

Reasons and Benefits of Adopting Internet

There has been substantial managerial interest in opportunities to use e-business technologies (Sanders, 2007) for many reasons. First of all, to create competitive advantage (Sanders, 2007)

through adopting new technologies (Chen et al., 2006). Cost reduction of the transactions is another reason for adopting Internet since most of the services would be provided with lower cost (Sanders, 2007; Chen et al., 2006).

In addition, as Boon & Ganeshan noted, e-Business technologies are digitally enabled and information technologies are used to accomplish business processes (Chen et al., 2006) by simplifying these process and reducing paper work, which result in time saving as well money. Moreover, they adopt Internet in order to increase and have greater knowledge about IT and participation in IS planning (Chen et al., 2006). One of the Important reason is to improve communication with staffs, customers, suppliers and other partner (Kula & Tatoglu, 2003).

Many organizations have gain many benefits through adopting Internet. For Instance, adopting Internet result in increasing sales and grate cost reduction (Lancioni et al., 2003) including Supply, marketing and administrative cost in many organization. In addition, it enhance the organization and business image among other competitors. Moreover, the Internet offers direct links with customers, suppliers and distributors and facilitates transactions, processes and information transfer through them.

Internet adoption enables companies to develop new products and services for existing and new customers and it offers opportunities for the companies to market their products around the world without physically contacting customers or advertising in other parts of the world as Karakaya observed. (Kula & Tatoglu, 2003) Another potential benefits of e-business technologies include, improved the speed and flexibility, higher customer service levels (Sanders, 2007) and Organizational collaboration and information sharing, in turn, are expected to improve organizational performance (Sanders, 2007).

Reasons and Challenges for Not Adopting Internet

As many companies around the world have adopted Internet to gain different advantages, many others still did not adopt internet usage in the organization for many reasons. One of the important reasons toward not adopting Internet is the lack of technical resource in the organization including the financial and technical resource. In addition, it requires a careful assessment of the needs and capabilities of the organization as well as the formulation of cost-effective adoption strategies (Chen et al., 2006).

Moreover, the lack of skill and knowledge in the organization is another reason as (10) emphasized that basic skills of workforces are an element of competitiveness for organizations because basic skills encompass personal development, occupational skills, and IT skills. Furthermore, as Chen et al. (2003) suggested that "IT skill set is one of the factors affecting adoption and diffusion of innovations for e-business systems" (Chen et al., 2006). Many of the companies concerned about security and protection issue as will as the difficulty of integrating IT systems.

Background on Oman

The Sultanate of Oman is a developing country, which is located on the south east of the Arabian Peninsula. Sultanate of Oman is the second largest country among the Gulf states after Saudi Arabia. It is spread over 309,500 square kilometres and has a 1,700-kilometre coastline. Since the accession of Sultan Qabbos in 1970 to the throne, there has been remarkable progress in different fields such as economy, politics, education, and the civil services. The modernization and restructuring of the administrative systems of the civil service as a result of the continuous progress have been vital in term of the changing circumstances and future requirements. The Sultanate of Oman enjoys a stable political, economic, and social system. Although Oman has achieved remarkable progress, both socially and economically with implementation of five-year Development plan, the country is watching closely the new challenges facing the country as the fluctuation of the oil prices. The country is sparsely populated with 8.6 inhabitants per kms. Oman has 2.7 million people. A very strong feature of the country is its young population; about 50% of the population is below the age of 15 years. According to the Ministry of National Economy – Oman (April, 2008), Oman's GDP has reached OMR 13,737 million in 2006. Oman's currency is the Rial (OMR) which is about USA $2.60 per unit.

ICT Sector in Oman

According to the United Nation 2008 E-Government Readiness Report, Oman has jumped up to 28 points in this ranking position from 112th position in 2005 to 84th position in 2008. Oman ranks 60th position in the E-participation Index (out of 192 countries) with an index value of 0.2045 (www.ameinfo.com). The number of Internet subscribers and mobile subscribers are rising dramatically over the past few years (Naqvi & Al-Shihi, 2009). According to the ministry of national economy- Oman (2008) statistical bulletin, the number of Internet subscribers is over 2.6 millions in 2007.

This rise is a reflection of "the pace of progress through initiatives' to build of ICT infrastructure, over electronic services and build capacity within the country to harness the power of technology" remarked by CEO of ITA.

Research Methodology

This research has been aimed at revealing the managerial expectations and attitudes towards adopting and not adopting Internet in the private organization in Oman. To obtain adequate information on these factors, a survey questionnaire was constructed drawing upon the prior literature reviewed and discussions.

The questionnaire was designed as two parts. The first part of the questionnaire was designed for the organization that have adopted Internet and E-business application and the second part was designed for the companies that have not adopted Internet.

The Questionnaires were sent to 15 organizations in Oman selected randomly. Only 7 questionnaires were returned, where the data shows that the large organizations 2 of the 7(about 28.5%) have more concern in adopting Internet.

Main Finding

Figure 1 shows that the main reasons for adopting Internet in the organizations in Oman are to simplify process, improve communication with staff, keep up with competitive and reduce paper. This is due the fact that the Omani organizations have lack of resources and are focusing on gain-ing advantages through the reducing the cost of application and transaction through less paper work and increasing the efficiency of the organization through enhancing the communication with the staff and external customers. In fact, that the cost and the efficiency is an important reason for Internet adoption.

Among the companies that adopted Internet they using an E-Marketing application and Customer relation management activities while none of them use supply chain management, secure on line ordering and e-auction as shown in Figure 2.

Figure 3 indicate that the main benefits for the organization which have adopted internet is the administrative cost reduction which a direct result of simplifying the business process and minimizing the scope of paper work. In addition the fact that the organizations want to built and enhances its image among the others. Increasing sales is one of the important benefits of adopting Internet as well as the other benefits.

Figure 1. Reasons for adopting Internet in Oman

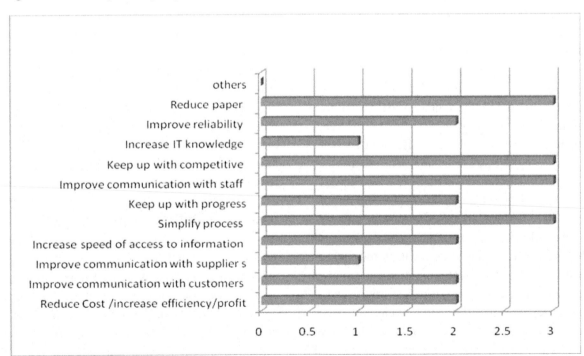

Figure 2. Internet /E-Business application

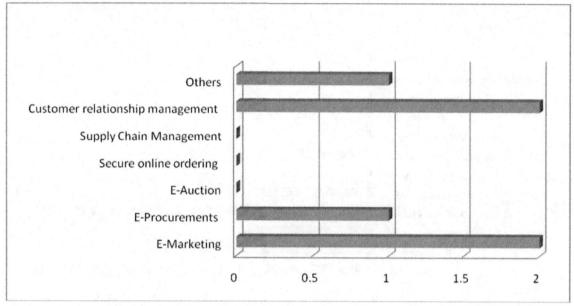

Figure 3. Benefits of adopting Internet in Oman

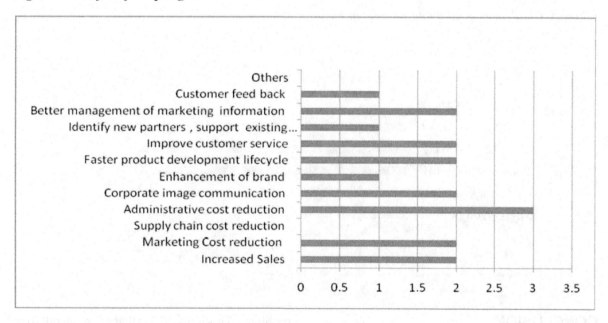

On the other hand, Figure 4 shows that the main reason for not adopting Internet is the set up cost. This is among the small organization with little resources while the other reason is the lack of skills among the staff. For some organization, system Integration and lack of knowledge play a big role for not adopting Internet application in an organization.

It is clear from Figure 5 that the main challenge in adopting internet in Oman is the issue of security problems and the lack of skills among the staff.

Figure 4. Reasons for not adopting Internet in Oman

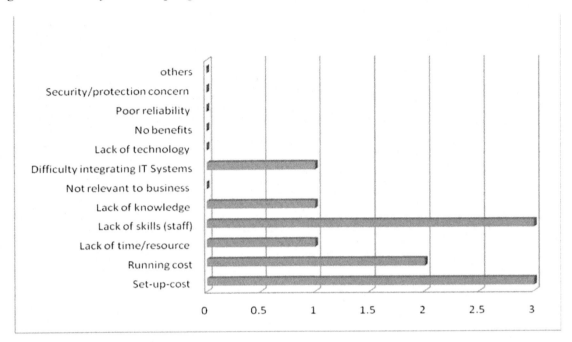

Figure 5. Challenges in adopting Internet in Oman

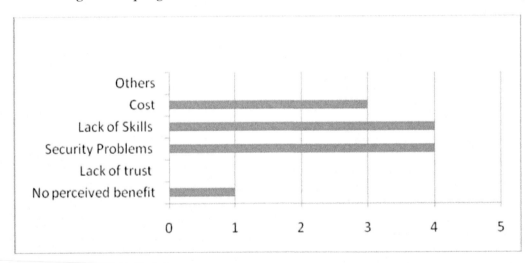

CONCLUSION

This paper found that the main reasons in adopting the Internet in Oman is the term of simplify process, improve communication with staff, keep up with competitive and reduce paper. In addition, the main challenge and reasons for not adopting Internet is the lack of skills of the staff and security problems. This is due to fact that adopting internet relay on the knowledge and skills of the staff to achieve the aimed benefits in adopting Internet. Due to the emergence of the Internet and Information technology in Oman many organization will enter the world of the new technology of the internet in the coming years.

REFERENCES

Chaffey, D. (2007). *E-Business and E-Commerce Management* (p. 4). Upper Saddle River, NJ: Prentice Hall.

Chen, A., Sena, S., & Shaoa, B. (2006). Strategies for effective Web services adoption for dynamic e-businesses. *Decision Support Systems, 42*(2), 789–809. doi:10.1016/j.dss.2005.05.011

Kula, V., & Tatoglu, E. (2003). An exploratory study of Internet adoption by SMEs in an emerging market economy. *European Business Review, 15*, 324–333. doi:10.1108/09555340310493045

Lancioni, R., Schau, H., & Smith, M. (2003). Internet impacts on supply chain management. *Industrial Marketing Management, 32*(3), 173–175. doi:10.1016/S0019-8501(02)00260-2

Ministry of National Econmy-Oman. (2008, April). *Monthly statistically bulletin, 19*(4).

Murnane, L. (n.d.). *E-Commerce and Internet Taxation*. Retrieved September 30, 2007 from http://www.infotoday.com

Naqvis. S. J., & AL-Shihi, H. (2009). M-Government Services Initiatives' in Oman. *Issue in Informing Science and Information Technology, 6.*

Navarroa, J., Jiménezb, D., & Conesac, E. (2007). Implementing e-business through organizational learning: An empirical investigation in SMEs. *International Journal of Information Management, 27*(3), 173–186. doi:10.1016/j.ijinfomgt.2007.01.001

Oman IT Executive Committee. (2002-2003) *Report, Sultanate of Oman.*

Porter, M. (2001, March). *Strategy and the Internet* (pp. 1-19). Boston, MA: Harvard Business Review.

Sanders, N. (2007). An empirical study of the impact of e-business technologies on organizational collaboration and performance. *Journal of Operations Management, 25*(6), 1332–1347. doi:10.1016/j.jom.2007.01.008

Wang, T., & Tadisina, S. (2007). Simulating Internet-based collaboration: A cost-benefit case study using a multi-agent model. *Decision Support Systems, 43*(2), 645–662. doi:10.1016/j.dss.2005.05.020

This work was previously published in International Journal of Technology Diffusion, Volume 1, Issue 2, edited by Ali Hussein Saleh Zolait, pp. 56-61, copyright 2010 by IGI Publishing (an imprint of IGI Global).

Chapter 11

Electronic Training Methods:
Relative Effectiveness and Frequency of Use in the Malaysian Context

Veeriah Sinniah
University of Malaya, Malaysia

Sharan Kaur
University of Malaya, Malaysia

ABSTRACT

This study comparatively examines the relative effectiveness and frequency of use of modern and conventional training methods, as much rhetoric has surrounded the use of techniques like distance learning and computer-based training methods. The responses from 200 employees suggest that no significant difference exists with respect to frequency of use, but a significant difference exists in terms of effectiveness. The result shows that on-the-job training (OJT) methods are widely used and are perceived as the most effective method, whereas distance learning is not widely used because it is perceived as less effective. This study also reveals that a significant difference exists between modern training methods and conventional training methods in terms of attaining training objectives. OJT is given the highest rating for attaining training objectives.

INTRODUCTION

A nation's competitiveness depends, to a great extent, on the quality of its human resources. The productivity of its workforce, the ability to learn, relearn, acquire new skills and competencies and the commitment to excellence will inevitably enhance national competitiveness. Thus, Malaysia continues to focus on improving its workforce through constant training and lifelong learning to stay competitive.

Investment in corporate training in Malaysia, which aims to build a world class workforce, has been given greater emphasis in the Ninth Malaysia Plan (2006-2010). The government has allocated RM 4792.6 million (Ninth Malaysian Plan 2006-2010) for corporate training, and this includes industrial, commercial and management

DOI: 10.4018/978-1-4666-1752-0.ch011

trainings, hence increasing the supply of educated and skilled human resource to support the expansion of education and training institutions.

The emphasis given by the government on corporate training is obvious due to its effect, direct or indirect on both employee motivation and organizational commitment (Meyer & Allen, 1991). Some organizations, planning for the long-term, invest in the development of new skills for their employees, so as to enable them to handle issues not currently present, but likely to come up in the future. Hence, the purpose of this study is to close the gap of employee's perceived effectiveness with respect to training methods used in the relevant literature, shedding more light into the relationship of perceived training effectiveness with regards to training methods. This study replicates the study by Sadler-Smith et al. (2000), also intends to explore the perceptions of management level employees to some of the 'modern' training methods and other more 'traditional' approaches employed in management training; as there is a gap between the rhetoric surrounding the supposed value of these methods, and the reality in terms of outcomes.

Learning and Development professionals have been faced with a number of challenges regarding the training and development of staff namely, increased numbers of employees to train; increased complexity in the type of work employees are required to perform (and the tools used at work); pressure on employees to learn and demonstrate new competencies faster and at a higher level; rapid changes in the business environment and limited funding to achieve all of the above. Many organizations have turned to modern methods of delivery which do not rely on conventional face-to-face contact between trainer and trainee. Companies are exploring the use of "e-Learning" courses, such as web-based, intranet-based, and CD-based training delivery systems to cut expenses and reduce their reliance on travel (Juptner, 2001). Today the level of development of computer-based training materials has risen dramatically as a consequence of the new and exciting opportunities provided by the World Wide Web (www).

New training delivery methods continue to expand because of the growth of the computing technology, increased information technology competencies, and reduced barriers to accessing and using the Internet. Effective strategies for technology-based training and instruction should focus on building virtual learning communities, making the technologies used to mediate communication as seamless and transparent as possible in order to efficiently and effectively reach as many learners as possible.

Today, the application of technology in both its "hard" (for example through computing technology) and "soft" (for example through instructional design) forms has enhanced the range of training methods available to practitioners. Many organizations have turned to modern methods of delivery. However, much rhetoric has surrounded the use of techniques such as distance learning and computer-based methods. Consequently, the purpose of this study is to explore the perceptions of employees to these "modern" training methods as compared to other more "conventional" training methods.

In reality the training methods used today are not so new-they are simply a better application of proven practices. Basically, organizations rely on the same fundamental training methods they have used; the instructional procedure and the discussion or conference procedure. If training practitioners indeed have responded to the exhortations of government and other attractive proponents of modern methods, it is argued that these should have been embraced, absorbed into the training mainstream and furthermore ought to have demonstrated their effectiveness. As such, this study will attempt to investigate the relative effectiveness of a number of different training delivery methods and their frequency of use based on employees' perspectives. Furthermore, an increasingly important issue is the relevance of particular training methods or approaches to small and medium sized organizations. Many of the researches have evolved from a large organizations' perspective of training and development and did not perceive the support of small organizations' training as part of their main role. One challenge for small organizations is reconciling modern training methods with the disparate needs of organizations. Thus, this study attempts to explore any significant differences in perceived effectiveness and frequency of use of training methods between small and large organizations.

The current study was undertaken to assess how employees perceive the relative effectiveness of alternative training methods to attain specific types of training objectives, whereby a part of this study is a replication of a research by Carroll et al. (1972). This study is important for two reasons. First, by comparing a number of training methodologies that are available today, insight may be gained as to alternative methods for effective and efficient management training delivery methods in the corporate environment. Identifying alternative modern training methods beyond the traditional instructor-led training method could greatly benefit Malaysian organizations.

Organizations need a training delivery method that achieves both transfer of training and reduction in travel costs. At the same time, the training method should be convenient and relevant for the learner, cost effective for the employer and motivational in helping the learner transfer skills and knowledge to the work environment. Thus, this study suggested that the challenge for HR practice is to successfully utilize and integrate modern and traditional methods, so as to build on the strengths of each and meet the needs of learners and businesses.

Secondly, this study is important because existing research and literature, in the Malaysian context, firmly establish the importance of workforce training, but what remains commonly debated is which forms of training and delivery methods are most effective. Most prevalent in this debate is the argument over choosing between traditional face-to-face training and that of emerging modern technology-based methods (which includes: Computer-based training, e-learning, On-line training, Web-based training, Distance Learning and Tele-training).

DEFINITION OF TRAINING

There appears to be various definitions of training. Some authors view training as activities or processes that provide individuals with the necessary skills to perform the duties required of their positions (Gomez-Mejia et al., 2004; Welber & Feinberg, 2002). Belcourt (2002) describe training as "any effort initiated by an organization to foster learning among its members" (p. 209). For the context of this study the researcher used the definition of Stolovitch and Keeps (2004) who believe training to be "structured activities focused on getting people to consistently reproduce behaviours without variation, but with increasingly greater efficiency (automatically) even if conditions around them change" (p. 5).

Most authors agree that the purpose of training is to generate a change in learners which is consistently reproduced without variation (Belcourt, 2002; Gomez-Mejia et al., 2004; Stolovitch & Keeps, 2004). This change in learners is generated through effective training programs. The most effective training programs are those that have a multi-perspective approach to instruction delivery (Belcourt, 2002; Granak et al., 2006). Companies need to structure their "training programs so that employees earn the greatest possible benefit from the training, thus benefiting the organization" (Whalen, 1997 p. 24).

MODERN TRAINING METHODS

There has been a tremendous increase and improvement in the use of electronic media to train management and most companies refer to this type of training as self-directed and distance learning programs or e-learning. "Self-directed learning refers both to the ability of learners to tailor training programs to their needs, and to the performance support tools developed for these learners. Distance learning is applied to materials and media that allow these learners to learn at a distance away for the source of expertise" (Harrison, 1998, p. 23). This training encompasses a wide range of different media: video and audio tools; computer based training; multimedia CD-ROM tools; intranet or Internet-based delivery; television delivery; as well as books, workbooks, and job aids.

Gloria Grey, known for her depth of knowledge in electronic means of instruction reminded corporate North America that the rapid advance of technology and the rapid depletion of an entry level skilled workforce, coupled with the removal of training and subject matter experts from direct contact with these workers, resulted in a crisis in performance for most work environment (1991). She made this strong statement in order to support the value of her proposal to use electronic performance support system to resolve this crisis.

Rossett (1996) listed some of the same factors that have driven corporations to look toward Electronic Performance Support Systems to meet training needs and two of the factors mentioned was "reengineering, … (which) has led to critical need for training provided through technology and nontraditional collaborations (and) … decentralization, which requires training to be as close as possible to where the work gets done" (p. 556-557).

Additional corporate factors listed by Rossett (1996) included less money for travel when training is needed most, which enforces the need for affordable desktop tools, training and systems that specify policies and perspectives and coach performance; improvement in technology which allows the ability to provide cost-effective training and support; and new integration of work

and support so that training can be embedded electronically within the workplace where the challenges and the customers reside.

COMPUTER-BASED TRAINING

In the early 1980's, it was the first time that computer- or "media–based instruction was able to take on the characteristics of a continuous dialogue between learner and program" (Craig, 1996, p. 540). The advantages include the potential to reduce the cost of training and/or increase the effectiveness of training, reduced cost: less student travel and living expenses, reduced length of training and more timely training (Dessler, 2008).

However, the 2001 Industry Report (Galvin, 2001) showed that the continued development of technology for computer based training had not significantly encouraged the increased use of it for training. "Telecommunications sector corporations reported that 76% still use Instructor led courses, 5% use remote Instructors (video and distance learning), 12% use Computer-based training, and 6% use other methods such as on-the-job, self-study manuals, or Videos" (p. 66).

WEB-BASED TRAINING

Compared to traditional training methods, web-based training features lower training development cost, simplify updating or material revision, and increase accessibility (Hall, 1997; Khan, 1997). Some advantages include developing training programs that can be accessed through the windows systems without requiring additional software as well as widely available internet connections and browsers. Moreover, most computer users have access to a browser, a company's intranet or the internet. Web-based training allows flexibility, accessibility and convenience. Trainees can do their training anytime, at any place, and at the amount they need. In other words, they control their training programs, hence making it cost effective and time saving. Travel costs will be eliminated because the internet can be accessed from any place. Another advantage is the ease of update. For example, when the training content needs to be updated, it can be done by simply uploading the changes to the server.

One disadvantage of web-based training, on the other hand, includes limited bandwidth. This limitation will affect the performance of sound, video, and graphics. In addition, web-based training takes more time with higher costs involved in developing it. Web-based training becomes a disadvantage when it requires learners to adapt to new methods. Moreover, in order to avoid a poor quality of content, it requires substantial infrastructure, which adds to the cost of training. However, Driscoll (1999) reported that "Web-based training has increased significantly with a projected growth rate of 95% between 1997 and 2002. Corporations were initially drawn to web-based instruction because of the cost savings as compared to centralized, instructor-led courses. Other strategic factors (that favour web-based training) include the ability to educate a global workforce, a reduction in turnaround from training to product deployment, an ability to meet continued training needs in a flattened organization with fewer job mentors, and an ability to meet the demand for technically skilled workers in a limited labor market" (pp. 21-22).

E-LEARNING

Some of the terms used to describe e-learning include computer-based training (CBT), technology-based training (TBT), online training, web-based training, multimedia-based training and distance training. With the exception of distance learning, Urdan and Weggen (2000) have commonly agreed with the interchangeable context of the various terms and they being collectively referred to as e-learning. Urdan considered e-learning a subset of distance learning. However, others purport that just-in-time learning is an advantage of e-learning but not of distance learning. Chute (1999) also included videoconferencing, teleconferencing, CDs, and corporate intranets as important e-learning mediums.

McCrea et al. (2000) also attributed the robust economy and the increasingly competitive global business environment as central to the e-learning movement. With the strategic importance of e-learning being unsurpassed by old corporate learning paradigms, the projected benefits are highly attractive. Urdan and Weggen (2000) stated that a higher retention of content through personalized learning is possible because technology-based (e-learning) solutions allow more room for individual differences in learning styles.

According to Chute et al. (1999), the potential financial savings associated with e-learning can be significant when compared to traditional methods of training. They stated that "e-learning can provide a cost-effective solution to the most demanding training and education needs by using acceptable media to deliver a variety training types" (Chute et al., 1999, pp. 81-88). A number of organizations also say that they have reduced training budgets by millions as a result of implementing e-learning programs. "Leading firms such as Motorola, MCI WorldCom, and Ford are already recognizing benefits associated with distributed learning" (Greengard, 1999).

COACHING

Coaching is a relatively new field in management training delivery, and it is not widely researched but the International Coach Federation reported a 100% growth in the field of coaching between 1996 and 2000 (Wilkins, 2000). According to Miller (2001), a recent survey found that coaching increased productivity for 53% of manager participants and quality for 48%. More importantly,

77% of managers said it had helped improve their working relationships with direct reports, and 71% said it had improved their relationship with their immediate supervisors. Coaching also impacted manager attitude, with 61% of managers reporting higher job satisfaction as a result of the coaching intervention.

Research suggests that the use of coaching after a traditional instructor-led training course is an effective way to increase skill retention and transfer of training (Showers, 1987). Showers studied the use of peer coaching to assist teachers transfer new knowledge acquired from an instructor-led teacher development workshop. The findings show that the participants retained and transferred 90% of the learnt skills when coaching was applied after training.

TRAINING IN SMALL AND MEDIUM SIZED ENTERPRISES (SMES)

Within SME research there are a number of studies examining the association of organizational characteristics with strategies, decision making, approaches to management and performance (see Carlson et al., 2006). In terms of training and development, however, empirical research is scarce. Although with the large firms, there is a great deal of consistent advice as to what managers should consider in the design and delivery of training interventions, there is lesser agreement as to what approaches can, and should, be adopted to ensure training success in SMEs.

Curran and Stanworth (1989, p. 18) highlighted the lack of research on the "character, availability and effectiveness" of small business education as being a weakness and argued that the assessment of training effectiveness in small firms is a major area for future work. Over the intervening decade there have been a number of important contributions to this debate (for example, Curran et al., 1989). However the distinctive nature of training in small firms has yet to be fully elucidated and the impact of newer training methods in small firms is largely unexplored from an empirical perspective.

A recent study by Jayawarna et al. (2007), suggest that the influences on training approach adopted by SMEs are likely to be influenced by specific firm characteristics (such as size), by product factors and market conditions (such as technology), and by the way responsibilities and management roles were apportioned (such as organizational structures). Previous research has also shown that family owned and operated firms often have different human resource management (HRM) strategies and commitment to training. For family businesses, HRM is a highly sensitive area, and improving the company knowledge base is not one of their business priorities. Matlay (2002) suggests that, in family businesses, HRM strategies tend to be reactive rather than proactive, and training is predominantly viewed as individual career development, which does not add value to the firm.

Sargeant (1996, p. 238) investigated the importance of a variety of factors influencing small firms' choice of external training provider. The physical location of the provider was significantly more important to small firms than to larger ones. Sargeant also compared the modes of training undertaken in large firms and SMEs: while the latter was less likely to undertake training.

Flexibility of delivery appears to be a crucial issue for smaller firms, to which open/distance/technology-based learning may present a viable solution. Curran and Stanworth (1989, p. 17) saw distance learning as an appropriate delivery mechanism for small businesses' " continuing education" since it could effectively overcome the barrier of the "resistance of small business owners to having any contact with formal educational institutions". Bassett-Jones (1991, p. 23) surveyed the use of different types of flexible learning media in a midlands' Training and Enterprise Council area. He found that "while large companies have been able to allocate resources to experiment with different modes of delivery, smaller companies find it more difficult and are reluctant to invest in innovation (in training delivery)". The higher the initial set up costs (for example, for computer-based methods and interactive video) the less likely it was that smaller firms would make this initial investment, irrespective of how appropriate such media are.

DEVELOPMENT OF HYPOTHESES

Training methods are the independent variable (applied to each hypothesis) consisting of seven different delivery methods. The methods were compared across each other and across firms' size to determine which method or methods demonstrated the greatest indications of effectiveness.

Whilst company commitment to training positively affects employee retention and leads to desirable outputs, there are many different categories and types of training (Switzer & Kleiner, 1996; Huang, 2001). To have positive results, organizational commitment, for example, must be closely related to appropriate effective training methods and training delivery mechanisms. In terms of training methodologies, what may be appropriate for one company (or employee) may not be for another company.

The use of technology-based training continues to increase worldwide with a wider adoption as technology deals with problems such as bandwidth limitations, technology costs and quality of content. Much of the content of the available literature concentrates on the advantages of modern learning methods. These are based around two main themes – the cost advantages and flexibility in delivery. The cost advantages centre on reduced training time, the costs saved in travel and time away from the job and the ability to serve large numbers at one time, or over time, with relatively little additional cost. Therefore, organizations with an understanding of the value in developing employees are more likely to invest in such

training-related technology, thus, the following hypothesis was developed to attest frequency of use among the Malaysian sample:

H1: There is a significant difference between modern and conventional training methods in terms of frequency of use.

Recent years have seen the range of training methods available to practitioners greatly enhanced through developments in the fields of instructional design and in computing and communications technologies. Many organizations have turned to modern methods of delivery hence modern methods have been acclaimed internationally. For example, in America, some organizations (including AT&T, Ford Motor Company, Intel Corporation, Aetna Life & Casualty and the US Government) have already seized opportunities that have placed them on the leading edge of successfully integrating technology into work-force training programs. These companies also are considered trend-setters when it comes to using high technology-based training ''(Leonard, 1996). Therefore, the following hypothesis is formed to determine the difference in effectiveness perceived by the sample:

H2: There is a significant difference between modern and conventional training methods in terms of effectiveness.

Bassett-Jones (1991, p. 23) surveyed the use of different types of flexible learning media in a midlands' Training and Enterprise Council area. He found that "while large companies have been able to allocate resources to experiment with different modes of delivery, smaller companies find it more difficult and are reluctant to invest in innovation [in training delivery]". The higher the initial set up costs (for example, for computer-based methods and interactive video) the less likely it was that smaller firms would make this initial investment, irrespective of how appropriate such media are, thus the third hypothesis:

H3: There is a significant difference between small firms, medium-sized and large firms in their use of training methods.

Carroll et al. (1971) conducted a study on the relative effectiveness of different training methods (Carroll et al., 1972). The study was designed to determine which training methods were best suited for different training objectives. Results of the study are reported in virtually all major human resources management texts in spite of the fact that the study is now over 30 years old. In 2000, two researchers replicated the study (Perdue & Woods, 2000) and a part of this study is a replication of the research by Carroll et al. (1972). The current study was undertaken to assess how employees perceive the relative effectiveness of alternative training methods to attain specific types of training objectives, in which case the following hypothesis was developed:

H4: There is a significant difference between modern training methods and conventional training methods in terms of attaining training objectives.

RESEARCH METHODOLOGY

This research provided the researcher with an opportunity to review the modern learning and training methods using a quantitative framework. In developing of hypotheses, training methods were the independent variable consisting of seven different delivery methods. The methods were compared across each other and across firms' size to determine which method or methods demonstrated the greatest indications of effectiveness.

In order to measure employees' perceptions towards training delivery methods, a self-reported data collection instrument was used to collect data in this study, and each respondent was asked to complete a questionnaire. The choice and adoption of the survey questionnaire items were based on the literature review and the purpose of this study. The survey had 46- items in four sections to test the research questions.

Training practices and methods were adopted from Sadler-Smith et al. (2000) while items relating to training objectives were adopted from Carroll et al. (1972). The first part of the questionnaire consisted of training practices which includes training needs analysis, design, delivery and evaluation. The second part of the questionnaire, which included seven training and development methods, was used to identify the relative effectiveness and frequency of use based on employees' perspectives. The third part of the questionnaire, which included seven training methods and five general training objectives, examined the relative effectiveness of training methods for achieving each of the five training objectives and these were scored as follows: very effective (5), effective (4), neutral (3), ineffective (2), and very ineffective (1). The final part of the questionnaire was the demographic profile.

The seven training methods used in this study are: Off-site Courses, On-site Courses, On-the-job training methods, Videos training methods, Distance learning, Computer-based methods and Coaching. In all of the construct ratings, five alternative degrees were put in order of Likert type scales.

Three hundred questionnaires were distributed to management level employees across different business sectors. Most of the respondents of this study were MBA part-students and employees who were working in different organizations and including employees at several government departments. Out of the 300 questionnaires distributed, 254 questionnaires were returned. However, 54 questionnaires were unacceptable because of various reasons such as partially complete or failed to follow instructions, so the total useable questionnaires were 200, hence giving a response rate of 66.67%. In order to analyze the research questions, the researcher applied the Statistical package for the Social Science (SPSS: version 15.0) in this study. The data analysis techniques included descriptive statistics, Pearson correlation, paired t-test, independent t-test, one way ANOVA and cross tabulation.

RESULTS

The demographic data of respondents were composed of: (a) gender (44% male and 56% female); (b) age (The majority age group was 26 to 30 years old at 44.3% followed by 31 to 35 years old at 25.1%); (c) ethnic background of respondents (35% Malays, 30% Chinese, and 24.1% Indians); (d) level of education (majority of the respondents have a bachelor's degree (67.5%); (e) employment duration (almost half of the employees were employed more than 1 year and up to 5 years at 48.7%); and (f) job position (senior executives or executives at 52.7% followed by managers at 32.0%).

. The majority of employees were from the service sector (57%) followed by manufacturing and construction sectors with equal representations of 21.5% respectively. With regards to the size of the firms, the number of respondents from less than 250 employees (regarded as small firms in this study) was 57.5% and large firms with more than 250 employees were 42.5%.

Construct reliability was evaluated using Cronbach's alpha with a score of .91 for training practices, .87 for training methods and the Cronbach alpha for training objectives was .90. The descriptive analysis conducted on training practices of organizations revealed that systematic training processes were well managed as most of the respondents stated each stage as important or very important. Almost more than half of the respondents stated training needs analysis, training design, training intervention, and training evaluation were important to their respective organizations.

Hypothesis 1 proposed a significant difference exists between modern training methods and conventional training methods in terms of frequency of use, however, the result showed that no significant difference exists between modern training methods (M=10.86, SD= 3.717) and conventional training methods (M= 10.91, SD=2.152) in terms of the frequency of use ($t =$ 1.146, df =199, p=.884). Therefore hypothesis 1 was not supported.

The analysis of data for frequency of use indicated that instructional-led conventional methods such as off-site courses and on-the-job training (OJT) ranked higher than modern technology-based methods. The frequency of use for OJT was 62.84%, off-site courses scored 61.85% and on-site courses are at 55.88%. For infrequent ratings, distance learning scored the highest at 47.48% (lowest mean) and this is followed by coaching at 35.85%.

Hypothesis 2 hypothesized that a significant difference exists between modern and conventional training methods in terms of effectiveness. The t-test result indicated that there is a significant difference between modern training methods (M=11.06, SD= 2.114) and conventional training methods (M= 12.09, SD=3.182) in terms of effectiveness (t = -4.257, df =199, p=.000). Therefore H2 was supported.

The data revealed that off-site courses, on-site courses and OJT, which were regarded as conventional training methods, scored higher percentages on effectiveness. OJT was the most preferred, with more than 75% (highest mean and lowest standard deviations) perceived it as effective or very effective, and ranked second was off-site courses with nearly 60%. Surprisingly, modern methods such as distance learning, computer-based, and coaching (including tele-coaching) were rated high on ineffectiveness. Computer-based ranked the most ineffective at 31.43% and followed by distance learning at 30.77%.

The correlations between frequency of use and effectiveness for conventional training methods revealed that there were significant correlations

($p < 0.01$). For OJT, the correlation between frequency of use (CF3) and effectiveness (CE3) ($r = .50, p < .01$) clearly indicated that those respondents who perceived the conventional training methods effective also used them frequently.

Analysis of data for correlations between frequency of use and effectiveness for modern training methods revealed that there were significant correlations ($p < 0.01$), which clearly indicated that those respondents who perceived the modern training methods effective also used them frequently. For example, the correlation between the frequency of use and effectiveness of computer-based training revealed an *r* value of .66 ($p < .01$).

Hypothesis 3 proposed that small firms (<250 employees) and large firms (>250employees) differ in their use of training methods. The t-test result shows that small firms (M=3.81, SD= .936) and large firms (M=3.85, SD=.982) are significantly not different in their use of OJT, (t = -.281, df = 198, p=.779). hence, the hypothesis was not supported.

In case of any significant differences between small and large firms in their perceived effectiveness with respect to OJTs, the t-test result shows that small firms (M=4.00, SD= .688) and large firms (M=4.11, SD=.817) are not significantly different in their perceived effectiveness of OJT, t = -.993, df = 198, p=.322).

According to the results, the off-site courses, on-site courses and OJT were used frequently or very frequently by all organizations. OJT reported to be the highest ranked with 70.43% for small organizations, and 70.59% for large organizations.

Over three quarters of all organizations reported OJT as effective or very effective: 82.60% of small organizations, and 82.35% of large organizations. Distance learning rated highest for ineffectiveness by all organizations, followed by computer-based training. Data revealed that 34.78% of small organizations and 44.71% of large organizations reported distance learning as ineffective or very ineffective and that there were no significant differences with respect to size of the organizations. The ANOVA results in Table 1

Table 1. Levene's test and One-Way ANOVA test results for firms' size and use of training methods

	Levene's Test	Variance source	Sum of Squares	df	Mean square	F	Sig.
Off-site Courses	1.68	Between Groups Within Groups Total	2.69 185.27 187.96	2 197 199	1.34 .94	1.43	.24
On-site Courses	.26	Between Groups Within Groups Total	.17 176.98 177.16	2 197 199	.09 .90	.10	.91
OJT	.47	Between Groups Within Groups Total	.22 180.66 180.88	2 197 199	.11 .97	.12	.89
Videos	.22	Between Groups Within Groups Total	2.13 250.22 252.36	2 197 199	1.07 1.03	.84	.43
Distance Learning	3.98	Between Groups Within Groups Total	2.06 278.82 280.88	2 197 199	1.03 1.42	.73	.49
Computer-based	2.89	Between Groups Within Groups Total	2.02 251.74 254.36	2 197 199	1.31 1.28	1.02	.36
Coaching	.79	Between Groups Within Groups Total	.66 239.56 240.22	2 197 199	.33 1.22	.27	.76

indicated no significant difference between size of firms in the use of training methods.

The final hypothesis hypothesized that a significant difference exists between modern training methods and conventional training methods in terms of attaining training objectives. In determining which training methods were most effective for attaining training objectives, respondents rated OJT as the highest for all training objectives, except for changing attitudes, coaching and OJT scored the same mean ($M_{Coaching}$ = 3.89, $SD_{Coaching}$ = .89; M_{OJT} = 3.88, SD_{OJT} = .85). As expected, distance learning was perceived as the least effective method for achieving training objectives ($M_{Distance\ Learning-Knowledge\ Acquisition}$ = 2.81, $M_{Distance\ Learning-Changing\ Attitudes}$ = 2.64, $M_{Distance\ Learning-Problem\ Solving}$ = 2.72, $M_{Distance\ Learning-Skill\ Development}$ = 2.80, $M_{Distance\ Learning-Knowledge\ Retention}$ = 2.79). Similarly, video and computer-based methods which represented modern methods had lower means ($M_{Video-Knowledge\ Acquisition}$ = 3.26, $M_{Video-Changing\ Attitudes}$ = 2.93, $M_{Video-Problem\ Solving}$ = 2.95, $M_{Video-Skill\ Development}$ = 3.00, $M_{Video-Knowledge\ Retention}$ = 3.02; $M_{Computer\ Based-Knowledge\ Acquisition}$ = 3.23, $M_{Computer\ Based-Changing\ Attitudes}$ = 2.80, $M_{Computer\ Based-Problem\ Solving}$ = 3.06, $M_{Computer\ Based-Skill\ Development}$ = 3.11, $M_{Computer\ Based-Knowledge\ Retention}$ = 3.15). The results showed that there is a significant difference between modern training methods (M=63.72, SD= 11.72) and conventional training methods (M= 57.02, SD=7.663) in term of effectiveness to accomplish various training objectives (t = -7.553, df =199, $p<0.5$). Hence, suggesting that H4 is supported.

SUMMARY OF THE FINDINGS

In sum, two out of the four hypotheses were supported. The first hypothesis that was not supported showed that there is no significant difference between modern and conventional training meth-ods in terms of frequency. However, the results support the second hypothesis, hence suggesting that a significant difference exists with respect to the effectiveness of conventional and modern methods. The third hypothesis, on the other hand, failed to be supported which indicated that there is no difference between small and large firms in their use of OJT.

The ratings of effectiveness of various training methods to attain specific training objectives were also analyzed, which resulted in a significant finding. This finding supported the fourth and final hypothesis which indicated that a significant difference exists between modern training methods and conventional training methods in terms of attaining training objectives. It was reported that OJT is the most effective training method to achieve all the objectives, except coaching, whereby it had a higher rating in terms of achieving the objective of changing attitudes. Modern technology-based methods, such as distance learning and computer-based, ranked the least effective in attaining all training objectives.

CONCLUSION

Contradictory to previous studies, this study found that all the organizations regardless of their size reported training activities very important or important to their organization. The use of the Internet, tele-matics, multimedia and other "virtual" realities is unlikely to supplant, as some seek to imply, "learning through doing" as epitomized by Revans (1983). This study does not seek to deny the value of modern learning methods. Efforts should be made to explore how they may best be exploited. Integrated mechanisms are required which utilize and exploit client-focused learning opportunities in the workplace to their fullest extent. The challenge for HR practice is to successfully utilize and integrate modern and traditional, OJT and off-job methods so as to build on the strengths of each and meet the needs of learners and businesses. Another direction for future research is the transfer of training of modern training methods. As indicated by Bhatti and Kaur (2009), the most vital impact is the transfer of training which leads to improvements in employee and organizational performance.

Finally, this study is without its limitation. The number of participants who took part in the questionnaire and convenient sampling limits this research paper. While 200 respondents represented three business sectors and various sizes of organizations, further research needs to be conducted with additional representatives from each sector and with different settings to determine whether the findings of this study can be generalized across the business sectors and industries. Furthermore, the respondents originated from organizations around the Klang Valley area, hence future research could consider getting representative samples from different regions of the country.

RECOMMENDATION

Employees should be included and actively involved in the planning process of training intervention. Future research is needed to investigate ways in which employee involvement of each stage of the training process affects training effectiveness. There is limited research, however, that reports on the nature of different types of interactive relationships and how various types of training methods can integrate into these relationships.

Technology-assisted training program delivery would be more effective if it was derived from partnerships with other businesses, professional associations, universities and training consultants in order to provide the expertise and technological support to develop and deliver effective and efficient business training. How distance learning can be incorporated into the mainstream of learning methods needs further exploration. There are advantages, as the rhetoric assures us, in using such methods (flexibility of time, place and pace) but they do not appear to be being exploited to their

fullest. How this may be achieved is a priority for investigations using more in-depth, qualitatively and meaningful approaches.

It should be noted that the views presented in this study are those of the employees and this is an acknowledged limitation; whether the views of the training managers would concur is an area for speculation and one which future research should seek to address. The review of literature reveals great gaps in knowledge about the effectiveness of various training methods. In addition, much more research needs to be focused on the personal and situational factors which moderate the effectiveness of alternative training methods.

Until now there has been no good guide that training practitioners could use to select the type of training methods which might be most useful to accomplish different training objectives. Future research on this subject is needed. Finally, the effectiveness of modern training methods needs to take into account the "aging work force". Research on this area should be done in the Malaysian context.

REFERENCES

Bassett-Jones, N. (1991). *Achieving Flexibility in Training*. Coventry: Coventry and Warwickshire Training and Enterprise Council.

Belcourt, M. (2002). *Managing human resources*. Scarborough, Ontario: Nelson Thompson Learning.

Bhatti, M. A., & Kaur, S. (2009). Factors affecting the transfer of training: A modern approach. *In Proceedings of the 12th IBIMA Conference*, Kuala, Lumpur.

Carlson, D. S., Upton, N., & Seaman, S. (2006). The impact of human resource practices and compensation design on performance: An analysis of family-owned SMEs. *Journal of Small Business Management, 44*, 531–543. doi:10.1111/j.1540-627X.2006.00188.x

Carroll, S. J., Paine, F. T., & Ivancevich, J. J. (1972). The relative effectiveness of training methods. *Personnel Psychology, 25*(4), 495–509. doi:10.1111/j.1744-6570.1972.tb00833.x

Chute, A., Melody, T., & Hancock, B. (1999). *The mcgraw-hill handbook of distance learning.* New York: McGraw-Hill.

Craig, R. L. (1996). *The ASTD training and development handbook, a guide to human resource development.* New York: McGraw-Hill.

Curran, J., & Stanworth, J. (1989). Education and training for enterprise: Some problems of classification, evaluation, policy and research. *International Small Business Journal, 7*(2), 11–22. doi:10.1177/026624268900700201

Driscoll, M. (1999, April). Web-based training in the workplace. *Adult Learning, 10*, 21–25.

Galvin, T. (2001). *Industry Report 2001.* Retrieved from http://www.eric.ed.gov/ERICWebPortal/custom/portlets/recordDetails/detailmini.jsp?_nfpb=true&_&ERICExtSearch_SearchType_o=no&accno=EJ632065

Gomez-Mejia, L. R., Balkin, D. B., Cardy, R. L., Dimick, D. E., & Templer, A. J. (2004). *Managing Human Resource.* Toronto, Ontario: Pearson Education Canada Inc.

Granak, A., Hughes, J., & Hunter, D. (2006). *Building the best: Lessons from inside Canada's best managed companies.* Toronto, Ontario: Penguin Group.

Greengard, S. (1999, February). Web-based training yields maximum returns. *Workforce, 78*, 95–96.

Grey, G. J. (1991). *Electronic performance support system.* Boston: Weingarten Pub.

Hall, B. (1997). *Web-based training cookbook.* New York: John Willey & Sons, Inc.

Huang, T.-C. (2001). The relation of training practices and organizational performance in small and medium size enterprises. *Education + Training, 43*(8-9), 437–444. doi:10.1108/00400910110411620

Jayawarna, D., Macpherson, A., & Wilson, A. (2007). Training commitment and performance in manufacturing SMEs: Incidence, intensity and approaches. *Journal of Small Business and Enterprise Development, 14*(2), 321–338. doi:10.1108/14626000710746736

Juptner, O. (2001). *Corporate e-Learning Market to Skyrocket.* Retrieved from http://www.e-gateway.net/infoarea/news/news.cfm?nid=1451

Leonard, B. (1996, April). Distance learning. Work and training overlap. *HR Magazine.*

Matlay, H. (2002). Training and HRM strategies in small, family-owned businesses: An empirical overview. In Fletcher, D. (Ed.), *Understanding the Small Family Business.* London: Routledge.

McCrea, F., Gay, R. K., & Bacon, R. (2000). *Riding the big waves: A white paper on B2B e-learning industry.* San Francisco, CA: Thomas Weisel Partners.

Meyer, J., & Allen, N. (1991). A three component conceptualization of organizational commitment. *Human Resource Management Review, 1*(1), 61–90. doi:10.1016/1053-4822(91)90011-Z

Miller, L. (2001, March). Coaching pays off. *Society of Human Resource Management, 46*, 16–17.

Ninth Malaysia Plan. *(2006-2010).* (2006). Retrieved from http://www.parlimen.gov.my/news/eng-ucapan_rmk9.pdf

Perdue, L. J., & Woods, R. H. (2000). The effectiveness of alternative training methods in college and university foodservice. *The Journal of the National Association of College and University Food Service, 22*(1), 64–70.

Revans, R. (1983). *The ABC of action learning.* Bromley, UK: Chartwell Bratt.

Rossett, A. (1996). Job aids and electronic performance support systems. In Craig, R. (Ed.), *The ASTD training and development handbook, a guide to human resource development* (pp. 554–578). New York: McGraw-Hill.

Sadler-Smith, E., Down, S., & Lean, J. (2000). Modern learning methods: rhetoric and reality. *Personnel Review*, *29*(4), 474–490. doi:10.1108/00483480010296285

Sargeant, A. (1996). Training for enterprise: what's so special about the small business? In *Proceedings of the 1996 Small Business & Enterprise Development Conference*. European Research Press: Shipley.

Showers, B. (1987). *Staff development handbook*. Columbia, South Carolina: South Carolina Department of Education.

Stolovitch, H. D., & Keeps, E. J. (2004). *Training ain't performance*. Alexandria, VA: ASTD.

Switzer, M., & Kleiner, B. H. (1996). New developments in training teams effectively. *Training for Quality*, *4*(1), 12–17. doi:10.1108/09684879610112819

Urdan, T., & Weggen, C. (2000). Corporate e-learning: Exploring a new frontier. *WR Hambrech Co*. Retrieved from http://www.educause.edu/asp/doclib/abstract.asp?ID=CSD1521

Welber, M., & Feinberg, J. (2002, September). Save by growing your own trainers. *Workforce*, *81*, 44.

Wilkins, B. (2000). *A grounded theory on personal coaching*. Unpublished doctoral Dissertation, University of Montana, Montana.

This work was previously published in International Journal of Technology Diffusion, Volume 1, Issue 2, edited by Ali Hussein Saleh Zolait, pp. 62-74, copyright 2010 by IGI Publishing (an imprint of IGI Global).

Chapter 12

Problems of Initiating International Knowledge Transfer:
Is the Finnish Living Lab Method Transferable to Estonia?

Katri-Liis Lepik
Estonian Business School, Estonia

Merle Krigul
Estonian Business School, Estonia

Erik Terk
Tallinn University, Estonia

ABSTRACT

Regional competitiveness is a policy priority of the European Union. This article explores cross-border knowledge transfer for regional integration and development. The focus of this research is the role of cross-border co-operation in development of innovative forms of co-operation, initiating and supporting knowledge transfer. The article presents a theoretical-methodological analysis of new complex tasks and theoretical paradigms emerging in the context of increasing integration and convergence of cross-border co-operation: method's innovation approach, knowledge and knowledge transfer. A cross-border co-operation organisation's potential model for enhancement of complex regional co-operation has also been described based on Helsinki-Tallinn Euregio's case. The article then focuses on investigating the international transferability of the Living Lab's method. The article concludes by presenting the opportunities and principles of activities of a cross-border co-operation organisation to support the knowledge transfer process.

DOI: 10.4018/978-1-4666-1752-0.ch012

INTRODUCTION

Regional competitiveness is among the policy priorities of the European Union as economy is international. As the population living in cross-border areas amounts to 181.7 million in the EU (37.5% of the total EU population), the cross-border co-operation is one of the main means to fulfill that objective. (Inforegio, 2009) In order to better promote the cross-border co-operation many regions in the EU have established cross-border co-operation (CBC) organisations/euroregions. The case of Helsinki-Tallinn Euregio which is one of those organisations established between the capitals and municipalities of the capital regions will be addressed throughout this article. Among the organisation's multiple tasks is diminishing disparities within the cross-border region by enhancing knowledge and competitiveness in the region. This article focuses on cross-border knowledge transfer for regional integration and development and usage of an innovative method Living Lab.

The articles aims at, firstly, analysing how knowledge management is used for development and management of CBC organisations with the task of building a knowledge region. Findings indicate that a knowledge transfer developed in one of the metropolitan regions will lead to an integration of that competence with other metropolitan region. Secondly, the article explores the knowledge transfer in cross-border co-operation organisations and the innovative method used in knowledge transfer – Living Labs. Thirdly, the article discusses the process of utilising the Living Labs concept in enhancing Helsinki-Tallinn metropolitan regional integration.

The article concludes by presenting how a cross-border knowledge organisation uses an innovative Living Labs' method for regional integration and development of the region.

METHODOLOGY

The present article is a research on knowledge transfer in cross-border co-operation. The case of two metropolitan regions – Helsinki and Tallinn are explored. Helsinki-Tallinn Euregio - a cross-border co-operation organisation which is a tool for promotion and initiation of is analysed.

The article presents a theoretical-methodological analysis of new complex tasks and theoretical paradigms emerging in the context of increasing integration and convergence of cross-border co-operation, frameworks which allow successfully tackle and solve such tasks: method's innovation approach in the frameworks of developing innovation theory, knowledge and knowledge transfer focused approaches. Thereafter a CBC organisation's potential model has been explained based on the investigation of 35 representatives of CBC organisations, its various options, advantages and disadvantages are described. Proceeding from the research focus of the present article, which is the role of CBC in development of innovative forms of co-operation, initiating and supporting knowledge transfer, the initial model has been developed based on the results of the interviews. The attempt has been made to formulate which characteristics of the model are suitable especially for enhancement of more complex regional co-operation. Following, the article focuses on investigating the international transferability of a concrete complex co-operation task, namely the living lab's method as one of the modern methodology of open innovation which is about to gain large popularity. For that purpose a special interview methodology was compiled and 14 in-depth interviews were conducted with persons who are involved or would potentially be involved in adoption of the living lab method in Tallinn and Helsinki. In the course of the interviews the prerequisites of the method's transfer, potential areas of usage and realisation options of the method were investigated. Based on the researched case some general conclusions were made about the factors hindering more complex international knowledge transfer. Finally, the conclusions were made about the opportunities and principles of activities of a CBC organisation to support the knowledge transfer process researched.

THEORETICAL FRAMEWORK

It is characteristic for regional co-operation that in addition to the movement of capital and goods also objects which are more difficult to be transferred or received/introduced like technology, skills and knowledge must move from one region to the other. When the co-operation deepens and the goals become more ambitious the role of immaterial components in co-operation increases compared to material ones. Instead of co-operation forms that can be dealt with separately (economic, cultural, administrative) complex tasks uniting several co-operation forms arise. Hence, the necessary circle of stake-holders required for fulfillment of co-operation tasks increases and becomes more complex, for instance, in economic co-operation projects universities and cultural institutions and often also citizens as potential users of the new systems must be included. The creativity of the co-operation increases. The simple, even algorithmic transfer, multiplying and copying will no longer be dominant which includes learning and changing of the behaviour mainly by the recipient, instead both parties must solve creative tasks while creating new systems and often the end results cannot be really forecasted.

The usefulness of the activity of CBC organisation depends on how well it can contribute to enhancement of such gradually more complex co-operation, support and initiates even more challenging forms of co-operation.

The previously described activity, the problems that might arise and ways of solution can be addressed in the framework of two paradigms. Firstly, the paradigm developed in the framework of innovation theory, and secondly, discussions

based on the term "knowledge" (knowledge creation, knowledge transfer, knowledge management). Following, we will try to show what kind of framework the two paradigms will constitute for the tasks we try to solve. We would like to stress that we deal with complementary rather than incompatible paradigms innovation related paradigm (Viia et al., 2007). In principle both are important but we will focus on more complex innovations in this article, meaning, on more radical innovations. Research done also in Estonia has shown that there are problems especially with this form of innovation. In Estonian companies, including those of Tallinn, the innovation intensity is not low according to international methodology (CIS-methodology, Community innovation Survey); at the same time the investment into radical innovations which would strongly change the situation are not sufficient. (Viia et al., 2007) The same result was received after analysing various development plans of Tallinn some years ago (Tafel & Terk, 2007). If we leave aside success in implementation of IT governance in the city, in case of which Tallinn is ahead of many other cities, the research has shown that despite large construction activities (assisted naturally by the economic boom) the majority of the urban development solutions and development plans included incremental, not radical innovations. International co-operation, especially when the partner is significantly well positioned in innovation charts like Southern-Finland could contribute to the change in this situation. At the same time no changes have occurred recently in Helsinki-Tallinn co-operation which could radically change the picture.

The intensity and making innovation more radical depends to a large extent on the spectrum of the source of innovative ideas. In addition to inherent sources of innovation like the direct clients and suppliers, other companies in the same field, and as co-operation partners, fairs, universities, research institutions, international literature, etc. are distinguished as sources of innovation in case of enterprises. (Viia et al., 2007) According to the approximate model the public sector institution's like city's sources of innovation "reservoir" can be described. The problem facing Estonian companies is the weak role of universities and research institutions as the source of innovative ideas and despite Estonian economy's (and society's) high level of general internationalisation, the cross-border innovation clusters including Estonia are not sufficiently developed. In some cases Estonian actors participate in them as fulfilling realisation functions rather than equal participants in innovation processes.

Significantly interesting tendency lies in such new developments in addressing innovation process like emergence of open innovation concept on the one hand, and convergence of ideology in development of innovation process and so called creative industries on the other hand.

The first one means transfer from innovation creation in a "lab" with a small number of people and publicising in co-operation with a large number of parties at a later stage, whereas the relations of the participants in the innovation process are not (only) strictly commercial. The motives can include opportunity for development of own ideas, new synergic effects hoping that they can be later commercialised in other business processes or in case of a city or a citizen just a wish to create surrounding living environment according to the local actors' versions and ideas. The second means logic which is characteristic for arts where one operates with meanings, symbols and identities rather than satisfies pragmatic needs and where instead of known achievement of results a creative and open ended process becomes important and spills over to other areas where the so called fordist logic was applied earlier.

The concept of innovation has been mostly discussed in literature as something related to technology and product innovation. In some cases innovation of organisation is also treated separately. However, the most difficult type of it is probably method's innovation. (Terk, 1986) However, in some cases the need to change meth-

ods of activities can be determined by the usage of new production or information technologies, to be so called automatic inevitability and in that case they get adopted quicker, at the same time such connection does not necessarily have to occur. There might occur situation where exactly the change of a method can open new opportunities for implementation of new technologies or for creation of new products. The usage of new methods requires in those cases very good demonstration and promotion activities, teaching and training. Massive breakthrough of new activity methods on some social environment can take even a generation, for instance, pedagogics. As a rule, successful innovation of the activity of some production-economic system requires inter-linked changes in products, technologies, organisation as well as people activity methods. (Terk, 1986) Such logic should also apply in case of other social systems.

Knowledge transfer adds new dimensions to innovation related to the social and institutional processes. In the present article we deal with innovation of innovation as we speak about Living Lab which is an innovative tool used for innovation and competitiveness.

Rogers (1964, 2003) proposes that adopters of any new innovation or idea can be categorised as innovators, early adopters, early majority, late majority and laggards, based on the mathematically-based Bell curve. These categories, based on standard deviations from the mean of the normal curve, provide a common language for innovation researchers. Each adopter's willingness and ability to adopt an innovation depends on their awareness, interest, evaluation, trial, and adoption. In case of Living Lab's only the awareness raising stage has been implemented so far and the practice is still very limited. The Living Lab method's innovation is more complex than a product, technology or any other type of innovation as in living Labs the technology and life-style are interwoven.

Knowledge and Knowledge Transfer

Knowledge transfer has abundantly been addressed in knowledge management literature.

The concept of knowledge has long fascinated scholars in many disciplines. This has contributed to making this concept extremely complex. Different perspectives have given rise to various methodologies by which knowledge can be studied and different ways for analysing, interpreting and managing knowledge. (Troilo, 2006; Firestone, 2001)

Regional competitiveness is based on its capabilities that impact its performance. Those capabilities are based on a fusion of effective goal-oriented business and management processes and skills, both of which are forms of knowledge. One of the best ways of understanding knowledge is to bring out the distinctions between information and knowledge. A common distinction is to note that information is anything that can be digitised. As such, if it can be stored in a database or attached to an e-mail, it is information.

There is no consensus on the nature of knowledge (Firestone, 2001). Definitions vary from "Justified true belief" (Nonaka & Takeuchi, 1995), "Knowledge, while made up of data and information, can be thought of as much greater understanding of a situation, relationships, causal phenomena, and the theories and rules (both explicit and implicit) that underlie a given domain or problem." (Bennet & Bennet, 1996) to "Knowledge is the capacity for effective action" (Karl-Erik Sveiby, 1999). This definition is the one favoured by the organisational learning community. Similarly, Tom Davenport and Larry Prusak contend that "knowledge can and should be evaluated by the decisions or actions to which it leads" (by Firestone, 2001).

Another important distinction is between tacit and explicit knowledge, introduced by Polanyi (1996): we can know more than we can tell or explain to others. Explicit knowledge is what we can express to others, while tacit knowledge comprises the rest of our knowledge - that which we cannot communicate in words or symbols. Much of our knowledge is tacit. Explicit knowledge, conversely, can be put in a form that can be communicated to others through language, visuals, models, diagrams or other representations. When knowledge is made explicit by putting it into words or other representations, it can then be digitised, copied, stored, and communicated electronically. It has become information. What is commonly termed explicit knowledge is information, while tacit knowledge is simply knowledge.

One way we can share our tacit knowledge with others is socialisation, where we converse directly, share experiences, and together work toward enhancing another person's or organisation's or local knowledge (Dawson, 2005). This is what happens in the process of cross-border co-operation.

Knowledge transfer seeks to organise, create, capture or distribute knowledge and ensure its availability for other users. In earlier literature knowledge transfer has been approached furthermost in the context of technology transfer. In case of some forms of technology transfer like direct investment from a strategic partner the recipient receives the technology and accompanying know-how relatively easily. In case of some other forms like buying of licences or patents of in case of "turn key" contract, it requires more learning from the recipient and in the third case when an international specialist is hired or own employee is sent abroad to study, not only technology but all knowledge in the person's head about the technology as well as its usage, organisational and other aspects moves (Lumiste, 2005). Knowledge management paradigm allows approaching the process deeply. The above-mentioned division between the tacit and explicit knowledge allows understanding that one part of knowledge, tacit knowledge, cannot be mechanically transferred from one person or body to another. It can be transferred in joint activity or the new group of people can create new and slightly different tacit knowledge than before.

We can assume that it is even more difficult to implement knowledge transfer in international co-operation than within one country because the hindering factors include national-organisational-cultural as well as economic situation's and economic environments' peculiarities, different institutional histories, etc.

Following we will test this hypothesis with one concrete innovative method, namely based on the analysis of the living lab method's transferability.

THE ROLE OF CROSS-BORDER CO-OPERATION ORGANISATION: CASE OF HELSINKI-TALLINN EUREGIO

CBC organisations are well informed about the local needs and problems of border territories and they are bearers of longstanding tradition of cross-border co-operation on the grass-root level. This knowledge and experience of the CBC organisations are valuable for discussions concerning crucial challenges of the region. Effective knowledge transfer in a cross-border organisation would contribute to developing regions' competitiveness. This means that knowledge creation, storage, and transfer are essential factors of raising regional competitiveness.

CBC organisations are important partners in knowledge transfer process, being collective agents of managing knowledge production, knowledge integration and knowledge transfer. They embody organisational process, combining information processing capacity of information technologies, and the creative and innovative capacity of human beings. CBCs use IT systems and change processes to generate ideas, transform the organisation or the problem into a new quality, manage change processes, use information, data and knowledge to achieve goals.

The present article presents the knowledge transfer from the cross-border co-operation perspective. The authors of the article presume that in the case, where the strategy, vision and mission

of a CBC organisation is focused on initiation and promotion of innovation and knowledge processes in the region, then knowledge transfer has to be in focus. One of such CBC promoters in the Baltic Sea area is Helsinki-Tallinn Euregio, an association of five partners: City of Helsinki, City of Tallinn, Uusimaa Regional Council, Union of Harju County Municipalities and Republic of Estonia, represented by Harju County Government. Helsinki-Tallinn Euregio started as a cross-border co-operation network in 1999 and was formalised into a non-profit association (NPA) in 2003. The mission of the Euregio is to enhance cross-border integration between Helsinki/Uusimaa region and Tallinn/Harju county. The role of Euregio is to promote and assist co-operation inside the twin-region as well as inter-regional development and competitiveness, aiming to strengthen the regional knowledge based economic development. Among its priorities are: increased interaction in spatial and regional planning, creation of an innovative and a barrier free region with common well-functioning markets, development of twin-region of arts and sciences. Twin-Region based on knowledge and culture is facilitated and supported via its activities.

The advantages and drawbacks of Euregio for being the promoter of regional knowledge transfer will be discussed based on the research carried out among the leaders of the 35 CBC organisations from the Baltic Sea Region. The detailed analyses of the characteristics and most crucial problems for cross-border co-operation institutions and ideas for addressing the problems are in the article "Euroregions as Mechanisms for Strengthening of Cross-border Cooperation in the Baltic Sea Region" (Trames, 2009 in process). The present interpretation relies on the material from the research but discusses the aspects of knowledge transfer which have not been previously dealt with.

Knowledge management as one of the management areas can be implemented in an organisation with developed structure and working culture. The investigation made evident that CBC organisations with partners from old EU member states and organisations established between new EU member states or member states and other countries differ significantly in their financial, institutional, organisational and managerial capabilities. According to its type and role Helsinki-Tallinn Euregio falls into the first category.

In first-mentioned CBC organisations the structures are developed and there tends to be a joint governing body or a secretariat and in new ones there tends to be no joint structure. In Euregio's case there is a cross-border office with employees from both sides, joint secretariat and joint board. The board consists of stake-holders from Estonia and Finland, both officials and politicians which is a crucial advantage in knowledge transfer processes as the involvement of political representatives (local, regional, national and European) is crucial for successful cross-border co-operation. Another advantage is involvement in long-term strategies of the development of the region. In CBC organisations with new EU member states the focus is often on solving concrete small-scale immediate border related problems rather than tackling larger regional challenges.

The most crucial challenge for several new CBC organisations with EU members states and new member states is absence of permanent funding and the required co-financing in projects. This also prevents them from having joint structures with common resources and they have to work merely on project bases rather than have permanent staff and long-term co-operation strategies in order to cover the costs of the activities and the office. Such funding scheme is unsustainable but the project management is of utmost importance since the goals of the organisations are achieved by implementing projects which support the strategy. As technical, administrative, financial and decision-making instruments are vital for lasting CBC activities, the results of the study allow presuming that advanced management systems are to be developed in the future. Another drawback in addition to the lack of funding in new CBC organisations is being understaffed as they are often one-or-two person led organisations. This is a disadvantage in involvement of large arena of stake-holders and leading larger knowledge transfer activities. A manager is expected to be competent in all areas of activities and processes on different sides of borders. She or he becomes a real knowledge bank – if the manager leaves, organisation is at risk of not being sustainable, as explicit knowledge consists basically of minutes of meetings, project descriptions and annual reports; good or bad working relations, unofficial networks, contexts and inside information are not described in the written form. Among various initiatives there is a need for better co-ordination of different institutions, demonstrations of the benefit of collective work and establishment of direct contacts to universities and business sector. This is not possible with one-person management that acts on project bases.

The importance of knowledge transfer has increased as today's successful regional and inter-regional co-operation is built on triple-helix model which forms a complicated system and requires various methods to be effectively implemented. The next step in the regional development process is the usage of an innovative tool - a Living Lab's method. The novelty of this research is to contribute to a successful use of Living Labs as a means for user involvement in public services by multiplying the Finnish experience to Estonia and developing the method further to be applied in cross-border context.

USAGE OF LIVING LABS' METHOD IN ENHANCING HELSINKI-TALLINN CROSS-BORDER CO-OPERATION AND METROPOLITAN REGIONAL INTEGRATION

Living Labs is a human-centric research and development approach in which new technologies are co-created, tested, and evaluated in the users' own private context (Samelin, 2007). Living Labs is societal innovation with technological innovation;

it includes creative processes for developing a new or innovative solution in co-operation with local authorities, technology companies and citizens.

The Living Lab phenomena can be viewed in two ways, as an environment, and, as a method or a concept or an approach.

In this article, the perspective taken is Living Lab as a method. Hence there is a noticeable lack of theories and methods supporting its actions. As a concept Living Lab is an innovative method with large potential but rather immature and there are many aspects that need to be studied and further explored to understand the phenomena in depth; hence, more insights into how Living Lab activities and contexts can be supported are needed (Stahlbröst 2008). Følstad (2008) argues that the most pressing challenge for research in Living Labs is related to the current lack of studies of Living Lab methods and tools.

Proceeding from the fourteen in-depth interviews carried out in 2008 with city officials, representatives of technology companies, experts of the fields that are internationally recognised as Living Labs testing grounds from Estonia and Finland, we may conceptualise the usage of the Living Lab's method in Helsinki-Tallinn cross-border concept.

Main research questions were:

a. Do those areas exist in Tallinn that requires Living Labs' method to introduce and develop new solutions?
b. Is there any potential and motivation of technology companies and universities, technology parks, research institutions to develop Living Labs' co-operation model?
c. Are the local authorities ready to work for developing new technologies and methods like Living Labs?
d. Are the citizens prepared for active participation (as the essence of the method presumes)?

As a result of the research two versions can be considered here.

1.   Transfer of the Method

This includes the spill-over effect when the experiences on the Finnish side should be creatively applied in Estonian context as direct copying is not possible due to different socio-economic context. Another aspect concerns the potential inclusion of the Finnish small and medium sized enterprises (SMEs). There are no economic or ideological limits to that but the problems may arise due to the local nature of the Living Lab. The prerequisites for a good Living Lab process are tight co-operation between SMEs while developing the ideas and services and it requires close ties and contacts with the city governments, citizens and environments. At the same time it is impossible to guarantee with detailed contracts between the SMEs and the city governments what benefits will be gained and what will be the profit earned as the nature of the final target services is not yet known. Therefore the authors perceive the usage of the SMEs of the neighbouring country in contributing to solving a problem of a local nature (meaning local during the testing period) as something exceptional and not a mainstream case. This applies to both, Estonian SMEs in Finland and Finnish ones in Estonia.

2.   Estonian-Finnish Joint Living Lab

The above mentioned limiting factor does not apply in the case when speaking about an affiliation of company (or an international company) located in the neighbouring country. The participation of a local affiliation of a Finnish mother company in Estonia would be more likely and therefore the authors would recommend this as an option while establishing a Living Lab in Tallinn. This naturally requires corresponding decision making of mother companies in Finland. In order to guarantee interest of Finnish SMEs towards such activity, several bonus schemes should be developed, e.g. giving shares of Tallinn Living Lab to Finnish counterparts. There is a need to deal with the awareness rising on the Living Lab's method. The prerequisite is that both sides need to profit from the activities.

Still, the study revealed barriers that need to be overcome:

a. Semantical: with no previous experiences, the method is just not understood or understood in an incorrect way;

b. Differences in institutional and organisational behaviours between Estonia and Finland, but also in-between different institutions in the same country;

c. Lack of co-operation culture between the public sector and entrepreneurs in Estonia;

d. Differences in democratic inclusion processes in Estonia and Finland;

e. Differences in priorities and innovation strategies in Helsinki and Tallinn.

   a. Regarding the areas for the use of the Living Lab's method in Tallinn, two areas were equally considered as having high potential: transport (also including logistics) and media. As far as media is concerned, it was sometimes considered as multimedia and sometimes as means of communication. Also the traditional media as well as interactive media were mentioned. Several respondents also favoured security and tourism. Two respondents favoured other areas (design and architecture, health care, energy sector). As far as technological tools used in those areas were concerned, the majority of the respondents mentioned ICT (in some cases ICT and in some cases IT, also as telecommunications and communication system). In some cases also several measuring and identifying systems as well as optics in relation to cameras were mentioned. In many cases also biotechnology was mentioned but its concrete usage in city areas were not covered.

b. Several, but not too many companies and also universities were interested in participation in developing the Living Lab's method, still one of the major obstacles is different understanding of the method itself and its realisation possibilities;

c. Some interested local leaders were identified in Tallinn with the same major obstacles as the differences in understanding of the method itself and its realisation possibilities;

d. Estonian citizens are interested and open to new technologies and ICT, hence citizens' and tourist' participation in developing of new solutions may presume to be existing. The problem includes different tradition of involving citizens in democratic participation processes that are different in Estonia and Finland.

In the case of implementing new cross-border methods the role of a cross-border organisation is significant. Helsinki-Tallinn Euregio is a suitable institution for cross-border knowledge transfer as its strategy includes promoting and assisting knowledge based co-operation inside the twin-region. Therefore a matchmaking organisation like Euregio would fill that gap. In the case of innovation the imago is important and here we can rely on the trustworthy Finnish reputation in this area.

DISCUSSION AND SUGGESTIONS FOR FUTURE RESEARCH

The authors of the article have identified some aspects of cross-border Living Lab that they believe are important to do more research about. These aspects are related to the need, capacity of the stake-holders, the focus of the environments and areas and the financial schemes of such processes.

Even today, the most advanced Living Labs are rather immature. Hence, there is a significant need for research and development to gain knowledge about how to organise a Living Lab with its inherent complexity as we are still in the awareness raising stage.

Potential environments and areas for the use of the Living Lab method in Tallinn, Estonia have two options. The first option includes environment as a unique object for a city (e.g., district Pasila in Helsinki) and development of a city district or creation of an important place or improvement of a transport system as the main value. The fact that an added value will emerge that can be multiplied in the future has a secondary value for a city government. The city government however should consider that the companies need to be interested in the object which is offered for the Living Lab. The second option is that the city government has some solutions tested in one district in order to multiply it to another districts in the future. Therefore the city government is also interested in having a typical environment for using the solution in the future.

Realisation of the Living Lab's method is institutionally a very challenging task. Proceeding from the interviews, there is a shared understanding regarding several public areas that the method can be implemented and also ideas were expressed which solutions can be adopted to enhance city life. There is also a small number of technology based small and medium size enterprises (SMEs) who could participate in implementation of the method, especially ICT SMEs. As a barrier the study brought out the lack of finances in some smaller companies and also the habit of investigating a process with an outcome not known beforehand. At the same time the ideas are not focused on a central idea around which a Living Lab could be built. Additionally, there is no clear understanding regarding the environment suitable for potential Living Labs. The city government and city departments have the strategic position in the implementation of the method in public services. If the city government is in the position of an initiator, they need to suggest the idea and provide financing for the process. A focused task and a well planned goal are the key success factors here and the SMEs should not start working on random ideas.

While selecting the appropriate environment and when following the "bottom-up" principle, it is decisive to have a sufficient number of "end-users" of citizens (in some cases also tourists) who would feel the need to develop or at least give feedback to a certain innovative technological and social service in a certain space in a certain way. At the same time in specific public service areas regarding large technology systems the Lab can exist in co-operation not directly with the citizen but a mediator like creator of transport or energy systems, organiser of waste treatment or traffic schemes. Then there might arise the question about the real representation of the needs and wishes of an end-user. An effect characteristic for open innovation can still be gained when some technological idea is tested and developed in multiple environments with different clients and their representatives from real life and with their active participation. In other words, it is not only *technology push* but also *demand driven* type process.

Concluding from the interviews the following steps should be taken: to investigate if the city government of Tallinn is ready to implement the method, to select the potential public service areas for creation of Living Labs, to focus on a couple of ideas by city departments and develop them further. The steps need to be followed with corresponding relevant financial commitments.

It is important to discuss the nature of the initiator of a cross-border Living Lab. Helsinki-Tallinn Euregio has direct access to relevant decision-makers in the region, however, the direct link to the companies is missing. The SMEs have been involved as partners so far but the involvement of representatives of the companies in the management structures of Euregio would need to be considered.

ACKNOWLEDGMENT

Research was supported by ETF grant 7537.

REFERENCES

Bennet, A., & Bennet, D. (2000). Characterizing the Next Generation Knowledge Organization. Knowledge and Innovation. *Journal of the KMCI, 1*(1), 8–42.

Dawson, R. (2005, May). *Leadership in Professiona services* (2ⁿᵈ ed., p. 416). Oxford, UK: Butterworth Heinemann Publications.

European Commission Regional Policy – Inforegio. (n.d.). Retrieved July 13, 2009 from http://ec.europa.eu/regional_policy/policy/object/index_en.htm

Firestone, J. M. (2001, April 15). Key issues in Knowledge Management. Knowledge and Innovation. *Journal of the KMCI, 1*(3).

Følstad, A. (2008). Living Labs for Innovation and Development of Information and Communication Technology: A Literature Review. *The Electronic Journal for Virtual Organizations and Networks, 10*, 100–131.

Lepik, K.-L. (2009). *Euroregions as Mechanisms for Strengthening of Cross-border Cooperation in the Baltic Sea Region.* Tartu, Estonia: Trames.

Malhotra, Y. (2001). *Knowledge Management and Business Model Innovation.* Hershey, PA: IGI Global.

Nonaka, I., & Takeuchi, H. (1995). *The Knowledge Creating Company.* New York: Oxford University Press.

Polanyi, M. (1966). *The Tacit Dimension.* London, UK: Routledge and Jegan Paul.

Possibilities to Use the Concept of Living Laboratories in Tallinn (Report) (2008). Tallinn, Estonia: Institute for Futures Studies

Rogers, E. M. (1964). *Diffusion of Innovations (p. 79/150).* Glencoe, IL: Free Press.

Rogers, E. M. (2003). *Diffusion of Innovation* (5th ed.). New York: Free Press.

Salmelin, B. (2007, May 21-22). *Open Innovation and eServices - Living Labs as facilitating environment.* Paper presented at the Conference of Co-Creative Research and Innovation to Connect the Lisbon Strategy to People: European Network of Living Labs Event, Guimarães, Portugal.

Ståhlbröst, A. (2008). *Forming Future IT - The Living Lab Way of User Involvement. Doctoral theses.* Sweden: Luleå University of Technology.

Sveiby, K.-E. (1999). *Welcome to the Knowledge Organisation!* Retrieved May 17, 2009 from http://www.sveiby.com/articles/K-era.htm

Szulanski, G. (1996). Exploring internal stickiness: Impediments to the transfer of best practice within the firm. *Strategic Management Journal, 17*(27-43), 151.

Tafel, K., & Terk, E. (2007). *Tallinna linna arengukavade analüüs ja arengu kavandamise täiustamise võimalused (Analysis of Development Plans of Tallinn City and Opportunities for Improvement of Planning).* Tallinn, Estonia: Estonian Institute for Futures Studies.

Terk, E. (1986). *Innovatsiooniteooria kasutamisvõimalustest. Kogumikus: Innovatsioon ja eksperimentika* (Opportunities of Using Innovation Theory. Publication: Innovation and experimenting).

Terk, E., & Lumiste, R. (2005). *Enterprises in technology-intensive business. Toolkit for coping with international environment and developing management competencies.* Tallinn, Estonia: Estonian Institute for Futures Studies.

Theoretical background of the Living Laboratories Concept and Overview of the Literature (Report) (2008). Tallinn, Estonia: Institute for Futures Studies.

Troilo, G. (2006). *Marketing knowledge management; managing knowledge in market oriented companies*. Cheltenham, UK: Edward Elgar.

Viia, A., Terk, E., Lumiste, R., & Heinlo, A. (2007). *Innovation in Estonian Enterprises*. Tallinn, Estonia: Enterprise Estonia.

Wiig, K. (2000). Knowledge Management in Innovation and R&D. In *Proceedings of the Aspen World 2000*. Cambridge, MA: Aspen Technologies.

Chapter 13

Mobile Commerce Use among UK Mobile Users Based on a Proposed Mobile Network Utilization Framework:
An Experimental Approach – Part 2

Asem Moqbel
Cardiff University, UK

Mirella Yani-Di-Soriano
Cardiff University, UK

Shumaila Yousafzai
Cardiff University, UK

ABSTRACT

This paper examines UK mobile users' perceptions of m-commerce utilization. For this purpose, the study has devised a Mobile Network Utilization Model that was empirically tested in experimental settings. The empirical findings revealed strong support for the capability of the proposed utilization model in measuring the concept of Mobile Task-Technology Fit (MTTF) and explaining the utilization of m-commerce services among UK mobile users. In particular, the research found that MTTF and m-commerce utilization are dependent on the interactions between the key components of a wider mobile network, that is mobile devices, mobile tasks, mobile operators, as well as mobile vendors. Fifteen factors were identified as a result of such interaction and the importance of these factors in explaining MTTF and the actual utilization of m-commerce services was empirically asserted.

DOI: 10.4018/978-1-4666-1752-0.ch013

INTRODUCTION

With slight variations mainly over the technological nature of the medium, m-commerce has been defined by a number of scholars as the trading of goods and services over mobile Internet devices. In their article, Wu and Hisa (2004) defined mobile commerce as a monetary-value transaction that is carried out over a wireless telecommunication network. Makki et al. (2002) asserted this view and attributed the growing demand on wireless Internet services to the increasing growth of wireless networks. Other scholars, however, have emphasized the broad dissemination of the mobile hardware when defining m-commerce. They argued for m-commerce as being the commercialization of services delivered over handheld devices such as mobile phones and Personal Digital Assistants (PDAs) (Sadeh, 2002; Mennecke & Strader, 2002; Dholakia & Dholakia, 2004; Shin et al., 2006). Still other scholars have favored a combination of the two views when defining m-commerce. Barnes (2002), for example, argued that "modern wireless communications represent the convergence of two key technology trends of the 1990s: portability and networking." In this view, the nature of m-commerce is multi-dimensional since its emergence is not only attributed to advancements in the Internet technologies but also to a corresponding set of inventions in the telecommunication technologies.

Clearly, the advent of m-commerce is a natural phenomenon of the wireless convergence. Many have regarded such a form of electronic trade as "a natural extension" of electronic commerce (Coursaris et al., 2003) or "a subset of e-commerce" (Dholakia & Dholakia, 2004; Ngai & Gunasekaran, 2007; Siau & Shen, 2003). Others have seen it as a totally different form of trade stressing the wireless nature of the medium and drawing on the distinction between wired and wireless Internet (Bhasin, 2005). The debate on the nature of m-commerce is still current since more technological advancements seem to add to its uniqueness as a newly emerging business model.

In the greatest part of the literature, there remains, however, a strong emphasis on the increasing importance of m-commerce as a thriving force with great future potential in the realm of electronic commerce. Bertrand et al. (2001) expect a possible surge in the mobile-based electronic commerce due to the growing number of value-added mobile services and the increasing world-wide adoption of mobile Internet. Successful adoption of m-commerce with particular reference to Nordic Countries (e.g., Kristoffersen & Ljungberg, 1999) and Japan's NTT DoCoMo (e.g., Bertrand et al., 2001; Anwar, 2002; Barnes, 2002; Funk, 2006) have been cited by many as examples to substantiate such a possible surge in m-commerce services in the years to come. Certain advanced regions and countries such as Western Europe and the USA, however, have been slow to embrace the m-commerce phenomenon. Scholars such as Makki et al. (2003) and Anckar and D'Incau (2002) have attributed such a slow response to the technical infrastructure, low speed wireless access links, as well as high costs associated with m-commerce implementation. This is also complicated by the absence of integration between mobile players' sophisticated infrastructure and applications development on the one hand and their wireless data service provision on the other (Seager, 2003).

The current paper, however, undertakes a consumer perspective as it utilizes a lab-based experiment to examine consumers' perceptions of m-commerce and explore the scope of its services adoption in the UK market. The experimental research aims to identify areas of interest in the mobile task-technology fit (MTTF) and ultimately measure users' utilization of m-commerce services. Building on some information system models, a conceptual framework was developed for the purpose of this research integrating relevant constructs perceived as central to answering the research questions and ultimately m-commerce adoption.

Theoretical Grounds

Frameworks and conceptual models of mobile information systems (Mobile IS) are very scant. The reasons are abound among which the novelty of the phenomenon, the non-commercial adoption of the innovation as a business model, as well as the interdependent nature of the medium exhibiting several players of contractual nature ranging from system manufacturers to service providers, mobile vendors, regulators, as well as mobile end users. Though the traditional information systems (IS) have witnessed the emergence of several models and frameworks attempting to explain its acceptance as well as usage (e.g., Davis, 1989), mobile information systems suffer from a shortage in such theoretical frameworks. Some of the existing mobile IS frameworks have entirely adopted traditional IS models in their endeavors to elucidate the adoption of mobile technologies (e.g., Junglas et al., 2008). Other models have either modified or extended such traditional IS frameworks to best fit the mobile information medium (e.g., Lee et al., 2007). Both streams, however, have reflected an understanding that mobile information systems are unique in their nature though the attempted elucidations of such uniqueness have predominately been based on traditional IS frameworks. They have also been pre-occupied with tackling the utilization of mobile information systems within organizational settings – an area in which such a medium is not fully utilized. Therefore, there has been an urging need for developing mobile IS frameworks to explain the adoption of mobile technologies and services among mobile end users being the societal sector mostly targeted with m-commerce services.

In their nature, mobile systems are mainly end user-centered, a phenomenon explained by the exponential diffusion of mobile devices among end users all over the globe. The existing m-commerce applications are mainly targeted to accommodate end users' needs and hence priority should be given to the development of mobile end user frameworks. To address such a shortcoming, a mobile system framework was developed to explain the nature of m-commerce services adoption among mobile end users.

THE RATIONALE FOR A MOBILE TECHNOLOGY FRAMEWORK

Mobile technology boosts a challenge for the information technology models designed for work settings. Such models were aimed at explaining the relationships between organizations' tasks and their informational systems in order to measure job-related constructs such as individual performance and system utilization. The ubiquitous nature of the mobile medium, however, has the potential to redefine such relationships between the constructs and might disclose layers of embedded interrelationships that remained unattended to within the research corpus of information systems. In addition, the mobile use context varies by the mobility of the medium and hence frames mobile users in various use situations requiring different cognitive responses to utilize the technology and perform the mobile task at that given time and place.

Being part of the mobile context, m-commerce is different from other technology innovations that are mainly characterized by restrictions to place, time, and use context. M-commerce operates in a mobile environment where the impact and interaction of mobile technology, mobile services, as well as mobile context frame the behavior of users and define their context of use. Hence, the requirements for utilizing m-commerce vary by context and the span of control imposed by the immediate context of use. For these reasons, theories such as the TAM (Davis, 1986) championing or implying perfect use conditions are not entirely applicable. Urbaczewski et al. (2002) confirm this view when they assert that any attempt to validate or invalidate theories such as the TAM in the mobile context would be premature if no effort is made to gain an understanding of the complex phenomenon of adoption of mobile technology as a complex socio-technical process. The underlying assumption of the TAM constructs of perceived usefulness (PU) and perceived ease of use (PEOU) is that their positive perception is the sole determinant of technology utilization. Hence, there is an apparent negligence of the impact of the multi-dimensionality of the use context. The TAM clearly implies the supremacy of its two major constructs as motivators freeing the user from the other opposing forces of the use context. In this sense, the TAM context is mainly organizational (Goodhue & Thompson, 1995; Dishaw & Strong, 1999) where job performance is the ultimate translation of technology acceptance – a phenomenon that is not entirely applicable to mobile technology and hence m-commerce where adopters are mainly end users.

The issue of job performance as a measure of technology acceptance has been widely criticized due to the relative absence of volitional use conditions in organizational settings (Stafford et al., 2004, cited in Lu et al., 2005). Voluntariness in usage was also an issue that has been criticized in the Theory of Reasoned Action (TRA) resulting in a modification of the theory's original model by adding the construct of perceived behavioral control as a determinant of behavioral intentions and use (Ajzen & Fishbein, 1973). This modification has come to be known as the Theory of Planned Behavior (TPB) (Ajzen, 1985, 1991). More recently, Venkatesh and Davis (2000) revised the original TAM proposing a TAM2 framework that included the construct of subjective norms as a determinant of PU.

Lu et al. (2005) further argue that the TAM related models focused on building a generic model for explaining general technology acceptance. A generic model may not accurately explain the process of adopting a specific system and tend to neglect one important variable – the impact of personal innovativeness on adoption (Ibid). A model such as the Task-Technology Fit (TTF)

(Goodhue & Thompson, 1995), on the other hand, includes user abilities as a core component, but the empirical research carried out by the authors did not explore the moderating nature of personal innovativeness as a mediating force between the two major parts of the model, namely, the task and technology. Our proposed framework accounts for the interaction effect resulting from the user moderating mobile tasks and mobile technology. We claim that a fit between the mobile task and technology is relative to an individual's personal innovativeness as well as the perception of and variation in the use context. Though studies such as Lee et al. (2004) have accounted for individual differences when measuring the TTF in use situations, they still share the commonality of applying the model to organizational settings in which the absence of volitional use is likely to distort the impact of TTF on both performance and use. Moreover, modeling the context of use to organizational settings could vary in extent and significance to that of end users'. These studies have also overlooked the impact of the use context on users' perception of the TTF and the inverse impact of such a use context on users' perceived abilities.

Though the TTF resembles the TAM in that they both presume perfect use conditions mainly in organizational settings, our proposed model for m-commerce adoption is not entirely pre-occupied with the technicalities of the system (i.e., the Technical Fit) but also extend to include a wider 'Network Fit' where the user is part of a bigger and interrelated network of technology developers, service providers, and service users. The two sub fit models (technical and network) are also integral parts of a larger socio-technical context. Moreover, beside the technical consideration of the medium and users' familiarity with the technology, the framework factors in the impact of the larger mobile use context as a determinant of technology utilization.

As an information system framework, however, the TTF enjoys an advantage over the TAM model.

While the former explicitly accounts for the information system task as a major determinant of the fit with the technological medium, the latter overlooks its criticality though its importance might implicitly be perceived as embedded under its construct of PU (Dishaw & Strong, 1999). After all, the two models were developed for stationary information systems and technologies.

Studies that have tested the TTF model on mobile information systems are very sparse. They are also pre-occupied with organizational tasks and the utilization of mobile technology in work settings. Gebauer and Shaw (2004), for example, applied the TTF to a newly implemented mobile e-procurement system introduced to aid the existing electronic procurement application of a Fortune 100 company. Gebauer et al. (2006) asserted that the existing studies on mobile information systems have addressed the basic concept of TTF but the concept has not been integrated systematically. In their research paper, the authors suggested the study of managerial tasks as the basis for analyzing mobile systems. Though the authors provided a systematic allocation of tasks based on their inherent nature of routineness and non-routineness, the study remained limited to managerial tasks whereby their performance was seen as part of the job rather than a voluntary choice (Dishaw & Strong, 1999).

Moreover, the study by Lee et al. (2007) explored the impact of individual differences among insurance agents on the performance of insurance tasks using the PDA technology. Although the study reported a major impact of individual differences on the performance of insurance tasks among the 238 surveyed insurance agents, it remained prone to the criticism that task performance in organizational settings is not entirely volitional. Besides, the study's organizational context distorted a precise measurement of the validity of the TTF and its applicability to mobile information systems though cognitive fit and computer self-efficacy were employed as explanatory measures of technology utilization and task performance.

Perhaps the more recent study by Junglas et al. (2008) has gone a step further in recreating a more authentic mobile context whereby tasks were divided on the basis of their sensitiveness and insensitiveness to location and technology was epitomized according to locatability and mobility. The major drawback of the study, however, was the deliberate elimination of the impact of individual differences as the study recruited its participants entirely from an information system class. By doing this, the study intended to test for the fit between mobile technology and mobile task without seeing individual abilities as having a major influence on moderating the fit between the task and technology. Furthermore, though the authors strived to provide ideal mobile context conditions to test for the fit between the proposed tasks and technologies, they overlooked the impact of the use context in determining the extent of fit between the tasks and technology used.

CONCEPTUAL MOBILE TECHNOLOGY FRAMEWORK AND HYPOTHESIZED RELATIONSHIPS

To address this urging need, we proposed a research framework for the utilization of mobile technology for m-commerce purposes incorporating constructs from information system models such as the TTF and our own. The conceptual framework employs the TTF model as a core component of a bigger network fit which is in turn incorporated into a larger socio-technical context. The logic for such a comprehensive framework is explained by the multi-dimensional nature of the mobile use context involving the existence and collaboration of many players forming an interrelated use network and assuming different but interlinked roles. The interaction between the constructs of individual fits within the framework have also been seen as crucial where, for example, individual differences are considered as having a moderation capability that affects the interaction between mobile task and mobile technology. The result is an extent of fit relative to the level of an individual's personal innovativeness. Similarly, the level of fit between the task and technology is impacted by the larger fit of the network in which the relative influence of mobile operators and vendors emerge as inevitable. Figure 1 presents a diagrammatic representation of our proposed framework along with the hypothesized inter-relationships.

To this end, the following can be hypothesized:

Technical Fit

Mobile Technology

H1: The characteristics of mobile devices contribute to the fit with mobile tasks and hence the actual use of m-commerce services and applications.

H1a: The input features of mobile devices affect MTTF and hence the actual use of m-commerce services and applications.

H1b: The output features of mobile devices affect MTTF and hence the actual use of m-commerce services and applications.

Mobile Users

H2: Mobile users' skills and abilities impact their perceptions of the difficulty of mobile tasks.

H3: Mobile users' skills and abilities impact their perceptions of mobile devices' compatibility with mobile tasks.

H4: Following from H2 and H3, mobile users' skills and abilities affect their perceptions of the mobile task-technology fit (MTTF).

Figure 1. Mobile Network Utilization Framework

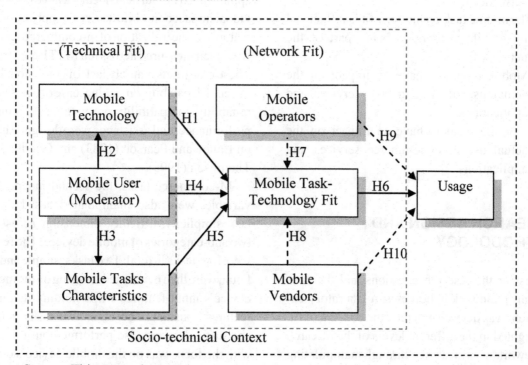

Source: This research
Note: Assumed indirect relationships are indicated with dotted lines.

Tasks Characteristics

H5: The characteristics of mobile tasks contribute to the fit with mobile devices and hence the actual use of m-commerce services and applications.

H5a: Simple mobile tasks are likely to reflect greater fit with mobile devices and hence affect the actual use of mobile m-commerce services and applications.

H5b: Complex mobile tasks are likely to reflect lesser fit with mobile devices and hence the actual use of m-commerce services and applications than simple mobile tasks.

Network Fit

H6: The mobile task-technology fit impacts the actual use of m-commerce services and applications.

H7: The mobile task-technology fit is influenced by mobile operators as being part of the network fit.

H8: The mobile task-technology fit is influenced by mobile vendors as being part of the network fit.

H9: Mobile operators have an impact on the actual use of m-commerce services and applications.

H10: Mobile vendors have an impact on the actual use of m-commerce services and applications.

RESEARCH DESIGN AND METHODOLOGY

To answer the research questions and the conceptual framework hypotheses, a laboratory experiment was devised whereby the concept of fit, highlighted in the different levels of the research framework, was measured through manipulating specific characteristics of the tested m-commerce tasks and mobile devices. These manipulations

in the characteristics of m-commerce tasks and mobile technology were aimed at measuring the impact of 'Technical Fit' on the utilization of m-commerce services and applications. Other elements of the framework such MTTF, mobile operators, and mobile vendors were also introduced as part of the experimental questionnaire in which subjects were asked to assess the impact of the wider 'Network Fit' on the utilization of m-commerce services.

Technology and Task Manipulations

Technology, as one of our independent variables, was manipulated through dividing mobile devices' characteristics into two sub-categories based on the mechanisms by which m-commerce tasks were performed. These sub-categories were mobile device input features and mobile device output features. The purpose of this was to test for the impact of mobile devices' hardware and software on the utilization of m-commerce services and applications (i.e. our dependent variable). The individual impact of mobile devices' input and output features on the utilization of m-commerce services were then measured across ten MTTF constructs. These constructs, namely lack of confusion, level of detail, locatability/meaning, ease of use, system reliability, compatibility, presentation, timeliness, performance, and assistance were designed based on Bailey and Pearson (1983) and Goodhue and Thompson (1995).

M-commerce tasks, the second independent variable, were also manipulated based on the task simplicity/difficulty dimension across the two sub-categories of mobile devices. The results were four tasks in total. Two tasks: simple and difficult, were then performed focusing on the mobile device's input features while holding its output features constant. The other two tasks: simple and difficult, were also performed but this time with the focus was on the mobile device's output features while holding the input features constant. The testing of task simplicity and difficulty was also carried out across the same ten constructs in an attempt to predict m-commerce tasks fit with mobile devices and ultimately the impact of this fit on m-commerce utilization.

The mobile task-technology manipulations resulted in four experimental groups to whom four m-commerce tasks were randomly assigned. Group 1 carried out 'Simple Task 1' (sending a text message with pre-defined parameters to a designated mobile phone number). In designing this simple task, an emphasis was placed on the ultimate utilization of mobile devices' input features so as to test them across the ten constructs set forth for this purpose. We attempted to control and minimize the impact of mobile devices' output features through focusing much of the subjects' attention on an input-oriented task where a considerable use of capitalizations, punctuations, characters, symbols, and numbers was emphasized. The purpose was to provide accurate measurements of 'the simple task versus mobile device's input features' dimension.

Experimental group 2 performed 'Simple Task 2' (navigating into the 'message inbox' of the mobile device and browsing through a pre-sent SMS. The design of this simple task was to test for the impact of mobile devices' output features (display and screen size) on the utilization of m-commerce services. The task aimed at controlling to a minimal level the use of mobile devices' input features as the task only involved reading a text message. Moreover, the emphasis on stimulating the subjects' minds to look for a flight booking confirmation number in the text message and to write it down on a sheet of paper was to encourage maximum utilization of the device output features (screen and display).

Experimental group 3 was asked to perform 'Difficult Task 3' (logging into a designated email account, re-typing and sending a pre-defined email to a designated email account). The testing of the mobile-device-mobile-task fit in task 3 was carried out along 'the difficult task versus mobile device input features' paradigm. The subjects

were requested to re-type and send a carefully designed email script the aim of which was to test the usability of the mobile device input features. As it was the case with Simple Task 1, the email script consisted of characters, numbers, symbols, punctuations, as well as capitalizations. 'Difficult Task 3' was designed with the same conditions of 'Simple Task 1' except for the level of task difficulty as opposed to task simplicity. The control and manipulation mechanisms are otherwise identical. Furthermore, the emphasis on performing 'Difficult Task 3' on the interface of an email service provider website was to increase the level of task difficulty and hence its performance on the interface. The standardization of the email interface to a single email service provider was also essential to eliminate the impact of differences in website layouts and designs on the performance of the task.

Experimental group 4 carried out 'Difficult Task 4' (logging into a standardized mobile Website, checking for weather forecasts according to pre-defined search parameters, and writing down weather details for task completion verification). The paradigm of testing the task was formulated around the dimension of 'difficult task versus mobile device output features.' For this experimental group, the task was designed so that maximum testing conditions of the usability of mobile devices' output features were to be attained. The weather checking process involved navigating through multiple Web pages within the standardized Website where browsing and scrolling through the mobile screen were inevitable. Moreover, the standardization of the mobile Website interface was to ensure accurate measurement of the task performance among the group subjects. Table 1 presents a tabular representation of the mobile experiment task-technology taxonomy.

Subjects

Subjects of the experiment were mainly students from various disciplines at a large UK university.

Table 1. Experimental task-technology taxonomy

TTF		Mobile Technology Characteristics	
		Device Input Features	**Device Output Features**
Mobile Task characteristics	**Simple**	Experimental Group 1 (Simple task 1)	Experimental Group 2 (Simple Task 2)
	Difficult	Experimental Group 3 (Difficult task 3)	Experimental Group 4 (Difficult task 4)

Source: This research

Though experiments involving students as the experimental subjects are often criticized of being unrepresentative of the general public due to lower external validity issues and hence their generalizable results are seen as less credible (Saunders et al., 2007), laboratory experiments can still provide accurate results considering the novelty of certain technology applications such as those of m-commerce which are not quite well known to the general public. Besides, lab-based experiments ensure greater control over the experiment variables and hence increase their internal validity which is crucial for testing novel innovations with which the general public is less familiar. Furthermore, subjects were paid for their participation in the experiment to encourage genuine participation. As being part of the research framework, subjects' impact on the concept of fit between mobile tasks and mobile technology was evaluated through measuring subjects' computer self-efficacy and analyzing their demographic data.

Mobile Operators and Vendors

Being part of the 'Network Fit,' both mobile operators and mobile vendors were hypothesized as having effect on users' perception of MTTF and ultimately on m-commerce task performance. Six mobile operator and five mobile vendor constructs were developed based on the literature review and our own so as to test for the claimed impact or the lack of it thereof. Table 2 shows the tested dimensions of mobile operators and mobile vendors.

Questionnaire Development

The questionnaire was carefully developed and designed as an integrated part of the experimental tool devised to answer the research questions and hypotheses. For the purpose of this research, questionnaires were used to collect data from the experiment. The strength of questionnaires lies in the fact that they enable the standardization of responses and hence more accurate analysis of the collected data (Saunders et al., 2007).

DATA ANALYSIS AND FINDINGS

Participants' Demographics

In total, forty participants took part in the experiment deployed for collecting data for the purpose of this study. The data collection process revealed an almost even split between male and female participants. Nineteen of the participants were males while the remaining twenty one were females accounting for 47.5 and 52.5 per cent respectively. Participants spread across three main age groups (18-25, 26-35, 36-45) out of four age groups used in the experiment-related questionnaire with 24 participants clustered around the 18-25 age group alone (60 per cent). Of the remaining participants, 32.5 per cent (i.e., 13 participants) belonged to the 26-35 age group while the other 7.5 per cent of participants (i.e., 3 participants) belonged to the 36-45 age group. A possible explanation of the absence of participants in the 'Over 46' age

Table 2. Characteristics of mobile operators and mobile vendors

Mobile Operator	Characteristics
	Network Coverage
	Connection Speed
	Range of services
	Pricing of services
	Level of integration with mobile devices, vendors, and users.
	Customers loyalty to mobile operator
	Characteristics
Mobile Vendor	Functionality of the mobile website
	Range of services
	Pricing of services
	Level of integration with mobile device, operators, and users.
	Customers loyalty to mobile vendor

Source: This research

group could be entailed to the weak representation of this age group among student population from which participants were mainly sampled. Table 3 summarizes the sample characteristics.

Reliability Analysis

The constructs of the research framework were tested using Cronbach's alpha for internal consistency and reliability. The analysis was carried out across the four experimental treatments to test for the 'Technical Fit' and 'Network Fit' of the research model. Table 4 presents the alpha values of the research framework constructs across the four experimental groups.

Though some scholars argue for an alpha value of 0.60 as marginally acceptable, the majority tend to emphasize a value of 0.70 or higher (Garson, 2008). As reflected in the table, the Cronbach's alpha values for the research framework constructs showed higher internal consistency levels except for mobile vendors' variables where the alpha value is 0.634 and hence might not be as reliable though marginally acceptable.

FACTOR ANALYSIS

To individually correlate an extensive number of constructs such as the ones deployed to test the several parts of the research framework can complicate the identification of patterns in the correlated relationships. To address this issue, the statistical reduction technique of factor analysis was employed to simplify and accurately identify the relationships between the research framework variables.

The Research Framework 'Technical Fit'

The 'Technical Fit' of the research framework comprised of three major parts as its core components: mobile device characteristics, mobile tasks characteristics, and mobile users.

Mobile Device Characteristics

The characteristics of mobile devices were examined using ten constructs across the dichotomous classification of Mobile Device Input Features and Mobile Device Output Features. Three factors

Table 3. Sample characteristics

Characteristic	Number of Sample	Percent
Gender		
Male	19	47.5
Female	21	52.5
Age		
18-25	24	60
26-35	13	32.5
36-45	3	7.5
Over 46	-	-
Education Level		
High School	-	-
Diploma	-	-
University Undergraduate	22	55
University Postgraduate	18	45
Income		
Unemployed	20	50
Under £10,000	8	20
£10,000 - £15,000	6	15
Over £15,000	6	15
Mobile Phone Ownership		
Yes	40	100
No	-	-
Number of Mobile Phones Owned		
One	28	70
Two	9	22.5
More than Two	3	7.5
Duration of Mobile Phone Ownership		
Under One Year	12	30
One to Two Years	4	10
Two to Three Years	4	10
Over Three Years	20	50

Source: This research

Table 4. Research Framework Reliability analysis

Research Framework Characteristic	Number of Constructs	Cronbach's Alpha Value
Mobile Device Input Features	10	0.805
Mobile Device Output Features	10	0.913
Simple Mobile Tasks	10	0.943
Difficult Mobile Tasks	10	0.935
Mobile Operators	6	0.772
Mobile Vendors	5	0.634
User's Computer self-efficacy	10	0.903

Source: This research

Their cumulative explanation potential of the variance between the tested original variables totaled to 68.726 per cent. Similarly, two eligible factors were extracted for mobile device output features. They were 'Mobile Device Output Features' Usability' and 'Mobile Device Output Features' Straightforwardness.' Table 5 and Table 6 show the factor analyses results for the ten constructs of mobile device input and output features.

MOBILE TASKS' CHARACTERISTICS

Mobile tasks characteristics were also dichotomously classified based on their level of difficulty into Simple Mobile Tasks and Complex/Difficult Mobile Tasks. As it was the case with mobile device features, the same ten constructs were used to measure the fit of the two types of mobile tasks with mobile devices.

The presence of high correlation values between the ten constructs used to test for the concept of fit of simple mobile tasks with mobile devices heralded the existence of inter-variable relationships. The results from factor analysis exhibited in Table 7 and Table 8 show that the high correlations (see appendix 1 and 2) across the variables are significant enough to enable

were extracted for mobile device input features with eigenvalues over the desired value of 1. They were 'Mobile Device Input Features' Usability,' 'Mobile Device Input Features' Efficiency,' and 'Mobile Device Input Features' Performance.'

Table 5. Factor analysis for Mobile Device Input Features

Original Variables	Mobile Device Input Features					
	Extracted Factors			Eigenvalue	% of Variance	Cumulative %
	F1- Mobile Device Input Features' Usability			3.839	38.390	38.390
		F2- Mobile Device Input Features' Efficiency		1.892	18.917	57.307
			F3- Mobile Device Input Features' Performance	1.142	11.418	68.726
	Variables' Loadings on Extracted Factors					
Lack of confusion	.097	-.821	-.219			
Level of Detail	.103	-.789	-.137			
Locatability	.681	-.402	-.078			
Ease of Use	.896	.240	-.042			
Reliability	-.007	.094	.929			
Compatibility	.563	-.091	.522			
Presentation	.523	-.164	.415			
Timeliness	-.298	-.754	.248			
Performance	.139	-.816	.123			
Assistance Level	.596	-.103	.034			

* Significant loading value over 0.44

the explanation of most of the variance between variables by a single extracted factor in the case of Simple Mobile Tasks (67.143%) and two factors in Complex Mobile Tasks (77.040%).

Evident from Table 7, all variables loaded positively on the simple mobile tasks' extracted factor. Hence, the name 'Mobile Tasks Straightforwardness' was attributed to the extracted factor as all original variables tackled mobile tasks simplicity from different perspectives. The two extracted factors of complex mobile tasks, on the other hand, reflected varying significance (see Table 8). Nine out of the original ten variables have positive significant loading values on factor 1. The remaining variable almost entirely loaded on factor 2. There are no relational cross-loading, which means that the two factors were fully dis-

tinct though they differed in their variance explanation strength of the overall ten variables. As the nine variables that loaded positively on factor 1 signify the difficulty level of mobile tasks, the name 'Mobile Tasks Complexity' can be attributed to extracted factor 1. Moreover, since factor 2 is solely concerned with the level of assistance required to accomplish the complex mobile task, the factor can therefore be named 'Complex Mobile Tasks Assistance Level.'

Mobile Users' Technological Characteristics

The research framework hypothesized that mobile users have a moderation impact on the perception of fit between m-commerce services and mobile

Table 6. Factor analysis for Mobile Device Output Features

Original Variables	Mobile Device Output Features				
	Extracted Factors		Eigenvalue	% of Variance	Cumulative %
	F1- Mobile Device Output Feature's Us-ability		5.777	57.771	57.771
		F2- Device Output Features' straightforwardness	1.284	12.839	70.610
	Variables' Loadings on Extracted Factors				
Lack of confusion	.797	.000			
Level of Detail	.875	.035			
Locatability	.597	.515			
Ease of Use	.604	.451			
Reliability	.751	-.288			
Compatibility	.731	.261			
Presentation	.898	-.176			
Timeliness	.774	-.006			
Performance	.721	.267			
Assistance Level	-.045	.943			

* Significant loading value over 0.44

Table 7. Factor analysis for Simple Mobile Tasks

Original Variables	Simple Mobile Tasks			
	Extracted Factors	Eigenvalue	% of Variance	Cumulative %
	F1- Mobile Tasks' Straightforwardness	6.714	67.143	67.143
	Variables' Loadings on Extracted Factor			
Lack of confusion	.787			
Level of Detail	.807			
Locatability	.770			
Ease of Use	.897			
Reliability	.899			
Compatibility	.892			
Presentation	.856			
Timeliness	.794			
Performance	.781			
Assistance Level	.687			

* Significant loading value over 0.44

Table 8. Factor analysis for Complex Mobile Tasks

Original Variables	Complex Mobile Tasks				
	Extracted Factors		Eigenvalue	% of Variance	Cumulative %
	F1- Mobile Tasks' Complexity		6.509	65.088	65.088
		F2- Complex Mobile Tasks' Assistance Level	1.195	11.952	77.040
	Variables' Loadings on Extracted Factors				
Lack of confusion	.978	-.239			
Level of Detail	.876	-.094			
Locatability	.671	.348			
Ease of Use	.950	-.289			
Reliability	.883	-.091			
Compatibility	.800	.291			
Presentation	.704	.310			
Timeliness	.713	.170			
Performance	.795	.234			
Assistance Level	.047	.916			

* Significant loading value over 0.44

devices. Two separate methods were designed to test for the significance of such a moderation effect. These were the duration of participants' technological exposure to the mobile context and their computer self-efficacy.

Descriptive Analysis of Participants' Technological Characteristics

This section will discuss some descriptive measures to check for the possible significance of the 'Duration of Mobile Device Ownership' variable on moderating mobile users' perception of MTTF. In general, the mean scores of the perception of fit between mobile devices and m-commerce tasks tended to be higher among participants who recorded an ownership of a mobile device(s) for over three years. However, for the purpose of this study, we ignored the impact of the two middle categories of 'The Duration of Mobile Device Ownership' variable (i.e., 'One to Two Years' and 'Two to Three Years') for two reasons. The first reason is that each category only recorded four

participants resulting in too a small percentage (10% each). The second reason is that the time span between the two middle categories was presumed as less significant as compared to the other two categories forming the extremes of the ordinal scale (Under One Year and Over Three Years). Besides, the 'Under One Year' and 'Over Three Years' recorded 12 and 20 participants respectively (i.e., 30% and 50%). Table 9 shows a projection of the mean and standard deviation scores of the ten constructs of mobile devices' input and output features for the ('Under One Year' and 'Over Three Years') categories.

As evident from the table, the higher mean and less standard deviation scores of the 'Over Three Years' category asserted that participants who owned a mobile device(s) for over three years reflected a tendency to perceive a higher fit rate between mobile devices and m-commerce tasks across the ten constructs as compared to participants who owned a mobile device(s) for less than one year. Similar higher mean and less standard deviations scores were also recorded among the

Table 9. Descriptive statistics for duration of mobile device ownership

Dependent Variable		No. of participants	Mean	Std. Deviation	Std. Error
Device Inputs Lack of Confusion	1 Under One Year	12	3.42	1.165	.336
	4 Over Three Years	20	3.55	.826	.185
Device Inputs Level of Detail	1 Under One Year	12	3.00	1.206	.348
	4 Over Three Years	20	3.35	.813	.182
Device Inputs Locatability	1 Under One Year	12	3.50	1.243	.359
	4 Over Three Years	20	3.75	.550	.123
Device Inputs Ease of Use	1 Under One Year	12	4.00	.853	.246
	4 Over Three Years	20	3.90	.788	.176
Device Inputs System Reliability	1 Under One Year	12	2.75	.754	.218
	4 Over Three Years	20	3.40	.883	.197
Device Inputs Compatibility	1 Under One Year	12	3.00	.853	.246
	4 Over Three Years	20	3.60	.883	.197
Device Inputs Presentation	1 Under One Year	12	3.50	.798	.230
	4 Over Three Years	20	3.80	.834	.186
Device Inputs Timeliness	1 Under One Year	12	3.00	1.206	.348
	4 Over Three Years	20	2.90	1.071	.240
Device Inputs Performance	1 Under One Year	12	3.00	1.348	.389
	4 Over Three Years	20	3.50	.889	.199
Device Inputs Assistance	1 Under One Year	12	4.58	.669	.193
	4 Over Three Years	20	4.00	.725	.162
Device Outputs Lack of Confusion	1 Under One Year	12	3.25	1.138	.329
	4 Over Three Years	20	3.80	.894	.200
Device Outputs Level of Detail	1 Under One Year	12	3.00	.953	.275
	4 Over Three Years	20	3.50	1.192	.267
Device Outputs Locatability	1 Under One Year	12	3.33	1.073	.310
	4 Over Three Years	20	3.20	1.005	.225
Device Outputs Ease of Use	1 Under One Year	12	3.58	.793	.229
	4 Over Three Years	20	3.50	1.000	.224
Device Outputs System Reliability	1 Under One Year	12	3.17	.835	.241
	4 Over Three Years	20	2.95	1.099	.246
Device Outputs Compatibility	1 Under One Year	12	3.17	.937	.271
	4 Over Three Years	20	3.25	.910	.204
Device Outputs Presentation	1 Under One Year	12	3.08	.996	.288
	4 Over Three Years	20	3.15	1.226	.274
Device Outputs Timeliness	1 Under One Year	12	2.75	1.288	.372
	4 Over Three Years	20	2.70	1.261	.282
Device Outputs Performance	1 Under One Year	12	3.33	.888	.256
	4 Over Three Years	20	3.15	1.089	.244
Device Outputs Assistance	1 Under One Year	12	4.33	.778	.225
	4 Over Three Years	20	3.80	.894	.200

Source: This research

Table 10. Descriptive statistics for duration of mobile device ownership across mobile tasks' two dimensions of simplicity and difficulty

Dependent Variable		No. of participants	Mean	Std. Deviation	Std. Error
Simple Task Lack of Confusion	1 Under One Year	12	3.92	.900	.260
	4 Over Three Years	20	4.10	.788	.176
Simple Task Level of Detail	1 Under One Year	12	3.83	.835	.241
	4 Over Three Years	20	4.05	.945	.211
Simple Task Locatability	1 Under One Year	12	3.58	.900	.260
	4 Over Three Years	20	3.55	.999	.223
Simple Task Ease of Use	1 Under One Year	12	3.75	1.055	.305
	4 Over Three Years	20	3.95	.826	.185
Simple Task System Reliability	1 Under One Year	12	3.67	1.073	.310
	4 Over Three Years	20	3.80	.951	.213
Simple Task Compatibility	1 Under One Year	12	3.58	1.084	.313
	4 Over Three Years	20	4.05	.826	.185
Simple Task Presentation	1 Under One Year	12	3.25	.965	.279
	4 Over Three Years	20	3.85	.933	.209
Simple Task Timeliness	1 Under One Year	12	3.58	1.379	.398
	4 Over Three Years	20	3.60	1.273	.285
Simple Task Performance	1 Under One Year	12	3.67	1.073	.310
	4 Over Three Years	20	3.90	.788	.176
Simple Task Assistance	1 Under One Year	12	4.50	.798	.230
	4 Over Three Years	20	4.15	.875	.196
Difficult Task Lack of Confusion	1 Under One Year	12	2.00	.953	.275
	4 Over Three Years	20	2.35	.933	.209
Difficult Task Level of Detail	1 Under One Year	12	2.33	.888	.256
	4 Over Three Years	20	2.60	1.095	.245
Difficult Task Locatability	1 Under One Year	12	2.50	.905	.261
	4 Over Three Years	20	2.30	.923	.206
Difficult Task Ease of Use	1 Under One Year	12	2.17	1.193	.345
	4 Over Three Years	20	2.20	1.005	.225
Difficult Task System Reliability	1 Under One Year	12	2.08	.996	.288
	4 Over Three Years	20	2.45	1.099	.246
Difficult Task Compatibility	1 Under One Year	12	2.58	1.311	.379
	4 Over Three Years	20	2.45	1.050	.235
Difficult Task Presentation	1 Under One Year	12	2.50	1.087	.314
	4 Over Three Years	20	2.75	1.118	.250
Difficult Task Timeliness	1 Under One Year	12	2.42	.996	.288
	4 Over Three Years	20	2.10	1.021	.228
Difficult Task Performance	1 Under One Year	12	2.75	1.138	.329
	4 Over Three Years	20	2.70	1.129	.252
Difficult Task Assistance	1 Under One Year	12	3.33	1.073	.310
	4 Over Three Years	20	2.85	1.040	.233

Source: This research

over-three-year mobile device owners than the under-one-year owners as far as mobile tasks are concerned (see Table 10). This means that the perception of m-commerce tasks fit with mobile devices was higher among participants who owned mobile phones for a longer period.

It can therefore be concluded from above that descriptive analysis substantiated the hypothesized impact of users' mobile technology skills on their perception of fit between mobile devices and m-commerce tasks. This is consistent with the moderation effect hypothesis of the research framework. Such a validation will be further ascertained by testing the perception of fit between mobile devices characteristics and m-commerce services against the possible impact of users' computer self-efficacy measures.

Mobile Users' Computer Self-Efficacy

Participants' computer self-efficacy (Compeau & Higgins, 1995) was tested using ten questions that asked participants to hypothetically assume ten different use situations. As the use of mobile device was constant throughout the ten use situations, the correlation values showed strong associations between the ten different use situations (see Table 11). This significance implied the possible impact of users' computer self-efficacy on the actual utilization of m-commerce services.

Factor analysis confirmed such strong associations and two factors were extracted as significant (see Table 12).

As can be seen from the table, factor 1 reflected greater significance with 5.666 eigenvalue and a variance explanation capability of 56.659 per cent. Factor 2, on the other hand, achieved a marginal significance value of 1.081 on the Eigen Test and a variance percentage of only 10.809 per cent. Altogether, the two factors projected a total variance explanation potential of 67.468 per cent among the ten variables.

Moreover, the loading use situations have split evenly between the two factors with use situations

1, 2, 3, 7, and 8 loading significantly to factor 1 and use situations 3, 5, 6, 9, and 10 loading significantly to factor 2 (see Table 13).

While all use situations loading to factor 1 shared the assumption that different mobile device self-help features were available during task performance, use situations loading to factor 2 were all assuming access to assistance from others – whether it be skillful people or customer service departments – to enable the performance of mobile tasks. Therefore, the two extracted factors can be named 'Mobile Device Self-Help Features' and 'Mobile Advice-based Help Features' respectively.

Furthermore, though the split was even in use situations, the variance explanation of factor 1 was almost six times as strong. The logic behind this is that participants' responses tended to be positively skewed towards the use situations with self-help features being available, thus reflecting higher confidence levels in their ability to handle mobile devices (factor 1). This also means that responses were negatively skewed towards the advice-based help features (factor 2) reflecting participants' reluctance to request for help in performing m-commerce services (Table 14).

REGRESSION ANALYSIS FOR THE NETWORK FIT AND M-COMMERCE UTILIZATION

In the research framework, the three components of the 'Network Fit,' namely MTFF, mobile operators, and mobile vendors were also hypothesized as having an impact on the utilization of m-commerce. As actual utilization of m-commerce cannot be recreated in experimental settings, perceived utilization circumstances were used to measure such an impact of the 'Network Fit' components. In this way, measured utilization can best resemble real use circumstances. Four constructs were used during the data collection process to test for the perceived utilization of m-

Table 11. Pearson's Product-Moment Correlation Coefficient for mobile users' computer self-efficacy variables

		User's Computer Self-Efficacy 1	User's Computer Self-Efficacy 2	User's Computer Self-Efficacy 3	User's Computer Self-Efficacy 4	User's Computer Self-Efficacy 5	User's Computer Self-Efficacy 6	User's Computer Self-Efficacy 7	User's Computer Self-Efficacy 8	User's Computer Self-Efficacy 9	User's Computer Self-Efficacy 10
User's Computer Self-Efficacy 1	Pearson Correlation	1	.505(**)	.640(**)	.506(**)	.179	.491(**)	.718(**)	.696(**)	.493(**)	.453(**)
User's Computer Self-Efficacy 2	Pearson Correlation	.505(**)	1	.560(**)	.540(**)	.189	.563(**)	.382(*)	.453(**)	.485(**)	.220
User's Computer Self-Efficacy 3	Pearson Correlation	.640(**)	.560(**)	1	.636(**)	.458(**)	.572(**)	.596(**)	.659(**)	.568(**)	.280
User's Computer Self-Efficacy 4	Pearson Correlation	.506(**)	.540(**)	.636(**)	1	.473(**)	.680(**)	.604(**)	.473(**)	.737(**)	.409(**)
User's Computer Self-Efficacy 5	Pearson Correlation	.179	.189	.458(**)	.473(**)	1	.479(**)	.360(*)	.246	.414(**)	.257
User's Computer Self-Efficacy 6	Pearson Correlation	.491(**)	.563(**)	.572(**)	.680(**)	.479(**)	1	.629(**)	.469(**)	.837(**)	.583(**)
User's Computer Self-Efficacy 7	Pearson Correlation	.718(**)	.382(*)	.596(**)	.604(**)	.360(*)	.629(**)	1	.702(**)	.702(**)	.564(**)
User's Computer Self-Efficacy 8	Pearson Correlation	.696(**)	.453(**)	.659(**)	.473(**)	.246	.469(**)	.702(**)	1	.454(**)	.377(*)
User's Computer Self-Efficacy 9	Pearson Correlation	.493(**)	.485(**)	.568(**)	.737(**)	.414(**)	.837(**)	.702(**)	.454(**)	1	.507(**)
User's Computer Self-Efficacy 10	Pearson Correlation	.453(**)	.220	.280	.409(**)	.257	.583(**)	.564(**)	.377(*)	.507(**)	1

** Correlation is significant at the 0.01 level (2-tailed).

* Correlation is significant at the 0.05 level (2-tailed).

Source: This research

Table 12. Factor analysis for mobile users' skills measures

Component	Initial Eigenvalues			Extraction Sums of Squared Loadings			Rotation Sums of Squared Loadings(a)
	Total	% of Variance	Cumulative %	Total	% of Variance	Cumulative %	Total
1	5.666	56.659	56.659	5.666	56.659	56.659	4.833
2	1.081	10.809	67.468	1.081	10.809	67.468	4.182
3	.917	9.167	76.634				
4	.740	7.399	84.033				
5	.443	4.428	88.462				
6	.322	3.216	91.678				
7	.278	2.778	94.455				
8	.266	2.663	97.118				
9	.176	1.757	98.876				
10	.112	1.124	100.000				

Source: This research

Table 13. Pattern Matrix for mobile users' skills measures

	Component	
	1	2
User's Computer Self-Efficacy 1	.953	-.114
User's Computer Self-Efficacy 2	.606	.129
User's Computer Self-Efficacy 3	.661	.248
User's Computer Self-Efficacy 4	.333	.626
User's Computer Self-Efficacy 5	-.226	.877
User's Computer Self-Efficacy 6	.273	.730
User's Computer Self-Efficacy 7	.686	.275
User's Computer Self-Efficacy 8	.920	-.106
User's Computer Self-Efficacy 9	.295	.697
User's Computer Self-Efficacy 10	.271	.448

Source: This research

commerce among participants. These constructs were the frequency of simple m-commerce services use over mobile devices, the frequency of difficult m-commerce services use over mobile devices, the impact of mobile operators' quality of services on m-commerce utilization, as well as the impact of mobile vendors' quality of services on

m-commerce utilization. The first two constructs were both designed to test for the MTTF impact on m-commerce use, while the third and fourth constructs aimed at measuring the effect of mobile operators and mobile vendors on the utilization of mobile services among participants respectively.

MTTF Impact on M-Commerce Utilization

The impact of MTTF on the use of m-commerce services was measured against two perceived utilization constructs, namely the frequency of usage of simple m-commerce services and the frequency of usage of complex m-commerce services over mobile devices. To test for such an impact, multiple regression and analysis of variance (ANOVA) were performed for each construct.

Evident from Table 15, there existed strong positive relationships (R, 0.617) between simple m-commerce services utilization (the dependent variable) and the extracted factors of MTTF (the independent variables). In addition, the coefficient of determination (R^2, 0.380) implied that 38 per cent of the variance in simple m-commerce ser-

Table 14. Factor analysis for Mobile Users' Computer Self-Efficacy

Original Variables	Mobile Users' Computer Self-Efficacy				
	Extracted Factors		Eigenvalue	% of Variance	Cumulative %
	F1- Mobile Device Self-Help Features		5.666	56.659	56.659
		F2- Mobile Device Advice-based Help Features	1.081	10.809	67.468
	Variables' Loadings on Extracted Factors				
User's Computer Self-Efficacy 1	.953	-.114			
User's Computer Self-Efficacy 2	.606	.129			
User's Computer Self-Efficacy 3	.661	.248			
User's Computer Self-Efficacy 4	.333	.626			
User's Computer Self-Efficacy 5	-.226	.877			
User's Computer Self-Efficacy 6	.273	.730			
User's Computer Self-Efficacy 7	.686	.275			
User's Computer Self-Efficacy 8	.920	-.106			
User's Computer Self-Efficacy 9	.295	.697			
User's Computer Self-Efficacy 10	.271	.448			

* Significant loading value over 0.44

vices utilization was explained by the perception of fit between m-commerce tasks and mobile devices. Moreover, the ANOVA reported an F-value of 2.379 at a significant level of $p<0.05$ purporting that there is less than five in a hundred chances that the significant difference between m-commerce utilization and mobile users' perception of MTTF occurred by chance.

As several extracted factors of MTTF were used, it is possible that not all of these factors contributed to the prediction of m-commerce services utilization. To test for this, the beta values of the standardized coefficients (see Table 16) were referred to as they usually state the contributions of independent variables in the explanation of variance in the dependent variable. Tradition-

ally, it is agreed that Beta values at a significant level less than $P<0.05$ report unique contributions of independent variables while Beta values with significance levels over $P>0.05$ do not make unique predictions of the dependent variable. Rather, they suggest overlapping with other independent variables (Miller, 2002).

In this context, only two MTTF extracted factors, namely Device Input Features' Usability and Mobile Tasks Complexity reported Beta values of 0.441 and 1.157 at significance levels of $p<0.05$ and $p<0.001$ respectively. The other independent variables greatly overlapped in their prediction of m-commerce utilization.

Similarly, a regression analysis and ANOVA of the effect of MTTF extracted factors on the

Table 15. Regression and ANOVA results of MTTF impact on m-commerce utilization (simple m-commerce services)

	R	R²	F	Sig.
Regression	.617(a)	.380	2.379	.040(a)

Source: This research

utilization of 'complex m-commerce services' were also conducted to test for the assumed relationship (see Table 17). As manifested in the following table, a coefficient R of 0.628 suggested a strong association between mobile users' perception of MTTF and the utilization of complex m-commerce services. In addition, almost 40 per cent of the variation in the utilization of complex m-commerce tasks was explained by mobile users' perception of fit between mobile devices and m-commerce tasks. Moreover, a significant F-Value of 2.521 at a significant level of $p<0.05$ was also evident in the ANOVA analysis:

This also confirms that there are less than five in a hundred chances that the significant difference between mobile users' utilization of complex m-commerce services and their perception of fit between mobile tasks and mobile devices was due to chance. However, as it was the case with simple m-commerce utilization, it is possible that the several independent variables might not all

be responsible for the unique difference. An investigation of the standardized Beta values in the Coefficients table (see Table 18) revealed that only the independent variable of 'Device Input Features' Performance' was responsible for the significant difference (B 2.048, $p<0.05$). The Beta values of the majority of independent variables, on the other hand, suggested significant overlapping in their impact on the utilization of complex m-commerce services.

It is, therefore, clear from above that the perception of fit between mobile tasks and mobile devices has an impact on mobile users' utilization of m-commerce services which is also consistent with the research framework hypothesis.

Mobile Operators' Impact on M-Commerce Utilization

The research framework also hypothesized the impact of mobile operators as part of the 'Network

Table 16. Coefficients of MTTF impact on m-commerce utilization (simple m-commerce services)

	Unstandardized Coefficients		Standardized Coefficients	t	Sig.
	B	Std. Error	Beta	B	Std. Error
Device Input Features Usability	.221	.099	.441	2.233	.033
Device Input Features Efficiency	.160	.114	.319	1.396	.173
Device Input Features Performance	-.145	.082	-.289	-1.770	.087
Device Output System Usability	-.322	.174	-.643	-1.851	.074
Device Output Features Straightforwardness	.066	.105	.132	.627	.535
Mobile Tasks Straightforwardness	-.085	.098	-.171	-.868	.392
Mobile Tasks Complexity	.579	.162	1.157	3.574	.001
Mobile Tasks Assistance Level	-.124	.098	-.247	-1.266	.215

Source: This research

Fit' on the actual use of m-commerce services. The two extracted factors (Mobile Operators' Quality of Services and Mobile Operators' Network Efficiency) out of the original six constructs were used as independent variables in the test for the assumed effect on the use of m-commerce services (the dependent variable).

As it is noticeable from Table 19, the coefficient (R, 0.422) revealed a tendency of a strong positive relationship between m-commerce utilization and participants' perception of mobile operators. The coefficient of determination R^2 also reported that participants' perception of mobile operators explained almost 18 per cent of the variance in m-commerce services use. Furthermore, the F-value of 4.014 at the acceptable significance level of $p < 0.05$ also asserted the existence of such an association well beyond the possibility of attributing it to mere chance.

To test for the source of the unique significance, however, the standardized Beta values for the two independent variables of mobile operators were computed (see Table 20). Mobile Operators' Network Efficiency (network coverage and connection speed) provided a larger positive Beta value of 0.409 at a significant level of $p < 0.05$ thus implying stronger unique contribution to the explanation of the variance in m-commerce utilization than that of Mobile Operators' Quality of Services variable. Therefore, it can be concluded that there existed a considerable positive impact of mobile users' perception of mobile operators (particularly in terms of network efficiency and connection speed) on the actual use of m-commerce services.

Mobile Vendors' Impact on M-Commerce Utilization

The research framework also hypothesized an impact of mobile vendors on the actual utilization of m-commerce services among mobile users. Out

Table 17. Regression and ANOVA results of MTTF impact on m-commerce utilization (complex m-commerce tasks)

	R	R^2	F	Sig.
Regression	.628(a)	.394	2.521	.031(a)

Source: This research

Table 18. Coefficients of MTTF impact on m-commerce utilization (complex m-commerce services)

	Unstandardized Coefficients		Standardized Coefficients	t	Sig.
	B	Std. Error	Beta	B	Std. Error
Device Input Features Usability	.060	.139	.084	.431	.669
Device Input Features Efficiency	-.065	.161	-.091	-.403	.690
Device Input Features Performance	.235	.115	.331	2.048	.049
Device Output System Usability	-.365	.244	-.513	-1.494	.145
Device Output Features Straightforwardness	-.029	.148	-.041	-.196	.846
Mobile Tasks Straightforwardness	.013	.138	.018	.092	.927
Mobile Tasks Complexity	-.116	.228	-.162	-.508	.615
Difficult Mobile Tasks Assistance Level	.191	.138	.269	1.391	.174

Source: This research

Table 19. Regression and ANOVA results of mobile operators' impact on m-commerce utilization

	R	R²	F	Sig.
Regression	.422(a)	.178	4.014	.026(a)

Source: This research

Table 20. Coefficients of mobile operators' impact on m-commerce utilization

	Unstandardized Coefficients		Standardized Coefficients	t	Sig.
	B	Std. Error	Beta	B	Std. Error
Mobile Operators' Quality Of Service	.036	.104	.052	.343	.734
Mobile Operators Network Efficiency	.281	.104	.409	2.689	.011

Source: This research

Table 21. Regression and ANOVA results of mobile vendors' impact on m-commerce utilization

	R	R²	F	Sig.
Regression	.438(a)	.192	9.044	.005(a)

Source: This research

of the original five mobile vendors' constructs used to test for the impact on MTTF, only one factor (Mobile Vendors' User Interface Functionality) was extracted using factor analysis. This variable was used as the independent variable in the regression analysis computed to measure the impact of mobile vendors on the utilization of m-commerce services (the dependent variable).

The coefficient R of 0.438 revealed a rather strong positive relationship between m-commerce utilization and participants' perception of mobile vendors. As also can be noticed from the coefficient of determination (R^2, 0.192), almost 20 per cent of the variance in m-commerce utilization can entirely be explained by the functionality of user interfaces of mobile vendors. Moreover, the F-value of (9.044, $p < 0.005$) in Table 21 confirmed such a unique significance.

The results from the table assert that there are less than five in a thousand chances that the significant relationship between mobile users' per-

ception of mobile vendors and the utilization of m-commerce can be attributed to chance. As also can be noticed from the Beta value (0.438) in Table 22, the functionality of mobile vendors' user interfaces reflected a strong contribution to the prediction of m-commerce utilization among participants.

It can also be concluded that the functionality of mobile vendors' user interfaces has a positive impact on the utilization of m-commerce services among mobile users which is also consistent with the research hypothesis.

CONCLUSION AND RECOMMENDATIONS

In general, the research proposed and empirically validated a Mobile Network Utilization Framework. More specifically, the research found that mobile users' utilization of m-commerce services

Table 22. Coefficients of mobile vendors' impact on m-commerce utilization

	Unstandardized Coefficients		Standardized Coefficients	t	Sig.
	B	Std. Error	Beta	B	Std. Error
Mobile Vendors' Interface Functionality	.281	.093	.438	3.007	.005

Source: This research

and applications is relative to their perceptions of the concept of fit between mobile devices, mobile services, mobile operators, as well as mobile vendors. It also found through empirical evidence that both the 'Technical Fit' and 'Network Fit' of the Mobile Network Utilization Framework are crucial elements of the mobile use context.

'Technical Fit' Findings

The research found supporting evidence for the interaction effect of the three main components of the research framework's 'Technical Fit,' namely mobile users, mobile devices, and mobile tasks.

Mobile Users

The research revealed that mobile users' perceptions of the concept of MTTF varied across the dimensions of users' exposure to mobile technology and their computer self-efficacy. As hypothesized, users' different skills and abilities have a moderation effect on their perceptions of fit between mobile devices and mobile services. It became clear from the analysis that mobile users with longer periods of exposure to mobile technology tended to perceive higher rates of fit between mobile devices and m-commerce services. Moreover, people with high computer self-efficacy showed tendency to adopt complex m-commerce tasks more than people with low computer self-efficacy.

In addition, the research disclosed two factors of mobile users' computer self-efficacy that are crucial to the concept of MTTF and the utilization of m-commerce services. These factors were

'Mobile Device Self-help Features' and 'Mobile Device Advice-based Help Features.' The majority of participants in the experiment revealed a higher tendency of adopting m-commerce services provided various self-help features such as built-in help features and mobile device manuals are available. Moreover, participants reflected more confidence in using mobile devices with the least amount of advice-based help from customer service departments or experienced users in the field. This is in line with the hypothesized positive impact of mobile users' exposure to mobile technology on MTTF. The perception of fit between mobile devices and m-commerce tasks tended to be higher among participants who recorded an ownership of a mobile device(s) for longer time periods.

Mobile Devices

The research found empirical evidence of the importance of the dichotomous classification of mobile devices characteristics into 'Input' and 'Output' Features. For the former, the study identified three important factors that are vital to measuring the impact of mobile devices' input features on the perception of fit with mobile tasks and ultimately m-commerce utilization. These factors were 'Mobile Device Input Features' Usability,' 'Mobile Device Input Features' Efficiency,' and 'Mobile Device Input Features' Performance.' This means that the importance of mobile devices' input features to the utilization of m-commerce services lay in their usability to mobile users; efficiency in accomplishing mobile services under different use circumstances; and capability of processing mobile services, i.e., performing mobile tasks. Similarly, the research also identified two factors spanning the criticality of mobile devices' output features to mobile users' perceptions of MTTF as well as the use of m-commerce services. These two factors were 'Mobile Device Output System's Usability' and 'Mobile Device Output Features' straightforwardness.' According to the empirical findings, these two factors were essential to the presentation and ultimately performance of m-commerce services on the device output mechanisms.

Mobile Tasks

The empirical research asserted the suitability of classifying mobile services according to their level of simplicity and difficulty. It also found that the level of simplicity or difficulty of mobile services is vital to mobile users' perception of fit between mobile technology and mobile tasks. It showed that the more complex the mobile service, the lower the fit rate between mobile devices and mobile services and vice versa. On these bases, the empirical test disclosed the factor of 'Mobile tasks' Straightforwardness' as very essential to perceiving higher fit rate between mobile devices and mobile services. This also held true for m-commerce services utilization. On the other hand, the perception of MTTF was seen to be lower among complex mobile services. Both the perception of fit between mobile devices and mobile tasks as well as the utilization of m-commerce services were found to be relative to two crucial factors that the research identified. These factors were 'Mobile Tasks Complexity' and 'Complex Mobile Tasks' Assistance Level.'

In general, mobile users reflected higher level of confidence in performing simple mobile services without the need for technical assistance. The findings also showed that mobile users exhibited reluctance to ask for help from others when performing mobile services particularly with the ones that were perceived as complex.

'Network Fit' Findings

The research experiment showed empirical evidence of the impact of the three components of the 'Network Fit,' namely, mobile operators, mobile vendors, and MTTF on the utilization of m-commerce services.

Mobile Operators

Data analysis reflected strong support for the impact of mobile operators on both mobile users' perception of MTTF and the utilization of m-commerce services. More specifically, the impact was evident in two major areas, that is, Mobile Network Efficiency and Mobile Operators' Quality of Services. Mobile users showed greater association between m-commerce utilization and mobile operators' network efficiency particularly their network coverage and connection speed. The quality of services such as the range of services and pricing were also seen as major elements in the actual performance of mobile services.

Mobile Vendors

Mobile vendors were also perceived as significant in the fit between mobile devices and mobile services as well as in the utilization of m-commerce services. Such a perceived influence was greatly present in mobile users' perception of mobile data presentation on mobile devices. The empirical test found that 'User Interfaces Functionality' was the most significant element of mobile vendors' impact on mobile users' utilization of m-commerce services. Moderate support was also found for the range of services and pricing.

Mobile Task-Technology Fit (MTTF)

The research empirical procedure also revealed direct impact of mobile users' perception of MTTF on the actual utilization of m-commerce services. In addition, strong empirical evidence of the overall effect of mobile users, mobile devices, mobile tasks, mobile operators, and mobile vendors on the formation of users' perception of MTTF was also witnessed. The empirical test further revealed that the concept of MTTF is dependent on the interaction between the key components of a wider mobile network, namely mobile users, mobile devices, mobile tasks, mobile operators, as well as mobile vendors (Table 23).

Table 23. Components and Extracted Factors of the Mobile Network Utilization Framework

Framework Components	Main Component	Sub Components	Extracted Factors
Technical Fit	Mobile Devices	Mobile Device Input Features	Mobile Device Input Features' Usability
			Mobile Device Input Features' Efficiency
			Mobile Device Input Features' Performance
		Mobile Device Output Features	Mobile Device Output Features' Usability
			Device Output Features' straightforwardness
	Mobile Tasks	Simple Mobile Tasks	Simple Mobile Tasks' Straightforwardness
		Complex Mobile Tasks	Mobile Tasks' Complexity
			Complex Mobile Tasks' Assistance Level
	Mobile Users' Skills	Mobile Users' Computer Self-Efficacy	Mobile Device Self-help Features
			Mobile Device Advice-based Help Features
Network Fit	Mobile Operators	Network Efficiency	Mobile Operators' Network Efficiency
		Services	Mobile Operators' Quality of Services
	Mobile Vendors	User Interfaces	Mobile User Interfaces' Functionality
		Services	Mobile Vendors' Quality of Services
	Mobile TTF	Mobile Devices	5 factors (3 Input Features factors + 2 Output Features factors)
		Mobile Tasks	3 factors (1 Simple Mobile Tasks factor + 2 Complex Mobile Tasks factors)
		Mobile Users' Skills	3 factors (2 Mobile Users' Computer Self-Efficacy factors + 1 Duration of Exposure to Mobile Technology factor)
Utilization	Technical Fit	Mobile Devices	5 factors (3 Input Features factors + 2 Output Features factors)
		Mobile Tasks	3 factors (1 Simple Mobile Tasks factor + 2 Complex Mobile Tasks factors)
		Mobile Users	3 factors (2 Mobile Users' Computer Self-Efficacy factors + 1 Duration of Exposure to Mobile Technology factor)
	Network Fit	Mobile Operators	2 factors (1 Mobile Network Efficiency + 1 Mobile Operators Quality of Services)
		Mobile Vendors	2 factors (1 Mobile User Interfaces' Functionality + 1 Mobile Vendors Quality of Services)
		Mobile TTF	11 factors (5 Mobile Devices factors where 3 are Input Features factors + 2 Output Features factors) + (3 Mobile Tasks factors where 1 Simple Mobile Tasks factor + 2 Complex Mobile Tasks factors) + (3 Mobile Users' factors where 2 Mobile Users' Computer Self-Efficacy factors + 1 Duration of Exposure to Mobile Technology factor)

Source: Author

Academic Contributions

This research has proposed and empirically validated a Mobile Network Utilization Model for measuring the actual utilization of m-commerce services among UK mobile end users. Unlike previous studies of mobile technologies adoption, the current study has emphasized through empirical evidence the importance of 'Network Fit' in explaining m-commerce utilization and its criticality to the overall mobile use context. Moreover, the study has identified fifteen factors that are vital elements of the Mobile Network Utilization Model. These factors are as follows:

1. Mobile Device Input Features' Usability
2. Mobile Device Input Features' Efficiency
3. Mobile Device Input Features' Performance
4. Mobile Device Output Features' Usability
5. Mobile Device Output Features' straightforwardness
6. Mobile Tasks' Straightforwardness
7. Mobile Tasks' Complexity
8. Complex Mobile Tasks' Assistance Level
9. Mobile Device Self-help Features
10. Mobile Device Advice-based Help Features
11. Mobile Operators' Network Efficiency
12. Mobile Operators' Quality of Services
13. Mobile Vendors User Interfaces' Functionality
14. Mobile Vendors' Quality of Services
15. Mobile Users' Duration of Exposure to Mobile Technologies.

Empirically speaking, the above factors reflected validated significance in explaining the utilization of m-commerce services. In fact, these factors defined the interaction process between the key players of the mobile network, namely mobile users, mobile devices, mobile tasks, mobile operators, as well as mobile vendors.

Managerial Implications

The study has validated a practical utilization model that can assist mobile key players in understanding mobile end users' perceptions of mobile devices and m-commerce services. The model can therefore be used to inform the development of mobile devices; the design of mobile applications; as well as the improvement of mobile services. It also provided insight into the crucial role of integration between key players in the mobile use context, namely mobile users through exposure to mobile technology; mobile manufactures through mobile devices' input and output features capabilities; mobile providers through network efficiency and quality of services; as well as mobile vendors through user interfaces' functionality and quality of services. The study has also identified fifteen crucial factors (see previous section) that can better aid mobile marketers in understanding both mobile services adopters and potential users. They can also be utilized in the design of m-commerce services and applications to better suit mobile end users.

Research Limitations

The tradeoff between internal and external validity is always present in experimental research (Zikmund, 2000). While this study recognized the importance of generalizable results, the internal validity was very essential to accurately measure m-commerce utilization. Moreover, the use of students as experimental subjects has often been criticized of being less representative of the general public. Yet, students were sampled randomly from across the university rather than a single class or department. Besides, participants were paid an agreed sum for their participation and use of own mobile devices. Unlike organizational settings where the use of information systems can be part of the actual job, choosing students as the subjects of the experiment ensured a voluntary atmosphere of participation. Overall, using students as experimental subjects was also helpful to ensure proper experimental settings to control for extraneous influences.

Directions for Future Research

The empirically tested Mobile Utilization Network Model provides opportunities for measuring the utilization of m-commerce services in different use contexts across different geographical, cultural, and socio-technical settings. It also provides scope for testing the impact of the model on mobile users' preferences of specific mobile devices and services. Moreover, the cultural aspect of mobile use can be explored as part of the socio-technical continuum.

The research has also identified a set of factors that are essential to the actual utilization of m-commerce services. Both the individual and collective impact of these factors can be investigated in areas such as the design of mobile user interfaces, the development of mobile applications, as well as improvements to mobile devices' current limitations. Further research can also be done on the 'Network Fit' where the impact of mobile operators and mobile vendors can be further studied. Since this study explored the actual utilization, the model can also be used to survey behavioral intentions of m-commerce adoption among potential mobile users.

REFERENCES

Ajzen, I. (1985). From intentions to actions: a theory of planned behavior. In Kuhi, J., & Beckmann, J. (Eds.), *Action-control: from cognition to behavior* (pp. 11–39). Heidelberg, Germany: Springer.

Ajzen, I. (1991). The theory of planned behavior. *Organizational Behavior and Human Decision Processes*, *50*(2), 179–211. doi:10.1016/0749-5978(91)90020-T

Ajzen, I., & Fishbein, M. (1973). Attitudinal and normative variables as predictors of specific behavior. *Journal of Personality and Social Psychology*, *27*, 41–57. doi:10.1037/h0034440

Anckar, B., & D'Incau, D. (2002). Value creation in mobile commerce: Findings from a consumer survey. *The Journal of Information Technology Theory and Application*, *4*(1), 43–64.

Anwar, S. T. (2002). DoCoMo and m-commerce: a case study in market expansion and global strategy. *Thunderbird International Business Review*, *44*(1), 139–164. doi:10.1002/tie.1043

Bailey, J. E., & Pearson, S. W. (1983). Development of a tool for measuring and analyzing computer user satisfaction. *Management Science*, *29*(5), 530–545. doi:10.1287/mnsc.29.5.530

Barnes, S. J. (2002). The mobile commerce value chain: analysis and future developments. *International Journal of Information Management*, *22*, 91–108. doi:10.1016/S0268-4012(01)00047-0

Bertrand, V., Caplan, A., Fernandez-Moran, E., & Letelier, C. (2001). M-commerce: who will reap the profits? In *Kellogg Tech Venture 2001*. Anthology.

Bhasin, M. L. (2005). E-Commerce and M-Commerce Revolution: Perspectives, Problems and Prospects. *The Chartered Accountant*, 824-840.

Compeau, D. R., & Higgins, C. A. (1995). Computer self-efficacy: development of a measure and initial test. *Management Information Systems Quarterly*, *19*(2), 189–211. doi:10.2307/249688

Coursaris, C., Hassanein, K., & Head, M. (2003). M-commerce in Canada: an interaction framework for wireless privacy. *Canadian Journal of Administrative Sciences*, *20*(1), 54–73.

Davis, F. (1986). *A technology acceptance model for empirically testing new end-user information systems: theory and results*. Unpublished doctoral dissertation, Sloan School of Management, Massachusetts Institute of Technology, Cambridge, MA.

Davis, F. (1989). Perceived usefulness, perceived ease of use, and end user acceptance of information technology. *Management Information Systems Quarterly, 13*(3), 318–339. doi:10.2307/249008

Dholakia, R. R., & Dholakia, N. (2004). Mobility and markets: emerging outlines of m-commerce. *Journal of Business Research, 57*, 1391–1396. doi:10.1016/S0148-2963(02)00427-7

Dishaw, M. T., & Strong, D. M. (1999). Extending the technology acceptance model with task–technology fit constructs. *Information & Management, 36*(1), 9–21. doi:10.1016/S0378-7206(98)00101-3

Fishbein, M., & Azjen, I. (1975). *Belief, attitude, intention, and behavior*. Reading, MA: Addison-Wesley.

Funk, J. L. (2006). The future of mobile phone-based Intranet applications: a view from Japan. *Technovation, 26*, 1337–1346. doi:10.1016/j.technovation.2005.08.009

Garson, D. (2008). *Scales and standard measures*. Retrieved July 18, 2008, from http://www2.chass.ncsu.edu/garson/pa765/standard.htm

Gebauer, J., & Shaw, M. J. (2004). Success factors and impacts of mobile business applications: results from a mobile e-procurement study. *International Journal of Electronic Commerce, 8*(3), 19–41.

Gebauer, J., Shaw, M. J., & Gribbins, M. L. (2006). *Task-Technology Fit for mobile information systems*. Retrieved July 15, 2008, from http://www.business.uiuc.edu/

Goodhue, D. L., & Thompson, R. L. (1995). Task-Technology Fit and individual performance. *Management Information Systems Quarterly, 19*(2), 213–236. doi:10.2307/249689

Junglas, I., Abraham, C., & Watson, R. T. (2008). Task-technology fit for mobile locatable information systems. *Decision Support Systems*. doi:10.1016/j.dss.2008.02.007

Kristoffersen, S., & Ljungberg, F. (1999). Making place" to make IT work: empirical explorations of HCI for mobile CSCW. In *Proceedings of the international ACM SIGGROUP conference on supporting group work*, Phoenix, AZ (pp. 276-285).

Lee, C. C., Cheng, H. K., & Cheng, H. H. (2007). An empirical study of mobile commerce in insurance industry: task–technology fit and individual differences. *Decision Support Systems, 43*, 95–110. doi:10.1016/j.dss.2005.05.008

Lee, Y. E., & Benbasat, I. (2004). A framework for the study of customer interface design for mobile commerce. *International Journal of Electronic Commerce, 8*(3), 79–102.

Lu, J., Yao, J. E., & Yu, C. S. (2005). Personal innovativeness, social influences and adoption of wireless Internet services via mobile technology. *The Journal of Strategic Information Systems, 14*(3), 245–268. doi:10.1016/j.jsis.2005.07.003

Makki, S. A. M., Pissinou, N., & Daroux, P. (2002). Mobile and wireless Internet access. *Computer Communications, 26*, 734–746. doi:10.1016/S0140-3664(02)00208-6

Miller, R. L., Acton, C., Fullerton, D. A., & Maltby, J. (2002). *SPSS for social scientists*. Hampshire, UK: Palgrave Macmillan.

Ngai, E. W. T., & Gunasekaran, A. (2007). A review for mobile commerce research and applications. *Decision Support Systems, 41*, 3–15. doi:10.1016/j.dss.2005.05.003

Sadeh, N. (2002). *M-Commerce: technologies, services, and business models*. New York: John Wiley & Sons.

Saunders, M., Lewis, P., & Thornhill, A. (2007). *Research methods for business students* (4th ed.). London: Prentice Hall.

Seager, A. (2003). M-commerce: an integrated approach. *Telecommunications International*, 36-38.

Shin, Y., Jeon, H., & Choi, M. (2006). Analysis of the consumer preferences toward m-commerce applications based on an empirical study. IEEE Computer Society. *International Journal on Hybrid Information Technology*, *1*, 654–659.

Siau, K., & Shen, Z. (2003). Building customer trust in mobile commerce. *Communications of the ACM*, *46*(4), 91–94. doi:10.1145/641205.641211

Urbaczewski, A., Wells, J., Sarker, S., & Koivisto, M. (2002). Exploring cultural differences as a means for understanding the global mobile Internet: a theoretical basis and program of research. In *Proceedings of the 35th Annual Hawaii International Conference on System Sciences (HICSS-35.02)*. Washington, DC: IEEE Computer Society.

Venkatesh, V., & Davis, F. R. (2000). A theoretical extension of the technology acceptance model: four longitudinal field studies. *Management Science*, *46*(2), 188–204. doi:10.1287/mnsc.46.2.186.11926

Wu, J.-H., & Hisa, T. (2004). Analysis of e-commerce innovation and impact: a hypercube model. *Electronic Commerce Research and Applications*, *3*, 389–404. doi:10.1016/j.elerap.2004.05.002

Zikmund, W. G. (2000). *Business research methods*. Fort Worth, TX: Dryden Press.

APPENDIX 1

Pearson's Product-Moment Correlation Coefficient for simple mobile tasks variables

		Simple Task Lack of Confusion	Simple Task Level of Detail	Simple Task Locatability	Simple Task Ease of Use	Simple Task System Reliability	Simple Task Compatibility	Simple Task Presentation	Simple Task Timeliness	Simple Task Perf/ Intrst/ Dedicat	Simple Task Assistance
Simple Task Lack of Confusion	Pearson Correlation	1	.771(**)	.574(**)	.625(**)	.650(**)	.623(**)	.579(**)	.550(**)	.583(**)	.503(**)
	Sig. (2-tailed)		.000	.000	.000	.000	.000	.000	.000	.000	.001
	N	40	40	40	40	40	40	40	40	40	40
Simple Task Level of Detail	Pearson Correlation	.771(**)	1	.543(**)	.643(**)	.664(**)	.646(**)	.641(**)	.506(**)	.714(**)	.481(**)
	Sig. (2-tailed)	.000		.000	.000	.000	.000	.000	.001	.000	.002
	N	40	40	40	40	40	40	40	40	40	40
Simple Task Locatability	Pearson Correlation	.574(**)	.543(**)	1	.721(**)	.685(**)	.729(**)	.591(**)	.601(**)	.338(*)	.508(**)
	Sig. (2-tailed)	.000	.000		.000	.000	.000	.000	.000	.033	.001
	N	40	40	40	40	40	40	40	40	40	40
Simple Task Ease of Use	Pearson Correlation	.625(**)	.643(**)	.721(**)	1	.723(**)	.849(**)	.830(**)	.706(**)	.647(**)	.546(**)
	Sig. (2-tailed)	.000	.000	.000		.000	.000	.000	.000	.000	.000
	N	40	40	40	40	40	40	40	40	40	40
Simple Task System Reliability	Pearson Correlation	.650(**)	.664(**)	.685(**)	.723(**)	1	.801(**)	.700(**)	.701(**)	.717(**)	.702(**)
	Sig. (2-tailed)	.000	.000	.000	.000		.000	.000	.000	.000	.000
	N	40	40	40	40	40	40	40	40	40	40
Simple Task Compatibility	Pearson Correlation	.623(**)	.646(**)	.729(**)	.849(**)	.801(**)	1	.737(**)	.643(**)	.634(**)	.589(**)

continued on following page

		Simple Task Lack of Confusion	Simple Task Level of Detail	Simple Task Locatability	Simple Task Ease of Use	Simple Task System Reliability	Simple Task Compatibility	Simple Task Presentation	Simple Task Timeliness	Simple Task Perf/ Intrst/ Dedicat	Simple Task Assistance
	Sig. (2-tailed)	.000	.000	.000	.000	.000		.000	.000	.000	.000
	N	40	40	40	40	40	40	40	40	40	40
Simple Task Presentation	Pearson Correlation	.579(**)	.641(**)	.591(**)	.830(**)	.700(**)	.737(**)	1	.711(**)	.684(**)	.491(**)
	Sig. (2-tailed)	.000	.000	.000	.000	.000	.000		.000	.000	.001
	N	40	40	40	40	40	40	40	40	40	40
Simple Task Timeliness	Pearson Correlation	.550(**)	.506(**)	.601(**)	.706(**)	.701(**)	.643(**)	.711(**)	1	.625(**)	.439(**)
	Sig. (2-tailed)	.000	.001	.000	.000	.000	.000	.000		.000	.005
	N	40	40	40	40	40	40	40	40	40	40
Simple Task Perf/Intrst/Dedicat	Pearson Correlation	.583(**)	.714(**)	.338(*)	.647(**)	.717(**)	.634(**)	.684(**)	.625(**)	1	.428(**)
	Sig. (2-tailed)	.000	.000	.033	.000	.000	.000	.000	.000		.006
	N	40	40	40	40	40	40	40	40	40	40
Simple Task Assistance	Pearson Correlation	.503(**)	.481(**)	.508(**)	.546(**)	.702(**)	.589(**)	.491(**)	.439(**)	.428(**)	1
	Sig. (2-tailed)	.001	.002	.001	.000	.000	.000	.001	.005	.006	
	N	40	40	40	40	40	40	40	40	40	40

** Correlation is significant at the 0.01 level (2-tailed).
* Correlation is significant at the 0.05 level (2-tailed).

197

APPENDIX 2

Pearson's Product-Moment Correlation Coefficient for difficult mobile tasks variables

		Difficult Task Lack of Confusion	Difficult Task Level of Detail	Difficult Task Locatability	Difficult Task Ease of Use	Difficult Task System Reliability	Difficult Task Compatibility	Difficult Task Presentation	Difficult Task Timeliness	Difficult Task Performance/ Interest/ Dedication	Difficult Task Assistance
Difficult Task Lack of Confusion	Pearson Correlation	1	.829(**)	.574(**)	.832(**)	.764(**)	.750(**)	.673(**)	.548(**)	.752(**)	.093
	Sig. (2-tailed)		.000	.000	.000	.000	.000	.000	.000	.000	.569
	N	40	40	40	40	40	40	40	40	40	40
Difficult Task Level of Detail	Pearson Correlation	.829(**)	1	.647(**)	.696(**)	.675(**)	.702(**)	.653(**)	.481(**)	.652(**)	.200
	Sig. (2-tailed)	.000		.000	.000	.000	.000	.000	.002	.000	.217
	N	40	40	40	40	40	40	40	40	40	40
Difficult Task Locatability	Pearson Correlation	.574(**)	.647(**)	1	.553(**)	.585(**)	.796(**)	.639(**)	.535(**)	.667(**)	.421(**)
	Sig. (2-tailed)	.000	.000		.000	.000	.000	.000	.000	.000	.007
	N	40	40	40	40	40	40	40	40	40	40
Difficult Task Ease of Use	Pearson Correlation	.832(**)	.696(**)	.553(**)	1	.797(**)	.734(**)	.483(**)	.671(**)	.620(**)	.078
	Sig. (2-tailed)	.000	.000	.000		.000	.000	.002	.000	.000	.632
	N	40	40	40	40	40	40	40	40	40	40
Difficult Task System Reliability	Pearson Correlation	.764(**)	.675(**)	.585(**)	.797(**)	1	.697(**)	.595(**)	.644(**)	.635(**)	.243
	Sig. (2-tailed)	.000	.000	.000	.000		.000	.000	.000	.000	.130
	N	40	40	40	40	40	40	40	40	40	40

continued on following page

		Difficult Task Lack of Confusion	Difficult Task Level of Detail	Difficult Task Locatability	Difficult Task Ease of Use	Difficult Task System Reliability	Difficult Task Compatibility	Difficult Task Presentation	Difficult Task Timeliness	Difficult Task Performance/ Interest/ Dedication	Difficult Task Assistance
Difficult Task Compatibility	Pearson Correlation	.750(**)	.702(**)	.796(**)	.734(**)	.697(**)	1	.677(**)	.673(**)	.729(**)	.510(**)
	Sig. (2-tailed)	.000	.000	.000	.000	.000		.000	.000	.000	.001
	N	40	40	40	40	40	40	40	40	40	40
Difficult Task Presentation	Pearson Correlation	.673(**)	.653(**)	.639(**)	.483(**)	.595(**)	.677(**)	1	.582(**)	.841(**)	.391(*)
	Sig. (2-tailed)	.000	.000	.000	.002	.000	.000		.000	.000	.013
	N	40	40	40	40	40	40	40	40	40	40
Difficult Task Timeliness	Pearson Correlation	.548(**)	.481(**)	.535(**)	.671(**)	.644(**)	.673(**)	.582(**)	1	.723(**)	.320(*)
	Sig. (2-tailed)	.000	.002	.000	.000	.000	.000	.000		.000	.044
	N	40	40	40	40	40	40	40	40	40	40
Difficult Task Performance/ Interest/ Dedication	Pearson Correlation	.752(**)	.652(**)	.667(**)	.620(**)	.635(**)	.729(**)	.841(**)	.723(**)	1	.367(*)
	Sig. (2-tailed)	.000	.000	.000	.000	.000	.000	.000	.000		.020
	N	40	40	40	40	40	40	40	40	40	40
Difficult Task Assistance	Pearson Correlation	.093	.200	.421(**)	.078	.243	.510(**)	.391(*)	.320(*)	.367(*)	1
	Sig. (2-tailed)	.569	.217	.007	.632	.130	.001	.013	.044	.020	
	N	40	40	40	40	40	40	40	40	40	40

** Correlation is significant at the 0.01 level (2-tailed).
* Correlation is significant at the 0.05 level (2-tailed).

This work was previously published in International Journal of Technology Diffusion, Volume 1, Issue 3, edited by Ali Hussein Saleh Zolait, pp. 1-33, copyright 2010 by IGI Publishing (an imprint of IGI Global).

Chapter 14

A Study on the Internet Security and its Implication for E-Commerce in Yemen

Ali Hussein Saleh Zolait
University of Malaya, Malaysia

Abdul Razak Ibrahim
University of Malaya, Malaysia

Ahmad Farooq
King Khalid University, Saudi Arabia

ABSTRACT

This study examines the use of the Internet for business purposes in Yemen, where main sectors of banking and private trade organizations are observed. Through interviews, a thorough study is performed concerning the Internet facilities available in Yemen, the literacy and use of Information Communication Technology (ICT) in organizations, the level of e-commerce adopted, the main hurdles in the adoption of e-commerce, and measures required to increase the adoption of e-commerce. The study finds that both organizations realize the importance of e-commerce for their business. The main causes in the delay of e-commerce adoption by some are the discrepancies in the infrastructure, high costing of the Internet facilities, bureaucratic hurdles in obtaining the facilities, and the non-availability of a secure environment. Beyond concerns about Internet security, their awareness of security hazards and protection measures is minimal. In light of the data collected, the study has come up with certain recommendations for the interested authorities to improve e-commerce in Yemen.

INTRODUCTION

With web II technology, firms are moving from traditional physical sales and service operations towards e-commerce as well as e-business. Electronic and dynamic websites in today's world of business are considered as the "click-and-mortar", "clicks-and-bricks" or "clicks and flips" of today's companies (Laudon & Traver, 2008). Yemen, over a long historical period, is a country of commerce and its people are famous for their trading and business activities. When the Internet project entered Yemen, the Yemeni business organizations faced challenging competition

DOI: 10.4018/978-1-4666-1752-0.ch014

to have a pronounced presence on the web. The aims behind this growing presence are commercial and for the purpose of reducing communication costs. Most of the companies in Yemen started to build their own websites on the web and started using them to communicate with both current and potential customers. In study conducted by Saeed et al. (2005), results show that firms with high electronic commerce competence exhibit superior performance and that customer value generated through Web site functionality partially mediates this relationship. Furthermore, firms have now started to realize the danger that comes from using this modern method of business, which is the difficulty of having a secure business. Laudon and Traver (2008) highlighted that the e-commerce environment holds threats for both consumers and merchants; therefore, unsecure operations can cause a firm to lose successful business.

Historical Background

In terms of business, Yemen historically was well known to the rest of the world as a country of trading and a central point for Asian goods that were re-exported to Europe and Africa, therefore; Yemen formed the central market that tied three continents countries: Asian countries with those of Europe and Africa. Its geographical and strategic commercial location enabled it to play a vital role in the past as a commercial route centre of world trade. History is going to repeat itself as Yemen is once again to be an international gateway to business opportunities in three continents – Asia, Europe, and Africa. In 1999 the new container port located in Aden commenced operation. It is located at the crossroads of the Red and Arabian Seas with the Indian Ocean. In addition, the Aden Free Zone will provide new regional trade and business opportunities. Yemen is also very rich in natural resources and cultural heritage. There are many traditional industries in Yemen, which have been handed down from generation to generation such as gem stones, souvenirs and traditional

weapons, traditional jewelers, antiques made of silver and gold, Yemeni national clothes and textiles, Yemeni handicrafts and other attractive local things that are characterized by their beauty and attractiveness. Interestingly, the majority of dealers online for those Yemeni local products are oversea companies.

With respect to the history of the Internet, in 1990, Cable & Wireless (C&W) of the UK entered into a joint venture agreement with the Public Telecommunications Corporation (PTC) to form TeleYemen, which is responsible for all of Yemen's international links and is also Yemen's mobile franchise carrier. The communication sector, has witnessed some improvements during the last ten years in terms of technology. Most Yemeni regions have been linked to the national telecom network. A fiber optics connection of more than 2,000 Km is now in service. The Internet service was introduced in 1996. TeleYemen initiated the service with a capacity of 2,000 subscribers (MPD, 2000). The demand for service has increased yearly reaching 295,215 subscribers in 2008, while subscribers to the Super Yemen Net (ADSL) service jumped to 24,442 (10,464). The number of Internet cafes across the republic rose from 925 in 2007 to 973 (ITU, 2009).

The WWW service of the Republic of Yemen is still facing troubles because of the absence of alternative competitors, as there are only two ISPs, government owned companies, which provides all the services to all Yemeni customers. In general, most Yemeni business companies are subscribers to the Internet service but the uses of the Internet for business purposes are limited to one aspect of Internet interaction facilities i.e., communication. Active Internet services in the business affairs of Yemeni banks and trade companies has not reached the required level at which the Yemeni business sector can benefit from participating in e-commerce activities. No evidence that any of business organizations are using the Internet for e-commerce purposes. Although hooking up to the Internet can also be a source of significant dangers and risks, most Yemeni business users today feel they will suffer a greater loss by not connecting to the Internet than they will face with security issues. The advances in Internet technology should go along the same lines as security. The banks in Yemen are lagging behind other geographical regions in the areas of technological interaction.

Literature Review

The use of the Internet in corporate organizations has continuously increased because the facilities that the Internet provides encourage many organizations to replace some of their traditional communications and methods for conducting business methods (Laudon & Traver, 2008). For instance, many organizations now communicate with their customers using Internet facilities such as e-mail services. Also, the Internet and web technology became the channel for publishing organizations' websites whereby organizations use it for promotion and offering online services and participating in e-commerce, including all operations concerning the selling of products and services over the Internet. Moreover, the Internet enables organizations to deliver an online catalogue and messages to a huge number of target consumers. Ahmed et al. (2006) highlighted three factors contributing to the growth of internet commerce. First is the continuous decline in the prices of computers and software's. Second, is the development of different platforms of internet browsers and third factor is the commercialization of the web itself with media-rich content and electronic commerce.

Importance of Security

Internet security applies to organizations that conduct online business operations over the Internet just like a national border. Only the permitted people who are holding official passports are allowed to pass and tour inside. Intruders should be met with hard strategic resistance to keep them far away from the target system buildings, PCs and database servers. The Internet does not provide built-in security. The messages and information sent via computer may be routed through many different systems before reaching their destination. Each different system introduces unwanted individuals who can access data; therefore, security is needed to protect organizations from unwanted damage, copying, or eavesdropping (Forcht et al., 1995). In line with this, gaining access to information on a website or eavesdropping on data, which is supposed to be restricted, can lead to misrepresentation of the organization and loss of information and open the door of vulnerability to many threats. Therefore, each organization is required to secure the content of its website (Stallings, 2000, p. 204). Once an organization decides to use the Internet or to establish their online business there are a few steps they should consider - business organizations must identify how it will use the Internet, they should be able to assess the risks involved, perform a cost/benefit analysis to determine if the benefits outweigh the potential costs, know very well the abilities of their auditor and systems administrator in controlling online change, a proper budget allocation should be assigned for security purposes, and management must view its computer system as it would any other company asset. It must be protected, especially when using the Internet for business. With appropriate caution, organizations should be able to successfully use the Internet to its full potential. Financial organizations should make sure they are involved in the process because their uses of the Internet are more sensitive and in the interim can cause bottom line loss. The Integrity of an organization's brand is a security problem that is also raised if the Internet is used for online business. It is what marketers are most concerned about when it comes to protecting online property rights; the logo of any e-business will be a vulnerable target too and many may be 'sniffed', especially those successful online business websites. If they fail to sniff they will try to cause trouble for the owner and users of these sites. The marketing manager has to be watchful about protecting the organization's brand by monitoring, either manually with search engines or via one of the many service companies that do it for them (Booker, 2000). A website host should have its own firewalls and other security technologies in place to protect hosted websites and customers' data from hackers and viruses. The website host must also operate servers that can support the technology with which a website has been developed (Cross, 2001).

Security Hazard

There are two types of security mechanisms that form the requisite preventive precautionary tool for organizations conducting online business. First, applying direct physical security to all system and network components is considered as a lock to minimize undesired disasters (the act of God). The second type are the intangible protective security measures of the system acting as the second line of defense, which are a way to enhance the capability of companies' security, enabling them to conduct a successful business over the Internet. For instance, firewalls with specialized software are placed between the organization LAN or WAN and the Internet, preventing unauthorized access to proprietary information stored on the intranet (Jessup & Valacich, 2008). Email is a security hazard and many bad things can happen to an individual's computer by simply previewing the message in a preview pane without even opening it. Although there are advances in terms of securing the networks against hackers, there are also advances developing in break-in and hacking tools too. It is very simple sometimes to break into other peoples and company's e-mails or sites and know everything available about them. Hackers can use very simple methods to reach you. Some of these methods do not require people experienced in programming. Hackers can use ready-made software produced by experts to enable them to reach organization's information by breaking into organization e-mail, company account and web

site. This ready-made software is widespread on the market, for example, spy log software and net pass. There is a lot that organizations should do to strengthen the security requirements to face the anticipated threat that can be posed to the company resources. They should think in advance, what will happen if someone gains access to any aspect of the company's resources.

Learn hacking tools - users of the organization online system should be trained to understand what hackers do and how they do it; because that is the only way they can protect themselves and know their enemy (Nelson, 2000). According to Totty (2001) companies must stay one step ahead of the hackers. Aldridge, (1997) recommended setting some precautionary conditions to be enforced and considered. Furthermore, Savage (2000) signals the learning from the security crises solutions of others. In addition, Totty, (2001) highlighted that organizations must use authentication software. Organizations must find certifying tools to measure the level of security (Verton, 2000), make sure that they have the skills and time to keep the round-the-clock vigils the software requires (Messmer, 2000), and establish an e-mail policy and enforce members to use it (Parker, 1999). Assuring the physical security of a website is similar to assuring the physical security of any other computer at any location. Restricting physical access to the machine is a preventative strategy that plays a useful role in securing the sensitive information from internal attackers. All security procedures should include telephone numbers and account numbers for all of organization potential vendors, and contact information for organization most critical employees. This information should be printed and made available in two separate locations. On other word, do not have organization online copy as your only copy (Garfinkeel, 1997). Business organizations should be very keen on understanding the elements of Internet security. Internet security is a combination of partial components that combine together to form a strong Internet security for doing business online. That means researchers should look to the Internet security for business as a group effort to securing the whole set of related contributing parties, which are: security of privacy, system privacy, user privacy, commerce transaction privacy and authentication of data (Lane, 1998). There are four security hazard mechanisms and strategies that will assist in keeping an organization's online transactions at least one-step ahead of intruders. According to Totty (2001) and Jessup and Valacich (2008), these four strategies are necessary to help the computing system in the organization at least to thwart online security breaches, which are;

a. Authentication (Are you who you say you are?)
b. Encryption (Hash up the data so no one without a key can read it)
c. Integrity (Has the information been tampered with?)
d. Firewalls are the door attendants who protect everyone's privacy.

Protection Measures

Some protective options available today are very easy and inexpensive, while others are more complicated and expensive. One inexpensive option is awareness; simply being more aware of the dangers out there and how to avoid them. More expensive and complicated measures include choosing more secure operating systems, imposing access restrictions and enforcing authentication procedures. Some of the protective methods are discussed in the following:

Systems Protection, the more a hacker knows about a system, the more likely he/she is to find loopholes. Creating a link to a sensitive area of the system and opening a hole for a hacker to enter is dangerous. A system administrator should check the system tools and Web logs regularly for any suspicious activity and make sure permissions are set correctly on the system files and on using the Internet. In addition, the administrator should make sure to disable any access to configure the system by users because users can make changes to the configuration file or document tree that could open up security holes (Aldridge et al., 1997).

Protecting Files and Data, this can be an effective protection measure once users avoid downloading from unknown sources such as bulletin board systems. These sources may contain damaging bugs or viruses. Even when downloading files from familiar sources, the program should run through some type of virus-protection software (Aldridge et al., 1997).

Backup Files, Copies and Archive Systems, create more than one backup copy of all-important files and store them in a different location so that it is easy to refer to the old version of the file either for comparisons, corrections or for confidential references. In addition, with backup files, the company can derive much benefit from adopting archive systems such as compromised data and reorganizing files that make it easy for retrieval. "The motivation to use archive systems comes from two issues. Server storage cannot be infinitely expanded without infinite money, power and space. In addition, the risk of having only one copy in a server leads to the natural impulse to make a backup copy" (Luff, 2002).

Information Security Officer (ISO), having a staff member to serve as an Information Security Officer (ISO) whose main responsibility is to enable the company to benefit from the Internet and network technologies in addition, supervising the environment and watching for anything unusual is important. The ISO role emphasis is on watching for any suspicious internal activities or external elements trying to get into the system by monitoring how many times a user is logged on and which files are being used. An ISO can also do careful monitoring. The ISO should be very well prepared and if it is possible hold a qualification of the GIAC (Security Officer Certification).

Implement Business-Intelligence Software, organizations need to use business-intelligence software interacting with user needs. The software can provide users - query and reporting tools, online analytical processing, and executive information systems and data mining.

Internet Performance

Drennan and McColl-Kennedy (2003) argued that to be competitive in today's "high tech" world, firms will need to offer specialized services and develop an innovative customer-focused strategy employing the new technologies. Although, there are some key challenges to do business over the internet in Arab countries but no one can stop it. For instance, the study by Ahmed et al. (2006) identified for Saudi's organizations are the continuing relying on face-to-face contact principles, information overload problems, expensive charges, technical support and expertise, management commitment and understanding the potential role of information technology (IT), and older people were more reluctant to use IT. Drennan and McColl-Kennedy (2003) research demonstrates that the performance of service firms appears to improve with Internet use. In particular, the more the firms use the Internet for e-mailing clients, obtaining customer feedback, searching for products or services, selling goods and services and paying for purchases, the better they perceive their performance to be. According to Drennan and McColl-Kennedy (2003), the Internet has impacted significantly in the services sector and large organizations such as banks, insurance providers and government organizations are prominent buyers of IT and tend to be involved in the initial design, financing and diffusion of the technology.

Methodology

The objective of the study is threefold – First, to recognize the attraction factors that will improve the use of the Internet for business, the benefit from this technology and avoidance of its serious drawbacks. Second, is to identify the main hurdles to the acceptance of e-business that hinder Yemeni business organizations from conducting online business activities, as well as the challenges facing the use of e-business by those organizations surveyed. Third, to explore the role of security in the adoption of online business - how secure is the Internet for the investigated organizations? In other words, how does the business community consider the security of the Internet in their work over the Internet? How do Yemeni firms treat the security aspect when they work online? The current study uses the quantitative approach whereby data collection is achieved by a survey questionnaire. In addition, individual interviews with the IT department officers of eighteen banks' head offices, ISP (Teleyemen) and the related public sectors like the Ministry of Planning and Development (MDP), Ministry of Telecommunication, GIT and TeleYemen were are one of the methods used to collect data. The focal population of the present study are "IT units and computer divisions" of the commercial Yemeni Banks and trade organizations in the capital city of the Republic of Yemen. The questionnaire items are mainly adopted from a review of previous literature. Pilot test was performed and the feedback received was used in finalizing the survey format. The questionnaire format selected covered three parts - care of the basic demographic information, investigate the willingness/usefulness to do business over the Internet and probe the expected problem of conducting online business by selected Yemeni organizations. There were 250 questionnaire forms self-administrated and distributed to the target sample. The responses received were 137 usable and completed forms from business organizations. There were 18 surveys from the main banks operating in Yemen. IT professionals and executive managers who were considered to be the decisions makers in these IT departments of both banks and trading organization were interviewed.

Table 1. Respondents profile (N= 137)

Capability	Frequency	Percent
Computerized systems	118	86.4
Microcomputer	70	56.9
Workstation	73	55.3
Subscribed to Internet	100	82.6
Have website	71	52.2
Have LAN	81	68.1
Have Intranet	20	17.9
Have WAN	16	14

Data Analysis

The preceding Table 1 indicates that 86% of organizations surveyed use computers in their daily business operations. Microcomputers (56.9%) and workstations (55.3%) are the common type of computers adopted by them. Also, 82.6% of them subscribed to the Internet and 52.2% have a website. WAN is not used extensively as the network connection technology (14.0%) also, 17.9% of them have their own Intranet

Usage of Internet

Although, the users of the Internet in Yemen are very few, study found that the Internet subscribers from the business sector represent 60% of Y.net customers. Whereas the data collected indicates that 82.6% of the selected sample are Internet subscribers. Table 2 displays the percentages of Internet usages in five business activities performed by surveyed organization.

The companies that use Internet facilities totally for their internal business affairs represent only 6.0%, while, 35% of the surveyed organizations agree that the Internet assists them to do 10% of their organization's internal daily business. A total of 49.6% of those surveyed agree on the range rate, from 10% to 25%, of their organization's external daily business affairs being assisted by the Internet. For marketing activity, 28.8% of the respondents agree that they do benefit 10% from using Internet for marketing activities. While 28.8% of the surveyed organizations agree that there is no use for the Internet to support marketing activities. For assistance in online activities 67.5% of the surveyed organizations agree that they have no use for the Internet to do online business activities, while 15.8% of them agree that they have benefited 25% from using the Internet to do online business.

Table 2. Percentage internet usage in business activities

Usage→	0%		10%		25%		50%		75%		100%	
Activity	Freq	%	Freq	%	Freq	%	Freq	%	Freq	%	Freq	%
Internal Business	21	17.9	41	35	24	20.5	15	12.8	9	7.7	7	6
External Business	21	17.6	29	24.4	30	25.2	11	9.2	14	11.8	14	11.8
Marketing	34	28.8	34	28.8	23	19.5	12	10.2	12	10.2	3	2.5
Job achievement	41	35.7	10	8.7	4	3.5	7	6.1	7	6.1	46	40
Online Activity	81	67.5	6	5	19	15.8	5	4.2	6	5	3	2.5

Table 3. Purposes of internet usage (N=137)

Purposes	Major Concern		Quite Well		Nothing	
	Freq	%	Freq	%	Freq	%
Communication	108	92.3	3	2.6	6	5.1
Find business opportunity	44	42.3	5	4.8	55	52.9
E-commerce	14	13.9	2	2.0	85	48.2
Policies publicity	52	50	3	2.9	49	47.1
Attract customers	44	41.5	3	2.8	59	55.7
Financial transactions	20	20.4	0	0	78	79
Research	31	31	1	.1	64	64
Learning	22	22	2	2	76	76

Online Business Propensity

Through the individual interviews with the Yemeni businessmen and their executives researchers gained a very positive feeling concerning how interested they are in doing e-business and how willing they are to accept and use the new concept. Table 3 shows the purposes of Internet usage.

Findings on using the Internet by the Yemeni business organizations show that 92.2% of the surveyed organizations commonly use the Internet for electronic communication purposes. There are 42.3% of the surveyed organizations agree that they use the Internet to assist them in finding business opportunities, while 52.9% do not use or do not know how to use the Internet for finding business opportunities. Using the Internet for doing e-commerce is represented by 13.9% of the

surveyed organizations, whereas organizations that do not participate in e-commerce were represented by 84.2%. Of the surveyed organizations 50% use the Internet to get publicity for the organization's policies, 41.5% of surveyed organizations use the Internet for the purpose of attracting new customers, 64.0% of respondents demonstrated they did not use the Internet for research purposes while 70.0% did not use the Internet for learning purposes.

The above Table 4 shows that 59.8% of the surveyed organizations have a major concern about wishing to use the Internet further to use e-mail, while 63.2% of the surveyed organizations have a wish to use the Internet further as a good source of business information. The findings show that 62.1% of the surveyed organizations are desirous to further the use of the Internet for online services

Table 4. Organization willingness to use the internet further (N=137)

Reasons to further use Internet	Major Concern		Considerable		Quite Well		Not Important		No Response	
	Freq	%	Freq	%	Freq	%	Freq	%	Freq	%
Provide service	64	62.1	0	.00	0	.00	19	18.4	20	19.4
Keep updated knowledge	61	59.8	0	.00	3	2.9	19	18.6	19	18.6
Reduce cost	72	67.9	4	3.8	8	7.5	7	6.6	15	14.2
Get customers	60	56.6	4	60.4	11	10.4	12	11.3	19	17.9
e-mail	64	59.8	6	5.6	8	7.5	8	7.5	21	19.6
Source of information	67	63.2	2	1.9	12	8.8	1	.7	24	22.6

while 59.8% of the organizations are willing to use the Internet further to update their knowledge and keep the organization updated. A total of 67.9% of organizations would like to use the Internet further to reduce the cost of their business. It also shows that 56.6% of the organizations would prefer to use the Internet further to bring more customers for their business.

Main Hurdles in Acceptance of Online Business

The acceptance of online business in Yemeni society needs the cooperation of all related parties to take it to a level where all participants are satisfied with Internet performance. Therefore, some hurdles to the acceptance of e-business should be investigated to find suitable solutions or at least to remove them from hindering any e-business projects (Table 5).

There are 40.6% of the surveyed organizations that do not use the web for business purposes because of the lack of expertise while 28.2% of

the surveyed organizations do not use the web for business purposes because it is costly. Of the organizations 57.5% do not use the web for business purposes because partners are not available, 45.2% because infrastructure is not available, 35.6% because organizations believe it is unsafe technology. There are 49.1% of the surveyed organizations that do not use the web for business purposes because their customers do not know how to use the Internet technology and 83.0% of them because government support for online business is not available. There are 45.6% of the surveyed organizations that think that documented papers (hardcopy) are practical, especially when used as evidence that can be certified. That means this will minimize the use of the Internet for the business purposes further. Of the organizations 56.1% think that the Internet is not a trustworthy medium to do online business while 21.8% of them think that undesired information on the Internet minimizes the use of the Internet further and 42.6% said it was not the undesired information on the Internet that minimized the

Table 5. Factors hindering online business by organization

Factors	Major Concern		Considerable		Quit Well		Not Important		No Response	
	Freq	%	Freq	%	Freq	%	Freq	%	Freq	%
Expertise	41	40.6	0	.00	0	.00	40	39.6	20	19.8
Cost	29	28.2	5	4.9	2	1.9	42	40.8	25	24.3
Partner availability	61	57.5	0	.00	0	.00	28	26.4	17	16.0
Infrastructure	47	45.2	4	3.8	3	2.9	33	31.7	17	16.3
Security	36	35.6	13	12.9	2	2.0	30	29.7	20	19.8
Customer cannot use	52	49.1	10	9.4	4	3.8	23	21.7	17	16.0
Government support	88	83.0	0	.00	0	.00	4	3.8	14	13.2
Professional Certification	47	45.6	10	9.7	1	1.0	28	27.2	17	16.5
Not a trustworthy tool	60	56.1	9	8.4	3	2.8	12	11.2	23	21.5
Fraudulent	22	21.8	12	11.9	4	4.0	43	42.6	20	19.8
Lack of cyber law	64	62.7	3	2.9	4	3.9	13	12.7	18	17.6
Undesired believed (Cyberterrorism)	21	21.0	0	.00	8	8.	40	40.0	31	31.0
Internet illiteracy	70	65.4	5	4.7	0	.00	13	12.1	19	17.8

use of the Internet. There are 62.7% of the organizations that think that the absence of cyber law (law on the Internet) is minimizing the use of the Internet further. However, 40.0% of them said, it is not making any difference to them to get undesirable beliefs (e.g., gambling, pornography, fraudulent, and non Halal products) and thought on the Internet. The undesirable beliefs and thought that the Internet can bring are minimizing the use of the Internet for business represented by 21.0% of the surveyed organizations. A total of 65.4% of them think that non-literate people are minimizing the use of the Internet further.

Security and E-business Adoption

Security is one of the hindering problems that thwart the further adoption of E-business even in the advanced countries and sometimes leads to a stop in any further online activities. The following low ratio for security tools use proves that security is a common reason preventing the adoption of e-business.

Results displayed in Table 6 reveal that only 12.4% of the surveyed organizations use a firewall as a security tool, and only 14.6% of them use encryption technology. Also, it was found that 61.31% of them do not use a firewall and 62.8% of them do not use encryption technology to enhance the security of data and systems. Also, that 21.9% of the surveyed organizations rely on proxy technology to scrutinize incoming

and receiving e-mails, while 56.2% of them do not use proxy. The table shows that 66.4% of the surveyed organizations do not use any sort of filtering for securitizing incoming and receiving e-mails, while 9.5% of them are using filtering to enhance the security of data and systems.

In addition to the low ratio recorded on the use of precaution measures of some security techniques researchers found that 10.2% of the surveyed organizations use integrity checker tools for securing their net, while 51.8% do not use integrity checker tools to provide such protection over the Internet (Table 7). Also it was found that 5.8% of the surveyed organizations are using intrusion detection tools for securing their net, while 53.3% do not use any intrusion detection tools. Business organizations do not do business on the Internet because of the security concern was tested to show the relationships with common internet security. The study shows that there is a significant relationship to denial of service (.010), to repeat disconnected (.021) and for the data and information integrity (.001). The study shows there is a significant relation between hacking .019 and for the data loss or damage, which is .053. There is no significant relation to viruses and fraud. This can have many interpretations including that although these organizations are familiar with dealing with virus problems, as it is a problem common to computing and networking regardless of whether they are connected to the Internet, the user assumes that hacking and

Table 6. Security methods activated by organization (N=137)

Security Technology	Technology Activated		Technology Not Activated		No Response	
	Freq	*%*	*Freq*	*%*	*Freq*	*%*
Firewall	17	12.4	84	61.3	36	26.2
Encryption	20	14.6	86	62.8	31	22.6
Proxy	30	21.9	77	56.2	30	21.9
Filtration	13	9.5	91	66.4	33	24.0
Other	18	13.1	84	61.3	35	25.5

Table 7. Use of precaution measures (N=137)

Precaution Measure	Measures Activated		Measures not Activated		No Response	
	Freq	%	Freq	%	Freq	%
Integrity checker	14	10.2	71	51.8	52	37.9
Intrusion Detection	8	5.8	73	53.3	56	40.9
Network monitoring software	75	54.7	13	9.5	49	35.8

fraud are problems brought by connection to the Internet. In testing the security implementation concern, the study shows a significant relation on companies that own a security policy on doing online business, which is .022. In addition, there is a significant relation to using such kinds of security software .001. The uses of integrity checker software (.004) and network monitoring software (.017) have a significant relation. Also, the study for organizations, which are interested in doing business on the Internet show that there is a significant relation between the organizations willingness to use the Internet further and providing online service (.038), also the organizations willingness to use the Internet further and communicate by e-mail as an efficient and reliable method of business interaction. Findings show that there is a significant relation between doing

business over the Internet and the Internet cost (.006), also, there is a strong significant relation with offering more security (.000). There is a significant relation on government support and using the Internet to do business (.005) and pushing prices of computer and its related components down (.048).

As can be seen (highlighted values in Figure 1, all three independent variables correlate statistically significant to doing online business; Security Hazard (r=.680***), Protection Measures (r =.760***), and Internet performance (r =.678***).

Discussion

E-business is a common trend of the third millennium towards further ease of business transactions.

Figure 1. The relationship between the independent variables and the dependent variable

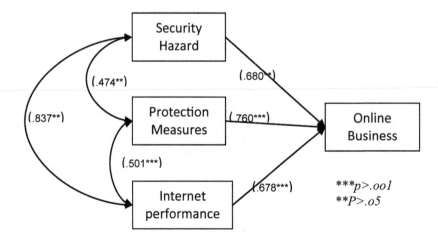

***p>.oo1
**P>.o5

Monopolizing a wide area of the international market is one of the factors that encourage electronic business. Internet use provides a shakeup of the business organizations in Yemen as most of their staff belong to the old generation before the Internet. This is the reason for being very late users of the Internet technology for business or for business by Yemeni firms. The study result shows that the business sector is a regular user of the Internet in Yemen in terms of numbers. The computerized system is already used by the majority of those organizations. The findings indicate that 86% of both commercial and bank organizations, which were investigated, are using computers to assist in their daily business operations. The past and current traditional methods of business face some difficulties. Some of them identified these problems as business and investment risks. Shall researchers in the current study assume that this new drive method of conducting business over the Internet is going to be treated similarly? Several researches conducted in this field signal the raise of security as a new problem to the e-business. This concept refers to the nature and the media this business run via it, by which researchers mean the Internet. Even though some Internet users feel that conducting business online is not easily attainable they have started applying this method as a new means for conducting business. For example you suggest to a layman friend to buy a book through the Internet they will of course will pose several questions to you, the question for the majority is about "how secure is the Internet to protect me against losing money?" Lack of experts, cost, lack of infrastructure and the absence of internal partners contribute in hindering the adoption of online business.

CONCLUSION

Although, IT infrastructure in Yemen is still an unknown phenomenon and the work concludes that this side has not been given much care from authorities in the communication department. In regard to banks and trade companies most of them have the computerized system and have a connection to the Internet. It is concluding that most of companies and banks are still unfamiliar with encryption technology and most of them do not use firewalls to protect the information assets that they possess. On other word, protective and preventive tools of security are not widely adapted by business organization in the country. The uses of the web technology and Internet are still limited and made web services available only to the mid-level managers; the use is also mostly limited to communication and to host some web pages. It is conclude that only few banks adopt ATM services and auto-bankers. Perfect security will never be reached; however, organizations and users will, hopefully, reach a level where everyone can live within this cyber age safely. For business organization, researchers can conclude that there are three groups of companies in terms of using the technology of computer networking and the Internet:

Companies Affiliated with International Business

To facilitate their business affairs this sort of company is adopting computerized systems and is fully connected to the World Wide Web but their appearance on the net is mainly dominated by promotional activities and the common use is for e- mail purposes.

Companies Affiliated with National Business

These sorts of trade companies own their computerized system, which enables them to drive the internal business. Some of them are connected to the net and others do not feel that the Internet has any importance for their business.

Trade Agencies and
Small Retail Stories

This kind of business seems to be in the middle of using this new technology for business. They have computers and they use them but in a limited way, for example, for office work some of them have started to adopt computerized systems.

Future work - the study revealed that the relationship between the Internet's security and doing online business over the Internet is not at the required level and it is not satisfactory at present for any business organization to start doing online business. It, consequently, cannot serve as a solid platform for the success of doing online business for Yemeni business organizations. This study suggests further work on the following aspects of the Internet security and e-business in Yemen:

- Difficulties and problems of e-commerce infrastructure in the Yemeni environment.
- Development of the concepts and principles of security in computing as a starting point for going into securing the local network for business purposes in Yemen.
- Development of Yemeni national backbone network.
- Development of the awareness and acceptance of IT for the Yemeni business society.

RECOMMENDATIONS

The work would like to make some recommendations that are considered important for government authorities, interested organizations and users of Internet technology in Yemen. The purpose of these recommendations is to make the Internet a meaningful way of doing business for companies and banks located in Yemen. The recommendations are categorized in four areas: increasing the awareness, making available the necessary infrastructure, easing the financial costing, and minimizing the bureaucratic hurdles. The details are provided in the following paragraphs.

Increasing Awareness - this goal can be achieved by offering opportunities to businesses interested in attending seminars on the Internet, e-business, and training session courses. Encourage the presence of Yemeni companies on the Internet and to participate in community service projects intended to increase Internet awareness and usefulness for improving the business.

Availability of Infrastructure - providing effective and efficient 'net' solutions to Yemeni business will be based on a complete and full infrastructure that covers all e-Services infrastructure components, e-security, Internet banking, ISP infrastructure, digital payment, gateways, Commerce Service Provider (CSP), Application Service Provider (ASP), Shared Processing Centre (SPC) and national Internet backbone.

Easing Financial Costing - this can be achieved through a good pricing policy that works to reduce the cost of the telephone and Internet subscription fees, taxes on the Internet and e-business hardware equipment and software. Also offer national expertise to those who can undertake to build local capacity in IT security, especially for the business sector and those demanding security on the Internet and provide consultancy at a low price.

Minimizing Bureaucratic hurdles - work hard to improve the legislative environment that assists in offering a good climate to further the use of the Internet in business through this general concept: Liberalization of information exchange, custom facilitation, liberalization of telecom and transport, Set out a general documented policy on the use of the Internet that encourages all people to use web services and e-business. Adopt e-banking through offering some online services, adoption of digital signature and e-contracting and encourage the creation of e-commerce companies.

REFERENCES

Ahmed, A. M., Zairi, M., & Alwabel, S. A. (2006). Global benchmarking for internet and e-commerce applications. *Benchmarking: an International Journal, 13*(1/2), 68–80. doi:10.1108/14635770610644583

Aldridge, A., White, M., & Forcht, K. (1997). Considerations of doing business via the Internet: Cautions to be considered. *Internet Research: Electronic Networking Applications and Policy, 7*(1), 9–15. doi:10.1108/10662249710159809

Booker, E. (2000). Protect online brand from unauthorized use. *B to B, 85*(18), 12- 39.

Cross, M. A. (2001). Set strategy before selecting a web site host. *Internet Health Care Magazine,* 42-43.

Drennan, J., & McColl-Kennedy, J. (2003). The relationship between Internet use and perceived performance in retail and professional service firms. *Journal of Services Marketing, 17*(3), 295–311. doi:10.1108/08876040310474837

Forcht, K. A., & Fore, R. E. (1995). Security issues and concern with the Internet. *Internet Research: Electronic Networking Applications and Policy of MCB, 5*(3), 23–31. doi:10.1108/10662249510104621

Garfinkel, S., & Spafford, G. (1997). *Web security & commerce* (1st ed.). New York: O'Reilly.

ITU. (2009). *International Telecommunication Union: News related to ITU Telecommunication/ ICT Statistics.* Retrieved July 31, 2009, from http:// www.itu.int/ITU-D/ict/newslog/Internet+Subscr ibers+Rise+36+In+2008+Yemen.aspx

Jessup, L., & Valacich, J. (2008). *Information Systems Today: Managing in the Digital World.* Upper Saddle River, NJ: Pearson education, Inc.

Lane, C. (1998). Five essential steps to privacy. *PC World, 16*(9), 116–117.

Laudon, K. C., & Traver, C. G. (2008). *E-commerce: Business, Technology and Society* (4th ed.). Upper Saddle River, NJ: Pearson Education.

Luff, J. (2002). Data archive systems. *Broadcast Engineering: Overland Park, 44*(3), 206.

Messmer, E. (2000). Security needs spawn services. *Network World, Framingham, 17*(14), 1–100.

Nelson, M. G. (2000). Hacker school teaches security. *Information Week, 779,* 137.

Parker, C. (1999). E-mail use and abuse. *Freelance journalist based in Cornwall, 48*(7), 257-260.

Saeed, K., Grover, V., & Hwang, Y. (2005). The Relationship of E-Commerce Competence to Customer Value and Firm Performance: An Empirical Investigation. *Journal of Management Information Systems, 22*(1), 223–256.

Savage, M. (2000). Attacks bring new security solutions. *Computing Research News, 884,* 44.

Stallings, W. (2000). *Network security essentials applications and standards.* Upper Saddle River, NJ: Prentice- Hall.

Totty, P. (2001). Staying One Step Ahead of the Hacker. *Credit Union Magazine, 67*(6), 39–41.

Verton, D. (2000). Co-op to certify tools to measure level of security. *Computerworld, 34*(49), 16.

This work was previously published in International Journal of Technology Diffusion, Volume 1, Issue 3, edited by Ali Hussein Saleh Zolait, pp. 34-47, copyright 2010 by IGI Publishing (an imprint of IGI Global).

Chapter 15

Supply Chain Management Practices and Firm Performance:
An Empirical Study of the Electronics Industry in Malaysia

Abdul Razak Ibrahim
University Malaya, Malaysia

Ali Hussein Zolait
University Malaya, Malaysia

Veera Pandiyan Sundram
University Malaya, Malaysia

ABSTRACT

Supply chain management (SCM) is the integration and strategic alliance involving all the value-creating elements in the supply, manufacturing, and distribution processes from raw material extraction, the transformation process, and end user consumption. This paper explores the SCM activities carried out by electronic manufacturing organizations in Malaysia and determines the correlation between SCM practices and firm performance. A self-administrated questionnaire based survey technique was employed to ascertain the status of SCM adoption and the practices in SCM that are significant for Malaysian electronics manufacturers. The findings suggest that the adoption of SCM activities is reasonably moderate.

INTRODUCTION

Supply chain management (SCM) is the term used to describe the management of the flow of materials, information, and funds across the entire supply chain; from suppliers to component producers to final assemblers to distribution (warehouses and retailers), and ultimately to the consumer. In fact, it often includes after-sales service and returns or recycling (Silver, Pyke, & Peterson, 1998; Johnson & Pyke, 2000). Supply chain management has generated much interest in recent years for a number of reasons. Many managers now realize

DOI: 10.4018/978-1-4666-1752-0.ch015

that actions taken by one member of the chain can influence the profitability of all others.

Objective of Study

The primary objective described in this paper is to explore SCM practices and the relationship with firm performance in the manufacturing sector in Malaysia. The research questions are "How widely are these SCM concepts implemented in practice?" and "How well do SCM practices correlate with firm performance?" For the purpose of this study, twenty-five commonly cited SCM practices from the literature were identified (Table 1) to describe the construct of SCM practices. These included practices relating to supply and materials management issues, operations, information technology and sharing, and customer service. In terms of the firm performance measurement, we examine whether the aggregate performance of a firm, as assessed by operations excellence, revenue growth, and customer relationships, is influenced by supply chain practices. Moreover the uniqueness of this study to our understanding and knowledge is implicit as there are no published studies on supply chain management practices in Malaysia.

Literature Review

The objective of this section is to perform a literature review of the issues relating to the practices and performance of SCM. Studies on supply chain management (SCM) practices in different industrial sectors allow special features to be distinguished to the applied practices, and a consequent improvement to SCM theories. In this context it is best to start with a few samples in this area from previous research that are regarded as very valuable. To date, studies have been conducted on various industrial sectors including pharmaceutical (Lurquin, 1996), apparel (Dapiran, 1992; Christopher & Peck, 1997), grocery (Fernie, 1995; Zairi, 1998), computer (Magretta, 1998), automobile (Helper, 1991; Choi & Hong, 2002),

chemical (Vlasimsky, 2003; Catalan & Kotzab, 2003), telecommunication (Reyes et al., 2000) and agriculture/food (Wilson, 1996; Cunningham, 2001). Most of the available literature on SCM is concerned with advocating SCM practices. Fox (1991) and Michael (1996) suggest that manufacturers should synchronize the entire supply chain as a single business entity and integrate the flows across the supply chain in order to reduce costs, improve customer service, and ward off impending competitive pressures in manufacturing. Balsmeier and Voisin (1996) highlighted the importance of SCM practices through strategic partnerships, information sharing and improved communications. Integrating the supply chain gives the business more options in competitive strategy. Ragatz et al. (1997) found that supplier memberships in new product development teams contributed significantly to the success of these teams. The mechanism through which SCM practices improve a firm's performance hinges on lead-time reduction (Towill, 1996). Literature suggests (Slywotzky et al., 2000) that a firm's aggregate performance relative to its competition comprises operations excellence, revenue growth, and customer relationships. Operations excellence is the extent of the focal firm's responsiveness to customers and improvements in productivity relative to its competition (Fisher, 1997; Simchi-Levi et al., 2000). Customer relationships focus on the bond and loyalty between a focal firm and its customers, and the focal firm's intimate knowledge about customer-related preferences (Groves & Valsamakis, 1998; Malhotra et al., 2005). Growth in revenues includes sales from existing products and from new products and markets (Kalwani & Naravandas 1995; Zahra & George 2002).

Methodology

A detailed description of the research method will be discussed, comprising research design, sampling method and type, measurement of concepts

Table 1. Descriptive analysis and reliability of SCM practices items

No	Scale Items	Mean	SD	Item–total correlation	Alpha if item deleted	Coeff. Alpha
	Supply Chain Management Practices					**0.81**
1	Improving the integration of activities across the supply chain.	4.66	0.48	0.45	0.79	
2	On-time delivery of own purchased materials directly to the firm's points of use.	4.62	0.49	-0.02	0.82	
3	On-time delivery of own firm's products directly to the customers' points of use.	4.50	0.51	0.01	0.82	
4	Increasing the firm's Just-In-Time (JIT) capabilities.	4.50	0.51	0.26	0.80	
5	Searching for new ways to integrate supply chain management activities.	4.50	0.51	0.02	0.82	
6	Determining customers' future needs.	4.34	0.48	0.35	0.80	
7	Contacting the end users of the products to get feedback on performance and customer service.	4.20	0.37	0.37	0.80	
8	Use of informal information sharing with suppliers and customers.	3.75	0.44	0.38	0.80	
9	Establishing more frequent contact with members of the supply chain.	3.75	0.44	0.38	0.797	
10	Communicating own firm's future strategic needs to the suppliers.	3.75	0.44	0.38	0.80	
11	Reducing response time across the supply chain.	3.72	0.46	0.31	0.80	
12	Creating a greater level of trust among the supply chain members.	3.53	0.51	0.26	0.80	
13	Participating in the marketing efforts of the customers.	3.38	0.49	-0.09	0.82	
14	Communicating customers' future strategic needs along the entire supply chain.	3.25	0.44	0.02	0.81	
15	Creating a compatible communication /information system with the suppliers and customers.	3.20	0.37	0.47	0.80	
16	Use of formal information sharing agreements with suppliers & customers.	3.20	0.37	0.47	0.80	
17	Aiding the suppliers to increase their JIT capabilities.	3.10	0.30	0.15	0.81	
18	Finding additional supply chains where the firm can establish a presence.	2.90	0.40	0.37	0.80	
19	Involving all members of the firm's supply chain in the product /service/ marketing plans.	2.75	0.44	0.53	0.79	
20	Participating in the sourcing decisions of the suppliers.	2.63	0.49	0.54	0.79	
21	Creating supply chain management teams that include members from different companies.	2.41	0.50	0.78	0.78	
22	Extending the supply chain to include members beyond immediate suppliers and customers.	2.34	0.48	0.68	0.78	
23	Locating closer to the customers.	2.34	0.48	0.68	0.78	
24	Use of a third-party supply chain management specialist.	2.19	0.59	0.61	0.78	
25	Requiring suppliers to locate closer to the firm.	1.84	0.68	0.35	0.80	

Source: Survey Result

and their operational definitions and finally the dimensions used to design the questionnaires.

Research Design: This is a descriptive and correlation study to understand the SCM practices and performance of the electronic manufacturing sector of the selected companies. The research was done in a non-contrived setting with no interference to the normal work routine of the population. It is a one-shot study, and the unit of analysis is manufacturing organization.

Sampling: A non-probability sampling method was used that specifically employed the convenience sampling technique. The data collection carried out encompassed managers from manufacturing organizations and distributors of manufactured products. The selected managers came from various firms and had a prominent role in the area of operations management and supply chain management.

Measurement and Scale: The practices of SCM are operationally defined as the level of commitment given by the organization in implementing the SCM activities. Therefore, the dimensions and elements used to measure the SCM practices were measured through the managerial and strategic commitment of the organization in total. A 5-point Likert scale was used to elicit responses from the respective respondents ranging from a continuum of very low, low, neutral, high to very high efforts.

Survey: Questionnaires, A survey instrument in the form of a questionnaire was used based on the constructs described in Table 1. We used the survey questionnaire adapted from Tan (1999) and Tan and Wisner (1999). This instrument has, thus, been tested and proven in terms of ambiguity, reliability, and validity. Respondents were asked to indicate, using a five point Likert scale, the importance of the twenty-five practices in

their firm's SCM efforts. Several other questions, including demographic information, were also presented in the questionnaire. A total of 75 questionnaires were distributed and collected.

Analysis: All the data was selected and processed by using the computer program "Statistical Package for Social Sciences (SPSS)" version 15.0. The statistical tools used in this study are descriptive statistical tools. To measure the primary objective of this study, that is, to identify the organizational adoption level of SCM practices, inferential statistical tools such as the one-sample t-test were employed. Pearson's correlation was used to reveal the underlining relationship between each supply chain practice and firm performance.

Findings

How extensively is SCM adopted in Malaysia? Businesses competing globally are under more intense competitive pressure to gain efficiency and efficacy in their supply and logistics systems. Thus, they could be expected to be on the leading edge of the implementation of SCM. To answer this question the respondents were presented with 25 SCM activities and asked to indicate the level of adoption in their business. The survey result was tested by a one sample T-Test to identify the organizational adoption in the practice of SCM activities.

Descriptive Analysis and Reliability Analysis

After the survey had been completed the reliability of the scale was further examined using coefficient alpha (Cronbach's alpha). All scales were found to exceed the minimum threshold of 0.7 suggested by Nunnally (1978) and cited by Panayides (2004). Convergent validity is indicated by a high Cronbach's alpha being attained when the individual variable scores are combined into a single scale. The actual result of the scale reliability analyses are reported in Table 1. The descriptive analysis (Table 1), mainly the measurement of central tendency (mean value and standard deviation), strongly indicate that on-time performance (including JIT), determining customers' needs and supply chain integration are the most highly adopted SCM practices. Whereas, choice of location within the vicinity of the suppliers/customers and extending the supply chain effort are generally less preferred by the selected respondents from the manufacturing firms.

One Sample T-Test to Determine the Extent of SCM Practices

The following presents the results of hypothesis testing through a one sample t-test, which indicates the extent or degree of practice of supply chain management among firms in the electronics sector in Malaysia. The hypothesis testing reveals that the mean value for overall SCM practices is significantly more than 3 ($\alpha = 5\%$). This confirms that selected respondents from the electronic manufacturing firms have adopted SCM practices. As such the above findings coincide with several other researchers' opinion (Berry, Towill, & Wadsley, 1994; Kim, 2006) on the importance of supply chain adoption, mainly by the manufacturers. The impetus for such supply chain adoption is due to several performance based factors, which range from firm level to performance of overall supply chain (Field & Meile, 2008; Forslund & Jonsson, 2007; Gunasekaran, Patel, & McGaughey, 2004). Furthermore, correlation test was performed to determine the relationship between SCM practices and firm performance and the result are shown in Table 2.

However, not all correlations were significant statistically. Although causality cannot be inferred from correlations, it appears that firms wishing to do well in operational excellence should focus on: increasing the firm's Just-In-Time (JIT) capabilities, contacting the end users of the products

to get feedback on performance and customer service, aiding suppliers to increase their JIT capability, and locating closer to the customers. To improve the revenue growth, firms would do well to ensure on-time delivery of own firm's products directly to the customers' points of use, increasing the firm's Just-In-Time (JIT) capabilities, contacting the end users of the products to get feedback on performance and customer service, participating in the sourcing decisions of the suppliers, locating closer to the customers, use of a third-party supply chain management specialist, and requiring suppliers to locate closer to the firm. This correlation between supply chain practices and organization effectiveness [operational excellence and revenue growth] is consistent with previous studies (Elmuti, 2002; Falah, Zairi, & Ahmed, 2003; Jharkharia & Shankar, 2006).

With respect to customer relationship levels, the activities to foster, i.e., the activities that statistically correlated with this performance measure were: on-time delivery of own firm's products directly to the customers' points of use, determining customers' future needs, contacting the end users of the products to get feedback on performance and customer service, participating in the marketing efforts of the customers, use of a third-party supply chain management specialist, and requiring suppliers to locate closer to the firm. These findings complement previous studies (Elmuti, 2002; Jharkharia & Shankar, 2006; Kim, 2006; Lau, Yam, & Tang, 2007) that found a positive relationship between supply chain management practices and customer relationship. The data also indicates that the main focus of SCM is on revenue growth levels: the number of statistically significant correlations with revenue growth levels is much more than the corresponding number for either of the two other firm performance measures.

Table 2. Correlation of SCM practices versus firm performance

Supply Chain Management Practices	Operational Excellence	Revenue Growth	Customer Relationship
	[μ= 3.15]	[μ= 3.77]	[μ= 3.35]
Aiding the suppliers to increase their JIT capabilities.	**0.393***	0.072	0.145
Locating closer to the customers.	**0.339***	**0.386***	0.060
Increasing the firm's Just-In-Time (JIT) capabilities.	**0.382***	**0.322***	0.274
Contacting the end users of the products to get feedback on performance and customer service.	**0.440***	**0.397***	**0.361***
On-time delivery of own firm's products directly to the customers' points of use.	0.115	**0.398***	**0.325***
Use of a third-party supply chain management specialist.	0.276	**0.426***	**0.326***
Requiring suppliers to locate closer to the firm.	0.052	**0.386***	**0.351***
Participating in the sourcing decisions of the suppliers.	0.106	**0.405***	0.251
Determining customers' future needs.	0.222	0.227	**0.374***
Participating in the marketing efforts of the customers.	0.191	0.114	**0.465***
On-time delivery of own purchased materials directly to the firm's points of use.	0.149	0.063	0.029
Improving the integration of activities across the supply chain.	0.118	0.004	0.037
Searching for new ways to integrate supply chain management activities.	0.141	0.142	0.007
Establishing more frequent contact with members of the supply chain.	0.180	0.038	0.195
Communicating own firm's future strategic needs to the suppliers.	0.180	0.271	0.195
Reducing response time across the supply chain.	0.111	0.038	0.195
Use of informal information sharing with suppliers and customers.	0.180	0.142	0.218
Creating a greater level of trust among the supply chain members.	0.245	0.012	0.157
Communicating customers' future strategic needs along the entire supply chain.	0.009	0.036	0.107
Creating a compatible communication /information system with the suppliers and customers.	0.041	0.036	0.107
Use of formal information sharing agreements with suppliers & customers.	0.041	0.096	0.134
Finding additional supply chains where the firm can establish a presence.	0.009	0.114	0.065
Involving all members of the firm's supply chain in the product /service/ marketing plans.	0.085	0.063	0.087
Creating supply chain management teams that include members from different companies.	0.124	0.088	0.155
Extending the supply chain to include members beyond immediate suppliers and customers.	0.124	0.088	0.155

Significant at α = 10%

CONCLUSION

The current research provides the supply chain management adoption level of selected firms in the electronics manufacturing sector in Malaysia, proving that the firms have adopted SCM activities at a statistically significant level. Nevertheless the adoption level is still at the moderate level. Even though the adoption of SCM in the Malaysian manufacturing industry is not very high, those firms who have made some progress in SCM practices have benefited from SCM regarding their performance, especially relating to revenue growth. This paper is a preliminary study, a pilot study, and was initiated to obtain an insight into the supply chain practices in the manufacturing industry and to explore the organizational effort and commitment towards the implementation of these supply chain management activities.

REFERENCES

Balsmeier, P. W., & Voisin, W. J. (1996). Supply Chain Management: A Time-based Strategy. *Industrial Management (Des Plaines)*, *38*(1), 24–27.

Berry, D., Towill, D. R., & Wadsley, N. (1994). Supply Chain Management in the Electronics Products Industry. *International Journal of Physical Distribution & Logistics Management*, *24*(10), 20–32. doi:10.1108/09600039410074773

Catalan, M., & Kotzab, H. (2003). Assessing the responsiveness in the Danish mobile phone supply chain. *International Journal of Physical Distribution & Logistics Management*, *33*(8), 668–695. doi:10.1108/09600030310502867

Choi, T. Y., & Hong, Y. (2002). Unveiling the structure of supply networks: case study in Honda, Acura, and DaimlerChrysler. *Journal of Operations Management*, *20*(5), 469–493. doi:10.1016/S0272-6963(02)00025-6

Christopher, M., & Peck, H. (1997). Managing logistics in fashion markets. *The International Journal of Logistics Management*, *8*(2), 63–73. doi:10.1108/09574099710805673

Cunningham, D. C. (2001). The distribution and extent of agrifood chain management research in the public domain. *Supply Chain Management*, *6*(5), 212–215. doi:10.1108/EUM0000000006040

Dapiran, P. (1992). Benetton – global logistics in action. *International Journal of Physical Distribution & Logistics Management*, *22*(6), 7–11. doi:10.1108/EUM0000000000416

Elmuti, D. (2002). The Perceived impact of Supply Chain Management on Organizational Effectiveness. *Journal of Supply Chain Management*, *38*(3), 49–57. doi:10.1111/j.1745-493X.2002.tb00135.x

Falah, K. A., Zairi, M., & Ahmed, A. M. (2003). The role of supply-chain management in world-class manufacturing-An empirical study in the Saudi context. *International Journal of Physical Distribution & Logistics Management*, *33*(5), 396–407. doi:10.1108/09600030310481979

Fernie, J. (1995). International comparison of supply chain management in grocery retailing. *The Service Industries Journal*, *15*(4), 134–147. doi:10.1080/02642069500000053

Field, J. M., & Meile, L. C. (2008). Supplier relations and supply chain performance in financial services processes. *International Journal of Operations & Production Management*, *28*(2), 185–206. doi:10.1108/01443570810846892

Forslund, H., & Jonsson, P. (2007). The impact of forecast information quality on supply chain performance. *International Journal of Operations & Production Management*, *27*(1), 90–107. doi:10.1108/01443570710714556

Fox, M. L. (1991). Logistics Planning: The Supply Chain as an Integrated Enterprise. *Production and Inventory Management*, *11*(7), 12–15.

Fynes, B., Voss, C., & Burca, S. d. (2005). The impact of supply chain relationship dynamics on manufacturing performance. *International Journal of Operations & Production Management*, *25*(1), 6–19. doi:10.1108/01443570510572213

Gunasekaran, A., Patel, C., & McGaughey, R. E. (2004). A framework for supply chain performance measurement. *International Journal of Production Economics*, *87*(1), 333–347. doi:10.1016/j.ijpe.2003.08.003

Helper, S. (1991). How much has really changed between US automakers and their suppliers? *Sloan Management Review*, *32*(1), 15–28.

Jharkharia, S., & Shankar, R. (2006). Supply chain management: some sectoral dissimilarities in the Indian manufacturing industry. *Supply Chain Management: an International Journal, 11*(4), 345–352. doi:10.1108/13598540610671798

Johnson, M. E., & Pyke, D. F. (Eds.). (2000). *Teaching Supply Chain Management*. Production and Operations Management Society.

Kim, S. W. (2006). Effects of supply chain management practices, integration and competition capability on performance. *Supply Chain Management: an International Journal, 11*(3), 241–248. doi:10.1108/13598540610662149

Lau, A. K. W., Yam, R. C. M., & Tang, E. P. Y. (2007). Supply chain product co-development, product modularity and product performance: Empirical evidence from Hong Kong manufacturers. *Industrial Management & Data Systems, 107*(7), 1036–1065. doi:10.1108/02635570710816739

Lurquin, M. G. (1996). Streamlining the Supply Chain in the Pharmaceuticals Industry. *Logistics Information Management, 9*(6), 6–10. doi:10.1108/09576059610148432

Magretta, J. (1998). The power of virtual integration: An interview with Dell Computers' Michael Dell. *Harvard Business Review, 76*(2), 72–83.

Michael, D. R. (1996). Is Manufacturing a Weak Link in Your Supply Chain? *Industrial Management (Des Plaines), 38*(6), 1–3.

Nunally, J. C. (1978). *Psychometric Theory*. New York: McGraw-Hill.

Ragatz, G., Handfield, R., & Scannell, T. (1997). Success Factors for Integrating Suppliers into New Product Development. *Journal of Product Innovation Management, 14*(1), 190–202. doi:10.1016/S0737-6782(97)00007-6

Reyes, P., Raisinghani, M., & Singh, M. (2000). Global supply chain management in the telecommunication industry: the role of information technology in integration of supply chain entities. *Journal of Global Information Technology Management, 5*(2), 48–67.

Silver, E. A., Pyke, D. F., & Peterson, R. (1998). *Inventory Management and Production Planning and Scheduling* (3rd ed.). New York: John Wiley & Sons.

Tan, K. C. (1999). *Supply Chain Management: Practices, Concerns, and Performance Issues* (Working Paper). Las Vegas, NV: University of Nevada, Department of Management.

Tan, K. C., & Wisner, J. D. (1999). *A Comparison of the Supply Chain Management Approaches of U.S. Regional and Global Businesses* (Working Paper). Las Vegas, NV: University of Nevada, Department of Management.

Towill, D. R. (1996). Time Compression and Supply Chain Management – a Guided Tour. *Logistics Information Management, 9*(6), 41–53. doi:10.1108/09576059610148694

Vlasimsky, S. (2003). Supply chain management: changing the status quo in chemicals. *Chemical Market Report, 294*(17), 29–30.

Wilson, N. (1996). Supply chain management: a case study of a dedicated supply chain for bananas in the UK grocery market. *Supply Chain Management, 1*(2), 25–28.

Zairi, M. (1998). Best practice in supply chain management: the experience of the retail sector. *European Journal of Innovation Management, 1*(2), 59–66. doi:10.1108/14601069810217239

This work was previously published in International Journal of Technology Diffusion, Volume 1, Issue 3, edited by Ali Hussein Saleh Zolait, pp. 48-55, copyright 2010 by IGI Publishing (an imprint of IGI Global).

Chapter 16
Traditional Job–Related Factors and Career Salience in IT–Based Workplace

Aminu Ahmad
Abubakar Tafawa Balewa University, Nigeria

Hartini Ahmad
Universiti Utara Malaysia, Malaysia

ABSTRACT

Despite growing academic and practical concerns about IT-transformed workplaces, little research empirically investigates these concerns. This paper adopts a unique approach to address these concerns by evaluating the appropriateness of traditional drivers of career salience in high IT working environments. Building on established measures of role stress, participation in decision making, job involvement and career salience, questionnaires were distributed to staff working in high IT organizations in Nigeria. Multiple regressions were run from a valid response of 223, resulting in the three traditional drivers accounting for 25% of the variance in career salience. Similarly, standardized β coefficients indicate on job involvement (0.46) makes unique significant contribution to career salience. This finding is in line with sociotechnical theory—that changes in technical sub-system affect the social sub-system and vice versa. The finding also provides indirect exploratory support for the decreasing importance of non-IT factors in the evolving digital workplace. Other implications, limitations and direction for future research are highlighted.

1. INTRODUCTION

Sociotechnical theory (STT) argued that organizational success relies on firms' ability to achieve good blend between its technical and social sub-systems (French & Ball, 1999). Hence,

understanding the right alignment between human resource and information technology (IT) is critical in today's IT transformed working environment (Tafti, Mithas, & Krishnan, 2007). Similarly, the importance of career salience (CS) in the increasingly changing working environment cannot be overstressed given the huge monetary expenditure

DOI: 10.4018/978-1-4666-1752-0.ch016

associated with losing employees (Sanjay, 2006) and high number (40%) of staff vigorously searching for new jobs (Maroney, 2007). Prominent among the list of factors redefining workplace is IT. As organizations become 'extremely dependent on computers and the communication devices' (Smith & Faley, 2001, p. 8), new workplace challenges emerge. Stanton and Stam (2003, p. 152) for example observed that firms often encroach on staff privacy via monitoring telephone records, web usage, email recipient addresses and email messages. Similarly, American Management Association (AMA) survey indicate 82% of employers engage in some form of e-monitoring, while globally around 27 million workers are under e-monitoring (Alder, Schminke, Noel, & Kuenzi, 2008). On the other hand increasing usage of IT (particularly internet) for job advertisement and recruitment makes it easy for employee to track and apply for employment online.

In addition, a number of theoretical gap underscores the need for research on job-related factors vis-à-vis CS in the evolving digital working environment. For example, even though 'traditional negotiation processes surrounding duties, rights, procedures, and policies including security and surveillance were redefined by the presence of the new IT system' (Stanton & Stam, 2003, p. 171) few research are conducted to study workers attitude to the new workplace atmosphere. Hence Danziger and Dunkle (2005, p. 3) observed 'despite the ever more pervasive presence of technology in the workplace, there have been few empirical studies of the effect of computer use on job satisfaction.' The limited literatures largely focused on strategies for avoiding defection, effects of personality traits on job/career satisfaction, or exclusively on e-monitoring such as Sanjay (2006), Lounsbury, Moffitt, Gibson, Drost, and Stevens (2007), and Alder et al. (2008) respectively. As a result this exploratory research aims to examine the empirical validity of these concerns by investigating the generic and specific influence of traditional job-related drivers of CS in IT-based work environ-

ment. A number of benefits can be drive from this research/approach. It will enable us know whether the traditional job-related drivers of CS are appropriate in increasingly IT-dependent working environment; which (if any) of the factor(s) is/are critical in today's IT-workplace; and hence offers inputs for a more comprehensive model that may explain greater variance of CS. The next parts of the paper include literature exploration, methodological issues, analysis, discussion and conclusion in that order.

2. CAREER SALIENCE AND IT CHALLENGE

STT provide a good theoretical premise for the research framework, in its simplest form the theory argued that organizations consist of two interdependent sub-systems, a social system and a technical system, and changes in one system significantly affects changes in the other (French & Ball, 1999). Accordingly, the social-sub system comprises of organizational employees as well as their knowledge, needs, interactions and commitments. The social sub-system is critical given that vast majority of IT failure is as a result of human/organizational setback not technological problems (Kontoghiorghes, 2005), as such Pasmore (1988) view the social sub-system to be the main source of organizational innovation and adaptation. It becomes imperative for organizations to cultivate employee creativity via participatory management, flattening hierarchies, feedback, and encouraging and rewarding team performance. Building on role theory, Lu and Lee (2007) argued that role conflicts and ambiguity (RCA) are key drivers of workplace stress, employee dissatisfaction and low productivity. Similarly, job involvement (JI) and participation in decision making (PDM) have long been empirically ascertained drivers of employee satisfaction and salience see for example (Dreher, 1980; Lawler,

1986; Loscocco & Roschelle, 1991) and (Daley, 1986; Spector, 1986; Soonhee, 2002) respectively.

Meanwhile, the technical sub-system of the organization consists of tools, techniques, procedures and knowledge used by organization (Kontoghiorghes, 2005). The technical sub-system is no less important as technological advances have radically altered the nature of work, the working environment, and employee–employer relationships (Alder et al., 2008, p. 481) and has direct effect on organizational productivity (Pasmore, 1988). Based on the foregoing, we hypothesize that the increasing infiltration and reliance on IT (the technical sub-system) has altered the social sub-system, and consequently redefine the key determinant of CS. The next part of the review dwells on human resource issues, commencing with a general outlook narrowing down to CS vis-à-vis IT.

Maroney (2007, p. 47) emphasized the need for staff retention in the light of time, expense and opportunity costs of attracting new employees. The research found comprehensive health-care coverage, bonus programs, compressed work-weeks and competitive salaries as the key drivers of job satisfaction. The study recommends firms to adopt clear, frequent, two-way communication; feedback; investing in training/education; leave time; child-care assistance; flexible scheduling and sick leave among others to avoid turnover. The research concur with STT that success depends on programs that 'balance the needs of employees (social) and business and use innovative technology (technical)' (Maroney, 2007, p. 50). Accordingly, organizations don't only lost employees but also the intangible cost of lost knowledge; future potential of departing employees (since only the brightest are desirable by others) as well as the possibility of sharing organizational secrets, methods, technology, customers, etc., with the new employer (Sanjay, 2006). As a solution Sanjay (2006) urged organizations to imbibe the culture of conducting anonymous internal survey to uncover employees' views about the man-

agement, policies and advancement potentials. With special reference to IT staff, Sanjay (2006) observe the need for Individual Development, Career Advancement, Recognition and Rewards, Empowerment among others to engender CS and hence increase retention.

In addition to the above traditional human resource challenges, Stanton and Stam (2003) observed that the continuous infiltration of IT in the work place has dramatically changed the traditional mode of interaction between employees and top management. For example, while mangers are excited with the possibilities of using IT to track workplace events closely and continuously via e-monitoring and surveillance. Employees on the other hand are less enthusiastic due to privacy issues and the possibility of presenting an inaccurate picture of work place dedication, as many employees do their office work at home in their free time, rising the issues of privacy, equity and fair play. In a related research, Smith and Faley (2001) observed the increasing introduction of technology vis-à-vis depersonalization of the workplace has compounded the already controversial issue of employee privacy. They argued that technology-enabled workplace surveillance has the tendency to deplete employee loyalty and heighten mistrust and fear of workplace privacy invasion.

Danziger and Dunkle (2005) utilized a framework with computing environment, organizational policies & practices and job characteristics on job satisfaction to investigate the relationship between excessive reliance on computers on workplace and job satisfaction. They conclude that autonomy/influence (operationalized as PDM) and continuous learning lead to positive job satisfaction. They however, found job stress (time pressure) does not negate job satisfaction even though job satisfaction negatively correlate to number of hours per day that the worker uses the computer. The research also found positive relationship between job satisfaction with information-rich environment (information availability, accessibility and up-to-date) and systems-rich environment (reliable computer systems and software stability) however there is no direct relation with technology uncertainty. In a similar research in non-profit organization Brown and Yoshioka (2003) found satisfaction and mission attachment to be both positively related with one another and intentions to stay with an organization.

Iscan and Naktiyok (2005) argued the increasing availability of new computer, internet and communication technologies have enable alternate arrangement from the traditional workplace setting via telecommuting with far reaching consequences on job satisfaction. They acknowledged telecommuting benefit to employee via working flexibility, ease of managing work-family conflict, reducing workplace stress as well as cost, time and hassle of commuting to/from office. Even though it is also perceived to derail career development, isolate staff and endangers poor commitment.

From the foregoing it is obvious that organizations today are facing both traditional human resource as well as IT induce workplace challenges, similarly the IT challenge are both internal (e.g., privacy issues) and external (e.g., easiness of getting new job). However, this research exclusively assesses the influence of three key traditional job related factors on CS in the evolving digital workplace environment.

3. METHODOLOGY

This research present a unique approach, instead of investigating IT job-related drivers of CS the research examine the traditional job-related (generic and specific) determinants of CS in order to evaluate their predictive power in the new IT-based working environment. This approach will enable the researchers not only to know whether the traditional model is suited to the new working place environment but also which of the factor(s) may be included in a propose model should the traditional model proved unsuited. A total of 500 questionnaires designed on 5-points likert scale (see appendix) were distributed to employees of organizations that heavily relies on IT in Nigeria. While 257 questionnaires were retrieved, only 223 were used for the final analysis after removing largely unfilled and morbidity responses and deleting univariate and multivariate outliers.

The demographic distribution of the data presented in Table 1 suggests the sample is a fair reflection of industries with high reliance on IT. For example banking/finance and Telecom firms-the largest users of IT represents over 54% of the respondents' place of work, another high IT group is the non-banking private firms representing almost 30%. Respondents from Education sector were largely drawn from university. Meanwhile both gender and age distributions are reflective of real marketplace figures, indicating sampling adequacy. Finally, respondent rank also presents a pro-rata representation across different positional level hence eliminating possible bias. By and large

Table 1. Sample characteristics

S/No.	Category	Sub-divisions/Frequencies/Percentage
1	Gender	Male 161(72.2%); Female 55(24.7%); 7(3.1%) Not indicated
2	Age	<18yrs 42(18.8%); 18-36yrs 137(61.4%); 37-55yrs 37(16.6%); >55yrs 7(3.1)
3	Rank	Clerks 41(18.4%); Officers 138(61.9%); Managerial Level 34(15.2%); Executive level 8(3.6%); 2(0.9%) Not Indicated
4	Sector	Banking/Finance 79(35.4%); Non-Banking 65(29.3%); Telecom 42(18.8%); Education 17(7.6%); Others 11(4.9%); Not indicated 9(4.0%)

the sample is a good representation of industries/ organizations that heavily rely on IT for the day to day running operations.

The questionnaire consists of 29 items adapted from previous literature: RCA, (Rizzo, House, & Lirtzman, 1970); PDM and JI (White & Ruh, 1973) and CS (Sekaran, 1986). While job satisfaction is often used as criterion variable, however CS represents overall summary of employees' perception of a lifetime of work and is found to relate with turnover in IT discourse (Lounsbury et al., 2007, p. 174), hence considered more appropriate for this research.

In line with Garson (2007) a standard multiple regression significance test of R^2 and standardized beta coefficient were used to determine the overall and relative predictive power of the three traditional job-related factors: All four constructs exhibit good internal consistency with the following cronbach's alpha values: RCA 0.79; PDM 0.63; JI 0.72 and CS 0.74 exceeding the benchmark of 0.6 (Bagozzi & Yi, 1988) and except PDM even the stricter 0.70 (Nunnally, 1978) acceptable cut-off point.

4. ANALYSIS AND DISCUSSION

Examination of the dataset indicates the data met both the size and statistical requirements for multiple regression. For example with 3 independent variables and a valid sample of 223 the sample met the size requirements of N >= 104 + 3 i.e., N > 107 (Tabachnick & Fidell, 2001, p. 117). In assessing the assumption of multivariate outliers, standardize residual values and Mahalanobis distance were examined. From the output of Casewise diagnostic and Mah_1 data file, two residual and multivariate outliers each were deleted. Afterward the dataset is free from outliers. In line with Sekaran (2003) the dataset is also free from multicollinearity as 0.4 is the highest correlation value among the independents constructs. This is further supported by acceptable tolerance values ranging from 0.94 for RCA to 0.81 for JI (see Table 2). Furthermore examination of residuals scatterplot and Normal Probability Plot of the regression standardised residuals further confirm the appropriateness of running multiple regression on the dataset. The next segment presents the result of the model.

The model summary presented in Table 2 indicates the three traditional job-related factors (RCA, PDM and JI) together explain 25% of the dependent variable (CS) which is significant (Sig. = .000 i.e., p<.0005) as indicated by the F-value of 25.54 (Table 2).

Although the model is significant and accounted for 25% of CS variance, however the output of this multiple regression call the traditional models predicting CS to question in technology-based industry. For example what other factors accounts for the remaining 75% of the variance? This may implies the traditional job related factors however significant are no longer the primary drivers of CS in high IT reliant firms. Inspection of β Sig. column revealed only JI makes significant unique contribution to the prediction of CS; accordingly JI makes the strongest contribution of 0.46 when

Table 2. Model summary, beta & collinearity statistics

	F	Sig.	R	R^2	Adjusted R^2
Model Summary	25.54	.000ᵃ	.511ᵃ	.261	.251
Predictors	RCA	PDM		JI	
Standardized β Coefficients	-0.088	.056		0.457	
β Sig.	.148	.382		.000	
Tolerance Level	.937	.832		.810	

the variance explained by all other variables in the model is controlled for. RCA (-0.088) and PDM (0.056) comes a distant second and third respectively without making unique significant contributions.

As expected RCA negatively correlate with CS, however unlike most traditional previous studies (see for example House & Rizzo, 1972; Miles & Perrault, 1976; Rizzo, House, & Lirtzaman, 1970; Schuler, Aldag, & Brief, 1977) it's insignificant to CS. This is quite interesting since RCA has been regarded as critical element of work stress for decades (see for example, Cooper & Dewe, 2004). The situation is similar with PDM. While this cannot be considered as conclusive evidence for the decreasing importance of these factors in IT-based workplace regime especially since the model did not account for other non–IT drivers of CS (such as medical policies, salaries/bonus, advancement), nevertheless β coefficients further indicate the factors (except JI) makes insignificant unique contribution to the variance of CS. At minimum the result supports the need for active search and inclusion of IT-related factors with a view to explaining larger and significant variance of CS.

In synopsis, finding of this research provide direct and indirect empirical support for STT and the growing academic concern for IT induce workplace drivers of CS respectively. Hence in order to identify the relative influence of IT and non-IT factors future models should include both factors. In line with the literature and this exploratory results non-IT factors such as JI, health-care policies, salaries/bonus, advancement and fairness/equity should be given serious consideration. While IT factors such as e-surveillance, privacy issues, restrictive IT usage, information/system-rich environment should be included.

5. CONCLUSION AND LIMITATION

Findings of this research emphasize the decreasing importance of the traditional job-related factors

and the need for a model involving varied and multiple factors to explain greater variance in CS in the new digital workplace. Practically, findings of this research caution organization on exclusive reliance on traditional job-related factors in today's IT influence workplace. Similarly, significant research insight can also be derived from this approach towards building a more apt model for explaining CS in IT-based working environment. However findings of this research should be use with caution given that the research relies on convenient sampling. Another point of caution is the non inclusion of other non IT drivers of CS in the model (for example health-care coverage, competitive salaries/bonus, advancement, and fairness/equity) even though β indicate except JI these factors do not make unique significant contribution to CS. As a follow-up therefore other research should try to include these factors in their models. Nevertheless, findings of this research provide exploratory support for both STT and growing number of literatures, that the rapidly IT induced working place is changing the key traditional determinants of CS.

REFERENCES

Alder, G. S., Schminke, M., Noel, T. W., & Kuenzi, M. (2008). Employee Reactions to Internet Monitoring: The Moderating Role of Ethical Orientation. *Journal of Business Ethics, 80,* 481–498. doi:10.1007/s10551-007-9432-2

Bagozzi, R. P., & Yi, Y. (1988). On the Evaluation of Structural Equation Models. *Journal of the Academy of Marketing Science, 16*(1), 74–94. doi:10.1007/BF02723327

Brown, W. A., & Yoshioka, C. F. (2003). Mission Attachment and Satisfaction as Factors in Employee Retention. *Nonprofit Management & Leadership, 14*(1), 5–18. doi:10.1002/nml.18

Cooper, C. L., & Dewe, P. J. (2004). *Stress: A Brief History*. Oxford, UK: Blackwell. doi:10.1002/9780470774755

Daley, D. M. (1986). Humanistic Management and Organizational Success: The Effect of Job and Work Environment Characteristics on Organizational Effectiveness, Public Responsiveness, and Job Satisfaction. *Public Personnel Management, 15*(2), 131–142.

Danziger, J., & Dunkle, D. (2005). Information Technology and Worker satisfaction. *Centre for Research on Information Technology and Organisations,* 1-12. Retrieved June 14, 2008, from www.repositories.cdlib.org

Dreher, G. F. (1980). Individual Needs as Correlates of Satisfaction and Involvement with a Modified Scanlon Plan Company. *Journal of Vocational Behavior, 17*(1), 80–94. doi:10.1016/0001-8791(80)90018-4

French, W., & Bell, C. (1999). *Organization development-Behavioral science interventions for organization improvement*. Upper Saddle River, NJ: Prentice-Hall.

Garson, G. D. (2007a). *Multiple Regression*. Retrieved November 28, 2007, from http://www2.chass.ncsu.edu/garson/PA765/ Multiple Regression

House, R. J., & Rizzo, J. R. (1972). Role Conflict and Ambiguity as Critical Variables in a Model of Organizational Behavior. *Organizational Behavior and Human Performance, 7*(3), 467–505. doi:10.1016/0030-5073(72)90030-X

Iscan, O. F., & Naktiyok, A. (2005). Attitudes towards telecommuting: the Turkish case. *Journal of Information Technology, 20*, 52–63. doi:10.1057/palgrave.jit.2000023

Kontoghiorghes, C. (2005). Key Organizational and HR Factors for Rapid Technology Assimilation. *Organization Development Journal, 23*(1), 26–39.

Lawler, E. E. (1986). *High Involvement Management: Participative Strategies for Improving Organizational Performance*. San Francisco, CA: Jossey-Bass.

Loscocco, K. A., & Roschelle, A. R. (1991). Influences on the Quality of Work and Nonwork Life: Two Decades in Review. *Journal of Vocational Behavior, 39*(2), 182–225. doi:10.1016/0001-8791(91)90009-B

Lounsbury, J. W., Moffitt, L., Gibson, L. W., Drost, A. W., & Stevens, M. (2007). An Investigation of personality traits in relation to job and career satisfaction of information technology professionals. *Journal of Information Technology, 22*, 174–183. doi:10.1057/palgrave.jit.2000094

Lu, L., & Lee, Y. (2007). The effect of supervision style and decision-making on role stress and satisfaction of senior foreign managers in international joint ventures in China. *International Journal of Commerce & Management, 17*(4), 284–294. doi:10.1108/10569210710844363

Maroney, J. (2007). Achieving the Balance: 10 Keys to Employee Satisfaction. *Workspan, 2*(8), 47–50.

Miles, R. H., & Perrault, W. D. (1976). Organizational Role Conflict: Its Antecedents and Consequences. *Organizational Behavior and Human Performance, 17*(1), 19–44. doi:10.1016/0030-5073(76)90051-9

Nunnally, J. L. (1978). *Psychometric Theory*. New York: McGraw-Hill.

Pasmore, A. W. (1988). *Designing effective organizations: The sociotechnical system perspective*. New York: Wiley & Sons.

Rizzo, J. R., House, R. J., & Lirtzaman, S. I. (1970). Role Conflicts and Ambiguity in Complex Organizations. *Administrative Science Quarterly, 15*(2), 150–163. doi:10.2307/2391486

Sanjay, A. (2006). *Retention in the IT industry* (White Paper). Project Perfect.

Schuler, R. S., Aldag, R. J., & Brief, A. P. (1977). Role Conflict and Ambiguity: A Scale Analysis. *Organizational Behavior and Human Performance*, *20*(1), 111–128. doi:10.1016/0030-5073(77)90047-2

Sekaran, U. (1986). *Dual-Career Families: Contemporary Organizational and Counseling Issues*. San Francisco, CA: Jossey Bass.

Sekaran, U. (2003). *Research Methods for Business. A Skill-Building*. New York: John Wiley & Sons.

Smith, A. D., & Faley, B. A. (2001). E-mail Workplace Privacy Issues in an Information- and knowledge-based Environment. *Southern Business Review*, *27*(1), 8–22.

Soonhee, K. (2002). Participative Management and Job Satisfaction: Lessons for Management Leadership. *Public Administration Review*, *62*(2), 231–241. doi:10.1111/0033-3352.00173

Spector, P. E. (1986). Perceived Control by Employees: A Meta- Analysis of Studies Concerning Autonomy and Participation at Work. *Human Relations*, *39*(11), 1005–1016. doi:10.1177/001872678603901104

Stanton, J. M., & Stam, K. R. (2003). Information Technology, Privacy, and Power within Organizations: a view from Boundary Theory and Social Exchange perspectives. *Surveillance & Society*, *1*(2), 152–190.

Tabachnick, B. G., & Fidell, L. S. (2001). *Using Multivariate Statistics*. Boston: Allyn and Bacon.

Tafti, A., Mithas, S., & Krishnan, M. S. (2007). Information technology and the autonomy–control duality: toward a theory. *Information Technology Management*, *8*, 147–166. doi:10.1007/s10799-007-0014-x

White, J. K., & Ruh, R. R. (1973). Effects of Personal Values on the relationship between Participation and Job attitudes. *Administrative Science Quarterly*, *18*(4), 506–514. doi:10.2307/2392202

APPENDIX I: RESEARCH INSTRUMENT

S/No.	Choose the statements that best describe the your job's of role stress	Strongly Disagree	Disagree	Neutral	Agree	Strongly Agree
1	I have to do things that should be done differently					
2	I work under incompatible policies and guidelines					
3	I receive an assignment without the manpower to complete it					
4	I have to skip a rule or policy in order to carry out an assignment					
5	I work with two or more groups who operate quite differently					
6	I receive incompatible requests from two or more people					
7	I receive an assignment without adequate resources and materials to execute it					
8	I work on unnecessary things					
S/No.	Choose the statements that best describe your participation in decision making	Strongly Disagree	Disagree	Neutral	Agree	Strongly Agree
1	In general, I have much say/influence on how I perform my work					
2	To a greater extend I am able to decide how to do my job					
3	In general, I have little or no say/influence on what goes on in my work group/place					
4	In general, I have much say/influence about decisions that affect my job					
5	My superiors are receptive to my ideas and suggestions					
S/No.	Choose the statements that best describe your Job Involvement	Strongly Disagree	Disagree	Neutral	Agree	Strongly Agree
1	My job means a lot more to me than just money					
2	The major satisfaction in my life comes from my job					
3	I am not interested in my work					
4	I would probably keep working even if I don't need the money					
5	The most important things that happen to me involves my work					
6	I will stay overtime to finish a job, even if I am not paid for					
7	For me, the first few hours of job really fly by					
8	I don't enjoy performing the daily activities that make up my job					
9	I really look forward to coming to work each day					
	Section C: Career Salience					
S/No.	Choose the statements that best describe your Career Salience	Strongly Disagree	Disagree	Neutral	Agree	Strongly Agree
1	My career choice is a good occupational decision for me					
2	My career enables me to make significant contributions to society					
3	The career I am in fits me and reflects my personality					
4	My education and training are not tailored for this career					
5	I don't intend changing careers					
6	All the planning and thought I gave for pursuing this career are a waste					
7	My career is an integral part of my life					

This work was previously published in International Journal of Technology Diffusion, Volume 1, Issue 3, edited by Ali Hussein Saleh Zolait, pp. 56-63, copyright 2010 by IGI Publishing (an imprint of IGI Global).

Chapter 17
The Impact of Technology Anxiety on the Use of Mobile Financial Applications

Cheon-Pyo Lee
Fairmont State University, USA

ABSTRACT

Mobile Commerce activities will not expand without the proper support of mobile financial applications (MFA), including mobile banking, mobile brokerage service, mobile money transfer, and mobile micro-payments. MFA is expected to have a great impact on the future of mobile commerce industries and makes purchasing activities more flexible and convenient, also creating new markets. However, despite the advent of these MFA technologies and the availability of various mobile services, the adoption of mobile financial applications across the globe is still relatively low. In this regard, this study investigates the role of technology anxiety (TA) in the adoption of MFA and resolves the discrepancy between the apparent interest in and low adoption of MFA. The results of a broad survey of 595 mobile payment users in Korea indicate TA negatively moderates the influence of intention on actual usage in addition to the direct negative influence on intention to use MFA. Also, the author found that TA significantly differs depending on the frequency of use and gender. However, contrary to a common notion that older people are more anxious in context to new technologies, TA has been found to be higher among young people.

INTRODUCTION

The convergence of mobile devices and wireless technologies in the last decade has brought a new type of technology-aided commerce, called mobile commerce (m-commerce). M-commerce refers to any transaction with a monetary value

DOI: 10.4018/978-1-4666-1752-0.ch017

- either direct or indirect - that is conducted over a wireless telecommunication network (Barnes, 2002) and is gaining rapid popularity across the globe. As e-commerce's next evolutionary stage, m-commerce has opened up new business opportunities in business-to-consumer (B2C) activities in addition to extending current operations in e-commerce and traditional brick and mortar businesses (Lee et al., 2003; Varshney & Vetter,

2002). M-commerce also provides customers with the anytime-anywhere connectivity of wireless device, which provides unique experiences and services (Figge, 2004; Zwass, 2003). Recently, in addition to the traditional voice and data-centric services, various m-commerce services, including mobile advertising, proactive service management, location-based services, mobile auction, mobile entertainment services, and wireless data center applications have emerged and are expected to attract more customers to the m-commerce market.

However, m-commerce activities will not expand without the proper support of mobile financial applications (MFA). MFA include mobile banking, mobile brokerage service, mobile money transfer, and mobile micro-payments which can enable a mobile device to become a business tool, replacing ATMs, and credit cards (Mallat et al., 2004; Varshney & Vetter, 2002). MFA not only makes purchasing activities more flexible and convenient, but also creates unimagined new markets. Thus, the use of MFA is expected to have a great impact on the future of mobile commerce industries. However, despite the advent of these advanced MFA technologies, and despite the availability of various mobile services, the adoption of mobile financial applications across the globe is still relatively low, and its growth appears much slower than anticipated (Mallat et al., 2004).

Many studies have supported that negative perceptions reside longer in users' memory and have more powerful effects on consequent variables such as intention and usage than positive perceptions (Baumeister et al., 2001; Hackbarth et al., 2003). Technology anxiety (TA) is one of frequently cited negative beliefs in prior studies, and it is defined as an individual's tendency to be uneasy, apprehensive, or fearful about the current or future use of a technology (Parasuraman & Igbaria, 1990). A significant body of research in IS has highlighted the importance of TA by demonstrating its influence on intention (Hackbarth et al., 2003; Verplanken et al., 1997) and on IT adoption (Meuter et al., 2003; Parasuraman & Igbaria, 1990). The purpose of this study is to investigate the role of technology anxiety (TA) in adoption of mobile financial applications and to resolve the discrepancy between the apparent interest in and low adoption of MFA.

LITERATURE REVIEW

Mobile Financial Applications

Mobile Payment

Mobile payment and mobile banking services are two of the most important mobile financial applications (MFA) (See Figure 1). Mobile payment (m-

Figure 1. Mobile financial services. Adapted from Varshney and Vetter (2002)

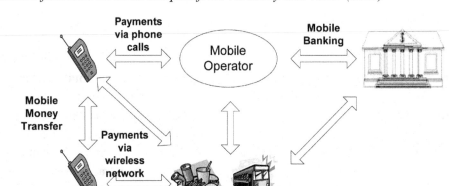

payment) is a point-of-sale payment made through a mobile device, such as a cellular telephone, a smartphone, or a personal digital assistant (PDA). Traditional payment technologies for the narrow sense of e-commerce (e-commerce), such as credit cards, store-valued card, or electronic cash, require a number of steps to complete, including payment authorization via the company's or third-party websites (Dutta et al., 2003). However, using m-payment, a person with a wireless device could pay for items in a store or settle a restaurant bill efficiently, and often without interacting with any staff member.

The introduction of m-payment technologies provides customers alternative payment methods and processes, which will influence consumers' purchase behaviors (Soamn, 2001). More customers tend to use these m-payment technologies, especially for small cash transactions (micro-payments) such as transit fares or vending machines (Kearney, 2004; Varshney, 2003). In some regions, such as Korea, Japan, Hong Kong, and Western Europe, the use of such mobile micro-payments have already grown to significant levels. For example, smart soda machines can transmit data back to company warehouses, triggering item restocking (Mendez-Wilson, 2000), and users can pay transit fare using their handsets. M-payment vendors predict that new types of content will fuel future demand for their products (Essex, 1999).

Mobile Banking

Mobile banking services, which are specifically designed for mobile devices and are conducted over wireless networks, provide customers with the capability to access a variety of financial services from anywhere at anytime and have become an essential part of m-commerce transactions. Mobile banking is the newest electronic delivery channel to be offered by banks in which technology has become an increasingly vital element, and it provides convenience and enhanced value to both

banks and customers (Suoranta & Mattila, 2004). Especially for banking, this new channel not only delivers new revenue streams but also minimizes or discontinues the provision of relatively old and cost-intensive distribution channels. Mobile banking is now gaining rapid popularity in European and Asian countries with the significant market penetration of mobile handsets and the optimally designed marketing tactics of service providers (Lee et al., 2003; Suoranta & Mattila, 2004). However, mobile banking is still marginally adopted across the globe, and, especially in the USA, the growth appears much slower than anticipated (Mallat et al., 2004).

Currently, various technologies have been tested and implemented in mobile banking systems including Short Message Service (SMS), Java, Wireless Application Protocol (WAP), i-mode, XHTML, and Integrated-Circuit (IC) chip (Kwon, 2004). Among them, SMS and WAP have been the most popular technologies for mobile banking systems in Europe and some Asia countries (Marenzi, 2004). Especially, SMS has dominated the market with its convenience and low cost for initial services (Lomax, 2002). However, i-mode and IC chip based mobile banking systems provide more secure and interactive banking services and are expected to be a primary banking technology in the future (Lee & Warkentin 2006).

Mobile Financial Applications Adoption

M-commerce adoption literatures have identified some of the significant features which differentiate MFA adoption from that of other previous information technology (IT). First, the average MFA user's characteristics differ from that of other IT, especially the narrow concept of e-commerce MFA users. According to Suoranta and Mattila (2004), unlike Internet banking which wealthier customers are more willing to adopt and use, the wealthier respondents were less willing to adopt the new mobile banking. One of the reasons explaining the

233

discrepancy is that the lack of fixed-line Internet is one of the major drivers of mobile banking adoption (Mattila, 2003). In other words, people using wired Internet banking heavily are less likely to adopt mobile banking.

Lee *et al.* (2003) found that increasing one's self-prestige is also an important driver of mobile financial applications adoption. Increased self-prestige from MFA adoption in turn may reduce the social risk or psychological risk of mobile banking adoption. However, the too early stage of development process (Mattila, 2003), the security issue of financial transaction (DeZoysa, 2001), and the cost and quality of the handset are still big barriers to MFA adoption. Moreover, many potential adopters intend to wait and get comments from other users in order to evaluate the performance

of the mobile banking services before an adoption decision is made (Lee et al., 2003).

Technology Anxiety

Anxiety concerning the use of technology, or technology anxiety (TA), is a common symptom of modern times and has received enormous attention from researchers and practitioners in such disciplines as marketing, psychology, education, and IS (Beckers & Schmidt, 2001; Chua et al., 1999; Meuter et al., 2003; Venkatesh, 2000). The emphasis of previous research has been on computer related anxiety (CA) due to the important role and impact of computers in our society (See Table 1). According to Brosnan (1998), TA is caused by the rapidly changing nature of new technology and the subsequent pressure for

Table 1. Technology anxiety studies and technologies tested

Study	Subjects	Technology Tested	Findings
Niemelä-Nyrhinen, 2007	620 baby boomers	Internet and SMS	Baby boomers (age between 50 and 60) shows low level of TA.
Meuter et al., 2003	823 consumers	Self-service Technologies	TA is a better predictor of SST usage than demographic characteristics.
Fagan et al., 2003	978 undergraduate students	General Computer	No relationship is found between CA and computer usage.
Gilbert et al., 2003	161 individuals	Mobile Internet Technology	TA correlates with demographic and psychological contexts.
Hackbarth et al., 2003	55 undergraduate students	Microsoft Excel	CA is a significant mediator of the effect of experience on ease of use.
Bozionelos, 2001	267 undergraduate students	Computer applications including software, hardware, and networking products.	Socio-economic background has an indirect relationship with CA.
Beckers & Schmidt, 2001	184 undergraduate students	General Computer	Training programs reduce CA.
Anderson, 1996	200 undergraduate students	Microcomputer, the DOS system, MS Word and Louts 123	Perceived knowledge rather than experience is a predictor of CA.
Scott & Rockwell, 1997	178 undergraduate Students	Wordprocessing, Email, Cellular Phones, ISDN, etc.	CA is correlated to a wide variety of new technologies.
Henderson et al., 1995	253 nursing and clerical staffs in a hospital	General Computer	The lower anxiety is found in the non-academic sample.
Brosnan, 1998	50 undergraduate students	Database	CA influences the task performance.
Kjerulff et al., 1992	219 nurses	Medical Equipment	Those who have TA feel more stress and are lower on job satisfaction.

social change. Surprisingly, 55% of Americans suffer from some degree of TA, and nearly five million American college students suffer from some type of TA (Scott & Rockwell, 1997). Also, about 50% of the British general public does not use a computer nor any form of new technology due to TA (Gilbert et al., 2003). Thus, TA has been a significant predictor for utilization and acceptance of technology (Hackbarth et al., 2003; Meuter et al., 2003; Venkatesh, 2000), and it has consequently influenced the performance and attitudes of people, such as students, teachers, and employees, who use information technology (IT) for certain tasks (Anderson, 1996; Brosnan, 1998; Kjerulff et al., 1992).

Technology anxiety is related to an individual's emotional feeling about new technologies. Users generally overcome their initial anxious feelings and develop favorable perceptions as they become familiar with technologies (Hackbarth et al., 2003). However, when individuals have less experience with a new technology, they are expected to rely upon their general beliefs regarding technologies and technology use and, therefore, their attitude may be highly anxious. Individuals with higher technology anxiety tend to automatically avoid the use of a particular new technology (Aarts et al., 1998). Even though younger people are gaining greater exposure to technologies, TA is fairly common to all ages of users (Williams, 1994). Users have higher levels of anxiety for newer technologies and higher risk technologies (Plouffe et al., 2001), even when they can see clear benefits. For example, many bank customers still prefer making deposits by placing checks into bank tellers hands even though a nearby ATM may be more convenient.

RESEARCH MODEL AND HYPOTHESES

Research Model

Numerous information technology (IT) adoption studies have employed intention-based models to explain how users decide to adopt a particular IT. These intention-based models have focused on individual characteristics to explain individual IT adoption behaviors, and the intention is regarded as the sole determinant of individual IT adoption (Heijden, 2003; Limayem et al., 2003). For example, TAM-based studies theorize that perceived usefulness and perceived ease of use are important determinants of an individual's intention to use IT (Davis, 1989), and a significant body of research has accumulated empirical support to show that it plays a critical role in predicting and determining an individual's technology adoption behavior (Venkatesh, 2000).

However, these TAM-based studies have also been criticized for their simplicity and lack of emphasis on attitudes (Legris et al., 2003; Tylor & Todd, 1995). In response, researchers have extended their search for factors that influence intentions with empirically tested models. Straub and Keil (1997) tested TAM on different cultural backgrounds, while others tested factors such as computer self-efficacy (Venkatesh & Davis, 1996), gender (Gefen & Straub, 1997), and habits (Gefen, 2003) on TAM. These intention-based IS adoption studies explain over 40 percent of the variance to individual actual use technology (Venkatesh et al., 2003), but they also have been criticized for disregarding some significant factors influencing intention and individual IT adoption behavior (Legris et al., 2003; Wang & Butler, 2003).

To understand the nature of the MFA adoption process and find impact of TA on the use of MFA, the present study uses TA as a determinant of intention to use MFA as well as a moderating factor which weaken the relationship between intention to use MFA and actual use. Also, since

Figure 2. Research model

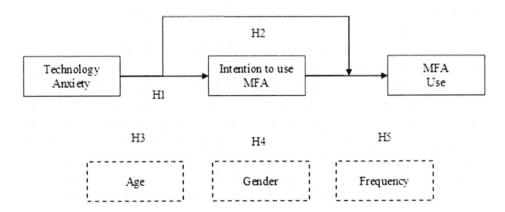

MFA is a new and payment-related technology, naturally there initially exists a higher level of technology anxiety about its use, though levels of such anxiety vary among users. Prior studies found various factors that correlate with TA, but gender, age, and experience have been the three most commonly examined correlates. Therefore, the present study also investigates the level of TA among users in different gender, age, and experience. The research model is illustrated in Figure 2.

HYPOTHESES DEVELOPMENT

An individual's intention to use IT and its antecedents have received enormous attention from researchers and practitioners and have become a main structure of IS adoption and utilization studies (e.g., Ajzen, 1991; Anol Bhattacherjee & Premkumar, 2004; Davis, 1989; Fishbein & Ajzen, 1975; Lewis et al., 2003). Such studies highlight that individual beliefs or perceptions about a new technology are significant determinants of intention to use IT (e.g., A Bhattacherjee, 2001; e.g., Marakas et al., 1998), and a significant body of research in IS has highlighted the importance of TA by demonstrating its influence on intention (Elasmar & Carter, 1996; Hackbarth et al., 2003; Verplanken et al., 1997). This suggests the following hypothesis:

H₁: Technology Anxiety is a significant determinant of intention to use of mobile financial applications.

Since MFA is a monetary-related technology, there initially exists a higher level of

TA about its use, though levels of such anxiety vary among users. Further, an individual's level of TA influences his or her habitual behavior to use IT. Based on the results from a person's inherent perceptions, such as habits in technology use (Verplanken et al., 1997), TA can be considered as playing a moderating role in the intention-adoption relationship by guiding individual intention to use a technology. Therefore, technology anxiety may weaken the relationship between intention and the use mobile financial applications. This suggests the following hypothesis:

H₂: Technology Anxiety negatively moderates the relationship between intention to use mobile financial applications and actual use.

It is commonly believed that older people are more anxious toward the use of technologies than young people, and many studies have supported this belief (i.e., Gilbert et al., 2003). However, many other studies also have found no relationship or an insignificant relationship between TA and age (Henderson et al., 1995). According to Chua et al.

(1999), the mixed results may be caused by the age range of population and sample. In other words, a wide range of target population consistently show a significant relationship of age and TA, but when the age range in population is narrow, the relationship is not significant. Since many prior studies used undergraduate students as a sample, the age range is narrow, and consequently the results are insignificant. However, a majority of m-commerce users are young people, and young people are early adopters of various m-commerce services. This suggests the following hypothesis:

H₃: Older people exhibit a higher degree of Technology Anxiety than younger people in the adoption of mobile financial applications.

Some studies suggested that gender is correlated to TA (Gilbert et al., 2003; Rosen & Weil, 1995), but many other studies also found that the relationship is not significant (Parasuraman & Igbaria, 1990; Scott & Rockwell, 1997); therefore, the relationship between TA and gender in prior studies is at best inconclusive. However, Gilbert et al. (2003) found that gender is a significant determinant of TA in mobile internet technology adoption. They conclude that females exhibit higher levels of TA than males. This suggests the following hypothesis:

H₄: Females exhibit a higher degree of Technology Anxiety than males in the adoption of mobile financial applications.

Prior studies consistently found TA could be reduced by exposing people to technologies. Some studies added that not only the exposure to technology, but also on the amount of the exposure time influences TA (Chua et al., 1999). According to the social cognitive theory (Bandura, 1986), enactive mastery attained through direct experience is the strongest source that raises an individual's confidence in attaining effective performance

level, and Venkatesh and Davis (1996) highlight that individuals without direct experience are more likely to base their perceptions on abstract criteria. This suggests the following hypothesis:

H₅: The frequency of mobile financial application use is negatively associated with Technology Anxiety.

RESEARCH METHODOLOGY AND RESULTS

Human Subjects and Instrument

The sample consists of 3,000 Korean mobile payment users. Instrument was developed to measure TA, mobile payment usage status, frequency of use, and demographic information including gender and age. To measure TA, the four-item TA scale developed in prior studies was used after modifying them to reflect TA in using mobile payment technology. The items were assessed on a seven-point likert scale with endpoints *strongly disagree* to *strongly agree*. Higher scores indicate higher levels of anxiety. The rest of the constructs were also adapted from prior studies and measured as the same as TA. Instrument was originally developed in English and translated to Korean. The survey instrument was placed on a web site where participants access and complete the survey. The email including survey information and URL were sent to 3000 randomly selected current and future mobile payment technologies users.

Survey Results

636 (21% response rate) surveys were collected and 595 usable surveys were used for data analysis. The respondents are comprised of more male (72.3%) than female, and the largest group of respondents are between the ages of 18 and 24 (59%). In terms of the status of mobile payment

Figure 3. Respondent's demographic distribution

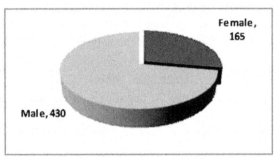
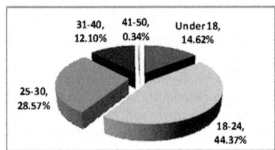

use, 70.6% of the respondents have used mobile payment systems, and 63.7% of the respondents use mobile payment systems one to three times in a month.

The reliability of the TA measure was verified with a Cronbach Alpha score of .807. This reliability is similar to the reliability in prior studies (.81) indicating that the modification of the items did not inhibit the effectiveness of the measure.

Regression was used to test hypotheses 1 and 2. Hypothesis 1 posits that TA is a significant determinant of intention to use of mobile financial applications. We found that the relationship between TA and intention to use mobile financial applications is significant (sig. = .000 and Adjusted R^2 = .263). We also found that TA indeed negatively moderates the relationship between intention and actual usage in addition to direct influence on intention to use MFA. R^2 with TA as a moderate variable was .258, little higher than without TA, .249.

ANOVA was used for Hypothesis 3, 4, and 5 to compare TA among the different groups of age, gender and frequent use. Contrary to our hypothesis, which posits that older people exhibit a higher degree of Technology Anxiety than younger people in the adoption of MFA, the result shows that younger people exhibit a higher degree of TA than older people. An additional Duncan test shows that TA among individuals over age 30 and those under age 30 is distinguished. The different sample size may influence the result of the oldest group,

but it is interesting that the mean of TA is getting lower as age is older. Hypothesis 4 contends that females exhibit a higher degree of TA than males in the adoption of mobile financial applications. Indeed, we found that TA among females (mean =3.57) is higher than males (mean = 3.26), and the relationship is significant. Hypothesis 5 posits that the frequency of mobile financial application use significantly influences TA. Indeed, we found that the more the individual uses mobile payment technology, the lower the individual's TA. The results of the Duncan test show that TA between daily users and light users or people who have never used mobile payment technologies is differentiated (See Table 2). The summary of research results is presented in Table 3.

DISCUSSION AND IMPLICATIONS

The first empirical finding of this study is that TA negatively moderates the influence of intention on actual usage, and further that TA exerts a direct negative influence on intention to use MFA. This implies that many users, even individuals who have an intention to adopt, decide not to use MFA due to TA. Therefore, IS training, which can reduce TA by either direct or vicarious experience, may be needed to expand the m-commerce market (Beckers & Schmidt, 2001).

The second empirical finding of this study of this research is that contrary to a common notion

Table 2. The result of duncan test for age and frequent use

	N	Subset for alpha=.05				N	Subset for alpha=.05	
AGE		1	2		**Frequency**		**1**	2
Over 30	74	2.9257			Daily use	31	**2.5726**	
25-30	264		3.3636		Often use	379		3.2691
18-24	170		3.3662		Never use	185		3.6419
Under 18	87		3.6293					

Table 3. The summary of test results

Hypothesis	Description	Result
H1	Intention to use adoption	Supported
H2	Moderate the relationship between intention and use	Supported
H3	Age	Not Supported
H4	Gender	Supported
H5	Frequency of use	Supported

that older people are more anxious toward the use of new technologies, this research found that TA is higher among younger people. Specifically, this study found that TA among individuals over age 30 is lower than those under age 30. The result implies that even though younger groups are larger customer groups, m-commerce practitioners should pay more attention to older groups who have more purchasing power and less technology anxiety.

Another finding of this study is that TA among females is higher than males. This finding is consistent with those of previous research that there exist some significant differences in information and communication technology use (e.g., Chou & Tsai, 2009). This finding implies that females are usually anxious about the monetary-related information technology. Finally, this study found that TA significantly differs depending on the frequency of use. This result confirms that users generally overcome their initial anxious feelings and develop favorable perceptions as they become familiar with technologies (Hackbarth et al., 2003) and that individuals with higher

technology anxiety tend to automatically avoid the use of a particular new technology (Aarts et al., 1998). Mobile transaction demonstration and education using websites and mobile devices may help individuals with higher technology anxiety and facilitate the use of MFA.

CONCLUSION

This study investigates the role of TA in the adoption of mobile financial applications (MFA) and resolves the discrepancy between the apparent interest in and low adoption rate of MFA. The result of this study will assist researchers and practitioners to find real reasons for slow growth of m-commerce and provide guidelines to expand m-commerce markets.

It is important to evaluate the study's results and contributions in light of its limitations. First, the use of subjects in only one country, Korea, may limit the generalizability of our findings to other countries which have different levels of mobile technology use and different cultures. Therefore, the countries which have more advanced or less advanced mobile technologies will yield different results. However, since South Korea has a highly advanced mobile technology infrastructure, this result can be a positive indication for many other countries that are currently developing mobile infrastructures.

This research has unique contributions for IS practitioners, especially for MFA developers and vendors. The slow growth of MFA is not caused by less advanced technologies but rather by rapid changes with insufficient consideration of users' reactions to IS. Therefore, developing and providing MFA which has greater appeal to users is a critical task for all practitioners. For academics, this study contributes to the knowledge base by empirically testing TA with mobile financial applications.

REFERENCES

Aarts, H., Verplanken, B., & Van Knippenberg, A. (1998). Predicting Behavior from Actions in Past: Repeated Decision Making or a Matter of Habit? *Journal of Applied Social Psychology*, *28*(15), 1355–1374. doi:10.1111/j.1559-1816.1998.tb01681.x

Ajzen, I. (1991). The Theory of Planned Behavior. *Organizational Behavior and Human Decision Processes*, *50*, 179–211. doi:10.1016/0749-5978(91)90020-T

Anderson, A. A. (1996). Predictors of Computer Anxiety and Performance in Information Systems. *Computers in Human Behavior*, *12*(1), 61–77. doi:10.1016/0747-5632(95)00019-4

Bandura, A. (1986). *Social Foundations of Thought and Action: A Social Cognitive Theory*. Upper Saddle River, NJ: Prentice-Hall.

Barnes, S. J. (2002). The mobile commerce value chain: Analysis and future developments. *International Journal of Information Management*, *22*(2), 91–108. doi:10.1016/S0268-4012(01)00047-0

Baumeister, R. F., Bratslavsky, E., Finkenauer, C., & Vohs, K. D. (2001). Bad is stronger than good. *Review of General Psychology*, *5*(4), 323–370. doi:10.1037/1089-2680.5.4.323

Beckers, J. J., & Schmidt, H. G. (2001). The structure of computer anxiety: A six-factor model. *Computers in Human Behavior*, *17*(1), 35–49. doi:10.1016/S0747-5632(00)00036-4

Bhattacherjee, A. (2001). Understanding Information Systems Continuance: An Expectation-Confirmation Model. *Management Information Systems Quarterly*, *25*(3), 351–370. doi:10.2307/3250921

Bhattacherjee, A., & Premkumar, G. (2004). Understanding Change in Belief and Attitude Toward Information Technology Usage: A theoretical Model and Longitudinal Test. *Management Information Systems Quarterly*, *28*(2), 229–254.

Brosnan, M. J. (1998). The impact of computer anxiety and self-efficacy upon performance. *Journal of Computer Assisted Learning*, *14*, 223–234. doi:10.1046/j.1365-2729.1998.143059.x

Chou, J., & Tsai, H. (2009). On-line learning performance and computer anxiety measure for unemployed adult novices using a grey relation entropy method. *Information Processing & Management*, *45*(2), 200–215. doi:10.1016/j.ipm.2008.12.001

Chua, S. L., Chen, D., & Wong, A. F. L. (1999). Computer anxiety and its correlates: A meta-analysis. *Computers in Human Behavior*, *75*, 609–623. doi:10.1016/S0747-5632(99)00039-4

Davis, F. A. (1989). Perceived Usefulness, Perceived Ease of Use, and User Acceptance of Information Technology. *Management Information Systems Quarterly, 13*, 319–339. doi:10.2307/249008

DeZoysa, S. (2001). *Who do you trust? Should banks or mobile operators be entrusted with m-commerce security?* Retrieved January 20, 2005, from http://www.telecommagazine.com/default.asp?journalid=2&func=articles&page=0112i13&year=2001&month=12

Dutta, R., Jarvenpaa, S., & Tomak, K. P. (2003). *Impact of feedback and usability of online payment processes on consumer decision making.* Paper presented at the Proceedings of the 24th International conference on Information Systems, Seattle, WA.

Elasmar, M., & Carter, M. (1996). Use of e-mail by College Students and Implications for Curriculum. *Journal of Mass Communications Education, 52*(2), 46–54.

Essex, D. (1999). Big dreams for tiny money. *Computerworld, 33*(50), 66.

Figge, S. (2004). Situation-dependent services - a challenges for mobile network operators. *Journal of Business Research, 57*(12), 1416–1422. doi:10.1016/S0148-2963(02)00431-9

Fishbein, M., & Ajzen, I. (1975). *Belief, Attitude, Intention and Behavior: An Introduction to Theory and Research.* Reading, MA: Addison-Wesley Publishing Company.

Gefen, D. (2003). TAM or just plain habit: A look at experienced online shoppers. *Journal of End User Computing, 15*(3), 1–13.

Gefen, D., & Straub, D. (1997). Gender differences in the perception and use of e-mail: An extension to the technology acceptance model. *Management Information Systems Quarterly, 21*(4), 389–400. doi:10.2307/249720

Gilbert, D., Lee-Kelley, L., & Barton, M. (2003). Technophobia, gender influences and consumer decision-making for technology-related products. *European Journal of Innovation Management, 6*(4), 253–263. doi:10.1108/14601060310500968

Hackbarth, G., Grover, V., & Yi, M. Y. (2003). Computer playfulness and anxiety: Positive and negative mediators of the system experience effect on perceived ease of use. *Information & Management, 40*(3), 221–232. doi:10.1016/S0378-7206(02)00006-X

Heijden, H. d. (2003). Factors influencing the usage of websites: the case of a generic portal in the Netherlands. *Information & Management, 40*, 541–549. doi:10.1016/S0378-7206(02)00079-4

Henderson, R., Deane, F., Barrelle, K., & Mahar, D. (1995). Computer anxiety: correlates, norms and problem definition in health care and banking employees using the Computer Attitude Scale. *Interacting with Computers, 7*(2), 181–193. doi:10.1016/0953-5438(95)93508-3

Kearney, A. T. (2004). *Mobinet 5.* Retrieved February 18, 2004, from http://www.atkearney.com/main.taf?p=5,4,1,60.

Kjerulff, K. H., Pillar, B., Mills, M. E., & Lanigan, J. (1992). Technology anxiety as a potential mediating factor in response to medical technology. *Journal of Medical Systems, 16*(1), 7–13. doi:10.1007/BF01674093

Kwon, S. H. (2004). *New technology in Mobile Banking.* Retrieved from http://www.etnews.co.kr/news/detail.html?id=200402040104.

Lee, C.-P., & Warkentin, M. (2006). Mobile Banking Systems and Technologies. In Khosrow-Pour, M. (Ed.), *Encyclopedia of E-Commerce, E-Government and Mobile Commerce* (pp. 754–759). Hershey, PA: IGI Global.

Lee, M. S. Y., McGoldrick, P. J., Keeling, K. A., & Doherty, J. (2003). Using ZMET to explore barriers to the adoption of 3G mobile banking services. *International Journal of Retail & Distribution Management, 31*(6/7), 340–348. doi:10.1108/09590550310476079

Legris, P., Ingham, J., & Collerette, P. (2003). Why do people use information technology? A critical review of the technology acceptance model. *Information & Management, 40*(3), 191–204. doi:10.1016/S0378-7206(01)00143-4

Lewis, W., Agarwal, R., & Sambamurthy, V. (2003). Sources of Influence on Beliefs about Information Technology Use: An empirical study of knowledge workers. *Management Information Systems Quarterly, 27*(4), 657–678.

Limayem, M., Cheung, C. M. K., & Chan, G. W. W. (2003). *Explaining information systems adoption and post-adoption: Toward an integrative model.* Paper presented at the 24th International Conference on Information Systems, Seattle, WA.

Lomax, V. (2002). WAP lash. *Financial World, 44.*

Mallat, N., Rossi, M., & Tuunainen, V. K. (2004). Mobile Banking Services. *Communications of the ACM, 47*(5), 42–46. doi:10.1145/986213.986236

Marakas, G. M., Yi, M. Y., & Johnson, R. D. (1998). The Multilevel and Multifaceted Character of Computer Self-Efficacy: Toward Clarification of the Construct and an Integrative Framework for Research. *Information Systems Research, 9*(2), 126–163. doi:10.1287/isre.9.2.126

Marenzi, O. (2004). *Will i-mode save Mobile Banking in Western Europe?* Retrieved February 10, 2005, from http://www.celent.com/PressReleases/20031023/MobileEurope.htm

Mattila, M. (2003). Factors affecting the adoption of mobile banking services. *Journal of Internet Banking and Commerce, 8*(1).

Mendez-Wilson, D. (2000). Goodbye cash and credit cards. *Wireless Week, 6*(44), 32.

Meuter, M. L., Ostrom, A. L., Bitner, M. J., & Roundtree, R. (2003). The influence of technology anxiety on consumer use and experiences with self-service technologies. *Journal of Business Research, 56*(11), 899–906. doi:10.1016/S0148-2963(01)00276-4

Niemelä-Nyrhinen, J. (2007). Baby boom consumers and technology: shooting down stereotypes. *Journal of Consumer Marketing, 24*(5), 305–312. doi:10.1108/07363760710773120

Parasuraman, S., & Igbaria, M. (1990). An examination of gender differences in the determinants of computer anxiety and attitudes toward microcomputers among managers. *International Journal of Man-Machine Studies, 32*(3), 327–340. doi:10.1016/S0020-7373(08)80006-5

Plouffe, C. R., Vandenbosch, M., & Hulland, J. (2001). Intermediating technologies and multigroup adoption: A comparison of consumer and merchant adoption intentions toward a new electronic payment system. *Journal of Product Innovation Management, 18,* 65–81. doi:10.1016/S0737-6782(00)00072-2

Rosen, L. D., & Weil, M. M. (1995). Computer availability, computer experience and technophobia among public school teachers. *Computers in Human Behavior, 11*(1), 9–31. doi:10.1016/0747-5632(94)00018-D

Scott, C. R., & Rockwell, S. C. (1997). The Effect of Communication, Writing, and Technology Apprehension on Likelihood to Use New Communication Technologies. *Communication Education, 46*(1), 44–62. doi:10.1080/03634529709379072

Soamn, D. (2001). Effects of Payment Mechanism on Spending Behavior: The Role of Rehearsal and Immediacy of Payments. *The Journal of Consumer Research, 27,* 460–474. doi:10.1086/319621

Straub, D., & Keil, M.. Testing the technology acceptance model across cultures: A three country study. *Information & Management, 33*(1), 1–11. doi:10.1016/S0378-7206(97)00026-8

Suoranta, M., & Mattila, M. (2004). Mobile banking and consumer behaviour: New insights into the diffusion pattern. *Journal of Financial Services Marketing, 8*(4), 354–366. doi:10.1057/palgrave.fsm.4770132

Tylor, S., & Todd, P. (1995). Understanding Information technology Usage: A Test of Competing Models. *Information Systems Research, 6*(2), 144–176. doi:10.1287/isre.6.2.144

Varshney, U. (2003). Wireless I: Mobile and Wireless Information Systems: Applications, Networks, and Research Problems. *Communications of the Association for Information Systems, 12*(11).

Varshney, U., & Vetter, R. (2002). Mobile Commerce: Framework, Applications and Networking Support. *Mobile Networks and Applications, 7*(3), 185–198. doi:10.1023/A:1014570512129

Venkatesh, V. (2000). Determinants of Perceived Ease of Use: Integrating Control, Intrinsic Motivation, and Emotion into the Technology Acceptance Model. *Information Systems Research, 11*(4), 342–365. doi:10.1287/isre.11.4.342.11872

Venkatesh, V. (2003). User acceptance of information technology: Toward a unified view. *Management Information Systems Quarterly, 27*(3), 425–478.

Venkatesh, V., & Davis, F. D. (1996). A model of the antecedents of perceived ease of use: Development and test. *Decision Sciences, 27*(3), 451–481. doi:10.1111/j.1540-5915.1996.tb01822.x

Verplanken, B., Aarts, H., & Van Knippenberg, A. (1997). Habits, Information Acquisition, and the Process of Making Travel Mode Choices. *European Journal of Social Psychology, 27*, 539–560. doi:10.1002/(SICI)1099-0992(199709/10)27:5<539::AID-EJSP831>3.0.CO;2-A

Wang, X., & Butler, B. S. (2003). Individual technology acceptance under conditions of change. In *Proceedings of the 24th International Conference on Information Systems*, Seattle, WA.

Williams, S. (1994). Technophobes Victims of Electronic progress. *Mobile Register*, 9E.

Zwass, V. (2003). Electronic Commerce and Organizational Innovation: Aspects and Opportunities. *International Journal of Electronic Commerce, 7*(3), 7–37.

This work was previously published in International Journal of Technology Diffusion, Volume 1, Issue 4, edited by Ali Hussein Saleh Zolait, pp. 1-12, copyright 2010 by IGI Publishing (an imprint of IGI Global).

Chapter 18
The Influence of Internet Security on E-Business Competence in Jordan:
An Empirical Analysis

Amin Ahmad Shaqrah
Alzaytoonah University of Jordan, Jordan

ABSTRACT

The purpose of this study is to investigate the relationship between internet security and e-business competence in Jordan. The proposed conceptual model examined the antecedents and consequences of e-business competence of its empirical validity, the sample of 152 banking and exchange firms, and tests the posited structural equation model. Results consistently support the validity of the proposed conceptual model, finding that both organizations realize the importance of e-business for their business and are willing to proceed further with e-business. In this regard, businesses are highly concerned about internet security, their awareness of security hazards, and minimal internet performance, concluding that public awareness of the ICT is very low. In light of the data collected, the study has proposed certain recommendations for the interested authorities to improve e-business in Jordan.

INTRODUCTION

Several studies suggested that the internet has become a popular delivery platform for electronic business (Sheshunoff, 2000; Oyegoke, 1999; Birch, 1999; Evans & Wurster, 1997). Electronic business offered an easy access to their accounts 24 hours per day, seven days a week. Regardless of this convenience, adoption rates of electronic business in most developed countries have been very low. Therefore, of interest to ascertain and understand the factors that drive using e-business applications. Jordan, over a long historical period, is a country of commerce and its people are famous for their trading and business activities. When the internet project entered Jordan, the Jordanian business organizations faced challenging

DOI: 10.4018/978-1-4666-1752-0.ch018

competition to have a pronounced presence on the web. The aims behind this growing attendance are commercial and for reducing communication costs. Most of the companies in Jordan started to build their own websites on the web and started using them to communicate with both current and potential customers.

Saeed et al. (2005) results illustrated that firms with high electronic commerce competence exhibit superior performance and that customer value generated through Web site functionality partially mediates this relationship. Additionally, firms have now started to realize the danger that comes from using this modern method of business, which is the difficulty of having a secure business. Laudon and Traver (2008) explained that the e-commerce environment holds threats for both consumers and merchants; therefore, unsecure operations can cause a firm to lose successful business. There are misconceptions must be overcome before it can be deemed suitable for electronic commerce. A few of the commonly expressed concerns include reliability, security, scalability, ease of use and payment (Ambrose & Johnson, 1998). Hence, security is one barrier but there is the real underlying factor.

Historical Background

The internet as an information and entertainment technology has affected on education, government, publishing, the retail industry, banking, broadcast services, and health care delivery. Therefore, the scope of internet applications and forces is to deliver the internet resource to business utility. Thus, the core indicators on accept and usage of internet by households and individuals should be used in parallel with flourish e-business activities as a starting point of Jordan that planning to implement the information society. In Jordan, the ICT sector has grown rapidly during the last years and enormous investments recently have made. Jordanian governments, ICT companies are also making efforts to involve more people in the adoption of their products and services. Current Jordanian stakeholders such as the government, internet Service Providers (ISPs), are making a lot of efforts and resources to speed up the adoption of e-commerce applications.

In general, most Jordanian business companies are subscribers to the internet service but the uses of the internet for business purposes are limited to one aspect of internet interaction facilities, i.e., communication. Active internet services in the business affairs of Jordanian banks and exchange companies has not reached the necessary level at which the Jordanian business sector can benefit from participating in e-commerce activities. Although the internet can also be a source of significant dangers and risks, most Jordanian business users today feel they will suffer a greater loss by not connecting to the internet than they will face with security issues. The advances in internet technology should go along the same lines as security. The banks in Jordan are covering behind other geographical regions in the areas of technological interaction. Table 1 shows the increased number of subscriber along the eight years.

In January 2008, the Government completed the sale of its Jordan Telecom shares. Such that 51% of company shares became own by France Telecom, and the rest of the shares distributed between the Social Security Corporation, the Nor Financial Investment Company (Nor), the armed forces and security agencies, leaving 7% available for exchange in Amman Stock Exchange market. In June 2008, telecommunication regularly commission "TRC" announced its intention to introduce 3G services in Jordan. Mid August 2009: TRC granted a third generation (3G) license to Orange Mobile Company.

Literature Review

The use of the internet in business organizations has continuously increased because the facilities that the internet provides push many organizations to replace some of their traditional com-

Table 1. Telecom market

Number of Subscribers: (000)	2001	2002	2003	2004	2005	2006	2007	2008
Fixed Phone	660	674	623	638	628	614	559	519
Mobile & Trunking	866	1200	1325	1624	3138	4343	4772	5,314
Internet (Subscribers)	66	62	92	111	197	206	228	229
Internet (Users)	238	279	399	537	720	770	1,163	1,500
Penetration Rate per 100 inhabitants (%)	2001	2002	2003	2004	2005	2006	2007	2008
Fixed Phone	13.1	13.4	11.3	11.9	11.6	11	10	8.9
Mobile & Trunking	16.7	22.9	24.2	30.4	57	78	83.3	91
Internet (Subscribers)	1.32	1.16	1.67	2.07	3.6	3.7	4	4
Internet (Users)	4.8	5.5	7.7	10	13.2	13.7	20	26
Volume of Investments: (Million JD)	2001	2002	2003	2004	2005	2006	2007	2008
Fixed Phone	90.1	38.2	11.5	10	12.3	12.7	12.2	23
Mobile & Trunking	89.2	93.3	91.9	100.3	137	139	92.5	65
Internet	5.5	3.5	1.5	0.7	5.6	2.3	11.1	22
Other Services	0.1	2.6	1.1	0.4	0.4	1.5	0.5	5
Total	184.9	137.6	106.0	111.4	155.3	155.4	116.3	115.0
Number of Employees:	2001	2002	2003	2004	2005	2006	2007	2008
Fixed Phone	4792	4548	3663	3048	2701	2432	2303	2212
Mobile & Trunking	1044	1168	1249	1641	2124	2251	2283	2079
Internet	457	408	294	353	450	415	498	644
Telephone Prepaid Calling Service	25	53	45	52	50	294	135	345
Total	6318	6177	5251	5094	5325	5392	5219	5280
Demography, Economy:	2001	2002	2003	2004	2005	2006	2007	2008
Population (000)	4,978	5,098	5,230	5,350	5,473	5,600	5,723	5,849
Households (000)	823	874	897	946	980	1037	1060	1104
Gross Domestic Product (GDP,Million JD) (Current Price)	6364	6794	7229	8081	9012	10109	11225	15058

munications and methods for conducting business methods (Laudon & Traver, 2008). For example, many Jordanian organizations now communicate with their customers using internet facilities such as e-mail services, communities, forum etc.... In addition, the internet and web technology turned into the channel for publishing organizations websites whereas organizations use it for promotion and offering online services and participating in e-commerce, including all operations concerning the selling of products and services over the internet. Moreover, the internet enables organizations to deliver an online catalogue and messages to a huge number of target consumers. A few steps should consider to use the internet or to establish online business: 1. Business organizations must recognize how it will use the internet 2. They should be able to assess the risks involved 3. Perform a cost/benefit analysis to determine if the benefits prevail over the potential costs 4. Know very well the capabilities of their auditor and systems administrator in controlling online change 5. An appropriate budget allocation for security purposes 6. Management must view its computer system as it would any other company asset.

Booker (2000) noted that with appropriate caution, organizations should be able to use the internet full potential. Jordanian organizations should make sure they are involved in the process because their uses of the internet are more sensitive and in the short-term can cause bottom line loss. It is what marketers are most concerned about when it comes to protecting online property rights; the logo of any e-business will be a vulnerable target too and many may be 'sniffed', especially those successful online business websites. If they fail to sniff, they will try to cause trouble for the owner and users of these sites. More specifically, the company's response time following a security related event is an indication of the organizational readiness towards external threats. Furthermore, when multiple sites suffer synchronously from advanced attacks, the response and recover time is a very important differentiator.

Cross (2001) stated website host must also operate servers that can support the technology with which a website developed. Website host should have its own firewalls and other security technologies in place to protect hosted websites and customers' data from hackers and viruses. According to Zolait et al. (2009) "internet security applies to organizations that conduct online business operations over the internet just like a national border." Ahmed et al. (2006) summarized three factors contributing to the growth of internet commerce. First is the constant decline in the prices of hardware and software's. Second, is the expansion of different platforms of internet browsers and third factor is the commercialization of the web itself with media-rich content and electronic commerce. Forcht et al. (1995) stated that information sent via computer might route through many different systems before reaching their destination. Each different system introduces unwanted individuals who can access data; therefore, security is vital to protect organizations from unwanted damage, copying, or eavesdropping (Zolait et al., 2009). Consequently, gaining access to information on a website or eavesdropping on

data, which is supposed to be restricted, can lead to misrepresentation of the organization and loss of information and open the door of vulnerability to many threats. Therefore, each organization is required to secure the content of its website.

The application of security policy must place in easy-to-reach locations, without requiring the user to consume considerable time to track down the links to these statements. Although the procedures and security mechanisms of the systems must be transparent in order not to discomfort the legitimate user, from a trust perspective the presence of the security mechanisms is essential. For example, the existence of a password policy could success with a respective web page educating the user about the password rules (e.g., minimum number of characters, denial of use of names, etc.).

Security Hazard

There are two types of security mechanisms for conducting online business. First, applying physical security mechanism to minimize the hazard. The second type are the intangible protective security measures of the system acting as the second line of defense, which are a way to enhance the capability of companies' security, enabling them to conduct a successful business over the internet. For example, firewalls with specialized software are placed between the organization LAN or WAN and the internet, preventing unauthorized access to proprietary information stored on the intranet (Jessup & Valacich, 2008). Email is a security hazard and many bad things can happen to an individual's computer by simply previewing the message in a preview window without even opening it (Zolait et al., 2009). Although there are advances in terms of securing the networks against hackers, there are also advances developing in break-in and hacking tools too. It is very simple sometimes to break into other peoples and company's e-mails or sites and know everything available about them (Zolait et al., 2009).

Hackers can use very simple methods to reach you; some of these methods do not require people experienced in programming. Hackers can use ready-made software produced by experts to enable them to reach organization's information by breaking into organization e-mail, company account, and web site. This ready-made software is widespread on the market, for example, spy log software and net pass. There is a lot that organizations should do to strengthen the security requirements to face the anticipated threat that cause company resources. They should think in advance, what will happen if someone gains access to any aspect of the company's resources (Garfinkel, 1997). According to Totty (2001) "companies must stay one-step ahead of the hackers". Users of the organization online system should train to understand what hackers do and how they do it; because that is the only way, they can protect themselves and know their enemy (Nelson, 2000). Aldridge (1997) recommended setting some preventive conditions to enforce. Furthermore, Savage (2000) pointed that the learning from the security crises solutions of others. In addition, Totty (2001) noted that organizations must use authentication software. Organizations must find certifying tools to measure the level of security (Verton, 2000), make sure that they have the skills and time to keep the round-the-clock vigils the software requires (Messmer, 2000), and establish an e-mail policy and enforce members to use it (Parker, 1999).

Assuring the physical security of a website is similar to assuring the physical security of any other computer at any location (Zolait et al., 2009). Restricting physical access to the machine is a preventative strategy that plays a useful role in securing the sensitive information from internal attackers. Business organizations should be eager to understanding the elements of internet security. Totty (2001), and Jessup and Valacich (2008) classified four strategies necessary to prevent online security breaches in the organization which are 1. Authentication 2. Encryption 3. Integrity 4.

Firewalls. Internet security is a combination of partial components that combine to form a strong internet security for doing business online. Lane (1998) concluded that internet security for business as a group effort to securing the whole set of related contributing parties, which are security of privacy, system privacy, user privacy, commerce transaction privacy and authentication of data. Although there are, risks associated with the use of the internet as the enabling technology for doing business, most of them can mitigate with an organized and systematic security investment, including both technology and organization. Since these risks depend on the security awareness and responsibility of the underlying e-business organization, it follows that trust should refer to the organization rather the internet itself.

Protection Measures

Protection measures implemented to protect organizations from different security attacks. To guarantee the security requirements of a given organization, it is essential to be able to evaluate the current security demands of an organization as well as the measures taken to achieve such requirements. Security weaknesses cause a negative impact on organizations such as financial loss, reputations, and loss of customer confidence (Kumar, 2008). Protection measures used in banking and exchange services to protect information security objectives. These measures will assist an evaluator to measure the security level. For example, the security level is high when an organization implements the most proper, updated measures, policies, and countermeasures to protect its security objectives. Organizations are required to take appropriate protection measures based on their requirements. Protection measures can group into three major groups: physical, personal, and network security measures. Each group employs several means for security protection. Within each group, security measures can classify into measures aimed at securing the confidentiality, integrity, and availability of the data and system. Banks, on the other hand, have high demand for data confidentiality.

Hence, the measures required to protect confidentiality are essential for banks. In essence, an organization may have different security requirements for information security objectives. Similarly, an organization may have different security requirements at different times. Some protective options available today are very easy and inexpensive, while others are more complicated and expensive. One inexpensive option is awareness; simply being more aware of the dangers out there and how to avoid them. More expensive and complicated measures include choosing more secure operating systems, imposing access restrictions and enforcing authentication procedures (Zolait et al., 2009). Information systems assets are tangible and intangible. Assets vary from one organization to another. Protecting information systems from breaches and preventing information theft done by defining the information systems assets. Each organization's information assets evaluated to determine their information security.

Dhillon (2006) mentioned that the purpose of defining and characterizing the organization's assets allows for better determination behind the threat. Documentation of the assets will be beneficial to an organization because it will know what to secure, and it will ensure updates of assets in the case of changes (Schou & Shoemaker, 2006). Security breaches appear due to the lack of documenting and characterizing the information system assets within organizations. According to Ciampa (2005), an organization not only protects its information by classifying its assets in order to protect them from any threat caused by crackers and hackers, but it also identifies its vulnerabilities. Automated measurements systems cannot measure the subjective elements. However, the objective elements measured successfully with the proper automated tools. When working from policy toward automated checks, a key intermediate deliverable is the platform specific checklist.

Sometimes these documents, often called 'security cookbooks' are already prepared and in use by systems administrators.

Internet Performance

Drennan and McColl-Kennedy (2003) summarized that the internet has affected significantly in the services sector such as banks, insurance providers, and government organizations. Ahmed et al. (2006) identified some key challenges to do business over the internet in Arab countries for Saudi's organizations are the continuing relying on face-to-face contact principles, information overload problems, expensive charges, technical support and expertise, management commitment and understanding the potential role of information technology (IT), and older people were more reluctant to use IT. Drennan and McColl-Kennedy (2003) concluded that organizations eager to offer specialized services and develop an innovative customer-focused strategy employing the new technologies to increase customer loyalty.

Web page download delay is a major factor affecting the performance of a site and ultimately a sites success can depend on how quickly a user can navigate its pages (Saiedian & Naeem, 2001). It is important for banking and exchange services to make every effort to ensure their sites are of a high quality with download times kept to a minimum to prevent surfers moving on elsewhere. This will do two things, compress it in size and ensure its colors are web safe (can be displayed properly). Compressing an image gets rid of redundant data from the image. For example, if a company is selling products online and they have not compressed their images, the extra download time required can distance a user. There needs to be a tradeoff between quality and download time if the company is to succeed.

Trust

Mayer et al. (1995) defined trust as "the willingness of a party to be vulnerable to the actions of another party." Trust based on the expectation performs a particular action important to the trust or, irrespective of the ability to monitor or control that other party. Internet security generally relied on users' mutual respect and honor, as well as their knowledge of conduct considered appropriate on the network. Trust based on the potential use of the technology to increase online business. Trust increases the probability of a trading partner's willingness to expand the amount of information sharing through EDI and explore new mutually beneficial arrangements (Hart & Saunders, 1997). Trust, especially among the banking and exchanges services in electronic commerce reinforces the prospect of continuity in a relationship and a commitment to extend an inter-organizational relationship. It implies that the online business is dependable and follows their promises, thus developing high levels of cooperation that will in turn reinforce trust (Cummings & Bromiley, 1996).

Both reliability and security are impaired when inconsistencies between words and actions among the trading partners increase. This decreases trust due to the lack of consistent and reliable behavior. Thus, trust only occurs when the trading partners assured of others willingness and ability to deliver on their obligations. Trust is vital not only in the pre-transaction and transaction phase (that is advertising, providing information about the product, ordering, purchasing, paying, and delivering the product), but also in the post-transaction phase in the form of warranties and refunds. internet security is depend on trust not only in the EC systems that provide efficient services and guarantee delivery of the messages, but also more importantly, that the message in actual fact came from an authorized person thus being authentic, having integrity, confidentiality

and unable of being repudiated. Hence, high levels of trust will likely result in high levels of security.

CIA Triad

To protecting banking online business, an information security professional must establish and maintain a strict security defense that ensures three requirements: The information keep confidential, integrity of the information is high, and the information is available when needed for authorized users. Bishop (2002) noted that confidentiality related to privacy, which means the sender, and its respective receiver should only share information, but unfortunately, TCP/IP has its own deficiencies. It is not able to guarantee data confidentiality while it flows in the system. This can easily lead us to logins, passwords deviation during a telnet session, for instance, data interception during a home-banking, commercial or even a personal transaction may result in serious hazards, and this kind of interference observed easily in e-mail operations, Web commercial transactions, and many other important data exchange. Such banking systems use long sequences of characters and complex algorithms to encode and decode information exchanged between computers with the appropriate application installed.

Integrity related to the verification performed by the internet security system against any kind of data loss, modification, and/or damage, which caused by intentional or casual reasons, such as prejudicial actions of hackers or normal electrical interference during data transference. Thus, the internet security system expected to assure that data received exactly the same way. Regardless of the original cause of losing data integrity, this loss will certainly be catastrophic in many ways. According to Ackermann (2001) "Data integrity may be affected without being noticed during storage or transmission, i.e., data may be altered due to inadequate access controls while located in one system, being then sent without any problem detection to the other end of the connection." Another fact considered is the possibility of intercepted during its transference, putting its integrity and/or confidentiality in doubt. Such tools detect non-authorized and/or unexpected data modification on those specific parts of the system.

Authenticity verification is directly related to the procedures the security system performs in order to establish how and where the data package was created, thus trying to assure the message or data received was really originated where it says it is coming from and sent by the one mentioned on its label (Brown,1999). The organization and coordination of operations in a net connection ruled by protocols - or a group of them, which may unfortunately add some problems as far as system security, is concerned. The most common group of protocols used in internet transactions is the TCP/IP. Brown (1999) elaborated that some security techniques, such as SSL, which stands for Secure Sockets Layer, include as part of their normal routines, procedures that try to provide some enhanced protection to lower layers of TCP/IP. Netscape SSL tries to protect all TCP/IP stack and provides a security structure in which application protocols may be executed safely. Actually, SSL gathers two protocols together. One specifically designed for real data transmission registry and other dedicated to handshake tasks, which supervises the duties accomplished, including authenticity and confidentiality.

Methodology

The objective of the study is First, to be familiar with attraction factors that will improve the use of the internet for business, the benefit from this technology and avoidance of its serious problems. Second, is to categorize the main obstacle to the acceptance of e-business that hinder Jordanian business organizations "banking sectors and exchange services" from conducting online business activities, as well as the challenges facing the use of e-business by those organizations surveyed. Third, to investigate the role of security in the adoption of online business -how secure is the internet for the investigated organizations? In other words, how does the business community consider the security of the internet in their work over the internet? How do Jordanian organizations "banking sectors and exchange services" treat the security aspect when they work online? The current study uses the quantitative approach whereby data collection attained by a survey questionnaire. In addition, individual interviews with the IT department officers of five banks' head offices, ISP "Jordan telecom, Tedata, Mada", and the related public sector Telecommunications Regularly Commission"TRC" were are one of the methods used to collect data. The focal population of the present study are "IT units and computer divisions" of the Arab bank, Cairo Amman bank, Housing bank, Islamic bank, Commercial bank, Al-alami for exchange, Jawdat for exchange, Abu-Allaban for exchange, and Jamal for exchange. The questionnaire items are mainly adopted from a review of previous literature. Pilot test was performed and the feedback received was used in finalizing the survey format. The questionnaire format selected covered three parts -care of the basic demographic information, investigate the willingness/usefulness to do business over the internet and probe the expected problem of conducting online business by selected Jordanian organizations. There were 200 questionnaire forms self-administrated and distributed to the purposive sample. The responses received were 152 usable and completed forms from business organizations. IT professionals and executive managers who were considered the decisions makers in these IT departments of both banks and trading organization were interviewed.

Data Analysis

Table 2 displays the percentages of internet usages in five business activities performed by surveyed organization. The companies that use internet facilities totally for their internal business affairs represent only 6.0%, while, 35% of the surveyed

Table 2. Percentage internet usage in business activities

Usage	0%	10%	25%	50%	75%	100%
Activity	%	%	%	%	%	%
Internal Business	17.9	35	20.5	12.8	7.7	6
External Business	17.6	24.4	25.2	9.2	11.8	11.8
Marketing	56.8	33.2	19.5	10.2	10.2	2.5
Job achievement	35.7	8.7	3.5	6.1	6.1	40
Online Activity	72.5	6	23.2	4.2	9	2.5

organizations agree that the internet assists them to do 10% of their organization's internal daily business. Fifty-two percent of surveyed agree on the range rate, from 10% to 25%, of their organization's external daily business affairs assisted by the internet. For marketing activity, 56.8% of the respondents agree that they do benefit 10% from using internet for marketing activities. While 33.2% of the surveyed organizations agree that, there is no use for the internet to support marketing activities. For assistance in online activities, 72.5% of the surveyed organizations agree that they have no use for the internet to do online business activities, while 23.2% of them agree that they have benefited 25% from using the internet to do online business. Online business inclination through the individual interviews with the Jordanian execu-

tives and their executives' researchers gained a very positive feeling concerning how interested they are in doing e-business and how willing they are to accept and use the new concept (Table 2).

Main Obstacles of E-Business Adoption

The acceptance of online business in Jordanian society needs the cooperation of all related parties to take it to a level where all participants are satisfied with internet performance. Therefore, Table 3 illustrated some obstacles to the acceptance of e-business should be considered to find suitable solutions.

There are 50.6% of the surveyed organizations didn't use the web for business purposes because of the lack of expertise, while 18.5% of the sur-

Table 3. Obstacles of e-business adoption

Factors	Major concern
	%
Expertise	50.6
Cost	18.5
Infrastructure	55.4
Security	66.5
Government support	85.0
Not a trustworthy tool	60.0
Fraudulent	21.0
Lack of cyber law	82.5
Undesired believed (Cyber terrorism)	33.0
Internet illiteracy	35.4

veyed organizations didn't use the web for business purposes because it is costly. 55.4% of the surveyed organizations did not use the web for business because infrastructure is not available. 66.5% of the surveyed organizations did not use the web for business because organizations believe it is unsafe technology. 85.0% of them did not use the web for business because government support for online business is not available. And 60.0% of the surveyed organizations didn't use the web for business because they think that the internet is not a trustworthy medium to do online business, while 21.0% of them think that undesired information on the internet minimizes the use of the internet. 82.5% of the organizations think the absence of cyber law (law on the internet) is minimizing the use of the internet further. The undesirable beliefs and thought that the internet can bring are minimizing the use of the internet for business represented by 33.0% of the surveyed organizations. 35.4% of them think that non-literate people are minimizing the use of the internet further.

Security is one of the hindering problems that prevent the further adoption of e-business even in the advanced countries and sometimes leads to a stop in any further online activities. The following low ratio for security tools use proves that security is a common reason preventing the adoption of e-business (see Table 4).

Results displayed in Table 4 revealed that only 32.5% of the surveyed organizations use a firewall as a security tool, and only 25.3% of them use encryption technology. In addition, 72.0% of surveyed organizations do not use a firewall and 50.8% of them do not use encryption technology to enhance the security of data and systems. In addition, that 37.7% of the surveyed organizations rely on proxy technology to scrutinize incoming and receiving e-mails, while 66.2% of them do not use proxy. The table showed that 70.0% of the surveyed organizations do not use any sort of filtering for securitizing incoming and receiving e-mails, while 17.0% of them are using filtering to enhance the security of data and systems.

Assessing the Measurement Model

A confirmatory factor analysis (CFA) using EQS was conducted to test the measurement model. The overall goodness-of-fit of the measurement model was examined using the following eight common model fit measures: X^2/DF ratio, GFI, AGFI, NFI, NNFI, CFI, RMSR, and RMSEA. The measurement model in the CFA was revised by removing items, one at a time that had large standardized residuals and/or weak correlations with other items. After removing items, as summarized in Table 1, the measurement model exhibited an overall good model fit, with the data collected from the respondents by meeting the acceptance levels commonly suggested by previous research. The exception was for the GFI level. GFI at 0.861 was slightly below but closer to the recommended level 0.90. Although the GFI level could be improved by dropping additional items, it was decided to stop the dropping procedure by considering the content of the measurement. Rec-

Table 4. Security methods activated by organization

Security Technology	Technology Activated	Technology Not Activated
	%	%
Firewall	32.5	72.0
Encryption	25.3	50.8
Proxy server	37.7	66.2
Filtering	17.0	70.0

Table 5. Fit indices

Fit	Recommended		Measurement	Structural
index	value		model	model
X^2	N/A		1401.89	388.17
Df	N/A		657	221
X^2/df	<	3.00	2.133	1.756
GFI	>	0.90	0.861	0.929
AGFI	>	0.80	0.835	0.912
NFI	>	0.90	0.971	0.980
NNFI	>	0.90	0.983	0.990
CFI	>	0.90	0.985	0.991
RMSR	<	0.10	0.043	0.046
RMSEA	<	0.08	0.051	0.041

ognizing the good model fit for the measurement model, further analysis was conducted to assess the psychometric properties of the scales; that is, for the construct validity of the research instruments. The construct validity has two important dimensions: convergent validity and discriminant validity (Table 5).

The convergent validity was assessed by three measures, as shown in Table 6: factor loading, composite construct reliability, and average variance extracted (Fornell & Larcker, 1981). In determining, the appropriate minimum factor loadings required for the inclusion of an item within a construct, factor loadings greater than 0.50 were considered highly significant (Hair et. al. 1998). A stricter recommendation of factor loading greater than 0.70 was also proposed (Fornell & Larcker, 1981). All of the factor loadings of the items in the measurement model were greater than 0.60, with most of them above 0.80. Each item loaded significantly ($p<0.01$ in all cases) on its underlying construct. The composite construct reliabilities were also within the commonly accepted range greater than 0.70 (Gefen et al., 2000). As a stricter criterion, the guideline with a minimum of 0.80 suggested by Nunnally and Bernstein (1994) was applied to determine the adequacy of the reliability coefficients obtained

for each construct. Finally, AVE measures the amount of variance captured by the construct in relation to the amount of variance due to measurement error (Fornell & Larcker, 1981). AVE was all above the recommended level of 0.50 (Hair et al., 1998) which meant that more than fifty percent of the variances observed in the items were explained by their underlying constructs. Therefore, all constructs in the measurement model had adequate convergent validity.

The discriminant validity was examined in two ways: comparing the inter-construct variances and average variances extracted and comparing the X^2 statistic of the original model against other models with every possible combination of two constructs. The shared variances between constructs were compared with the average variance extracted of the individual constructs (Fornell & Larcker, 1981). To confirm discriminant validity, the average variance shared between the construct and its indicators should be larger than the variance shared between the construct and other constructs. As shown by comparing the inter-construct variances and average variances extracted in Table 7, all constructs share more variance with their indicators than with other constructs. Discriminant validity of the constructs was further validated by combining the items

Table 6. Convergent validity test

Constructs*	Items	Factor loading	Composite reliability	AVE
SH	SH1	0.798	0.862	0.612
	SH2	0.650		
	SH3	0.786		
	SH4	0.879		
PM	PM1	0.735	0.848	0.583
	PM2	0.851		
	PM3	0.753		
	PM4	0.707		
IP	IP1	0.802	0.835	0.560
	IP2	0.775		
	IP3	0.758		
	IP4	0.649		
T	T1	0.727	0.868	0.687
	T2	0.893		
	T3	0.858		
CIA	CIA1	0.822	0.904	0.701
	CIA 2	0.864		
	CIA 3	0.822		
	CIA 4	0.840		

*SH: Security Hazard, PM: Protection Measures, IP: Internet Performance, T: Trust, CIA: Confidentiality; Integrity; Availability

between various constructs and then re-estimating the modified model (Segars, 1997). That is, comparing the X^2 statistic of the original model with its all constructs against other models with every possible combination of two constructs was conducted. Significant differences in the X^2 statistic of the original and alternative models imply high discriminant validity. As reported in Table 7, the X^2 statistic of the original model was signifi-

cantly better than any possible combination of any two constructs, confirming discriminant validity. Therefore, these results revealed no violation of the criteria for the discriminant validity of the constructs in the research model. To confirm the multidimensionality for the constructs of organizational commitment and attitude toward change, a second order CFA for these constructs was conducted. All of coefficients and the factor load-

Table 7. Discriminant validity test using AVE comparison

Constructs	SH	PM	IP	T	CIA
SH	0.612				
PM	0.513	0.583			
IP	0.444	0.349	0.560		
T	0.162	0.078	0.124	0.687	
CIA	0.277	0.156	0.166	0.674	0.701

ings of the items were greater than 0.60, with most of them above 0.80, and all the paths are significant ($p<0.01$ in all cases). In addition, the second order factor model exhibited an overall good model fit with the data collected from the respondents, by meeting the commonly recommended levels. These results confirmed the multidimensionality of the above two constructs.

Assessing the Structural Model

A structural equation modeling technique called Partial Least Squares (PLS) was chosen for analyzing the research model (Wold, 1985). PLS is a technique that uses a combination of principal components analysis, path analysis, and regression evaluated theory and data simultaneously (Wold, 1985). The path coefficients in a PLS structural model are standardized regression coefficients, while the loadings can be interpreted as factor loadings. PLS is ideally suited to the early stages of theory development and testing - as is the case here - and has been used by a growing number of researchers from a variety of disciplines (e.g., Birkinshaw et al., 1995; Green et al., 1995; Higgins et al., 1992). The explanatory power of the model is tested by examining the size, sign, and statistical significance of the path coefficients between constructs in the model. The predictive

capacity of a PLS model can also be evaluated by examining the variance explained (i.e., R^2) in the dependent (or endogenous) constructs. The objective of a PLS analysis is to explain variance in the endogenous constructs, rather than to replicate the observed covariance matrix as is the case with covariance structure techniques (such as LISREL). One consequence of using a variance-minimization objective is the absence of overall fit t statistics for PLS models (Hulland, 1999).

The model explained 32% of the variance in the use of online business construct. Overall, the amount of variance explained by the model appeared reasonable. The exogenous variables would likely be only some of many things affecting the endogenous construct, resulting in the relatively modest R^2 value as can be seen in Figure 1. All three exogenous variables have direct effect correlate statistically significant to doing online business; security hazard (path coefficient=0.55), protection measures (path coefficient =0.61), internet performance (path coefficient =0.57), trust (path coefficient =0.72), and CIA Triad (path coefficient =0.65). The construction of the model by induction from quantitative data may set a limit to its applicability. A more accurate verification of the model by using our qualitative data from conducted in-depth interviews is included in Figure 1. Another limitation of this model is that

Figure 1. Testing the research model

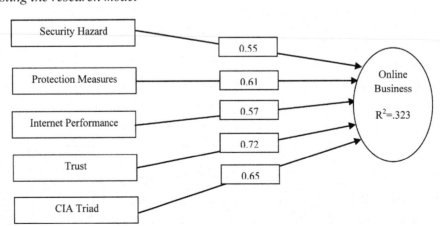

its data is derived from one sample, and has not been tested with different organization groups. While non-users and users differ in many parts, the factors in the model may have quite different loadings for different segments.

CONCLUSION

This study concluded that the business sector is a regular user of the internet in Jordan in terms of numbers. The majority of those organizations already use the computerized system. The findings indicate that 96% of both exchange and bank organizations, which were investigated, are using computers to assist in their daily business operations. Researcher in the current study assumes that this new drive method of conducting business over the internet is going to be treated similarly. Several researches conducted in this field signal the raise of security as a new problem to the e-business. This concept refers to the nature and the media this business run via it, by which researchers mean the internet. Although some internet users feel that conducting business online is not easily attainable, they have started applying this method as a new means for conducting business.

Most of companies and banks are still unfamiliar with encryption technology and most of them do not use firewalls to protect the information assets that they possess. On other word, protective and preventive tools of security are not widely adapted by business organization in the Jordan. Researcher concluded that there are a company affiliated with international business, to facilitate their business affairs this arranges of company is adopting computerized systems. In addition, there are companies affiliated with national business, these variety of trade companies own their computerized system, which enables them to drive the internal business. Some of them are connected to the net and others do not feel that the internet has any importance for their business.

Future work suggested exposed that the relationship between the internet's security and doing online business over the internet is not at the required level and it is not satisfactory at present for any business organization to start doing online business. It, consequently, cannot serve as a solid platform for the success of doing online business for Jordanian business organizations. The recommendations are:

- Increasing awareness by offering opportunities to businesses interested in attending seminars on the internet, e-business, and training session courses. Encourage the presence of Jordan companies to participate in community service projects intended to increase internet awareness and usefulness for improving the business.
- Reduce the cost of the telephone and internet subscription fees, taxes on the internet and e-business hardware equipment and software. Also, offer national expertise to those who can undertake to build local capacity in IT security, especially for the business sector and those demanding security on the internet and provide consultancy at a low price.
- Adopt e banking through offering some online services, adoption of digital signature and e contracting and encourage the creation of e-commerce companies.

The purpose of these recommendations is to make the internet a meaningful way of doing business for exchanges and banks located in Jordan.

REFERENCES

Ackermann, R., Schumacher, M., Roedig, U., & Steinmetz, R. (2001). Vulnerabilities and Security Limitations of Current IP Telephony Systems. In *Proceedings of the Conference on Communications and Multimedia Security* (pp. 53-66).

Ahmed, A., Zairi, S., & Alwabel, S. (2006). Global benchmarking for Internet and e-commerce applications. *Benchmarking International Journal, 13*(2), 68–80. doi:10.1108/14635770610644583

Aldridge, A., White, M., & Forcht, K. (1997). Considerations of doing business via the internet: Cautions to be considered. *Internet Research: Electronic Networking Applications and Policy, 7*(1), 9–15. doi:10.1108/10662249710159809

Ambrose, P., & Johnson, G. (1998). A Trust Model of Buying Behavior in Electronic Retailing. In *Proceedings of the Association for Information Systems, Americans Conference*, Baltimore (pp. 263-265).

Birch, D. (1999). Mobile finance services: the Internet is not the only digital channel to consumers. *Journal of Internet Banking and Commerce, 4*(1), 20–29.

Birkinshaw, J., Morrison, A., & Hulland, J. (1995). Structural and competitive determinants of a global integration strategy. *Strategic Management Journal, 16*(8), 637–655. doi:10.1002/smj.4250160805

Bishop, M. (2002). *Computer Security: Art and Science*. Reading, MA: Addison-Wesley.

Booker, E. (2000). Protect online brand from unauthorized use. *B to B Chicago, 85*(18), 12-39.

Brown, F., Divietri, J., Diaz, G., & Fernandez, E. (1999). The Authenticator Pattern. In *Proceedings of PLoP*.

Ciampa, M. (2005). *Security+ Guide to network security fundamentals* (2nd ed.). Boston: Course Technology.

Cross, M. (2001). Set strategy before selecting a web site host. *Internet Health Care Magazine*, 42-43.

Cummings, L., & Bromiley, P. (1996). The Organizational Trust Inventory (OTI): Development and Validation. In Kramer, R. M., & Tyler, T. R. (Eds.), *Trust in Organizations: Frontiers of Theory and Research* (pp. 220–302). Thousand Oaks, CA: Sage Publications.

Dhillon, G. (2006). *Principles of information systems security: Texts and Cases* (1st ed.). Hoboken, NJ: Wiley.

Drennan, J., & McColl-Kennedy, J. (2003). The relationship between internet use and perceived performance in retail and professional service firms. *Journal of Services Marketing, 17*(3), 295–311. doi:10.1108/08876040310474837

Evans, P., & Wurster, T. (1997). Strategy and the new economics of information. *Harvard Business Review, 9*(10), 71–82.

Forcht, K., & Richard, E. (1995). Security issues and concern with the internet. *Internet Research: Electronic Networking Applications and Policy of MCB, 5*(3), 23–31. doi:10.1108/10662249510104621

Fornell, C., & Larcker, D. (1981). Evaluating Structural Equation Models with Unobservable Variables and Measurement Error. *Management Science, 40*(4), 440–465.

Garfinkel, S., & Spafford, G. (1997). *Web security & commerce* (1st ed.). New York: O'Reilly & Associates, Inc.

Gefen, D., Straub, D., & Boudreau, M. (2000). Structural Equation Modeling and Regression: Guidelines for Research Practice. *Communications of the Association for Information Systems, 4*(7), 1–70.

Green, D., Barclay, D., & Ryans, A. (1995). Entry strategy and long-term performance: conceptualization and empirical examination. *Journal of Marketing, 59*(4), 1–16. doi:10.2307/1252324

Hair, T., Anderson, R., Tatham, R., & Black, W. (1998). *Multivariate Data Analysis* (5th ed.). Upper Saddle River, NJ: Prentice Hall.

Hart, P., & Saunders, C. (1997). Power and Trust: Critical Factors in the Adoption and Use of Electronic Data Interchange. *Organization Science, 8*(1), 23–41. doi:10.1287/orsc.8.1.23

Higgins, C., Duxbury, L., & Irving, R. (1992). Work-family conflict in the dual-career family. *Organizational Behavior and Human Decision Processes, 51*(1), 51–75. doi:10.1016/0749-5978(92)90004-Q

Hulland, J. (1999). Use of partial least squares in strategic management research: a review of four recent studies. *Strategic Management Journal, 20*(2), 195–204. doi:10.1002/(SICI)1097-0266(199902)20:2<195::AID-SMJ13>3.0.CO;2-7

Jessup, L., & Valacich, J. (2008). *Information Systems Today: Managing in the Digital World.* Upper Saddle River, NJ: Pearson.

Kumar, R., Park, S., & Subramaniam, C. (2008). Understanding the value of countermeasures portfolios in information systems security. *Journal of Management Information Systems, 25*(1), 241–279. doi:10.2753/MIS0742-1222250210

Lane, C. (1998). Five essential steps to privacy. *PC World, 16*(9), 116–117.

Laudon, K., & Traver, C. (2008). *E-commerce: Business, Technology, and Society* (4th ed.). Upper Saddle River, NJ: Pearson Education Inc.

Messmer, E. (2000). Security needs spawn services. *New World (New Orleans, La.), 17*(14), 1–100.

Nelson, M. (2000). *Hacker school teaches security.* Information Week.

Nunnally, J., & Bernstein, I. (1994). *Psychometric Theory.* New York: McGraw-Hill.

Oyegoke, A. (1999). Surfing Europe. *The Banker, 1*(2), 72–73.

Parker, C. (1999). E-mail use and abuse. *Freelance journalist based in Cornwall, 48*(7), 257-260.

Saeed, K., Grover, V., & Hwang, Y. (2005). The Relationship of E-Commerce Competence to Customer Value and Firm Performance: An Empirical Investigation. *Journal of Management Information Systems, 22*(1), 223–256.

Saiedian, M., & Naeem, M. (2001). Understanding, and reducing web delays. *IEEE Computer Journal, 34*(12), 30–37.

Savage, M. (2000). *Attacks brings new security solutions.* Computer Reseller News.

Schou, C., & Shoemaker, D. (2006). *Information assurance for the enterprise: A roadmap to information security.* New York: McGraw-Hill Irwin.

Segars, A. (1997). Assessing the Unidimensionality of Measurement: a Paradigm and Illustration within the Context of Information Systems Research. *Omega, 25*(1), 107–121. doi:10.1016/S0305-0483(96)00051-5

Sheshunoff, A. (2000). Internet banking, un update from the frontlines. *ABA Banking Journal, 92*(1), 51–55.

Totty, P. (2001). Staying One Step Ahead of the Hacker. *Credit Union Magazine, 67*(6), 39–41.

TRC. (2010). *Telecommunication Regularly Commission.* Retrieved January 5, 2010, from http://www.TRC.Jo

Verton, D. (2000). Co-op to certify tools to measure level of security. *Computerworld, 34*(49), 16.

Wold, H. (1985). Systems analysis by partial least squares. In Nijkamp, P., Leitner, L., & Wrigley, N. (Eds.), *Measuring the Unmeasurable* (pp. 221–251). Dordrecht, The Netherlands: Marinus Nijhoff.

Zoliat, A., Ibrahim, A., & Farooq, A. (2009). A Study on the Internet Security and its Implication for e-Commerce in Yemen. In *Proceedings of the Conference on Knowledge Management and Innovation in Advancing Economies* (pp. 911-922).

This work was previously published in International Journal of Technology Diffusion, Volume 1, Issue 4, edited by Ali Hussein Saleh Zolait, pp. 13-28, copyright 2010 by IGI Publishing (an imprint of IGI Global).

Chapter 19
Human Talent Forecasting using Data Mining Classification Techniques

Hamidah Jantan
Universiti Teknologi MARA (UiTM), Malaysia & Universiti Kebangsaan Malaysia (UKM), Malaysia

Abdul Razak Hamdan
Universiti Kebangsaan Malaysia (UKM), Malaysia

Zulaiha Ali Othman
Universiti Kebangsaan Malaysia (UKM), Malaysia

ABSTRACT

Talent management is a very crucial task and demands close attention from human resource (HR) professionals. Recently, among the challenges for HR professionals is how to manage organization's talents, particularly to ensure the right job for the right person at the right time. Some employee's talent patterns can be identified through existing knowledge in HR databases, which data mining can be applied to handle this issue. The hidden and useful knowledge that exists in databases can be discovered through classification task and has been widely used in many fields. However, this approach has not successfully attracted people in HR especially in talent management. In this regard, the authors attempt to present an overview of talent management problems that can be solved by using this approach. This paper uses that approach for one of the talent management tasks, i.e., predicting potential talent using previous existing knowledge. Future employee's performances can be predicted based on past experience knowledge discovered from existing databases by using classification techniques. Finally, this study proposes a framework for talent forecasting using the potential Data Mining classification techniques.

INTRODUCTION

Human capital is a definitely critical issue and it demands close attention from the top management and Human Resource (HR) professionals in any organization. Human Resource Management (HRM) that deals with human capital aims to facilitate organizational competitiveness; enhances productivity and quality; promotes individual growth and development; and complies with legal and social obligation (DeNisi & Griffin, 2005). Besides that, an organization needs to struggle

DOI: 10.4018/978-1-4666-1752-0.ch019

effectively in term of cost, quality, service and innovation in order to achieve organization's target. All these depend on having enough right people, with the right skills, employed in the appropriate locations at appropriate points in time. Recently, among the challenges for HR professionals is managing talent, especially to ensure the right person for the right job at the right time. These tasks involve a lot of managerial decisions, which are sometimes very ambiguous, uncertain and difficult. On the other hand, HR decision practices depend on various factors such as human experience, knowledge, preference and judgment. These factors cause inconsistence, inaccuracy, inequality and unforeseen decisions. Consequently, in promoting individual growth and development, this situation can often make people sense injustice and this can also influence the productivity of an organization. In talent management, to identify the existing talent for the right job is the topmost challenge for HR professional (A TP Track Research Report, 2005); and at present, most of the determination processes use human experience knowledge that is supported with evidence to justify the potential talent.

The advancement of technology has proposed some new approaches that can be used to solve some decision making problems. Data mining (DM) and also known as Knowledge Discovery in Database (KDD) approach is a computer technology that can be used to handle some talent management issues. DM is one of the Artificial Intelligent (AI) technologies that have been developed for exploration and analysis in large quantities of data to discover meaningful patterns and rules. In HRM, HR data can provide a plenty of resource for knowledge discovery and decision support tools. Therefore, the application using DM approach has not attracted much attention in HRM field (Ranjan, 2008) compared to other fields such as in marketing, financial, manufacturing, medical and many others. DM approach has several tasks such as classification and prediction; concept description; association; cluster analysis; outlier

analysis; trend and evaluation analysis; statistical analysis and others. Over the years, data mining has evolved various techniques to perform tasks including database oriented techniques, statistic, machine learning, pattern recognition, neural network, rough set and etc. Classification and prediction technique is among the popular task in DM. For that reason, in this article we attempt to use DM classification techniques for managing talent tasks especially to identify existing talent by predicting the performance using past experience knowledge. Finally, this study aims to suggest the framework for talent forecasting using selected DM classification techniques.

This paper is organized by describing related work on HR decision system that uses Artificial Intelligent technology. Next, some issues in talent management are discussed while reviewing HR researches that use the DM approach. Then DM classification techniques are discussed followed by an explanation on how talent management tasks use the DM approach in their problems solving and suggests framework for talent forecasting using DM classification techniques. Finally, the paper ends with the concluding remarks and future research directions are also identified.

HR DECISION APPLICATION

Nowadays, HR has been linked to improve productivity, good customer service, greater profitability and on the whole organizational survival. Successively to reach such link, management must not only face contemporary issues of human resource but also deal with future challenges to HRM effectively (Stavrou-Costea, 2005). HRM tasks involve a lot of managerial decisions and professionals that are highly needed to focus the goal for each of HR activities such as: staffing task is to locate and secure competent employees; training and development task to adapt competent workers to the organization and help them obtain up-to date skill, knowledge and abilities;

motivation task to provide competent and adapt employees who have up-to date skill, knowledge and abilities with an environment that encourage them to exert high energy level; and maintenance task is to help competence and adapt employees who have up-to date skill, knowledge and abilities and exert high level energy level to maintain their commitment and loyalty to the organization (DeCenZo & Robbins, 2005).

Among the challenges for HRM professionals are issues regarding health, managing talent, employee rewards, retention, training and development, technology innovation, tribalism, nepotism and corruption. However, among the major potential prospects for HRM is technology's innovation, selection and implementation (Okpara & Wynn, 2008). In addition, the benefits of technology applications and innovation in HRM are to easily deliver information from the top to bottom workers in an organization, easily to communicate with employees and it is easier for HR professionals to formulate managerial decisions. Nowadays, HR decision application can be widely used in any type of decision making tasks as contribution to the achievement of HR goals. The potentials of HR decision applications are to increase the productivity, consistent in performance and the institutionalized expertise where the system capabilities are embedded into the specific programs (Hooper, Galvin, Kilmer, & Liebowitz, 1998).

The technology's innovation in HRM can help HR manages and makes decision in some decision making process especially for decisions which involved human judgment. Artificial Intelligent technology is a current and useful technology that can be embedded with any HR decision making tool towards producing more precise decision in decision making process. In fact, there are many techniques or approaches in Artificial Intelligent that can be used in a development of the advance decision making tools. Besides that, this technology was adopted in many fields such as in manufacturing, management, development, plan-

ning, finance, medical and many others (Jantan, Hamdan, & Othman, 2008b). Most studies in the HR decision application that use Artificial Intelligent techniques focus only on the specific HRM domains such as in personnel selection, training, scheduling and job performance (Table 1). Besides that, the advance computer technologies used for most of the HR decision applications are expert system or Knowledge-based system (KBS), and focuses especially on HR personnel selection and training tasks. The commercial emergence of KBS information technology applications represents a tremendous opportunity to improve the practice of HRM (Martinsons, 1995). The KBS benefits are more permanent, easier to duplicate, less expensive and automatically documented. On the other hand, the limitations of KBS systems are difficult to capture informal knowledge; knowledge has not been documented and difficult to verbalize. The techniques used to verify and validate the conventional systems are considered to be insufficient and KBS-specific methods are still immature. Due to these reasons, currently, the new HR decision application researches use other computer technology approaches especially that are related to Artificial Intelligent technologies. In this case, for personnel selection, they use Data Mining (Chien & Chen, 2008; Tai & Hsu, 2005) and Neural Network approaches (Liang Chih Huang, Huang, Huang, & Jaw, 2004; Huang, Wu, Kuo, & Huang, 2001) (Table 1).

However, in this study, there are very few researches that use Artificial Intelligent techniques and do research in HR decision application field. Besides that, the focus domains are also limited to the specific problem such as in personnel selection and training activities. Recently, in information technology era, advance HR decision applications that are supported by Artificial Intelligent techniques can be used as a tool to help human resource managers in their decision making problems.

Table 1. HR decision applications using AI technology

Category	Techniques used
Staffing Personnel Selection	*Expert system/* *Knowledge-based system (Hooper et al., 1998) and (Mehrabad & Brojeny, 2007)* *Data Mining (Huang, Tsou, & Lee, 2006) and (Chien & Chen, 2008)* *Artificial Neural Network (Liang Chih Huang et al., 2004)and (Huang et al., 2006)*
Training and Development Training Development	*Knowledge-based system (Liao, 2007)* *Expert System (Chen, Chen, Wu, & Lee, 2007)* *Rough Set Theory (Chien & Chen, 2007)*
Motivation Job Attitudes Performance appraisal	*Artificial Neural Network (Tung, Huang, Chen, & Shih, 2005)* *Fuzzy logic (Ruskova, 2002)*
Administration Meeting scheduling	*Software agent (Glenzer, 2003)*

TALENT MANAGEMENT

In any organization, talent management has become an increasingly crucial method of approaching HR functions (American Management Association, 2009; Hart, 2006; Hiltrop, 1999; Personneltoday, 2008; PricewaterhouseCoopers, 2008; SuccessFactors, 2007; Wilkins, 2008). Talent management involves human resource planning that regards processes for managing people in organization especially to develop existing talent and forecasting talent needs (A TP Track Research Report, 2005; Taleo Research, 2009). In other studies, talent management can be defined as an outcome to ensure the right person for the right job; process to ensure leadership continuity in key positions and encourage individual advancement; and decision to manage supply, demand and flow of talent through human capital engine (Cubbingham, 2007). Failures in talent management are an ongoing source of pain for executives in modern organization and it will cause surpluses to shortfalls of talent (Cappelli, 2008). Talent is considered as any individual who has the capability to make a significant difference to the current and future performance of the organization (Lynne, 2005). However, talent can also be categorized as valuable, rare and difficult

to-imitate but the specific prescription regarding talent are not always clear. Besides that, talent is critical because it is the role of a strong HR function to manage everyone for high performance and business trends now place talent in general more valuable (Lewis & Heckman, 2006). In HRM, talent management is very important and needs full attentions from HR professionals since this task deals with organization's valuable asset. Nowadays, most organizations concentrate on how they can attract and retain talent to achieve organization target. Figure 1 shows some issues related to talent management; and the top talent management challenges (A TP Track Research Report, 2005), and one of them is to identify the existing talent which is closely related to talent forecasting (Jantan, Hamdan, & Othman, 2008a).

Recently, in modern organization, a new way to think about talent management is by looking at manufacturing sector. In that case, we can say how forecasting product demand is very important in manufacturing, which is comparable to forecasting talent needs in an organization. In talent management, talent is an organization product, which is how employee advance through development jobs and experiences are remarkably similar to how products move through a supply chain; reducing bottlenecks the block advancement,

Figure 1. Talent management challenges

Forecasting talent needs, gaps and surpluses (CHINA UPDATE, 2007)

Attracting and retaining the right people went to the very top of the list of executives' business concerns, where it remains today (Cappelli, 2008)

Top talent management challenges (TP TRACK RESEARCH REPORT, 2005)

❖ Developing existing talent
❖ Forecasting talent needs, gaps and surpluses over next three to five years
❖ Attracting and retaining the right leadership talent
❖ Engaging talent
❖ **Identifying existing talent**
❖ Retaining the right key contributor/technical talent
❖ Deploying existing talent
❖ Attracting and retaining the right key contributor/technical talent
❖ Lack of leadership capability at senior levels
❖ Ensuring a diverse talent pool

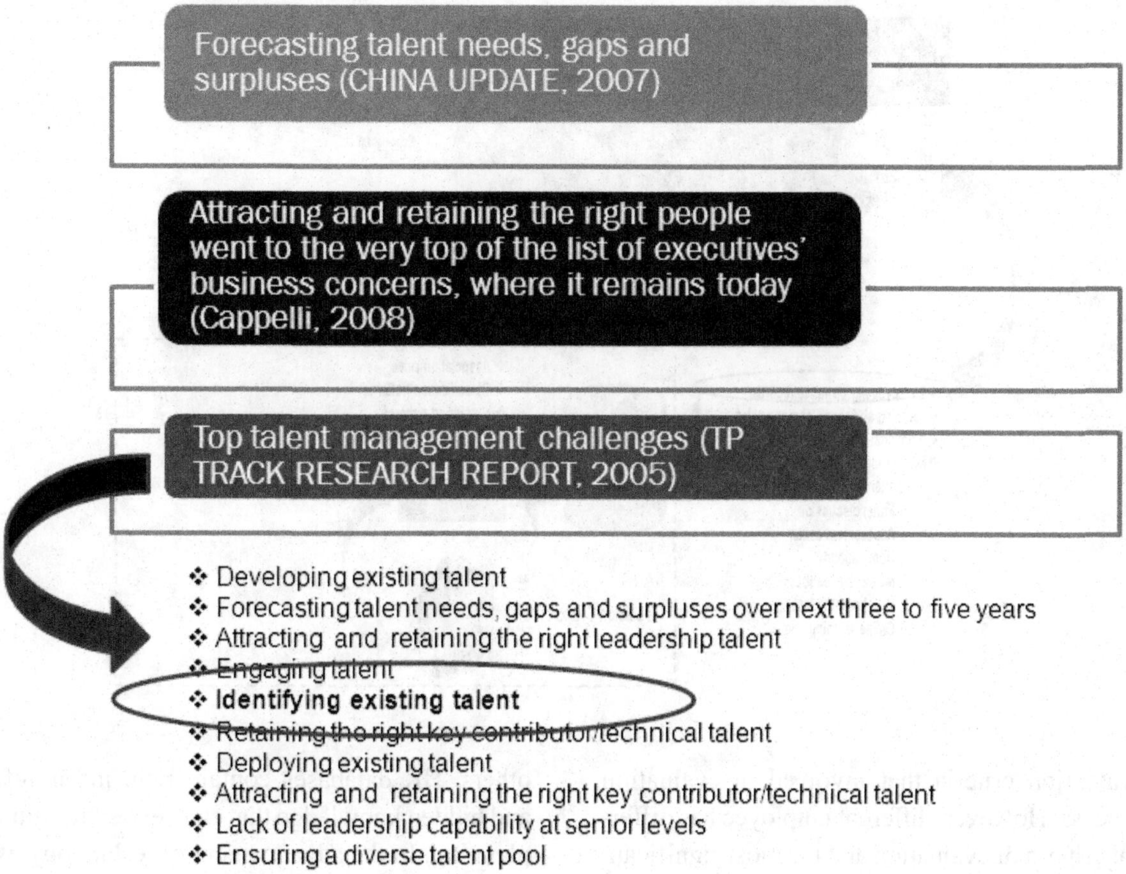

speeding up processing time, improving forecast to avoid mismatches (Cappelli, 2008). For those reasons, we can apply the same approach to identify existing talent in an organization by using forecasting idea. Figure 2 shows processes involved to identify the people in the organization who constitute the key talents using some common evaluation approaches (Cubbingham, 2007; Taleo Research, 2009). Besides that, it also demonstrates how Knowledge Discovery in Database (KDD) approach can be used to solve some talent management problems.

Furthermore, forecasting future talent for an organization is similar to forecasting product demand in business field. In other words, we can apply any suitable prediction approaches to predict future talent. In the literature study, prediction approaches can be categorized into two approaches; the first approach is statistical approach and the second one is intelligent approach which is concerned with Artificial Intelligent technology. There are many intelligent approaches are used in prediction application such as KDD, Artificial Neural Network, Artificial Immune System (AIS), Support Vector Machine (SVM) and many others (Jantan et al., 2008b). Due to that reason, this study attempts to apply KDD approach for talent identification which is regarding the key talent in an organization. The employee performance and talent records that are stored in databases will be used to discover talent patterns and prediction model for selected category of employee in an organization. The talents of employee in general are according to the

Figure 2. Talent management and KDD approach

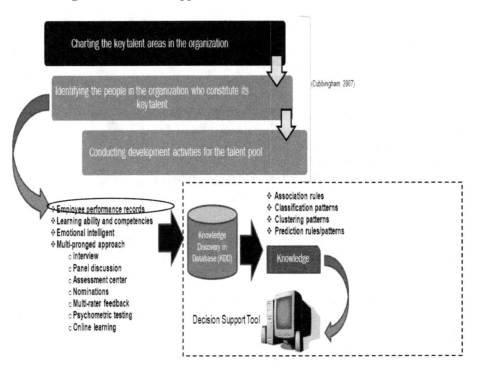

evaluation criteria that involved in evaluation process. However, different employee has different criteria of evaluation and the most significant factor involved in evaluating employee's performance is individual factor. In that factor, the work outcome; knowledge and skill; individual quality; and activities and contribution area are among the main criteria especially for management talent (Adobor, 2004). Besides that, in management and professional performance evaluation, the competency-based criteria are used and it involves skill, knowledge and attitude factors. The competency-based evaluation criteria can be categorized into four main components; supervisory, cognitive; administrative; and communication (Executive-Brief, 2008). Each of the components contains performance criteria that should be considered in the evaluation process, as stated in Figure 3.

In many organizations, information regarding employee's performance can be gathered through affiliated sections in HR department, such as personnel, training, employee development and

others. HR databases contain rich, meaningful and hidden knowledge that can be used for future planning. In the advancement of technology, we can get all information especially related to employee's performance through the respective HR databases. The selected data that are used for prediction is associated to the factors involved in prediction. In Data mining process, all evaluation criteria for each factor will be represented as attribute. The attribute contains information regarding data that we have. KDD or Data mining approach can be used to discover the hidden and meaningful knowledge for the existing data and that will be discussed in the next section.

DATA MINING IN HRM

DM and Knowledge Discovery in Database (KDD) are used interchangeable in this article. DM is a step to KDD and currently receives great attention and is recognized as a newly emerging

Figure 3. Talent factors in evaluation process

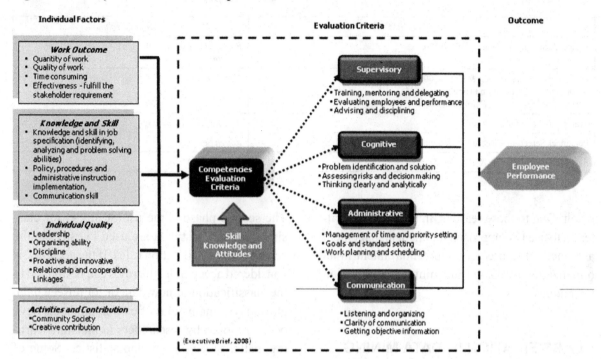

analysis tool (Tso & Yau, 2007). Recently, DM has given a great deal of concern and attention in the information industry and in society as a whole. This is due to the wide accessibility of enormous amounts of data and the important need for turning such data into useful information and knowledge (Han & Kamber, 2006). Data mining is a machine learning approach, which has several tasks such as classification and prediction; concept description; association; cluster analysis; outlier analysis; trend and evaluation analysis; statistical analysis and others. Computer application interfaces with DM tool can help executives to make more informative and objective decisions. Besides that, it can help managers to retrieve, summarize and analyze decision related data to make wiser and more informed decisions. Over the years, DM has involved various techniques including statistics, neural network, decision tree, genetic algorithm, and visualization techniques. Moreover, DM has been applied in many fields such as finance, marketing, manufacturing, health care, customer

relationship and etc. Nevertheless, its application in HRM is rare (Chien & Chen, 2008) (Table 2).

Nowadays, there are some interests on solving HRM problems using DM approach (Ranjan, 2008); and Table 2 lists some of the HR tasks that use DM techniques as a tool to solve some HR problems. There are very few studies related to prediction application in HR that uses this approach. However this approach is quite popular in HR personnel selection problems. From the literature study, prediction applications in HRM are infrequent, there are some examples such as to predict the length of service, sales premiums, to persistence indices of insurance agents and analyze mis-operation behaviors of operators (Chien & Chen, 2008). In Data mining researches, classification and prediction techniques are among the popular task. The classification techniques are known as supervised learning, where the class level or classification target is already identified. In that case, we can classify the new data with classification target as our prediction

Table 2. Human resource researches that use data mining techniques

Activity in HRM	Data Mining Techniques
Project Assignment (Huang et al., 2006)	*Fuzzy Data Mining and Fuzzy Artificial Neural Network*
Personnel selection (Chien & Chen, 2008), Job attitudes classification (Tung et al., 2005) Performance Evaluation (Xin, 2008)	*Decision tree*
Training (Chen et al., 2007)	*Association rule mining*
Personnel Selection – Recruit and Retain Talents (Chien & Chen, 2007)	*Rough Set Theory*
Personnel Selection (Tai & Hsu, 2005)	*Fuzzy Data Mining*

result. Due to these reasons, in this study, we attempt to use DM approach for talent management as a method to predict the potential talent in an organization by using Data mining classification techniques.

CLASSIFICATION IN DATA MINING

DM tasks are generally categorized as clustering, association, classification and prediction(Chien & Chen, 2008; Ranjan, 2008). DM has involved various techniques to perform tasks including database oriented techniques, statistic, machine learning, pattern recognition, neural network, rough set and etc. Databases or data warehouse are rich with hidden information that can be used to provide intelligent decision making. Intelligent decision refers to the ability to make automated decision that is quite similar to human decision. In other words, prediction and classification techniques are among the methods that can be used to produce intelligent decision. Prediction and classification in Data mining are two forms of data analysis that can be used to extract models describing important data classes or to predict future data trends (Han & Kamber, 2006). Besides that, classification process has two phases; the first phase is learning process where the training data are analyzed by classification algorithm (Figure 4). The learned model or classifier is presented in the form of classification rules or patterns.

The second phase is the use of model for classification and, test data are used to estimate the accuracy of classification rules. If the accuracy is considered acceptable, the rules can be applied to the classification of new data or for unseen data. Nowadays, many classification methods have been proposed by researchers in machine learning, pattern recognition, and statistics. Some of the techniques that are used for classification in Data mining are decision tree, Bayesian methods, Bayesian networks, rule-based algorithms, neural network, support vector machine, association rule mining, k-nearest-neighbor, case-based reasoning, genetic algorithms, rough sets and fuzzy logic. Thus, decision tree and neural network are found useful in developing predictive models in many fields (Tso & Yau, 2007). Some of the techniques that are used for data classification are decision tree, Bayesian methods, Bayesian network, rule-based algorithms, neural network, support vector machine, association rule mining, k-nearest-neighbor, case-based reasoning, genetic algorithms, rough sets, fuzzy logic. In this study, our discussion focuses on three classification techniques, i.e., decision tree, neural network and Nearest-neighbor that shown in Table 3.

Decision tree and neural network are found useful in developing predictive models in many fields (Tso & Yau, 2007). The advantage of decision tree technique is that, it does not require any domain knowledge or parameter setting, and is appropriate for exploratory knowledge discovery.

Figure 4. Classification in data mining process

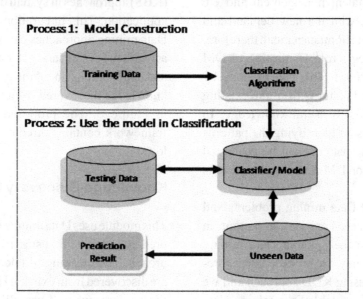

Table 3. Potential data mining classification techniques

Data Mining Techniques	Classification Algorithm
Decision Tree	**C4.5** *(Decision tree induction – the target is nominal and the inputs may be nominal or interval. Sometimes the size of the induced trees is significantly reduced when a different pruning strategy is adopted).* **Random forest** *(Choose a test based on a given number of random features at each node, performing no pruning. Random forest constructs random forest by bagging ensembles of random trees).*
Neural Network	**Multi Layer Perceptron** *(An accurate predictor for underlying classification problem. Given a fixed network structure, we must determine appropriate weights for the connections in the network).* **Radial Basic Function Network** *(Another popular type of feed forward network, which has two layers, not counting the input layer, and differs from a multilayer perceptron in the way that the hidden units perform computations).*
Nearest Neighbor	**K*Star** *(An instance-based learning using distance metric to measure the similarity of instances and generalized distance function based on transformation*

The second technique is neural-network which has high tolerance of noisy data as well as the ability to classify pattern on which they have not been trained. It can be used when we have little knowledge of the relationship between attributes and classes. The Nearest-neighbor technique is an instance-based learning that uses distance metric to measure the similarity of instances. All these three classification techniques have their own advantages and disadvantages and depend on the type of data used. Due to this reason, we attempt to explore selected techniques from three main classification techniques in the next experiment.

TALENT MANAGEMENT USING DATA MINING

In the literature studies, most of the DM researches in HR problems focus on personnel selection and very few discussions in other activities such as planning, training, talent management and etc (Table 1). Recently, with the new demand and increased visibility of HR management, therefore, HRM seeks a strategic role by turning to DM methods (Ranjan, 2008). This can be done by identifying generated patterns from the existing data in HR databases to useful knowledge. In this article, we focus on identifying the patterns related to talent. The patterns can be generated by using some major DM techniques and it is shown in Figure 5.

The matching of Data mining problems and talent management needs are very important, in a way to determine the suitable Data mining techniques. In this study, we propose talent forecasting framework using KDD approach and we attempt to hybrid the suitable Data mining classification technique and knowledge-based system

(KBS) approaches in system development for HR application. This integration between KBS and Data mining approaches can allow users to interact with the system and get the forecasting results and explanations about the decision made by the knowledge discovered from the database shown in Figure 6. The proposed talent forecasting framework contains three main modules as follows:

Knowledge Discovery in Database

This module uses Data mining approach to develop predictive model by using machine learning approach. The meaningful talent pattern and rules are discovered from existing HR database system. In this case, we will use HR databases that are related to talent performance such as data from

Figure 5. Data mining for talent management

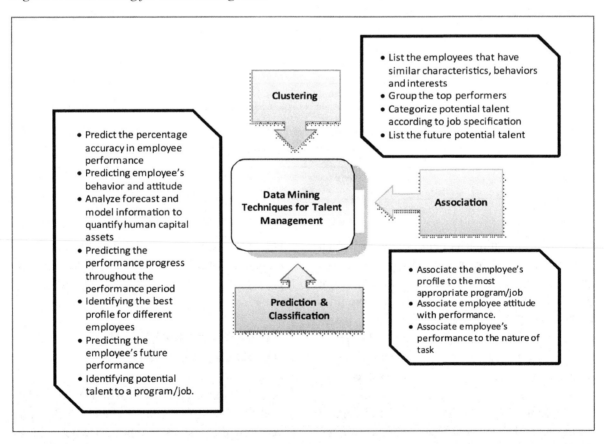

Figure 6. Suggested framework for talent forecasting

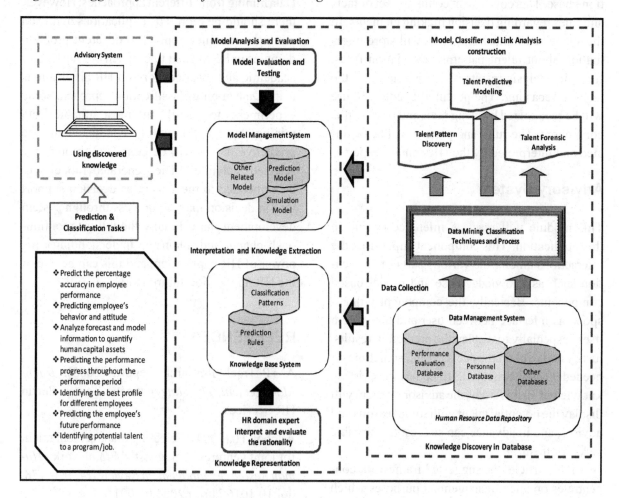

personnel, training, administrative, performance evaluation data and other related databases. The selected databases need to be evaluated through data preprocessing process. This process is a major task in Data mining. Data preprocessing have data cleaning, data integration, data transformation and data reduction processes.

Besides that, all these processes involved tasks such as dataset selection, dealing with missing values, reducing data dimension and complexity; and data enrichment. The relevant data will be transformed into useful knowledge as predictive model through talent predictive modeling, generated rules by talent pattern discovery and extracted patterns to find unusual data elements by forensic

analysis. All these hidden and meaningful knowledge are very useful for talent management tasks.

Model and Knowledge Based System

The model based system is used to store constructed model, existing simulation model and any related models that can be used in decision making process especially related to talent forecasting. In fact, before we can embed the talent performance predictive model in this application, the model must be evaluated and tested through model analysis and evaluation phase that involves the domain experts. The knowledge based system is known as interpretation and knowledge extraction phase. This component contains a set of facts and rules regarding decision making elements. In the suggested framework, KBS will store information about talent patterns, association rules, forensic analysis results which is related to the talent forecasting. The potential talent in future will be recognized by using facts and rules in this component. The rules and pattern will be evaluated and interpreted by the HR domain experts.

Advisory System

This module will react as inference engine in this application. This component supervises the interactions among the various parts of application such as knowledge-base and model based components. Basically, the component will respond as interface between user and the system itself, especially to display the prediction results, justify and explain the decision and sometimes if needed it can instruct KBS to update the existing knowledge. In this study, the advisory system will display the potential talent with some reasons and advises, and in advance can suggest the possible tasks for them.

In this article, the suggested framework concentrates on talent management purposes which are used to identify the potential talent that is suitable with the talent management needs. On the other hand, this framework can also be applied to other DM tasks such as association, and clustering to solve some talent management problems.

CONCLUSION

This article has described the significance of the study and discussed issues in talent management and Data mining approach in HR application. As a result, we propose a HR application framework using Data mining classification technique for talent forecasting to identify potential talent in an organization. From the literature study, most researchers have discussed HR applications using Data mining from different approaches. However, there should be more HR applications and Data mining techniques applied to different problem domains in HRM field to broaden our horizon of academic and practice work on HR applications using Data mining classification approach. Some experiments to identify the most suitable Data mining classification will be conducted and the predictive model will be generated through the selected technique. The generated model will be embedded to the system as decision support tool in decision making process through system development phase. Finally, the ability to continuously change and obtain new understanding is the power of HR application, and this can be one of the HR application future works.

REFERENCES

A TP Track Research Report. (2005). *Talent Management: The State of the Art*: Towers Perrin HR Services.

Adobor, H. (2004). Selecting management talent for joint ventures: A Suggested Framework. *Human Resource Management Review, 14*, 161–178. doi:10.1016/j.hrmr.2004.05.001

American Management Association. (2009). *Talent Management*. Retrieved November 5, 2009, from http://www.amanet.org/seminars/seminar.cfm?basesemno=8116

Cappelli, P. (2008). Talent Management for the Twenty-First Century. *Harvard Business Review*, 1–9.

Chen, K. K., Chen, M. Y., et al. (2007). *Constructing a Web-based Employee Training Expert System with Data Mining Approach*. Paper presented at the 9th IEEE International Conference on E-Commerce Technology and the 4th IEEE International Conference on Enterprise Computing, E-Commerce and E-Services (CEC-EEE 2007).

Chien, C. F., & Chen, L. F. (2007). Using Rough Set Theory to Recruit and Retain High-Potential Talents for Semiconductor Manufacturing. *IEEE Transactions on Semiconductor Manufacturing, 20*(4), 528–541. doi:10.1109/TSM.2007.907630

Chien, C. F., & Chen, L. F. (2008). Data mining to improve personnel selection and enhance human capital: A case study in high-technology industry. *Expert Systems with Applications, 34*(1), 380–290. doi:10.1016/j.eswa.2006.09.003

Cubbingham, I. (2007). Talent Management: Making it real. *Development and Learning in Organizations, 21*(2), 4–6. doi:10.1108/14777280710727307

DeCenZo. D. A., & Robbins, S. P. (2005). *Fundamentals of Human Resource Management* (8ᵗʰ ed.). New York: John Wiley & Sons Inc.

DeNisi, A. S., & Griffin, R. W. (2005). *Human Resource Management*. New York: Houghton Mifflin Company.

ExecutiveBrief. (2008). *12 Competencies: Which Ones Should Your People Have*. Retrieved November 13, 2008, from http://www.executivebrief.com

Glenzer, C. (2003). A conceptual model of an interorganizational intelligent meeting-scheduler (IIMS). *Strategic Information Systems, 12*(1), 47–70. doi:10.1016/S0963-8687(02)00034-3

Han, J., & Kamber, M. (2006). *Data Mining: Concepts and Techniques*. San Francisco: Morgan Kaufmann Publisher.

Hart, D. M. (2006). Managing the global talent pool: Sovereignty, treaty, and intergovernmental networks. *Technology in Society, 28*, 421–434. doi:10.1016/j.techsoc.2006.09.002

Hiltrop, J.-M. (1999). The Quest for the Best: Human Resource Practices to Attract and Retain Talent. *European Management Journal, 17*(4), 422–430. doi:10.1016/S0263-2373(99)00022-5

Hooper, R. S., & Galvin, T. P. (1998). Use of an Expert System in a personnel selection process. *Expert Systems with Applications, 14*(4), 425–432. doi:10.1016/S0957-4174(98)00002-5

Huang, L. C., Huang, K. S., et al. (2004). Applying fuzzy neural network in human resource selection system. In *Proceedings of the NAFIPS '04, IEEE Annual Meeting of the Fuzzy information*.

Huang, L. C., & Wu, P. (2001). A neural network modeling on human resource talent selection. *International Journal of Human Resources Development and Management, 1*(2-4), 206–219.

Huang, M. J., & Tsou, Y. L. (2006). Integrating fuzzy data mining and fuzzy artificial neural networks for discovering implicit knowledge. *Knowledge-Based Systems, 19*(6), 396–403. doi:10.1016/j.knosys.2006.04.003

Jantan, H., Hamdan, A. R., et al. (2008a). *Data Mining Techniques for Performance Prediction in Human Resource Application*. Paper presented at the 1st Seminar on Data Mining and Optimization, Bangi, Selangor.

Jantan, H., Hamdan, A. R., et al. (2008b). Potential Intelligent Techniques in Human Resource Decision Support System (HR DSS). In *Proceedings of the 3rd International Symposium on Information Technology*, Kuala Lumpur.

Lewis, R. E., & Heckman, R. J. (2006). Talent Management: A Critical Review. *Human Resource Management Review, 16*, 139–154. doi:10.1016/j.hrmr.2006.03.001

Liao, S.-H. (2007). A knowledge-based architecture for implementing collaborative problem-solving methods in military e-training. *Expert Systems and Applications*.

Lynne, M. (2005). *Talent Management Value Imperatives: Strategies for Execution*. Paper presented to the Conference Board.

Martinsons, M. G. (1995). Knowledge-based systems leverage human resource management expertise. *International Journal of Manpower, 16*(2), 17–34. doi:10.1108/01437729510085747

Mehrabad, M. S., & Brojeny, M. F. (2007). The development of an expert system for effective selection and appointment of the jobs applicants in human resource management. *Computers & Industrial Engineering, 53*(2), 306–312. doi:10.1016/j.cie.2007.06.023

Okpara, J. O., & Wynn, P. (2008). Human resource management practices in a transition economy: Challenges and prospects. *Management Research News, 31*(1), 57–76. doi:10.1108/01409170810845958

Personneltoday. (2008). *Talent management is most critical HR challenge worldwide*. Retrieved June 7, 2008 from http://www.personneltoday.com

PricewaterhouseCoopers. (2008). *Managing People*. Retrieved June 7, 2008, from http://www.pwc.com/

Ranjan, J. (2008). Data Mining Techniques for better decisions in Human Resource Management Systems. *International Journal of Business Information Systems, 3*(5), 464–481. doi:10.1504/IJBIS.2008.018597

Ruskova, N. A. (2002). *Decision Support System for Human Resource Appraisal and Selection*. Paper presented at the Paper in First International IEEE Symposium on Intelligent Systems.

Stavrou-Costea, E. (2005). The challenges of human resource management towards organizational effectiveness A comparative study in Southern EU. *Journal of European Industrial, 29*(2), 112–134. doi:10.1108/03090590510585082

SuccessFactors. (2007). *Performance & Talent Management Trend Survey*. Retrieved November 5, 2009, from http://www.successfactors.com/docs/performance-management-trends/2007/

Tai, W. S., & Hsu, C. C. (2005). *A Realistic Personnel Selection Tool Based on Fuzzy Data Mining Method*. Retrieved September 1, 2008, from www.atlantis-press.com/php/download_papaer?id=46

Taleo Research. (2009). *Talent Management Processes*. Retrieved July 12, 208, from http://www/taleo.com/research/articles/talent/don-miss-the-next-strategic-turn-115.html

Tso, G. K. F., & Yau, K. K. W. (2007). Predicting electricity energy consumption: A comparison of regression analysis, decision tree and nerural networks. *Energy, 32*, 1761–1768. doi:10.1016/j.energy.2006.11.010

Tung, K. Y., & Huang, I. C. (2005). Mining the Generation Xer's job attitudes by artificial neural network and decision tree - empirical evidence in Taiwan. *Expert Systems with Applications, 29*(4), 783–794. doi:10.1016/j.eswa.2005.06.012

Wilkins, D. (2008). *Talent Management Perspectives*. Retrieved July 12, 2008, from http://www.talentmgt.com/talent.php?pt=a&aid=701

Xin, Z. (2008). *An Empirical Study of Data Mining in Performance Evaluation of HRM*. Paper presented at the International Symposium on Intelligent Information Technology Application Workshops.

This work was previously published in International Journal of Technology Diffusion, Volume 1, Issue 4, edited by Ali Hussein Saleh Zolait, pp. 29-41, copyright 2010 by IGI Publishing (an imprint of IGI Global).

Chapter 20
Computing Gamma Calculus on Computer Cluster

Hong Lin
University of Houston-Downtown, USA

Jeremy Kemp
University of Houston-Downtown, USA

Padraic Gilbert
University of Houston-Downtown, USA

ABSTRACT

Gamma Calculus is an inherently parallel, high-level programming model, which allows simple programming molecules to interact, creating a complex system with minimum of coding. Gamma calculus modeled programs were written on top of IBM's TSpaces middleware, which is Java-based and uses a "Tuple Space" based model for communication, similar to that in Gamma. A parser was written in C++ to translate the Gamma syntax. This was implemented on UHD's grid cluster (grid.uhd.edu), and in an effort to increase performance and scalability, existing Gamma programs are being transferred to Nvidia's CUDA architecture. General Purpose GPU computing is well suited to run Gamma programs, as GPU's excel at running the same operation on a large data set, potentially offering a large speedup.

HIGHER-LEVEL PARALLEL COMPUTING - IMPLICIT PARALLELISM

Higher level parallel programming models express parallelism in an implicit way. Instead of imposing programmers to create multiple tasks that can run concurrently and handle their communications and synchronizations explicitly, these models allow programs to be written without assumptions of artificial sequenciality. The programs are naturally parallel. Examples of such kind of models include the Chemical Reaction Models (CRMs) (Banatre & Le Metayer, 1990, 1993), Linda (Carriero & Gelernter, 1989), and Unity (Chandy & Misra, 1988; Misra, 1989). These models are created to address higher level programming issues such as formal program specification, program synthesis, program derivation and verification, and software architecture. Efficient implementation

DOI: 10.4018/978-1-4666-1752-0.ch020

of these models has limited success and therefore obscures its direct applications in software design (Creveui, 1991; Gladitz, 1996). Despite this limitation, efforts have been made in both academic and industrial settings to avail these models in real-world programming. For example, Unity has been used in industrial software design and found successful; execution efficiency of Linda has been affirmed by experiments and it is implemented by IBM Tuple Space. Recent discussions of these models in multi-agent system design have also been found in literature (Cabri, 2000). In the following discussion, we focus on the Chemical Reaction Models and its applications.

The Chemical Reaction Models describe computation as "chemical reactions". Data (the "solution") are represented as a multiset. A set of "reaction" rules is given to combine elements in the multiset and produce new elements. Reactions take place until the solution becomes inert, namely there are no more elements can be combined. The results of computation are represented as the inert multiset. Gamma is a kernel language in which programs are described in terms of multiset transformations. In Gamma programming paradigm, programmers can concentrate on the logic of problem solving based on an abstract machine and are free from considering any particular execution environment. It has seeded follow-up elaborations, such as Chemical Abstract Machine (Cham) (Berry & Boudol, 1992), higher-order Gamma (Le Metayer, 1994; Cohen & Muylaert-Filho, 1996), and Structured Gamma (Fradet & Le Metayer, 1998). While the original Gamma language is a first-order language, higher order extensions have been proposed to enhance the expressiveness of the language. These include higher-order Gamma, hmm-calculus, and others. The recent formalisms, γ-Calculi, of Gamma languages combine reaction rules and the multisets of data and treat reactions as first-class citizens (Banâtre, Fradet, & Radenac, 2004, 2005a, 2005b). Among γ-Calculi, γ_0-Calculus is a minimal basis for the chemical paradigm; γ_c-Calculus extends γ_0-Calculus by

adding a condition term into γ-abstractions; and γ_n-Calculus extends γ_0-Calculus by allowing abstractions to atomically capture multiple elements. Finally, γ_{cn}-Calculus combines both γ_c-Calculus and γ_n-Calculus. For notational simplicity, we use γ-Calculus to mean γ_{cn}-Calculus from this point on.

The paper will be organized as follows. In the second section, we give a brief introduction to γ-Calculus. In the third and the fourth section, we discuss the method for implementing γ-Calculus in IBM Tuple space and in OpenCL, respectively. Experimental results are presented thereafter. We conclude in the last section.

γ-CALCULUS

The basic term of a Gamma program is molecules (or γ-expressions), which can be simple data or programs (γ-abstractions). The execution of the Gamma program can be seen as the evolution of a solution of molecules, which react until the solution becomes inert. Molecules are recursively defined as constants, γ-abstractions, multisets or solution of molecules. The following is their syntax:

M::= 0 | 1 | ... | 'a' | 'b' | ... ; constants

| γP[C].M ; γ-abstraction

| M_1, M_2 ; multiset

| <M> ; solution

The multiset constructor "," is associative and commutative (AC rule). Solutions encapsulate molecules. Molecules can move within solutions but not across solutions. γ-abstractions are elements of multisets, just like other elements. They can be applied to other elements of the same solution if a match to pattern P is found and condition C evaluates to true and therefore facilitate the chemical reaction. The pattern has the following syntax:

P::= x | P, P | <P>

where x is a variable. In addition, we allow for the use of tuples (written $x_1:...:x_n$) and names of types. For example, γ-abstraction

$$\gamma(x: Int, y: Int)[x \geq y].x$$

can be interpreted as: replace x, y by x if $x \geq y$, which is equivalent to finding the maximum of two integers.

The semantics of γ-Calculus is defined as the following:

$(\gamma p[c].m_1), m_2 = \phi m_1$ if match$(p/ m_2) = \phi$ and ϕc ; γ-conversion

$m_1, m_2 = m_2, m_1$; commutativity

$m_1, (m_2, m_3) = (m_1, m_2), m_3$; associativity

$E_1 = E_2 => E[E_1] = E[E_2]$; chemical law

The γ-conversion describes the reaction mechanism. When the pattern p matches m_2, a substitution ϕ is yielded. If the condition ϕc holds, the reactive molecules $\gamma p[c].m_1$ and m_2 are consumed and a new molecule ϕm_1 is produced. match(p/m) returns the substitution corresponding to the unification of variables if the matching succeeds, otherwise it returns fail.

Chemical law formalizes the locality of reactions. $E[E_1]$ denotes the molecule obtained by replacing holes in the context E[ ] (denoted by [ ]) by the molecule E_1. A molecule is said to be inert if no reaction can be made within:

Inert(m) $\Leftrightarrow$

$(m \equiv m'[(\gamma p[c].m_1), m_2] => match(p/m_2) = fail)$

A solution is inert if all molecules within are inert and normal forms of chemical reactions are inert γ-expression. Elements inside a solution can be matched only if the solution is inert. Therefore, a pattern cannot match an active solution. This ensures that solutions cannot be decomposed before they reach their normal form and therefore permits the sequentialization of reactions. The following inference rule governs the evolution of γ-expressions:

$$\frac{E_1 \to E_2 \quad E \equiv C[E_1] \quad E' \equiv C[E_2]}{E \to E'}$$

This high level language can be implemented in Java using IBM's TSpaces server and Java package. The method is detailed in the following section.

IMPLEMENTATION IN IBM TUPLE SPACE

IBM Tuple Space was originally invented as an implementation of Linda computational model. While version 3.0 is only available after obtaining a site license, version 2.12 is freely available. Installing TSpaces is as easy as unpackaging the TSpaces package on the networked file system (NFS), adding its directory to the users classpath, and starting the server in a GNU Screen session.

Data Structures and Methods

A TSpaces program uses more of a client/server model, with each node only communicating with a 'host' or any machine with a known name, which on a cluster would usually be the head node. And although TSpaces is flexible enough to assign global names and ranks to each node, micro-managing the communications, this would defeat the purpose of having the abstraction layer TSpaces offers you. Data in a TSpaces program is shared through Tuples, a tuple is a data structure that wraps all other data structures in a tuplespace, this can include data primitives, as well as standard java classes and user defined classes. Every tuple is in a TuplesSpace, and every TupleSpace has a host(actually a fully qualified host name).

The TSpaces methods used to obtain tuples are: read(), waitToRead(), take(), waitToTake(). The read() and take() methods vary in that the read() method leaves the tuple returned to the program in the tuplespace, and the take() method removes it from the tuplespace. The waitTo versions wait until a tuple appears in a tuplespace, and then takes it; these are good for synchronization, and can be set to time out in order to prevent the program from hanging indefinitely. These methods take Tuples as arguments, and return the first tuple from the tuplespace that matches either the data types you specified, or specific values. There is also the scan() method, which works like read() except it returns all values that match the tuple specified. There are other Tspace methods that allow you more control over your program; countN() returns all the matching tuples and delete() removes all matching tuples. There are many other advanced features that allow you to manipulate TSpaces with a great deal of precision.

Another bonus of using a platform that runs on Java is being able to run these programs on any OS, and even inside a web browser using an applet. Such applets are ideal for being able to monitor or visualize a reaction that is running.

Synchronization

The most difficult task in writing a CRM/gamma program in Tspaces is synchronization. Synchronization is needed to determine when to terminate the program, or when the molecules stop reacting.

One program acts as one molecule, and different programs can read from the same tuplespace, but in order to test that the reaction of a molecule is exhausted, a program must run through the entire data space. So, reactions that involve more then

one molecule type should be run in a cycle, the first program reacting all of the molecules from the original tuplespace, and writing the resulting tuples, as well as all of the unused tuples to the next tuplespace. The next program acts on this tuplespace until it is stable with regard to the molecule it represents, leaving the tuples in a third tuplespace. This continues until all of the programs that represent molecules have had a chance to run, and then it starts over. Termination occurs when the programs cycle through all of the programs without any changes to the tuples.

Molecules that reduce tuplespaces to a single solution are the simplest. They require only one tuplespace and no synchronization. The max number finder and the tuple adder are examples of this, they simply react until there is only one element left, then they are done.

After some further thought (but not further programming) a relation of numbers of tuplespaces to input and output elements of the gamma function can be noticed. In order to use the style of synchronization used in the sorting program, a program with X input molecules and Y output molecules requires X tuplespaces for the input and Y tuplespaces for the output. In order to detect stability, it will have to empty the input tuples 1 time with no changes and empty the output tuplespace 1 time.

The sorting program is an example of this; the method it uses involves alternating between comparing two tuples of the form (even index n, dataValue), (n +1, dataValue) and (odd index m, dataValue), (m+1, dataValue), and incrementing a counter tuple whenever a change occurs. This allows a comparison after the last tuples are removed from the tuplespace and into another tuplespace to determine if any changes have been made. If two consecutive changeless runs occur, then every data element is in order, and the program terminates.

There is a complication with programs where number of inputs is not equal to the number of outputs. The indexing must be handles specially or removed entirely; with numbers removed, there will be n + 1 elements missing, and with numbers added, there will be elements that need to be added somewhere, these can usually be appended to the end?

If there are more inputs then outputs, then the tuplespace will eventually be reduced to the number of outputs for the one molecule. These types of programs can use the termination style of the max element and tuple adder programs; simply running until there are Y elements left, and then stopping. The only synchronization required is when emptying a tuplespace(or set of tuplespaces), and to prevent deadlock when (number of elements) < (number of processors) * (number of inputs), but this can be handled by detecting null reads and random timeouts on the waitToRead() calls.

Although Tuple Space was initially implemented to support Linda computation model, its functions well suite in the operational semantics of the chemical reactions models. We propose implementing γ-Calculus on Tuple Space. In the following, we demonstrate two sample programs in γ-Calculus and their Tuple Space implementations.

Max Number Finder

Given a set of values of an ordered type M, this program returns the maximum number of the set. The following γ-abstraction compares two randomly selected values. If the first value is greater than or equal to the second, it removes the second value from the set:

select = γ(a: M, b: M)[a $\geq$ b]. a: M, select

No global control is imposed on the way multiset elements are selected to ignite the reaction. If select is placed in an initial set M_0 of values, it will compare two values and erase the smaller at a time till the maximum is left. So the maximum number program can then be written as:

Max M_0 = <select, M_0>

If the multiset M_0 is represented as a tuple space, this program can be converted into one that finds and displays the greatest tuple inside a tuple space. It works with each node taking two tuples from the tuple space, comparing them, and placing the greatest one back to the tuple space. This process repeats itself until the termination condition is met, that is, when there is only one tuple left in the tuple space. When a node picks tuples up, if both tuples happen to be the same size, it simply places one of them back in the tuplespace while discarding the other one. If a node happens to take only one tuple because another node already picked the last remaining ones in the tuple space, this puts it back and repeats the process. This ensures that by the next check, a node will be able to take two tuples and perform the remaining operations to find the greatest tuple. If a node sees no tuples in the tuple space, this displays a message and terminates. If a node sees only one tuple in the tuple space, it assumes the greatest tuple was already found, displays a message and terminates.

Figure 1 shows the flowchart of the tuple space maximum number finder program

Sorter

If a list is represented by multiset M = {(a, i) | a is value and i an index and i's are consecutive}, the following recursive γ-abstraction replaces any ill-ordered pairs by two other pairs:

sigma = γ((a, i): M, (b, j): M)[i < j $\wedge$ a > b]. (b, i): M, (a, j): M, sigma

It specifies that any two selected pairs (a, i) and (b, j) that satisfy the condition, i < j $\wedge$ a > b are replaced by two other pairs (b, i) and (a, j), and a copy of itself. If sigma is placed in an initial set M_0 of pairs, it will replace ill-ordered pairs until the entire list is sorted. So a sorting program can be defined as:

Sort M_0 = <sigma, M_0>

In a tuple space, a similar process will happen. The program will sort all of the tuples in a tuple space in ascending order. Each tuple has an index and a value in the following format: (index, value). When two tuples, (i, x) and (j, y) from said tuple space S are taken by a node, it first checks whether x > y & i < j. If this happens to be true, then the following swap is performed: (i, y), (j, x) they are put back in the tuple space, and the tuples are in order. This process repeats itself until no more swaps can be performed, that is, when all of the tuples in a tuple space are arranged in ascending order.

As mentioned above, multiple tuplespaces are required to synchronize this 'single pool' abstraction, in this case four tuplespaces were used. There is a primary pool, where the data is initially stored and an alternate pool where the data is written as it is being processed. Each of these pools is broken in to an even and an odd pool

The primary feature of this programming model is that it can utilize up to $n/2$ processing nodes, where n is the number of data items being sorted.

We have tested the above TSpace programs on a PC cluster and observed the computation in multiple nodes, and how the increase of nodes divides the number of comparisons per node, and increases speed; all of this thanks to the abstractions and portability offered by TSpaces. Figure 2 shows the performance statistics of the sorting program.

Figure 1. Maximum number finder in TSpace

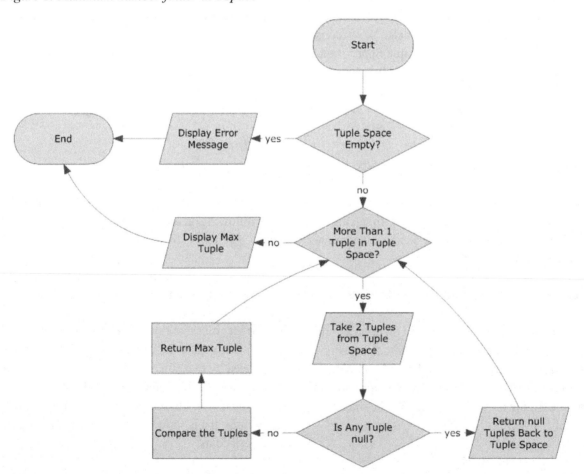

Figure 2. The performance of a Gamma sorting program on TSpace

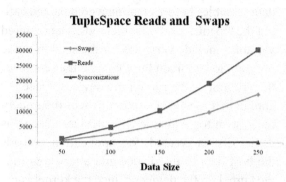

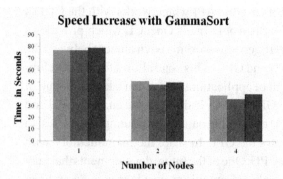

(a) A graph of number of swaps, reads and synchronizations vs the number of data elements.

(b) A graph of the number of nodes vs time.

We want to point out that when converting a γ-Calculus program into a TSpace program, details must be added to make a working program. However, through the above examples, we can see the conversion is straightforward in sense of the computation model. Therefore, it is technically feasible to design an automatic conversion system that can parse γ-Calculus and convert the program into a TSpace program and this is the next goal of our ongoing project.

IMPLEMENTATION IN OPENCL

The second part of the project was to implement programs modeled as closely as possible to the Gamma paradigm and run these models on three C1060 Tesla GPUs. The Tesla Cards are made by NVIDIA and designed specifically for general purpose GPU computation. The first step to modeling Gamma programs required setting up the necessary API to communicate with the GPUs. The possible APIs were narrowed down to CUDA for C or OpenCL. The next step was determining a sequential language which the API would extend and compile from. It was decided best to use a langue that was most compatible with the API but maintained an easy input/output system. The third

step in this project was learning the selected API and developing ways to adapt the chosen Gamma programs to the APIs environment. This research project was successful in the implementation of these programs.

OpenCL API

OpenCL stands for Open Computing Language and works as an extension for many sequential languages. Java, C++, C, and Ruby are a few examples of successful implementations of the API extension. OpenCL was created by Apple™ to take advantage of multiple core CPUs and provide GPU computation outside the realm of graphics processing. The designers at Apple have continued to take their graphics technology towards a GPGPU industry and therefore needed a language which provided computer applications access to CPUs and GPUs and graphics memory. GPGPU stands for General Purpose Graphics Processing Unit. Until the development of the CUDA SDK by NVIDIA, the general purpose programming accessibility for the average graphics processor was very limited. GPUs were only used to offset load of floating point operations required by running an application. CUDA for C is an API developed by NVIDIA allows programmers to write applications that take advantage of GPU processing power. Another GPU API which works with the CUDA driver is Apple Inc.'s OpenCL which provides a heterogeneous working environment between the CPU and GPU. This zone allows for the development of applications which can take advantage of the GPU and CPU directly and enables GPU and CPU computing parallel computing. OpenCL also allows the GPU to share the main memory with the CPU. One of the future developments that may take place from this project is creating a multiset in main memory and assigning several GPUs a set of abstractions that affect that multiset. This project's goal, however, is only to aimed to reach the first step in Gamma abstraction development.

OpenCL with C++

The OpenCL API is a framework for writing programs which operate across a heterogeneous zone of platforms, including CPUs, GPUs, and Cell processors. Included in the API is a C99 based language used for writing kernels. Kernels are device driven functions which operate in a SIMD/MIMD format. Since the OpenCL API is a recent development most of the example code and tutorials available for it are written in C. NVIDIA released an OpenCL SDK and example codes written entirely in C in September of 2009. Most of the OpenCL functions used in developing the Gamma models for this project were referenced from these examples. Though the C language was the target language for use with OpenCL, we decided C++ is easier to work with in terms of input and output and inherits most of the C language's properties.

There are three parts to an OpenCL program. The first part is the host section which is run by the CPU. The second part is the OpenCL context which gives access to the devices that will be used, in the case of this research project; the devices are the C1060 Tesla GPU cards. The last part of an OpenCL program is the Kernel code which is compiled and ran from the devices. The host

processor creates the application and all required data variables before creating a context and calling the OpenCL compiler methods. The required variables include variables for the section of the program to be run on the CPU and the section of the program to be run on the devices. Once the application creates a context, it will then query the system for available GPU devices. Once this device list is created, the application uploads the host data to the device and afterwards runs the kernel on the devices. Since the kernel is the function that operates on the data, we modeled the kernel after the Gamma abstractions.

Techniques for using the OpenCL Kernel to Model a Gamma Program

The OpenCL Kernel is made of a multidimensional grid which in turn is consists of multidimensional work groups. Each work group contains an application specified dimension and number of work items. The work items are what manipulate the data in an OpenCL kernel. The programs we are creating have to model the Gamma abstractions for adding two matrixes (named "Add") and finding the maximum number (named "Max"). With OpenCL the application will have to upload the multiset to the devices before the kernel can manipulate the data pool. Most OpenCL applications upload variables that hold the data to be computed along with variables that read in the results of those calculations. Because of this, we had to decide whether to upload a single multiset to the devices or a multiset for each argument in the abstractions. For example, the "Add" abstraction reads two elements and replaces them with the sum of those elements.

Once the kernel is called it will run its specified operations on each item of data only once, assigning the results to one of its arguments and closing. This leads to another issue: Without a way to make the kernel continually work on the data and not close until there is no longer a set of elements that fit the conditions, the application will have to repeatedly call the kernel after every operation. From this repeated call the modeled abstractions will be much more sequential than is desired and much less efficient than a real Gamma program. In addition to the excessive sequentiality in the application, requiring the host part of the application to subdivide the multiset after every return from the kernel call adds an element of unwanted artificial sequentiality.

IMPLEMENTING THE "ADD" GAMMA ABSTRACTION

A kernel could read two subset arrays and easily add any pair of elements inside the array. Figure 3 shows the "Add" program and its data mapping on GPU.

To implement the "Add" program, we created a kernel function which takes three arguments: arrayA, arrayB, arrayC. The arguments consisted of the two subsets, arrayA and arrayB, which are derived from the multiset and the third argument, arrayC, which holds the resulting computation. The results are assigned by adding each individual element in arrayA to its counter element in arrayB and saving the results in arrayC. The

application simply loads the kernel with the three arguments and then requests the results once the device is finished with the program. Then the application checks if the resulting array has more than one element to determine if it should continue calling the kernel to perform the "Add" program on the array. Figure 4 shows the kernel implementation of the "Add" abstraction.

Implementing the "Max" Gamma Abstraction

To implement the "Max" program all that had to be done was a slight adjustment the kernel function. The function is renamed to Max and reads the same arguments as the Add function did. The only difference between "Add" and "Max" is that "Max" compares element pairs to see which is greater and stores the greater element in the third array, arrayC. Figure 5 contains the "Max" Gamma and OpenCL kernel function "max" modeled after it.

Figure 3. The GPU "Add" program

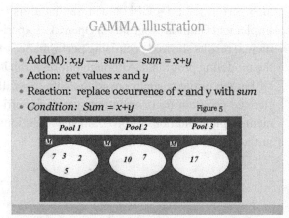

(a) A matrix addition program

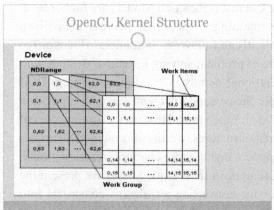

(b) Data mapping

Figure 4. OpenCL kernel Add.cl and the Gamma abstraction it's modeled after

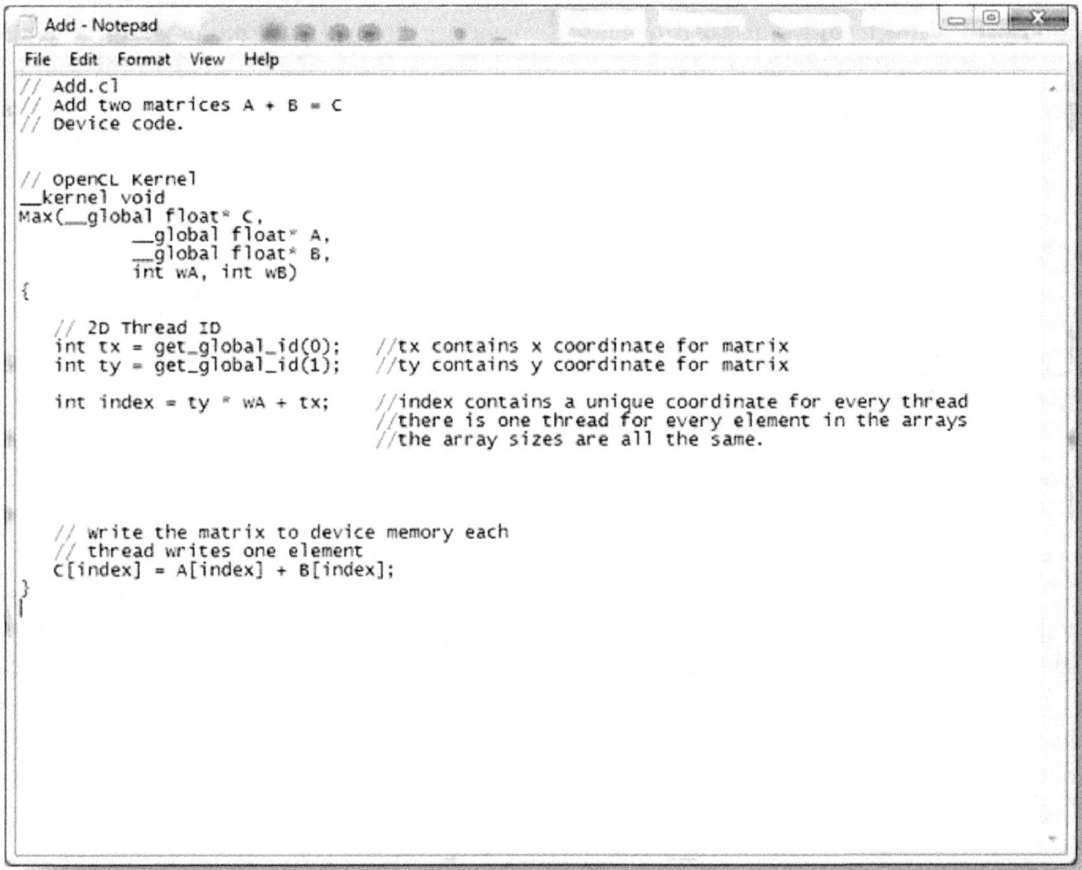

```
Add - Notepad

File  Edit  Format  View  Help
// Add.cl
// Add two matrices A + B = C
// Device code.


// OpenCL Kernel
__kernel void
Max(__global float* C,
        __global float* A,
        __global float* B,
        int wA, int wB)
{

    // 2D Thread ID
    int tx = get_global_id(0);    //tx contains x coordinate for matrix
    int ty = get_global_id(1);    //ty contains y coordinate for matrix

    int index = ty * wA + tx;     //index contains a unique coordinate for every thread
                                  //there is one thread for every element in the arrays
                                  //the array sizes are all the same.



    // write the matrix to device memory each
    // thread writes one element
    C[index] = A[index] + B[index];
}
```

CONCLUSION

The Chemical Reaction Models are higher level programming models that address parallelism implicitly and allows programmers to focus on the logic of problem solving instead of dealing with operational details in parallel computing. IBM Tuple Space supports client/server computation based on Linda model that uses a similar concept for data structures. We discuss a method for implementing a higher order chemical reaction model, γ-Calculus, in IBM Tuple Space. We present the rules for converting γ-Calculus constructs into TSpace codes and discuss the critical techniques such as synchronizations. Our work shows that the conversion is practical. Experiments are also conducted on a computer cluster. Research is also performed on a GPU machine that aims to implement Gamma programs in OpenCL. Experimental results showed promising performance of the modeling programs. Although our research is still in the initial stage, it paved the path to a full fledged program transformation system for efficient implementations of program specifications in the Chemical Reaction Models.

Figure 5. Max kernel modeled after the "Max" Gamma abstraction

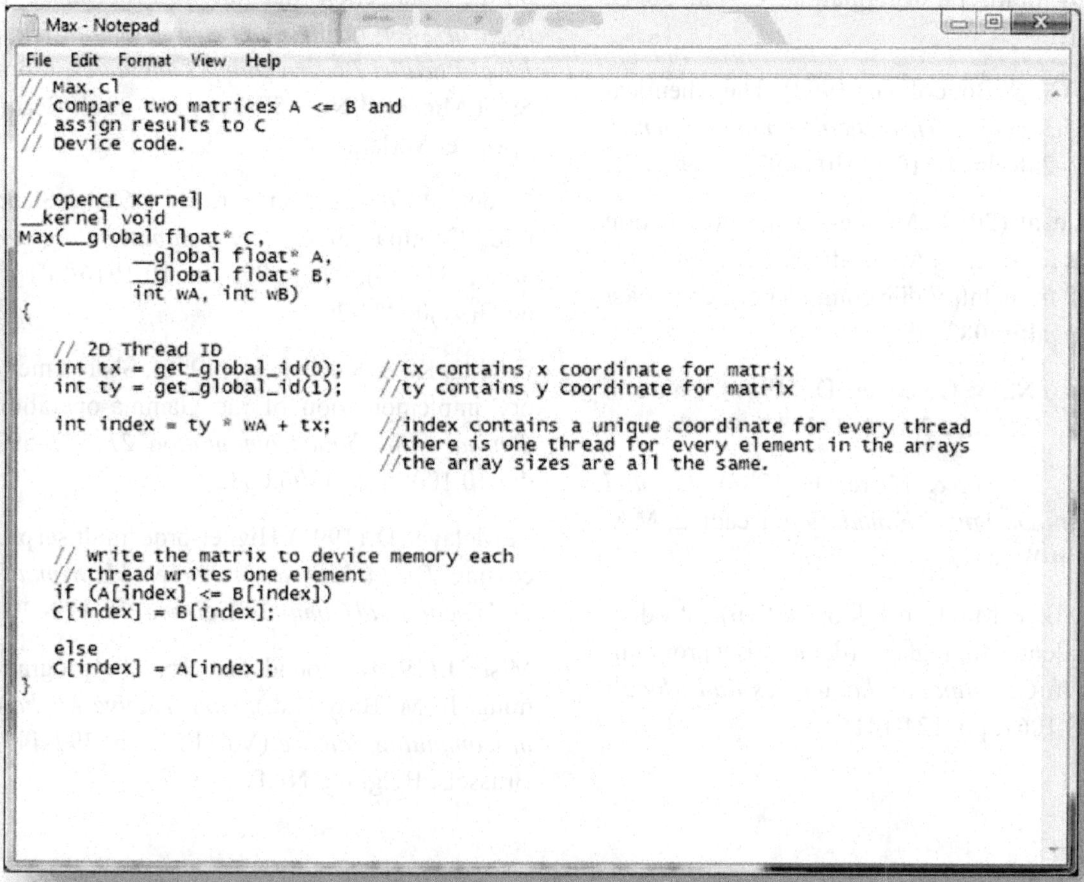

```
Max - Notepad

File  Edit  Format  View  Help
// Max.cl
// Compare two matrices A <= B and
// assign results to C
// Device code.

// OpenCL Kernel
__kernel void
Max(__global float* C,
        __global float* A,
        __global float* B,
        int wA, int wB)
{

    // 2D Thread ID
    int tx = get_global_id(0);    //tx contains x coordinate for matrix
    int ty = get_global_id(1);    //ty contains y coordinate for matrix

    int index = ty * wA + tx;     //index contains a unique coordinate for every thread
                                  //there is one thread for every element in the arrays
                                  //the array sizes are all the same.




    // write the matrix to device memory each
    // thread writes one element
    if (A[index] <= B[index])
    C[index] = B[index];

    else
    C[index] = A[index];
}
```

ACKNOWLEDGMENT

This research is partially supported by NSF grant "Acquisition of a Computational Cluster Grid for Research and Education in Science and Mathematics" (#0619312).

REFERENCES

Banâtre, J.-P., Fradet, P., & Radenac, Y. (2004). Chemical specification of autonomic systems. In *Proceedings of the 13th International Conference on Intelligent and Adaptive Systems and Software Engineering (IASSE'04)*.

Banâtre, J.-P., Fradet, P., & Radenac, Y. (2005a). Principles of chemical programming. In S. Abdennadher & C. Ringeissen (Eds.), *Proceedings of the 5th International Workshop on Rule-Based Programming (RULE'04)* (pp. 133-147).

Banâtre, J.-P., Fradet, P., & Radenac, Y. (2005b). Higher-order Chemical Programming Style. In *Proceedings of Unconventional Programming Paradigms* (LNCS 3566, pp. 84-98). Berlin: Springer Verlag.

Banatre, J.-P., & Le Metayer, D. (1990). The Gamma model and its discipline of programming. *Science of Computer Programming, 15*, 55–77. doi:10.1016/0167-6423(90)90044-E

Banatre, J.-P., & Le Metayer, D. (1993). Programming by multiset transformation. *CACM, 36*(1), 98–111.

Berry, G., & Boudol, G. (1992). The Chemical Abstract Machine. *Theoretical Computer Science, 96*, 217–248. doi:10.1016/0304-3975(92)90185-I

Cabri., et al. (2000). Mobile-Agent Coordination Models for Internet Applications. *Computer*. Retrieved from http://dlib.computer.org/co/books/co2000/pdf/r2082.pdf

Carriero, N., & Gelernter, D. (1989). Linda in context. *CACM, 32*(4), 444–458.

Chandy, K. M., & Misra, J. (1988). *Parallel Program Design: A Foundation*. Reading, MA: Addison-Wesley.

Cohen, D., & Muylaert-Filho, J. (1996). Introducing a calculus for higher-order multiset programming. In *Coordination Languages and Models* (LNCS 1061, pp. 124-141).

Creveuil, C. (1991). Implementation of Gamma on the Connection Machine. In *Proceedings of the Workshop on Research Directions in High-Level Parallel Programming Languages*, Mont-Saint Michel (LNCS 574, pp. 219-230). Berlin: Springer Verlag.

Fradet, P., & Le Metayer, D. (1998). Structured Gamma. *Science of Computer Programming, 31*(2-3), 263–289. doi:10.1016/S0167-6423(97)00023-3

Gladitz, K., & Kuchen, H. (1996). Shared memory implementation of the Gamma-operation. *Journal of Symbolic Computation, 21*, 577–591. doi:10.1006/jsco.1996.0032

Le Metayer, D. (1994). Higher-order multiset processing. *DIMACS Series in Discrete Mathematics and Theoretical Computer Science, 18*, 179–200.

Misra, J. (1989). A foundation of parallel programming. In M. Broy (Ed.), *Constructive Methods in Computing Science* (Vol. F55, pp. 397-443). Brussels, Belgium: NATO.

This work was previously published in International Journal of Technology Diffusion, Volume 1, Issue 4, edited by Ali Hussein Saleh Zolait, pp. 42-52, copyright 2010 by IGI Publishing (an imprint of IGI Global).

Chapter 21
Determinants of the Use of Knowledge Sources in the Adoption of Open Source Server Software

Kris Ven
University of Antwerp, Belgium

Jan Verelst
University of Antwerp, Belgium

ABSTRACT

Previous research suggests that the adoption of open source server software (OSSS) may be subject to knowledge barriers. In order to overcome these barriers, organizations should engage in a process of organizational learning. This learning process is facilitated by exposure to external knowledge sources. Unfortunately, this leaves open the question of which factors determine which knowledge sources are used by organizations. In this study, the authors have performed an exploratory study on the determinants of the use of knowledge sources in the adoption of OSSS. The conceptual model developed in this study was based on the absorptive capacity theory. Data was gathered from 95 organizations to empirically investigate this model. Results provide a quite consistent view on how external knowledge sources are used by organizations in the adoption of OSSS. Moreover, results provide more insight into the context in which the adoption of OSSS takes place.

INTRODUCTION

Over the past 10 years, open source software (OSS) has become a viable solution for organizations. Although OSS used to be developed by a community of volunteer developers, an increasing number of commercial software companies have started to offer support and other OSS-related services and products (Fitzgerald, 2006). This increased commercial support has had a positive effect on the adoption of OSS (Dedrick & West, 2003; Fitzgerald & Kenny, 2003; Morgan & Finnegan, 2007). Many OSS products have indeed already

DOI: 10.4018/978-1-4666-1752-0.ch021

widely diffused through organizations. Recently, an increasing number of studies on the adoption of OSS have been conducted. The aim of most of these studies is to identify the factors that influence the adoption of OSS. Several of these studies have suggested that the availability of external support is an important concern in the adoption of OSS (Dedrick & West, 2003; Fitzgerald & Kenny, 2003; Morgan & Finnegan, 2007; Ven & Verelst, 2006; Li, Tan, Teo, & Siow, 2005). A lack of external support may be a barrier to the adoption of OSS, (Morgan & Finnegan, 2007; Li et al., 2005), while the availability of external support can provide some reassurance to organizations (Fitzgerald & Kenny, 2003). These findings suggest that IT managers are rather reluctant to adopt OSS in the absence of external support, fearing that they cannot rely on the support that is offered by the OSS community or on the internal resources of the organization.

In our previous research, we have investigated the adoption of *open source server software (OSSS)*. OSSS is a term that is used to refer to OSS products that are primarily used on server-side platforms, such as operating systems, web servers and mail servers. Results indicated that the adoption of OSSS may be subject to *knowledge barriers* (Ven, 2008). Organizations can overcome knowledge barriers by engaging in a process of organizational learning (Attewell, 1992; Cohen & Levinthal, 1990). This learning process is dependent on the organization's *absorptive capacity*, namely the ability of the organization to acquire and assimilate new knowledge (Cohen & Levinthal, 1989). Exposure to external knowledge sources allows organizations to increase their absorptive capacity (Cohen & Levinthal, 1989; Cohen & Levinthal, 1990; Zahra & George, 2002).

The external support options for OSSS represent the external knowledge sources that are available to organizations to facilitate the organizational learning process. However, it has been noted that organizations differ in which types of external support are used (Morgan & Finnegan,

2007; Ven & Verelst, 2006). At the moment, it is unclear which factors influence the decision of the organization to make use of one of these external knowledge sources. Yet, this is a crucial question since organizations that face high knowledge barriers may not be aware of the best way to obtain the knowledge required to adopt and implement an innovation. It is the aim of this study to gain more insight into this issue. To this end, we conducted an exploratory study into which knowledge sources are used by organizations in the adoption of OSSS. Our approach is grounded in the absorptive capacity theory.

THEORETICAL BACKGROUND

Previous studies have shown that the adoption of complex technologies may be subject to *knowledge barriers* (Attewell, 1992; Fichman & Kemerer, 1997). According to this view, organizations will defer adoption until sufficient knowledge about the technology has been assimilated (Attewell, 1992; Fichman & Kemerer, 1997). The adoption and diffusion of such technologies are primarily influenced by the ease with which organizations can obtain the knowledge required to adopt and implement these technologies. Therefore, organizations that can obtain this knowledge more effectively are expected to exhibit more innovative behavior (Cohen & Levinthal, 1990; Attewell, 1992). In order to overcome the knowledge barriers involved with adopting new technologies, organizations have to engage in a process of *organizational learning* (Levitt & March, 1988; Attewell, 1992).

Organizational learning is dependent on the organization's *absorptive capacity* (Kim, 1998). The concept of *absorptive capacity* was developed by Cohen and Levinthal (1989), and was defined as *"the firm's ability to identify, assimilate, and exploit knowledge from the environment"* (Cohen & Levinthal, 1989, p. 569). Organizations that have a higher absorptive capacity will be better able to learn about new technologies, or in other words, will be better able to acquire and exploit new knowledge (Cohen & Levinthal, 1989; Cohen & Levinthal, 1990). Organizations that engage in a learning process will further develop their absorptive capacity, which in turn will stimulate and facilitate future learning (Lane, Koka, & Pathak, 2006).

In order to sustain the learning and innovation process within organizations, it is critical that organizations are exposed to external sources of knowledge (Cohen & Levinthal, 1990; Van Den Bosch, Volberda, & De Boer, 1999; Zahra & George, 2002; Todorova & Durisin, 2007). Exposure to a variety of external knowledge sources allows organizations to further develop their absorptive capacity (Zahra & George, 2002; Jansen, Bosch, & Volberda, 2005). Although internal knowledge is also an important determinant of an organization's absorptive capacity, failing to acquire new knowledge from external sources may prevent the organization from exploring new technologies (Zahra & George, 2002). This can lead to competence-traps in which the organization becomes locked out from trying new technologies that become available (Levitt & March, 1988).

The concept of absorptive capacity has received much attention in literature. In fact, Lane et al. (2006) report that the construct has been used in over 900 papers. Their literature review showed that the absorptive capacity theory has been studied from three main angles: the antecedents or outcomes of absorptive capacity, the relationship of absorptive capacity with related concepts (i.e., organizational learning, interorganizational learning, and innovation), and definitions and measurements of absorptive capacity (Lane et al., 2006). Although previous research has investigated the effect of the use of various knowledge sources on absorptive capacity, to our knowledge no study so far has investigated the factors that determine which external knowledge sources are used when learning about a new technology. In this study, we aim to address this gap in literature within the context of the adoption of OSSS.

CONCEPTUAL MODEL

Many types of OSS products are available today. These can be roughly classified in server, desktop, and enterprise applications. The knowledge required for adopting and implementing these types of OSS differs significantly, and may pose different knowledge barriers to the organization (e.g., an organization may be very familiar with Linux for server applications, but may not be familiar with open source ERP products). As a result, the organization may need to rely on different knowledge sources depending on the type of OSS. In order to increase the validity of our study, we restricted the scope of our research to OSSS. The choice for our focus on OSSS was motivated by the fact that this type of OSSS is most frequently adopted by organizations and also has the most knowledge available on the market. Special attention will be given to the adoption of Linux. Linux is a very important product since it is the most often adopted OSSS product. Moreover, organizations that have adopted Linux can be considered to be using OSSS as platform. Other types of OSSS—such as Apache or Sendmail—can also run on the Microsoft Windows or Unix operating system. Considering those organizations that have adopted OSSS without adopting OSSS is less interesting for the purpose of our study since they are not using OSSS as a platform and may be confronted with fewer and other knowledge requirements.

We consider this study to be exploratory since no prior study has investigated which factors influence the use of knowledge sources in the adoption of IT. Based on the absorptive capacity theory, we constructed a conceptual model that describes 8 knowledge-related variables that may have an impact on the use of knowledge sources in the adoption of OSSS. This conceptual model is shown in Figure 1. We will first discuss the dependent variables in our model, after which we will elaborate on the independent variables.

We distinguish between three external knowledge sources that are available to organizations

Figure 1. Conceptual model

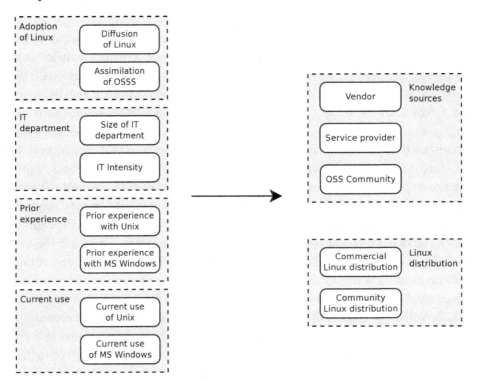

in the adoption of OSSS. First of all, commercial support is offered by *software vendors*. A number of enterprise Linux versions are available that ship with a support contract (e.g., RedHat Enterprise Linux and SUSE Linux Enterprise). Hence, when difficulties occur with these OSSS products, organizations can rely on the knowledge offered by these OSS vendors. Second, knowledge on OSSS is also provided by independent service providers, consultants or other third parties (from now on referred to as *service providers*) that assist the organization in installing and maintaining their OSSS infrastructure. Such service providers offer on-site services and may be especially useful when the organization's internal IT staff is not able to undertake these tasks itself. Many local businesses currently offer OSS-related services. These two external knowledge sources represent the commercial support options available to organizations. The availability of this commercial support has been shown to be an important factor in the adoption of OSSS (Dedrick & West, 2003; Fitzgerald & Kenny, 2003; Morgan & Finnegan, 2007; Ven & Verelst, 2006). Finally, the organization can also rely on the knowledge offered by the *OSS community*. The support offered by the OSS community can provide a quick, free and effective solution to problems that organizations experience. On the negative side, the support offered by the OSS community is not guaranteed, does not provide organizations with a single point-of-contact, and may require more searching to find the correct solution to a problem (Ven & Verelst, 2006).

The Linux distribution used by organizations may also reflect the type of support used. We can distinguish between two main types of Linux distributions. First, *commercial distributions* are offered by a vendor and generally come with a support contract so that organizations can rely on the services of a vendor for support. Therefore, the use of vendor support seems related to the use of a commercial Linux distribution. Examples in this category include RedHat Enterprise Linux and SUSE Linux Enterprise. Second, *community distributions* are maintained by non-profit organizations. Support is offered by the OSS community on mailing lists and discussion forums. Hence, we expect that the factors that influence the choice for a community Linux distribution will be similar to those influencing the use of the OSS community. Examples in this category include Fedora, CentOS, Ubuntu, and Debian. Although the use of a Linux distribution cannot be considered a direct external knowledge source, we would expect that the factors that influence the choice for a commercial or community Linux distribution will be similar to those influencing the use of vendor support or community support respectively. Therefore, we will also explore which factors influence the use of a commercial or community Linux distribution using two additional dependent variables.

Research has shown that organizations differ in which types of support are used (Ven, Verelst, & Mannaert, 2008; Morgan & Finnegan, 2007). The use of external support—such as vendors and consultants—represent external knowledge sources that can be used by organizations to acquire knowledge about new technologies (Attewell, 1992; Cohen & Levinthal, 1990). Several authors have emphasized that exposure to external knowledge sources is important to increase the absorptive capacity of organizations (Lane et al., 2006; Cohen & Levinthal, 1990; Zahra & George, 2002). The level of absorptive capacity of an organization is dependent on the *prior knowledge* available within the organization (Cohen & Levinthal, 1990; Kim, 1998). Hence, based on the absorptive capacity theory, we posit that the decision to use a particular external knowledge source—or type of Linux distribution—is dependent on the prior knowledge of the organization. We therefore need to identify various knowledge-related factors that reflect the relevant prior knowledge of the organization. These factors are the independent variables in our conceptual model. We have identified 4 groups of factors that may influence

the use of the knowledge sources: *adoption of Linux, characteristics of the IT department, prior experience with related technologies*, and *current use of related technologies*. We will now discuss each of these groups of factors in more detail.

Adoption of Linux

Several authors have emphasized that a key element of absorptive capacity consists of exploitation, i.e., being able to apply the assimilated knowledge in a practical setting (Cohen & Levinthal, 1989; Cohen & Levinthal, 1990; Van Den Bosch et al., 1999; Lane et al., 2006; Zahra & George, 2002). Within the context of knowledge-intensive technologies, adoption can be considered to be a learning process for organizations (Fichman & Kemerer, 1997; Attewell, 1992). As organizations learn about the technology, they will overcome the knowledge barriers associated with the technology, and will be able to adopt and implement the technology. Organizations that have progressed further in the assimilation of a technology can therefore be considered to have assimilated more knowledge about that innovation. The level of adoption will therefore be reflective of the knowledge that has been assimilated and that can be exploited by the organization. The level of adoption may therefore influence which external knowledge sources are used by organizations. It has indeed been argued that organizations are expected to seek complementarily in the external knowledge they source since already acquired knowledge does not have to be re-acquired from external sources (Zahra & George, 2002).

A first measure we consider relevant in this context is the *diffusion of Linux*. Diffusion can be defined as "*the extent of use of an innovation across people, projects, tasks, or organizational units*" (Fichman, 2001, p. 454). It therefore reflects how many people in the organization are affected by the innovation. The more people that are exposed to the technology, the more internal knowledge that is likely to have been accumulated. Since

Linux is a server platform, its diffusion within the organization reflects the relative importance of OSSS in the organization, to which degree the organization bases its infrastructure on OSSS, and how much knowledge of OSSS that has actually been assimilated by the organization.

In addition, we consider the influence of the *assimilation of OSSS*. Assimilation refers to *"the process spanning from an organization's first awareness of an innovation to, potentially, acquisition and widespread deployment"* (Fichman & Kemerer, 1997, p. 1346). By considering the assimilation of OSSS, we also capture the amount of knowledge that has been acquired and assimilated on other OSSS products.

Characteristics of the IT Department

We expect that two characteristics of the IT department may determine which knowledge sources are used by organizations in the adoption of OSSS. First, we consider the *size of the IT department*, in terms of the number of IT staff members. The level of an organization's absorptive capacity is formed by the absorptive capacity of the individuals within the organization (Cohen & Levinthal, 1990; Lane et al., 2006). Hence, the knowledge possessed by the organization is dependent on the knowledge held by the individuals within the organization. Since we are concerned with the use of OSSS, relevant knowledge will be possessed by the IT staff. The size of the IT department will therefore reflect the knowledge that has been assimilated by the organization.

Second, we consider the influence of *IT intensity*. Some organizations make more intensive use of IT to support their daily operations compared to other organizations. Organizations in which IT staff members are more involved in the IT tasks in the organization could exhibit a higher absorptive capacity (Kim, 1998). For example, organizations in which IT is considered crucial may develop more IT-related knowledge to be able to identify opportunities for using new technologies more quickly, or to be better able to support the IT infrastructure.

Prior Experience with Related Technologies

Next, we consider the influence of *prior experience with related technologies*. In order to facilitate learning, the organization should also possess prior knowledge related to the innovation (Cohen & Levinthal, 1990; Lane et al., 2006). Given this cumulative nature of knowledge creation, the acquisition of knowledge is often path-dependent (Cohen & Levinthal, 1990; Lane et al., 2006). Organizations can therefore be said to follow a certain path of competence development (Teece, Pisano, & Shuen, 1997). This implies that the capabilities of an organization today are influenced by its technology and knowledge-related decisions it has made in the past (Teece et al., 1997; Lane et al., 2006; Cohen & Levinthal, 1990). Prior related knowledge reflects with which technologies the organization has had experience in the past. Through the use of these technologies, the organization will have assimilated specific knowledge. This knowledge may influence which knowledge sources will be used in the adoption of OSSS. Given our focus on Linux as the use of OSSS as a platform, related prior knowledge that is relevant in this context is the previous use of other server platforms. Two other operating systems for server-side use with a dominant market share are Unix and Microsoft Windows. Hence, we expect that previous use of any of these two operating systems may also influence the external knowledge sources used in the adoption of OSSS.

Current Use of Related Technologies

Finally, we consider the influence of the *current use of related technologies*. Not only is the previous experience of the organization with related technologies important: its current experience also reflects the absorptive capacity of the organization. This is related to the diversity of knowledge held by the organization. Diversity of knowledge contributes to increasing absorptive capacity, since it exposes the organization to a larger number of knowledge sources and provides access to broader range of related technologies, and allows the organization to more easily recognize the value of new innovations that become available (Cohen & Levinthal, 1990). Therefore, the current use of related technologies may also determine which external knowledge sources are used by organizations. Similar to the existence of prior related knowledge, we consider the fact whether the organization currently uses Unix or Microsoft Windows to be relevant in determining which external knowledge sources are used.

RESEARCH METHOD

In order to investigate the impact of potential antecedents on the use of external knowledge sources during the assimilation of OSSS by organizations, we performed a field study using the survey method. A self-administered web survey was used to collect the data for our study. Before administering the web survey, the survey instrument was subjected to a qualitative pretest involving 7 experts (3 academics and 4 practitioners). The aim of the pretest was to identify any issues in the survey design including, but not limited to, wording of the questions, and ease of understanding and answering of the questions in the survey. Five experts were asked to complete the survey and note any remarks or comments they had with respect to the questions. In order to elicit additional feedback on the survey design, we also used the *cognitive interviewing* technique (Willis, 2005) with two of our experts. No major issues were discovered during this pretest, but some minor adjustments were made in the formulation of some questions.

Data Collection

The target population for our study consisted of all Flemish organizations that had servers installed. Organizations were sampled from a database of a market research bureau that collects IT-related information on a regular basis from 25,000 organizations from various sectors in Belgium, The Netherlands and the Grand Duchy of Luxembourg. Organizations from different sectors and sizes were represented in our sample. The target person in each organization was the IT decision maker, commonly the CIO or IT manager. A sample consisting of 332 organizations was selected to participate in the survey. A total of 111 replies were received to the survey, corresponding with a response rate of 33.4%. We belief this response rate can be attributed to several factors. First, each respondent was personally contacted by telephone to ask for his or her participation. We observed that this had a very favorable influence on the tendency to cooperate. Second, we asked respondents if they were willing to participate in the survey—providing them with the possibility to decline—before sending an invitation. Finally, a number of reminders were sent if respondents did not complete the survey within two weeks. Given the purpose of our research, we were primarily interested in the organizations that have adopted OSSS as a platform. Therefore, our sample was reduced to those organizations that indicated to be using Linux to at least some degree. A total of 95 cases remained available for further analysis.

Operationalization

In this section, we discuss the operationalization of the dependent and independent variables.

Our three main dependent variables are concerned with the use of a *vendor*, a *service provider*, and the *OSS community* as a knowledge source. Three dichotomous variables were used to measure whether the organization made use of each knowledge source. The use of a commercial and community Linux distribution was also measured using two dichotomous variables. Respondents were asked to select from a list which Linux distributions were used in their organization. Organizations that indicated to be using RedHat Enterprise Linux, SUSE Linux Enterprise or Xandros were classified as using a commercial Linux distribution. Those organizations that indicated to be using any of the other Linux distributions (e.g., Fedora, Ubuntu, or Debian) were marked as using a community Linux distribution. Therefore, organizations could be using commercial and community Linux distributions simultaneously.

The *diffusion of Linux (LINUX)* was measured using a 7-point Likert scale ranging from "*no usage*" to "*to a very large extent*", with each point labeled.

The *assimilation of OSSS (ASSIMILATION)* was measured by using the measurement scale developed by Fichman and Kemerer (1997). It uses a Guttman scale to classify organizations in 7 possible assimilation stages through which organizations may progress (i.e., not aware, aware, interest, evaluation/trial, commitment, limited deployment, and general deployment). In order to ensure that each respondent interpreted the term OSSS the same way, respondents were provided with an explicit definition. Similar to Fichman and Kemerer (1997), we constructed an exhaustive list of 7 well-known OSS products consisting of Linux, BSD, Apache, Bind, Sendmail, Postfix and Samba. Respondents were instructed that the term OSSS referred to this specific list of OSS products.

The *size of the IT department (ITSIZE)* was measured by counting the number of employees within the IT department. Since examination of our data showed that this measure was skewed, the natural logarithm of this value was used in subsequent analyses.

The *IT intensity (ITINTENSITY)* was measured similar to Waarts, Everdingen, and Hillegersberg (2002) by dividing the number of servers by the size of the organization (measured by the number of employees). Since the measures for the number of

employees and the number of servers was skewed, the natural logarithm from both measures was taken before calculating the IT intensity measure.

The *prior experience with Unix (PRIORUNIX)* and *prior experience with Microsoft Windows (PRIORWINDOWS)* were each measured using a dichotomous variable, indicating whether the organization ever replaced a Unix or Microsoft Windows system, respectively, with Linux.

The *current use of Unix (USEUNIX)* and *current use of Microsoft Windows (USEWINDOWS)* were each measured using a dichotomous variable, indicating whether the organization made use of Unix or Microsoft Windows servers, respectively.

EMPIRICAL ANALYSIS

Given the nature of the dependent and independent variables, we decided to make use of logistic regression to analyze our data. Although logistic regression is relatively free of restrictions, we subjected our data to a careful screening process to check for the existence of univariate or multivariate outliers, and the presence of missing values. The Box-Tidwell transformation showed no issues with respect to linearity in the logit (Hosmer & Lemeshow, 2000; Tabachnick & Fidell, 2001). Multicollinearity was tested for by investigating the variance inflation factors (VIF). The maximum value was 2.23, which is well below the cut-off of 10 recommended in literature (Neter, Wasserman, & Kutner, 1990). These tests showed no issues with respect to our data set.

Use of External Knowledge Sources

We started our analysis by examining which factors impact the use of external knowledge sources by performing a series of logistic regressions in SPSS. To evaluate the significance of each independent variable, SPSS reports the results of the Wald test. However, the use of this statistic has been criticized in literature. It has been shown that the

Wald test sometimes results in too conservative estimates, which lead to increased chances of a Type II error (i.e., failing to find a relationship that actually exists) (Tabachnick & Fidell, 2001; Menard, 1997). Instead, it is recommended to evaluate the contribution of a variable by comparing the model fit of the full model to the model where the variable is removed from the model (Tabachnick & Fidell, 2001; Menard, 1997). The difference in the log-likelihood statistic reflects the contribution of each variable to the model. This result can be converted into a χ^2-statistic with 1 degree-of-freedom by using the following formula (Tabachnick & Fidell, 2001; Menard, 1997):

$$\chi^2 = 2 [\text{log-likelihood\_full\_model} - \text{log-likelihood\_model\_with\_variable\_removed}]$$

This method is computational intensive since it requires that each variable is consecutively removed from the model, but results in better estimates for the significance of the weights of the independent variables in the regression analysis (Tabachnick & Fidell, 2001; Menard, 1997). Therefore, we adopted the method described above to determine the significance of all weights. To this end, for each dependent variable, 10 logistic regressions were performed (1 with all variables included, 8 with one independent variable removed, and 1 without including the constant in the model). Hence, a total of 50 regression analyses were performed.

We performed 3 series of logistic regressions to see which independent variables had a significant impact on the use of a vendor, a service provider, or the OSS community. Table 1 shows that both *LINUX* and *PRIORUNIX* have a significant positive impact on the use of a vendor. The model fit was evaluated based on a number of statistics. First, the overall model evaluation using the commonly used χ^2 log-likelihood test indicates whether the set of predictors included in the model are good predictors for the outcome variable. As can be seen in Table 1 under "*overall model evaluation*", the

χ^2-value of the model is significant, which means that the model performs significantly better than a constant-only model. A second test that is more robust than—and preferred over—the traditional χ^2-test, is the *Hosmer and Lemeshow chi-square test of goodness of fit*, which tests whether the model fits the data at an acceptable level. As shown in Table 1, the Hosmer and Lemeshow χ^2-value is not significant, which leads us to accept the null hypothesis that the model provides an adequate fit. In addition, analogue statistics to R^2 have been proposed for logistic regression. It must, however, be noted that the R^2-values for logistic regression should not be interpreted as the percent of variance explained by the model, but rather as an approximation of it (Tabachnick & Fidell, 2001). A first statistic is the Cox and Snell R^2-statistic. The disadvantage of this measure is that it can never achieve a maximum value of 1, making it difficult to interpret. The Nagelkerke R^2 is based on the Cox and Snell value and ensures that values range between 0 and 1 by dividing the Cox and Snell R^2-value by the maximum possible R^2-value. These two R^2-statistics are reported in Table 1, and amount to .197 and .272 respectively, which suggests that the model performs rather well. Finally, the correct classification rate for the model is shown in Table 1. The correct classification rate for the constant-only model indicates the percentage of cases that would be correctly classified when all observations were assigned to the category with the most cases. It can be seen that the full model increases the correct classification rate with 3.9%, which is a modest improvement. Overall, it can be concluded that the model exhibits a good model fit.

The results for the use of a service provider are shown in Table 2. Two variables, *ITINTEN-SITY* and *PRIORWINDOWS*, were found to have a significant negative impact on the use of a service provider. The traditional χ^2-test indicates a rather poor model fit, although the Hosmer and Lemeshow test shows that the model fits the data at an acceptable level. Both R^2-values are some-

Table 1. Model statistics for the use of a vendor

Variable	Beta	Std.Err.	chi²	df	Sig		Exp(Beta)
ASSIMILATION	.209	.235	.804	1	.370		1.232
LINUX	.416	.214	4.162	1	.041	*	1.516
ITSIZE	.402	.287	2.052	1	.152		1.494
ITINTENSITY	-1.056	1.754	2.971	1	.085		.348
PRIORUNIX	1.100	.660	3.879	1	.049	*	3.003
PRIORWINDOWS	-.996	.767	3.483	1	.062		.369
USEUNIX	-.060	.626	.009	1	.924		.942
USEWINDOWS	1.851	1.227	2.809	1	.094		6.365
constant	-5.354	1.664	13.293	1	.000	***	.005
Model Evaluation			chi²	df	Sig		
Overall model evaluation			16.921	8	.031	*	
Hosmer and Lemeshow goodness of fit			8.029	8	.431		
Pseudo R² values							
Cox & Snell R²			.197				
Nagelkerke R²			.272				
Correct classification rate							
Constant only model			64.9%				
Full model			68.8%				

what lower than the previous model, but still show acceptable values. It can also be seen that the model offers a considerable increase by 14.3% in the correct classification rate. Therefore, we can conclude that the model offers a good fit.

Table 3 shows the results for the logistic regression investigating the use of the OSS community. Three variables, *ASSIMILATION, PRIORWINDOWS* and *USEWINDOWS*, were found to have a significant positive impact on the use of the OSS community. Both model evaluation tests showed that the model exhibited a good fit, and both R²-values were quite high compared to the previous two models. The full model also offers a correct classification rate of 82.7%, which is a considerable improvement over the constant-only model. Hence, this model showed very strong support in terms of model fit.

Use of Linux Distributions

Subsequently, we performed a similar analysis to investigate which independent variables have an impact on the use of a commercial or community Linux distribution. Hence, we performed two series of logistic regressions with as dependent variable the use of a commercial or community Linux distribution respectively.

The results for the use of a commercial Linux distribution are shown in Table 4. It showed that only *PRIORUNIX* has a significant positive influence. Model evaluation showed that the model exhibits a good fit with our data. The R²-values

Table 2. Model statistics for the use of a service provider

Variable	Beta	Std.Err.	chi²	df	Sig		Exp(Beta)
ASSIMILATION	.227	.226	1.020	1	.313		1.254
LINUX	.082	.184	.200	1	.655		1.085
ITSIZE	.073	.260	.080	1	.777		1.076
ITINTENSITY	-3.153	1.738	5.618	1	.018	*	.043
PRIORUNIX	.609	.574	3.150	1	.076		1.838
PRIORWINDOWS	-.501	.707	4.670	1	.031	*	.606
USEUNIX	.480	.563	.731	1	.393		1.616
USEWINDOWS	-.908	1.248	.581	1	.446		.403
constant	.607	1.587	.152	1	.697		1.835
Model Evaluation			chi²	df	Sig		
Overall model evaluation			12.753	8	.121		
Hosmer and Lemeshow goodness of fit			8.203	8	.414		
Pseudo R² values							
Cox & Snell R²			.153				
Nagelkerke R²			.204				
Correct classification rate							
Constant only model			54.5%				
Full model			68.8%				

also provide acceptable values. On the other hand, the increase in the correct classification rate is limited over the constant-only model, suggesting that the model offers relatively little insight into the data. Nevertheless, the correct classification rate of 75.9% is still very good. Therefore, we can conclude that this model provides a good fit with our data.

The results for the use of a community Linux distribution can be found in Table 5. Results showed that *ITINTENSITY* and *PRIORWINDOWS* had a significant positive impact on the use of a community Linux distribution. Model evaluation statistics showed that the model exhibited a good fit. The R²-values are also rather high, as well as the correct classification rate. The model also shows a considerable increase of 25.0% in the

correct classification rate over the constant-only model. Hence, this model also provides a good fit with our data.

Summary

A final overview of our results is presented in Table 6. It provides a synthesis of which relationships were found to be significant in the various logistic regression analyses. A positive or negative sign means the independent variable has a significant positive or negative impact on the dependent variable respectively. All significant relationships are also graphically presented in Figure 2.

Table 3. Model statistics for the use of the OSS community

Variable	Beta	Std.Err.	chi²	df	Sig		Exp(Beta)
ASSIMILATION	1.046	.409	9.594	1	.002	**	2.848
LINUX	.245	.295	.681	1	.409		1.278
ITSIZE	.566	.438	1.825	1	.177		1.760
ITINTENSITY	-2.708	2.478	3.097	1	.078		.067
PRIORUNIX	-1.459	1.064	3.655	1	.056		.233
PRIORWINDOWS	1.623	.891	3.965	1	.046	*	5.067
USEUNIX	1.576	.899	3.488	1	.062		4.837
USEWINDOWS	2.995	1.524	4.615	1	.032	*	19.990
constant	-8.076	2.396	16.631	1	.000	***	.000
Model Evaluation			chi²	df	Sig		
Overall model evaluation			50.352	8	.000	***	
Hosmer and Lemeshow goodness of fit			4.885	7	.674		
Pseudo R² values							
Cox & Snell R²			.489				
Nagelkerke R²			.657				
Correct classification rate							
Constant only model			57.3%				
Full model			82.7%				

DISCUSSION AND IMPLICATIONS

The aim of our exploratory study was to investigate whether the use of knowledge sources in the adoption of OSSS is influenced by various knowledge-related factors. The results of our statistical analysis have shown that some factors indeed have a significant effect on the use of the various knowledge sources. These results also provide interesting insights into the way organizations adopt OSSS. We will now discuss our results in more detail.

The use of vendor support was positively related to the extent of Linux adoption and previous experience with Linux. Organizations that exhibit a high extent of Linux diffusion were found to be more likely to be using vendor support. As the extent of Linux adoption increases in the organization, it is likely that the importance of Linux to the organization will increase as well, and that Linux will become more critical to the operation of the organization. In that case, the organization will require a reliable support contract as a kind of insurance. Such a support contract can be provided by vendors such as RedHat and SUSE (Ven et al., 2008; Morgan & Finnegan, 2007). In addition, organizations that have previous experience with Unix were found to be more likely to have a support contract in place. Organizations that migrate from Unix to Linux seem to request the same level of support for Linux as for Unix, possibly because these systems are used for mission-critical applications. In this respect, they

Table 4. Model statistics for the use of a commercial Linux distribution

Variable	Beta	Std.Err.	chi²	df	Sig		Exp(Beta)
ASSIMILATION	-.064	.280	.052	1	.820		.938
LINUX	.428	.229	3.780	1	.052		1.535
ITSIZE	.488	.356	2.043	1	.153		1.628
ITINTENSITY	.216	2.135	1.029	1	.310		1.241
PRIORUNIX	2.174	.803	13.511	1	.000	***	8.795
PRIORWINDOWS	-.030	.826	1.623	1	.203		.970
USEUNIX	-1.195	.729	2.853	1	.091		.303
USEWINDOWS	.388	1.436	.071	1	.790		1.475
constant	-2.103	1.777	1.324	1	.250		.122
Model Evaluation			chi²	df	Sig		
Overall model evaluation			21.299	8	.006	**	
Hosmer and Lemeshow goodness of fit			7.699	8	.463		
Pseudo R² values							
Cox & Snell R²			.236				
Nagelkerke R²			.345				
Correct classification rate							
Constant only model			73.4%				
Full model			75.9%				

exchange the Unix platform for Linux, but do not alter their attitude towards support considerably.

The use of a third party is negatively related to the IT intensity of the organization and the prior use of Microsoft Windows. Hence, organizations that make intensive use of IT were found to be less likely to make use of a third party in the adoption of OSSS. Organizations that are more IT intensive are more involved in IT, and may have a larger IT staff relative to their IT infrastructure. Given the importance of IT for their daily operation, such organizations may also prefer to be able to handle most tasks internally to avoid being dependent on an external party. This obviously reduces the need to rely on a service provider. It is also interesting to note that organizations that migrate from Microsoft Windows to Linux

are less likely to use a service provider. At first sight, this seems counter-intuitive since it could be expected that organizations with prior experience with Microsoft Windows would need to rely on a service provider in the initial stages, since they lack the internal knowledge on OSSS. Instead, our data suggests that such organizations rather prefer to rely on internal knowledge. Previous research has shown that the adoption of OSSS is frequently driven by boundary spanners (Ven & Verelst, 2008; Dedrick & West, 2003; Lundell, Lings, & Lindqvist, 2006). These are employees with knowledge on OSSS that was acquired outside the workplace. It therefore appears that these boundary spanners are able to provide the required expertise in organizations.

Table 5. Model statistics for the use of a community Linux distribution

Variable	Beta	Std.Err.	chi²	df	Sig		Exp(Beta)
ASSIMILATION	-.318	.274	1.444	1	.229		.728
LINUX	.309	.216	2.068	1	.150		1.362
ITSIZE	-.040	.354	.012	1	.913		.961
ITINTENSITY	1.522	2.076	3.904	1	.048	*	4.581
PRIORUNIX	-.160	.719	1.293	1	.255		.852
PRIORWINDOWS	3.492	.912	26.733	1	.000	***	32.857
USEUNIX	1.314	.721	3.708	1	.054		3.721
USEWINDOWS	1.755	1.239	2.060	1	.151		5.785
constant	-4.825	1.919	7.836	1	.005	**	.008
Model Evaluation			chi²	df	Sig		
Overall model evaluation			37.491	8	.000	***	
Hosmer and Lemeshow goodness of fit			11.733	8	.164		
Pseudo R² values							
Cox & Snell R²			.374				
Nagelkerke R²			.502				
Correct classification rate							
Constant only model			56.3%				
Full model			81.3%				

Table 6. Summary overview of results

		Vendor	Third party	OSS Community	Commercial Linux	Community Linux
Adoption of Linux	LINUX	+				
	ASSIMILATION			+		
IT department	ITSIZE					
	ITINTENSITY		-			+
Prior experience	PRIORUNIX	+			+	
	PRIORWINDOWS		-	+		+
Current use	USEUNIX					
	USEWINDOWS			+		
Legend: +/-: independent variable has positive/negative impact						

The use of the OSS community is positively related to the assimilation of OSSS, as well as the prior and current use of Microsoft Windows. The fact that the organizations that have progressed fur-ther in the assimilation of OSSS are more likely to make use of the OSS community seems to indicate that organizations have to learn how support from the OSS community can be effectively obtained,

Figure 2. Results of the empirical analysis

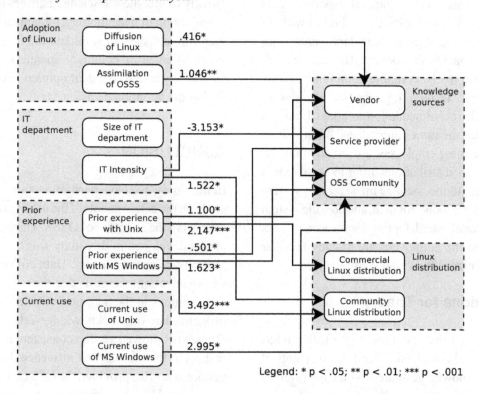

Legend: * p < .05; ** p < .01; *** p < .001

and that a certain learning process is required. This also suggests that the OSS community is not used to resolve minor issues related to the installation and configuration of OSS products that occur when the organization is starting to implement OSSS. It rather seems that the OSS community is used to resolve specific and complex technical issues. In those cases, only a few experts may be able to provide a reliable answer, and those experts can be found in the globally distributed OSS community. It is also remarkable that organizations with both prior and current experience with Microsoft Windows are more likely to make use of the OSS community, since Linux and Microsoft Windows are considered to be rather incompatible concerning the knowledge required by both (Dedrick & West, 2003; Ven & Verelst, 2006). This seems to further confirm the importance of boundary spanners in these organizations. Since boundary spanners will have assimilated OSS-related knowledge outside their work environment, they are already familiar with the way in which support can be obtained from the OSS community.

The use of a commercial Linux distribution is positively related to the prior use of Unix. Hence, organizations that have replaced Unix with Linux are more likely to make use of a commercial Linux distribution. This seems to further confirm the findings with respect to the use of vendor support. In addition, it suggests that organizations that migrate from Unix to Linux are not really concerned with savings in license fees that could possibly be realized by opting for a community Linux distribution. There are indeed indications that such migrations are primarily undertaken to lower the hardware costs (Ven et al., 2008; Ven & Verelst, 2006; Dedrick & West, 2003).

Interestingly, the use of a community Linux distribution is positively influenced by the IT intensity of the organization and the prior use of Microsoft Windows, which is opposite to the use of a third party. This further suggests that boundary spanners are important to provide the organization with some level of internal expertise. This allows them to use a Linux distribution without commercial support. Since boundary spanners are likely to try out OSSS products at home, they will resort to the freely available community Linux distributions. If their organization decides to follow their recommendation to adopt Linux, it is likely that the same Linux distribution will be used, since these employees are already familiar with it. Linux distributions differ to some extent with respect to the package management system being used, the tools provided, and how the system should be configured. Opting for the same Linux distribution the employees are already familiar with minimizes the overall learning effort.

Implications for Theory

The main contribution of this paper is that it has identified and examined several determinants of the use of knowledge sources in the adoption of OSSS. Previous research has investigated which factors influence the absorptive capacity of organizations, but has not considered which factors influence which knowledge sources can be used by organizations in this process. Nevertheless, this is a critical issue, since in order to develop absorptive capacity, the organization needs to be exposed to external knowledge sources. This study therefore addresses this gap in literature.

Implications for Practice

The results of this study may be useful to IS managers who consider adopting OSSS. Our results provide more insight into which external knowledge sources are used in the adoption of OSSS, depending on the organization's knowledge characteristics. The results can therefore help decision makers to take appropriate actions to further increase the organization's absorptive capacity. In addition, our results suggest that boundary spanners play an important role in this learning process. By having access to boundary spanners, organizations will be able to more

quickly overcome knowledge barriers related to the adoption of a technology. Organizations may therefore consider to stimulate the formation of informal roles of boundary spanners around a technology and to take their opinion into account during the adoption decision.

CONCLUSION

In this study, we have performed an exploratory study on the determinants of the use of knowledge sources in the adoption of OSSS. The conceptual model developed in this study was based on the absorptive capacity theory. Data collected from 95 organizations suggests that the use of knowledge sources in the adoption of OSSS is indeed influenced by various knowledge-related factors. Our results showed a rather consistent image with respect to the reasons that influence the use of a vendor, a service provider, the OSS community, a commercial Linux distribution, and a community Linux distribution. Our results not only provide more insight into which external knowledge sources are used by organizations; they also provide more insight into how OSSS is currently being adopted by organizations. Hence, we believe that investigating the use of knowledge sources by organizations may provide more insight into the context surrounding the adoption of innovations. Given the exploratory nature of this study, future studies could further build upon the results of this study to address some of its limitations. For example, this study was focused on the use of knowledge sources in the adoption of OSSS. Future studies could be performed in the context of the adoption of other technologies.

REFERENCES

Attewell, P. (1992). Technology diffusion and organizational learning: The case of business computing. *Organization Science*, *3*(1), 1–19. doi:10.1287/orsc.3.1.1

Cohen, W. M., & Levinthal, D. A. (1989). Innovation and learning: The two faces of R&D. *The Economic Journal*, *99*(397), 569–596. doi:10.2307/2233763

Cohen, W. M., & Levinthal, D. A. (1990). Absorptive capacity: A new perspective on learning and innovation. *Administrative Science Quarterly*, *35*(1), 128–152. doi:10.2307/2393553

Dedrick, J., & West, J. (2003). Why firms adopt open source platforms: A grounded theory of innovation and standards adoption. In J. L. King & K. Lyytinen (Eds.), *Proceedings of the workshop on standard making: A critical research frontier for information systems*, Seattle, WA (pp. 236-257).

Fichman, R. G. (2001). The role of aggregation in the measurement of IT-related organizational innovation. *Management Information Systems Quarterly*, *25*(4), 427–455. doi:10.2307/3250990

Fichman, R. G., & Kemerer, C. F. (1997). The assimilation of software process innovations: An organizational learning perspective. *Management Science*, *43*(10), 1345–1363. doi:10.1287/mnsc.43.10.1345

Fitzgerald, B. (2006). The transformation of open source software. *Management Information Systems Quarterly*, *30*(3), 587–598.

Fitzgerald, B., & Kenny, T. (2003). Open source software in the trenches: Lessons from a large scale implementation. In S. T. March, A. Massey, & J. I. DeGross (Eds.), *Proceedings of 24th international conference on information systems (ICIS 2003)*, Seattle, WA (pp. 316-326). Atlanta, GA: Association for Information Systems.

Hosmer, D. W., & Lemeshow, S. (2000). *Applied logistic regression* (2nd ed.). New York: Wiley. doi:10.1002/0471722146

Jansen, J. J. P., & Bosch, F. A. J., Van den, & Volberda, H. W. (2005). Managing potential and realized absorptive capacity: how do organizational antecedents matter? *Academy of Management Journal*, *48*(6), 999–1015.

Kim, L. (1998). Crisis construction and organizational learning: Capability building in catching-up at hyundai motor. *Organization Science*, *9*(4), 506–521. doi:10.1287/orsc.9.4.506

Lane, P. J., Koka, B. R., & Pathak, S. (2006). The reification of absorptive capacity: a critical review and rejuvenation of the construct. *Academy of Management Review*, *31*(4), 833–863.

Levitt, B., & March, J. G. (1988). Organizational learning. *Annual Review of Sociology*, *14*, 319–340. doi:10.1146/annurev.so.14.080188.001535

Li, Y., Tan, C.-H., Teo, H.-H., & Siow, A. (2005). A human capital perspective of organizational intention to adopt open source software. In D. Avison, D. Galletta, & J. I. DeGross (Eds.), *Proceeding of the 26th annual international conference on information systems (ICIS 2005)*, Las Vegas, NV (pp. 137-149). Atlanta, GA: Association for Information Systems.

Lundell, B., Lings, B., & Lindqvist, E. (2006). Perceptions and uptake of open source in Swedish organisations. In Damiani, E., Fitzgerald, B., Scacchi, W., Scotto, M., & Succi, G. (Eds.), *Open source systems, IFIP working group 2.13 foundation on open source software, Como, Italy* (Vol. 203, pp. 155–163). Boston: Springer.

Menard, S. W. (1997). *Applied logistic regression analysis* (No. 106, 2nd ed.). Thousand Oaks, CA: Sage Publications.

Morgan, L., & Finnegan, P. (2007). How perceptions of open source software influence adoption: An exploratory study. In H. Österle, J. Schelp, & R. Winter (Eds.), *Proceedings of the 15th european conference on information systems (ECIS 2007)*, St. Gallen, Switzerland (pp. 973-984). St. Gallen, Switzerland: University of St. Gallen.

Neter, J., Wasserman, W., & Kutner, M. H. (1990). *Applied linear statistical models: Regression, analysis of variance, and experimental designs* (3rd ed.). Homewood, IL: Irwin.

Tabachnick, B. G., & Fidell, L. S. (2001). Logistic regression. In Tabachnick, B. G., & Fidell, L. S. (Eds.), *Using multivariate statistics* (4th ed., pp. 517–581). Boston: Allyn and Bacon.

Teece, D. J., Pisano, G., & Shuen, A. (1997). Dynamic capabilities and strategic management. *Strategic Management Journal, 18*(7), 509–533. doi:10.1002/(SICI)1097-0266(199708)18:7<509::AID-SMJ882>3.0.CO;2-Z

Todorova, G., & Durisin, B. (2007). Absorptive capacity: Valuing a reconceptualization. *Academy of Management Review, 32*(3), 774–786.

Van Den Bosch, F. A. J., Volberda, H. W., & De Boer, M. (1999). Coevolution of firm absorptive capacity and knowledge environment: Organizational forms and combinative capabilities. *Organization Science, 10*(5), 551–568. doi:10.1287/orsc.10.5.551

Ven, K. (2008). The Organizational Adoption of Open Source Server Software: An Information Systems Innovation Perspective. Unpublished PhD dissertation, University of Antwerp, Antwerp, Belgium

Ven, K., & Verelst, J. (2006). The organizational adoption of open source server software by Belgian organizations. In Damiani, E., Fitzgerald, B., Scacchi, W., Scotto, M., & Succi, G. (Eds.), *Open source systems, IFIP working group 2.13 foundation on open source software, Como, Italy* (*Vol. 203*, pp. 111–122). Boston: Springer.

Ven, K., & Verelst, J. (2008). The organizational adoption of open source server software: A quantitative study. In W. Golden, T. Acton, K. Conboy, H. van der Heijden, & V. Tuunainen (Eds.), *Proceedings of the 16th European conference on information systems (ECIS 2008)*, Galway, Ireland (pp. 1430-1441).

Ven, K., Verelst, J., & Mannaert, H. (2008). Should you adopt open source software? *IEEE Software, 25*(3), 54–59. doi:10.1109/MS.2008.73

Waarts, E., Everdingen, Y. M. v., & van Hillegersberg, J. (2002). The dynamics of factors affecting the adoption of innovations. *Journal of Product Innovation Management, 19*(6), 412–423. doi:10.1016/S0737-6782(02)00175-3

Willis, G. B. (2005). *Cognitive interviewing: A tool for improving questionnaire design*. London: Sage Publications.

Zahra, S. A., & George, G. (2002). Absorptive capacity: a review, reconceptualization, and extension. *Academy of Management Review, 27*(2), 185–203. doi:10.2307/4134351

This work was previously published in International Journal of Technology Diffusion, Volume 1, Issue 4, edited by Ali Hussein Saleh Zolait, pp. 53-70, copyright 2010 by IGI Publishing (an imprint of IGI Global).

Compilation of References

ATP Track Research Report. (2005). *Talent Management: The State of the Art*: Towers Perrin HR Services.

Aarts, H., Verplanken, B., & Van Knippenberg, A. (1998). Predicting Behavior from Actions in Past: Repeated Decision Making or a Matter of Habit? *Journal of Applied Social Psychology*, *28*(15), 1355–1374. doi:10.1111/j.1559-1816.1998.tb01681.x

Ackermann, R., Schumacher, M., Roedig, U., & Steinmetz, R. (2001). Vulnerabilities and Security Limitations of Current IP Telephony Systems. In *Proceedings of the Conference on Communications and Multimedia Security* (pp. 53-66).

Adams, D. A., Nelson, R. R., & Todd, P. A. (1992). Perceived usefulness, ease of use and usage of information technology: A replication. *Management Information Systems Quarterly*, *16*(2), 227–247. doi:10.2307/249577

Adobor, H. (2004). Selecting management talent for joint ventures: A Suggested Framework. *Human Resource Management Review*, *14*, 161–178. doi:10.1016/j.hrmr.2004.05.001

Agrawal, D., Abbadi, A., Singh, A., & Yurek, T. (1997). Efficient View Maintenance at Data Warehouse. *SIGMOD Record*, *26*(2), 417–427. doi:10.1145/253262.253355

Aguayo, R. (1990). *Dr. Deming the American who taught the Japanese about quality*. New York: Lyle Stuart.

Ahmed, A. M., Zairi, M., & Alwabel, S. A. (2006). Global benchmarking for internet and e-commerce applications. *Benchmarking: an International Journal*, *13*(1/2), 68–80.. doi:10.1108/14635770610644583

Ahmed, A., Zairi, S., & Alwabel, S. (2006). Global benchmarking for Internet and e-commerce applications. *Benchmarking International Journal*, *13*(2), 68–80. doi:10.1108/14635770610644583

Ajzen, I. (1985). From intentions to actions: a theory of planned behavior. In Kuhi, J., & Beckmann, J. (Eds.), *Action-control: from cognition to behavior* (pp. 11–39). Heidelberg, Germany: Springer.

Ajzen, I. (1991). The theory of planned behavior. *Organizational Behavior and Human Decision Processes*, *50*(2), 179–211. doi:10.1016/0749-5978(91)90020-T

Ajzen, I., & Fishbein, M. (1973). Attitudinal and normative variables as predictors of specific behavior. *Journal of Personality and Social Psychology*, *27*, 41–57. doi:10.1037/h0034440

Akao, Y. (1990). *Quality function deployment: Integrating customer requirements in product design*. Cambridge, MA: Productivity Press.

Akao, Y. (1991). *Hoshin kanri: Policy deployment for successful TQM*. Cambridge, MA: Productivity Press.

Akther, M. S., Onishi, T., & Kidokoro, T. (2007). E-Government in a developing: Citizen-centric approach for success. *International Journal of Electronic Governance*, *1*(1). doi:10.1504/IJEG.2007.014342

Al Ismaily, S. (2004). *The Goals and A Progress Report*. DIGITAL OMAN.

Alder, G. S., Schminke, M., Noel, T. W., & Kuenzi, M. (2008). Employee Reactions to Internet Monitoring: The Moderating Role of Ethical Orientation. *Journal of Business Ethics*, *80*, 481–498. doi:10.1007/s10551-007-9432-2

Aldridge, A., White, M., & Forcht, K. (1997). Considerations of doing business via the internet: Cautions to be considered. *Internet Research: Electronic Networking Applications and Policy*, *7*(1), 9–15. doi:10.1108/10662249710159809

Al-Gahtani, S. S. (2001). The Applicability of TAM Outside North America: An Empirical test in the United Kingdom. *Information Resources Management Journal*, *14*(3), 37–46.

Alshawi, S., Irani, Z., & Baldwin, L. (2003). Benchmarking Information Technology Investment and Benefits Extraction. *Benchmarking*, *10*(4), 414–423. doi:10.1108/14635770310485015

Ambrose, P., & Johnson, G. (1998). A Trust Model of Buying Behavior in Electronic Retailing. In *Proceedings of the Association for Information Systems, Americans Conference*, Baltimore (pp. 263-265).

Ambrose, M.L., & Kulik, C.T. (1999). Old friends, new faces: Motivation research in the 1990s. *Journal of Management*, *25*, 231–292. doi:. doi:10.1177/014920639902500302

American Management Association. (2009). *Talent Management*. Retrieved November 5, 2009, from http://www.amanet.org/seminars/seminar.cfm?basesemno=8116

Amin, H. (2007). An analysis of mobile credit card usage intentions. *Information Management & Computer Security*, *15*(4), 260–269. doi:10.1108/09685220710817789

Amoako-Gyampah, K., & Salam, A. (2004). An extension of the technology acceptance model in an ERP implementation environment. *Information & Management*, *41*(6), 731–745. doi:10.1016/j.im.2003.08.010

Anckar, B., & D'Incau, D. (2002). Value creation in mobile commerce: Findings from a consumer survey. *Journal of Information Technology Theory and Application*, *4*(1), 43–64.

Anckar, B., & D'Incau, D. (2002). Value creation in mobile commerce: Findings from a consumer survey. *The Journal of Information Technology Theory and Application*, *4*(1), 43–64.

Anderson, G. L., Herr, K., Nihlen, A. S., & Noffke, S. E. (2007). *Studying your own school: An educator's guide to practitioner action research*. Thousand Oaks, CA: Corwin Press.

Anderson, A. A. (1996). Predictors of Computer Anxiety and Performance in Information Systems. *Computers in Human Behavior*, *12*(1), 61–77. doi:10.1016/0747-5632(95)00019-4

Anwar, S. T. (2002). DoCoMo and m-commerce: a case study in market expansion and global strategy. *Thunderbird International Business Review*, *44*(1), 139–164. doi:10.1002/tie.1043

Arauz, R., & Suzuki, H. (2004). ISO 9000 performance in Japanese industries. *Total Quality Management*, *15*(1), 3–33.

Armstrong, R. (2007), When and Why to Put What Data Where. Teradata Corporation White Paper, 1-5.

Artkinson, D. R. (2003). *Network government for the digital age*. Washington, DC: Progressive Police Institute.

Attewell, P. (1992). Technology diffusion and organizational learning: The case of business computing. *Organization Science*, *3*(1), 1–19. doi:10.1287/orsc.3.1.1

Bagozzi, R. P., & Yi, Y. (1988). On the Evaluation of Structural Equation Models. *Journal of the Academy of Marketing Science*, *16*(1), 74–94. doi:10.1007/BF02723327

Bailey, J. E., & Pearson, S. W. (1983). Development of a tool for measuring and analyzing computer user satisfaction. *Management Science*, *29*(5), 530–545. doi:10.1287/mnsc.29.5.530

Baldwin, E., & Curley, M. (2007). *Managing it innovation for business value: Practical strategies for it and business managers*. Intel Press.

Balsmeier, P. W., & Voisin, W. J. (1996). Supply Chain Management: A Time-based Strategy. *Industrial Management (Des Plaines)*, *38*(1), 24–27.

Balutis, A. P. (2001). E-government 2001, Part I: Understanding the challenge and evolving strategies. *Public Management*, *30*(1), 33–37.

Banâtre, J.-P., Fradet, P., & Radenac, Y. (2004). Chemical specification of autonomic systems. In *Proceedings of the 13th International Conference on Intelligent and Adaptive Systems and Software Engineering (IASSE'04)*.

Banâtre, J.-P., Fradet, P., & Radenac, Y. (2005a). Principles of chemical programming. In S. Abdennadher & C. Ringeissen (Eds.), *Proceedings of the 5th International Workshop on Rule-Based Programming (RULE'04)* (pp. 133-147).

Banâtre, J.-P., Fradet, P., & Radenac, Y. (2005b). Higher-order Chemical Programming Style. In *Proceedings of Unconventional Programming Paradigms* (LNCS 3566, pp. 84-98). Berlin: Springer Verlag.

Banatre, J.-P., & Le Metayer, D. (1990). The Gamma model and its discipline of programming. *Science of Computer Programming*, *15*, 55–77. doi:10.1016/0167-6423(90)90044-E

Banatre, J.-P., & Le Metayer, D. (1993). Programming by multiset transformation. *CACM*, *36*(1), 98–111.

Bandura, A. (1986). *Social Foundations of Thought and Action: A Social Cognitive Theory*. Upper Saddle River, NJ: Prentice-Hall.

Bannister, F., & Remenyi, D. (2000). Acts of Faith: Instinct, Value and IT Investment Decisions. *Journal of Information Technology*, *15*(3), 231–241. doi:10.1080/02683960050153183

Bannister, F., & Remenyi, D. (2005). Why IT Continues to Matter: Reflections on the Strategic Value of IT. *Electronic Journal Information Systems Evaluation*, *8*(3), 159–168.

Barnes, S. J. (2002). The mobile commerce value chain: Analysis and future developments. *International Journal of Information Management*, *22*(2), 91–108. doi:10.1016/S0268-4012(01)00047-0

Barrick, M. R., Parks, L., & Mount, M. K. (2005). Self-monitoring as a moderator of the relationships between personality traits and performance. *Personnel Psychology*, *58*(2), 745–767. doi:10.1111/j.1744-6570.2005.00716.x

Bassett-Jones, N. (1991). *Achieving Flexibility in Training*. Coventry: Coventry and Warwickshire Training and Enterprise Council.

Bauer, H. H., Reichardt, T., Barnes, S. J., & Neumann, M. M. (2005). Driving consumer acceptance of mobile marketing: A theoretical framework and empirical study. *Journal of Electronic Commerce Research*, *6*(3), 181–192.

Baumeister, R. F., Bratslavsky, E., Finkenauer, C., & Vohs, K. D. (2001). Bad is stronger than good. *Review of General Psychology*, *5*(4), 323–370. doi:10.1037/1089-2680.5.4.323

Beccalli, E. (2007). Does IT Investment Improve Bank Performance? Evidence from Europe. *Journal of Banking & Finance*, *31*(7), 2205–2230. doi:10.1016/j.jbankfin.2006.10.022

Becker, K. H., & Seidl, D. (2007). Different kinds of openings of Luhmann's Systems Theory: A reply to la Cour et al. *Organization*, *14*(6), 939–944. doi:10.1177/1350508407082268

Beckers, J. J., & Schmidt, H. G. (2001). The structure of computer anxiety: A six-factor model. *Computers in Human Behavior*, *17*(1), 35–49. doi:10.1016/S0747-5632(00)00036-4

Belcourt, M. (2002). *Managing human resources*. Scarborough, Ontario: Nelson Thompson Learning.

Bennet, A., & Bennet, D. (2000). Characterizing the Next Generation Knowledge Organization. Knowledge and Innovation. *Journal of the KMCI*, *1*(1), 8–42.

Berry, D., Towill, D. R., & Wadsley, N. (1994). Supply Chain Management in the Electronics Products Industry. *International Journal of Physical Distribution & Logistics Management*, *24*(10), 20–32. doi:10.1108/09600039410074773

Berry, G., & Boudol, G. (1992). The Chemical Abstract Machine. *Theoretical Computer Science*, *96*, 217–248. doi:10.1016/0304-3975(92)90185-I

Bertrand, V., Caplan, A., Fernandez-Moran, E., & Letelier, C. (2001). M-commerce: who will reap the profits? *Kellogg Tech Venture 2001 Anthology*.

Bertrand, V., Caplan, A., Fernandez-Moran, E., & Letelier, C. (2001). M-commerce: who will reap the profits? In *Kellogg Tech Venture 2001*. Anthology.

Beszedes, A. (2003). Survey of Code-Size Reduction Methods. *ACM Computing Surveys, 35*(3), 223–267. doi:10.1145/937503.937504

Bettencourt, L. A., & Ulwick, A. W. (2005). The customer centered innovation map. *Harvard Business Review, 86*(5), 109–114.

Bhasin, M. L. (2005). E-Commerce and M-Commerce Revolution: Perspectives, Problems and Prospects. *The Chartered Accountant*, 824-840.

Bhattacherjee, A. (2001). Understanding Information Systems Continuance: An Expectation-Confirmation Model. *Management Information Systems Quarterly, 25*(3), 351–370. doi:10.2307/3250921

Bhattacherjee, A., & Premkumar, G. (2004). Understanding Change in Belief and Attitude Toward Information Technology Usage: A theoretical Model and Longitudinal Test. *Management Information Systems Quarterly, 28*(2), 229–254.

Bhatti, M. A., & Kaur, S. (2009). Factors affecting the transfer of training: A modern approach. *In Proceedings of the 12ᵗʰ IBIMA Conference,* Kuala, Lumpur.

Birch, D. (1999). Mobile finance services: the Internet is not the only digital channel to consumers. *Journal of Internet Banking and Commerce, 4*(1), 20–29.

Birkinshaw, J., Morrison, A., & Hulland, J. (1995). Structural and competitive determinants of a global integration strategy. *Strategic Management Journal, 16*(8), 637–655. doi:10.1002/smj.4250160805

Bishop, M. (2002). *Computer Security: Art and Science.* Reading, MA: Addison-Wesley.

Booker, E. (2000). Protect online brand from unauthorized use. *B to B Chicago, 85*(18), 12-39.

Brady, M. K., Cronin, J. J., & Brand, R. R. (2002). Performance only measurement of service quality: A replication and intention. *Journal of Business Research, 55*, 17–31. doi:10.1016/S0148-2963(00)00171-5

Brosnan, M. J. (1998). The impact of computer anxiety and self-efficacy upon performance. *Journal of Computer Assisted Learning, 14*, 223–234. doi:10.1046/j.1365-2729.1998.143059.x

Brown, F., Divietri, J., Diaz, G., & Fernandez, E. (1999). The Authenticator Pattern. In *Proceedings of PLoP.*

Brown, W. A., & Yoshioka, C. F. (2003). Mission Attachment and Satisfaction as Factors in Employee Retention. *Nonprofit Management & Leadership, 14*(1), 5–18. doi:10.1002/nml.18

Brynjolfsson, E. (1993). The Productivity Paradox of Information Technology. *Communications of the ACM, 36*(12), 67–77. doi:10.1145/163298.163309

Brynjolfsson, E., & Hitt, L. M. (1996). Paradox Lost? Firm-level Evidence on the Returns to Information Systems Spending. *Management Science, 42*(4), 541–558. doi:10.1287/mnsc.42.4.541

Brynjolfsson, E., & Hitt, L. M. (1998). Beyond the Productivity Paradox. *Communications of the ACM, 41*(8), 49–55. doi:10.1145/280324.280332

Brynjolfsson, E., & Hitt, L. M. (2000). Beyond Computation: Information Technology, Organizational Transformation and Business Performance. *The Journal of Economic Perspectives, 14*(4), 23–48.

Brynjolfsson, E., & Hitt, L. M. (2003). Computing Productivity: Firm-Level Evidence. *The Review of Economics and Statistics, 85*(4), 793–808. doi:10.1162/003465303772815736

Brynjolfsson, E., & Yang, S. (1996). Information Technology and Productivity: A Review of the Literature. *Advances in Computers, 43*, 179–214. doi:10.1016/S0065-2458(08)60644-0

Burden, R. L., & Fairs, J. D. (2001). *Numerical Analysis* (7th ed.). Pacific Grove, CA: Brooks/Cole.

Bynner, W. (1944). *The way of life: According to Lao Tzu.* New York: Capricorn Books.

Byrd, T. A., Lewis, B. R., & Bryan, R. W. (2006). The Leveraging Influence of Strategic Alignment on IT Investment: An Empirical Examination. *Information & Management, 43*(3), 308–321. doi:10.1016/j.im.2005.07.002

Cabri., et al. (2000). Mobile-Agent Coordination Models for Internet Applications. *Computer.* Retrieved from http://dlib.computer.org/co/books/co2000/pdf/r2082.pdf

Canadian International Development Agency. (2007). *Knowledge-Sharing Plan.* Retrieved February 2009 from http://www.acdi-cida.gc.ca/CIDAWEB/acdicida.nsf/En/EMA-218122154-PR4

Cappelli, P. (2008). Talent Management for the Twenty-First Century. *Harvard Business Review*, 1–9.

Carey, M. J., Jauhari, R., & Livny, M. (1989), Priority in DBMS Resource Scheduling, In Proceedings of the 15th international conference on Very Large Data Bases, Amsterdam, The Netherlands (pp. 397 – 410).

Carlson, D. S., Upton, N., & Seaman, S. (2006). The impact of human resource practices and compensation design on performance: An analysis of family-owned SMEs. *Journal of Small Business Management*, *44*, 531–543. doi:10.1111/j.1540-627X.2006.00188.x

Carriero, N., & Gelernter, D. (1989). Linda in context. *CACM*, *32*(4), 444–458.

Carr, N. G. (2003). IT Doesn't Matter. *Harvard Business Review*, *81*(5), 41–49.

Carroll, S. J., Paine, F. T., & Ivancevich, J. J. (1972). The relative effectiveness of training methods. *Personnel Psychology*, *25*(4), 495–509. doi:10.1111/j.1744-6570.1972.tb00833.x

Carter, L., & Belanger, F. (2004). *Citizen adoption of electronic government initiatives*. Paper presented at the 37th Hawaii International Conference on System Sciences.

Catalan, M., & Kotzab, H. (2003). Assessing the responsiveness in the Danish mobile phone supply chain. *International Journal of Physical Distribution & Logistics Management*, *33*(8), 668–695. doi:10.1108/09600030310502867

Chaffey, D. (2007). *E-Business and E-Commerce Management* (p. 4). Upper Saddle River, NJ: Prentice Hall.

Chan, O. J. (2005). Enterprise information systems strategy and planning. *The Journal of American Academy of Business, 2*.

Chandy, K. M., & Misra, J. (1988). *Parallel Program Design: A Foundation*. Reading, MA: Addison-Wesley.

Chang, F. C. (2006). Inverse of a perturbed matrix. *Applied Mathematics Letters*, *19*, 169–173. doi:10.1016/j.aml.2005.04.004

Chan, S., & Lu, M. (2004). Understanding Internet banking adoption and use behaviour: A Hong Kong perspective. *Journal of Global Information Management*, *12*(3), 21–43.

Chao, C. (2004). Incremental Maintenance of Object Oriented Data Warehouse. *Information Sciences*, *1*(4), 91–110. doi:10.1016/j.ins.2003.07.014

Chaudhuri, S., & Dayal, U. (1997). An Overview of Data Warehousing and OLAP Technology. *SIGMOD Record*, *26*(1). doi:10.1145/248603.248616

Chen, K. K., Chen, M. Y., et al. (2007). *Constructing a Web-based Employee Training Expert System with Data Mining Approach*. Paper presented at the 9th IEEE International Conference on E-Commerce Technology and the 4th IEEE International Conference on Enterprise Computing, E-Commerce and E-Services (CEC-EEE 2007).

Chen, A., Sena, S., & Shaoa, B. (2006). Strategies for effective Web services adoption for dynamic e-businesses. *Decision Support Systems*, *42*(2), 789–809. doi:10.1016/j.dss.2005.05.011

Chen, Y., & Zhu, J. (2004). Measuring Information Technology's Indirect Impact on Firm Performance. *Information Technology and Management*, *5*(1-2), 9–22. doi:10.1023/B:ITEM.0000008075.43543.97

Chien, C. F., & Chen, L. F. (2007). Using Rough Set Theory to Recruit and Retain High-Potential Talents for Semiconductor Manufacturing. *IEEE Transactions on Semiconductor Manufacturing*, *20*(4), 528–541. doi:10.1109/TSM.2007.907630

Chien, C. F., & Chen, L. F. (2008). Data mining to improve personnel selection and enhance human capital: A case study in high-technology industry. *Expert Systems with Applications*, *34*(1), 380–290. doi:10.1016/j.eswa.2006.09.003

Chirkova, R., Li, C., & Li, J. (2006). Answering Queries using Materialized Views with Minimum Size. *The VLDB Journal*, *15*(3), 191–210. doi:10.1007/s00778-005-0162-8

Choi, T. Y., & Hong, Y. (2002). Unveiling the structure of supply networks: case study in Honda, Acura, and DaimlerChrysler. *Journal of Operations Management, 20*(5), 469–493. doi:10.1016/S0272-6963(02)00025-6

Chou, J., & Tsai, H. (2009). On-line learning performance and computer anxiety measure for unemployed adult novices using a grey relation entropy method. *Information Processing & Management, 45*(2), 200–215. doi:10.1016/j.ipm.2008.12.001

Christopher, M., & Peck, H. (1997). Managing logistics in fashion markets. *The International Journal of Logistics Management, 8*(2), 63–73. doi:10.1108/09574099710805673

Chua, S. L., Chen, D., & Wong, A. F. L. (1999). Computer anxiety and its correlates: A meta-analysis. *Computers in Human Behavior, 75*, 609–623. doi:10.1016/S0747-5632(99)00039-4

Chute, A., Melody, T., & Hancock, B. (1999). *The mcgraw-hill handbook of distance learning.* New York: McGraw-Hill.

Ciampa, M. (2005). *Security+ Guide to network security fundamentals* (2nd ed.). Boston: Course Technology.

Cohen, D., & Muylaert-Filho, J. (1996). Introducing a calculus for higher-order multiset programming. In *Coordination Languages and Models* (LNCS 1061, pp. 124-141).

Cohen, W. M., & Levinthal, D. A. (1989). Innovation and learning: The two faces of R&D. *The Economic Journal, 99*(397), 569–596. doi:10.2307/2233763

Cohen, W. M., & Levinthal, D. A. (1990). Absorptive capacity: A new perspective on learning and innovation. *Administrative Science Quarterly, 35*(1), 128–152. doi:10.2307/2393553

Collins, J., & Millen, R. (1995). Information systems outsourcing by large American industrial firms: Choices and impacts. *Information Resources Management Journal, 8*(1), 5–13.

Compeau, D. R., & Higgins, C. A. (1995). Computer self-efficacy: development of a measure and initial test. *Management Information Systems Quarterly, 19*(2), 189–211. doi:10.2307/249688

Cook, C. W., & Hunsaker, P. L. (2001). *Management and organisational behaviour.* New York: McGraw-Hill.

Cook, R. E., & Scott, W. R. (2000). *The quality movement & organizational theory.* Thousand Oaks, CA: Sage.

Cooper, (2000). Data Warehousing Supports Corporate Strategy at First American Corporation. *Management Information Systems Quarterly, 24*(4), 547–567. doi:10.2307/3250947

Cooper, C. L., & Dewe, P. J. (2004). *Stress: A Brief History.* Oxford, UK: Blackwell. doi:10.1002/9780470774755

Coursaris, C., Hassanein, K., & Head, M. (2003). M-commerce in Canada: an interaction framework for wireless privacy. *Canadian Journal of Administrative Sciences, 20*(1), 54–73.

Craig, R. L. (1996). *The ASTD training and development handbook, a guide to human resource development.* New York: McGraw-Hill.

Crawford, R. (1991). *In the era of human capital.* New York: HarperBusiness.

Credit Union League and CUNA and Affiliates. (1994). *Total Quality Management.* Dubuque, IA: Kendall/Hunt Publishing.

Creveuil, C. (1991). Implementation of Gamma on the Connection Machine. In *Proceedings of the Workshop on Research Directions in High-Level Parallel Programming Languages,* Mont-Saint Michel (LNCS 574, pp. 219-230). Berlin: Springer Verlag.

Cronk, M. C., & Fitzgerald, E. P. (1999). Understanding IS Business Value: Derivation of Dimensions. *Logistics Information Management, 12*(1/2), 40–49. doi:10.1108/09576059910256240

Cross, M. (2001). Set strategy before selecting a web site host. *Internet Health Care Magazine,* 42-43.

Cross, M. A. (2001). Set strategy before selecting a web site host. *Internet Health Care Magazine,* 42-43.

Csikszentmihalyi, M. (1993). *The evolving self.* New York: Harper Perennial.

Cubbingham, I. (2007). Talent Management: Making it real. *Development and Learning in Organizations, 21*(2), 4–6. doi:10.1108/14777280710727307

Cummings, L., & Bromiley, P. (1996). The Organizational Trust Inventory (OTI): Development and Validation. In Kramer, R. M., & Tyler, T. R. (Eds.), *Trust in Organizations: Frontiers of Theory and Research* (pp. 220–302). Thousand Oaks, CA: Sage Publications.

Cunningham, D. C. (2001). The distribution and extent of agrifood chain management research in the public domain. *Supply Chain Management, 6*(5), 212–215. doi:10.1108/EUM0000000006040

Curran, J., & Stanworth, J. (1989). Education and training for enterprise: Some problems of classification, evaluation, policy and research. *International Small Business Journal, 7*(2), 11–22. doi:10.1177/026624268900700201

Curtis, G. A., Melnicoff, R. M., & Mesoy, T. (2003). Value Discovery: A Better Way to Prioritize IT Investments. *Accenture Outlook Journal*.

Daley, D. M. (1986). Humanistic Management and Organizational Success: The Effect of Job and Work Environment Characteristics on Organizational Effectiveness, Public Responsiveness, and Job Satisfaction. *Public Personnel Management, 15*(2), 131–142.

Danziger, J., & Dunkle, D. (2005). Information Technology and Worker satisfaction. *Centre for Research on Information Technology and Organisations,* 1-12. Retrieved June 14, 2008, from www.repositories.cdlib.org

Dapiran, P. (1992). Benetton – global logistics in action. *International Journal of Physical Distribution & Logistics Management, 22*(6), 7–11. doi:10.1108/EUM0000000000416

Dardan, S., Stylianou, A., & Kumar, R. (2006/2007). The Impact of Customer-Related IT Investments on Customer Satisfaction and Shareholder Returns. *Journal of Computer Information Systems, 47*(2), 100–111.

Davis, F. (1986). *A technology acceptance model for empirically testing new end-user information systems: theory and results.* Unpublished doctoral dissertation, Sloan School of Management, Massachusetts Institute of Technology, Cambridge, MA.

Davis, F. (1989). Perceived usefulness, perceived ease of use, and end user acceptance of information technology. *Management Information Systems Quarterly, 13*(3), 318–339. doi:10.2307/249008

Davis, F. A. (1989). Perceived Usefulness, Perceived Ease of Use, and User Acceptance of Information Technology. *Management Information Systems Quarterly, 13*, 319–339. doi:10.2307/249008

Davis, F. D., Bagozzi, R. P., & Warshaw, P. R. (1992). Extrinsic and intrinsic motivation to use computers in the workplace. *Journal of Applied Social Psychology, 22*(1), 1111–1132. doi:10.1111/j.1559-1816.1992.tb00945.x

Davision, M. R., Wagner, C., & Ma, C. K. L. (2005). From government to e-government: A transition model. *Information Technology & People, 18*(3), 280–299. doi:10.1108/09593840510615888

Dawes, S. S. (2002). *The future of e-government.* Retrieved March 20, 2009, from http://www.vinnova.se/upload/EPiStorePDF/vri-06-11.pdf

Dawson, R. (2005, May). *Leadership in Professiona services* (2nd ed., p. 416). Oxford, UK: Butterworth Heinemann Publications.

Dayal, U., Kuno, H., Wiener, J.L., Wilkinson, K., Ganapathi, A. & Krompass, S. (2009), Managing Operational Business Intelligence Workloads. ACM SIGOPS Operating Systems Review archive, 43 (1), 92-98.

Dearstyne, D. (2001). E-business, e-government & information proficiency. *Information Management Journal, 35*(4), 16–24.

DeCenZo. D. A., & Robbins, S. P. (2005). *Fundamentals of Human Resource Management* (8th ed.). New York: John Wiley & Sons Inc.

Dedrick, J., & West, J. (2003). Why firms adopt open source platforms: A grounded theory of innovation and standards adoption. In J. L. King & K. Lyytinen (Eds.), *Proceedings of the workshop on standard making: A critical research frontier for information systems,* Seattle, WA (pp. 236-257).

Dedrick, J., Gurbaxani, V., & Kraemer, K. L. (2003). Information Technology and Economic Performance: A Critical Review of the Empirical Evidence. *ACM Computing Surveys, 35*(1), 1–28. doi:10.1145/641865.641866

Deming, W. E. (1986). *Out of the Crisis.* Cambridge, MA: MIT CAE.

Demirhan, D. (2005). Factors Affecting Investment in IT: A Critical Review. *Journal of Information Technology Theory and Application, 6*(4), 1–13.

DeNisi, A. S., & Griffin, R. W. (2005). *Human Resource Management.* New York: Houghton Mifflin Company.

Dey, D., Zhang, Z., & De, P. (2006). Optimal Synchronization Policies for Data Warehouse. *Information Journal on Computing, 18*(2), 229–242.

DeZoysa, S. (2001). *Who do you trust? Should banks or mobile operators be entrusted with m-commerce security?* Retrieved January 20, 2005, from http://www.telecommagazine.com/default.asp?journalid=2&func=articles&page=0112i13&year=2001&month=12

Dhillon, G. (2000). Interpreting Key Issues in IS/IT Benefits Management. In *Proceedings of the 33rd Annual Hawaii International Conference on System Sciences,* Maui, Hawaii (Vol. 7, pp. 7036).

Dhillon, G. (2006). *Principles of information systems security: Texts and Cases* (1st ed.). Hoboken, NJ: Wiley.

Dholakia, R. R., & Dholakia, N. (2004). Mobility and markets: emerging outlines of m-commerce. *Journal of Business Research, 57,* 1391–1396. doi:10.1016/S0148-2963(02)00427-7

Diamond, J. (1999). *Guns, germs, and steel: The fates of human societies.* New York: W. W. Norton.

Diamond, J. (2005). *Collapse: How societies choose to fail or succeed.* New York: Penguin Books.

Digital Society. (2002). *Executive summary.* Muscat, Oman: Government of Oman.

Dishaw, M. T., & Strong, D. M. (1999). Extending the technology acceptance model with task–technology fit constructs. *Information & Management, 36*(1), 9–21. doi:10.1016/S0378-7206(98)00101-3

Dongarra, J. J., & Eijkhout, V. (2000). Numerical linear algebra algorithms and software. *Journal of Computational and Applied Mathematics, 123,* 489–514. doi:10.1016/S0377-0427(00)00400-3

Dos Santos, B., & Sussman, L. (2000). Improving the Return on IT Investment: The Productivity Paradox. *International Journal of Information Management, 20*(6), 429–440. doi:10.1016/S0268-4012(00)00037-2

Doyle, S. (2000). Software review: Using short messaging services as a marketing tool. *Journal of Database Marketing, 8*(3), 273–277. doi:10.1057/palgrave.jdm.3240043

Dreher, G. F. (1980). Individual Needs as Correlates of Satisfaction and Involvement with a Modified Scanlon Plan Company. *Journal of Vocational Behavior, 17*(1), 80–94. doi:10.1016/0001-8791(80)90018-4

Drennan, J., & McColl-Kennedy, J. (2003). The relationship between internet use and perceived performance in retail and professional service firms. *Journal of Services Marketing, 17*(3), 295–311. doi:10.1108/08876040310474837

Driscoll, M. (1999, April). Web-based training in the workplace. *Adult Learning, 10,* 21–25.

Drucker, P. F. (2007). *People and performance.* Boston: Harvard Business School Press.

Dul, J., & Hak, T. (2007). *Case study methodology in business research.* Oxford, UK: Butterworth-Heinemann.

Dung, X. T., Rahayu, W., & Taniar, D. (2007). A high performance integrated web data warehousing. *Cluster Computing, 10,* 95–109. doi:10.1007/s10586-007-0008-9

Durand, R., & Calori, R. (2006). Sameness, otherness? Enriching organizational change theories with philosophical considerations on the same and the other. *Academy of Management Review, 31*(1), 93–114.

Durant, W., & Durant, A. (1968). *The lessons of history.* New York: Simon and Schuster.

Dutta, R., Jarvenpaa, S., & Tomak, K. P. (2003). *Impact of feedback and usability of online payment processes on consumer decision making.* Paper presented at the Proceedings of the 24th International conference on Information Systems, Seattle, WA.

Ebrahim, Z., & Irani, Z. (2005). E-government adoption: architecture and barriers. *Business Process Management Journal, 11*(5), 589–611. doi:10.1108/14637150510619902

Ehrlick, C. (2006). The EFQM-model and work motivation. *Total Quality Management, 17*(2), 131–140.

Ejaz, A., & Kenneth, R. (2004), Utilizing Staging Tables in Data Integration to Load Data into Materialized Views. In Proceedings of the First International Symposium on Computational and Information Science (CIS'04), Shanghai, China, (pp. 685-691).

Elasmar, M., & Carter, M. (1996). Use of e-mail by College Students and Implications for Curriculum. *Journal of Mass Communications Education, 52*(2), 46–54.

Elmuti, D. (2002). The Perceived impact of Supply Chain Management on Organizational Effectiveness. *Journal of Supply Chain Management, 38*(3), 49–57. doi:10.1111/j.1745-493X.2002.tb00135.x

Elnaffar, S. S. (2002), A methodology for auto-recognizing DBMS workloads. In Proceedings of the 2002 conference of the Centre for Advanced Studies on Collaborative research, Toronto, Ontario, Canada.

El-Nawawy, M. A., & Ismail, M. M. (1999). Overcoming Deterrents and Impediments to e-commerce in Light of Globalization: The Case of Egypt. In proceedings of INET99, June 22-25, San Jose, California.

Epstein, M. J., & Buhovac, A. R. (2006). What's in IT for You (and Your Company)? *Journal of Accountancy, 201*(4), 69–75.

Essex, D. (1999). Big dreams for tiny money. *Computerworld, 33*(50), 66.

European Commission Regional Policy – Inforegio. (n.d.). Retrieved July 13, 2009 from http://ec.europa.eu/regional_policy/policy/object/index_en.htm

European Commission. (2003). *Linking-up Europe: The importance of interoperability for e-Government services.* Retrieved July 20, 2009, from http://europa.eu.int/ISPO/ida/

Evans, P., & Wurster, T. (1997). Strategy and the new economics of information. *Harvard Business Review, 9*(10), 71–82.

Evermann, J. (2008). An Exploratory Study of Database Integration Processes. *IEEE Transactions on Knowledge and Data Engineering, 20*(1). doi:10.1109/TKDE.2007.190675

ExecutiveBrief. (2008). *12 Competencies: Which Ones Should Your People Have.* Retrieved November 13, 2008, from http://www.executivebrief.com

Falah, K. A., Zairi, M., & Ahmed, A. M. (2003). The role of supply-chain management in world-class manufacturing-An empirical study in the Saudi context. *International Journal of Physical Distribution & Logistics Management, 33*(5), 396–407. doi:10.1108/09600030310481979

Fan, H., & Poulovassilis, A. (2003), Using AutoMed Metadata in Data Warehousing Environments. In Proceedings of the 6th ACM international workshop on Data warehousing and OLAP, New Orleans, Louisiana, USA, 86 - 93.

Farbey, B., Land, F., & Targett, D. (1992). Evaluating Investments in IT. *Journal of Information Technology, 7*(2), 109–122. doi:10.1057/jit.1992.16

Farooq, A., & Hamid, K. (2010). An efficient and simple algorithm for matrix inversion. *International Journal of Technology Diffusion, 1*(1), 20–27.

Fearon, C., & Philip, G. (1999). An Empirical Study of the Use of EDI in Supermarket Chains Using a New Conceptual Framework. *Journal of Information Technology, 14*(1), 3–21. doi:10.1080/026839699344719

Fernie, J. (1995). International comparison of supply chain management in grocery retailing. *The Service Industries Journal, 15*(4), 134–147. doi:10.1080/02642069500000053

Fichman, R. G. (2001). The role of aggregation in the measurement of IT-related organizational innovation. *Management Information Systems Quarterly*, 25(4), 427–455. doi:10.2307/3250990

Fichman, R. G., & Kemerer, C. F. (1997). The assimilation of software process innovations: An organizational learning perspective. *Management Science*, 43(10), 1345–1363. doi:10.1287/mnsc.43.10.1345

Field, J. M., & Meile, L. C. (2008). Supplier relations and supply chain performance in financial services processes. *International Journal of Operations & Production Management*, 28(2), 185–206. doi:10.1108/01443570810846892

Figge, S. (2004). Situation-dependent services - a challenges for mobile network operators. *Journal of Business Research*, 57(12), 1416–1422. doi:10.1016/S0148-2963(02)00431-9

Fill, J., & Fishkind, D. E. (1997). Moore-Penrose generalized inverse for sums of matrix. *Annual Mathematical Statistics, 18*.

Firestone, J. M. (2001, April 15). Key issues in Knowledge Management. Knowledge and Innovation. *Journal of the KMCI, 1*(3).

Fishbein, M., & Ajzen, I. (1980). *Understanding Attitudes and Predicting Social Behavior*. Upper Saddle River, NJ: Prentice-Hall.

Fishbein, M., & Ajzen, I. (1975). *Belief, Attitude, Intention and Behavior: An Introduction to Theory and Research*. Reading, MA: Addison-Wesley Publishing Company.

Fitzgerald, B., & Kenny, T. (2003). Open source software in the trenches: Lessons from a large scale implementation. In S. T. March, A. Massey, & J. I. DeGross (Eds.), *Proceedings of 24th international conference on information systems (ICIS 2003),* Seattle, WA (pp. 316-326). Atlanta, GA: Association for Information Systems.

Fitzgerald, B. (2006). The transformation of open source software. *Management Information Systems Quarterly*, 30(3), 587–598.

Fitzgerald, G. (1998). Evaluating Information Systems Projects: A Multidimensional Approach. *Journal of Information Technology*, 13(1), 15–27. doi:10.1080/026839698344936

Følstad, A. (2008). Living Labs for Innovation and Development of Information and Communication Technology: A Literature Review. *The Electronic Journal for Virtual Organizations and Networks, 10*, 100–131.

Forcht, K. A., & Fore, R. E. (1995). Security issues and concern with the Internet. *Internet Research: Electronic Networking Applications and Policy of MCB*, 5(3), 23–31. doi:10.1108/10662249510104621

Forcht, K., & Richard, E. (1995). Security issues and concern with the internet. *Internet Research: Electronic Networking Applications and Policy of MCB*, 5(3), 23–31. doi:10.1108/10662249510104621

Forde, C., Slater, G., & Spencer, D. A. (2006). Faring the worst? Threat, participation and workplace productivity. *Economic and Industrial Democracy*, 27(3), 369–398. doi:10.1177/0143831X06065961

Fornell, C., & Larcker, D. (1981). Evaluating Structural Equation Models with Unobservable Variables and Measurement Error. *Management Science*, 40(4), 440–465.

Forslund, H., & Jonsson, P. (2007). The impact of forecast information quality on supply chain performance. *International Journal of Operations & Production Management*, 27(1), 90–107. doi:10.1108/01443570710714556

Fox, M. L. (1991). Logistics Planning: The Supply Chain as an Integrated Enterprise. *Production and Inventory Management*, 11(7), 12–15.

Fradet, P., & Le Metayer, D. (1998). Structured Gamma. *Science of Computer Programming*, 31(2-3), 263–289. doi:10.1016/S0167-6423(97)00023-3

Francalanci, C., & Galal, H. (1998). Information technology and worker composition: Determinants of productivity in the life insurance industry. *Management Information Systems Quarterly*, 22(2), 227–241. doi:10.2307/249396

Freedman, R. (2003). Helping Clients Value IT investments. *Consulting to Management*, 14(3), 33–39.

French, W., & Bell, C. (1999). *Organization development-Behavioral science interventions for organization improvement*. Upper Saddle River, NJ: Prentice-Hall.

Funk, J. L. (2006). The future of mobile phone-based Intranet applications: a view from Japan. *Technovation, 26*, 1337–1346. doi:10.1016/j.technovation.2005.08.009

Furlow, G. (2001), The Case for Building a Data Warehouse. IT Professional, 3(4,), 31-34.

Fynes, B., Voss, C., & Burca, S. d. (2005). The impact of supply chain relationship dynamics on manufacturing performance. *International Journal of Operations & Production Management, 25*(1), 6–19. doi:10.1108/01443570510572213

Gable, G. (1994). Integrating Case Study and Survey Research Methods: an Example in Information Systems. *European Journal of Information Systems, 3*(2), 112–126. doi:10.1057/ejis.1994.12

Galvin, T. (2001). *Industry Report 2001*. Retrieved from http://www.eric.ed.gov/ERIC-WebPortal/custom/portlets/recordDetails/detailmini.jsp?_nfpb=true&_&ERICExtSearch_SearchType_o=no&accno=EJ632065

Ganguly, S., Hasan, W., & Krishnamurthy, R. (1992), Query Optimization for Parallel Execution. In Proceedings of the 1992 ACM SIGMOD international conference on Management of data, San Diego, California, United States, 9 - 18.

García-García, J., & Ordonez, C. (2010). Extended aggregations for databases with referential integrity issues. *Data & Knowledge Engineering, 69*, 73–95. doi:10.1016/j.datak.2009.08.008

Gardner, S. R. (1998). Building the Data Warehouse. *Communications of the ACM, 41*(9). doi:10.1145/285070.285080

Garfinkel, S., & Spafford, G. (1997). *Web security & commerce* (1st ed.). New York: O'Reilly & Associates, Inc.

Garson, D. (2008). *Scales and standard measures*. Retrieved July 18, 2008, from http://www2.chass.ncsu.edu/garson/pa765/standard.htm

Garson, G. D. (2007a). *Multiple Regression*. Retrieved November 28, 2007, from http://www2.chass.ncsu.edu/garson/PA765/ Multiple Regression

Gebauer, J., Shaw, M. J., & Gribbins, M. L. (2006). *Task-Technology Fit for mobile information systems*. Retrieved July 15, 2008, from http://www.business.uiuc.edu/

Gebauer, J., & Shaw, M. J. (2004). Success factors and impacts of mobile business applications: results from a mobile e-procurement study. *International Journal of Electronic Commerce, 8*(3), 19–41.

Gefen, D. (2003). TAM or just plain habit: a look at experienced online shoppers. *Journal of End User Computing, 15*(3), 1–13.

Gefen, D., Karahanna, E., & Straub, D. W. (2003). Trust and TAM in online shopping: An integrated model. *Management Information Systems Quarterly, 27*(1), 51–90.

Gefen, D., & Straub, D. (1997). Gender differences in the perception and use of e-mail: An extension to the technology acceptance model. *Management Information Systems Quarterly, 21*(4), 389–400. doi:10.2307/249720

Gefen, D., Straub, D., & Boudreau, M. (2000). Structural Equation Modeling and Regression: Guidelines for Research Practice. *Communications of the Association for Information Systems, 4*(7), 1–70.

Georgieva, T. (2008). Discovering Branching and Fractional Dependencies in Databases. *Data & Knowledge Engineering, 66*, 311–325. doi:10.1016/j.datak.2008.04.002

Ghazal, A., Seid, D., Bhashyam, R., Crolotte, A., Koppuravuri, M., & Vinod, G. (2009), Dynamic Plan Generation for Parameterized Queries. In Proceedings of SIGMOD'09, Providence, RI, USA.

Gichoya, D. (2005). Factors affecting the successful implementation of ICT projects in government. *Electronic. Journal of E-Government, 3*(4), 175–184.

Gilbert, C. (2003). *Guidelines for an information sharing policy*. Bethesda, MD: SANS Institute.

Gilbert, D., Lee-Kelley, L., & Barton, M. (2003). Technophobia, gender influences and consumer decision-making for technology-related products. *European Journal of Innovation Management, 6*(4), 253–263. doi:10.1108/14601060310500968

315

Gilligan, R., & Heinzmann, P. (2004). *Exploring how cultural factors could potentially influence ICT use: An Analysis of European SMS and MMS use* (Cultural Difference Workgroup COST 269 Rep. No. 4). Ljubljana, Slovenia: COST.

Gitlow, H. S., & Gitlow, S. J. (1987). *The Deming guide to quality and competitive position.* Englewood Cliffs, NJ: Prentice-Hall.

Gladitz, K., & Kuchen, H. (1996). Shared memory implementation of the Gamma-operation. *Journal of Symbolic Computation, 21,* 577–591. doi:10.1006/jsco.1996.0032

Gladwell, M. (2002). *The tipping point: How little things can make a big difference.* New York: Little Brown and Company.

Glenzer, C. (2003). A conceptual model of an interorganizational intelligent meeting-scheduler (IIMS). *Strategic Information Systems, 12*(1), 47–70. doi:10.1016/S0963-8687(02)00034-3

Golfarelli, M., Rizzi, S., & Cella, I. (2004). *Beyond data warehousing: what's next in business intelligence?* DOLAP.

Gomez-Mejia, L. R., Balkin, D. B., Cardy, R. L., Dimick, D. E., & Templer, A. J. (2004). *Managing Human Resource.* Toronto, Ontario: Pearson Education Canada Inc.

Goodhue, D. L., & Thompson, R. L. (1995). Task-Technology Fit and individual performance. *Management Information Systems Quarterly, 19*(2), 213–236. doi:10.2307/249689

Gottschalg, O., & Zollo, M. (2007). Interest alignment and competitive advantage. *Academy of Management Review, 32*(2), 419–437.

Granak, A., Hughes, J., & Hunter, D. (2006). *Building the best: Lessons from inside Canada's best managed companies.* Toronto, Ontario: Penguin Group.

Grant, A. (2008). Does intrinsic motivation fuel the prosocial fire? Motivational synergy in predicting persistence, performance, and productivity. *The Journal of Applied Psychology, 93*(1), 48–58. doi:10.1037/0021-9010.93.1.48

Grant, A. (2008). The significance of task significance: Job performance effects, relational mechanisms, and boundary conditions. *The Journal of Applied Psychology, 93*(1), 108–124. doi:10.1037/0021-9010.93.1.108

Grayson, C. J., & O'Dell, C. (1988). *American business: A two-minute warning.* New York: Free Press.

Green, D., Barclay, D., & Ryans, A. (1995). Entry strategy and long-term performance: conceptualization and empirical examination. *Journal of Marketing, 59*(4), 1–16. doi:10.2307/1252324

Greengard, S. (1999, February). Web-based training yields maximum returns. *Workforce, 78,* 95–96.

Grewal, D., Monroe, K. B., & Krishnan, R. (1998). The effects of price comparison acquisition value, transaction value and behavioral intentions. *Journal of Marketing, 62*(2), 46–59. doi:10.2307/1252160

Grey, G. J. (1991). *Electronic performance support system.* Boston: Weingarten Pub.

Grover, V., Teng, J. T. C., & Fiedler, K. D. (1998). IS Investment Priorities in Contemporary Organizations. *Communications of the ACM, 41*(2), 40–48. doi:10.1145/269012.269019

Gunasekaran, A., Patel, C., & McGaughey, R. E. (2004). A framework for supply chain performance measurement. *International Journal of Production Economics, 87*(1), 333–347. doi:10.1016/j.ijpe.2003.08.003

Hackbarth, G., Grover, V., & Yi, M. Y. (2003). Computer playfulness and anxiety: Positive and negative mediators of the system experience effect on perceived ease of use. *Information & Management, 40*(3), 221–232. doi:10.1016/S0378-7206(02)00006-X

Hackman, J. R., & Wageman, R. (2000). Total quality management: Empirical, conceptual, and practical issues. In R. E. Cole & W. R. Scott (Eds.), *The Quality Movement & Organization Theory* (pp. 23-48). Thousand Oaks, CA: Sage.

Haefner, J. J. (2008, July). *Beyond theory Z: Motivation in the knowledge-value era.* Poster session presented at the Walden University Ph. D. Summer Session Academic Residency Research Symposium.

Haefner, J. J., & Bartel, T. J. (1993). A structured approach. *The TQM Magazine, 3*(5), 19–26.

Hair, T., Anderson, R., Tatham, R., & Black, W. (1998). *Multivariate Data Analysis* (5th ed.). Upper Saddle River, NJ: Prentice Hall.

Halberstam, D. (1986). *The reckoning.* New York: William Morrow and Company.

Hall, B. (1997). *Web-based training cookbook.* New York: John Willey & Sons, Inc.

Han, J., & Kamber, M. (2006). *Data Mining: Concepts and Techniques.* San Francisco: Morgan Kaufmann Publisher.

Hanson, J. H., & Willshire, M. J. (1997), Modeling a faster data warehouse. International Database Engineering and Applications Symposium (IDEAS 1997).

Haricharan, S. (2005). *Knowledge management in the South African public sector.* Retrieved July 5, 2009, from http://www.ksp.org.za/holonl03.htm

Harris, P., Rettie, R., & Cheung, C. C. (2005). Adoption and usage of m-commerce: A cross-cultural comparison of Hong Kong and the United Kingdom. *Journal of Electronic Commerce Research, 6*(3), 210–224.

Hart, D. M. (2006). Managing the global talent pool: Sovereignty, treaty, and intergovernmental networks. *Technology in Society, 28*, 421–434. doi:10.1016/j.techsoc.2006.09.002

Hart, P., & Saunders, C. (1997). Power and Trust: Critical Factors in the Adoption and Use of Electronic Data Interchange. *Organization Science, 8*(1), 23–41. doi:10.1287/orsc.8.1.23

Hassan, S. Z., & Saeed, K. A. (1999). A Framework for Determining IT Effectiveness: An Empirical Approach. In *Proceedings of the 32nd Annual Hawaii International Conference on System Sciences* (Vol. 7, pp. 7034).

Hawkins, P. (2007). *Blessed unrest.* New York: Viking.

Heeks, R. (2002). *eGovernment in Africa: Promise and practice* (iGovernment Working Paper Series Paper No. 13). Manchester, UK: University of Manchester.

Heeks, R. (2003). *e-Government Special – Does it Exist in Africa and what can it do?* Retrieved September 8, 2009, from http://www.balancingact-africa.com/news/back/balancing-act93.html#headline

Heijden, H. d. (2003). Factors influencing the usage of websites: the case of a generic portal in the Netherlands. *Information & Management, 40*, 541–549. doi:10.1016/S0378-7206(02)00079-4

Helper, S. (1991). How much has really changed between US automakers and their suppliers? *Sloan Management Review, 32*(1), 15–28.

Henderson, R., Deane, F., Barrelle, K., & Mahar, D. (1995). Computer anxiety: correlates, norms and problem definition in health care and banking employees using the Computer Attitude Scale. *Interacting with Computers, 7*(2), 181–193. doi:10.1016/0953-5438(95)93508-3

Hendricks, K. B., Singhal, V. R., & Stratman, J. K. (2007). The Impact of Enterprise Systems on Corporate Performance: A study of ERP, SCM, and CRM System Implementations. *Journal of Operations Management, 25*(1), 65–82. doi:10.1016/j.jom.2006.02.002

Herrnstein, R. J., & Murray, C. (1994). *The bell curve.* New York: Free Press Paperbacks.

Higgins, C., Duxbury, L., & Irving, R. (1992). Work-family conflict in the dual-career family. *Organizational Behavior and Human Decision Processes, 51*(1), 51–75. doi:10.1016/0749-5978(92)90004-Q

Hill, G., & Ross, A. (2009). Reducing outer joins. *The VLDB Journal, 18*, 599–610. doi:10.1007/s00778-008-0110-5

Hiltrop, J.-M. (1999). The Quest for the Best: Human Resource Practices to Attract and Retain Talent. *European Management Journal, 17*(4), 422–430. doi:10.1016/S0263-2373(99)00022-5

Hitt, L. M., & Brynjolfsson, E. (1996). Productivity, Business Profitability, and Consumer Surplus: Three Different Measures of Information Technology Value. *Management Information Systems Quarterly, 20*(2), 121–142. doi:10.2307/249475

Holze, M., & Ritter, N. (2007), Towards Workload Shift Detection and Prediction for Autonomic Databases. In Proceedings of PIKM'07, Lisbon, Portugal.

Hooper, R. S., & Galvin, T. P. (1998). Use of an Expert System in a personnel selection process. *Expert Systems with Applications, 14*(4), 425–432. doi:10.1016/S0957-4174(98)00002-5

Hosmer, D. W., & Lemeshow, S. (2000). *Applied logistic regression* (2nd ed.). New York: Wiley. doi:10.1002/0471722146

House, R. J., & Rizzo, J. R. (1972). Role Conflict and Ambiguity as Critical Variables in a Model of Organizational Behavior. *Organizational Behavior and Human Performance, 7*(3), 467–505. doi:10.1016/0030-5073(72)90030-X

http://www.ameinfo.com/147106.html#story

Huang, L. C., Huang, K. S., et al. (2004). Applying fuzzy neural network in human resource selection system. In *Proceedings of the NAFIPS '04, IEEE Annual Meeting of the Fuzzy information.*

Huang, L. C., & Wu, P. (2001). A neural network modeling on human resource talent selection. *International Journal of Human Resources Development and Management, 1*(2-4), 206–219.

Huang, M. J., & Tsou, Y. L. (2006). Integrating fuzzy data mining and fuzzy artificial neural networks for discovering implicit knowledge. *Knowledge-Based Systems, 19*(6), 396–403. doi:10.1016/j.knosys.2006.04.003

Huang, T. H. (2005). A Study on the Productivities of IT Capital and Computer Labor: Firm-level Evidence from Taiwan's Banking Industry. *Journal of Productivity Analysis, 24*(3), 241–257. doi:10.1007/s11123-005-4933-4

Huang, T.-C. (2001). The relation of training practices and organizational performance in small and medium size enterprises. *Education + Training, 43*(8-9), 437–444. doi:10.1108/00400910110411620

Hulland, J. (1999). Use of partial least squares in strategic management research: a review of four recent studies. *Strategic Management Journal, 20*(2), 195–204. doi:10.1002/(SICI)1097-0266(199902)20:2<195::AID-SMJ13>3.0.CO;2-7

Hunt, M. (2007). *The story of psychology.* New York: Anchor Books.

Hussin, B. (2005, August 9). A sure thing. *The Sun (Baltimore, Md.)*, 9.

Hwang, D. H., & Kang, H. (2005). XML View Materialization with Deferred Incremental Refresh: the Case of a Restricted Class of Views. *Journal of Information Science and Engineering, 21*, 1083–1119.

IDC. (2007). *The Economic Impact of IT, Software, and the Microsoft Ecosystem on the Global Economy.* Microsoft.

Ifinedo, P. (2005). Measuring Africa's e-readiness in the global networked economy: A nine-country data analysis. *International Journal of Education and Development Using ICT, 1*(1).

Impact Consulting. (2007). *A CLICK AWAY: The benefits of managing programme information electronically.* Retrieved November 8, 2009, from http://www.sangonet.org.za/conference2007

Infodev. (2002). *The E-Government handbook for developing countries.* Retrieved September 30, 2009, from http://www.egovbarriers.org

Isaacs, S. (2007). *Survey of ICT and education in Africa: Aimbabwe country report.* Retrieved November 8, 2009, from http://www.infodev.org/en/Document.437.pdf

Iscan, O. F., & Naktiyok, A. (2005). Attitudes towards telecommuting: the Turkish case. *Journal of Information Technology, 20*, 52–63. doi:10.1057/palgrave.jit.2000023

Ishikawa, K. (1982). *Guide to Quality Control.* Tokyo: Asian Productivity Organization.

ITU. (2009). *International Telecommunication Union: News related to ITU Telecommunication/ICT Statistics.* Retrieved July 31, 2009, from http://www.itu.int/ITU-D/ict/newslog/Internet+Subscribers+Rise+36+In+2008+Yemen.aspx

Jansen, J. J. P., & Bosch, F. A. J., Van den, & Volberda, H. W. (2005). Managing potential and realized absorptive capacity: how do organizational antecedents matter? *Academy of Management Journal, 48*(6), 999–1015.

Jantan, H., Hamdan, A. R., et al. (2008a). *Data Mining Techniques for Performance Prediction in Human Resource Application.* Paper presented at the 1st Seminar on Data Mining and Optimization, Bangi, Selangor.

Jantan, H., Hamdan, A. R., et al. (2008b). Potential Intelligent Techniques in Human Resource Decision Support System (HR DSS). In *Proceedings of the 3rd International Symposium on Information Technology,* Kuala Lumpur.

Jayawarna, D., Macpherson, A., & Wilson, A. (2007). Training commitment and performance in manufacturing SMEs: Incidence, intensity and approaches. *Journal of Small Business and Enterprise Development, 14*(2), 321–338. doi:10.1108/14626000710746736

Jessup, L., & Valacich, J. (2008). *Information Systems Today: Managing in the Digital World.* Upper Saddle River, NJ: Pearson education, Inc.

Jessup, L., & Valacich, J. (2008). *Information Systems Today: Managing in the Digital World.* Upper Saddle River, NJ: Pearson.

Jharkharia, S., & Shankar, R. (2006). Supply chain management: some sectoral dissimilarities in the Indian manufacturing industry. *Supply Chain Management: an International Journal, 11*(4), 345–352. doi:10.1108/13598540610671798

Johnson, M. E., & Pyke, D. F. (Eds.). (2000). *Teaching Supply Chain Management.* Production and Operations Management Society.

Joshi, K., & Pant, S. (2008). Development of a Framework to Assess and Guide IT Investments: An analysis based on a Discretionary-Mandatory Classification. *International Journal of Information Management, 28*(3), 181–193. doi:10.1016/j.ijinfomgt.2007.09.002

Jung, C. G. (1958). *The undiscovered self.* New York: Signet.

Junglas, I., Abraham, C., & Watson, R. T. (2008). Task-technology fit for mobile locatable information systems. *Decision Support Systems.* .doi:10.1016/j.dss.2008.02.007

Juptner, O. (2001). *Corporate e-Learning Market to Skyrocket.* Retrieved from http://www.e-gateway.net/infoarea/news/news.cfm?nid=1451

Juran, J. M., & Gryna, F. M. (1951). *Juran's quality control handbook.* New York: McGraw-Hill.

Kaaya, J. (2004). Implementing e-government services in east africa: assessing status through content analysis of government websites. *Electronic. Journal of E-Government, 1*(2).

Kanungo, S., Duda, S., & Srinivas, Y. (1999). A Structured Model for Evaluating Information Systems Effectiveness. *Systems Research and Behavioral Science, 16*(6), 495–518. doi:10.1002/(SICI)1099-1743(199911/12)16:6<495::AID-SRES238>3.0.CO;2-R

Karakasidis, A., Vassiliadis, P., & Pitoura, E. (2005), ETL Queues for Active Data Warehousing. In Proceedings of the 2nd International Workshop on Information Quality in Information Systems, IQIS 2005, Baltimore, MD, USA.

Kark, R., & Kijk, D. V. (2007). Motivation to lead, motivation to follow: the role of self-regulatory focus in leadership processes. *Academy of Management Review, 22*(2), 500–528.

Katic, N., Quirchmayr, G., Schiefer, J., Stolba, M., & Tjoa, A. M. (1998). *A Prototype Model for Data Warehouse Security Based on Metadata.* IEEE Xplore.

Kearney, A. T. (2004). *Mobinet 5.* Retrieved February 18, 2004, from http://www.atkearney.com/main.taf?p=5,4,1,60.

Keller, M. (1989). *Rude awakening: The rise, fall, and struggle for recovery of General Motors.* New York: William Morrow and Company.

Khalid, S., & Affisco, J. (2002, June 23-25). *Reporting on E-Government Initiatives in Canada and the United States.* Paper presented at the Third Annual Global Information Technology Management (GITM) World Conference, New York.

Kim, H. W., Chan, H. C., & Gupta, S. (2005). Value based adoption of mobile Internet: An empirical investigation. *Decision Support System.*

Kim, J. K., Xiang, J. Y., & Lee, S. (2008). The Impact of IT Investment on Firm Performance in China: An Empirical Investigation of the Chinese Electronics Industry. *Technological Forecasting and Social Change, 76*(5), 678–687. doi:10.1016/j.techfore.2008.03.008

Kim, L. (1998). Crisis construction and organizational learning: Capability building in catching-up at hyundai motor. *Organization Science, 9*(4), 506–521. doi:10.1287/orsc.9.4.506

Kim, S. W. (2006). Effects of supply chain management practices, integration and competition capability on performance. *Supply Chain Management: an International Journal, 11*(3), 241–248. doi:10.1108/13598540610662149

Kim, T., Kim, J., & Lcc, H. (2000). *A Metadata-Oriented Methodology for Building Data warehouse: A Medical Center Case.* Seoul, Korea: Informs & Korms.

King, B. (1989). *Hoshin planning: The developmental approach.* Methuen, MA: Goal/QPC.

Kivijarvi, H., & Saarinen, T. (1995). Investment in Information Systems and the Financial Performance of the Firm. *Information & Management, 28*(2), 143–163. doi:10.1016/0378-7206(95)94022-5

Kjerulff, K. H., Pillar, B., Mills, M. E., & Lanigan, J. (1992). Technology anxiety as a potential mediating factor in response to medical technology. *Journal of Medical Systems, 16*(1), 7–13. doi:10.1007/BF01674093

Kocabiyikoglu, A., & Popescu, I. (2007). Managerial motivation dynamics and incentives. *Management Science, 53*(5), 834–848. doi:10.1287/mnsc.1060.0640

Kock, N. (2008). *Levels of adoption in organizational implementation of e-collaboration technologies.* Hershey, PA: IGI Publishing.

Kodama, F. (1991). *Analyzing Japanese high technologies.* London: Pinter Publishers.

Kohli, R., & Devaraj, S. (2003). Measuring Information Technology Payoff: A Meta-Analysis of Structural Variables in Firm-level Empirical Research. *Information Systems Research, 14*(2), 127–145. doi:10.1287/isre.14.2.127.16019

Kohli, R., & Grover, V. (2008). Business Value of IT: An Essay on Expanding Research Directions to keep up with the Times. *Journal of the Association for Information Systems, 9*(1), 23–39.

Kontoghiorghes, C. (2005). Key Organizational and HR Factors for Rapid Technology Assimilation. *Organization Development Journal, 23*(1), 26–39.

Kristoffersen, S., & Ljungberg, F. (1999). "Making place" to make IT work: empirical explorations of HCI for mobile CSCW. In *Proceedings of the International ACM SIGGROUP Conference on Supporting Group Work,* Phoenix, AZ (pp. 276-285).

Krompass, S., Kuno, H., Dayal, U., & Kemper, A. (2007), Dynamic Workload Management for Very Large Data Warehouses – Juggling Feathers and Bowling Balls. In Proceedings of the 33rd international conference on Very large data bases, Vienna, Austria, 1105-1115.

Krompass, S., Kuno, H., Wiener, J. L., Wilkinson, K., Dayal, U., & Kemper, A. (2009), Managing Long-Running Queries. In Proceedings of the 12th International Conference on Extending Database Technology: Advances in Database Technology, Saint Petersburg, Russia, 132-143.

Kudyba, S., & Diwan, R. (2002). Research Report: Increasing Returns to Information Technology. *Information Systems Research, 13*(1), 104–111. doi:10.1287/isre.13.1.104.98

Kuhn, L. (2007). Why use complexity theories in social inquiry? *World Futures, 63,* 156–175. doi:10.1080/02604020601172525

Kula, V., & Tatoglu, E. (2003). An exploratory study of Internet adoption by SMEs in an emerging market economy. *European Business Review, 15,* 324–333. doi:10.1108/09555340310493045

Kumar, R., Park, S., & Subramaniam, C. (2008). Understanding the value of countermeasures portfolios in information systems security. *Journal of Management Information Systems, 25*(1), 241–279. doi:10.2753/MIS0742-1222250210

Kumar, S., Ressler, T., & Ahrens, M. (2005). Systems thinking, a consilience of values and logic. *Human Systems Management, 24*(4), 259–274.

Kumar, V., Mukerji, B., Butt, I., & Persaud, A. (2007). Factors for Successful e-Government Adoption: a Conceptual Framework. *Electronic. Journal of E-Government, 5*(1), 63–76.

Kwon, S. H. (2004). *New technology in Mobile Banking.* Retrieved from http://www.etnews.co.kr/news/detail.html?id=200402040104.

la Cour, A., Vallentin, S., Hojlund, H., Thyssen, O., & Rennison, B. (2007). Opening systems theory: A note on the recent special issue of Organization. *Organization, 14*(6), 929–938. doi:10.1177/1350508407082267

Labio, W., Yang, J., Cui, Y., Garcia-Molina, H., & Widom, J. (2000), Performance issues in Incremental Warehouse Maintenance. In Proceedings of the VLDB, Cairo, Egypt.

Lai, T. T. (2004). Service quality and perceive value's impact on satisfaction, intention and usage of short message service. *Information Systems Frontiers, 6*(4), 353–368. doi:10.1023/B:ISFI.0000046377.32617.3d

Lam, K., & Lee, V. C. S. (2006). On Consistent Reading of Entire Databases. *IEEE Transactions on Knowledge and Data Engineering, 18*(4).

Lancioni, R., Schau, H., & Smith, M. (2003). Internet impacts on supply chain management. *Industrial Marketing Management, 32*(3), 173–175. doi:10.1016/S0019-8501(02)00260-2

Land, G. T. L. (1973). *Grow or die: The unifying principle of transformation.* New York: Dell Publishing.

Lane, C. (1998). Five essential steps to privacy. *PC World, 16*(9), 116–117.

Lane, P. J., Koka, B. R., & Pathak, S. (2006). The reification of absorptive capacity: a critical review and rejuvenation of the construct. *Academy of Management Review, 31*(4), 833–863.

Langfred, K., & Moye, N. A. (2004). Effects of task autonomy on performance: An extended model considering motivation, informational, and structural mechanisms. *The Journal of Applied Psychology, 89*(6), 934–945. doi:10.1037/0021-9010.89.6.934

Laszlo, E. (1996). *The systems view of the world.* Cresskill, NJ: Hampton Press.

Lau, A. K. W., Yam, R. C. M., & Tang, E. P. Y. (2007). Supply chain product co-development, product modularity and product performance: Empirical evidence from Hong Kong manufacturers. *Industrial Management & Data Systems, 107*(7), 1036–1065. doi:10.1108/02635570710816739

Laudon, K. C., & Traver, C. G. (2008). *E-commerce: Business, Technology and Society* (4th ed.). Upper Saddle River, NJ: Pearson Education.

Laudon, K., & Traver, C. (2008). *E-commerce: Business, Technology, and Society* (4th ed.). Upper Saddle River, NJ: Pearson Education Inc.

Lawler, E. E. (1986). *High Involvement Management: Participative Strategies for Improving Organizational Performance.* San Francisco, CA: Jossey-Bass.

Layne, K., & Lee, J. (2001). Developing fully functional E-government: A four stage model. *Government Information Quarterly, 18*(2), 122–136. doi:10.1016/S0740-624X(01)00066-1

Le Metayer, D. (1994). Higher-order multiset processing. *DIMACS Series in Discrete Mathematics and Theoretical Computer Science, 18,* 179–200.

Lee, K. Y., & Kim, M. H. (2005), Optimizing the Incremental Maintenance of Multiple Join Views. In Proceedings of the 8th ACM International Workshop on Data Warehousing and OLAP (DOLAP'05), Bremen, Germany.

Lee, K. Y., Son, J. H., & Kim, M. H. (2001), Efficient Incremental View Maintenance in Data Warehouses. In Proceedings of the Tenth International Conference on Information and Knowledge Management (CIKM'01), Atlanta, Georgia, USA.

Lee, B., & Menon, N. M. (2000). Information Technology Value through Different Normative Lenses. *Journal of Management Information Systems, 16*(4), 99–119.

Lee, C. C., Cheng, H. K., & Cheng, H. H. (2007). An empirical study of mobile commerce in insurance industry: task–technology fit and individual differences. *Decision Support Systems, 43,* 95–110. doi:10.1016/j.dss.2005.05.008

Lee, C.-P., & Warkentin, M. (2006). Mobile Banking Systems and Technologies. In Khosrow-Pour, M. (Ed.), *Encyclopedia of E-Commerce, E-Government and Mobile Commerce* (pp. 754–759). Hershey, PA: IGI Global.

Lee, M. S. Y., McGoldrick, P. J., Keeling, K. A., & Doherty, J. (2003). Using ZMET to explore barriers to the adoption of 3G mobile banking services. *International Journal of Retail & Distribution Management, 31*(6/7), 340–348. doi:10.1108/09590550310476079

Lee, Y. E., & Benbasat, I. (2004). A framework for the study of customer interface design for mobile commerce. *International Journal of Electronic Commerce, 8*(3), 79–102.

Lee, Y., Lee, I., Kim, J., & Kim, H. (2002). A cross-cultural study on the value structure of mobile Internet usage: comparison between Korea and Japan. *Journal of Electronic Commerce Research, 3*(4), 227–239.

Legris, P., Ingham, J., & Collerette, P. (2003). Why do people use information technology? A critical review of the technology acceptance model. *Information & Management, 40*(3), 191–204. doi:10.1016/S0378-7206(01)00143-4

Leidner, D., & Jarvenpaa, S. (1993). The information Age Confronts Education: Case studies on Electronic Classrooms. *Information Systems Research, 4*(1), 24–54. doi:10.1287/isre.4.1.24

Leleur, S. (2007). Systemic planning: Dealing with complexity by a wider approach to planning. *E:CO, 9*(1/2), 2-10.

Lemonides, J. S. (2007). Toward an Adlerian approach to organizational intervention. *Journal of Individual Psychology, 63*(4), 399–413.

Leonard, B. (1996, April). Distance learning. Work and training overlap. *HR Magazine*.

Lepik, K.-L. (2009). *Euroregions as Mechanisms for Strengthening of Cross-border Cooperation in the Baltic Sea Region.* Tartu, Estonia: Trames.

Levitt, B., & March, J. G. (1988). Organizational learning. *Annual Review of Sociology, 14*, 319–340. doi:10.1146/annurev.so.14.080188.001535

Lewis, R. E., & Heckman, R. J. (2006). Talent Management: A Critical Review. *Human Resource Management Review, 16*, 139–154. doi:10.1016/j.hrmr.2006.03.001

Lewis, W., Agarwal, R., & Sambamurthy, V. (2003). Sources of Influence on Beliefs about Information Technology Use: An empirical study of knowledge workers. *Management Information Systems Quarterly, 27*(4), 657–678.

Li, Y., Tan, C.-H., Teo, H.-H., & Siow, A. (2005). A human capital perspective of organizational intention to adopt open source software. In D. Avison, D. Galletta, & J. I. DeGross (Eds.), *Proceeding of the 26th annual international conference on information systems (ICIS 2005),* Las Vegas, NV (pp. 137-149). Atlanta, GA: Association for Information Systems.

Liao, S.-H. (2007). A knowledge-based architecture for implementing collaborative problem-solving methods in military e-training. *Expert Systems and Applications*.

Liker, J. K. (2004). *The Toyota way: 14 management principles from the world's greatest manufacturer.* New York: McGraw-Hill.

Limayem, M., Cheung, C. M. K., & Chan, G. W. W. (2003). *Explaining information systems adoption and post-adoption: Toward an integrative model.* Paper presented at the 24th International Conference on Information Systems, Seattle, WA.

Lin, W. T., & Shao, B. B. M. (2000). Relative Sizes of Information Technology Investments and Productive Efficiency: Their Linkage and Empirical Evidence. *Journal of the Association for Information Systems,* 1-35.

Lin, B. W. (2007). Information Technology Capability and Value Creation: Evidence from the US Banking Industry. *Technology in Society, 29*(1), 93–106. doi:10.1016/j.techsoc.2006.10.003

Liu, B., Chen, S., & Rundensteiner, E. A. (2002), Batch Data Warehouse Maintenance in Dynamic Environments. In CIKM'02, 68-75.

Liu, P. L., & Tsai, C. H. (2007). Effect of Knowledge Management Systems on Operating Performance: An Empirical Study of Hi-Tech Companies using the Balanced Scorecard Approach. *International Journal of Management, 24*(4), 734–743.

Lomax, V. (2002). WAP lash. *Financial World,* 44.

Lord, R. L., & Farrington, P. A. (2006). Age-related differences in the motivation of knowledge workers. *Engineering Management Journal, 18*(3), 2026.

Loscocco, K. A., & Roschelle, A. R. (1991). Influences on the Quality of Work and Nonwork Life: Two Decades in Review. *Journal of Vocational Behavior, 39*(2), 182–225. doi:10.1016/0001-8791(91)90009-B

Lounsbury, J. W., Moffitt, L., Gibson, L. W., Drost, A. W., & Stevens, M. (2007). An Investigation of personality traits in relation to job and career satisfaction of information technology professionals. *Journal of Information Technology, 22*, 174–183. doi:10.1057/palgrave.jit.2000094

Lounsbury, M., & Ventresca, M. (2004). The new structuralism in organization theory. *Organization, 10*(3), 457–480. doi:10.1177/13505084030103007

Love, P. E. D., Irani, Z., & Edwards, D. J. (2004). Industry-Centric Benchmarking of Information Technology Benefits, Costs and Risks for Small-To-Medium Sized Enterprises in Construction. *Automation in Construction, 13*(4), 507–524. doi:10.1016/j.autcon.2004.02.002

Lu, J., Yu, C., Liu, C., & Yao, J. (2004). Technology Acceptance Model for wireless Internet. *Internet Research: Electronic networking application and Policy, 13*(3), 206-222.

Luff, J. (2002). Data archive systems. *Broadcast Engineering: Overland Park, 44*(3), 206.

Luhmann, N. (2006). System as difference. *Organization, 13*(1), 37–57. doi:10.1177/1350508406059638

Lu, J., Yao, J. E., & Yu, C. S. (2005). Personal innovativeness, social influences and adoption of wireless Internet services via mobile technology. *The Journal of Strategic Information Systems, 14*(3), 245–268. doi:10.1016/j.jsis.2005.07.003

Lu, L., & Lee, Y. (2007). The effect of supervision style and decision-making on role stress and satisfaction of senior foreign managers in international joint ventures in China. *International Journal of Commerce & Management, 17*(4), 284–294. doi:10.1108/10569210710844363

Luling, D. (2001). Taking it online: Anyway, anyplace. Tennessee anytime. *Journal of Government Financial Management, 50*(2), 42–49.

Lundell, B., Lings, B., & Lindqvist, E. (2006). Perceptions and uptake of open source in Swedish organisations. In Damiani, E., Fitzgerald, B., Scacchi, W., Scotto, M., & Succi, G. (Eds.), *Open source systems, IFIP working group 2.13 foundation on open source software, Como, Italy* (*Vol. 203*, pp. 155–163). Boston: Springer.

Lurquin, M. G. (1996). Streamlining the Supply Chain in the Pharmaceuticals Industry. *Logistics Information Management, 9*(6), 6–10. doi:10.1108/09576059610148432

Lussier, R. N. (2000). *Management fundamentals: Concepts, applications, skill development.* Springfield, MA: Springfield College.

Lynne, M. (2005). *Talent Management Value Imperatives: Strategies for Execution.* Paper presented to the Conference Board.

MacDonald, S., Anderson, P., & Kimbel, D. (2000). Measurement or Management?: Revisiting the Productivity Paradox of Information Technology. *Quarterly Journal of Economic Research, 69*(4), 601–617.

Magretta, J. (1998). The power of virtual integration: An interview with Dell Computers' Michael Dell. *Harvard Business Review, 76*(2), 72–83.

Makki, S. A. M., Pissinou, N., & Daroux, P. (2002). Mobile and wireless Internet access. *Computer Communications, 26*, 734–746. doi:10.1016/S0140-3664(02)00208-6

Malhotra, Y. (2001). *Knowledge Management and Business Model Innovation.* Hershey, PA: IGI Global.

Mallat, N., Rossi, M., & Tuunainen, V. K. (2004). Mobile Banking Services. *Communications of the ACM, 47*(5), 42–46. doi:10.1145/986213.986236

Marakas, G. M., Yi, M. Y., & Johnson, R. D. (1998). The Multilevel and Multifaceted Character of Computer Self-Efficacy: Toward Clarification of the Construct and an Integrative Framework for Research. *Information Systems Research, 9*(2), 126–163. doi:10.1287/isre.9.2.126

Marche, S., & McNiven, J. D. (2003). E-Government and E-Governance: The Future isn't what it used to be. *Canadian Journal of Administrative Sciences, 20*(1), 74–86.

Marenzi, O. (2004). *Will i-mode save Mobile Banking in Western Europe*? Retrieved February 10, 2005, from http://www.celent.com/PressReleases/20031023/Mo-bileEurope.htm

Maroney, J. (2007). Achieving the Balance: 10 Keys to Employee Satisfaction. *Workspan, 2*(8), 47–50.

Martin, P., & Powley, W. (2007), An Approach to Managing the Execution of Large SQL Queries. In Proceedings of the 2007 conference of the center for advanced studies on Collaborative research, Richmond Hill, Ontario, Canada, 268 - 271.

Martinsons, M. G. (1995). Knowledge-based systems leverage human resource management expertise. *International Journal of Manpower, 16*(2), 17–34. doi:10.1108/01437729510085747

Maslow, A. H. (1968). *Toward a psychology of being.* New York: John Wiley & Sons.

Maslow, A. H. (1998). *Maslow on Management.* New York: John Wiley & Sons.

Mathieson, K. (1991). Predicting user intentions: Comparing the technology acceptance with the theory of planned behavior. *Information Systems Research, 2*(3), 173–191. doi:10.1287/isre.2.3.173

Matlay, H. (2002). Training and HRM strategies in small, family-owned businesses: An empirical overview. In Fletcher, D. (Ed.), *Understanding the Small Family Business.* London: Routledge.

Matsumoto, K. (1993). *The rise of the Japanese corporate system.* New York: Kegan Paul International.

Mattila, M. (2003). Factors affecting the adoption of mobile banking services. *Journal of Internet Banking and Commerce, 8*(1).

McBride, N., & Fidler, C. (2003). An Interpretive Approach to Justification of Investment in Executive Information Systems. *Electronic Journal of Information Systems Evaluation, 6*(1).

McCrea, F., Gay, R. K., & Bacon, R. (2000). *Riding the big waves: A white paper on B2B e-learning industry.* San Francisco, CA: Thomas Weisel Partners.

McKinsey Global Institute. (2001). *US Productivity Growth, 1995-2000.* Retrieved from http://www.mckinsey.com/mgi/publications/us/index.asp

Mehrabad, M. S., & Brojeny, M. F. (2007). The development of an expert system for effective selection and appointment of the jobs applicants in human resource management. *Computers & Industrial Engineering, 53*(2), 306–312. doi:10.1016/j.cie.2007.06.023

Melville, N., Kraemer, K., & Gurbaxani, V. (2004). Review: Information Technology and Organizational Performance: An Integrative Model of IT Business Value. *Management Information Systems Quarterly, 28*(2), 283–322.

Menard, S. W. (1997). *Applied logistic regression analysis* (No. 106, 2nd ed.). Thousand Oaks, CA: Sage Publications.

Mendez-Wilson, D. (2000). Goodbye cash and credit cards. *Wireless Week, 6*(44), 32.

Menezes, L. M., & Wood, S. (2006). The reality of flexible work systems in Britain. *International Journal of Human Resource Management, 17*(1), 106–138.

Merono-Cerdan, A. L. (2008). Groupware Uses and Influence on Performance in SMEs. *Journal of Computer Information Systems, 48*(4), 87–96.

Messmer, E. (2000). Security needs spawn services. *Network World. Framingham, 17*(14), 1–100.

Meuter, M. L., Ostrom, A. L., Bitner, M. J., & Roundtree, R. (2003). The influence of technology anxiety on consumer use and experiences with self-service technologies. *Journal of Business Research, 56*(11), 899–906. doi:10.1016/S0148-2963(01)00276-4

Meyer, J. P., Becker, T. E., & Vandenberghe, C. (2004). Employee commitment and motivation: A conceptual analysis and integrative model. *The Journal of Applied Psychology, 89*(6), 991–1007. doi:10.1037/0021-9010.89.6.991

Meyer, J., & Allen, N. (1991). A three component conceptualization of organizational commitment. *Human Resource Management Review, 1*(1), 61–90. doi:10.1016/1053-4822(91)90011-Z

Michael, D. R. (1996). Is Manufacturing a Weak Link in Your Supply Chain? *Industrial Management (Des Plaines)*, *38*(6), 1–3.

Michaelson, C. (2005). Dialogue. *Academy of Management Review*, *30*(2), 235–238.

Midgley, G. (2003). Five sketches of postmodernism: Implications for systems thinking and operational research. *Journal of Organisational Transformation & Social Change*, *1*(1), 47–62. doi:10.1386/jots.1.1.47/0

Mikkawy, M. E., & Karawia, A. (2006). Inversion of general tridiagonal matrices. *Applied Mathematics Letters*, *19*, 712–720. doi:10.1016/j.aml.2005.11.012

Miles, R. H., & Perrault, W. D. (1976). Organizational Role Conflict: Its Antecedents and Consequences. *Organizational Behavior and Human Performance*, *17*(1), 19–44. doi:10.1016/0030-5073(76)90051-9

Miller, L. (2001, March). Coaching pays off. *Society of Human Resource Management*, *46*, 16–17.

Miller, R. L., Acton, C., Fullerton, D. A., & Maltby, J. (2002). *SPSS for social scientists*. Hampshire, UK: Palgrave Macmillan.

Miller, R. L., Acton, C., Fullerton, D. A., & Maltby, J. (2002). *SPSS for social scientists*. Hampshire, UK: Palgrave Macmillan.

Ministry of National Econmy-Oman. (2008, April). *Monthly statistically bulletin*, *19*(4).

Misencik, K. (2004). *Introduction to Freud*. Retrieved March 3, 2008, from http://classweb.gmu.edu/nclc130/s04/s04KMFreud.ppt

Misra, J. (1989). A foundation of parallel programming. In M. Broy (Ed.), *Constructive Methods in Computing Science* (Vol. F55, pp. 397-443). Brussels, Belgium: NATO.

Mizuno, S. (1984). *Company-wide total quality control*. Tokyo: Asian Productivity Association.

Mohania, M., & Kambayashi, Y. (2000). Making Aggregate Views Self-Maintainable. *Journal of Data and Knowledge Engineering*, *32*(1), 87–109. doi:10.1016/S0169-023X(99)00016-6

Morcol, G. (2005). A new systems thinking: Implications of the sciences of complexity for public policy and administration. *Public Administration Quarterly*, *29*(3/4), 297–320.

Morgan, L., & Finnegan, P. (2007). How perceptions of open source software influence adoption: An exploratory study. In H. Österle, J. Schelp, & R. Winter (Eds.), *Proceedings of the 15th european conference on information systems (ECIS 2007)*, St. Gallen, Switzerland (pp. 973-984). St. Gallen, Switzerland: University of St. Gallen.

Murnane, L. (n.d.). *E-Commerce and Internet Taxation*. Retrieved September 30, 2007 from http://www.infotoday.com

Najafi, H. S., & Solary, M. S. (2006). Computational algorithms for computing the inverse of a square matrix, quasi-inverse of a non-square matrix and block matrices. *Applied Mathematics and Computation*, *183*, 539–550. doi:10.1016/j.amc.2006.05.118

Nakamura, S. (1991). *The new standardization: Keystone of continuous improvement in manufacturing*. Portland, OR: Productivity Press.

Naqvis. S. J., & AL-Shihi, H. (2009). M-Government Services Initiatives' in Oman. *Issue in Informing Science and Information Technology*, *6*.

Navarroa, J., Jiménezb, D., & Conesac, E. (2007). Implementing e-business through organizational learning: An empirical investigation in SMEs. *International Journal of Information Management*, *27*(3), 173–186. doi:10.1016/j.ijinfomgt.2007.01.001

Ndou, V. (2004). E-Government for Developing Countries: Opportunities and Challenges. *Electronic Journal on Information Systems in Developing Countries*, *18*(1), 1–24.

Nelson, M. (2000). *Hacker school teaches security*. Information Week.

Nelson, M. G. (2000). Hacker school teaches security. *Information Week*, *779*, 137.

Neter, J., Wasserman, W., & Kutner, M. H. (1990). *Applied linear statistical models: Regression, analysis of variance, and experimental designs* (3rd ed.). Homewood, IL: Irwin.

Ngai, E. W. T., & Gunasekaran, A. (2007). A review for mobile commerce research and applications. *Decision Support Systems*, *41*, 3–15. doi:10.1016/j.dss.2005.05.003

Nicolaou, A. I., & Bhattacharya, S. (2006). Organizational Performance Effects of ERP Systems Usage: The Impact of Post-Implementation Changes. *International Journal of Accounting Information Systems*, *7*(1), 18–35. doi:10.1016/j.accinf.2005.12.002

Niemelä-Nyrhinen, J. (2007). Baby boom consumers and technology: shooting down stereotypes. *Journal of Consumer Marketing*, *24*(5), 305–312. doi:10.1108/07363760710773120

Ninth Malaysia Plan. *(2006-2010)*. (2006). Retrieved from http://www.parlimen.gov.my/news/eng-ucapan_rmk9.pdf

Nonaka, I., & Takeuchi, H. (1995). *The Knowledge Creating Company*. New York: Oxford University Press.

Nunally, J. C. (1978). *Psychometric Theory*. New York: McGraw-Hill.

Nunnally, J., & Bernstein, I. (1994). *Psychometric Theory*. New York: McGraw-Hill.

Nysveen, H., Pedersen, P., Thorbjornsen, H., & Berthon, P. (2005). Mobilizing the brand- The effects of mobile services on brand relationship and main channel use. *Journal of Service Research*, *7*(3), 257–276. doi:10.1177/1094670504271151

Okpara, J. O., & Wynn, P. (2008). Human resource management practices in a transition economy: Challenges and prospects. *Management Research News*, *31*(1), 57–76. doi:10.1108/01409170810845958

Oman IT Executive Committee. (2002-2003) *Report, Sultanate of Oman.*

Oman IT Executive Committee. (2002-2003). *Report, Sultanate of Oman.* Muscat, Oman: Government of Oman.

Osei-Bryson, K. M., & Ko, M. (2004). Exploring the Relationship between Information Technology Investments and Firm Performance Using Regression Splines Analysis. *Information & Management*, *42*(1), 1–13.

Ouchi, W. G. (1981). *Theory Z: How American business can meet the Japanese challenge.* New York: Avon.

Oyegoke, A. (1999). Surfing Europe. *The Banker*, *1*(2), 72–73.

Oz, E. (2005). Information Technology Productivity: In Search of a Definite Observation. *Information & Management*, *42*(6), 789–798. doi:10.1016/j.im.2004.08.003

Parajuli, J. (2007). A content analysis of selected government web sites: A case study of Nepal. *Electronic.Journal of E-Government*, *5*(1).

Parasuraman, A., Zeithaml, V. A., & Berry, L. L. (1988). SERVQUAL: A multiple item scale for measuring consumer perception of service quality. *Journal of Retailing*, *64*(1), 12–40.

Parasuraman, S., & Igbaria, M. (1990). An examination of gender differences in the determinants of computer anxiety and attitudes toward microcomputers among managers. *International Journal of Man-Machine Studies*, *32*(3), 327–340. doi:10.1016/S0020-7373(08)80006-5

Parker, C. (1999). E-mail use and abuse. *Freelance journalist based in Cornwall, 48*(7), 257-260.

Pasmore, A. W. (1988). *Designing effective organizations: The sociotechnical system perspective.* New York: Wiley & Sons.

Payton, F. & Handfield, R. (2004, Spring), Strategies for Data Warehousing. MIT Sloan Management Review.

Perdue, L. J., & Woods, R. H. (2000). The effectiveness of alternative training methods in college and university foodservice. *The Journal of the National Association of College and University Food Service*, *22*(1), 64–70.

Personneltoday. (2008). *Talent management is most critical HR challenge worldwide.* Retrieved June 7, 2008 from http://www.personneltoday.com

Pinker, S. (2002). *The blank slate.* New York: Penguin Books.

Plouffe, C. R., Vandenbosch, M., & Hulland, J. (2001). Intermediating technologies and multi-group adoption: A comparison of consumer and merchant adoption intentions toward a new electronic payment system. *Journal of Product Innovation Management*, *18*, 65–81. doi:10.1016/S0737-6782(00)00072-2

Polanyi, M. (1966). *The Tacit Dimension*. London, UK: Routledge and Jegan Paul.

Porter, M. (2001, March). *Strategy and the Internet* (pp. 1-19). Boston, MA: Harvard Business Review.

Possibilities to Use the Concept of Living Laboratories in Tallinn (Report) (2008). Tallinn, Estonia: Institute for Futures Studies

Powley, W., Martin, P., & Bird, P. (2008), DBMS Workload Control using Throttling: Experimental Insights. In Proceedings of the 2008 conference of the center for advanced studies on collaborative research, Ontario, Canada.

PricewaterhouseCoopers. (2008). *Managing People*. Retrieved June 7, 2008, from http://www.pwc.com/

Pyzdek, T. (2001). *The six sigma handbook*. New York: McGraw-Hill.

Quigley, N. R., Tesluk, P. E., Locke, E. A., & Bartol, K. M. (2007). A multilevel investigation of the motivational mechanisms underlying knowledge sharing and performance. *Organization Science*, *18*(1), 71–88. doi:10.1287/orsc.1060.0223

Ragatz, G., Handfield, R., & Scannell, T. (1997). Success Factors for Integrating Suppliers into New Product Development. *Journal of Product Innovation Management*, *14*(1), 190–202. doi:10.1016/S0737-6782(97)00007-6

Ragowsky, A., Stern, M., & Adams, D. A. (2000). Relating Benefits from Using IS to an Organization's Operating Characteristics: Interpreting Results from Two Countries. *Journal of Management Information Systems*, *16*(4), 175–194.

Rahman, N. (2005), Intelligent Metadata Model in a Teradata Warehousing Environment. The 2005 Teradata PARTNERS User Group Conference and Expo, Orlando, FL, USA.

Rahman, N. (2007). Refreshing Data Warehouses with Near Real-Time Updates. *Journal of Computer Information Systems*, *47*(3), 71–80.

Ram, P., & Do, L. (2000), Extracting Delta for Incremental Data Warehouse Maintenance. In Proceedings of the 16th International Conference on Data Engineering, San Diego, CA.

Rami, R., & Nabila, B. A. (2002), Query-based Data Warehousing Tool. ACM Fifth International Workshop on Data Warehousing and OLAP (DOLAP 2002) McLean, VA, USA.

Ranjan, J. (2008). Data Mining Techniques for better decisions in Human Resource Management Systems. *International Journal of Business Information Systems*, *3*(5), 464–481. doi:10.1504/IJBIS.2008.018597

Rao, C., & Mitra, S. K. (1971). Generalized inverse of matrices and its applications. New York: Wiley.

Rei, C. M. (2004). Causal Evidence on the "Productivity Paradox" and Implications for Managers. *International Journal of Productivity and Performance Management*, *53*(1/2), 129–142. doi:10.1108/17410400410515034

Renkema, T. J. W., & Berghout, E. W. (1997). Methodologies for Informaiton Systems Investment Evaluation at the Proposal Stage: A Comparative Review. *Information and Software Technology*, *39*(1), 1–13. doi:10.1016/0950-5849(96)85006-3

Revans, R. (1983). *The ABC of action learning*. Bromley, UK: Chartwell Bratt.

Reyes, P., Raisinghani, M., & Singh, M. (2000). Global supply chain management in the telecommunication industry: the role of information technology in integration of supply chain entities. *Journal of Global Information Technology Management*, *5*(2), 48–67.

Richardson, K. A. (2004). Systems theory and complexity: Part 1. *E:CO*, *6*(3), 75-79.

Richardson, K. A. (2004). Systems theory and complexity: Part 2. *E:CO*, *6*(4), 77-82.

Richardson, K. A. (2005). Systems theory and complexity: Part 3. *E:CO*, *7*(2), 104-114.

Richardson, K. A. (2007). Systems theory and complexity: Part 4. *E:CO*, *9*(1/2), 166.

Riley, T. B. (2004). *E-government, the digital divide and information sharing: Examining the issue*. Commonwealth Centre for E-Governance.

Rivarda, S., Raymond, L., & Verreault, D. (2006). Resource-based View and Competitive Strategy: An Integrated Model of the Contribution of Information Technology to Firm Performance. *The Journal of Strategic Information Systems*, *15*(1), 29–50. doi:10.1016/j.jsis.2005.06.003

Rizzo, J. R., House, R. J., & Lirtzaman, S. I. (1970). Role Conflicts and Ambiguity in Complex Organizations. *Administrative Science Quarterly*, *15*(2), 150–163. doi:10.2307/2391486

Robinson, L. (2009). *Understanding diffusion of innovations.* Retrieved February 20, 2009, from http://www.enablingchange.com.au

Rogers, E. M. (1962). *Diffusion of Innovations.* New York: Free Press.

Rogers, E. M. (1995). *Diffusion of Innovations* (4th ed.). New York: Free Press.

Rogers, E. M. (1964). *Diffusion of Innovations (p. 79/150).* Glencoe, IL: Free Press.

Rogers, E. M. (2003). *Diffusion of Innovation* (5th ed.). New York: Free Press.

Rosen, L. D., & Weil, M. M. (1995). Computer availability, computer experience and technophobia among public school teachers. *Computers in Human Behavior*, *11*(1), 9–31. doi:10.1016/0747-5632(94)00018-D

Rossett, A. (1996). Job aids and electronic performance support systems. In Craig, R. (Ed.), *The ASTD training and development handbook, a guide to human resource development* (pp. 554–578). New York: McGraw-Hill.

Ross, J. W., & Beath, C. M. (2002). Beyond the Business Case: New Approaches to IT investment. *MIT Sloan Management Review*, *43*(2), 51–59.

Ruhode, E., Owei, V., & Maumbe, B. (2008, May). *Arguing for the Enhancement of Public Service Efficiency and Effectiveness Through e-Government: The Case of Zimbabwe.* Paper presented at the IST-Africa Conference, Windhoek, Namibia.

Ruskova, N. A. (2002). *Decision Support System for Human Resource Appraisal and Selection.* Paper presented at the Paper in First International IEEE Symposium on Intelligent Systems.

Saad, Y., & Vorst, H. A. (2000). Iterative solution of linear systems in the 20th century. *Journal of Computational and Applied Mathematics*, *123*, 1–33. doi:10.1016/S0377-0427(00)00412-X

Sadeh, N. (2002). *M-Commerce: technologies, services, and business models.* New York: John Wiley & Sons.

Sadler-Smith, E., Down, S., & Lean, J. (2000). Modern learning methods: rhetoric and reality. *Personnel Review*, *29*(4), 474–490. doi:10.1108/00483480010296285

Saeed, K., Grover, V., & Hwang, Y. (2005). The Relationship of E-Commerce Competence to Customer Value and Firm Performance: An Empirical Investigation. *Journal of Management Information Systems*, *22*(1), 223–256.

Saiedian, M., & Naeem, M. (2001). Understanding, and reducing web delays. *IEEE Computer Journal*, *34*(12), 30–37.

Sakaiya, T. (1991). *The knowledge-value revolution.* New York: Kodonsha International.

Salmelin, B. (2007, May 21-22). *Open Innovation and eServices - Living Labs as facilitating environment.* Paper presented at the Conference of Co-Creative Research and Innovation to Connect the Lisbon Strategy to People: European Network of Living Labs Event, Guimarães, Portugal.

Sanders, N. (2007). An empirical study of the impact of e-business technologies on organizational collaboration and performance. *Journal of Operations Management*, *25*(6), 1332–1347. doi:10.1016/j.jom.2007.01.008

Sanjay, A. (2006). *Retention in the IT industry* (White Paper). Project Perfect.

Sargeant, A. (1996). Training for enterprise: what's so special about the small business? In *Proceedings of the 1996 Small Business & Enterprise Development Conference.* European Research Press: Shipley.

Saunders, M., Lewis, P., & Thornhill, A. (2007). *Research methods for business students* (4th ed.). London: Prentice Hall.

Savage, M. (2000). Attacks bring new security solutions. *Computing Research News*, *884*, 44.

Sayer, A. (1992). *Method in social science: A realist approach.* New York: Routledge.

Schou, C., & Shoemaker, D. (2006). *Information assurance for the enterprise: A roadmap to information security.* New York: McGraw-Hill Irwin.

Schuler, R. S., Aldag, R. J., & Brief, A. P. (1977). Role Conflict and Ambiguity: A Scale Analysis. *Organizational Behavior and Human Performance, 20*(1), 111–128. doi:10.1016/0030-5073(77)90047-2

Schwarz, H., Wagner, R., & Mitschang, B. (2001), Improving the Processing of Decision Support Queries: The Case for a DSS Optimizer. In proceedings of the International Database Engineering & Applications Symposium. (IDEAS '01).

Scott, C. R., & Rockwell, S. C. (1997). The Effect of Communication, Writing, and Technology Apprehension on Likelihood to Use New Communication Technologies. *Communication Education, 46*(1), 44–62. doi:10.1080/03634529709379072

Seager, A. (2003). M-commerce: an integrated approach. *Telecommunications International,* 36-38.

Seddon, P. B. (2005). *Are ERP systems a source of competitive advantage?* New York: John Wiley & Sons.

Segars, A. (1997). Assessing the Unidimensionality of Measurement: a Paradigm and Illustration within the Context of Information Systems Research. *Omega, 25*(1), 107–121. doi:10.1016/S0305-0483(96)00051-5

Sekaran, U. (1986). *Dual-Career Families: Contemporary Organizational and Counseling Issues.* San Francisco, CA: Jossey Bass.

Sekaran, U. (2003). *Research Methods for Business. A Skill-Building.* New York: John Wiley & Sons.

Senge, P. M. (1990). *The fifth discipline: The art and practice of the learning organization.* New York: Doubleday.

Sharaf, M. A., & Chrysanthis, P. K. (2009), Optimizing I/O-Intensive Transactions in Highly Interactive Applications. In Proceedings of the 35th SIGMOD international conference on Management of data, Providence, Rhode Island, USA, 785-798.

Sheshunoff, A. (2000). Internet banking, un update from the frontlines. *ABA Banking Journal, 92*(1), 51–55.

Shin, B. (2003). An Exploratory Investigation of System Success Factors in Data Warehousing. *Journal of the Association for Information Systems, 4,* 141–170.

Shin, Y., Jeon, H., & Choi, M. (2006). Analysis of the consumer preferences toward m-commerce applications based on an empirical study. IEEE Computer Society. *International Journal on Hybrid Information Technology, 1,* 654–659.

Showers, B. (1987). *Staff development handbook.* Columbia, South Carolina: South Carolina Department of Education.

Shu, W., & Strassmann, P. A. (2005). Does Information Technology Provide Banks with Profit? *Information & Management, 42*(5), 781–787. doi:10.1016/j.im.2003.06.007

Siau, K., & Shen, Z. (2003). Building customer trust in mobile commerce. *Communications of the ACM, 46*(4), 91–94. doi:10.1145/641205.641211

Silcock, R. (2001). What is e-government? *Parliamentary Affairs, 54,* 88–101. doi:10.1093/pa/54.1.88

Silver, E. A., Pyke, D. F., & Peterson, R. (1998). *Inventory Management and Production Planning and Scheduling* (3rd ed.). New York: John Wiley & Sons.

Simitsis, A., Vassiliadis, P., & Sellis, T. (2005), Optimizing ETL Processes in Data Warehouses. In Proceedings of the 21st International Conference on Data Engineering (ICDE'05).

Singh, N. (2008, July). *Moving from silos to virtual government.* Paper presented at the GoveTech 2008 Conference, Durban, South Africa.

Sircar, S., Turnbow, J. L., & Bordoloi, B. (2000). A Framework for Assessing the Relationship between Information Technolgy Investments and Firm Performance. *Journal of Management Information Systems, 16*(4), 69–97.

SKMM. (2007). *Hand Phone Users Survey 2007.* Selangor, Malaysia: Author.

Skyttner, L. (2001). *General systems theory: Ideas and application.* River Edge, NJ: World Scientific Publishing.

Smith, A. D., & Faley, B. A. (2001). E-mail Workplace Privacy Issues in an Information- and knowledge-based Environment. *Southern Business Review*, 27(1), 8–22.

Soamn, D. (2001). Effects of Payment Mechanism on Spending Behavior: The Role of Rehearsal and Immediacy of Payments. *The Journal of Consumer Research*, 27, 460–474. doi:10.1086/319621

Sohal, A. S., Moss, S., & Ng, L. (2001). Comparing IT Success in Manufacturing and Service Industries. *International Journal of Operations & Production Management*, 21(1/2), 30–45. doi:10.1108/01443570110358440

Sohal, A. S., & Ng, L. (1998). The Role and Impact of Information Technology in Australian Business. *Journal of Information Technology*, 13(3), 201–217. doi:10.1080/026839698344846

Solow, D., & Szmerekovsky, J. G. (2007). The role of leadership: What management science can give back to the study of complex systems. *E:CO*, 8(4), 52-60.

Soonhee, K. (2002). Participative Management and Job Satisfaction: Lessons for Management Leadership. *Public Administration Review*, 62(2), 231–241. doi:10.1111/0033-3352.00173

Soror, A. A., Minhas, U. F., & Aboulnaga, A. (2008), Automatic Virtual Machine Configuration for Database Workloads. In Proceedings of the 2008 ACM SIGMOD international conference on Management of data, Vancouver, Canada, 953-966.

Spector, P. E. (1986). Perceived Control by Employees: A Meta- Analysis of Studies Concerning Autonomy and Participation at Work. *Human Relations*, 39(11), 1005–1016. doi:10.1177/001872678603901104

Ståhlbröst, A. (2008). *Forming Future IT - The Living Lab Way of User Involvement. Doctoral theses*. Sweden: Luleå University of Technology.

Stake, R. E. (1995). *The Art of Case Study Research*. Thousand Oaks, CA: Sage Publications.

Stallings, W. (2000). *Network security essentials applications and standards*. Upper Saddle River, NJ: Prentice- Hall.

Stanton, J. M., & Stam, K. R. (2003). Information Technology, Privacy, and Power within Organizations: a view from Boundary Theory and Social Exchange perspectives. *Surveillance & Society*, 1(2), 152–190.

Stavrou-Costea, E. (2005). The challenges of human resource management towards organizational effectiveness A comparative study in Southern EU. *Journal of European Industrial*, 29(2), 112–134. doi:10.1108/03090590510585082

Stedman, C. (1998). Warehousing Projects Hard to Finish. *Computerworld*, 32(12), 29.

Steele, M. D. (2003). Margins count: Systems thinking and cost. *AACE International Transactions*, 1-5.

Stiroh, K. J. (2002). Information Technology and the U.S. Productivity Revival: What Do the Industry Data Say? *The American Economic Review*, 92(5), 1559–1576. doi:10.1257/000282802762024638

Stolovitch, H. D., & Keeps, E. J. (2004). *Training ain't performance*. Alexandria, VA: ASTD.

Storey, V. C., & Goldstein, R. C. (1993). Knowledge-Based Approaches to Database Design. *Management Information Systems Quarterly*, 17(1), 25–46. doi:10.2307/249508

Straub, D., & Keil, M.. Testing the technology acceptance model across cultures: A three country study. *Information & Management*, 33(1), 1–11. doi:10.1016/S0378-7206(97)00026-8

SuccessFactors. (2007). *Performance & Talent Management Trend Survey*. Retrieved November 5, 2009, from http://www.successfactors.com/docs/performance-management-trends/2007/

Suoranta, M., & Mattila, M. (2004). Mobile banking and consumer behaviour: New insights into the diffusion pattern. *Journal of Financial Services Marketing*, 8(4), 354–366. doi:10.1057/palgrave.fsm.4770132

Sveiby, K.-E. (1999). *Welcome to the Knowledge Organisation!* Retrieved May 17, 2009 from http://www.sveiby.com/articles/K-era.htm

Svendsen, G. B., & Johnsen, J. A. K. (2006, January 4-7). *Use of SMS in office environment.* Paper presented at the 39th Annual Hawaii International Conference on System Science, Kauai, Hawaii.

Swierczek, F. W., & Shrestha, P. K. (2003). Information Technology and Productivity: A Comparison of Japanese and Asia-Pacific Banks. *The Journal of High Technology Management Research, 14*(2), 269–288. doi:10.1016/S1047-8310(03)00025-7

Switzer, M., & Kleiner, B. H. (1996). New developments in training teams effectively. *Training for Quality, 4*(1), 12–17. doi:10.1108/09684879610112819

Szulanski, G. (1996). Exploring internal stickiness: Impediments to the transfer of best practice within the firm. *Strategic Management Journal, 17*(27-43), 151.

Tabachnick, B. G., & Fidell, L. S. (2001). Logistic regression. In Tabachnick, B. G., & Fidell, L. S. (Eds.), *Using multivariate statistics* (4th ed., pp. 517–581). Boston: Allyn and Bacon.

Tabachnick, B. G., & Fidell, L. S. (2001). *Using Multivariate Statistics.* Boston: Allyn and Bacon.

Tafel, K., & Terk, E. (2007). *Tallinna linna arengukavade analüüs ja arengu kavandamise täiustamise võimalused (Analysis of Development Plans of Tallinn City and Opportunities for Improvement of Planning).* Tallinn, Estonia: Estonian Institute for Futures Studies.

Tafti, A., Mithas, S., & Krishnan, M. S. (2007). Information technology and the autonomy–control duality: toward a theory. *Information Technology Management, 8*, 147–166. doi:10.1007/s10799-007-0014-x

Tai, W. S., & Hsu, C. C. (2005). *A Realistic Personnel Selection Tool Based on Fuzzy Data Mining Method.* Retrieved September 1, 2008, from www.atlantis-press.com/php/download_papaer?id=46

Taleo Research. (2009). *Talent Management Processes.* Retrieved July 12, 208, from http://www.taleo.com/research/articles/talent/don-miss-the-next-strategic-turn-115.html

Tan, K. C. (1999). *Supply Chain Management: Practices, Concerns, and Performance Issues* (Working Paper). Las Vegas, NV: University of Nevada, Department of Management.

Tan, K. C., & Wisner, J. D. (1999). *A Comparison of the Supply Chain Management Approaches of U.S. Regional and Global Businesses* (Working Paper). Las Vegas, NV: University of Nevada, Department of Management.

Tangpong, C. (2008). IT-Performance Paradox Revisited: Resource-Based and Prisoner's Dilemma Perspectives. *Journal of Applied Management and Entrepreneurship, 13*(1), 35–49.

Tapscott, D. (1995). Leadership needed in age of networked intelligence. *Boston Business Journal, 11*(24).

Taufer, M., Stricker, T., & Weber, R. (2002), Scalability and Resource Usage of an OLAP Benchmark on Clusters of PCs. In Proceedings of SPAA'02, Winnipeg, Manitoba, Canada.

Teece, D. J., Pisano, G., & Shuen, A. (1997). Dynamic capabilities and strategic management. *Strategic Management Journal, 18*(7), 509–533. doi:10.1002/(SICI)1097-0266(199708)18:7<509::AID-SMJ882>3.0.CO;2-Z

Tellis, W. (1997). Introduction to Case Study. *Qualitative Report, 3*(2).

Terk, E. (1986). *Innovatsiooniteooria kasutamisvõimalustest. Kogumikus: Innovatsioon ja eksperimentika* (Opportunities of Using Innovation Theory. Publication: Innovation and experimenting).

Terk, E., & Lumiste, R. (2005). *Enterprises in technology-intensive business. Toolkit for coping with international environment and developing management competencies.* Tallinn, Estonia: Estonian Institute for Futures Studies.

Thatcher, M. E., & Oliver, J. R. (2001). The Impact of Technology Investments on a Firm's Production Efficiency, Product Quality, and Productivity. *Journal of Management Information Systems, 18*(2), 17–45.

Thatcher, M. E., & Pingry, D. E. (2007). Modeling the IT Value Paradox. *Communications of the ACM, 50*(8), 41–45. doi:10.1145/1278201.1278204

Theoretical background of the Living Laboratories Concept and Overview of the Literature (Report) (2008). Tallinn, Estonia: Institute for Futures Studies.

Tiernan, C., & Peppard, J. (2004). Information Technology: Of Value or a Vulture? *European Management Journal, 22*(6), 609–623. doi:10.1016/j.emj.2004.09.025

Tillquist, J., & Rodgers, W. (2005). Using Asset Specificity and Asset Scope to Measure the Value of IT. *Communications of the ACM, 48*(1), 75–80. doi:10.1145/1039539.1039542

Timmer, M. P., & Arky, B. (2005). Does Information and Communication Technology Drive EU-US Productivity Growth Differentials? *Oxford Economic Papers, 57*(4), 693–716. doi:10.1093/oep/gpi032

Todorova, G., & Durisin, B. (2007). Absorptive capacity: Valuing a reconceptualization. *Academy of Management Review, 32*(3), 774–786.

Totty, P. (2001). Staying One Step Ahead of the Hacker. *Credit Union Magazine, 67*(6), 39–41.

Towill, D. R. (1996). Time Compression and Supply Chain Management – a Guided Tour. *Logistics Information Management, 9*(6), 41–53. doi:10.1108/09576059610148694

TRC. (2010). *Telecommunication Regularly Commission*. Retrieved January 5, 2010, from http://www.TRC.Jo

Trochim, W. M. K., & Cabrera, D. (2005). The complexity of concept mapping for policy analysis. *E:CO, 7*(1), 11-22.

Troilo, G. (2006). *Marketing knowledge management; managing knowledge in market oriented companies*. Cheltenham, UK: Edward Elgar.

Tsai, W., Chen, C., & Liu, H. (2005). An integrative modeling linking employee positive moods and task performance. *Academy of Management Best Conference Paper, OB,* H1-H6.

Tso, G. K. F., & Yau, K. K. W. (2007). Predicting electricity energy consumption: A comparison of regression analysis, decision tree and nerural networks. *Energy, 32*, 1761–1768. doi:10.1016/j.energy.2006.11.010

Tung, K. Y., & Huang, I. C. (2005). Mining the Generation Xer's job attitudes by artificial neural network and decision tree - empirical evidence in Taiwan. *Expert Systems with Applications, 29*(4), 783–794. doi:10.1016/j.eswa.2005.06.012

Turban, E., King, D., Lee, J. K., & Viehland, D. (2006). *Electronic Commerce - A Managerial Perspective* (4th ed.). Upper Saddle River, NJ: Pearson-Prentice Hall.

Tylor, S., & Todd, P. (1995). Understanding Information technology Usage: A Test of Competing Models. *Information Systems Research, 6*(2), 144–176. doi:10.1287/isre.6.2.144

Uchimaru, K., Okamoto, S., & Kurahara, B. (1993). *TQM for technical groups.* Portland, OR: Productivity Press.

UN. (2008). *E-Government Survey Report*. Retrieved June 10, 2009, unpan1.un.org/intradoc/groups/public/documents/UN/UNPAN028607.pdf

Urbaczewski, A., Wells, J., Sarker, S., & Koivisto, M. (2002). Exploring cultural differences as a means for understanding the global mobile Internet: a theoretical basis and program of research. In *Proceedings of the 35th Annual Hawaii International Conference on System Sciences (HICSS-35.02).* Washington, DC: IEEE Computer Society.

Urdan, T., & Weggen, C. (2000). Corporate e-learning: Exploring a new frontier. *WR Hambrech Co.* Retrieved from http://www.educause.edu/asp/doclib/abstract.asp?ID=CSD1521

Urwiler, R., & Frolick, M. N. (2008). The IT Value Hierarchy: Using Maslow's Hierarchy of Needs as a Metaphor for Gauging the Maturity Level of Information Technology Use within Competitive Organizations. *IS Management, 25*(1), 83–88.

Uzoka, F. E., Shemi, A. P., & Seleka, G. G. (2007). Behavioural influences on e-commerce adoption in a developing country context. *Electronic Journal of Information Systems in Developing Countries, 31*(4), 1–15.

Vajargah, B. F. (2007). New advantage to obtain accurate matrix inversion. *Applied Mathematics and Computation..* doi:10.1016/j.amc.2006.12.060

Van Den Bosch, F. A. J., Volberda, H. W., & De Boer, M. (1999). Coevolution of firm absorptive capacity and knowledge environment: Organizational forms and combinative capabilities. *Organization Science, 10*(5), 551–568. doi:10.1287/orsc.10.5.551

Varshney, U. (2003). Wireless I: Mobile and Wireless Information Systems: Applications, Networks, and Research Problems. *Communications of the Association for Information Systems, 12*(11).

Varshney, U., & Vetter, R. (2002). Mobile Commerce: Framework, Applications and Networking Support. *Mobile Networks and Applications, 7*(3), 185–198. doi:10.1023/A:1014570512129

Ven, K. (2008). The Organizational Adoption of Open Source Server Software: An Information Systems Innovation Perspective. Unpublished PhD dissertation, University of Antwerp, Antwerp, Belgium

Ven, K., & Verelst, J. (2008). The organizational adoption of open source server software: A quantitative study. In W. Golden, T. Acton, K. Conboy, H. van der Heijden, & V. Tuunainen (Eds.), *Proceedings of the 16th European conference on information systems (ECIS 2008),* Galway, Ireland (pp. 1430-1441).

Ven, K., & Verelst, J. (2006). The organizational adoption of open source server software by Belgian organizations. In Damiani, E., Fitzgerald, B., Scacchi, W., Scotto, M., & Succi, G. (Eds.), *Open source systems, IFIP working group 2.13 foundation on open source software, Como, Italy* (*Vol. 203*, pp. 111–122). Boston: Springer.

Ven, K., Verelst, J., & Mannaert, H. (2008). Should you adopt open source software? *IEEE Software, 25*(3), 54–59. doi:10.1109/MS.2008.73

Venkatesh, V. (2000). Determinants of Perceived Ease of Use: Integrating Control, Intrinsic Motivation, and Emotion into the Technology Acceptance Model. *Information Systems Research, 11*(4), 342–365. doi:10.1287/isre.11.4.342.11872

Venkatesh, V. (2003). User acceptance of information technology: Toward a unified view. *Management Information Systems Quarterly, 27*(3), 425–478.

Venkatesh, V., & Davis, F. D. (1996). A model of the antecedents of perceived ease of use: Development and test. *Decision Sciences, 27*(3), 451–481. doi:10.1111/j.1540-5915.1996.tb01822.x

Venkatesh, V., & Davis, F. R. (2000). A theoretical extension of the technology acceptance model: four longitudinal field studies. *Management Science, 46*(2), 188–204. doi:10.1287/mnsc.46.2.186.11926

Verplanken, B., Aarts, H., & Van Knippenberg, A. (1997). Habits, Information Acquisition, and the Process of Making Travel Mode Choices. *European Journal of Social Psychology, 27,* 539–560. doi:10.1002/(SICI)1099-0992(199709/10)27:5<539::AID-EJSP831>3.0.CO;2-A

Verton, D. (2000). Co-op to certify tools to measure level of security. *Computerworld, 34*(49), 16.

Viia, A., Terk, E., Lumiste, R., & Heinlo, A. (2007). *Innovation in Estonian Enterprises*. Tallinn, Estonia: Enterprise Estonia.

Vlasimsky, S. (2003). Supply chain management: changing the status quo in chemicals. *Chemical Market Report, 294*(17), 29–30.

von Bertalanffy, L. (1968). *General system theory.* New York: George Braziller.

Waarts, E., Everdingen, Y. M. v., & van Hillegersberg, J. (2002). The dynamics of factors affecting the adoption of innovations. *Journal of Product Innovation Management, 19*(6), 412–423. doi:10.1016/S0737-6782(02)00175-3

Walton, M. (1990). *Deming management at work.* New York: Perigree Books.

Wang, X., & Butler, B. S. (2003). Individual technology acceptance under conditions of change. In *Proceedings of the 24th International Conference on Information Systems*, Seattle, WA.

Wang, C., Hsu, Y., & Fang, W. (2004). Acceptance of technology with network externalities: An empirical study of Internet instant messaging services. *Journal of Information Technology Theory and Application, 6*(4), 15–28.

Wang, T. W. (2004). From general system theory to total quality Management. *The Journal of American Academy of Business, 4*(1/2), 394–400.

Wang, T., & Tadisina, S. (2007). Simulating Internet-based collaboration: A cost-benefit case study using a multi-agent model. *Decision Support Systems, 43*(2), 645–662. doi:10.1016/j.dss.2005.05.020

Wang, Y., Wang, Y., Lin, H., & Tang, T. (2003). Determinants of user acceptance of Internet banking: An empirical study. *International Journal of Service Industry Management, 14*(5), 501–519. doi:10.1108/09564230310500192

Wanjiku, R. (2008, September). Still waiting for Madaraka PC. *ComputerWorld Kenya*.

Ward, J. (1990). A Portfolio Approach to Evaluating Information Systems Investments and Setting Priorities. *Journal of Information Technology*, 5(4), 222–231. doi:10.1057/jit.1990.46

Ward, J., Daniel, E., & Peppard, J. (2008). Building Better Business Cases for IT Investments. *MIS Quarterly Executive*, 7(1), 1–15.

Weber, M. (2002). The protestant ethic and the "spirit" of capitalism: And other writing. New York: Penguin Books.

Weill W., Subramani, M. & Broadbent, M. (2002, Fall), Building IT Infrastructure for Strategic Agility. MIT Sloan Management Review.

Weill, P. (1992). The Relationship between Investment in Information Technology and Firm Performance: A Study of the Valve Manufacturing Sector. *Information Systems Research*, 3(4), 307–333. doi:10.1287/isre.3.4.307

Weill, P., & Olson, M. H. (1989). Managing Investment in Information Technology: Mini Case Example and Implications. *Management Information Systems Quarterly*, 13(1), 3–17. doi:10.2307/248694

Welber, M., & Feinberg, J. (2002, September). Save by growing your own trainers. *Workforce*, 81, 44.

White, J. K., & Ruh, R. R. (1973). Effects of Personal Values on the relationship between Participation and Job attitudes. *Administrative Science Quarterly*, 18(4), 506–514. doi:10.2307/2392202

Widom, J. (1995), Research Problems in Data Warehousing. In proceedings of the 4th Int'l Conference on Information and Knowledge Management (CIKM).

Wiig, K. (2000). Knowledge Management in Innovation and R&D. In *Proceedings of the Aspen World 2000*. Cambridge, MA: Aspen Technologies.

Wilkins, B. (2000). *A grounded theory on personal coaching*. Unpublished doctoral Dissertation, University of Montana, Montana.

Wilkins, D. (2008). *Talent Management Perspectives*. Retrieved July 12, 2008, from http://www.talentmgt.com/talent.php?pt=a&aid=701

Williams, S. (1994). Technophobes Victims of Electronic progress. *Mobile Register*, 9E.

Willis, G. B. (2005). *Cognitive interviewing: A tool for improving questionnaire design*. London: Sage Publications.

Wilson, N. (1996). Supply chain management: a case study of a dedicated supply chain for bananas in the UK grocery market. *Supply Chain Management*, 1(2), 25–28.

Wixom, B. H., & Watson, H. J. (2001). An Empirical Investigation of the Factors Affecting Data Warehousing Success. *Management Information Systems Quarterly*, 25(1), 17–41. doi:10.2307/3250957

Wold, H. (1985). Systems analysis by partial least squares. In Nijkamp, P., Leitner, L., & Wrigley, N. (Eds.), *Measuring the Unmeasurable* (pp. 221–251). Dordrecht, The Netherlands: Marinus Nijhoff.

Wong, C. C., & Hiew, P. L. (2005). *The Current State and the Evolutionary Pathway of Telcos in Malaysia*. Paper presented at the 2005 Hawaii International Conference on Business.

Wu, J.-H., & Hisa, T. (2004). Analysis of e-commerce innovation and impact: a hypercube model. *Electronic Commerce Research and Applications*, 3, 389–404. doi:10.1016/j.elerap.2004.05.002

Xin, Z. (2008). *An Empirical Study of Data Mining in Performance Evaluation of HRM*. Paper presented at the International Symposium on Intelligent Information Technology Application Workshops.

Yan, J. (2006). Effective and Efficient Dimensionality Reduction for Large-Scale and Streaming Data In Preprocessing. *IEEE Transactions on Knowledge and Data Engineering*, 18(3).

Yin, R. (1994). *Case Study Research Design and Methods* (2nd ed.). Newbury Park, CA: Sage.

Yin, R. K. (2003). Case study research design and methods. *Applied Social Research Methods Series, 5*.

Yorukoglu, M. (1998). The Information Technology Productivity Paradox. *Review of Economic Dynamics*, 1(2), 551–592. doi:10.1006/redy.1998.0016

Zahra, S. A., & George, G. (2002). Absorptive capacity: a review, reconceptualization, and extension. *Academy of Management Review, 27*(2), 185–203. doi:10.2307/4134351

Zairi, M. (1998). Best practice in supply chain management: the experience of the retail sector. *European Journal of Innovation Management, 1*(2), 59–66. doi:10.1108/14601069810217239

Zhang, M., Martin, P., & Powley, W. (2008), Using Economic Models to Allocate Resources in Database Management Systems. In Proceedings of the 2008 conference of the center for advanced studies on collaborative research, Ontario, Canada.

Zhuge, Y., García-Molina, H., Hammer, J., & Widom, J. (1995), View Maintenance in a Warehousing Environment. In Proceedings of the 1995 ACM SIGMOD International Conference on Management of Data (SIGMOD'95), San Jose, CA USA.

Zhuge, Y., Wiener, J. L., & Garcia-Molina, H. (1997), Multiple View Consistency for Data Warehousing. In Proceedings of the Thirteenth International Conference on Data Engineering, Birmingham U.K.

Zikmund, W. G. (2000). *Business research methods*. Fort Worth, TX: Dryden Press.

Zoliat, A., Ibrahim, A., & Farooq, A. (2009). A Study on the Internet Security and its Implication for e-Commerce in Yemen. In *Proceedings of the Conference on Knowledge Management and Innovation in Advancing Economies* (pp. 911-922).

Zwass, V. (2003). Electronic Commerce and Organizational Innovation: Aspects and Opportunities. *International Journal of Electronic Commerce, 7*(3), 7–37.

About the Contributors

Ali Hussein Saleh Zolait (Known Dr. Zolait) is the Assistant Professor of Management Information Systems (MIS) at the College of Information Technology – Department of Information System – University of Bahrain. Dr. Zolait is considered a prominent scholar and leader in the field of innovation diffusion and technology acceptance. He has published more than 30 articles on aspects of information security, internet banking, mobile application, supply chain integration, information systems performance in organization, web maturity evaluation, information systems, performance analysis and instructional technologies, and e-commerce application. His work has been published in leading international journals such as *Government Information Quarterly, Behaviour & Information Technology, Journal of Systems and Information Technology,* and *Journal of Financial Services Marketing*. He is the Editor-in-Chief of the *International Journal of Technology Diffusion* (IJTD). Before coming to University of Bahrain, he was the Stoops distinguished Assistant Professor of E-commerce and Management Information Systems at Graduate School of Business- University of Malaya - Malaysia which is ranked one of top 100 universities in the world. Dr. Zolait also serves as the Visiting Research at the University of Malaya at Faculty of Business and Accountancy (2008). He has excellent communication skills, a collegial approach to faculty and student interactions, and a sincere appreciation of cultural diversity. He literally developed hundreds of students at all levels- undergraduate, MBA, MM, executive development, and Doctoral.

* * *

Farooq Ahmad is Professor of Computer Science at King Khalid University, Abha, Saudi Arabia. He did his PhD at Strathclyde University, Glasgow, UK in 1991. He has been teaching at various universities in Pakistan, Malaysia and Saudi Arabia. His research interests covers Artificial Intelligence and Linear Programming.

Joseph J. Haefner (ABD, MSIE) is the quality manager for the three production facilities of OEM Fabricators, OEM Micro-Machining, and Midwest Mechanics (design and creation of heavy fabricated assemblies for experimental research) in West Central Wisconsin, USA. He is currently completing his dissertation at Walden University in applied management and decision sciences with specialization in engineering management for Globally Competitive Product and Services. Haefner has taught statistics in the College of Engineering at the University of Wisconsin – Madison and worked for many years in industry to improve processes and launch new products such as automotive air bags and automotive cam phasing. He has also led Credit Union National Association – Card Services Group to win the Wisconsin

Quality Network Award by improving in every category of the Malcolm-Baldrige Award. Haefner has presented at conferences, and published papers about integrated planning, design of experiments, and total quality management. His research interest is improving worker productivity and well-being. He is also working on the 20/20 Survey for assessing organizational capacity to adapt. Joe can be reached at haefnerjjh@aol.com

Hamid Khan is Assistant Professor in Mathematics at FAST- National University of Computer & Emerging Sciences, Peshawar Campus, Pakistan. He did his M. Phil from Kohat University of Science & Technology, Kohat, Pakistan in 2007. He has a teaching experience of more than 8 years. His research interests covers Linear Algebra and Set Theory.

Cheon-Pyo Lee is an Assistant Professor of Information Systems at Fairmont State University. He received his Ph.D. in Management Information Systems degree from Mississippi State University and MS/CIS degree from Georgia State University. His research interests include organizational information technology adoption, mobile commerce, and business value of information technology. He has authored several articles, books, and chapters including European Journal of Information Systems (EJIS), Communications of the Association for Information Systems (CAIS), Journal of Information Technology Theory and Application (JITTA), Information Technology and People (IT & People), and Journal of Internet Banking and Commerce (JIBC). He has also presented at conferences such as the Americas Conference on Information Systems (AMCIS), Decision Sciences Institute (DSI) Conference, and International Resource Management Association (IRMA) Conference.

Christos Makrigeorgis (PhD, MS) is an analytics manager at Microsoft Corporation (TX, USA). He has over 17 years of industry experience in the development and application of quantitative models for a number of verticals including airlines, consumer packaged goods and process supply chains, supply chain software and business intelligence and analytics. His is also a part-time faculty at Walden University where he teaches quantitative methodology to doctoral students. His primary interests are in the application of operations research and statistical methodologies to real-world problems including manpower scheduling and resource allocation. He holds several training certifications in project and people management and computer and business applications. He has published several articles and presented several papers at international conferences on airline models, production, inventory and distribution planning and manpower planning.

Asem Y. A. Moqbel holds a BA from Aden University, Yemen, MA from Central Connecticut State University, USA, and MBA from Cardiff University, UK. His research interests include mobile and electronic commerce, Technology Use in Business, Business Information Systems, Interactive Marketing, Internet Marketing and Advertising, Consumer Behavior, as well as Gender and Culture issues in Internet and Marketing. Besides working for the private sector and international organizations in Yemen, he taught at various places including Aden University and the University of Science and Technology, Yemen.

Nayem Rahman is a Senior Application Developer in Enterprise Data Warehouse Engineering (EDWE) - ETL, Intel Corporation. He has implemented several large projects using data warehousing technology for Intel's mission critical enterprise DSS platforms and solutions. He holds an MBA in Management

Information Systems (MIS), Project Management, and Marketing from Wright State University, Ohio, USA. He is a Teradata Certified Master. He is also an Oracle Certified Developer and DBA. His most recent publications on Data Warehousing appeared in proceedings of the 14th Americas Conference on Information Systems (AMCIS 2008) and the Journal of Computer Information Systems. His principal research areas are Active Data Warehousing, Changed Data Capture and Management in Temporal Data Warehouses, Change Management and Process Improvement for Data Warehousing projects, Decision Support System, Data Mining for Business Analysts, and Sustainability of Information Technology.

Amin A. Shaqrah is currently Assistant Professor of Management Information Systems at Al Zaytoonah University of Jordan. He holds a PhD in MIS from Arab Academy for Banking and Financial Sciences, and received MA in MIS from Amman Arab University for Graduate Studies. He is a Certified e-business Consultants and a KM Professional. He is affiliated with a number of international professional societies on KM, E-business, and a member of editorial review boards for a number of International Journals. He had a leadership role in the design and implementation of MIS program at the undergraduate level. His research interests are mainly knowledge sharing and transfer, organizational knowledge theory, knowledge culture, CRM value strategies, data mining techniques, Innovative work environment, human and Social implications of Enterprise systems (ERP, CRM, SCM). His work appears in number international Journals and conferences.

Sharan Kaur Garib Singh, PhD. is a senior lecturer at the Faculty of Business & Accountancy, University of Malaya, Malaysia. Her areas of interests are Strategic Management and Human Resource Management.

Veeriah Sinniah is a MBA graduate of the Faculty of Business & Accountancy, University of Malaya, Malaysia.

Ainin Sulaiman is the dean and a professor of MIS at the Faculty of Business and Accountancy, University of Malaya. Research interests are management information systems, technology diffusion and adoption and E-Commerce.

Mirella Yani-De-Soriano is a Lecturer in Marketing at Cardiff Business School. Her research focuses on cross-cultural consumer behavior in three main areas: the interplay of emotions, cognitive style and behavior in consumer choice, attitudes and behavior in a societal marketing context, and technology-based-services consumer behavior.

Shumaila Yousafzai is a Lecturer in Marketing at Cardiff Business School. Her research focuses on consumer behavior in the following areas: Fair Trade consumption, Islamic finance, Addictive online consumption among young University Students and technology-based-services consumer behavior. She has published various articles in Journals including Psychology & Marketing, Technovation, and Service Industries Journal.

Index

A

absorptive capacity 287-289, 291-293, 302-304
American Management Association (AMA) 223
analysis of variance (ANOVA) 97, 185
Application Service Provider (ASP) 212
Artificial Immune System (AIS) 265
Artificial Intelligent (AI) 262
Authentication 76, 203-204, 248-249
autopoiesis 65

B

batteries-per-person (bpp) 60
behavioural intention (BI) 47
bijections 113
business-to-consumer (B2C) 231

C

Cable & Wireless (C&W) 201
career salience (CS) 222
Chemical Abstract Machine (Cham) 276
Chemical Reaction Models (CRMs) 275
cognitive interviewing 293, 304
Commerce Service Provider (CSP) 212
commercial distributions 290
Complex Mobile Tasks 83, 89, 91, 102-103, 172, 176-177, 179, 190-191
Complex Mobile Tasks Assistance Level 177
computer-based training (CBT) 144
computer self-efficacy 82, 86, 91, 93, 95, 97, 101, 106, 170, 174, 178, 182-183, 185, 189, 194, 235, 242
confirmatory factor analysis (CFA) 253
Cronbach's alpha 87, 148, 175, 217, 226
cross-border co-operation (CBC) 155
Customer Relationship Managenement (CRM) 11

D

database management system (DBMS) 119
Data mining (DM) 262
Data warehousing 118-121, 123-124, 126, 129-132
demand driven 163
Democratic Republic of the Congo (DRC) 10
depersonalization 224
deterrence orientation 56-58, 60, 68
deterrent management orientation 63
Diffusion of Innovations Theory (DOI) 3
discriminant validity 254-255
Distance Learning 140-145, 147-152
Duration of Mobile Device Ownership 91-92, 94, 178, 180-181

E

e-Business 73, 77, 133-137, 139, 200, 202, 205, 207-212, 244-245, 247-248, 251-253, 257
E-Government Readiness Report 76, 135
Eigen Test 93, 182
electronic commerce competence 201, 245
E-Marketing 136
Encryption 204, 209, 211, 248, 253, 257
engineer 60-61
enterprise data warehouse (EDW) 120
Enterprise Resource Planning (ERPs) 11
E-participation Index 76, 135
explicit knowledge 158, 160
extent of usage (EU) 50-51
extract-transform-load (ETL) 119

F

firewalls 203-204, 211, 247-248, 257
Firm Performance 30-31, 36-37, 39-42, 213-215, 217-219, 259
fuzzy logic 268

G

Gamma program 276, 278, 282-283
Generalized Inverses 112
Global Network 134
Government-to-Business (G2B) 74
Government-to-Citizen (G2C) 74
Government-to-Employee (G2E) 74
Government-to-Government (G2G) 74

H

Human Resource (HR) 261
Human Resource Management (HRM) 145, 261

I

Individual Development 224
Information Security Officer (ISO) 204
IT Business Value 29, 31, 33-35, 38, 41
IT Evaluation 29
IT intensity 292, 294, 299, 301
IT Investment 29-40, 42
IT Productivity Paradox 29, 31-33, 35

J

job involvement (JI) 223
Just-In-Time (JIT) 218

K

knowledge barriers 287-289, 291, 302
Knowledge-based system (KBS) 263, 270
Knowledge Discovery in Database (KDD) 262, 265-266
Knowledge transfer 154-160, 162

L

Linear Algebra 21, 112, 117
Living Lab 154-155, 157, 159-164
Local Area Network (LAN) 7

M

Malaysian Communications and Multimedia Commission (MCMC) 45
Matrix Inversion 21-22, 27-28, 112-113, 117
megawatts (MW) 10
Ministry of Planning and Development (MDP) 205
Mobile banking 231-234, 241-243

Mobile Device Input Features 84-85, 87, 89, 98, 102-103, 172-173, 175, 177, 190-191
mobile information systems (Mobile IS) 79, 168
Mobile Operators' Network Efficiency 99-100, 102-103, 187, 190-191
Mobile Operators' Quality of Services 97, 99-100, 102-103, 182, 187, 190-191
Mobile Tasks Complexity 91, 98, 102, 177, 186, 190
mobile task-technology fit (MTTF) 78-79, 83, 103, 166-167, 171, 191
Mobile vendors 78-79, 84, 86-87, 96-97, 100-103, 105, 166, 168, 172, 174-175, 182, 184, 188-191, 193
Mobile Vendors' User Interface Functionality 188
modern information technology (MIT) 74
Motivational Saturation 56-57, 66-69
Motivation Bonus 56, 60
Motivation Theory 56, 67
multiset elements 279

N

National Aids Council (NAC) 9
National Blood Services of Zimbabwe (NBSZ) 6
National Social Security Authority (NSSA) 7
networked file system (NFS) 277
Network Fit 81-82, 84, 86-87, 96, 99, 101-103, 105, 169-170, 172, 174-175, 182, 187, 189-191, 193
non-profit association (NPA) 159

O

one sample t-test 217-218
online transaction processing (OLTP) 123
on-the-job training (OJT) 140, 148
Open Computing Language (OpenCL) 281
open source server software (OSSS) 287-288
open source software (OSS) 287
open systems theory 56, 58
organizational learning 139, 287-289, 302-303

P

Partial Least Squares (PLS) 256
participation in decision making (PDM) 223
Perceived Ease of Use (PEOU) 47, 80, 169
Perceived Usefulness (PU) 47, 80, 169
Personal Computers (PCs) 7
personal digital assistants (PDA) 45
physical security 203, 247-248

postal and telecommunications regulatory authority of Zimbabwe (POTRAZ) 13
practically wise 68
prior knowledge 291-292
progressive mechanization 64, 68
Protection measures 200, 204, 210, 248, 255-256
Pseudo Inverse 21, 112
Public Telecommunications Corporation (PTC) 201

R

research and development (R&D) 12
role conflicts and ambiguity (RCA) 223

S

scalability 132, 245, 275
security hazard 203-204, 210, 247, 255-256
Security Officer Certification (GIAC) 204
Shared Processing Centre (SPC) 212
Short Message Service (SMS) 233
Simple Mobile Tasks 83, 89-90, 108, 172, 176-177, 179, 196
Small and Medium Sized Enterprises (SMES) 145
Sociotechnical theory (STT) 222
software vendors 290
Statistical Package for Social Sciences (SPSS) 217
Supply chain management (SCM) 214-215
Supply Chain Practices 214-215, 218, 220
Support Vector Machine (SVM) 265
Synchronization 129, 278-279
Systemic Motivation 56-57, 60-61

T

tacit knowledge 158
Task-Technology Fit (TTF) 81, 169
Technical Fit 81, 83-84, 87, 101, 169, 171-172, 175, 189
Technology anxiety (TA) 231-232, 234
technology-based training (TBT) 144
technology push 163
telecommunication regularly commission (TRC) 245
telecommunication technology (TT) 74
Tele-training 142
TeleYemen 201, 205
Theory of Planned Behavior (TPB) 81, 169
Theory of Reasoned Action (TRA) 81, 169
third generation (3G) 245
tipping point 65, 70
training delivery method 142

V

variance inflation factors (VIF) 294

W

wide area network (WAN) 7
Wireless Application Protocol (WAP) 45, 233
World Health Organisation (WHO) 7

Z

Zimbabwe Aids Network (ZAN) 9